Visual C# .NET
Developer's Handbook

Visual C#™ .NET Developer's Handbook™

John Paul Mueller

SYBEX

San Francisco · London

Associate Publisher: Richard Mills
Acquisitions and Developmental Editor: Denise Santoro Lincoln
Editor: Colleen Wheeler Strand
Production Editor: Kylie Johnston
Technical Editor: Ross Russell Mullen
Graphic Illustrator: Tony Jonick
Electronic Publishing Specialist: Nila Nichols
Proofreaders: Amey Garber, Dave Nash, Laurie O'Connell, Yariv Rabinovitch, Nancy Riddiough
Indexer: Ron Strauss
CD Coordinator: Dan Mummert
CD Technician: Kevin Ly
Cover Designer: Carol Gorska/Gorska Design
Cover Photographer: Glen Allison/PhotoDisc

Library of Congress Card Number: 2002103166

ISBN: 0-7821-4047-5

Manufactured in the United States of America

10 9 8 7 6 5 4 3 2 1

This book is in loving memory of Esther Darneal
(1916–2002).

Acknowledgments

Thanks to my wife, Rebecca, for working with me to get this book completed during an exceptionally difficult time. I really don't know what I would have done without her help in researching and compiling some of the information that appears in this book (especially the Glossary). She also did a fine job of proofreading my rough draft and page-proofing the final result.

Russ Mullen deserves thanks for his technical edit of this book. He greatly added to the accuracy and depth of the material you see here. I really appreciated the time he devoted to checking my code for accuracy. Russ also supplied some of the URLs you see in the book and other helpful tips and hints.

Matt Wagner, my agent, deserves credit for helping me get the contract in the first place and taking care of all the details that most authors don't really consider. I always appreciate his help. It's good to know that someone wants to help.

Finally, I would like to thank Denise Santoro Lincoln, Kylie Johnston, Colleen Strand, and the rest of the Sybex production staff, including Nila Nichols, Kevin Ly, and Dan Mummert, for their assistance in bringing this book to print. It's always nice to work with such a great group of professionals.

Contents at a Glance

Contents

Introduction

Frustration! It's one word that I've used to describe many of my development experiences.

Anyone who's worked with Visual Studio fully knows about the two-language dilemma that it poses. At the one end of the development experience, Visual Basic makes development relatively easy and fast, but it lacks the low-end connectivity I often need without performing a lot of additional programming. At the other end of the development continuum, Visual C++ makes it relatively easy to gain low-level access to anything in the Windows environment, but development is a time-intensive task requiring Machiavellian expertise.

What most developers need is a Reese's Peanut Butter Cup programming experience—two tastes in one. C# provides that flavor-combining programming experience in many ways; you gain the rapid application development environment of Visual Basic combined with the low-level language support of Visual C++. One of the main purposes of this book is to share that two-tastes-in-one experience with you.

Take the Grand Tour

I'm assuming that many of you have already programmed in Visual Basic or Visual C++ (or perhaps even both) and found the experience lacking in some fundamental way. C# is a great development language, but it's by no means perfect. I'll still use Visual C++ to develop native unmanaged applications and components that need that last ounce of performance. Visual Basic is still my development language of choice for quick prototyping and some database management tasks. However, for the vast majority of my programming needs, C# fills a need that the other two languages can't (without a lot of extra effort). Of course, the trick is learning where C# fits into your language toolkit.

We'll take the grand tour of C# programming capabilities in this book. I won't bore you with fundamentals such as basic code construction or learning how to create programming loops. We will discuss everything from basic utility applications to complex database applications that use OLE-DB, ODBC.NET, ADO, or ADO.NET as a basis for communication. Some of the applications will provide a view of the local programming environment, while others will provide a view of the Internet and distributed application development in all its glory. By the time you finish Chapter 17, you'll know that C# is a language for every environment—from the desktop to the PDA.

Some Extras to Consider

You'll also find three interesting appendices in the back of the book. The first two will help those of you who are used to working with Visual C++ or Visual Basic make the adjustment to C#. You'll learn how C# differs from these two languages and about some of the common problems that other developers have faced when making the transition. The third appendix will show how you can create a complex application that Microsoft doesn't even mention in the Visual Studio .NET help files—the Microsoft Management Console (MMC) snap-in. I placed this example in an appendix because it isn't a pure C# application—some applications still require the use of Visual C++ to make some underlying connections, and this is one of them.

C# is a new programming language. While it does resemble languages of the past, it's truly a new language for a new age of application development. This book is your guide to a larger world of C# application development. You'll learn how to create many types of applications, but more importantly, you'll learn how unique C# is and how it can help you overcome modern application development problems that older languages are ill equipped to handle.

Who Should Read This Book?

I'll begin by saying that, as I write this, there are many good books for novices on the market, and I have consequently decided not to discuss the same issues that those other texts already cover. This book specifically addresses the needs of those who already know something about C# or at least those who have decided to move from another Visual Studio language such as Visual C++ or Visual Basic. If you've never programmed before, you'll probably find that you'll get lost by the time you reach the end of the first chapter.

As mentioned in the first part of the Introduction, this book provides the grand tour of C#. I've designed it to show you how to put a variety of application types together in a short time and with little effort. We'll explore the capabilities of C# by looking at a wealth of programming examples. Every chapter has several examples, most of which show a specific set of C# features. Most intermediate-to-expert level developers who have some experience in other languages and want to learn what C# can do for them will gain something by reading this book.

Some experts will find that this book doesn't answer every question. If you have already read every C# book on the market and regularly develop complex applications using C#, I don't have a lot to offer in the way of truly strange development tricks (unless you consider the example in Appendix C). This is a book that shows how to perform typical programming tasks. For example, the database examples show how to create multiple views of the same data, add, remove, and update records, and perform some mandatory tasks such as printing.

The example won't show you how to create a complex connection between your mainframe, a minicomputer, and several web server farms—I simply don't get into that much detail.

Tools Required

There are some assumptions that I've made while writing the application programming examples in this book. You need at least two machines: a workstation and a server. This two-machine setup is the only way that you'll see C# in action and truly know it works as anticipated. In addition, your development workstation and server must meet the minimum .NET requirements (and hopefully provide more than the minimum). You might experience problems with the database and other large examples if you're running a minimal machine configuration.

During the writing of this book, I used a Windows 2000 and Windows XP workstation. There's no guarantee that any of the code in the book will work with Windows 9x, although most of it will. The server was loaded with Windows 2000 Server with the latest patches and service packs installed. You'll need a Pocket PC–compatible PDA to work with the examples in Chapter 17. You must install the latest service packs for all products before the examples will work properly. .NET is a new technology and relies on the latest versions of many DLLs and the .NET Framework.

> **NOTE** Many of the concepts you'll learn in this book won't appear in your online documentation. Some of it's so new that it only appears on selected websites. You'll find either a tip or a note alerting you to the location of such information throughout the book. In addition, Microsoft made some material available only through selected channels like MSDN subscriptions. Other pieces of information are simply undocumented, and you won't find them anywhere except within a newsgroup when someone finds a feature accidentally.

I tested all of the examples in this book with Visual Studio .NET Enterprise Architect Edition. None of these examples are guaranteed to work with any other programming language products and none of them will work with the educational versions of Visual Studio.

Some of the example programs rely on a database manager. I used Microsoft Access for many of the examples in this book for the sake of simplicity. Other examples rely on SQL Server 2000 so that you can see the power C# when working in the database management environment. The CD contains copies of all of the Access databases and scripts for reproducing the SQL Server 2000 databases used in this book.

Conventions Used in This Book

It always helps to know what the special text means in a book. In this section we'll cover usage conventions. This book uses the following conventions:

`Inline Code`   Some code will appear in the running text of the book to help explain application functionality. The code appears in a special typeface that makes it easy to see. This monospaced font also makes the code easier to read.

`Inline Variable`   As with source code, variables that appear inline will also use a special typeface that makes them stand out from the rest of the text. When you see monospaced text in an italic typeface, you can be sure it's a variable of some sort.

`User Input`   Sometimes I'll ask you to type something and designate it with this typeface. For example, you might need to type a particular value into the field of a dialog box. This special font helps you see what you need to type.

`[Filename]`   When you see square brackets around a value, switch, or command, it means that it's an optional component. You don't have to include it as part of the command line or dialog field unless you want the additional functionality that the value, switch, or command provides.

`Filename`   A variable name is a value that you need to replace with something else. For example, you might need to provide the name of your server as part of a command-line argument. Because I don't know the name of your server, I'll provide a variable name instead. The variable name you'll see usually provides a clue as to what kind of information you need to supply. In this case, you'll need to provide a particular filename.

File ➤ Open   Menus and the selections on them appear with a special menu arrow symbol. "File ➤ Open" means "Access the File menu and choose Open."

italic   You'll normally see words in italic if they have special meaning or this is the first use of the term and its accompanying definition. Always pay special attention to words in italic, because they're unique in some way.

`monospace`   Some words appear in a monospace font because they're easier to see, they require emphasis of some type, or to immediately let you know they aren't standard English words. For example, all filenames in the book appear in a monospace font to make them easier to read.

URLs   URLs will normally appear highlighted so that you can see and refer back to them with greater ease. The URLs in this book provide sources of additional information designed to make your development experience better. URLs often provide sources of interesting information as well.

Notes, Tips, and Warnings

This book contains many notes, tips, and warnings to provide you with particularly significant information. The following paragraphs describe the purpose of each.

NOTE Notes tell you about interesting facts that don't necessarily affect your ability to use the other information in the book. I use note boxes to give you bits of information that I've picked up while using C#, Windows 9x, Windows 2000, or Windows XP.

TIP Everyone likes tips because they tell you new ways of doing things that you might not have thought about before. A tip box might also provide an alternative way of doing something that you might like better than the first approach I provided.

WARNING Warnings almost always tell you about some kind of system or data damage that'll occur if you perform a certain action (or fail to perform others). Make sure you understand a warning thoroughly before you follow any instructions that come after it.

You'll also find that I use notes and tips to hold amplifying information. For example, many of the URLs in this book appear as part of a note or a tip. The Internet contains a wealth of information, but finding it can be difficult, to say the least. URLs within notes and tips help you find new sources of information on the Internet that you can use to improve your programming or to learn new techniques. You'll also find newsgroup URLs that tell where you can find other people to talk with about C#. Finally, URLs will help you find utility programs that'll make programming faster and easier than before.

About the Author

I really enjoy learning computer technology and telling others what I have learned. So far, I've produced 54 books and over 200 articles that help other people understand computers and the computer industry. The topics I've covered range from networking to artificial intelligence and from database management to heads-down programming. Variety is the spice of life, so I've also written a number of user-level books. As part of my personal development, I've helped over 25 of my fellow authors by technically reviewing their books. Besides providing technical editing services to both Data Based Advisor and Coast Compute magazines, I've also contributed articles to magazines like *SQL Server Professional*, *Visual C++ Developer*, and *Visual Basic Developer*. I'm currently the editor of the .NET electronic newsletter for Pinnacle Publishing.

When I'm not working at the computer, you can find me in my workshop, enjoying wood-working and candle-making. On any given afternoon, I might be working at a lathe or putting the finishing touches on a bookcase. One of my newest craft projects is glycerin soap making, which comes in handy for gift baskets.

How to Contact the Author

You can e-mail me with your suggestions and comments at `JMueller@mwt.net`. I'm also setting up a website at `http://www.mwt.net/~jmueller/`. Feel free to look and make suggestions on how I can improve it. One of my current projects is creating book FAQ sheets that should help you find the book information you need much faster.

PART I

An Overview of C#

CHAPTER 1

Introduction to C#

- Why Introduce Another Language?

- Design Goals for C#

- An Overview C# and the .NET Platform

- Understanding the Benefits of Using C#

- When C# Isn't the Right Choice

M ost developers have at least heard about C#, and many have already written a "Hello World" application or two with it. C# is the newest language in the developer's toolbox. This is an exciting language because it fixes problems that developers have had with older languages when working in the distributed application environment. Microsoft designed C# from the ground up for use in a distributed application environment of the sort that developers use today. You'll find that C# combines the ease-of-use features of Visual Basic with the low-level programmability of C++. This chapter provides you with a brief overview of why C# is important and when you would use it. You can easily skip this chapter if you want to start coding right away.

Why Introduce Another Language?

One of the biggest questions that developers need to answer is why they need yet another language. The computer world is literally swimming in computer languages of various types. You can find a language to do just about anything today, and some of them do more than one task well. However, the problem isn't one of a need for new language constructs. Languages such as Visual Basic, Java, and C++ have the bases covered in that arena. In fact, C# detractors rightly point out that C# is the Microsoft version of Java, although we'll see that the similarities are superficial as the book progresses.

C# is an answer to a new problem: developers need a language that works well in a distributed programming environment. Applications no longer sit alone on local area networks (LANs) or in remote access scenarios between satellite offices. The application you build today might be in use on a partner corporation desktop tomorrow. The biggest problem developers face is that they really don't know where the application will end up. The application they create at design time may end up performing other tasks later on. The decision to move the application comes later, long after you've finished writing it. Consequently, the application has to be robust enough to work in remote settings across company boundaries.

Companies also force developers to complete applications faster today. In days gone by, it wasn't unusual for an application development cycle to last a few years. Today, companies measure application delivery schedules in months, and the developer doesn't get many of them. C# helps developers produce more code more quickly than ever before. However, producing code quickly doesn't buy you much on its own; the code must also be free of bugs, and C# helps answer that need as well.

NOTE   Don't believe all the hype about C#—it doesn't free you from every bug that ever existed and the presence of a debugger in Visual Studio .NET is confirmation of this fact. Microsoft has made vast improvements in debugging and application automation with C#. However, bugs are an ever-present enemy of the developer, and it's unlikely this situation will change any time soon. It's true that C# reduces the chance of a memory error because the .NET Framework provides management resources in this area. Unfortunately, the need to access existing API functionality means you don't always gain the full .NET Framework functionality, and the .NET Framework introduces new problems such as non-deterministic finalization—the inability of the developer to determine when the .NET Framework will destroy an object. Bugs *are* part of C#, they just have a new form.

In some respects, Microsoft is attempting to create that mystical language that serves all needs for everyone. When they first began to talk about C#, Microsoft presented it as a wonder language. The truth is that C# sits somewhere between Visual Basic and Visual C++ in capabilities. You gain the programming environment of Visual Basic with C#. Developing an application is no longer a painful experience fraught with odd coding techniques that create even odder bugs. On the other hand, you also gain much of the low-level functionality of C++. Unlike Visual Basic, where every attempt to use the Windows API is a major development experience, C# provides the same level of access that C++ does.

The question is whether C# is actually the wonder language that Microsoft thinks it is. For the most part, C# is a vast improvement over previous languages and it has many new features to offer. You'll find that it's a valuable addition to your programmer toolkit. However, I'd stop short of saying it's a one-size-fits-all language. For one thing, you can't create a native EXE file with C#, which is a problem for certain types of application development. In short, C# is a new addition to your existing toolkit, but you'll probably want to keep Visual C++ and Visual Basic around as well.

Design Goals for C#

Like any other development scenario, Microsoft had specific goals in mind when it created C#. The programmers at Microsoft realized that current languages lacked features that developers needed when writing applications for distributed environments. In addition, existing development needs, like tools for creating components, were often slow and cumbersome because of a lack of language functionality. In short, one of the overriding goals for C# was to create a language that would allow developers to become more productive. C# is a language that will allow fast development of today's applications. The following list looks at some of the other design goals for C#.

Improved productivity   Visual C++ is one of the most widely used languages for low-level development and in application development where flexibility is key. Unfortunately, that flexibility comes at the price of developer productivity. For example, writing a component in Visual C++ requires easily three or four times the amount of code than that of a comparable Visual Basic component. While you gain better control over the component code execution, you pay for it with extra code and the time/complexity that comes with that extra code. The goal of C# is to provide the same level of flexibility with increased developer productivity. (C# won't work for native EXEs; see the "Native Executable Development" section for details.)

Reduced complexity   Developers need to remember too many arcane facts right now. For example, data conversions can become a major source of problems for any developer. Because C# is a true object-oriented language, elements such as variables are treated like objects in most cases—especially during data conversion. This means you can use methods like `ToString()`, `Convert()`, and `Parse()` to convert between data types, even for data normally treated as values. The developer doesn't need to worry about memory management as much, since the Garbage Collector automatically frees memory used by variables. C# variables are also type safe and automatically initialized. In short, Microsoft looked for common development errors and attempted to find ways to resolve them. Accomplishing this goal makes C# more accessible to developers than a language like C++.

NOTE   We'll discuss the Garbage Collector several times in the book. The Garbage Collector provides the memory management features found in .NET. Whenever the Garbage Collector runs, it looks for and frees unused objects and resources. The Garbage Collector is one tool that .NET uses to reduce application errors, especially those related to memory.

Web standard support   Not every application created today will interact with the Internet, but a lot of them do. While you can use existing languages to create applications that will work on the Internet, most don't provide full support for web standards like eXtensible Markup Language (XML) and Simple Object Access Protocol (SOAP). The lack of web standards support makes applications run poorly, introduces security problems, or creates other hazards. Web support comes in other ways with C# as well. For example, you can use C# to write web services—a technique for sharing applications over the Internet. Of course, all of the other .NET languages provide XML and SOAP support, so this isn't a C# only feature. (Interestingly enough, you can't use Visual C++ for scripting in places such as web pages.)

Online Resources for SOAP and XML

SOAP and XML are new technologies that are in a state of flux. Consequently, you'll want to know where you can locate the latest information online. There are many useful online resources for SOAP and XML. The following list tells you about some of the more useful sites.

`http://www.soap-wrc.com/webservices/default.asp`   is a site where you'll find great SOAP information.

`http://msdn.microsoft.com/nhp/default.asp?contentid=28000523`   also has information about the SOAP specification.

`http://xml.org/`   is one of the better places to find XML information.

`http://msdn.microsoft.com/xml/default.asp`   also has good XML information.

`http://www.xml.com/axml/axml.html`   has an annotated version, which can be good when you find the XML specification a little hard to understand.

`http://www.webservices.org`   is of the better places to look for web services information in general. This site includes SOAP, XML, and .NET resources, as well as information about products and services from other companies.

Existing application interpretability   Your company has a lot invested in existing applications. Any new programming language will have to produce applications that can interact with those existing applications. While you can't use C# to write code for existing applications, you can extend those applications through components. A component written in C# will look just like any other component to older applications.

NOTE   You do need to register the component using RegAsm to make the component accessible. In addition, you need to either place the component in the application directory or use GacUtil to place a reference to the component in the Global Assembly Cache (GAC). A component requires less work than controls. If you want to create a managed control for use in an unmanaged application, you'll also need to add special interfaces, make registry entries, and perform additional testing to ensure that the control works as intended on the various Form Designer displays.

Short learning curve   Visual C++ programmers will see many familiar constructs in C#. Except for learning a few new rules and ways of performing tasks, C++ developers will be able to start using C# immediately. Visual Basic developers will see some familiar elements, but the learning curve will be a little higher. Fortunately, gaining access to low-level programming functionality is well worth the price.

Reliability   At one time, IT professionals looked at PCs as toys. Enlightened IT professionals might have looked at PCs as something useful for workgroup applications, but certainly not for anything mission critical. Today, developers do use the PC for mission-critical applications. The application has to work all the time and act in a predictable manner. The problem is that older languages don't tend to promote reliable application execution. In many cases, these languages leave fault detection as an exercise for the developer. C# changes all of this by taking a proactive approach to error detection and resolution.

Improved performance   This is one area where the way you use C# will affect the benefit you receive. Microsoft's goal is to make distributed applications run faster, not all applications as a whole. Features like mapping XML data directly to C# structs, rather than relying on classes, will make web-based applications run faster. In addition, you'll gain performance benefits from C# scripts compiled as part of ASP.NET pages. The use of features like Code Behind makes creating ASP.NET pages easier than ASP, and you can use mixed languages within the scripts (if desired).

Application and component versioning   Anyone who's gone through DLL hell will understand the importance of this feature. DLL hell occurs when you have two applications—both require the same DLL, but different versions of that DLL. The need to specifically override methods within a C# application reduces the problem of DLL hell by making the developer aware of the potential risks. Versioning support isn't automatic, but the goal, in this case, is to make the developer savvy about application interactions and what can happen when a method is overwritten.

NOTE   You'll find the .NET Framework in the \WINNT\Microsoft.NET\Framework folder of your machine. This folder contains one folder for each version of the .NET Framework installed on your machine. An application uses the version of the .NET Framework that was in use when the developer created the application. While keeping multiple copies of the .NET Framework on the user's machine does increase the hard drive requirements for .NET; it also eliminates the problem of DLL hell. The application packaging process includes adding a copy of the version of the .NET Framework used to create the application. The resulting package is larger than a native EXE package (by as much as 45MB), but definitely complete. The .NET Framework is only installed if the client machine lacks the proper version of the .NET Framework for the application.

Metadata Support   The goal, here, is to document and augment component behaviors so they reflect real-world processes. In many cases, there isn't any connection between a real-world behavior and the component implementing the behavior using older programming languages. By using metadata as a documentation technique, C# developers can create components that better reflect the business processes they're supposed to support.

An Overview C# and the .NET Platform

C# and the .NET Platform are closely coupled. In fact, every application you create will begin with a connection to the .NET Framework—the developer access portion of the .NET Platform. Yes, you can write unmanaged code under certain circumstances, but most people are going to want to use C# for its intended purpose of writing distributed applications. The easiest way to write managed code with C# is to use the .NET Framework.

NOTE   C# does support work with unmanaged code. In fact, C# uses the `unsafe` keyword to enable developers to create unmanaged code within their applications. Normally, you'll restrict use of unsafe code to methods that use pointers. However, the `unsafe` keyword is a powerful feature that you could use for a broad range of purposes. So, how do you gain access to the .NET Framework from within C#? Create any program and you'll see that this line of code appears in every case: `using System`.

This line of code provides ready access to a specific level of .NET Framework services added through a reference in your code. If you want to access other portions of the .NET Framework, you'll add other `using` statements to the beginning of the application. In some cases, you might also need to use the Project ➤ Add Reference command to display the Add Reference dialog box shown in Figure 1.1. This dialog box provides access to the various DLLs used to add functionality to your application.

FIGURE 1.1:

The Add Reference dialog box provides access to .NET, COM, and Project components.

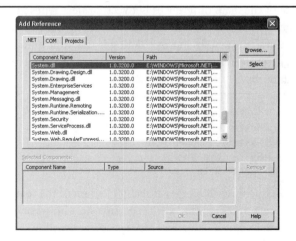

The .NET Framework uses a hierarchical list of services. Figure 1.2 shows a partial listing of these services as found in the .NET Framework SDK documentation. C# uses the same method (a menu entry) that Visual Basic does for adding references to these services. Adding the using System statement to your code means you don't have to write as much code—the compiler knows to look at the referenced service for methods it can't resolve normally.

FIGURE 1.2:

The .NET Framework relies on a hierarchical list of services.

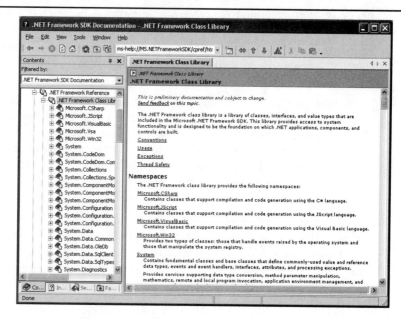

One of the main differences between project types in C# is the number and type of .NET Framework references automatically added to the project for you. The single reference shown in the examples in this briefing is the minimum for a console application. C# uses a more extensive list of .NET Framework services for even a small Windows application, as shown here:

```
using System;
using System.Drawing;
using System.Collections;
using System.ComponentModel;
using System.WinForms;
using System.Data;
```

Component developers will really like one of the features that the .NET Framework provides—easy access to the event log. Anyone who's worked with the event log in Visual Basic knows that while making an entry is easy, controlling the contents of the entry is frustrating at best because you don't have full access to the event log entries. Many Visual C++ developers don't even realize that you can make event log entries using API calls, and those who do wish for an easier way. Yes, you get full control over the event log entry in Visual C++, but the coding effort is a painful experience. When using C#, all you need is a reference to the System.Diagnostics namespace. The EventLog class provides complete access to the event log and with very little effort on the part of the developer.

As you can see, there's a tight connection between C# and the .NET Framework. You'll find that using the .NET Framework for your applications makes coding almost simple. As a result, the development cycle for C# projects is going to be much shorter than Visual C++ projects, once your development staff becomes familiar with the product.

Assemblies

An assembly is a complete compiled application entity. It contains the code and data for your application. The assembly also contains a manifest that lists the contents of the assembly and some of the assembly features. For example, the manifest contains the name of the company that developed the assembly. To gain a better understanding of an assembly, imagine creating the simple application containing two buttons. The application would display a simple message if you clicked one button and would close if you clicked the second. (You'll find this simple application in the \Chapter 01\Simple2 folder of the source code CD.)

Figure 1.3 shows the disassembly of the simple application. You can obtain this same view using the ILDASM (Intermediate Language Disassembler) utility to open the Simple2 application. As the figure shows, the assembly consists of the manifest and a `Sample` namespace. Under the `Sample` is the `SimpleDialog` class, which contains the buttons and other elements of the application.

FIGURE 1.3:

An assembly contains several elements, including a manifest.

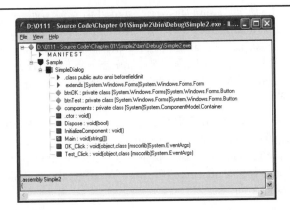

We'll dissect other applications as the book progresses because you can find out interesting information by disassembly and studying the IL created for your application. (See the "Working with a Common Language Base" section of Chapter 2 for details.) The point is that assemblies are an ordered method of packaging an application or an application unit such as a component.

Attributes

Attributes are special features that enable you to describe an application that would normally require code. For example, you can use an attribute to define an event receiver or an event source. A single word or short set of words serves to augment some code within an application or a component.

So, why is this feature so important? Imagine writing the components you always have in the past, but with as little as 25% of the code you use today. Less code means fewer potential errors and a shorter development time. Programmers from all walks are finding they have a hard time meeting delivery dates, and are given shorter deadlines and increasing application complexity. Any technology that promises to reduce development time using a tool that you're already familiar with is a welcome relief.

We'll use attributes a lot throughout the book. Attributes are such a useful feature that using them is an essential part of learning C#. Once you learn how to use the built-in attributes, we'll also discuss creating custom attributes. Using custom attributes can significantly improve an already great feature. (See the section titled "An Attribute Example" in Chapter 3 for details.)

Other Language Interoperatiblity

All of the .NET languages are designed to work together with relative ease. In fact, you can use a mixed language environment when scripting. A component you create in C# will work with Visual Basic because both use the same IL. Mixing and matching languages that rely on the .NET Framework doesn't require much work. If you want to use a Visual Basic component in your C# application, simply place the component in the project folder or register the component in the GAC.

Working with non-.NET languages is a little harder, but not impossible. You can use your managed component in an unmanaged application, or your unmanaged component in a managed application. Microsoft provides a special namespace: `System.Runtime.InteropServices` and some special attributes to make interoperability easier. We'll discuss this topic further as the book progresses.

Understanding the Benefits of Using C#

In the previous sections of the chapter, you learned what C# is and what it has that you didn't have before. This is important, but some developers will still say, "So what?" Yes, C# does solve many problems that developers have with older languages, but experienced developers already know how to get around those issues and may see C# as yet another language to learn.

The fact is that C# has a lot to offer developers from a personal perspective. I wouldn't say any of these features are earth shattering, and you've probably heard these promises for other languages in the past. C# actually delivers on these promises and makes life easier for the developer. Will C# make you a better programmer? Yes, in some ways. For example, it helps you catch more errors before they become problems. However, only experience creates great programmers.

Most developers will find that C# makes them faster and more efficient programmers. You'll spend less time figuring out how to code something due to an ambiguity in the development environment. In many cases, you'll also find that you spend less time searching for just the right API call or switch that isn't documented.

Now that you have some idea of what you have to gain from C#, let's discuss the topic in detail. The following sections answer the question, "What will C# do for me?" You'll learn why C# is such an important improvement in the development community.

Developer Productivity Enhancements

There's one overriding reason to use C#—it's the language of choice for many developers who work extensively with COM or other object-based development technologies. Spending even a small amount of time on the `microsoft.public.dotnet.csharp.general`, `microsoft.public.dotnet.vb.general`, and `microsoft.public.dotnet.vc.general` newsgroups shows widespread developer interest in C# as a language. (You can find all of these newsgroups on the `news://news.microsoft.com` server, if you can't find them on your local ISP.) Many developers on these newsgroups already plan to move to C# because it alleviates so many application development problems. In addition, Microsoft has submitted C# to the European standards group, ECMA (`http://www.ecma.ch/`), which means that the language will benefit from the efforts of a standards committee. (The `http://www2.hursley.ibm.com/tc39/` website contains a better description of the standards effort.) Finally, more than one company is interested in C#, which could mean some level of platform independence for the language. The high interest in this language, coupled with a standards-oriented approach, means that developers will want to adopt C# relatively quickly.

Now that we've covered the main reason to move to C#, let's talk about all of the reasons to use it. The following sections will tell you about the benefits of C#, the prototyping and development speed, and how you can use C# to create better COM+ applications.

Simplicity

C# adds simplicity to the development environment in several ways. We've already talked about how Microsoft has simplified the data types by consolidating some and adding others. For example, you no longer need to worry about which char data type to use—there's only one. Likewise, the new decimal data type will greatly reduce programming complexity.

The use of the .NET Framework will simplify matters as well. The hierarchical structure of namespaces will make it easier to find methods that you need. In addition, more system resources are available as methods, rather than API calls. For example, with C# you can now write event log entries using a simple method call, rather than using the convoluted method for Visual C++.

One item I haven't mentioned yet is the IDE provided with Visual Studio .NET. Microsoft has added a variety of automation features to the product. For example, when you type a statement name, the IDE will automatically add the required braces for you. This feature won't necessarily save a lot of time, but it should reduce the number of simple coding errors that programmer will have to find before an application compiles.

Managed environments simplify programming tasks. For example, C# will greatly reduce memory leaks using garbage collection. Of course, the use of garbage collection will also reduce debugging time because the programmer will have fewer errors to find. Since memory leaks are notoriously difficult to find and fix, most developers will find that garbage collection greatly reduces the amount of debugging time for a given project.

Consistency

There are many new types of consistency within C#. However, three forms deserve special mention because they have such a great impact on the development environment.

Everything is an object.   C# even treats variables as objects. The runtime environment "boxes" variables into an object when you need to perform a task like data conversion. Once the data conversion is finished, the variable is unboxed. The point is that you can access everything in the same way—there aren't any special rules to remember.

The .NET Framework ensures function call consistency.   Instead of having to remember a lot of very odd API calls, you just follow a hierarchy of namespace entries to the method you need to perform a specific task. Since every call is handled in the same way, the developer only needs to worry about the task at hand, rather than try to remember the odd exception to the rule that an API call might require.

Error trapping is easier than ever before.   Unlike Visual C++ and Visual Basic where there are a number of ways to detect errors, C# uses a single standard method. This means that developers can standardize error-trapping routines and reduce the complexity of finding and eradicating problems like data entry errors.

Modern Development Options

Visual C++ and other languages were developed at a time when the Desktop was king. Vendors updated these languages with moderate success for the world of client/server programming.

In the past few years, Internet development has become the area where most developers spend their time. Updates to these older languages now feel like kludges added to compensate for a development environment that vendors never designed these languages to address.

Given the need for distributed applications today, it's time for a new language that's designed to better meet the needs of modern developers. C# is that language. The use of a modern IDE and programming techniques will allow developers to gain the level of operating system access they require. We've talked about all of these features throughout this briefing, so I won't cover them again here.

Object Orientation

Unlike Visual C++ and Visual Basic, C# provides true object orientation. Everything is an object. This language does make some concessions for the sake of performance, but even in these areas, C# provides the means to use objects. For example, C# stores and uses variables in the same way that Visual C++ and Visual Basic have in the past. The difference is that C# can box a variable within an object, making it easy to access the variable as an object when needed. This means that C# provides the same level of object orientation that languages like Eiffel and Smalltalk do, but without the performance penalties.

C# also embraces the COM+ virtual object system. This means that all objects execute within a context. You can assign role-based security to objects, which means that you can allow user interaction based on the role the user has within an organization. In short, you have much finer control over the component execution environment.

Finally, C# gets rid of the global variables, methods, and constants. Everything appears within a class. This means there are fewer chances for naming conflicts and the data contained within variables remains safer. While it will take some developers time to get used to the new method of handling data, the result is more reliable components and applications.

Compatibility

C# provides an environment that's compatible with everything that has gone before. If you really want to use the old APIs that you used in C programs long ago, C# provides a means to access them. Likewise, you have access to standard COM and OLE Automation through the APIs you've used in the past. C# provides access to all of the required data types through the COM+ runtime.

Flexibility

You'll find that C# is extremely flexible. It can't quite do everything that Visual C++ can. For example, if you need a native code output such as a DLL or EXE, then Visual C++ is the only choice when using Visual Studio .NET. However, in all other ways, C# is more flexible than anything that has gone before. You obtain all of the best features of Visual Basic and Visual C++ in one package.

Faster Prototyping and Development

To provide an honest evaluation in this section, you have to separate the benefits of using the new Visual Studio .NET IDE from the benefits of using C#. For example, everyone has access to the autocomplete and help features that the Visual Studio .NET IDE provides. While the new IDE does help you work faster, you'd also receive this benefit when using other languages.

C# provides its own set of productivity features. The way Microsoft put the language together means you'll spend less time guessing and more time writing code. You don't have to worry about pointers any longer. That alone should save both development and debugging time.

You'll also find that the organizational benefits of C# help you prototype and develop applications faster. The consistent look of every class you create means you spend less time worrying about structure and more time coding your project. However, as with any other new product, you'll spend some time overcoming the C# learning curve before you actually see the benefits of the new way of creating classes.

When C# Isn't the Right Choice

Developers are always looking for the silver bullet—the solution that works every time. Unfortunately, there aren't any silver bullets in the computer industry. While you can bend a computer language to your will and force it to perform a task, some tasks naturally work better with some languages. C# has limitations—some architectural and some as a matter of convenience. The following sections tell you about the areas where C# isn't necessarily the best language choice.

Native Executable Development

C# is the language of choice for many types of managed application development, those types of applications that rely upon the .NET Framework. However, C# can't provide native executables, those that rely exclusively on the underlying operating system. In fact, the only way to generate native executables with Visual Studio .NET is by using Visual C++. The lack of native code development potential means you can't use C# in situations where native executables are the only answer. The following list provides some ideas on when you should avoid using C# because of native code development requirements:

- Older versions of Windows

- Drivers and other low-level programming

- Downloadable components

It's especially important to consider your knowledge of the client for application services. Many existing Windows platforms lack .NET Framework support, which means they can't run managed applications. Consider the fact that the client would need to download such support before using your component if you used managed code when a native EXE would work better.

Older Application Support

Most companies have a wealth of existing code that they can ill afford to move to another development environment. These older applications might work fine as they are today or require small tweaks in order to keep pace with current technology. Even if you decide to build part of the application in a mixed environment (part managed and part unmanaged code), it's often better to continue using the current language. Continuing with Visual C++ or Visual Basic makes sense from a developer learning curve and code maintenance perspective when an application already relies on these products and has nothing to gain from using C#.

However, you should differentiate a local monolithic application from a distributed application on the Internet. Developing new services for an existing application using C# could make sense if the service is used for generalized access. For example, a web service that provides support to a company database for your company and several partners might make a good candidate for C#.

Older Platform Support

Microsoft has been touting platform independence as the reason to use .NET, yet the .NET Framework doesn't even run on all Windows platforms yet. As of this writing, there aren't any plans to port the .NET Framework to older Windows platforms, and the deafening quiet from third parties indicates that .NET won't appear on your local Linux machine either. In short, .NET is very much platform dependent, and you need to consider this limitation as part of your upgrade plans.

If you're working with smaller clients that still own a mix of older and newer operating systems, then C# might not be a very good choice for application upgrades. A native EXE application upgrade that runs on fine on a Windows 95 machine is unlikely to work with managed code. Microsoft simply doesn't consider the Windows 95 platform viable any longer and hasn't made the .NET Framework usable with it.

Where Do You Go From Here?

This chapter has helped you discover some of the reasons that C# is such a great addition to your toolbox. You've learned why so many people are excited about this new language and have decided to use it for some types of projects. Of course, there's a negative side to most new technologie,s and this chapter has helped you learn about the areas where C# doesn't quite match the hype. You've also learned that C# doesn't fulfill every need, so it should be just one selection in your developer toolbox.

If you need more general information about C# before you move on to the programming examples that follow, make sure you check out the websites listed in this chapter. Two additional websites include C# Help (http://www.csharphelp.com/) and C# Corner (http://www.c-sharpcorner.com/). Both websites provide articles, tips, hints, and assorted source code. You might also want to spend time on the newsgroups talking to other C# developers. In addition, check out *Mastering Visual C# .NET* by Jason Price and Charles Caison (ISBN: 0-7821-2911-0; published by Sybex). This book covers the fundamentals of the C# language and how it works within the .NET Framework. It also covers the essentials for using ASP, ADO, and XML with Visual C# .NET.

Chapter 2 tells you about the .NET architecture. You'll learn about the underpinnings of C#—how it enables you to create Windows applications. The .NET Framework is an essential part of all managed application development in Visual Studio, no matter which language you use.

Working with the .NET Architecture

- An Overview of .NET

- How Will .NET Change Development?

- Understanding the Common Language Runtime for Visual Studio

- Advantages and Disadvantages of Using Managed Code

- .NET Forms and User Interface Support

- An Overview of the Visual Studio .NET Designers

Many developers who are reading this chapter have already worked with other languages under Windows. In the past, developers used the Windows API to access the operating system and the underlying hardware. The problem with this approach is that it's platform-specific. In addition, this old technique requires that the developer manage memory and perform other tasks. In many cases, the additional responsibilities are the source of bugs and memory leaks in the resulting application.

The .NET Framework represents a new, managed method for accessing the operating system and underlying hardware. It reduces the need for the developer to worry about "housekeeping" tasks and allows the developer to focus on the application development tasks at hand. Microsoft divides the .NET Framework into namespaces and classes contained within the namespaces. The hierarchical structure enables developers to locate .NET Framework resources faster and in a consistent manner across all .NET languages.

An Overview of .NET

What is .NET all about? It's a question that developers ask even after they begin using the product. The problem is that Microsoft's marketing staff sends out conflicting messages with documentation that promises whatever the marketing staff thinks the public needs at the moment. However, .NET doesn't have to be a mystery. For C# developers, .NET is a combination of these elements:

- .NET Framework
- Attributed programming
- Use of an Intermediate Language (IL)
- Common Language Runtime (CLR)

We'll discuss these elements in detail as the book progresses. For example, you'll find a discussion of IL in the "Creating the Custom Attribute" section of Chapter 6. We'll also discuss IL as part of the "Working with a Common Language Base" section of this chapter. However, it pays to have an overall understanding of what these elements do for you, before we begin to work with C# in earnest.

The .NET Framework is a bundling of routines. As you'll discover in "An Overview of the .NET Framework Namespaces," later in this chapter, the Visual Studio package includes two main namespaces. The first (Microsoft) contains Microsoft Windows–specific classes, while the second (System) contains classes designed for generic use. All .NET languages have equal access to the .NET Framework, and you'll find that there are few differences in calling the same methods from Visual Basic, Visual C++, and C#. (You do need to adjust the calls to factor language-specific features, such as the differences in the way Visual C++ and C# handle calling syntax.)

In pre-.NET languages, many developers were used to writing a lot of code to accomplish even the smallest task. Some developers reduced the amount of coding necessary for common tasks using macros or other productivity aids. .NET provides a productivity aid in the form of attributes. An attribute augments the code by providing a precise meaning for coding elements or by describing them in some way. We'll discuss attributes in detail in the "An Overview of Reflection" section of Chapter 6.

As described in Chapter 1, the Intermediate Language (IL) is the output of the C# compiler and linker. When you create a managed executable (EXE or DLL), you're really creating an IL file. All managed applications consist of IL that the Just-In-Time (JIT) compiler transforms into a native (machine language) executable. The main reason for using IL is platform independence. Theoretically, if you have a CLR for a platform, a managed executable will run on it, even if you created the executable on another platform.

NOTE   The use of IL to ensure platform independence is theoretical. Microsoft recently released a compact framework for the Pocket PC. Not only won't the compact framework run on every Pocket PC, but the compact framework also places restrictions on the calls you can use within an application. In short, if you create an application for a desktop machine, there's no guarantee that this application will run on every Pocket PC, even though it should in theory. (Some Pocket PCs have different processors than others, and different versions of Windows CE have quirks that prevent some common software from running.)

CLR (pronounced "clear") is the engine for interpreting IL. CLR uses a stack-based approach to working with data—there aren't any registers. If an application wants to add two numbers, it must first load the two numbers on the stack, then call the add routine. The add routine will pop the two numbers from the stack, add them, and then push the result back onto the stack. The application retrieves the result by popping it from the stack. Of course, CLR also relies on memory (the heap) to store objects—only values appear on the stack. The IL discussion in Chapter 6 will better show how CLR works on an application.

NOTE   It's important to understand that an application need only use CLR once. After the JIT compiler creates a native executable, the operating system will use it. However, if the operating system sees a change in the IL file, it uses the JIT compiler to create a new version of the native executable. As a developer, this means you're more apt to see worst-case performance on a continual basis.

Understanding the Common Language Runtime for Visual Studio

It's essential to understand CLR because it forms the basis of how you interact with .NET. Consider CLR as the new operating system for your applications, because it fulfills that role in certain ways. Your application will run on CLR, which in turn runs on the operating system. However, as far as your application is concerned, all it sees is CLR unless you specifically add unmanaged functionality to your application (and run in unsafe mode).

The following sections discuss four elements of CLR. You can summarize the sections as follows:

- Understanding the CLR DLLs and associated architectural details.

- Using the common language base as input to CLR.

- Defining the common elements of the .NET Framework (including namespaces).

- Learning to use the common .NET components.

What Is CLR?

The Common Language Runtime (CLR) is the engine behind managed applications created with Visual C++ .NET. In the "An Overview of .NET" section of the chapter, we discussed how CLR uses a stack-based approach to managing applications. In other words, the IL file contains directives for loading data onto the stack, performing an operation on the data, and then storing the data into memory. Because IL uses generalized instructions, the same file could potentially work on any platform. However, this is a theoretical advantage now because the only place you'll find .NET is as part of Windows (and not even all Windows, such as Windows 9x, support it).

The central part of CLR is MSCOREE.DLL. Every managed application contains a reference to this DLL. MSCOREE.DLL performs a lot of work on behalf of the application by managing memory and enabling the developer to discover every aspect of every type (not just those that are exported from objects, as in COM). CLR calls all standalone components or functional applications assemblies, and each assembly contains one or more types. COM uses a separate 128-bit key to identify each type. CLR uses a 128-bit key for the assembly, then refers to each type within the assembly using a strong name. The effect of both techniques is the same, just different; every type has a unique identifier, but CLR uses a different method to provide this identifier.

One of the advantages of using CLR is that it doesn't discriminate between languages. For example, under the old COM system, Visual Basic developers used one method (IDispatch) to define types and Visual C++ developers used a different technique (IDL). These language differences caused a number of problems for COM developers when working in mixed language environments. CLR uses a single technique to describe types. The binary format enables all languages to gain access to type information using the same methodologies. Here's the same interface described using C#:

```
namespace MathStuff
{
    interface IDoMath
    {
        short DoAdd(short Value1, short Value2);
    };
}
```

Anyone who's worked with components in an unmanaged environment knows about IUnknown and the VARIANT type. The first is the root type for all objects, while the second is the root type for all values. Both of these root types no longer exist under .NET. CLR uses a single root type, System.Object, for all types. Checking against a system or a user-defined type enables you to detect the type of an incoming value, which is more convenient and error-proof than previous techniques.

Given the number of differences between CLR and unmanaged code, MSCOREE must provide some means for translating between the two environments. Every time an application passes a value beyond the MSCOREE boundary, MSCOREE must translate that value in some way. The method used for objects is to create a Runtime Callable Wrapper (RCW) or a COM Callable Wrapper (CCW), depending on the direction of data flow. A RCW acts as a proxy for unmanaged applications, while a CCW acts as a proxy for managed applications. Values are treated differently from objects. MSCOREE can marshal all of the values in the following list directly:

- Single
- Double
- SByte
- Byte
- Int16
- UInt16
- Int32
- UInt32
- Int64
- UInt64
- Single dimensional arrays containing any of the previous types

MSCOREE can't marshal some values directly—it must translate them before use. In most cases, this means conversion to a Win32 compatible type. Table 2.1 shows the values that require translation and describes the common method for translating them.

TABLE 2.1: Common Value Translation Methods between Managed and Unmanaged Applications

Value	Translation Method
Multi-Dimension Array	Marshals as a safearray, in most cases, or an interface in others.
Array of Complex Types	Marshals as an interface, in most cases, but can also use a safearray.
Boolean	Converted to a value of type VARIANT_BOOL or Win32 BOOL. The conversion depends on remote object requirements.
Char	Converted to CHAR for 8-bit values or WCHAR for multi-byte values.
String	Converted to BSTR whenever possible. Converted to LPSTR for 8-bit values or LPWSTR for multi-byte values if BSTR isn't possible. LPTSTR is supported for platform invoke (PInvoke) calls, but not for COM interoperation. Other conversions include ByValTStr and TBStr.
Object	Converted to a VARIANT for COM interoperation only.

Sometimes the translation type for a value isn't clear at the outset. In this case, if you need a specific translation type, you can use the [MarshalAs] attribute to achieve a proper conversion. One of the most flexible types in this regard is the String. The following code shows how you can marshal strings as various types.

```
public static extern void MyFunction(
    [MarshalAs(UnmanagedType.LPStr)] String lpString,
    [MarshalAs(UnmanagedType.LPWStr)] String lpwString,
    [MarshalAs(UnmanagedType.LPTStr)] String lptString,
    [MarshalAs(UnmanagedType.BStr)] String bstrString);
```

As you can see, CLR not only runs your managed applications, but also enables you to create a mixed environment with relative ease and data compatibility. CLR is the basis for running applications under the .NET Framework and it therefore pays to know how to work with it. In at least a few cases, this means knowing how to translate data between the managed and unmanaged environments—at least until Microsoft adds full development capabilities to the .NET Framework.

NOTE   Not every attribute is accessible using the default application or DLL settings provided by the IDE. For example, you must include the System.Runtime.InteropServices namespace to use the [MarshalAs] attribute.

What happens when CLR completely fails to provide a needed service? It's at this point that the whole idea of a managed environment breaks down. At some point, you'll find yourself importing parts of the Windows API using the [DllImport] attribute. We'll discuss the use of various attributes in Chapter 3.

Working with a Common Language Base

One of the elements of the .NET Architecture that takes developers by surprise is the use of a common language base. IL is the common language base for all .NET languages. In fact, it's quite possible to develop an application using IL if desired. The ILASM utility accepts IL files as input and compiles them into assemblies that CLR can read. Of course, this would be an extremely painful way to develop applications.

The best way to learn about IL is to take some applications apart and see how the IL code compares to the code you write. Listing 2.1 shows the source code for a modified version of the Simple2 application from Chapter 1. As you can see, it performs some very basic operations that are perfect for examining CLR at work.

Listing 2.1   **A Simple Coding Example Reveals How IL Works**

```
protected void Test_Click(object sender, System.EventArgs e)
{
    String   Message; // Display Message.
    int      Value1;  // First value.
    int      Value2;  // Second value.
    int      Total;   // Total of two values.

    // Initialize and add the two values.
    Value1 = 1;
    Value2 = 2;
    Total = Value1 + Value2;

    // Create a message.
    Message = "The total of the two values is: " + Total.ToString();

    // Display the message.
    MessageBox.Show(this, Message,
                "Adding Two Values",
                MessageBoxButtons.OK,
                MessageBoxIcon.Information);
}
```

The complete application source code is on the CD, but Listing 2.1 shows the essential code we'll examine in this section. Figure 2.1 shows the ILDASM view of the application. Notice that there are entries for every component described for the application.

FIGURE 2.1:

Every managed application contains a manifest, namespace entries, and entries for each data type.

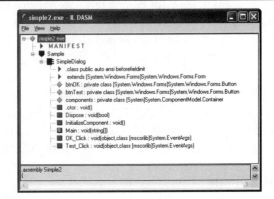

Double-click on any of these entries and you'll see the disassembled version of that entry. For example, Figure 2.2 shows the disassembled code for the Test_Click() event handler. As you can see, the output really does look similar to assembly language.

FIGURE 2.2:

Disassembling the code reveals the method used to convert C# code to IL.

```
SimpleDialog::Test_Click : void(object,class [mscorlib]System.EventArgs)
.method family hidebysig instance void  Test_Click(object sender,
                                           class [mscorlib]System.EventArgs e) cil manage
{
  // Code size      43 (0x2b)
  .maxstack  5
  .locals init ([0] string Message,
           [1] int32 Value1,
           [2] int32 Value2,
           [3] int32 Total)
  IL_0000:  ldc.i4.1
  IL_0001:  stloc.1
  IL_0002:  ldc.i4.2
  IL_0003:  stloc.2
  IL_0004:  ldloc.1
  IL_0005:  ldloc.2
  IL_0006:  add
  IL_0007:  stloc.3
  IL_0008:  ldstr      "The total of the two values is: "
  IL_000d:  ldloca.s   Total
  IL_000f:  call       instance string [mscorlib]System.Int32::ToString()
  IL_0014:  call       string [mscorlib]System.String::Concat(string,
                                                     string)
  IL_0019:  stloc.0
  IL_001a:  ldarg.0
  IL_001b:  ldloc.0
  IL_001c:  ldstr      "Adding Two Values"
  IL_0021:  ldc.i4.0
  IL_0022:  ldc.i4.s   64
  IL_0024:  call       valuetype [System.Windows.Forms]System.Windows.Forms.DialogResult [System

  IL_0029:  pop
  IL_002a:  ret
} // end of method SimpleDialog::Test_Click
```

At the top of disassembly, you'll see the local variable initialization. Each variable receives a number that IL uses for reference. For example, the very first call reads: ldc.i4.1. You can break this down as load the 32-bit integer constant marked 1 with a value of 1. The second instruction stores this constant in the memory location reserved for local variable 1. The same steps occur for local variable 2. The code shows that the next step is to push the values in local variable slots 1 and 2 onto the stack, call the add routine, then store the result (pop the value from the stack) into the memory location for local variable 3.

Manipulating the local string variable, Message, requires more work. Notice the routine begins by loading the string value onto the stack. It then loads the local value named Total. The routine then makes two calls. The first converts Total into a string value. Note that the string equivalent returns on the stack, so we end up with just two values on the stack: the Message string and the Total value converted to a string. Another call concatenates these two values. The final step is to store the result in the Message string memory location.

The final portion of this disassembly contains a single call to MessageBox.Show() method. The call requires four arguments in this case. Look at Figure 2.2. The LD* instructions load the stack with the data required for the call to MessageBox.Show(). The final call is to the MessageBox.Show() method. This call is rather long and you can't see the result in Figure 2.2. Figure 2.3 shows the disassembled version of that call. Notice that instead of the constants values loaded in Figure 2.2, you can now see the actual values for the icon and button used within the dialog box.

FIGURE 2.3:

The MessageBox .Show() method requires four input values.

This section also demonstrates a potential problem with .NET: Many developers fear that third parties will steal their code by disassembling it. Worst still, some developers see the potential for crackers to distribute virus-ridden code in their name. Hopefully, Microsoft will find a cure for this problem in the near future. We'll see later in the book that there's a partial solution for the problem now using strong names. You create a strong name by adding a key value to the AssemblyInfo.CS file of a component or application.

NOTE   For the purposes of this book, the term *cracker* will always refer to an individual who is breaking into a system on an unauthorized basis. This includes any form of illegal activity on the system. On the other hand, a *hacker* will refer to someone who performs low-level system activities, including testing system security. In some cases, you need to employ the services of a good hacker to test the security measures you have in place, or suffer the consequences of a break-in. This book will use the term hacker to refer to someone who performs these legal forms of service.

An Overview of the .NET Framework Namespaces

You can look at the .NET Framework in many ways. However, there's one undeniable use of the .NET Framework that all developers can appreciate: The .NET Framework is a method of organizing code to make it easier to access and use. Given the disorganized state of the Windows API, making the move to .NET makes sense even if your only reason is to gain a little sanity in the development environment.

NOTE   Microsoft promises a lot from the .NET Framework, but doesn't always deliver precisely what developers want. The .NET Framework is a work in progress. You'll discover that the .NET Framework doesn't provide complete coverage at this point, so you'll need to access the Windows API to perform selected tasks. For example, if you want 3D graphics, you'll need to access the Windows API or use DirectX—the .NET Framework offers nothing to meet your needs. We'll discuss some of these problem areas as the book progresses.

As you begin creating your own applications, you'll develop libraries of routines that you can use in more than one application. C# has no rule stating that you must place these classes within namespaces, but namespaces are a great organizational tool, especially if you plan to share this code with anyone. Using a company namespace helps prevent confusion in shared code. If two companies create a class or method of the same name, using a namespace can provide the distinction needed to avoid problems with application code.

Microsoft provides two namespaces with the .NET Framework. The first namespace, Microsoft, contains access to what you might term as Windows-specific functionality. For example, this is the namespace that contains the Registry classes and you'll use classes in this namespace to manage power. The second namespace is System. The System namespace contains framework-generic classes. For example, this is the namespace that defines the data types used within C#.

The Microsoft Namespace

The Microsoft namespace contains everything that isn't directly related to the .NET Framework. For example, this is the namespace where you'll find Registry classes. It's also the namespace used to hold language-specific namespaces such as the Microsoft.CSharp namespace. (Visual C++ .NET is a special case because it can produce native executable files, so you won't see a Microsoft.VC++ namespace in the list.) As other vendors introduce additions to the Visual Studio .NET environment, you'll likely see namespaces added under these other names.

> **TIP**   You can access any namespace desired within your applications. This feature means you can theoretically create mixed language applications by using more than one language namespace within your application file. The wizards automatically add a reference to the base language you're using for the application, but you can easily add others as needed. The only problem with mixing languages within a single file is the confusion it would create for developers who modify the code after you.

The most important namespace is `Microsoft.Win32`. This namespace provides you with limited access to the Windows 32-bit API. Always check this namespace for an API feature before you resort to using PInvoke to gain access to a Windows API feature. (Make sure you check the System namespace as well—some Windows API features are hidden in arcane places.)

Unfortunately, you'll find a limited number of Windows API features in this version of the .NET Framework. However, the features you do have are important. For example, you can access the Registry as shown in Listing 2.2. (Note that the full source for this example appears on the CD—the listing only shows the core code for the example.) Figure 2.4 shows the dialog box used for this example. The four buttons have names of `btnOK`, `btnAddEntry`, `btnDeleteEntry`, and `btnReadEntry`. The textbox control uses a name of `txtRegEntry`.

FIGURE 2.4:

The Registry example test form

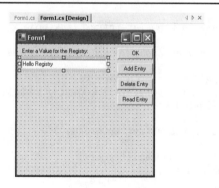

⊃ **Listing 2.2**   **Accessing the Registry with .NET**

```csharp
private void btnOK_Click(object sender, System.EventArgs e)
{
    // Close the application.
    Close();
}

private void btnAddEntry_Click(object sender, System.EventArgs e)
{
```

```
   RegistryKey oReg;     // Hive Registry Key
   RegistryKey oSub;     // Company storage key.

   // Open the HKEY_LOCAL_MACHINE\Software key for writing.
   oReg = Microsoft.Win32.Registry.LocalMachine.OpenSubKey(
            "Software",
            true);

   // Write the company subkey.
   oReg.CreateSubKey("MyCompany");

   // Write the default value.
   oSub = Microsoft.Win32.Registry.LocalMachine.OpenSubKey(
            "Software\\MyCompany",
            true);
   oSub.SetValue(null, txtRegEntry.Text);

   // Close the registry keys.
   oReg.Close();
   oSub.Close();

   // Enable the read and delete buttons after we add a new
   // registry entry.
   btnReadEntry.Enabled = true;
   btnDeleteEntry.Enabled = true;
}

private void btnDeleteEntry_Click(object sender, System.EventArgs e)
{
   RegistryKey oSub; // Company storage key.

   // Delete the MyCompany key.
   oSub = Microsoft.Win32.Registry.LocalMachine.OpenSubKey(
      "Software",
      true);
   oSub.DeleteSubKey("MyCompany");

   // Close the registry key.
   oSub.Close();

   // Enable the read and delete buttons after we add a new
   // registry entry.
   btnReadEntry.Enabled = false;
   btnDeleteEntry.Enabled = false;
}

private void btnReadEntry_Click(object sender, System.EventArgs e)
{
   RegistryKey oSub;     // Company storage key.
   String      RValue;   // Stored key value.
```

```
    // Read the stored value and display it.
    oSub = Microsoft.Win32.Registry.LocalMachine.OpenSubKey(
        "Software\\MyCompany");
    RValue = (String)oSub.GetValue(null);
    MessageBox.Show(RValue,
                    "Stored Registry Value",
                    MessageBoxButtons.OK,
                    MessageBoxIcon.Information);

    // Close the registry keys.
    oSub.Close();
}
```

Each of the buttons works in a similar fashion, but each shows a distinct part of working with the Registry. The RegistryKey class enables you to work with Registry objects. However, you'll use the Registry class to gain access to one of the six main Registry divisions, as shown in Table 2.2.

TABLE 2.2: Registry Class Instances

Instance	Associated Registry Key
ClassesRoot	HKEY_CLASSES_ROOT
CurrentUser	HKEY_CURRENT_USER
LocalMachine	HKEY_LOCAL_MACHINE
Users	HKEY_USERS
CurrentConfig	HKEY_CURRENT_CONFIG
PerformanceData	HKEY_PERFORMANCE_DATA
DynData	HKEY_DYN_DATA

The btnAddEntry_Click() event handler actually creates two Registry key objects. To add a new key, you must first open the parent key, then use the CreateSubKey() method to create the sub key. Once the sub key exists, the code creates a second Registry key object that points to the new sub key. You can't change the existing parent key to point to the new location, so the second key is a requirement.

The SetValue() and GetValue() methods enable you to write and read Registry values. Note that you can only write to the Registry if you enable write access. The various Registry methods assume you want read-only access unless you specify write access as part of the OpenSubKey() method call by supplying *true* as the second argument. Figure 2.5 shows the results of the btnAddEntry_Click() event handler code.

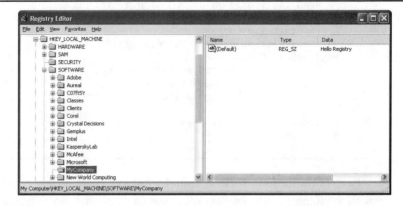

Every Registry routine must end in the same way. Use the Close() method to signify that you no longer require the RegistryKey object. In addition, Close() flushes the Registry changes to the Registry—ensuring the Registry records them. This is an especially important consideration when working with remote Registry entries.

Another consideration when working with the Registry is that many calls assume generic objects. The use of generic types methods means you'll need to perform type conversions in many cases. For example, look at the GetValue() method call found in the btnRead-Entry_Click() event handler. As you can see, the return of a generic object means converting the value to a string.

The System Namespace

The System namespace contains the bulk of the namespaces and classes you'll use to create an application. In fact, this namespace is too vast to even summarize properly in a single section. We'll discuss this namespace in detail as the book progresses. In general, anything that more than one programming language could use on more than one platform will appear in this namespace (at least, that's the theory). This namespace includes all type, data access, drawing, data communication (including XML and XML derivatives), component, storage, service, and management classes. The System namespace also includes diagnostic, debug, and trace namespaces used to make application development easier.

You do need to know about some System namespaces to begin programming. Of course, everything you create will contain a reference to the System namespace, but there are other common namespaces. For example, every application you create will include the following namespaces because they're used to begin the application design process.

- System.Drawing
- System.Collections

- `System.ComponentModel`
- `System.Windows.Forms`
- `System.Data`

The Application Wizard also includes the associated DLL support within your application when you define it. For example, the `System.Drawing` namespace appears within the `System.Drawing.DLL` file, not within the standard system files. You don't need drawing support to create a component, so keeping this functionality in a separate DLL makes sense.

Most projects contain a reference to the `System.ComponentModel` namespace, because this namespace contains basic control and component behavior classes. For example, this namespace contains the various `License` classes used to enable and verify licensing for the third-party components and controls used in your application. This namespace also contains the Toolbox classes required to support controls and components in the Toolbox.

The `System.Windows.Forms` namespace contains classes associated with Windows forms. If you want to display any type of information on a form, you need this namespace in your application. In fact, you can't display so much as a message box without it (unless you want to go the PInvoke route). This namespace also contains all of the controls normally associated with forms such as `Button` and `DataGrid`.

In many cases, you can actually create applications without the `System.Data` namespace. This namespace includes support for many types of data access (ODBC.NET is an exception). The reason the wizard includes this namespace is to enable support for the DataGrid and other data bound controls. You can remove this support for smaller, non-database applications and save some memory. However, the gains you obtain by omitting the namespace are small, because Visual Studio .NET optimizes applications to use only the namespaces they actually reference.

Developers will want to learn about the `System.Diagnostics` namespace because it contains classes that enable you to learn more about problems in your application. We'll use the `Trace` and `Debug` classes relatively often in the book. The `EventLog` class should also be on the top of your list because it helps you record component errors in a place where the network administrator will see them.

In the past, working with the `EventLog` could be a painful experience. Visual C++ required a lot of obscure code to work with the `EventLog`, while Visual Basic provided incomplete support (which meant incomplete and often useless entries). Listing 2.3 shows a typical example of event log entry code for a .NET application. (You'll find the complete source in the \Chapter 02\Diagnose folder on the CD.)

Listing 2.3 **Working with Event Logs in .NET**

```
private void btnTest_Click(object sender, System.EventArgs e)
{
    // Create some raw data to store with the log entry.
    byte    []RawData = {82, 97, 119, 32, 68, 97, 116, 97};

    // Open the Application log.
    EventLog AppLog = new EventLog("Application");
    AppLog.Source = this.ToString();

    // Write the event to the Application log.
    AppLog.WriteEntry("This is a test entry",
                      EventLogEntryType.Information,
                      200,
                      100,
                      RawData);

    // Close the log.
    AppLog.Close();
}
```

The first thing you should notice is the array of byte in the form of the RawData variable. In this case, the RawData variable actually contains "Raw Data" (as we'll see later). You must convert all text to byte values, which could prove time-consuming if you don't have a function for doing so, especially when you use the event log regularly and need to convert long strings. In this case, the entry is short, so using a direct conversion makes sense.

Even though the documentation says you don't need to provide a string with the Event-Log() constructor, it usually pays to provide at least the log name, as shown in Listing 2.3. Adding the log name ensures the event entries go to the right log on the machine. Other constructor overrides enable you to assign both a source and a machine name to the log entry.

If you don't provide the source as part of the EventLog() constructor, you must set the Source property separately, as shown in Listing 2.3. Notice that the example uses this .ToString() instead of a string. Using this technique produces an interesting result that we'll see during the example test.

You'll use the WriteEntry() method to create a new event log entry. The method accepts an error message string, the type of event log entry (Warning, Error, or Information), an EventID, category, and some raw data. Other overrides enable you to provide less information than shown.

Finally, make sure you close the event log before you exit the application. The Close() method frees resources and ensures the data is flushed to the log. Flushing the data is especially important for remote machine scenarios.

When you run the application and click Test, it makes an event log entry. Figure 2.6 shows the Event Viewer display. Notice that the Source column contains the name of the application class, as well as the text from the form's title bar. The reason that this is such as valuable way to make an event log entry is that you gain a better understanding into the source of the error.

FIGURE 2.6:

The Event Viewer shows the results of creating an event log entry.

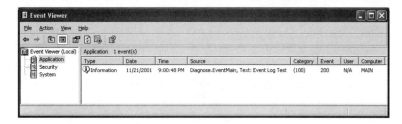

Double-clicking the event log entry reveals the details shown in Figure 2.7. Notice that the event log entry contains the raw data we added to the `WriteEntry()` call. You can also see the error description. Of course, you'll want to make a real entry far more useful by including complete diagnostic information.

FIGURE 2.7:

The Event Properties dialog contains detailed information about the event.

Working with .NET Components

One of the biggest concerns that Microsoft has tried to address in .NET is the problem of DLL hell. The use of separate folders for each version of the .NET Framework, the Global Assembly Cache (GAC), and other versioning measures have made it a lot easier to avoid DLL hell. In fact, a developer would have to work at creating a DLL hell situation—the development environment tends to support application versioning.

What does this new level of support mean to the application developer? In the past, every component you created ended up in the Registry because the IDE registered the component as part of the build process. The .NET Framework no longer relies on the Registry to store component data. The information is stored within the assembly as part of the component. While this technique certainly avoids confusion caused by old Registry entries, it begs the question of how an application will find the component support it will require.

.NET provides two methods for working with components. The first is the private component method. Simply copy the components you need to the application's BIN folder. The application will look in this folder for any components it needs so there's no requirement for a central information store. Because the component contains all the information that used to appear within the Registry as part of the assembly, the Registry is superfluous. This technique also avoids DLL hell by keeping a copy of the component required for application execution with the application.

The second method is to create a public entry for the component in the GAC. If an application can't find a copy of the component it needs in the BIN folder, it automatically looks for the component in the GAC. Note that the GAC stores the version and strong name information for the component as part of the entry as shown in Figure 2.8. (The GAC normally appears in the \Windows\Assembly folder as shown in the figure.)

FIGURE 2.8:

The GAC provides centralized storage for public components.

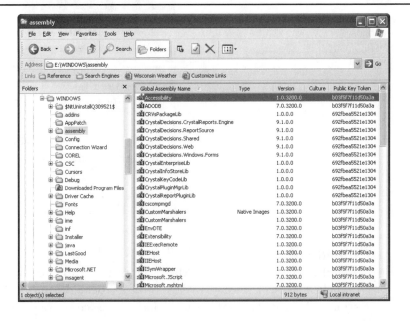

The application will look for the specific version of the component used to create the application in the GAC. The GAC can also contain multiple versions of the same component to help ensure compatibility. Notice that the GAC display also makes provision for the component type and the culture (locale) information. You can include several copies of a component based on locale, even if the components are the same version. The Public Key Token field relates to the assignment of a strong name to the component. We'll discuss this issue in detail in Chapter 6. For now, all you need to know is that the key provides a unique way to identify the component and ensures that .NET will detect any tampering by a third party. In short, using a strong name not only ensures uniqueness, but aids in maintaining security as well.

.NET Forms and User Interface Support

One overriding goal of .NET is to make application development easier, especially distributed application development. Developers no longer have time to spend researching arcane function calls in the Windows API and even more time figuring out that the documentation is simply wrong. In addition, the Windows API doesn't even come close to providing an environment for distributed applications. The Windows environment of old assumes that every piece of code you create will execute locally and therefore have access to a standard display.

Creating a user interface, a really functional user interface, has been the topic of many books. It's not an easy task under the best of circumstances. However, .NET does reduce the complexity of creating a great user interface. The following sections will look at the ways that you can use the features that .NET provides to create an easy to use and understand interface for your next application in a short amount of time.

Active Server Pages

Active Server Pages (ASP) support is old news .NET. Developers have used ASP for several years now. During that time, developers have created a wish list of those new features they consider essential. This is the basis for the improved form of ASP found in Visual Studio .NET—ASP .NET.

You can still use all of your existing ASP files with ASP .NET. Unlike some parts of the .NET upgrade (such as ADO .NET, discussed later in the book), ASP .NET provides full backward compatibility. However, it also provides all of those new features that developers want.

Two of the most important features are Code Behind and ASP controls. One of the biggest problems with ASP files right now is that they mix code and HTML elements. The mixture makes ASP files somewhat difficult to read. Code Behind rids the developer of this problem by placing the script code for a page in a separate file. This technique also makes it easier to reuse existing code, because the code exists separately from the HTML elements used to render the results on screen.

Another problem with ASP is that it relies heavily on plain HTML tags to get the job done. The problem with HTML tags is they don't work like the controls found in desktop applications and they come with a wealth of limitations. ASP controls eliminate this problem by providing full control support for ASP development. The client still sees HTML tags, but the server-side entity is a control. In short, ASP controls enable the developer to create applications faster and with better functionality, without requiring anything new on the part of the user.

Let's consider a very simple example consisting of a Test pushbutton and a label. When you click the Test pushbutton, the web server displays a message within the label. Listing 2.4 shows the ASPX (ASP eXtended) page required for this example. (You'll find this project in the \Chapter 02\SimpleASP folder of the CD.)

Listing 2.4   A Simple ASP .NET Example

```
<%@ Page language="c#" Codebehind="WebForm1.aspx.cs"
    AutoEventWireup="false" Inherits="SimpleASP.WebForm1" %>
<!DOCTYPE HTML PUBLIC "-//W3C//DTD HTML 4.0 Transitional//EN" >
<HTML>
    <HEAD>
        <title>WebForm1</title>
        <meta name="GENERATOR" Content="Microsoft Visual Studio 7.0">
        <meta name="CODE_LANGUAGE" Content="C#">
        <meta name="vs_defaultClientScript" content="JavaScript">
        <meta name="vs_targetSchema"
            content="http://schemas.microsoft.com/intellisense/ie5">
    </HEAD>
    <body MS_POSITIONING="GridLayout">
        <form id="Form1" method="post" runat="server">
            <asp:Label id="lblOutput"
                    style="Z-INDEX: 101;
                    LEFT: 20px;
                    POSITION: absolute;
                    TOP: 16px"
                    runat="server"
                    Width="173px">
            </asp:Label>
            <asp:Button id="btnTest"
                    style="Z-INDEX: 102;
                    LEFT: 20px;
                    POSITION: absolute;
                    TOP: 55px"
                    runat="server"
```

```
                    Text="Test">
            </asp:Button>
        </form>
    </body>
</HTML>
```

Notice the page begins with a reference to `WebForm1.aspx.cs`. This is the glue that binds the web page to the associated script. We'll discuss the whole issue of bonding between the various ASP .NET elements in Chapter 15. All you need to know for now is that the connection exists.

You should already recognize the tabs within the `<HEAD>`. These tags remain unchanged from ASP for the most part. However, when you get to the `<BODY>` you'll notice that some things have changed. The page now contains `<asp:>` tags that enable you to describe the page elements using the same properties you would use on a standard desktop application. In fact, when you work with the pages in the IDE, you'll use the same Toolbox that you would for a desktop application. The feel of designing for the web is the same as it is for the desktop.

The code behind page, `WebForm1.aspx.cs`, looks similar to any desktop application you create with C#. The application does use some namespaces we haven't discussed yet and you'll find the control display code is missing, but otherwise it looks like a standard desktop application (see the file on the CD for details). Here's the simple event handler for displaying the test text within the label.

```
private void btnTest_Click(object sender, System.EventArgs e)
{
    // Output some text.
    lblOutput.Text = "Hello ASP .NET";
}
```

As you can see, the code looks the same as the code any desktop application would use. The only real difference is that it appears on a web page.

Control Additions and Modifications

Developers have had control support in the IDE for quite a few versions of Visual Studio, so controls as an entity aren't anything new. However, controls of the past have always provided an inconsistent interface and contrasting levels of functionality. Part of the problems with controls was the different types of interface support required by each language. We've already discussed the benefit of .NET with regard to uniform interface support. However, there are other issues to consider.

The first issue is one of functionality for existing controls. You'll find that all controls provide a basic level of support for common features, making the controls easier to use because they have a shorter learning curve. For example, all controls support basic properties such as Text. You'll also find common event support for common events such as Click. Finally, every control supports certain methods such as ToString() and you'll find they all use the same method for adding event handlers.

The second issue is new controls that are needed to address the requirements for distributed and data-oriented programming environments. For example, the new DataGrid control provides better data handling support. You can access both local and remote sources of information with little difference in programming approach. In addition, the same control appears in both Windows Forms and Web Forms, which means the knowledge you gain learning to use the control for local applications will also apply for remote applications.

Crystal Reports

Reports are the most important part of any database application. The only way that some people (like management) will ever interact with your application is by viewing the reports that it creates. That's why it's important that your application produce functional, easy-to-read, and great looking reports. Crystal Reports is one way to obtain great-looking reports with less work than creating the report from scratch using hand coding techniques.

Crystal Reports is especially important for database applications, so we'll discuss this utility as part of the database sections of the book. However, it's important to remember that you can use Crystal Reports for any type of data from any application.

Formatting Data

Data formatting is one of those simple, but nagging, issues for many developers—which method to use for converting data from one format or type to another. Of course, the easiest and most common conversion is to a string using the ToString() method. However, what if the ToString() method of producing a simple string isn't what you want? You can also use the Format() method found in the System.String namespace as shown here:

```
// The single integer value used for all conversions.
int myInt = 2345;

// Begin by displaying actual value.
string myString = "Actual Value:\t" + myInt.ToString();
// Currency format.
myString = myString +
    String.Format("\n\nCurrency:\t{0:C}", myInt);
// Decimal format.
myString = myString +
    String.Format("\nDecimal:\t\t{0:D}", myInt);
// Exponential format.
```

```
myString = myString +
    String.Format("\nExponential:\t{0:E}", myInt);
// Fixed point format.
myString = myString +
    String.Format("\nFixed Point:\t{0:F}", myInt);
// General format.
myString = myString +
    String.Format("\nGeneral:\t\t{0:G}", myInt);
// Numerical format (with commas).
myString = myString +
    String.Format("\nNumerical:\t{0:N}", myInt);
// Hexadecimal format.
myString = myString +
    String.Format("\nHexadecimal:\t{0:X}", myInt);
```

You also have access to all of the features of the `System.Convert` namespace. This namespace contains methods such as `ToDateTime()`, `ToBoolean()`, and `ToInt32()` that make it easy to convert from one type to another. The following code shows a conversion from a string to an integer.

```
// Create a string.
string myString = "234";

// Convert it to an integer.
int myInt = System.Convert.ToInt32(myString);

// Display the result.
MessageBox.Show(this, myInt.ToString());
```

You can also use the `Int32.Parse()` method to convert a string into its numeric counterpart. It turns out that there are other `Parse()` methods available such as `Int16.Parse()`. The point is that you have multiple ways to convert one value to another when working with .NET. Note that you can find all of these conversion techniques in the \Chapter 02\Convert example.

Understanding Boxing and Unboxing

The only native data types that are objects are the string and the object. C# considers all objects reference types and allocates them from the heap. Otherwise, whenever you look at a variable, you're looking a value. C# allocates all values from the stack. Generally, values are more efficient than references, but sometimes you need a reference to perform a specific task.

Continued on next page

C# calls the process of converting a value to a reference *boxing*, while going in the other direction is *unboxing*. Generally, you won't have to box or unbox values manually; C# will do it for you automatically as needed. However, you may run into situations when you need to box or unbox a value manually. The following example shows how to box and unbox a value. (Note that this example also appears in the \Chapter 02\Box_and_Unbox folder.)

```
// Create an integer value.
int myInt = 25;

// Box it to an object and display the type.
object myObject = myInt;
MessageBox.Show(this, myObject.GetType().ToString());

// Unbox it into a value and display the contents.
int newInt = (int)myObject;
MessageBox.Show(this, newInt.ToString());
```

When you run this code, the first message will tell you that the object type is still a System.Int32, while the second will show that C# preserves the value during the boxing and unboxing process. Everything about the value remains the same as before. The only thing that's happened is that C# literally places the value in a box. You can operate on boxed values as you would any other object. Note that you can use this technique to make structs appear as objects as needed.

GDI+

Anyone who's developed graphics applications under Windows knows that it's an error-prone process. You need to gain access to a device context, allocate memory, and remember to give it all up when you're finished. The Graphical Device Interface (GDI) calls are especially troublesome because they seldom follow the same syntax from call to call. GDI+ rids the developer of these problems by enabling access to the graphical environment through managed programming techniques.

Don't get the idea that GDI+ is a complete solution. Microsoft still has a lot of problems to iron out in this area. The biggest problem is the lack of support for anything but 2D graphics primitives at this point. Many developers, even those that work primarily with business software, require 3D graphics today. Business users need presentations with pizzazz to garner the level of interest needed to win new accounts or develop interest in a new idea. The lack of 3D graphics is a major concern.

Another problem is that GDI+ is slow compared to GDI and even worse when compared to DirectX. The reason that Microsoft developed DirectX is that developers complained the current graphics environment was too slow. The need for high-speed graphics doesn't disappear simply because the developer begins to use a new programming environment.

These two problems are just the tip of the iceberg, but they are significant problems that most developers will encounter when using GDI+. The choice you have to make is one of ease-of-use versus capability and execution speed. GDI+ removes the source of many bugs, but the cost is high. If you're working with relatively simple graphics and don't require 3D, the choice is relatively easy to make. GDI+ has a lot to offer to the low-end graphics developer.

An Overview of the Visual Studio.NET Designers

Visual Studio .NET includes a designer feature. A *designer* is a new name for something that's existed since the first versions of Visual Studio. It's the visual part of the IDE that enables you to create the user interface for your application, using what amounts to dragging and dropping controls onto a form. However, the support for visual development in Visual Studio .NET has changed.

The new designer support uses a componetized approach that enables you to use more than one interface for creating the user interface for your application. The idea is that you can use the set of tools that best match the requirements of the user interface. A web page has different design requirements than a desktop application does, so it makes sense to use an interface with the web environment in mind. In addition, this approach enables third-party developers to create additional designers for specific situations.

The three designers that come with Visual Studio .NET include one for Web (HTML) design, a second for Windows design, and a third for working with XML schemas. All three designers look approximately the same and work the same, but the type of display they create is different. When you work with the Windows designer, you'll create a form for a desktop application. The HTML designer creates a web page. The XML schema designer shows the relationship between XML entries including elements, attributes, and types.

The Windows designer contains a single tab because it doesn't have to hide any details from the viewer. The HTML designer contains two tabs, one labeled Design for the graphic view of the web page and a second labeled HTML that enables you to view the resulting HTML code. Likewise, the XML schema designer contains a Schema tab (graphical representation) and an XML tab (actual output).

You'll also find that you populate the forms for the three designers using the controls on the Toolbox or the data from the Server Explorer. We'll discuss both of these elements more as the book progresses and you create more applications. Visual Studio .NET provides methods for customizing both the Toolbox and Server Explorer, which means that you have a great deal of flexibility in the appearance of these two tabs. The tabs slide out of view when you don't need them so you have better access to the design area.

NOTE   The Web or Windows designer might not appear when you first open an application. To open a designer, highlight the appropriate form in Class View, then use the View ➢ Designer command to display the designer on screen. The same command works for both types of forms. Visual Studio .NET automatically chooses the correct designer for your needs.

The HTML and Windows designers begin in grid view. Most developers find the grid helps them design forms quickly, but some find the grid actually gets in the way and obscures their view of the control layout. You can also turn on the Snap to Grid feature. Whenever you move a control, it snaps to the grid. While the Snap to Grid feature does enable you to create neat forms quickly, it does hinder precise placement of controls on screen. You can override the current designer settings by opening the Options dialog using the Tools ➢ Options command, and then choosing the correct designer entry.

Where Do You Go From Here?

This chapter has helped you discover more about .NET. We've spent time looking at both the .NET Framework and CLR, both of which affect Windows development in profound ways. You've also learned about the various interface support mechanisms.

One of the things you can do to improve your .NET experience is to spend some time looking at the various .NET Framework namespaces. This is a new technology and you might not always find classes you need in the obvious places. In addition, learning about the .NET Framework helps you design your own namespaces—a requirement for projects of any complexity.

Chapter 3 will begin the process of creating complex applications. We'll discuss classes in detail. Of course, this includes a few class basics as well as programming considerations such as non-deterministic finalization (the fact that you can't determine in advance when C# will release a resource). You'll learn about such programming features as delegates and attributes. We'll create custom attributes, and you'll learn how to use reflection.

CHAPTER 3

A Quick View of Classes

- Class Basics

- Class Life Cycle

- Base Classes

- Delegates

- Attributes

C# is a true object-oriented language; we've seen many examples of this orientation in the book so far. As a result, classes are an especially important part of working with C#. You must create classes that the system uses to create objects. A class is simply a description of how to build an object. As shown in Chapter 2, C# treats all entities as values or references, both of which can appear in the form of objects.

This chapter discusses classes from a C# perspective. Experienced developers will find a few changes from Visual C++ or Visual Basic. The lack of global variables makes a difference in the way you design C# classes. You must pass every piece of data between classes through properties, fields, or structures. There's no concept of global data in C#, so you have to design classes to provide robust application support.

We'll also discuss the class life cycle. Garbage collection (along with other .NET Framework features) changes class construction techniques. You'll find that you don't have to implement certain class components such as a destructor. Working with C# also means learning to deal with problems such as nondeterministic finalization (an inability to determine when the system destroys an object).

Class Basics

Classes encapsulate code and the data the code manipulates. It's important to understand that the data and the code are never separate in C#. The C# approach means leaving behind some coding techniques you might have used in the past. However, you'll also find that the C# approach reduces the complexity of many coding scenarios, makes bugs less likely, and makes your code easier to read.

C# extends the idea of modularity and organization by extending it to the application as a whole. A C# application uses hierarchical design to an extreme. In fact, the Visual Studio IDE is designed to accommodate this feature so that you can view your application from several different "levels" using IDE (features we'll discuss as the section progresses). The idea is that you can view your application in an outline mode that makes design flaws easier to see and fix. More importantly, you can move from one area of the application to another with greater ease by viewing the code at a higher level.

Class construction means knowing how to use existing code, providing safe code access, and creating complex classes with the least amount of code. As part of creating classes, you need to know about working with base classes, delegates, and attributes.

Base classes   The concept of the base class is universal to all languages with object-oriented design capabilities. In many ways, this is the most generic of the C# class creation features. When creating a new class, you can inherit the capabilities of a base class.

Depending on the construction of the base class, you can customize class behavior by over-riding base class methods.

Delegates   Delegates are simply a new way to handle function pointers. However, the term delegate isn't simply a replacement for function pointer. You'll find that delegates have differences from function pointers that make class creation simultaneously easier and more difficult. The delegate object encapsulates a reference to a method within a class.

Attributes   Attributes are a means to augment the capabilities of your class. You can use attributes for a number of purposes and even create your own attributes to meet special needs. We'll discuss attributes throughout the book, but this chapter will introduce the attributes that you'll use on a regular basis.

The following sections will lead you through the process of creating simple (example) classes. We'll begin with the easiest console application class you can create and move onto examples that use additional C# features. The idea of this section is to show you how classes work in the C# world. We won't build complex applications or even delve very far into Windows applications. All of the examples rely on the console or are simple Windows application types.

Application Structure

Let's begin by looking at the structure of a C# application. Every C# application contains certain elements. The application begins with the hierarchical levels, listed here in order of appearance.

1. Namespace
2. Class
3. Method

Every application begins with a namespace that has the same name as the project. Of course, you can change the namespace to anything you like in order to maintain compatibility with other projects. We'll discuss the implications of namespaces in the "Working with Namespaces" section of the chapter.

Below the namespace level is the class level. The name of this class varies. If you create a console application, then C# assigns the class a name of Class1; Windows applications begin with a class name of Form1.

Classes normally contain one or more methods. Every C# application has at least one method in it called Main(). This is the method that C# uses as a starting point for execution. Every C# application has to have an entry point, and some types of C# projects often have more than one. For example, a DLL commonly has more than one entry point. Figure 3.1 shows a basic C# application.

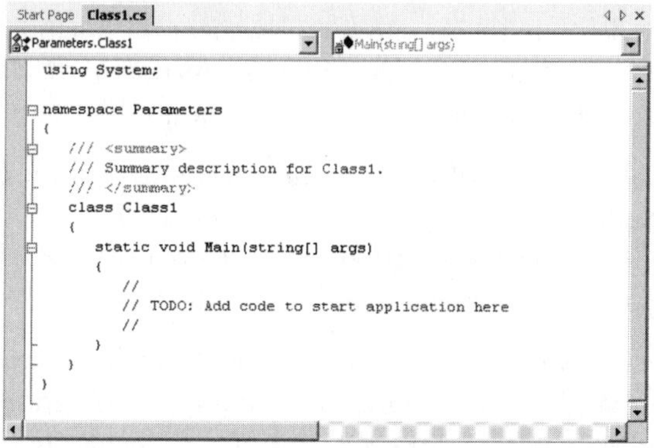

FIGURE 3.1:

Every C# application begins with the same hierarchical structure.

Sometimes it's hard to see the structure of your application. Even the basic Windows application contains a lot of "boilerplate" or default code. Look at Figure 3.1 again and you'll notice some minus signs next to each major code area. Click the minus sign, and you'll see that section contract. Using this technique enables you to see the structure of an application with greater ease. Figure 3.2 shows an example of a typical Windows application.

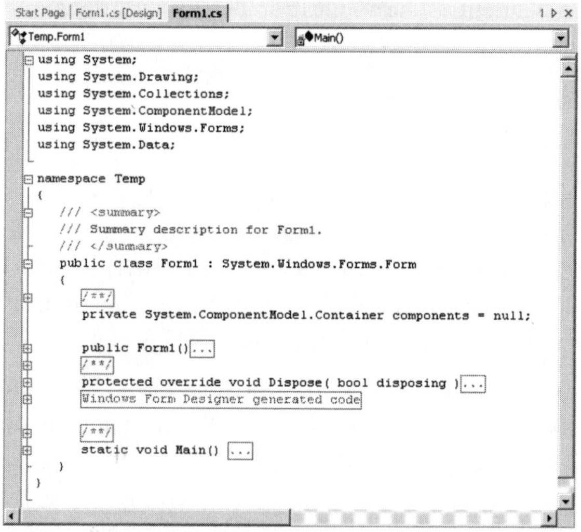

FIGURE 3.2:

You can use the IDE to help you see the structure of an application.

As you can see from Figure 3.2, a Windows application has the same elements as a console application. It contains a namespace, class, and at least one method. In this case, Main() doesn't accept parameters, but you can change this behavior. `Main()` does call on the application to create an instance of `Form1` as part of the startup process. A Windows application also includes a `Form()` method to display the graphical interface and a `Dispose()` method for releasing resources.

Figure 3.2 also shows the effect of using the IDE to display the application hierarchy. The ellipses next to each entry tell you that the application contains more code; you just can't see it now. Clicking the plus sign reveals the code for that area of the application.

Working with Parameters

It's not uncommon for class constructors to accept input parameters that configure the class in some way. In fact, many classes provide several overrides that enable the developer to select the most convenient method for creating the class. For example, a constructor might provide overrides that accept no parameters, a string, and an integer for the same class. Some overrides enable the developer to choose which optional parameters to provide with the constructor call.

We'll explore general class parameters in more detail in several sections of this chapter and throughout the book. For example, the "Working with the *Out* and *Ref* Keywords" section describes how you can pass values by reference. You'll also learn some parameter passing techniques in the "Understanding Methods, Properties, and Events" section.

This section of the book examines a special type of parameter passing—the type that occurs when you start an application. Many applications require input parameters (the type entered at the command line). For example, you can start Notepad with input parameters that automatically load a file or print a selected file. The use of parameters enables an application to automate certain tasks and make it user friendly. In some cases, you must include parameter support to enable your application to work with Windows utilities such as the Task Scheduler.

Adding command-line parameter support to your application isn't difficult. All you need to do is change the `Main()` method to accept the parameters, then pass the parameters to the initial class for your application. Listing 3.1 shows the essential parts of the Parameters example found in the \Chapter 03\Parameters folder on the CD. Note that this is just one of several methods for handling command-line parameters.

Listing 3.1   **One Method of Handling Command-Line Parameters**

```
static void Main(string[] args)
{
   string   []NoArg = {"No Argument Supplied"};

   // Determine the correct string to pass to the constructor.
```

```
        if (args.Length > 0)
            Application.Run(new Param(args));
        else
            Application.Run(new Param(NoArg));
    }

    public Param(string[] InputValue)
    {
        // Required for Windows Form Designer support
        InitializeComponent();

        // Process the input parameters one at a time.
        foreach (string Argument in InputValue)
        {
            this.InputValue.Text += Argument;
            this.InputValue.Text += "\r\n";
        }

    }
```

Notice the addition of the `string[] args` parameter to the `Main()` method. This is the entry point for data into the application. However, the user isn't under any obligation to pass any arguments, so the code needs to detect the presence of command-line arguments. You can perform this task in one of two ways. Listing 3.1 shows a technique where you detect the command-line parameters in the `Main()` method. A second method is to create two constructors. The first accepts parameters, and the second doesn't. C# automatically selects the correct constructor at runtime.

The example performs simple processing of the command-line parameters. It separates each parameter, adds it to a text box on screen, and then adds a carriage return so it's easy to see the individual command-line parameters. Figure 3.3 shows some typical output from the application.

FIGURE 3.3:

An example of
command-line
processing

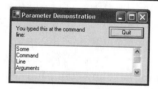

It's convenient to add the command-line parameters directly to the project so you don't have to keep a command prompt open for testing purposes. To add a set of command-line parameters to your test environment, right click Parameters in Class View and choose Properties from the context menu. Select the Configuration Properties ➢ Debugging folder. You can type the command-line options that you want to use in the Command Line Arguments field, as shown in Figure 3.4.

FIGURE 3.4:

Use the Command Line Arguments field to hold any parameters you need for testing.

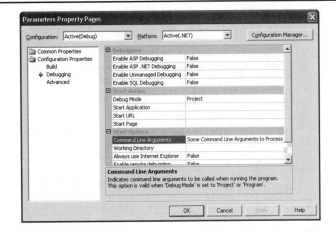

Working with the *Out* and *Ref* Keywords

C# makes a distinction between values and references. Any variable that keeps its value on the stack is a value. Examples of values include int and short. Any variable that maintains a pointer on the stack and its value on the heap is a reference. Examples of references include strings. We've discussed this issue several times in the book so far, but it's important to understand the distinction when it comes to the Out and Ref keywords.

> **NOTE**   You'll find the full source code for the examples in this section in the \Chapter 03\Reference folder on the CD. The listings show just the demonstration code.

When you pass a reference to a method in your class, any changes the class makes will appear in the reference when the call returns. However, when you pass a value to a method in your class, the value remains unchanged when the call returns. The Ref keyword enables you to change this behavior. If you add the Ref keyword to a method's parameter list, then the value reflects any changes made during the call. Listing 3.2 shows an example of this technique.

Listing 3.2   **Using the Ref Keyword to Affect Parameter Return Value**

```
private void DoReference(int Value1, ref int Value2)
{
    // Increment the two values.
    Value1++;
    Value2++;
```

```
    }

    private void btnRefTest_Click(object sender, System.EventArgs e)
    {
        // Create two variables and assign them values.
        int   Value1 = 1;
        int   Value2 = 1;

        // Call a function using a reference for one and standard
        // calling technique for the other.
        DoReference(Value1, ref Value2);

        // Display the results.
        MessageBox.Show("Value1 Results: " + Value1.ToString() +
                        "\r\nValue2 Results: " + Value2.ToString(),
                        "Output of Reference Test",
                        MessageBoxButtons.OK,
                        MessageBoxIcon.Information);
    }
```

Notice that the first value is passed normally, while the second value uses the ref keyword. Both values are int and initialized to 1. However, on return to the call from DoReference(), Value2 contains 2, not 1 as normal. Figure 3.5 shows the output from this example.

FIGURE 3.5:

Using the Ref keyword properly can help you extend the flexibility of your applications.

NOTE One rule you must observe when using the Out and Ref keywords is that the keyword must appear at both the calling and receiving methods. C# will remind you to add the keywords if you fail to include them on one end of the call.

The Out keyword serves a different purpose from the Ref keyword. In this case, it enables you to pass an uninitialized value to a method and receive it back initialized to some value. You gain three benefits when using this technique.

- Slight performance gain by passing the value once
- Less code
- Slightly lower memory cost

You won't see huge gains by using the Out keyword, but they're real nonetheless. The point of this keyword is that you can create the value locally, but expect the called method to perform all of the work for you. Listing 3.3 shows a quick example of the Out keyword.

Listing 3.3   Using the Out Keyword to Affect Parameter Initialization

```
private void DoOut(out int Value1)
{
   // Initialize the value.
   Value1 = 3;
}

private void btnOutTest_Click(object sender, System.EventArgs e)
{
   // Create a variable, but don't initialize it.
   int   Value1;

   // Call a function using the Out keyword.
   DoOut(out Value1);

   // Display the result.
   MessageBox.Show("Value1 Results: " + Value1.ToString(),
                   "Output of Out Test",
                   MessageBoxButtons.OK,
                   MessageBoxIcon.Information);
}
```

As you can see, the calling routine creates Value1, but doesn't initialize it. DoOut() performs the task of initializing Value1. Of course, this is a very simple example of how the Out keyword works. Figure 3.6 shows the output from this example.

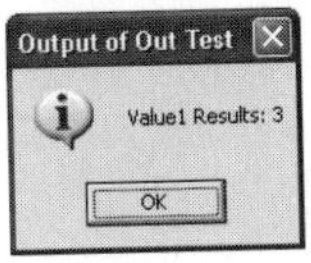

FIGURE 3.6:

The Out keyword allows you to pass uninitialized values to a method.

Working with Namespaces

Nothing in the C# standard says you *must* use namespaces. You can create classes by themselves and use them as needed. The point behind using namespaces is organization. Using a namespace enables you to gather all of the classes you create in one place, even if they exist in separate files. In addition, using namespaces helps avoid potential name clashes between vendors. If two vendors choose the same name for a class, then C# will constantly flag ambiguous references in your code.

The namespace isn't a one-level phenomenon. You can use several levels of namespaces to organize your code. In fact, Microsoft followed this procedure when creating the .NET Framework. Look at the System namespace and you'll see it contains several levels of other namespaces.

Creating multiple levels of namespaces in your own code is relatively easy. All you need to do is define a namespace within the confines of another namespace as shown here:

```
namespace Sample
{
    public class Class0
    {
        public Class0()
        {
        }
    }
    namespace MyFirstNamespace
    {
        public class Class1
        {
            public Class1()
            {
            }
        }
    }
    namespace MySecondNamespace
    {
        public class Class2
        {
            public Class2()
            {
            }
        }
    }
}
```

Notice that the Sample namespace contains a combination of classes and namespaces. You can mix and match classes and namespaces as needed to achieve your organizational goals. The important consideration is keeping the classes organized so they're easy to find.

The namespaces use a dot syntax. If you want to access Class1 in the previous example, you need to access it through Sample.MyFirstNamespace. Figure 3.7 shows the Object Browser view of this set of namespaces and classes. Of course, a read class library would contain more classes within the namespaces than are shown in the example.

FIGURE 3.7:

Use namespaces to
organize your code.

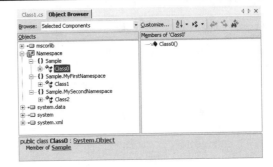

Understanding Methods, Properties, and Events

Methods, properties, and events are the three essential constructs of COM classes. All three elements still exist in .NET, but you'll find that some of the rules for creating and using them have changed. In addition, .NET introduces an event substitute called the delegate that we'll discuss in the "Delegates" section of the chapter. In short, you need to be aware of some changes in the way that you work with classes.

You've already seen several examples of methods in the chapter. Methods have changed the least from the days of COM. The only rule you need to remember beyond those used in the past is that a method must exist within a class. You can't create a global method as you could in previous versions of Visual Studio.

The placement of methods within the class affects the visibility of the method. The visibility of the class also affects the external visibility of the method. However, the class still has a visibility indicator that tells its internal visibility. Table 3.1 shows how internal and external visibility interact to create specific method visibility conditions. The table also tells which combinations the Common Language Specification (CLS) supports directly.

TABLE 3.1: Member Access Specifiers for Managed Code

External Access	Internal Access	CLS	Result
public	public	public	Accessible by any code that accesses the class.
public	protected	famorassem	Limits accessibility to types in the same assembly or types derived from the containing type. A derived type doesn't have to appear in the same assembly.
public	private	assem	Only types within the same assembly have access.
protected	public	N/A	Accessible by code in any derived type and within the containing type. A derived type doesn't have to appear in the same assembly.

Continued on next page

TABLE 3.1 CONTINUED: Member Access Specifiers for Managed Code

External Access	Internal Access	CLS	Result
protected	protected	family	Accessible by code in any derived type. A derived type doesn't have to appear in the same assembly.
protected	private	famandassem	Only accessible by code in a derived type if the code appears in the same assembly.
private	public	N/A	Fully accessible from code within the containing type and subclasses.
private	protected	N/A	Fully accessible from code within the containing type and visible to subclasses.
private	private	private or privatescope	When used with a method, only accessible from code within the containing type. When used with a static variable, the member isn't accessible at all.

Creating a property is easy in C#. Like methods, properties have a visibility indicator that defines how other objects interact with them. You use the Property keyword to create a property. In addition, you can make properties read-only, write-only, or read/write. Here's a short example of a property (the full component code appears in the \Chapter 03\Example folder on the CD, while the test application appears in the \Chapter 03\Property folder).

```
// Create the private field used to hold the data.
private string _Hello;

// Create the public property used to manipulate
// the data.
public string Hello
{
    get
    {
        return _Hello;
    }
    set
    {
        _Hello = value;
    }
}
```

Notice that the class hides the variable used to hold the data. Someone who wants to work with the property must use the public property. The get method enables read access, while the set method enables write access. The read/write state of a property depends on whether you implement either or both get and set. Note, also, that this is all the code you need to make the property persistent. Anyone who's spent hours trying to get COM to cooperate in storing values will appreciate the way .NET handles this issue.

When you add a property to your class, you'll see a special icon for it in Class View, like the one shown in Figure 3.8. Notice that Class View shows both the private field and the public property. A lock on the _Hello field indicates the private state of this variable.

FIGURE 3.8:

Look for the special symbol for a property and its associated field in Class View.

Creating Interfaces

An interface is a contract between the client and server that determines how the two will interact. The interface specifies the methods, properties, and events used for communication, without actually providing an implementation of any of these elements. In short, you should look at an interface as a blueprint for communication. In some respects, an interface is similar to an abstract class. The difference is that an abstract class is used as a base class to create other classes, while an interface is mixed in an inheritance tree that determines the behavior of a new class.

Creating interfaces is important when a developer wants to provide more than one implementation but ensure the contract between client and server always remains the same. The best example of interface use is in components and controls. Both rely on the use of interfaces to define their behavior. In fact, the interface is essential in determining how the client will react to the component or control. While the implementation of the interface varies by component or control, the usage of the interface remains the same, which allows client and server to interact using a standardized method.

NOTE   It's traditional to start an interface name with the letter I, as shown in the example code in this section. Using an I also provides a visual cue to anyone working with your code. However, the I is a convention and the interface will work just fine if you don't include it.

Defining an interface is relatively easy. You create a class-like structure that includes the Interface keyword and a description of the events, methods, and properties the interface supports (without any implementation). Here's a quick example of an interface.

```
namespace Sample
{
```

```
// Create a simple interface.
public interface ISimple
{
   // Methods only need to show an argument list.
   void MyMethod(int Variable);

   // Add properties without implementation,
   // but always include get and/or set.
   int MyProperty
   {
      get;
      set;
   }
}
```

As you can see, an interface contains a complete description of the implementation without the implementation details. A server implementing the interface will provide the implementation details. An interface also has a special appearance in Class View, making it easy to see. Figure 3.9 shows the interface created by the example code. You could also view the interface within Object Viewer. Because interfaces are so important to components and controls, we'll discuss this topic in detail in Chapter 6.

FIGURE 3.9:

The Visual Studio .NET IDE provides a special presentation of interfaces.

Class Life Cycle

Every class has a life cycle. An application creates an object based on the class using a constructor, uses it for a while, and then discards it. At some point, the garbage collection system will locate the object created from the class and free the resources that it used. In a few instances, the Garbage Collector will also call upon a destructor to free unmanaged resources, such as those needed for COM interoperability.

Understanding the class life cycle is important because there are some problems that you'll need to diagnose based on this understanding. For example, your application might experience memory problems if it creates a large number of short-lived objects. While Microsoft has tuned the Garbage Collector to prevent problems of this sort, you need to know when the Garbage Collector is to blame for a memory problem (and what you can do to fix it). Of course, the most basic fix is to dispose of your objects (a procedure that isn't recommended, in most cases, because using dispose indiscriminately can cause performance problems).

The following sections contain a description of the life cycle of a class. They help you understand some of the requirements for working with classes under .NET. The reason this section is so important is because .NET has a class life cycle that's essentially different from the process used in the past.

Working with Constructors

Any class you create should include a constructor, even if the constructor is empty. A constructor enables a client to create an instance of the object that the class defines. The constructor is the starting point for your class. We've already looked at several constructors in the chapter. As you've seen, constructors never provide a return value, but they can accept one or more input parameters.

One of the issues we haven't discussed is the use of multiple constructors. Classes with multiple constructors are quite common because the multiple constructors enable a client to create objects in more than one way. In addition, many classes use overrides as a means for handling optional parameters. One of the better examples of this second form of constructor is the MessageBox.Show() method, which has 12 overrides that enable you to use different types of optional parameters. Here's an example of an application that relies on a class with multiple constructors. (You'll find the source code in the \Chapter 03\Constructor folder on the CD.)

```
public TestForm()
{
   // Call the Form Designer code.
   InitializeComponent();
}

public TestForm(String FormName)
{
   // Call the Form Designer code.
   InitializeComponent();

   // Set the form name.
   Text = FormName;
}

public TestForm(String FormName, String WelcomeLabel)
{
```

```
    // Call the Form Designer code.
    InitializeComponent();

    // Set the form name.
    Text = FormName;

    // Set the welcomd text.
    lblWelcome.Text = WelcomeLabel;
}
```

The example application uses these three constructors to open three versions of a secondary form. As you can see, each constructor adds another optional parameter. The example works equally well with any of the constructors. However, adding more information results in a more functional display. The three buttons (Plain, Name, and Welcome) on the first example form exercise the three constructors, as shown here.

```
private void btnPlain_Click(object sender, System.EventArgs e)
{
    // Create the form using the first constructor,
    // then display it.
    TestForm Dlg = new TestForm();
    Dlg.ShowDialog();
}

private void btnName_Click(object sender, System.EventArgs e)
{
    // Create the form using the second constructor,
    // then display it.
    TestForm Dlg = new TestForm("A Test Form Name");
    Dlg.ShowDialog();
}

private void btnWelcome_Click(object sender, System.EventArgs e)
{
    // Create the form using the third constructor,
    // then display it.
    TestForm Dlg = new TestForm("Test Form with Welcome",
                                "Hello, this is a Welcome label.");
    Dlg.ShowDialog();
}
```

When you click Welcome, you'll see the full output of the secondary dialog, as shown in Figure 3.10. Of course, this is a simple example of the types of constructors we'll create as the book progresses. The idea is to use constructors carefully to ensure the developer has the right combination of flexibility and ease-of-use. Too many constructors would make the decisions of which constructor to use difficult at best. Also note that the constructors are arranged in order from least to most complex, making it easier to find the correct constructor.

FIGURE 3.10:

Using a series of con-
structors can help you
create multiple effects
using a single class.

TIP The example in this section uses multiple forms. When working with complex class additions, make sure you use the C# Class Wizard to aid your efforts. You open the C# Class
Wizard by right-clicking the Project entry in Class View, then choosing Add ➢ Add Class.
Type a class name in the Class Name field on the Class Options tab. In the Base Class
tab, choose System.Windows.Forms in the Namespace field and Form in the Base Class
field. Select other options as needed for the dialog that you want to create, then click Finish. The new class will contain rudimentary support for essential form elements, saving
you some typing time.

Working with Destructors

Given the way that C# applications work, you'll almost never need to add a destructor to any
code. A destructor works differently in the .NET environment than in previous Windows
environments in that you can't be sure when the destructor will get called. The Garbage Collector frees class resources, at some point, after the class is no longer needed. See the
"Understanding Non-Deterministic Finalization" section for further details.

The C# specification does allow for a destructor. The destructor can't have any return
value, nor can it accept any input values. This means you can't override the destructor, so
there's at most one destructor for any given class. In addition, a class can't inherit a destructor, which means you must create a unique destructor for each class you create (if one is
desired).

Destructors should avoid making time-critical changes to the user environment, and they
should not use resources that might not be available at the time the destructor is called. For
example, you wouldn't want to display a completion message from the destructor because the
user might be engaged in some other activity. Likewise, you wouldn't want to attempt to
close a file handle from the destructor because the file resource might not exist.

Despite problems using destructors in managed applications, you can use them for some types of non-time-critical purposes. For example, services and server-side components often place a message in the Event Log to signal a successful shutdown or to register shut down errors. You could perform this task with a destructor, provided the destructor doesn't rely on any external resources.

The one essential use of destructors is when you include unmanaged resources in your application. For example, you might create a device context for creating a 3D drawing in your application. If the device context is global to the class, you could use the destructor to free it before the application ends. However, a better memory management technique is to keep as many unmanaged resources as possible within the method call in which they're used, so you can free the resource immediately after use. Here's a simple example of a destructor (you'll find the full source in the \Chapter 03\Destructor folder on the CD).

```
// A simple class that includes both constructor
// and destructor.
public class DoTest
{
    public DoTest()
    {
        // Display a message when the class is destroyed.
        MessageBox.Show("The class has been created!",
            "Destructor Test Message",
            MessageBoxButtons.OK,
            MessageBoxIcon.Exclamation);
    }

    ~DoTest()
    {
        // Display a message when the class is destroyed.
        MessageBox.Show("The class has been destroyed!",
            "Destructor Test Message",
            MessageBoxButtons.OK,
            MessageBoxIcon.Exclamation);
    }
}
```

This code will eventually run; however, you might end up waiting quite a while unless your machine is short on resources. (Make sure you click Quit for the first test in the example program.) The Garbage Collector only runs as needed, and that isn't as often as you might think on a well-designed development machine. As part of the testing process for this book, I ended up waiting a full minute for the Garbage Collector to run on at least one machine. The message always appears, but this example serves to point out that relying on a destructor under .NET is an error-prone and time-consuming process at best. Of course, you can speed the process up, if desired, but only if you're willing to give up some of the performance benefits of the Garbage Collector.

NOTE   One of the interesting features of this example is that the second message box (the one signifying the destructor was called) will close by itself because the class that pointed to the dialog box is no longer available. Wait a few seconds after the clicking Quit, and you'll see the dialog box close automatically. However, if you force garbage collection (as described in the paragraph that follows), the dialog box remains in place until you specifically close it because the garbage collection mechanism keeps the class in place.

Every C# program has access to the GC (Garbage Collector) object. You can tell the Garbage Collector to run when it's convenient for you. However, the garbage collection process doesn't just involve your application. If you start the garbage collection process, the Garbage Collector will examine the resources for every running application—a huge performance penalty in some situations. The garbage collection could also occur at an inconvenient time. Time-critical processes could get interrupted when you force a garbage collection at the wrong time. The following code shows how to force a garbage collection, but you should use this feature with extreme care.

```
private void btnGC_Click(object sender, System.EventArgs e)
{
    // Create the test class.
    DoTest   MyTest;
    MyTest = new DoTest();

    // Free the resource.
    MyTest = null;

    // Force a garbage collection.
    GC.Collect();
    GC.WaitForPendingFinalizers();

    // Display a success message.
    MessageBox.Show("Garbage collection has succeeded.",
                    "Garbage Collection Test",
                    MessageBoxButtons.OK,
                    MessageBoxIcon.Information);

    // Exit the application.
    Close();
}
```

Understanding Non-Deterministic Finalization

Anyone who's worked with unmanaged code in the past knows that classes always contain a constructor (for creating an instance of the class) and a destructor (for cleaning up after the class is no longer needed). The world of .NET works differently from code you might have used in the past. Classes still contain constructions, as shown in previous examples, but they no longer contain destructors because the Garbage Collector determines when an object is no longer needed. This loss of ability to determine when a class is no longer needed is called *non-deterministic finalization.*

Behind the fancy term is a simple explanation. The developer loses the ability to determine when an object is going to go away. The object doesn't go away immediately—it may go away after the application terminates. This is a problem if you're using the destructor in an object to perform post-component processing. For example, you may leave a file open the whole time you use a component and close it only when the component no longer needs file access. Using the destructor to close the file is no longer an option in .NET, so you need to use some other method to handle the problem.

NOTE   You can read more about this particular problem at `http://www.devx.com/free/press/2000/102500.asp`. Fortunately, there are workarounds for this problem, most of which are addressed by following good coding practice. In some cases, however, the Garbage Collector will cost some performance, because you'll need to open and close files more often.

Delegates

Delegates are the new event class for .NET. Using a delegate is somewhat different from an event. In some respects, using delegates is more flexible than using events. However, given the differences between delegates and events, even the most experienced programmers find them confusing to say the least.

NOTE   Delegates can take many forms. This section presents one of the easiest to understand forms that a delegate can take. In addition, delegates often provide support for multiple handlers. This section will look at two forms of handler, but we'll discuss them separately. In a multiple handler scenario, the delegate actually receives a linked list of handlers that it calls in order. We'll discuss more complex forms of delegates as the book progresses because this is such as useful feature.

You begin creating a delegate by declaring the form the delegate must take. The `Delegate` keyword creates a special type of class that enables you to define delegate prototypes. Here's the code you'll normally use to declare a delegate. (The source code for this section appears in the \Chapter 03\Delegate folder of the CD.)

```
// Define a delegate for the example.
public delegate void DisplayMessage(String Subject, String Title);
```

As you can see, the code is relatively simple. You define the return value (normally void), the delegate name, and any arguments the delegate will require. It's important to note that this one line of code represents an entire class. C# creates the class for you behind the scenes. As a result, the delegate definition normally appears within a namespace, but outside of a class.

Delegates require an external entity that stores data for processing and the list of handlers for the delegate. These entities normally appear in separate classes. The class could provide something as complex as database manipulation or as simple as managing a list in memory. (For that matter, you can keep track of a single data member at a time, but that technique doesn't demonstrate the power of delegates fully.) Here's the ProcessMessageClass for the example.

```
// Define a message processor.
public class ProcessMessageClass
{
    // Using this struct makes it easier to store the
    // Subject and Title values.
    private struct Message
    {
        public   String   Subject;
        public   String   Title;

        public Message(String _Subject, String _Title)
        {
            Subject = _Subject;
            Title = _Title;
        }
    }

    // Create an array to hold the message values.
    private ArrayList   Msg = new ArrayList();

    public void add_Message(String Subject, String Title)
    {
        // Add new messages to the list when requested.
        Msg.Add(new Message(Subject, Title));
    }

    public void ProcessMessage(DisplayMessage Del)
    {
```

```
        // Process each message in the message list.
        foreach (Message Item in Msg)
           Del(Item.Subject, Item.Title);
     }
  };
```

As you can see, the example uses a struct named `Message` to act as a means for storing the data elements exposed to the handlers. The example will store a message subject (content) and title. The `ArrayList` data member `Msg` is the in memory database for the example. It holds every addition the code makes to the list of messages the user wants processed. The final piece of the database is `add_Message()`. This method adds new messages to `Msg`.

`ProcessMessage()` is the active part of the delegate-processing mechanism. It receives an implementation of the delegate we discussed earlier (the handler) and sends the handler the data in `Msg` to process. `ProcessMessage()` has no idea at the outset if it will receive one or multiple handlers, nor does it care which handler processes the data. In short, it's completely disconnected from the client portion of the application until the code creates the required connection.

Let's discuss the process of adding entries to the database. The following code shows how the application sends the information contained in two textboxes on the form to the database for processing.

```
// Create an instance of the ProcessMessageClass.
ProcessMessageClass  MyMsg = new ProcessMessageClass();

private void btnAddMessage_Click(object sender, System.EventArgs e)
{
   // Add new messages to the message list.
   MyMsg.add_Message(txtSubject.Text, txtTitle.Text);
}
```

First we need to create an instance of the data handling class, `ProcessMessageClass`. Whenever the user clicks Add, the application calls `add_Message()` with the values from the two textboxes. The `add_Message()` method adds these entries to the `ArrayList`, `Msg`.

At this point, we have a delegate, a database, and a means for handing the data off for processing. The handlers come next. A handler is an implementation of the delegate we discussed earlier. The following code demonstrates that it's the form of the handler, not the code inside that's important.

```
// Create a dialog-based message handler.
private void PrintMessage(String Subject, String Title)
{
```

```
    // Display the message.
    MessageBox.Show(Subject,
                    Title,
                    MessageBoxButtons.OK,
                    MessageBoxIcon.Information);
}

// Create a list filling message handler.
private void ListMessage(String Subject, String Title)
{
    // Add the output to the list.
    txtOutput.AppendText(Subject + "\t" + Title + "\r\n");
}
```

These two handlers don't do anything spectacular, but they do process the data. The first displays a message box for every data element in the database. The second places each data element on a separate line of a multiple-line textbox.

The handler and the data processing elements exist, but there's no connection between them. We need something to fire the event. The following code shows this last part of the puzzle.

```
private void btnFireMessage_Click(object sender, System.EventArgs e)
{
    // Fire the event and put the message handler into action.
    MyMsg.ProcessMessage(new DisplayMessage(PrintMessage));
}

private void btnFireList_Click(object sender, System.EventArgs e)
{
    // Clear the list box before we fill it.
    txtOutput.Clear();

    // Fire the event and put the list message handler into action.
    MyMsg.ProcessMessage(new DisplayMessage(ListMessage));
}
```

As you can see, the code calls ProcessMessage() with the handler of choice. Notice how we pass the name of the handler to the delegate as if we're creating a new object. This process is how delegates create the connection. Figure 3.11 shows typical output from this example.

FIGURE 3.11:

Using delegates
enables you to fire
one or more events
that process one or
more pieces of data at
a time.

Attributes

Attributes augment your applications in a number of ways. In fact, there are so many prede-fined attributes provided with Visual Studio .NET, that it's unlikely you'll find a single list containing them all. Most developers categorize attributes to make it easier to figure out which one to use.

It's important to know that each attribute affects application functionality at a specific level. For example, some attributes affect the way the compiler looks at the code during the compilation process. Attributes can allow certain types of optimizations to occur that the compiler may not normally use. They can also prevent inadvertent bugs by shutting off com-piler optimizations in areas where the optimization may have unexpected results. With this in mind, let's look at the various kinds of attributes that C# will place at your disposal.

> **NOTE**   This chapter doesn't contain a complete list of .NET attributes; it contains an overview of some of the more interesting ones. We'll discuss many more of the predefined attributes as the book progresses. In addition, you'll learn how to create user-defined attributes in some sections of the book, such as the "Creating the Custom Attribute" section of Chap-ter 6, where you'll also learn the importance of attributes in creating components and controls.

COM

If you've ever had to deal with the vast number of macros required to create a component, you know that they can become confusing. While the C# wizards attempt to write as much of the code for you that they can, there are always additions that you need to make yourself. Unfortunately, figuring out where to make the entries and how to format them is often more in line with the black arts than with science. In addition, if you make a mistake in filling out the wizard entries, trying to overcome the problem can prove difficult, because the wizard-generated code is difficult to read. The COM attributes overcome these problems by replacing large numbers of macro entries with easier to read attributes. Consider this example:

```
[ progid("CAgClass.coclass.1"), aggregates(__uuidof(CAgClass) ]
class CmyClass
{
    void MyMethod(void);
};
```

The progid attribute specifies the program identifier—the human readable dot syntax name of an object. The compiler uses this information to locate information about the object in the Registry and learn more about it. You'll use this attribute when creating external references to other objects on the client machine.

The aggregates attribute allows you to aggregate an existing component into the current component. In this case, CAgClass will become part of CMyClass. Notice that we use the __uuidof() function to obtain the universally unique identifier (UUID) of the existing class from the Registry. You could also enter the UUID directly.

TIP   You can't use the aggregates attribute alone—this attribute is always preceded by the coclass, progid, or vi_progid attributes. (If you use one of the three, the compiler will apply all three.) The progid and vi_progid descriptions appear in Table 3.2. However, it's important to realize that some attributes have dependencies—you can't use them alone. Always check for dependencies before using an attribute in your code.

The COM attributes represent one of the more complex attribute groups. They also represent one of the best ways to improve developer productivity when working in mixed language environments. You'll find that these attributes will at least halve the amount of code you write for even simple code and make your code infinitely easier to understand. Table 3.2 provides a list of common COM attributes and associated descriptions.

TABLE 3.2: COM Attributes

Attribute	Description
aggregatable	Determines whether another control can aggregate this control. A component can disallow aggregation, allow both standalone and aggregated use, or require aggregated use.
aggregates	Shows that this control is aggregating another control.
com_interface_entry	Adds an interface to the current class. You define the interface separately from the class code. (We'll discuss this issue in the IDL section.)

Continued on next page

TABLE 3.2 CONTINUED: COM Attributes

Attribute	Description
implements_category	Identifies component categories implemented by the target class—in other words, the areas of functionality that the component supports.
progid	Specifies the program identifier of a control.
rdx	Creates or modifies a Registry key. The parameters for this attribute include the key, value, and value type.
registration_script	Allows execution of a custom registration script.
requires_category	Identifies component categories required by the target class. In other words, the areas of functionality that a container must provide to use this component.
support_error_info	Specifies that the component will return detailed context-sensitive error information using the IErrorInfo interface.
synchronize	Synchronizes access to a method within the target class.
threading	Determines which threading model a class uses. Standard values include apartment, neutral, rental, single, free, and both.
vi_progid	Specifies the version independent program identifier of a control.

Compiler

You won't currently find compiler attributes that control every aspect of compiler behavior. However, you'll find attributes that provide access to the functionality of .NET and reduce the complexity of changing some features. Unfortunately, this attribute category only works in a managed code environment. C# does provide a managed code environment by default, but many developers will also use C# to work with unmanaged code in a mixed language environment. In short, the compiler attributes only affect certain compiler operations, but they're very important operations. Many of these attributes appear at the beginning of the file or in conjunction with specialty classes. Table 3.3 contains a list of the compiler attributes.

TABLE 3.3: Compiler Attributes

Attribute	Description
emitidl	Determines if the compiler generates an IDL file based on IDL attributes. There are four possible emission conditions: true (the IDL is generated), false (the IDL isn't generated), restricted (allows IDL attributes without a module attribute—no IDL file generated), and forced (overrides the restricted condition and forces the file to contain a module attribute).
event_receiver	Creates an event receiver. The event receiver can use the native, COM, or managed models for receiving events. The managed option will enforce .NET Framework requirements such as use of the Garbage Collector.

Continued on next page

TABLE 3.3 CONTINUED: Compiler Attributes

Attribute	Description
event_source	Creates an event source. The event source can use the native, COM, or managed models for sending events. The managed option will enforce .NET Framework requirements such as use of the Garbage Collector.
export	Places the target union, typedef, enum, or struct in the IDL file.
importidl	Allows placement of the target IDL file within the generated IDL file.
includelib	Defines the name of an IDL or H file that you want to place within the generated IDL file.
library_block	Places a construct, such as an interface description, within the generated IDL file. This ensures the construct is passed to the type library, even if you don't reference it.
no_injected_text	Prevents the compiler from injecting text as the result of using attributes within the code. This option assumes that the text is either not needed or that you injected it manually. For example, the /Fx compiler option uses this feature when creating merge files.
satype	Specifies the data type for a SAFEARRAY structure.
version	Specifies a class version number.

OLE-DB Consumer

Database management is a mainstay of most developers. Somewhere along the way, most developers end up spending at least some time working with databases. That's why the inclusion of OLE-DB consumer attributes is so important. Using attributes in a database application can greatly reduce the amount of coding you need to do to perform simple and common tasks. Here's a simple example of what you might see within a method designed to work with databases.

```
HRESULT MyDataAccess()
{
   [ db_source(
      db_source="DSN=FoodOrdersData",
      name="FoodOrder",
      hresult="hr" ]

   if (FAILED(hr))
      return hr;

   [ db_command(
      db_command="SELECT * FROM FoodOrders",
      name="FoodOrderRowset",
      sourcename="FoodOrder",
```

```
        hresult="hr" ]

    if (FAILED(hr))
        return hr;

    return S_OK;
  }
```

In this case, data access consists of a db_source and a db_command attribute. The db_source attribute allows us to gain access to the database connection defined by the FoodOrdersData data source name (DSN). The connection receives a name of FoodOrder and the result of the call appears in hr. Note that we don't create hr—C# automatically creates the HRESULT variable. The db_command attribute accepts a standard SQL command. The results of this command appear in FoodOrderRowset. Access to the database requires a connection, which is supplied by the sourcename parameter.

Microsoft has gone to great lengths to simplify database access in C# by using attributes. In fact, you'll find that most activities require only two or three of the six database attributes. Table 3.4 lists the attributes and describes them for you.

TABLE 3.4: DB-OLE Consumer Attributes

Attribute	Description
db_accessor	Binds the columns in a rowset to the corresponding accessor maps. You must provide an accessor number as the first parameter. The second parameter can contain a Boolean value that determines if the application automatically retrieves the accessor.
db_column	Binds a column to a rowset. You must provide a column name or the ordinal number of the column within the rowset to use for binding. Optional parameters include the data type, precision, scale, status, and length of the data.
db_command	Allows execution of database commands on an open connection. You must provide a database command as the first parameter. Optional parameters include the rowset name, source name, return value variable name, bindings value, and bulk fetch value.
db_param	Creates a connection between a member variable and an input or output parameter. You must provide a column name or the ordinal number of the column within the rowset to use for binding. Optional parameters include the parameter type, data type, precision, scale, status, and length of the data.
db_source	Opens a connection to a data source using a data provider. You must provide the name of a data source. Optional parameters include a name for the connection and the name of a return value variable. The connection string can take a number of forms—it's not necessary to use a DSN.
db_table	Opens an OLE-DB table. You must provide the name of the table you want to open. Optional parameters include a name for the table that the call returns, a data source name, and the name of a variable to receive the results of the operation.

An Attribute Example

You'll use some attributes more often than you will others. For example, anyone who builds components will want to know how to work with component attributes. One of the attributes you'll use most often is [Description] because it provides visual documentation of methods, events, and properties within your component. Another useful attribute is [Category] because it helps you organize the properties that a component supports. Here's a quick example of the [Description] and [Category] attributes at work.

```
// Create the public property used to manipulate
// the data.
[Description("A simple property for saying Hello.")
 Category("Special")]
 public string Hello
{
   get
   {
      return _Hello;
   }
   set
   {
      _Hello = value;
   }
}
```

When you apply the [Description] attribute to a property, the component user sees descriptive text when they select the property in the Properties window. If the user also chooses to display the properties in category order, the [Category] attribute determines where the property appears in the list. Figure 3.12 shows how the descriptive text would appear in the Properties window. Note that the string will automatically break at word boundaries if it's too long for the window area. The property also appears in the Special category because the window is in Categorized mode.

FIGURE 3.12:

Some attributes make your components easier for other developers to use.

Where Do You Go From Here?

The essential lesson to learn in this chapter is that C# uses classes for everything. You won't find global variables or functions that sit by themselves. Everything is part of a class and you access the code using objects based on the class template. Consequently, you need to know more about class creation in C# than any other language that you might have used in the past. Fortunately, C# makes creating classes relatively easy. It even does some of the coding for you.

Every class has three hierarchical levels as a minimum that include namespace, class, and method. You can nest levels. For example, an application could include more than one level of methods. Each level can also contain multiple sublevels. For example, a namespace could host more than one class or other namespaces.

This chapter provides a lot of information in a very small space. It provides at least one source on the Internet that you'll want to check out. Make sure you spend time learning the basics. For example, it's important to know how to create properties and work with delegates. You'll also want to spend some time learning about attributes. Using attributes can save you an immense amount of time and effort.

At this point, you should have a better idea of how to build basic classes. These are fully functional classes, but they lack some of the polish you could obtain using advanced coding techniques. You've learned how to pass data, create methods, and handle events. We'll discuss advanced class construction techniques, like sealed classes, in Chapter 4.

CHAPTER 4

Advanced Class Topics

- Application Techniques

- Error Handling

- Advanced Class Creation Techniques

As mentioned in other areas of the book, classes are the foundation of creating applications of any type in .NET. Gone are the freestanding bits of code and data that used to permeate applications in the past. Knowing how to work with classes isn't just a nice topic to know in .NET, it's an essential skill.

In Chapter 3, we discussed some of the basics of creating classes. This chapter builds on those techniques that you learned in that chapter. We'll discuss how you can perform some advanced programming with classes in .NET. For example, you'll learn about new ways to work with the command line using multiple constructors (and then to do something with the data once you receive it). We'll also visit error handling—a required skill that many developers ignore at the user's displeasure. Finally, you'll learn how to create alternative class types, including the mysterious sealed class.

Application Techniques

Many developers begin learning about a new language by creating small applications to test various language features. It turns out, that's the best way to learn about classes as well. Creating small classes that you can build quickly and see the results of instantly helps you learn more about how .NET works.

The following sections demonstrate some class techniques by creating small applications to demonstrate them. For example, the command-line example not only shows you how to enhance your next application with command-line processing, it also shows you how to create multiple constructors for your form class. You'll also learn how to perform various types of parsing within .NET.

Processing the Command Line

Processing the command line is an important feature in all but the smallest applications. At the very least, you want users to have access to the print capabilities of an application without opening it. In addition, creating command-line processing capabilities is an essential part of making your application script and task scheduler friendly. These application environments often need to provide direct input to the application in order to open files and perform other tasks. In short, knowing how to work with the command line is an essential task for everyone to learn.

We created a basic command-line processing example in Chapter 3. In that example, the Main() method determined if the user passed any command-line parameters, then adjusted the method it used to instantiate the Param class to match the input. However, this isn't necessarily the best way to handle the situation. Main() should be able to instantiate the form class without worrying about the command-line parameters.

This section of the chapter shows an example of how you can use multiple constructor overrides to provide a better class interface for your application. Main() won't need to know about the command-line parameters at all. It will simply pass them along and the form constructor will take care of the rest. In addition, this example will demonstrate how to parse and use the command-line parameters to perform useful work.

NOTE   The example in the \Chapter 04\CommandLine2 folder might seem a tad incomplete because it only contains the Open, Print, and Exit commands on the File menu. The focus of this example is the command line, so we don't need to address other file-handling issues until the next chapter.

Parsing the Command Line

One of the difficult considerations for an application that parses the command line and performs some tasks with the input is that the command-line features will almost certainly duplicate menu functionality. You must consider at the outset which parts of the menu portion of the command to duplicate and which portions to place in a common function. For example, the process of reading a file will be the same whether you do it from the command line or from within a menu. The menu version will require a user interface, but you can separate that portion of the command into menu code. On the other hand, printing might require more processing when working from within the application and the command-line version will almost certainly want to exit immediately after the print job is complete. In this case, the command-line version of the code and the menu version of the code could be at odds, making it less time consuming, especially with regard to debugging, to write duplicate code instead.

As previously mentioned, the example will contain two constructors for the form. The first is a simple constructor that doesn't accept any command-line input. The second constructor will accept any number of input arguments, but the code is constructed such that only two parameters will actually do any work. The application will accept the name of an existing file and the /p argument for printing. Anything else is neatly disposed of by the code during parsing. Listing 4.1 shows the two constructors for this example. (You'll find the source code for this example in the \Chapter 04\CommandLine2 folder of the CD.)

Listing 4.1   **Multiple Constructors Used for Command-Line Parsing**

```
public Form1()
{
    // Required for Windows Form Designer support
    InitializeComponent();

    // We don't want to exit the application.
```

```
      CommandLineOnly = false;
}

// Determines if we're using command line processing alone.
private bool CommandLineOnly;

public Form1(String[] args)
{
   FileInfo        FInfo = null;              // File Information
   int             Count;                     // Command Line Argument
   bool            DoPrint = false;           // Print Document?
   PrintDocument   PD = new PrintDocument();  // Document Rendering

   // Required for Windows Form Designer support
   InitializeComponent();

   // We don't want to exit the application yet.
   CommandLineOnly = false;

   // Process each command line argument in turn. Look for a
   // filename and the /P parameter. Ignore anything else.
   for (Count = 0; Count < args.Length; Count++)
   {

      // Check if there is a document to open.
      try
      {
         // Only try this until we find a file.
         if (File2Open == null)
            FInfo = new FileInfo(args[Count]);
      }
      catch
      {
      }
      if (File2Open == null && FInfo != null)
         if (FInfo.Exists)
            File2Open = args[Count];

      // Check if the argument is /P.
      if (args[Count].ToUpper() == "/P")
         DoPrint = true;
   }

   // Open the document if one exists.
   if (FInfo.Exists)
   {

      DoFileOpen(File2Open);

      // Print the document if requested.
      if (DoPrint)
      {
```

```
        // Object containing document to print.
        Doc2Print = new StringReader(txtEdit.Text);

        // Add an event handler for document printing details.
        PD.PrintPage += new PrintPageEventHandler(PD_PrintPage);

        // Set up the document for printing.
        PD.DocumentName = File2Open;

        // Print the document.
        PD.Print();

        // Exit the application.
        CommandLineOnly = true;
    }
}
else

    // The file wasn't found, so the command line constructor
    // won't do any useful work in this case.
    MessageBox.Show("Invalid Filename or File Not Found\r\n" +
                    "(Always supply a path for the filename.)",
                    "Command Line Argument Error",
                    MessageBoxButtons.OK,
                    MessageBoxIcon.Error);
}
```

As you can see from Listing 4.1, the standard constructor initializes the components and sets the *CommandLineOnly* field to false. The example requires some means of detecting when it should open the file, print it, and then exit. This field enables the application to perform the additional processing without too many problems. In most cases, you'd use such a variable only if you wanted to provide some form of automatic processing, such as printing. This enables the user to schedule the print job and not worry about finding a number of active application copies when the background tasks complete. (You'll learn how this processing works later in this section.)

The command-line version of the constructor accepts a string array named *args* as input. After it performs the same processing as the standard version of the constructor, the command-line version of the constructor begins parsing the command-line parameters. Notice the technique used to parse the command line for a filename. It uses the *File2Open* field to determine when to stop looking for a valid filename. The *File2Open* field is only set to a filename if the *FInfo* object contains a valid filename.

Notice the bit of code where we create a new FileInfo() object based on the *args* string. The entire process is placed within a try...catch structure, because any attempt to open an invalid file will result in an exception. So the purpose of this construction is to catch the error, if it occurs. However, the application doesn't really care if the user passes an invalid filename, because the application will simply ignore it. Consequently, the catch portion of the structure is blank. We'll discuss the try...catch structure in more detail in the "Using Try and Catch" section of the chapter.

TIP   Use default command-line switches whenever possible to make your application easier to use and faster for users to learn. For example, if you plan to provide command-line help, always support /?. Likewise, printing normally uses the /p switch. The best way to find the default command-line switches—those used by the majority of Windows applications—is to check Windows Help and Microsoft resources for the functionality you want to include in your application. Unfortunately, Microsoft has never published a list of recommended application switches.

Parsing out the /p command-line argument is easy. The only consideration is ensuring you capture the argument by setting the input to uppercase so you don't need to check for numerous forms of capitalization. If the constructor detects a /p entry in *args*, it sets *DoPrint* to true.

If the user has provided a filename that exists, the constructor calls DoFileOpen() with the name of the valid filename the user provided. This is a situation when the command-line version and the menu version of a function are similar, so using the same common function makes sense.

The else clause of the file existence check displays an error message. The only problem with this approach is that you don't know if the user is around to see the error message. You have several other options in this case. The application could simply exit and not do anything at all. However, this technique is unfriendly because the user will have every expectation that the task completed successfully. Another technique is to write an entry into the event log. Of course, the user has to know to look in the event log for errors to make this method work. Finally, because you're using this method at the command line, the application could write an informative message to the command line and exit. Of course, the command line might not exist after the application exists, so again, you're facing a situation where the user might not see the error message. The remaining code determines if the user wants to load the file or print it. If the user wants to print the file, the constructor provides a custom print routine that doesn't rely on any user interaction. This means the application uses defaults for every aspect of the print job. Notice the last task the code performs is setting the *CommandLineOnly* field to true. The following code shows how the *CommandLineOnly* field affects application operation.

```
private void Form1_Activated(object sender, System.EventArgs e)
{
    // Exit the application if we're using the commandline
```

```
    // only for printing.
    if (CommandLineOnly)
        Close();
}
```

As you can see, the code closes the form if the user has chosen to use the command-line version of the application to print a file. However, at first glance it's easy to think you could simply close the application from the constructor. The truth is that the application isn't active at this point—the constructor is creating the form. Attempting to close the application in the constructor won't work because there's nothing to close. The Activated event occurs after the constructor returns to the call in Main(), shown here.

```
static void Main(string[] args)
{
    if (args.Length == 0)

        // Use the standard constructor.
        Application.Run(new Form1());
    else

        // Use the command line constructor.
        Application.Run(new Form1(args));
}
```

In short, the command-line version of the constructor opens the file, prints it if necessary, and then returns to the Application.Run(new Form1(args)) statement in Main(). At this point, the application becomes active, and you can close it if desired. The first place you can close the application is in the Form1_Activated() method. It's one of those odd concepts to twist your brain around, but an important concept to remember.

Displaying the Text

Displaying text on screen is a multiple part process. Of course, you have to begin with the proper controls on your form. The example uses a RichTextBox so it can display both plain text and formatted RTF text files. The application will allow you to edit the text, but you can't save it. We'll also use a menu for this application instead of the pushbuttons of the past.

Once you have a user interface to work with, you can create the menu command required to start opening a file. The user begins by selecting a file to open. The code opens the file, reads it, then passes the data to the edit control. Listing 4.2 shows this entire process.

Listing 4.2   Opening and Displaying a File

```
private   String   File2Open;   // Selected Filename

private void menuFileOpen_Click(object sender, System.EventArgs e)
```

```
{
    OpenFileDialog Dlg = new OpenFileDialog();   // File Open Dialog

    // Set up the File Open Dialog
    Dlg.Filter = "Rich Text Format (*.rtf)|*.rtf|" +
                 "Text Files (*.txt)|*.txt";
    Dlg.DefaultExt = ".rtf";
    Dlg.Title = "Open File Dialog";

    // Display the File Open Dialog and obtain the name of a file and
    // the file information.
    if (Dlg.ShowDialog() == DialogResult.OK)
    {
        File2Open = Dlg.FileName;
    }
    else
    {
        // If the user didn't select anything, return.
        return;
    }

    // Open the document.
    DoFileOpen(File2Open);
}

private bool DoFileOpen(String Filename)
{
    Stream        FileStrm;              // File Data Stream
    FileInfo      FInfo;                 // File Information
    String        FileExt;               // File Extension

    // Determine the file type.
    FInfo = new FileInfo(File2Open);
    FileExt = FInfo.Extension.ToUpper();

    // Set the name of the file on the Title bar.
    if (Form1.ActiveForm != null)
        Form1.ActiveForm.Text = "Command Line Example - Editing: " +
                                File2Open;

    // Open the file and display it.
    FileStrm = new FileStream(File2Open, FileMode.Open);
    if (FileExt == ".RTF")
        txtEdit.LoadFile(FileStrm, RichTextBoxStreamType.RichText);
    else
        txtEdit.LoadFile(FileStrm, RichTextBoxStreamType.PlainText);

    // Close the file.
    FileStrm.Close();

    return true;
}
```

Notice that this portion of the example relies on the *File2Open* field to perform the same function as it did in the constructor—keep track of the open file. It's essential to provide such a field in an application where multiple methods rely on the filename.

TIP

Never place any unnecessary spaces in the Filter property for a common dialog. Otherwise, the dialog may think that you want the added space in the filter specification. An entry of `"*.txt"` could become `"*.txt "` if you add an extra space, making the filter useless.

The `menuFileOpen_Click()` method begins by creating a File Open dialog box. The `OpenFileDialog` class takes care of many details for you. However, you still need to provide some input. The example shows a minimal implementation. Setting changes include creating a filter, a default file extension, and a title for the dialog box. If the user selects a file and clicks Open, the application places the filename in *File2Open* for future use. If the user clicks any other button, the method returns without doing anything.

This is all the code you need to create the user interface portion of the file opening process. Figure 4.1 shows the File Open dialog created by the code in this example. The example code calls `DoFileOpen()`, the same method called by the command-line version of the constructor. It's time to discuss the common function used by both the command-line and the menu versions of the file-opening process.

FIGURE 4.1:

C# requires little code to create an interesting and useful File Open dialog box.

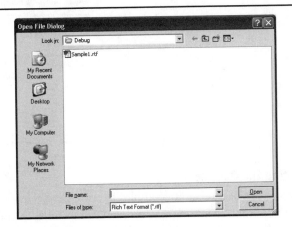

`DoFileOpen()` begins by performing some housekeeping chores. First, it determines the file type and assigns it to *FileExt* for later use. Second, the code places the current file name (along with other text) in the form title bar. Using the title bar this way ensures the user always knows the current filename.

After it completes the housekeeping chores, DoFileOpen() creates *FileStrm*, which contains the data displayed in the form. Notice that we use the LoadFile() method to load the data into *txtEdit*. The default RichTextEdit control provides support for plain text, rich text, plain text with OLE support, rich text without OLE support, and Unicode. You could override this control to provide other forms of support. For example, you could choose to display binary data in a hexadecimal format. Each type of data loading requires a different constant so RichTextEdit will know how to handle it. The example supports plain text and rich text without any of the other permutations. You must check for the RTF extension for the rich text file. However, the plain text form of LoadFile() will support anything, including binary files. Of course, you won't be able to read the data displayed, but LoadFile() won't display an error message either.

The example code ends by closing the file stream. If you've opened the file stream for read/write access, you don't necessarily have to close it at this point. In fact, you might want to leave the file opened and locked to prevent another user from modifying the data. However, adding this support also increases the complexity of the application, so you need to decide how likely it is that the application will see use as a means to modify shared data on a network. Figure 4.2 shows what the application looks like with the sample file (located in the \Chapter 04\CommandLine2\bin\Debug folder) loaded.

FIGURE 4.2:

The example application can load both plain text and rich text files.

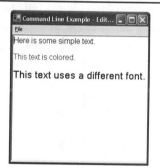

Printing the Document

Printing can become quite complex because most data files lend themselves to more than one form of output. In addition, users require flexibility in configuring the output. Finally, most print jobs need to support multiple output scenarios. The three common scenarios include:

- Screen (display)
- Printer
- File

Each of these common scenarios will often support multiple subtypes. For example, the user might call upon your application to provide one level of support for monotone printers (black and white) and another level for color printers. Screen displays often require support for zoom, in-place editing, and other conveniences. In short, it's easy to lose sight of the purpose of the code because you're mired in options.

The printing for this example is simple. The application supports one type of output—a monotone printer. The example is purposely simple so you can see the mechanics of printing before the book becomes mired in supporting all of the options typical applications will require. Listing 4.3 shows the example code for printing.

Listing 4.3   Printing a Document Displayed on Screen

```csharp
private StringReader   Doc2Print;   // Reads document line by line.

private void menuFilePrint_Click(object sender, System.EventArgs e)
{
    PrintDialog     Dlg = new PrintDialog();   // Print Dialog
    PrintDocument   PD = new PrintDocument();  // Document Rendering

    // Object containing document to print.
    Doc2Print = new StringReader(txtEdit.Text);

    // Add an event handler for document printing details.
    PD.PrintPage += new PrintPageEventHandler(PD_PrintPage);

    // Set up the Print Dialog.
    Dlg.PrinterSettings = new PrinterSettings();

    // Obtain the print parameters.
    if (Dlg.ShowDialog() == DialogResult.OK)
    {
        // Set up the document for printing.
        PD.PrinterSettings = Dlg.PrinterSettings;
        PD.DocumentName = File2Open;

        // Print the document.
        PD.Print();
    }
    else
    {
        // Exit if the user selects Cancel.
        return;
    }
}

private void PD_PrintPage(object sender, PrintPageEventArgs ev)
{
    String   TextLine = null;  // Current line of text.
```

```
Font     docFont;          // Printing Font
float    yPos;             // Position of text on page.
int      Line = 2;         // Current print line w/margin.
float    LinesPerPage;     // Number of lines per page.

// Create the font.
docFont = new Font("Arial", 12);

// Calculate the number of lines on a page.
LinesPerPage = ev.MarginBounds.Height / docFont.GetHeight();

// Continue printing as long as there is space on the page and
// we don't run out of things to write.
while ((Line - 2 < LinesPerPage &&
        (TextLine = Doc2Print.ReadLine()) != null))
{
    // Determine the Y position of the print area.
    yPos = Line * docFont.GetHeight();

    // Go to the next line.
    Line++;

    // Print the line of text.
    ev.Graphics.DrawString(TextLine,
                           docFont,
                           Brushes.Black,
                           40,
                           yPos);
}

// Determine if we need to print more text.
if (TextLine != null)
    ev.HasMorePages = true;
else
    ev.HasMorePages = false;
}
```

As you can see, the printing process requires use of two methods: a menu handler (menuFilePrint_Click()) and a print event handler (PD_PrintPage()). Both methods rely on a StringReader field, *Doc2Print*, to hold the data the application will print. Note that *Doc2Print* contains the raw data, not the data formatted for printing. The example also ignores any native formatting the raw data might contain.

The menuFilePrint_Click() method begins by creating a Print dialog box. The only configuration issue that you must consider is the *PrinterSettings* property. The example doesn't do much with the Print dialog box, but it is functional. Figure 4.3 shows the output you'll see.

FIGURE 4.3:

The Print dialog
requires little configu-
ration to provide a
usable display.

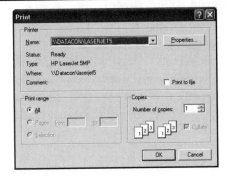

If the user clicks OK, the application will send the data to the printer. Notice that you can still select Print to File in the Print dialog. Windows handles this feature for you. However, the output is a printer-ready file, not data in a user-friendly format. If you want user-friendly file output, you'll need to create it as part of the application.

The Print dialog provides input for the `PrintDocument` object, *PD*. Notice that *PD* also requires an entry for the *PrinterSettings* property. However, you derive this value from the Print dialog so that any user changes appear in the final document. You also need to provide a filename so the user knows which document is printing.

Earlier, the code used the `PrintPageEventHandler(PD_PrintPage)` method call to assign the `PD_PrintPage()` method as a print event handler to *PD*. The `PD.Print()` method invokes `PD_PrintPage()`. In short, you set up the printer document and then fire an event to show that it's ready to print. However, the printer document contains setup information, not data.

NOTE   The reason for using a print event handler is to enable background printing. Windows will continue to call the print routine in the background until there are no more pages to print. This technique helps the user to get back to work more quickly.

The `PD_PrintPage()` method creates the printed output by combining *PD* (the settings) with *Doc2Print* (the data). Creating printer output means working with graphic methods. The example shows the simplest possible print routine for text. The code begins by defining a font and determining print boundaries. It then creates the graphic output line-by-line. Notice that the `PrintPageEventArgs` variable, *ev*, provides the device context used to create the output. Notice that the code always assigns a value to *ev.HasMorePages* so the application knows whether it needs to call `PD_PrintPage()` to output the next page of text. You must set this value to `true` after each page or Windows will assume you don't have any more data to print.

Using Preprocessing Directives

Anyone who's used Visual C++ will know the value of preprocessing directives. C# provides a limited number of preprocessing directives that control the flow of compilation, but don't provide the same level of functionality that Visual C++ provides because C# lacks a true preprocessor. In short, you can use the preprocessor to add or subtract features based on the current configuration, but you can't perform some of the other tasks that Visual C++ can perform. For example, you can't use the directives to create macros. Table 4.1 shows the preprocessor directives that C# supports and provides a short definition for them.

> **NOTE**   We'll look at how C# differs from the Visual Studio languages of old. Appendix A contains an analysis of how C# differs from Visual C++, while Appendix B performs the same analysis for Visual Basic users.

TABLE 4.1: Preprocessing Directives Supported by C#

Directive	Meaning for C#	Short Example
#define	Creates a symbol used for conditional statements such as #if. Never use a variable name for a #define.	#define DEBUG
#elif	Enables conditional compilation if the selected condition is true and the associated #if condition is false. Use this directive in place of #else if you need to test more than one condition. Uses the same operators as the #if directive.	#elif (DEBUG)
#else	Enables conditional compilation if the associated #if condition is false.	#else
#endif	Ends conditional compilation started with an #if directive.	#endif
#endregion	Ends a region created with the #region directive.	#endregion
#error	Generates an error message. This directive is normally associated with the #if directive to turn the error generation on and off.	#error This is an error message.
#if	Enables conditional compilation if the selected condition is true. You can test for equality (==) and inequality (!=). The #if directive also supports both and (&&) and or (||). Using #if without operators tests for the existence of the target symbol.	#if (DEBUG)
#line	Modifies the current line number. You can also add an optional filename. Using default in place of a number returns the embedded numbering system to its default state.	#line 200 or #line default or #line 20 "MyFilename"

Continued on next page

TABLE 4.1 CONTINUED: Preprocessing Directives Supported by C#

Directive	Meaning for C#	Short Example
#region	Creates a region block within the IDE. Each region block has an associated collapse feature so you can hide of display the region. You can't overlap a region with an #if directive. However, the #if can contain the region or the region can contain the #if.	#region MyRegionName
#undef	Deletes a symbol created with the #define directive.	#undef DEBUG
#warning	Generates a warning message. This directive is normally associated with the #if directive to turn the error generation on and off.	#warning This is a warning message.

As you can see, the list isn't long, but the directives definitely make it easier to work with your code. Listing 4.4 shows a short example of all the directives in use.

Listing 4.4   Using Directives within a C# Application

```
#define MyDefine
#undef MyUndef

using System;

namespace Preprocess
{
   class Class1
   {
      [STAThread]
      static void Main(string[] args)
      {
         #region MyDefine area of code
         #if (MyDefine)
         #error MyDefine is defined
         #else
         #error MyDefine isn't defined
         #endif
         #endregion

         #line 1 "Sample Filename"

         #region MyUndef area of code
         #if (!MyDefine && !MyUndef)
         #warning Neither MyDefine nor MyUndef are defined.
         #elif (MyDefine && !MyUndef)
         #warning MyDefine is defined, but MyUndef is undefined.
```

```
        #elif (!MyDefine && MyUndef)
        #warning MyDefine is not defined, but MyUndef is defined.
        #else
        #warning Both MyDefine and MyUndef are defined.
        #endif
        #endregion

        #line default
    }

  }
}
```

The #define and #undef directives shown in this example create two symbols that appear as part of the #if and #elif directives later. Notice that the example code contains two regions. The reason regions are such a good idea is that you can see just the parts of your code you want. The collapsed areas contain descriptive text, as shown in Figure 4.4.

FIGURE 4.4:

Use regions to provide collapsible areas in your code.

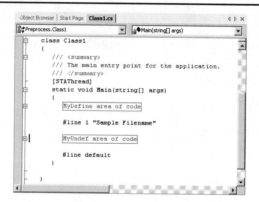

As shown in Figure 4.4, the #region directive creates collapsible areas within the Main() method. This provides you with better flexibility in viewing your code, especially if a method contains a lot of code.

The #warning and #error directives appear in the output when you compile the code. Figure 4.5 shows the result of compiling the sample code. Notice that the #error entry contains an exclamation mark to make it easier to find. You should also observe that the #warning output contains a line number based on the #line directive entry in the code shown in Listing 4.4. The filename is different as well.

FIGURE 4.5:

The #warning and #error directives provide output you can use as a reminder.

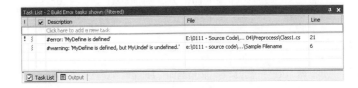

Calling Native DLLs

It's important to use the .NET Framework for as much of your coding as possible because it provides a managed environment. However, sometimes you'll find that the .NET Framework doesn't provide a service that you need for your application. In this case, you need to resort to the Win32 API to service the application requirement. You'll hear this technique called by a variety of names, but the most common is Platform Invoke, or PInvoke for short.

The main idea behind using PInvoke is to create a connection between your managed code and the unmanaged code of the Win32 API. Microsoft suggests that you create one or more classes to hold the PInvoke calls so that you can use them with multiple applications. Given the importance of some of these calls, expect to see third-party libraries containing the required classes for you. Fortunately, using PInvoke isn't difficult, as shown in Listing 4.5.

Listing 4.5   Use PInvoke to Access Win32 API Functions

```csharp
// Make sure you include the InteropServices namespace.
using System;
using System.Windows.Forms;
using System.Runtime.InteropServices;


namespace PInvokeDemo
{
   class Class1
   {
      // Import the MessageBeep function so we can use it.
      [DllImport("User32", EntryPoint = "MessageBeep")]
      static extern bool MessageBeep(int uType);

      [STAThread]
      static void Main(string[] args)
      {
         // Play the default beep.
         MessageBox.Show("Should hear default beep.");
         MessageBeep(-1);

         // Play the asterisk sound.
         MessageBox.Show("Should hear asterisk sound.");
```

```
        MessageBeep((int)MessageBoxIcon.Asterisk);
    }
  }
}
```

Always add the `System.Runtime.InteropServices` namespace if you plan to use an external DLL. This namespace adds the support you need to work with PInvoke.

The second step is to add the `[DllImport]` attribute to your code along with a method declaration. The example uses the `MessageBeep()` function found in the `User32.DLL` file. Notice that you must declare `MessageBeep()` as `static extern`, as shown in the listing, or the application won't compile. The `MessageBeep()` declaration indicates the function will accept an integer value as input and provide a `bool` output (true when successful).

When using the `MessageBeep()` function, you can supply a value for a specific kind of beep based on the message box icons, or you can provide a value of −1 for the default beep. Normally, you'd need to provide a list of constants for the beep values; but, in this case, we can use the .NET Framework–supplied values. Notice the `(int)MessageBoxIcon.Asterisk` entry for the asterisk sound. You'll find that the `int` cast works just fine for this example and many other examples you might want to create. Of course, you can't use the .NET Framework values directly—you must perform the cast in order to prevent problems when making the Win32 API call.

Error Handling

Most applications today contain some form of error handling. Unfortunately, the level and quality of error handling varies greatly. Some applications provide so much error handling that the application constantly raises alarms, even if the user provides the correct input. Other applications provide error handling that only a developer could love—the messages are replete with jargon and the data is useful only if you designed the application. Still other applications provide one-size-fits-all error handling that simply tells the user an error occurred without saying what error it was or how to fix it. The following sections will demonstrate various error-handling techniques. We'll also visit this topic regularly throughout the book.

Using Try and Catch

You'll use the `try...catch` statement regularly for error handling. In fact, you saw one example of the `try...catch` statement earlier in the chapter when we discussed using multiple constructors to handle command-line input. The purpose of the `try...catch` statement is to allow you to handle application errors so the user won't see the usual incomprehensible Windows error message. Even if you can't handle the error, it's helpful to provide a detailed and understandable message. Generally, the try...catch statement takes the form shown here.

```
private void btnThrow1_Click(object sender, System.EventArgs e)
{
    object   MyObject = null;  // Create an object.

    // Create the try...catch... structure.
    try
    {
        // The call will fail because of a bad cast.
        MyBadCall1((int)MyObject);
    }
    catch (Exception error)
    {
        // Display an error message.
        MessageBox.Show("Source:\t\t" + error.Source +
                        "\r\nMessage:\t\t" + error.Message +
                        "\r\nTarget Site:\t" + error.TargetSite +
                        "\r\nStack Trace:\t" + error.StackTrace,
                        "Application Error",
                        MessageBoxButtons.OK,
                        MessageBoxIcon.Error);
    }
}
```

In this case, the example code will fail because the method we're calling expects an integer. The invalid cast will cause an error even though C# compiles the example without so much as a warning. Notice that this try...catch statement uses the general Exception variable. Using Exception enables the application to catch all errors. We'll see in the next section that you can provide more selective error handling.

The exception object, *error*, contains a wealth of information. The example shows some of the common items you'll use to diagnose problems with your application. Here's the output you'll see when working with this example.

FIGURE 4.6:

The error object contains a wealth of information about the problem with the application.

As you can see, the output is the usual incomprehensible gibberish that Windows produces by default. We'll see in the next section that you can improve on the Windows messages by catching errors and handling them yourself. Using this technique enables you to create better error messages.

Throwing an Exception

Sometimes you'll want to detect an error in your application and provide custom support for it. However, you might not be able to handle the error at the level at which the error occurs. In this case, you need to throw an exception. The exception will travel to the next level in the application hierarchy. Listing 4.6 shows an example of throwing an exception.

Listing 4.6   Throw an Exception When Necessary

```
private void btnThow2_Click(object sender, System.EventArgs e)
{
   try
   {
      // The call will fail because we've thrown an exception.
      MyBadCall1(12);
   }
   catch (InvalidOperationException error)
   {
      // Display an error message.
      MessageBox.Show("Invalid Exception Error" +
                      "\r\nSource:\t\t" + error.Source +
                      "\r\nMessage:\t\t" + error.Message +
                      "\r\nTarget Site:\t" + error.TargetSite +
                      "\r\nStack Trace:\t" + error.StackTrace,
                      "Application Error",
                      MessageBoxButtons.OK,
                      MessageBoxIcon.Error);

      // Display the inner error message as well.
      Exception   InnerError = error.InnerException;
      MessageBox.Show("Inner Error Message" +
                      "\r\nSource:\t\t" + InnerError.Source +
                      "\r\nMessage:\t\t" + InnerError.Message +
                      "\r\nTarget Site:\t" + InnerError.TargetSite +
                      "\r\nStack Trace:\t" + InnerError.StackTrace,
                      "Application Error",
                      MessageBoxButtons.OK,
                      MessageBoxIcon.Error);
   }
}

private void MyBadCall1(int AnInt)
{
   object   MyObject = null;

   try
```

```
    {
        // Create an error condition.
        AnInt = (int)MyObject;
    }
    catch (Exception error)
    {
        // Throw an exception.
        throw(new
            InvalidOperationException("This is an error message!",
                                        error));
    }
}
```

MyBadCall1() creates an error condition by attempting to cast an object as an int. This is the same error as in the first example. However, MyBadCall1() is one level lower in the hierarchy, so we catch the error and pass it up to the calling method, btnThow2_Click(). Notice the technique used to create a new exception of a different type and to pass the existing exception up to the next highest level.

The catch portion of btnThow2_Click() looks for a specific error. In this case, it looks for an InvalidOperationException object. However, you could use the same techniques shown here for any other specific error. The two MessageBox.Show() calls display the error information. The first call contains the custom message shown in Figure 4.7. The second call contains the same error information you saw in Figure 4.6 (with appropriate changes for error location).

FIGURE 4.7:

A custom error message can provide better input than the Windows default message.

Using the *Finally* Keyword

The finally keyword is an addition to the try...catch statement. You can use it in addition to, or in place of, the catch keyword. Any code that appears as part of the finally portion of the statement will run even after an error occurs. This keyword comes in handy when you want to attempt to reduce the damage of an error. For example, you might need to close a file to ensure a graceful failure of your application. Here's an example of the finally keyword in use.

```
private void btnThrow3_Click(object sender, System.EventArgs e)
{
```

```
try
{
    // The call will fail because we've thrown an exception.
    MyBadCall1(12);
}
catch
{
    // Display an error message.
    MessageBox.Show("Invalid Exception Error",
                    "Application Error",
                    MessageBoxButtons.OK,
                    MessageBoxIcon.Error);

    // Try to return.
    return;
}
finally
{
    // The example must run this code.
    MessageBox.Show("Must Run This Code",
                    "Finally Code",
                    MessageBoxButtons.OK,
                    MessageBoxIcon.Information);
}

// The example will try to run this code, but won't
// because of the exception.
MessageBox.Show("This Code Won't Run",
                "Code Outside Try//Catch",
                MessageBoxButtons.OK,
                MessageBoxIcon.Information);
}
```

As you can see, we're using MyBadCall1() again to generate an error. In this case, the catch portion of the try…catch statement will generate a simple message telling you of the error. The message in the finally portion of the try…catch statement will also appear, despite the return statement in the catch portion. The finally code will always run. However, because of the return statement, the message box outside the try…catch statement will never appear.

Advanced Class Creation Techniques

By now, you should know that classes are extremely flexible. However, we haven't looked at some of the advanced development techniques for classes. For example, you can nest one class within another. The parent class can see and use the child class, but you can hide this class from the outside world if desired.

The following sections look at several helpful class creation techniques. You might not use these techniques every day, but you'll find them essential when you do. For example, not every class requires variable length parameter lists, but knowing how to create a class that does can keep you from creating an odd assorting of class overrides to fulfill certain needs. We'll also discuss how you can create class versions and implement special class conditions.

Creating Variable Length Parameter Lists

There are some situations when you don't know the precise number of parameters that a user will pass to your method. For example, you might create a method that adds a list of numbers, but you not know how many numbers the user might need to add. C# provides help in this situation in the form of the params keyword. The params keyword can only appear once in a list of arguments for a method and must appear at the end of the list. Here's an example of the params keyword in use.

```
private void btnTest_Click(object sender, System.EventArgs e)
{
    // Test the variable argument list.
    MessageBox.Show("The Result Is: " + MyVar(1, 2).ToString());
    MessageBox.Show("The Result Is: " + MyVar(1, 2, 3).ToString());
    MessageBox.Show("The Result Is: " + MyVar(1, 2, 3, 4).ToString());
}

private int MyVar(int Value1, params int[] Value2)
{
    int   Temp;    // Temporary Value Holder
    int   Count;   // Loop Count

    // Transfer Value 1 to Temp.
    Temp = Value1;

    // Keep adding until done.
    for (Count = 0; Count < Value2.Length; Count++)
        Temp = Temp + Value2[Count];

    // Return the value.
    return Temp;
}
```

In this example, MyVar() requires a minimum of two numbers to add. However, if you want to add more numbers, MyVar() will accept them, as shown in btnTest_Click(). As you can see, you must add the params keyword to the last argument in the list. The argument must also consist of an array told hold the variable number of input values.

The example shows how you could use an `int` array. However, this technique works even better with strings or objects because you can send data of various types and convert them within the method. The biggest disadvantage of this technique is that Intellisense can't help the user. For example, the user will only receive helps on the first two arguments in the example code.

Creating Class Versions

Most of the classes in the .NET Framework follow a hierarchy. A derived class uses a base class as a means of getting started. In most cases, the base class is perfectly usable as a class in its own right. However, there are exceptions to the rule that we'll discuss in the "Implementing Special Class Conditions" section that follows. Some classes are only usable as base classes and you can't derive from others.

The act of evolving a class over time is called *versioning*. Almost every class you build will go through several versions, because usage will demonstrate the need for added functionality. The act of creating new versions of existing methods is common practice—many companies will simply append a number to the end of the method name to avoid problems.

You can also apply the term versioning to derived classes. The derived class is a new version of an existing class. In some languages, the act of deriving new classes mixed with the need of the base class to evolve causes problems. For example, whenever a developer adds a new method to a base class, there's a chance that the new method will conflict with methods in a derived class.

While a well-designed class will retain the same interface for existing methods, adding new methods usually doesn't break applications—that is, unless the addition creates a conflict. Derived classes are an essential part of the object-oriented programming paradigm. A developer writes a base class with some simple functionality, then refines the intended behavior within a derived class. Consequently, developers require access to both new versions of existing classes and derived classes that augment the behavior of the base class. Conflicts seem inherent and unavoidable in such an environment.

To prevent problems with versions, C# forces the derived class to declare its intent using one of several keywords. The first keyword is `new`. If you declare a method in a derived class with the same name as the base class, but add the word `new` to the declaration, then C# treats the method as a new addition. The new method doesn't override or block the method in the base class—users can see both methods when they use the derived class.

In some cases, the derived class does need to override the method found in the base class. Perhaps the implementation of the method in the base class won't work with the derived class. In this case, the developer adds the `override` keyword to the method declaration in the derived class. The user of the derived class will only see the method that appears in the derived class—the method in the base class is blocked from view. Listing 4.7 shows an example of the new and override keywords in use.

Listing 4.7   **Using the *New* and *Override* Keywords**

```
using System;

namespace ClassVersion
{
    class Base
    {
        // Create the conflicting method.
        public virtual void Conflict(int Value)
        {
            Console.WriteLine("This is from Base: {0}", Value);
        }
    }

    class Derived1 : Base
    {
        // This method won't hide the one in Base.
        public new virtual void Conflict(int Value)
        {
            Console.WriteLine("This is from Derived1: {0}", Value);
        }
    }

    class Derived2 : Base
    {
        // This method does hide the one in Base.
        public override void Conflict(int Value)
        {
            Console.WriteLine("This is from Derived2: {0}", Value);
        }
    }

    class Class1
    {
        [STAThread]
        static void Main(string[] args)
        {
            // Create three objects based on the classes.
            Base  MyBase = new Base();
            Derived1 MyDerived1 = new Derived1();
            Derived2 MyDerived2 = new Derived2();

            // Output values based on the Conflict method.
            MyBase.Conflict(1);
            MyDerived1.Conflict(1);
            MyDerived2.Conflict(1);
```

```
        }
      }
    }
```

As you can see, all three classes contain the same method. When you call on them in the Main() function, they all display the results you expect. Each call to Conflict() uses the version specifically designed for that class.

An interesting thing happens if you make the Conflict() method in Derived1 private. The application still compiles, but you'll see the output from the Base class, not Derived1. Because Derived1 doesn't hide the Base class version of Conflict(), the application assumes you want to use the Base class version. On the other hand, if you try to make the version of Conflict() in Derived2 private, the application will register an error telling you that you can't make virtual methods private. The reason for the difference is that Derived2 hides the version of Conflict() in the Base class.

Implementing Special Class Conditions

All classes don't come in the same form. So far, we've dealt with classes that are basically open for any activity. You can inherit from them, instantiate them, and generally use them as needed. However, not every class is a good candidate for such global use. For example, you might want to create a class that serves only as a template for creating other classes. This is the infamous base class that you've heard so much about. To create a base class, you need to know about abstract classes. The following list describes each special class condition in a little more detail.

Sealed   Sealed classes always provide a full implementation of all the methods they contain. You can instantiate a sealed class and use the result object as you would any other object. However, other classes can't inherit from a sealed class. In addition, all methods within a sealed class are static, which means that they can't be changed or overridden in any way. Sealed classes are useful because they enable you to create a specific class implementation without concern that someone else will misuse the class in some unforeseen way.

Abstract   Abstract classes are very close to interfaces. You can't instantiate an abstract class and the class doesn't need to provide implementations for any of the methods it contains. However, unlike an interface, an abstract class has the option of providing some implementation details. In addition, while a class can inherit from multiple interfaces, it can inherit from only one class. This means that an abstract class provides the perfect means to create a base class—one that you'd never use, except to create other classes.

NOTE   You might hear the term *virtual* in conjunction with classes. In C#, the `virtual` keyword only appears with methods and properties. The keyword enables developers to override the method or property in a derived implementation of the associated class. In short, any interface or class that contains virtual members could be considered virtual, but the keyword has no meaning in this context.

Where Do You Go From Here?

When you complete this chapter, you should have a better idea of how to work with classes with C#. One of the central ideas is that the class is the center of everything in .NET. We've explored classes in many ways, including specialty class types used to create other classes.

One of the best ways to use the information in this chapter is to look at any existing code you might have written in .NET or design some new code using the principles in Chapters 3 and 4. Make sure you consider how best to write the code so that it requires the least effort. For example, you'll want to use attributes and directives to perform some work automatically, rather than write all of the code by hand.

The problem that you hear about the most today is bugs in code. Yes, there's the age-old argument that users are their own worst enemy, but a good developer realizes this and builds the application accordingly. A large part of the solution for errant code is good error handling. This chapter has introduced you to some new solutions for error handling provided by .NET. Now might be a good time to see how your existing code stacks and use the information in this chapter to improve it.

Chapter 5 is going to explore the application that all of us have written at one time or another—the desktop application. The chapter will tell you about the basic application types you can create with C#, how to use various resources, and then how to write the various applications. We'll also discuss an essential topic for developers—debugging techniques. The Visual Studio .NET IDE makes this task easier than ever before.

PART II

Standard Application Development with C#

CHAPTER 5

Building Desktop Applications

- Desktop Application Types

- Writing Console Applications

- Resource Essentials

- Writing Windows Applications

- Application Debugging

With all of the emphasis on distributed applications that only appear on the Internet, it's easy to forget that not every application ever created appears on someone's website. Distributed application development is extremely important—we'll spend a considerable part of this book discussing that topic. However, the desktop application hasn't gone away and it's unlikely to go away in the near future. The simple fact is that desktop applications serve the needs of many computer users who don't need access to the Internet, much less access to a business partner's network.

You can create a vast assortment of application types with C#, including desktop applications. We've already looked at a simple example of a desktop application in Chapters 3 and 4 (Parameters and CommandLine2). This chapter is going to build on your knowledge of desktop applications and show you how to create several application types including dialog-based, single document interface (SDI), and multiple document interface (MDI).

Desktop Application Types

Desktop applications come in a variety of shapes and sizes. C# is quite capable of creating any application you can imagine (and perhaps a few that you can't). However, there are five application types that exemplify desktop applications as a whole, and that's what we'll concentrate on first.

Console applications   Represent those situations when you don't need a full-fledged interface for the user to work with. Many console applications appear as part of script, task scheduler, or remote machine access applications.

Dialog-based applications   Are normally reserved for utilities or applications that are too small to require complete menuing systems. Many dialog-based applications provide informational displays, and they're known for their small memory footprint.

Single-document applications   Are representative of simple applications that work with their own data, like note takers or small database front ends. These applications also require a menuing system of some type. A single-document application works with one document at a time.

Multiple-document applications   Include full-fledged applications like word processors and spreadsheets. When you think about it, they represent that fringe area of C# programming where you need to weigh the flexibility of C# against the development speed offered by RAD programming environments like Visual Basic. Multiple-document applications can work with more than one document at a time and could work with multiple document types simultaneously.

HTML-based applications   Work with data of some type (like single-document or multiple-document applications) but with browser twist. Instead of a standard editor, your user will see what amounts to a web browser front end. The data normally appears formatted as a web page.

NOTE   Remember that we're talking about desktop applications in this chapter. C# is capable of creating all kinds of different code. You can use it to create DLLs, ActiveX controls, components, background executing programs like screensavers, and even extensions to C# itself. We're only talking about general applications in this chapter, but we'll cover many of these other possibilities as the book progresses. Two notable exceptions from the C# repertoire include ISAPI Extensions and device drivers.

Console

I made some statements previously that gave you an overall sense of what a console application is, but they were too sweeping to really tell you what a console application is all about. A console application has a DOS window look rather than the more familiar Windows-style appearance. It uses monospaced font, just like you'd see in a DOS window, and you can use special input/output functions such as `Console.WriteLine()` and `Console.Read()`. However, internally, the program is a Windows application.

One of the early reasons for using console applications was to move a utility from DOS to Windows. Developers and network administrators owned a wealth of management applications that worked well at the command prompt. The high end user didn't require a user interface and appreciated the efficiency boost that a console application could provide. Working at the command line is still a major part of the network administration experience, but many network administrators are moving from the command line to large windowed management applications such as the Microsoft Management Console (MMC).

TIP   Interestingly enough, some developers are still moving their DOS utilities to Windows. It's safe to assume that you'll be able to move the "business logic" of your DOS application to Windows using a console application. You may also be able to move some of the display and printing elements. However, it's never safe to assume that you'll be able to maintain one set of code for both DOS and Windows by using a console application—the two environments are different enough that you'll always have to make changes in the move from DOS to Windows.

Today, console applications serve a different purpose. Network administrators commonly look to console applications as a means to automate maintenance tasks. A console application is a perfect solution for scripting and task scheduling. Because a console application doesn't require a GUI interface, a network administrator can use it across a network connection from a command prompt. Console applications also support pipes and other means of redirecting output to a file. In fact, the console application is so important in this role that Microsoft actually added more command-line tools to Windows XP for the sole purpose of network and system management.

Console applications serve other purposes as well. For example, many user-level utilities either support a command-line interface or use a console interface. Many developers use console applications for experimentation. Console applications offer a clarity of coding that's often obscured by the GUI code in a Windows application.

Standard Windows

The standard Windows format is still the main method for creating desktop applications. Windows applications typically come in three styles: dialog-based, SDI, and MDI. Each of these styles serves a different purpose. A developer won't want to suffer the encumbrance of an MDI application when a dialog-based application will do. On the other hand, a dialog-based application is ill suited to present large quantities of textual or graphic information. You need an SDI or MDI application to perform most types of large-scale data manipulation.

Many programming languages differentiate between the various Windows application types. For example, Visual C++ has separate wizard settings for each type of application. C# doesn't provide a real differentiation between the three types of Windows application—every application begins as a dialog-based application. The presentation of the information and use of controls changes the application type. For example, the CommandLine2 application in Chapter 4 began as a dialog-based application, but the addition of a RichTextEdit control and a menu changed the application's appearance to the SDI model. The following sections describe the uses for the various Windows application types, as well as presentation concerns that you need to consider as you develop the application.

Dialog-Based Applications

Many people associate dialogs with configuration screens, About boxes, and other adjuncts to a full-fledged application. Dialog-based applications have a place, too. They're extremely useful for utility-type applications where you need to display a fairly minimal amount of data and you require minimal user input. The main advantages of using a dialog-based application include:

- Quick prototyping
- Short development cycle
- Small memory footprint

TIP When deciding whether to build a dialog-based or window-based application, think utility. If your application fits into the utility category, it's probably a good candidate for a dialog-based interface. On the other hand, if you're thinking about adding a lot of features or allowing the user to interact with the application heavily, you may want to look at an SDI or MDI application. Make sure you take future expansion into account when making your decision—a bad choice today could cost you a lot in rework time tomorrow.

So, what makes a dialog-based application better than a full-fledged window-based application? One of the more important factors is size. You can create two versions of the same application, one that uses a dialog front end and another that depends on a window. The dialog version will be smaller every time. In addition to conserving resources, you may find that the dialog version loads faster. A dialog-based application is simply more efficient than its window-based counterpart.

You may find that building a dialog-based application is faster as well. Dialog-based applications are meant to be small and efficient. If you find that you're adding a lot of bells and whistles to this kind of application, perhaps you've used the wrong kind of application to start with. Dialog-based applications normally eschew menus and other paraphernalia that a window-based application requires in order to provide a user-friendly front end. Fewer bells and whistles spell reduced development and debugging time for the programmer. Obviously, anything that speeds the programmer along is worth looking at.

The only real problem with dialog-based applications is that some programmers feel they can stuff one to the point of breaking. I've seen some dialog-based applications that are so filled with gizmos that you really can't tell what they're supposed to do. While a dialog-based application may look a little more cramped than its SDI or MDI counterpart, you shouldn't have it so crammed that no one can use it.

TIP You can reduce clutter on a dialog-based application by using tabbed pages, just like a property dialog used by Windows for configuration purposes. Each tab should have a specific purpose, and you should limit the number of tabs to those that can fit comfortably in the default dialog frame.

Single Document Interface (SDI)

A single-document application is one like Notepad or Microsoft Paint. It's designed to handle one document at a time, which reduces programming complexity and the amount of resources required for running the application. You'd use this kind of windowed application for something small, like a text editor or perhaps a small graphics editor. A single-document application allows users to interact fully with the document that you want them to create, but it's usually less robust than an application designed to work with multiple documents. In addition, the single-document application usually has a minimum of one less menu than a multiple-document application would—the Window menu that's used to select the document you want to edit.

SDI applications also use controls that tend to support object linking and embedding (OLE). For example, the RichTextEdit control offers modes that support use of the control as an OLE container. An OLE container can act as a receptacle for data from other applications. For example, OLE enables a user to place a graphic image within a text document. Unlike some Visual Studio languages, you'll find that you need to develop OLE server capabilities in C# through manual programming techniques—none of the wizards offer to set this feature up for you.

Unfortunately, single-document window-based applications can suffer from the same problem as a dialog-based application—too much complexity. I still remember problems trying to use older versions of Corel Draw. Every time I wanted to look at a drawing, I had to close the currently open document before doing so. This limitation made Corel Draw a little harder to use than it needed to be. For example, I wasted a lot of time trying to compare one drawing against another. (Fortunately, Corel Corporation has corrected this oversight in current versions of Corel Draw.)

TIP   The single-document, window-based application works surprisingly well when it comes to database management systems. The reason is fairly simple. Very few (if any) of your users will need to open more than one database at a time. Even if they do, the rules for working with databases would make it less desirable to allow the user to access multiple databases by themselves. You'll normally want to control all access to the various database elements programmatically and display the results to the user.

Multiple Document Interface (MDI)

Now we're down to the multiple-document application. You'd use this kind of window-based application to create something like a word processor or spreadsheet application. If you think about it for a second, a text editor has a limited appeal simply because it can only open one document at a time. People need to be able to compare one document to another; that's why multiple-document applications aren't only nice, but required in so many situations.

Multiple-document applications also tend to be feature rich. (You can still go overboard; just look at all the people complaining about the bloated feature sets of major products produced by vendors today.) A text editor may provide a very simple find function and not offer any means for replacing occurrences of text. A full-fledged word processor provides both search and replace as standard features.

The failings of a multiple-document application begin with the fact that it can handle multiple documents. The capability of handling more than one document at a time means a lot of additional programming. You don't just have to keep track of all the open documents. There's the Window menu to manage, and special program features like split-screen to consider as well. You'll also need to decide whether the user will be allowed to display more than one document at once. Things like minimizing one document while keeping another maximized require additional code as well. In sum, you'll need to be prepared for some major programming time before you even start a multiple-document application.

Of course, multiple-document applications have plenty of other disadvantages as well. For example, if you've ever tried to use Word for an OLE server, you know all about the frustration of waiting for this behemoth application to open every time you click on a link in another application. You've probably experienced the serious consequences of running out of memory as well. Until recently, every time you wanted to use OLE, you had to have enough memory to run both applications (the client and the server). Fortunately, Microsoft has reduced this requirement somewhat by allowing the server to take over the client's window; now the server only has to worry about working with the document itself. The client window provides a framework for the server's menus and toolbar, so there isn't any extra memory wasted.

Web-Based Applications

Web-based applications are becoming more popular as more companies require distributed application support. Combining a web page front end with data delivered using SOAP or some other XML technology makes sense in a world where developers don't even know what platform will run the application. However, before you begin thinking that a browser is the only way to create a Web-based application, consider the fact that Visual Studio supports other types of web-based application development, some of which are completely invisible to the end user. For example, the help files provided with Visual Studio .NET rely on web technology, but the interface looks like a typical desktop application. The first clue that Visual Studio .NET is using an HTML-based front end is when you need something found on Microsoft's website and the application looks for an Internet connection.

TIP   You'll find Microsoft Help URLs placed throughout the book. All of these URLs begin with `ms-help://`. You can enter the URL in the Address Bar for Visual Studio Help, or you can open a copy of Internet Explorer and enter the URL there. One of the benefits of using Internet Explorer is that you can see an unencumbered view of the information. Of course, you lose the ability to search the rest of Visual Studio .NET Help when using Internet Explorer as your browser. However, you'll find the loss of search capability minimal when viewing lists of information, such as the list of WMI hardware classes discussed in the "Script-Based Example for Batch Jobs" section of the chapter.

From a development perspective, you can divide web-based applications into two categories: those that rely on a browser and those that use an HTML-based front end. The browser application is more flexible because you can place it on any machine with a compatible browser. For example, it's possible to develop SOAP applications on your desktop machine that will ultimately run on a PDA using the browser application. The HTML-based front end has the advantage of functionality. You can combine standard desktop elements with HTML elements to create a type of hybrid application.

So, what good is an HTML-based document application? Think about the advantages of creating your own custom web browser. You could set it to view the company website automatically and restrict users from viewing non-business-oriented sites on the Web. Since a custom browser need not carry all of the generic features of a full-fledged browser, it would consume less memory and less disk space as well. In other words, you could create an environment that provides all of the functionality of a browser with none of the problems (at least from a company website access perspective).

However, this new application type is more valuable than you may initially think. For example, you could add HTML-enabled components to an existing application to allow it to access a web server–based help desk. Instead of creating a standard help file and adding it to your application, you can create a very specialized Web browser and add it instead. (This is precisely the route that Microsoft took with Visual Studio .NET.)

The advantages of HTML-based help are clear. Using the older help files meant that you couldn't easily update the help files for your application once you sent the application to a customer or distributed it throughout the company. Updating HTML help is as easy as changing a file on your web server. In addition, working with Microsoft Help Workshop isn't easy—many developers found deciphering the arcane language used in help files akin to learning a new programming language. HTML-based help requires no compiler or special tools, just a text editor. (Theoretically, you'll want an editor designed to work with HTML before writing a huge help file.)

There are disadvantages to HTML help as well. For one thing, it's a lot of more difficult to build adequate search capability into HTML-based help. Since finding the information the user wants is just as important as creating it in the first place, HTML-based help may not be the answer of choice for novice users. In addition, HTML-based help necessitates an Internet (or, at least, an intranet) connection. If your company has many users on the road, trying to find an Internet connection may not be practical. Of course, you could always create a local copy of the required HTML files, but that would create the same problem as you had before—out-of-date help files.

Writing Console Applications

As previously mentioned, console applications are useful for a number of tasks, so knowing how to create a console application is important. Most of the applications so far have relied on a dialog-based presentation because the dialog presentation is good for shorter example code. The following sections show how to create two examples that you could use to work with your machine from the command prompt. The goal is to create applications that can execute in the foreground, as part of a script, as a scheduled task, or even as part of another application.

Simple Example

You can create new console applications by selecting the Console Application project in the New Project dialog box shown in Figure 5.1. The resulting project is bare. It includes only a namespace and class declaration with an empty `Main()` method. As previously mentioned, console applications are designed to provide their functionality with a minimum of memory and resource usage.

FIGURE 5.1:

The New Project dialog box contains a special icon for console applications.

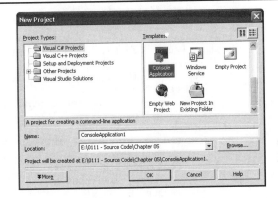

Console applications generally eschew graphics of any kind. In fact, console applications can access the `System.Console` class for all input and output requirements. For example, if you want to output some text to the command prompt display, you could use either of these two methods:

```
Console.WriteLine("Method 1");
Console.Out.WriteLine("Method 2");
```

The first method will always output the string to the screen. The output destination of the second method depends on where you set the application output. While the default setting uses the console screen, you can use the `Console.SetOut()` method to select another location, such as a file. You can also use the techniques for the Diagnose example in Chapter 2 to output messages to the event logs. This is a favorite technique for console applications designed to run as part of a script or of the Task Scheduler on a server.

Part of writing a console application is to know how to process the environmental data. You don't worry about this information in a standard Windows application as much because the application isn't running at the command line. Listing 5.1 shows a simple example of reading all of the environment variables on the current machine and sending them to the console display. (You can also find this code in the \Chapter 05\SimpleConsole folder on the CD.)

Listing 5.1 **Processing the Environment Variables**

```
using System;
using System.Diagnostics;

namespace SimpleConsole
{
   class CheckEnvironment
   {
      [STAThread]
      static void Main(string[] args)
      {
         int    Counter;        // Loop counter.
         bool   NoPause = false;  // Should the application pause?

         // Determine if the user asked for help.
         if (args.Length > 0)
            for (Counter = 0; Counter < args.Length; Counter++)
               if (args[Counter] == "/?")
               {
                  Console.WriteLine("Displays system environment " +
                     "variables.");
                  Console.WriteLine("Use the /NoPause switch to " +
                     "display without a pause.");
                  return;
               }

         // Create an instance of the process information.
         ProcessStartInfo  MyInfo = new ProcessStartInfo();

         // Process each environment variable.
         foreach(String Key in MyInfo.EnvironmentVariables.Keys)
         {
            // Write the current key and key value.
            Console.WriteLine("The current key is: {0}", Key);
            Console.WriteLine(MyInfo.EnvironmentVariables[Key]);
            Console.WriteLine();
         }
```

```
        // Determine if we need to pause.
        if (args.Length > 0)
            for (Counter = 0; Counter < args.Length; Counter++)
                if (args[Counter].ToUpper() == "/NOPAUSE")
                    NoPause = true;

        // Only needed so application pauses.
        if (!NoPause)
        {
            Console.Write("Press any key when ready...");
            Console.ReadLine();
        }
    }
  }
}
```

The code begins by checking for the /? command-line switch. Any console application you write should include at least a modicum of help for those who want to use it. Generally, you'll want to include a short description of application function and any command-line switches.

After checking for the /? command-line switch, the code creates a new `ProcessStartInfo` object, `MyInfo` object. This object contains a wealth of information about the application's starting environment, including the environment variables. You access the environment variables using `MyInfo.EnvironmentVariables[]`. The index is a string containing the name of the key.

The only problem with using the `MyInfo.EnvironmentVariables[]` index is that you don't know the key names when the application starts because every machine can have a different set of environment variables. That's where the `foreach` loop comes in handy. This loop accesses the `MyInfo.EnvironmentVariables.Keys` collection, which contains the name of every key defined on the user's machine. C# excels at working with collections using the technique shown in Listing 5.1.

The application ends by checking for the /NoPause command-line switch. Notice the use of the `ToUpper()` method to ensure the code finds the switch in the `args` list no matter how the user capitalizes the switch. The *NoPause* variable determines if the application exits directly or pauses for user input. The addition of a pause enables the user to access the application from within Windows or from the command prompt with equal ease.

This is actually a handy maintenance utility to have around because you can use the Task Scheduler to output the user's environment to a known location on the server using redirection like this:

```
SimpleConsole /NoPause >> Temp.txt
```

Some applications insist on adding environment variables to the system and then don't remove them later. As the system gets more clogged with weird environment entries, it can slow. In some cases, a bad environment string can also cause some applications to fail (or, at least, not behave very well). It's also helpful to have an application parse the environment variables looking for development needs. For example, a simple script could detect the presence of path entries for the .NET environment and provide you with a simple "Ready" or "Not Ready" indicator of system setup.

Script-Based Example for Batch Jobs

Many console applications begin and end their existence at the command line because the developer doesn't need them for any other purpose. However, as network administrators begin to write more script applications, the need for console applications that can perform some type of generic low-level work increases. The console application becomes a "black box" that accepts some input from the network administrator, then provides a single output in the form of a return value. Often, the return value indicates only success or failure, but it can offer more.

The example in this section accepts a Windows Management Instrumentation (WMI) query and a text filename as input. The application outputs selected data about the query to a text file. The return value of the application is the number of devices of the requested type. If the application returns 0, then none of the requested devices exists and the text file is blank. Listing 5.2 shows the source code for this example.

Listing 5.2   **WMI Provides an Interesting Basis for a Console Application**

```
static int Main(string[] args)
{
    int                       Counter;     // Loop Counter
    ManagementObjectSearcher  MOS;         // WMI Query Object
    ManagementObjectCollection MOCollect;  // Query Result Collection.
    string                    Query;       // Query Request String
    TextWriter                SendOut;     // Output File Object.
    bool                      Verbose;     // Output to file and screen.
    bool                      Clear;       // Clear the old output file.
    string                    OutFile;     // Output Filename

    // Verify the user has provided input.
    if (args.Length == 0)
    {
        Console.WriteLine("You must supply a query or request" +
            "help using the /? switch.");
        return 1;
    }
```

```
// Handle help requests.
if (args.Length > 0)
   for (Counter = 0; Counter < args.Length; Counter++)
      if (args[Counter] == "/?")
      {
         Console.WriteLine("Displays system information " +
            "using Windows Management Instrumentation (WMI).");
         Console.WriteLine();
         Console.WriteLine("Command Line:");
         Console.WriteLine("\tConsoleScript /Query:<Query> " +
            "/Out:<Filename> [/V] [/Clear]");
         Console.WriteLine();
         Console.WriteLine("/Query:<Query>\tProvide a query " +
            "string as input.");
         Console.WriteLine("\t\tAn example query would be, \"" +
            "SELECT * FROM Win32_LogicalDisk\"");
         Console.WriteLine("/Out:<Filename>\tName of the " +
            "file you want to use for output.");
         Console.WriteLine("/V\t\tDisplays the output on " +
            "screen as well as outputting to the\r\n\t\tfile.");
         Console.WriteLine("/Clear\t\tClear the output file " +
            "before writing to it.\r\n\r\n");
         Console.WriteLine("Return values:");
         Console.WriteLine("\t0 - Success");
         Console.WriteLine("\t1 - No Input Provided");
         Console.WriteLine("\t2 - No Query Found");
         Console.WriteLine("\t3 - Device Access Error");
         return 0;
      }

// Locate the query.
for (Counter = 0; Counter < args.Length; Counter++)
   if (args[Counter].Length > 7)
   {
      if (args[Counter].Substring(0, 7).ToUpper() == "/QUERY:")
         break;
   }
   else
      if (Counter == args.Length - 1)
      {
         Console.WriteLine("No Query Found");
         return 2;
      }

// Place the query in a string.
Query = args[Counter].Substring(7) + " ";
Counter++;
while (args[Counter].Substring(0 , 1) != "/")
{
   Query = Query + args[Counter] + " ";
   Counter++;
```

```csharp
      if (Counter == args.Length)
         break;
}

// Locate the output filename.
OutFile = "";
for (Counter = 0; Counter < args.Length; Counter++)
   if (args[Counter].Length > 5)
      if (args[Counter].Substring(0, 5).ToUpper() == "/OUT:")
      {
         OutFile = args[Counter].Substring(5);
         break;
      }
      else
         if (Counter == args.Length - 1)
         {
            Console.WriteLine("Using Default Filename");
            OutFile = "Temp.TXT";
         }

// Create the output file.
Clear = false;
for (Counter = 0; Counter < args.Length; Counter++)
   if (args[Counter].ToUpper() == "/CLEAR")
      Clear = true;
if (Clear)
   SendOut = new StreamWriter(OutFile, false);
else
   SendOut = new StreamWriter(OutFile, true);

// Determine if we need console output.
Verbose = false;
for (Counter = 0; Counter < args.Length; Counter++)
   if (args[Counter].ToUpper() == "/V")
      Verbose = true;

try
{
   // Create a WMI query based on user input.
   MOS = new ManagementObjectSearcher(Query);

   // Get the query results and place them in a collection.
   MOCollect = MOS.Get();

   // Output the data.
   foreach( ManagementObject MO in MOCollect )
   {
      SendOut.Write("Caption: {0} Description: {1}\r\n",
         MO["Caption"], MO["Description"]);
      if (Verbose)
         Console.WriteLine("Caption: {0} Description: {1}\r\n",
```

```
                MO["Caption"], MO["Description"]);
        }

        // Close the output file.
        SendOut.Close();
    }
    catch (System.Management.ManagementException e)
    {
        // Output error information as needed.
        Console.WriteLine("Error Accessing Device");
        Console.WriteLine(e.ErrorCode);
        Console.WriteLine(e.ErrorInformation);
        Console.WriteLine(e.Message);
        Console.WriteLine(e.Source);
        return 3;
    }

    // No errors, so standard return.
    return 0;
}
```

As you can see, this console application is a little more complex than the previous example. The first thing you should notice is that the return value of Main() has changed from void to int to allow a return value. The batch file used to test this example relies on the return value to print a message.

The code begins by ensuring the user has provided command-line input. At the very least, the application requires a query to perform any function at all. The user can also request help using the /? command-line switch. The help for this example is more extensive, because the console application can perform more work.

The next two sections of code work with the query string, *Query*. First, the code needs to locate the /Query switch within the command-line arguments. Second, the code builds the query string. The application continues processing the arguments until it runs into another switch or comes to the end of the command line. The content of *Query* looks much like a SQL statement and follows some of the same logic. A simple query always includes four elements: Select *<What to Select>* From *<WMI class name>*. For example, if you wanted to query the logical disks on your system, you'd use a string similar to, "Select * From Win32_LogicalDisk." The ManagementObjectSearcher object also allows you to filter the output using a WHERE clause such as "WHERE DriveType = 3." In this case, we'd be looking for all local drives and filtering out the network drives.

TIP   You can find a list of WMI classes in the Computer System Hardware Classes help topic (`ms-help://MS.VSCC/MS.MSDNVS/wmisdk/r_32hard1_9v77.htm`). Each class lists the types of information you can retrieve about the hardware in question. Some types of information, such as Description, are generic for any hardware class. Other pieces of information, such as the Compressed Value for Win32_LogicalDisk, are specific to the hardware class in question.

After it creates a query string, the code locates the output filename. Even though the help lists the /Out switch as required, it can recover from input errors by creating a default filename. The application does output a message stating it's using a default filename instead of using one provided by the user. The code checks for the /Clear switch, then creates the file using the StreamWriter() constructor. The second argument of this constructor is true if you want to append data to the existing file. The resulting object assumes you want to use the local directory, if you don't supply a path as part of the filename.

At this point, the code enters a try block. Error handling is nice in other areas of the application, but it's required here. Otherwise, the application will fail on a number of WMI supported devices, even if the device is installed and functional. The problem is one of recognition. Depending on the BIOS provided with the machine, the method used to support WMI, and Windows ability to see the device, some devices might not appear on the list.

It's time to obtain the WMI information from the system. The code performs three steps to complete this process.

1. The code creates the query. The query will normally succeed unless the input string is malformed.

2. The code executes the query and places the result in a collection. If this step fails, the collection will contain a null value, but won't fail.

3. The code uses a foreach loop to view each collection member. This step always fails if the device is inoperative, unrecognized, or unavailable. The example provides two forms of output. The first is to a file, while the second is an optional screen output.

Before you can compile this application, you need to add the usual using statements to the beginning of the file (see the source code in the \Chapter 05\ConsoleScript folder on the CD for details). You also need to add a reference to the System.Management component by selecting the Project ➤ Add Reference command. You'll see an Add Reference dialog box similar to the one shown in Figure 5.2. Highlight the System.Management entry, click Select, then click OK to add the reference to your project.

FIGURE 5.2:

Use the Add Reference dialog box to add the System.Management component to your application.

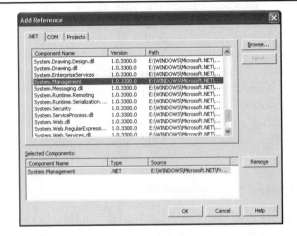

You'll find a simple batch file named Test.BAT in the \Chapter 05\ConsoleScript\bin\ Debug folder. It accepts a simple query as input and provides some output based on the ConsoleScript invocation results. Here's the Test.BAT code.

```
ECHO OFF

REM Run the application.
ConsoleScript %1 %2 %3 %4 %5 %6 %7

REM Test the output.
If ErrorLevel 3 Goto DeviceErr
If ErrorLevel 2 Goto NoQuery
If ErrorLevel 1 Goto NoInput

REM If no error, exit.
Goto Success

REM Error Message Output.
:NoInput
ECHO No Input Provided
GOTO END
:NoQuery
ECHO Always provide an /Query input.
GOTO END
:DeviceErr
ECHO Device error - is it installed?
GOTO END

:Success
```

```
ECHO Task Completed Successfully!

:END
ECHO ON
```

Of course, you could easily use the ConsoleScript application with a script file or as part of a Task Scheduler entry. The point is that console applications help you automate many tasks and perform others in the background or at a command prompt. A console application isn't a good choice when you need to provide a large amount of user interaction, but it does fill a needed gap in the network administrator's Toolkit.

Resource Essentials

You won't write many applications that can function without resources of some type. Resources include menus, accelerators, bitmaps, special controls, accessibility features, and web-access support. Resources also include fonts, brushes, and pens—the drawing tools we've used in other areas of the book. (See the CommandLine2 example in Chapter 4 for an example of a print routine that uses the drawing tools.) Your code interacts with the resources to present information to the user in a helpful manner.

The following sections will discuss many of the resources we haven't yet covered fully or at all. We'll work with these resources extensively as the book progresses. For example, you'll find some graphics examples later in the chapter. This chapter will also show one way to use timers in your applications. The Resources example found in the \Chapter 05\Resource folder on the CD also contains some examples of using resources within an application.

Accelerators and Menus

Menus come in a variety of shapes and sizes. All SDI and MDI applications require a main menu. This menu normally contains a File entry, as well as some form of Help. However, Visual Studio .NET provides you with a clean slate when you create a menu, so the contents are completely up to you. Following the pattern used by existing applications is good practice because using a standard menu template makes it easier for others to learn your application.

Another typical menu type is the context menu. Most Windows objects provide a context menu so the user knows how to interact with that object. Dialog applications use context menus frequently, and you'll find context menus in SDI and MDI applications. The menu you see in an application that resides in the Taskbar tray is a context menu, as is the menu you see when you click within the work area of an SDI or MDI application.

The main and context menus for an application are different controls: `MainMenu` and `ContextMenu`. An application can have multiple context menus, but it can contain only one main menu. The main menu attaches itself to the form where you create it and normally remains visible. In most cases, you can hide the main menu by setting the *Menu* property of the form to a null (blank) value. Here's an example of two context menu commands that will hide and show the main menu.

```
private void HideMainMenu_Click(object sender, System.EventArgs e)
{
    // Hide the main menu.
    Menu = null;
}

private void ShowMainMenu_Click(object sender, System.EventArgs e)
{
    // Show the main menu.
    Menu = mainMenu1;
}
```

It's interesting to note that you can use this same technique for changing between predefined main menus, rather than build each main menu by scratch. Many applications disable the menu entries the user can't access given the current environment, but sometimes it pays to create multiple main menus during design time for a quick swap during runtime. Of course, you can only use one main menu at a time.

You need to attach a context menu to an object using the object *ContextMenu* property to make it accessible. The context menu is only visible when the user right-clicks on the object or you make the menu visible in some other way. Unlike a main menu, context menus contain only one main entry. However, you can create as many submenus as needed to complete a given task.

Despite their differences, creating a main menu and a context menu is essentially the same. You'll begin with a blank menu where you type the various menu entries, as shown in Figure 5.3. Notice the use of the ampersand to create underlines. A user can type the underlined character to access the menu entry, so you need to make the entries unique for a given menu level.

Visual Studio .NET uses a nondescript naming technique for menus—menuItem followed by a number. Most developers use a naming scheme that follows the menu hierarchy. For example, a developer might name the Exit option of the File menu mnuFileExit for easy identification.

FIGURE 5.3:

Main and context menus follow essentially the same design process.

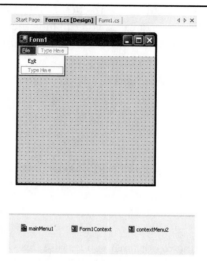

This brings us to the topic of accelerators or shortcut keys (the term you use likely depends on the environment in which you started working). You assign an accelerator to an object using the *Shortcut* property. An accelerator enables a user to access a menu or other command using a key combination, rather than the menu hierarchy. Like menu setups, most applications use specific accelerators for the same task. For example, you can usually access the print feature of an application by pressing Ctrl+P.

One of the interesting characteristics of the C# IDE is that you can't see the accelerator you assign to a menu entry until the application is running. This means you have to assign the accelerator judiciously. Otherwise, the same accelerator could appear on two different menu entries, as shown in Figure 5.4. Experimentation shows that the first menu item to receive the accelerator key will normally use it, which means you might receive unexpected results with conflicting accelerators.

FIGURE 5.4:

Always use accelerators carefully to avoid conflicts.

C# doesn't limit you to using accelerators for menu entries. Some controls such as the DataGrid come with built-in accelerators. You can also create accelerators with labels to access the associated control faster. Type an ampersand next to the letter in the label that you want to use for access. When you press Alt+<*Letter*>, the application automatically selects the control (normally a textbox) associated with the label. Some controls, such as the pushbutton, allow you to add the accelerator directly by typing the ampersand as part of the control text.

Accessibility Features

The best way to make your application friendly is to use a sensible layout, add plenty of help, and use features such as accelerators. These features help a lot; but, in some cases, they aren't enough. That's where the accessibility features come into play. Visual Studio .NET provides the means to add accessibility cues to your applications. For example, these cues could help someone who might not be able to see the application to make more sense out of what they hear about the application.

The three accessibility cues are associated with control properties. The following list tells you about each property and tells how you'd use it to increase the information about your application.

AccessibleDescription   This property provides a better description of the use of an application control than might be apparent from the control itself. For example, if you use a picture button, someone with normal vision might understand that a stop-sign symbol enables them to stop the current operation. However, you'd also want to provide an AccessibleDescription that tells how to use the button.

AccessibleName   This property contains the short name for a control. You'd use it when you need to provide a more descriptive name for the control than space will allow on a form, but don't require a complete description. For example, this property might contain a value of "OK Button," so someone with a screen reader would know that it's a button with the word OK on it.

AccessibleRole   This property to is used to define the type of control interface. For example, you can define the role of a button or button-like control as a PushButton. Visual Studio appears to use the Default setting for all controls, even when it's easy to determine the type of control. All screen readers will use this property, even the readers that come with the various versions of Windows. Telling the user that they're working with a push-button is helpful, especially when the pushbutton had a unique shape or other feature. (Think about the odd buttons on the skin for the Windows Media Player.)

In addition to filling out the accessibility properties for all of the controls in your application, you can also support some accessibility features directly. For example, one of the accessibility features that many users need is high contrast. This feature is indispensable when working on some laptops, because it provides the extra information needed to see the screen in sunlight. While some people use this feature all of the time, others use it at the end of the day to reduce eyestrain.

Your application can detect when the system goes into high contrast mode by monitoring the `SystemInformation.HighContrast` property. Of course, you'll still need to select high contrast color combinations (with black and white providing the best contrast). The point is that some screens that look great in color look terrible when put into high contrast mode. If you don't detect this property, the high contrast mode that should help the user might end up causing problems.

Graphics

In some respects, graphics haven't changed for Windows developers since the days of Window 3.*x*. Visual Studio still provides access to the same three graphic resources: icons (ICO), bitmaps (BMP), and cursors (CUR). The only change for Visual Studio .NET is an increase in the number of colors you can use. Unlike previous versions, you can now create your graphics in something more than 256 colors. You'll also find that icons and cursors now come in a 96 × 96–bit size.

Adding a new graphic image has changed in Visual Studio .NET. The fastest way to add a new graphic is to right-click the project entry in Solution Explorer and choose Add ➤ Add New Item from the Context menu. Select the Resources category and you'll see a list of resources similar to the one shown in Figure 5.5.

FIGURE 5.5:

Visual Studio .NET provides access to enhanced forms of the graphics files you've always used.

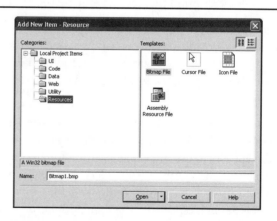

Once you create the new graphic, you'll see a typical bit level drawing area that includes a color selection toolbar and a second toolbar with drawing tools. Anyone who's used Paint in the past will feel comfortable with the tools in Visual Studio .NET.

Bitmap files contain only one image, so if you need different resolutions of the same bitmap, you'll need to create individual bitmap files. However, cursor and icon files can both contain multiple images that vary by resolution and color depth. In fact, you'll need to define multiple images when working with icons to obtain the best display, because Windows will select the best image automatically. This is especially important in Windows XP, because this new operating system uses 64×64–bit icons and greater color depth. To add a new image to the list for an icon, right-click the drawing area and choose New Image Type from the Context menu. You'll see a New Icon Image Type dialog box from which you can choose a new type. Context menu options also enable you to select from an existing image type or delete one that you no longer need.

Graphic resources aren't limited to the three you can access directly in Visual Studio .NET. We'll see later that you can use the Bitmap object to import graphics that Visual Studio never supported in the past. This includes using resources such as GIFs in your applications. Anyone who's designed a web page knows the value of animated GIFs in dressing up a display so it looks attractive to visitors. In fact, we'll create a desktop application that makes use of an animated GIF later in the "SDI Example" section of this chapter.

Timers

Timers help you keep track of time. A timer is actually one of the easiest controls to use in Windows. All you need to do is set the *Interval* property for the number of milliseconds between each *Tick* event. You create an event handler for the tick that tracks events or performs other tasks based on the time. Look in the "Dialog-Based Example" section of the chapter for an example of an application that uses timers to keep track of your typing time.

Toolbars

Toolbars are a required resource for SDI and MDI applications because they provide a shortcut to essential application functionality. For example, users have become very dependent on the three icons used to manage documents in most SDI and MDI applications: New, Open, and Save.

In the past, developers would drop a toolbar on their application, then drop buttons on the toolbar. Visual Studio .NET takes a slightly different approach, with a vastly improved ToolBar control. Unlike previous versions, the buttons are now part of a collection that resides with the toolbar. However, adding a button isn't quite as obvious as it might be, so some people are still using the old approach of dropping buttons on the toolbar.

Click the *Buttons* property on the ToolBar control and you'll see the word (*Collection*). Click the ellipsis button and you'll see a ToolBarButton Collection Editor dialog box similar to the one shown in Figure 5.6. (Note that the figure shows a toolbar with buttons already

defined—your toolbar will start out buttonless.) This dialog box is the only method for
defining the properties for the buttons.

FIGURE 5.6:

Use the ToolBarButton
Collection Editor to
modify the appear-
ance of the ToolBar
control.

> **NOTE**   If you want to create picture buttons for your `ToolBar` control, you'll want to create an
> `ImageList` control first and fill it with the images that you'll need. Associate the `Image-`
> `List` with the `ToolBar` using the *ImageList* property. The *ImageIndex* property found in
> the ToolBar Collection Editor dialog box enables you to choose a specific icon from the
> `ImageList` for the current `ToolBarButton`.

This brings us to the problem of working with a `ToolBar` that has embedded `ToolBarBut-`
`tons`, rather than standard buttons placed over the `ToolBar`. When you use standard buttons,
you can access the individual button events. However, when working with embedded `Tool-`
`BarButtons`, you only have access to the `ToolBar` events.

One of the `ToolBar` events is `ButtonClicked`. When you create an event handler for this
event, the application passes you a copy of the information for the button. Unfortunately,
this information doesn't include the button name. To make it possible to identify the button,
you must assign the button a *Tag* property value. Once you have the *Tag* property value, you
can pass the `ToolBar` button handling onto the associated menu event handler as shown in
the following code.

```
private void mnuFileNew_Click(object sender, System.EventArgs e)
{
    // Display a helpful message.
    MessageBox.Show("Clicked File | New");
}
```

```
private void toolBar1_ButtonClick(object sender,
    System.Windows.Forms.ToolBarButtonClickEventArgs e)
{
    // Display a message for the button.
    MessageBox.Show("Clicked the " +
                    e.Button.Tag.ToString() +
                    " button.");

    // Do something special for the New button.
    if (e.Button.Tag.ToString() == "New")
        mnuFileNew_Click(this, e);
}
```

Writing Windows Applications

Most of the applications you'll create with C# will likely have a GUI. Windows applications use a GUI to make the user experience better, reduce training time, and enable the user to work more efficiently. As previously mentioned, the standard Windows application types include dialog-based, SDI, and MDI. Within those three categories are an infinite array of subtypes. For example, a dialog-based application can act as a training aid or as a utility application.

The following sections examine several types of Windows applications. These examples are unique in some way—they don't necessarily follow the business-focused applications we'll discuss as the book progresses. For example, the dialog-based example also shows you how to create a utility that appears within the Taskbar Tray (Notification Area) instead of the Taskbar. This example also serves to demonstrate some of the ways in which Microsoft has improved Visual Studio .NET. Creating such an application in the previous version of Visual Studio would have required substantially more work.

Dialog-Based Example

Although we've already viewed several in the book, one type of dialog-based example that we haven't discussed is the use of the Taskbar Tray for keeping utility applications active and out of the way. Previous versions of Visual Studio tended to make it difficult to create such an application. Visual Studio .NET provides several new components and controls, plus some additional form settings, that make the task almost trivial. This example is a basic timer application. It displays a message at specific intervals that remind you to take a break from typing. The source code for this example is in the \Chapter 05\TypingBuddy folder on the CD.

This example name is Typing Buddy. It appears in the Taskbar Tray until the predefined interval elapses. At that moment, the program displays a message box advising the user it's time for a break. You'll need to use three special controls to make this application work properly:

- NotifyIcon
- ContextMenu
- Timer

In addition to adding new components and controls to the application, you'll also need to configure the main form differently from other projects. Make sure you set the *ShowIn-Taskbar* property to false so the application moves to the Taskbar Tray when minimized. You'll also want to start the application minimized using the `WindowState` property so it waits in the background without bothering the user. Figure 5.7 shows the form configuration for this example.

FIGURE 5.7:

The Typing Buddy example includes some basic configuration controls.

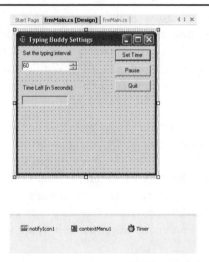

This type of application relies on a certain level of automation. You want the application to start automatically when the machine starts and continue operation until the user shuts the machine down. Of course, you also need to be sure the user configures the application properly for use. The solution is to check for an existing set of configuration options, and then create them if needed. Listing 5.3 shows the `frmMain_Load()`, which is responsible for getting the application running.

Listing 5.3   **Creating the Initial Application Configuration**

```
private void frmMain_Load(object sender, System.EventArgs e)
{
```

```
        // See if the user has worked with this program before.
        if (!InRegistry())
        {
            // If not, display a welcome message and the configuration
            // screen.
            MessageBox.Show("Welcome to Typing Buddy!\r\n" +
                "You need to set an initial typing value by " +
                "entering a time interval and clicking Set.",
                "Welcome Message",
                MessageBoxButtons.OK,
                MessageBoxIcon.Information);
            WindowState = FormWindowState.Normal;
        }
        else
            // Start the timer.
            Timer.Start();
    }

    private bool InRegistry()
    {
        RegistryKey oSub;              // Typing Buddy storage key.

        // Check for the application key; null if not available.
        oSub = Microsoft.Win32.Registry.LocalMachine.OpenSubKey(
            "Software\\TypingBuddy");

        // Check to see if the key exists.
        if (oSub != null)
        {
            // Set the timer value.
            TimeLeft = (int)oSub.GetValue("TimeSet");

            // Close the registry keys.
            oSub.Close();

            // Return a success value.
            return true;
        }

        // Return a failure value.
        return false;
    }
```

The main job of frmMain_Load() is to ensure the application has settings to use when it begins running. The choice is one of displaying the configuration screen if this is the first use of the application or starting the timer so the application begins running in the background without user interaction. The means for making this determination is the InRegistry() method.

The `InRegistry()` uses the simple technique of opening the application's registry entry. If *oSub* is null, then the registry key doesn't exist and the application isn't configured for use. On the other hand, if the registry key does exist, `InRegistry()` reads the contents of the *TimeSet* value and places them in *TimeLeft*.

You might wonder why `InRegistry()` doesn't start the timer as well. The current coding enables the application to use `InRegistry()` from various locations to check the configuration state of the application. We'll also use this method when configuring the application.

It's time to look at the code for the three buttons shown in Figure 5.7. The Pause context menu option also relies on this code. All three buttons and the context menu control that state of the application. Listing 5.4 shows you how.

Listing 5.4   The Set Time, Pause, and Quit Buttons Control Application State

```
private void btnSet_Click(object sender, System.EventArgs e)
{
    RegistryKey oReg; // Hive Registry Key
    RegistryKey oSub; // Company storage key.

    // Set the controls.
    TimeLeft = (Int32)TimerValue.Value * 60;
    Timer.Start();

    // Add the information to the registry.

    if (!InRegistry())
    {
        // Open the HKEY_LOCAL_MACHINE\Software key for writing.
        oReg = Microsoft.Win32.Registry.LocalMachine.OpenSubKey(
            "Software",
            true);

        // Write the company subkey.
        oReg.CreateSubKey("TypingBuddy");

        // Close the registry key.
        oReg.Close();
    }

    // Write the default value.
    oSub = Microsoft.Win32.Registry.LocalMachine.OpenSubKey(
        "Software\\TypingBuddy",
        true);
    oSub.SetValue("TimeSet", TimeLeft);

    // Close the registry keys.
    oSub.Close();
}
```

```csharp
bool  IsPaused;    // Is the timer paused?

private void btnPause_Click(object sender, System.EventArgs e)
{
   if (IsPaused)
   {
      // Start the timer.
      IsPaused = false;
      Timer.Start();

      // Display status information.
      btnPause.Text = "Pause";
      mnuPause.Text = "Pause";
   }
   else
   {
      // Stop the timer.
      IsPaused = true;
      Timer.Stop();

      // Display status information.
      btnPause.Text = "Restart";
      mnuPause.Text = "Restart";
      notifyIcon1.Text = "Timer is Paused";
   }
}

private void btnQuit_Click(object sender, System.EventArgs e)
{
   DialogResult   RetValue;   // Users selection.

   // Display an exit message.
   RetValue = MessageBox.Show("Are you sure you want to exit?" +
      "\r\n(Program will minimize if you select No.)",
      "Exit Application",
      MessageBoxButtons.YesNo,
      MessageBoxIcon.Question,
      MessageBoxDefaultButton.Button2);

   if (RetValue == DialogResult.Yes)
      // Exit the application.
      Close();
   else
      // Minimize the form.
      WindowState = FormWindowState.Minimized;
}
```

The `btnSet_Click()` begins by setting the control values for the application and starting the timer. This ensures the user will see changes immediately and won't need to wait for registry operations to complete.

The next task is to determine if the registry already contains settings for the control. If the registry doesn't contain the required entries, the application makes them, and then closes the registry key. The final step is to write the new timer value into the registry so that it's ready for the next time the user starts the application.

The `btnPause_Click()` method toggles the application between two operational states. The paused state sets the timer off and changes the buttons and notification icon balloon help to reflect the change. Likewise, when the application starts again, the timer state is changed and so are the buttons. The notification icon balloon help changes automatically as part of the timer functionality, so there's no need to change it here. The *IsPaused* field keeps track of the current state.

Normally, when the user selects Quit, the application exits. However, some users don't realize that minimizing the application removes the dialog display from view. Because of this problem, you'll want to write a special routine for the `btnQuit_Click()` method. Notice that this is one of the first times we've used the return value from the `MessageBox.Show()` method to control application flow. In addition, the example shows how to create a default button for the dialog box associated with the `MessageBox.Show()` call.

The return value determines if the application ends or merely minimizes. Notice the use of various built-in values for this example. You'll use the special `DialogResult` type to hold the user selection and compare it to values in the `DialogResult` class. The `FormWindowState` enumeration also enables you to set the *WindowState* property of the form with ease. Note that we use the `FormWindowState` enumeration for the `notifyIcon1_DoubleClick()` method as well (see the source code on the CD for details).

The "heartbeat" of this application is the system clock referenced by the Timer control. This control has a single event associated with it, `Tick`. Listing 5.5 shows the code for the `Timer_Tick()` method.

Listing 5.5   **The *Timer_Tick()* Method is Central to Typing Buddy Operation**

```
private void Timer_Tick(object sender, System.EventArgs e)
{
   DialogResult   RetVal;  // Return value from dialog.

   // Set the timer value.
   TimeLeft–;

   // See if the timer has expired.
   if (TimeLeft == 0)
```

```
{
    // Reset the controls.
    TimeLeft = (Int32)TimerValue.Value * 60;
    Timer.Stop();

    // Display the stop typing message.
    RetVal = MessageBox.Show("Time to stop typing! Relax!" +
        "\r\nPress OK to Restart" +
        "\r\nor Cancel to exit program.",
        "TypingBuddy Alert",
        MessageBoxButtons.OKCancel,
        MessageBoxIcon.Hand);

    if (RetVal == DialogResult.OK)
        // Restart the timer.
        Timer.Start();
    else
        // Exit the application.
        Close();
}
else
{
    // Update the time left indicator.
    TypingTime.Text = TimeLeft.ToString();
    notifyIcon1.Text = "Time Left in Seconds: " +
                        TimeLeft.ToString();
}
}
```

As you can see, the operation isn't complex. During a normal update cycle, the Timer_Tick() method decrements the *TimeLeft* field and performs a comparison to see if *TimeLeft* is at 0. Normally, the comparison will fail, so the Timer_Tick() method will update the text values for the *TypingTime* text box (shown in Figure 5.7) and *notifyIcon1*. Updating the *notifyIcon1.Text* property changes the value of the balloon help, so the user can hover their mouse over the icon to see how much time they have until their next break.

When *TimeLeft* does make it to 0, Timer_Tick() resets the *TimeLeft* field and turns off the timer. It displays a "break" message to the user. When the user clicks OK, the whole timing process begins again. Of course, the user can always select Cancel to end the application.

SDI Example

At one time, it was sufficient for an application to provide an appealing display of data located on either the user's hard drive or the company network. In fact, many users were happy if they could understand the display and use it to do something useful. Today, a user wants more in the way of presentation and feedback. Many applications today use simple animation to get a point across to the user.

Microsoft is at the forefront of the changes to the user interface—at least in some areas. For example, Windows Explorer uses animations to show a file moving from one location to another. The presence of action gives the user a feeling of comfort about the application, even when it doesn't do anything other than display the animated sequence.

Unfortunately, creating animations is difficult in Windows if you use the traditional methods. Fortunately, some solutions make it easy to add animation to websites and now those animations can appear on the desktop as well. One of many ways to create animations it to use an animated GIF file. Animated GIFs have been around for quite some time. You see them all the time on the Internet. All of those little animations you see on websites are very likely animated GIFs. An animated GIF file works by placing multiple images in a single file. Timing and presentation commands separate the images. Each command tells the displaying application how to present the next frame of the animation and how long to present it.

TIP   You can see animated GIFs in action on many Internet sites. One of the more interesting places to look is `http://www.wanderers2.com/rose/animate.html`. The site offers an index of sites you can visit to see various kinds of animated GIFs. Looking at a variety of sites will help you understand what works and what doesn't. You can also download an animated GIF Wizard, make your own animated GIF online, and learn all about how to make animated GIFs.

Most developers know that Visual Studio doesn't support the GIF file format as a standard graphic—at least, Visual Studio didn't provide GIF support in the past. If you tried loading an animated GIF to your project, you'd receive an error message saying the GIF was damaged or simply incorrect. The Visual Studio .NET IDE still doesn't support GIF files directly. Even if you can view the GIF inside Internet Explorer, Visual Studio .NET will steadfastly refuse to load it.

TIP   You'll find many applications you can use to create an animated GIF for your application. I designed the animated GIF for the example using the GIF Construction Set from Alchemy Mind Works. You can download this product from several places. The best place is from the vendor at `http://www.mindworkshop.com/alchemy/gifcon.html`. Another good alternative is Paint Shop Pro 7 from JASC (`http://www.jasc.com`). Note that earlier versions of the product don't include this feature and that the current product isn't quite as capable as the GIF Construction Set.

The good news is that you can combine the new `Bitmap` object with the `Animator` object to load and support animated GIFs within your application—even desktop applications. The `Bitmap` object acts as a container for the graphic, while the `Animator` provides the means to page through each image and presents it in turn. When you combine the two objects, you see the animation sequence on screen without resorting to the odd programming techniques of the past. Listing 5.6 shows the code you'll need to make this application work. (The full source code for this example appears in the \Chapter 05\AniDisplay folder on the CD.)

Listing 5.6 **Adding Animation to the Desktop Isn't Hard in Visual Studio .NET**

```
private  String    File2Open;   // Selected Filename
private  Bitmap    AniGIF;      // Animated GIF to Display
private  int       DrawSelect;  // Drawing mode.
private  bool      Animated;    // Animation active.

private void mnuFileOpen_Click(object sender, System.EventArgs e)
{
    OpenFileDialog Dlg = new OpenFileDialog();    // File Open Dialog

    // Set up the File Open Dialog
    Dlg.Filter = "Graphics Interchange Format File (*.gif)|*.gif";
    Dlg.DefaultExt = ".gif";
    Dlg.Title = "Open File Dialog";

    // Display the File Open Dialog and obtain the name of a file and
    // the file information.
    if (Dlg.ShowDialog() == DialogResult.OK)
    {
        File2Open = Dlg.FileName;
    }
    else
    {
        // If the user didn't select anything, return.
        return;
    }

    // Open the document.
    AniGIF = new Bitmap(File2Open);

    // Set the drawing mode.
    DrawSelect = 2;
    Animated = false;

    // Change the title bar.
    Form1.ActiveForm.Text = "GIF Animation Example - " + File2Open;

    // Force a redraw of the display area.
    DisplayArea.Invalidate();
}

private void DisplayArea_Paint(object sender,
    System.Windows.Forms.PaintEventArgs e)
{
    // Can't draw the image if the bitmap is null.
```

```
    if (AniGIF != null)
    {
        switch (DrawSelect)
        {
            case 1:
                // Animate the GIF file.
                ImageAnimator.UpdateFrames();
                e.Graphics.DrawImage(AniGIF,
                                     4,
                                     4,
                                     AniGIF.Width,
                                     AniGIF.Height);
                break;


            case 2:
                // Draw a graphic normally.
                e.Graphics.DrawImage(AniGIF,
                                     4,
                                     4,
                                     AniGIF.Width,
                                     AniGIF.Height);
                break;
        }
    }
}

private void mnuAnimationStart_Click(object sender, System.EventArgs e)
{
    // Initialize the animating the first time the user selects it.
    if (!Animated)
    {
        ImageAnimator.Animate(AniGIF,
                              new EventHandler(NextFrame));
        Animated = true;
    }

    // Select a drawing mode.
    DrawSelect = 1;
}

private void mnuAnimationStop_Click(object sender, System.EventArgs e)
{
    // Select a drawing mode that stops the animation.
    DrawSelect = 2;
}

private void NextFrame(object sender, System.EventArgs e)
{
    // Force OnPaint() to redraw the animation.
    DisplayArea.Invalidate();
}
```

The application requires the use of four fields, as shown in the listing. It's important to make the bitmap resources universally available within the class to ensure you can perform all of the required timing for the animation. However, nothing outside the class should require access to the bitmap. If so, you should use properties to ensure you can track everything that affects the bitmap and animation.

When the user opens the application, they'll see a typical SDI display. The first task is to open a file. (See the CommandLine2 example in Chapter 4 for code that grabs the filename from the command line.) The code shown in `mnuFileOpen_Click()` looks much the same as the code for the CommandLine2 example.

Near the end of the `mnuFileOpen_Click()` method, you'll see five lines of code that load the bitmap into the drawing area. The four fields now contain the values needed to present the bitmap on screen. The `DisplayArea.Invalidate()` call forces a redraw of the `DisplayArea` panel so that you can see the bitmap loaded.

The `DisplayArea_Paint()` method can present the bitmap in two ways. The method of choice when the bitmap first loads is as a static image. As you can see from the `case 2` code, `System.Windows.Forms.PaintEventArgs` provides the application with a drawing area that it uses to display the bitmap on screen. All the code has to specify is the `Bitmap` object (`AniGIF`) and the drawing rectangle. (We'll discuss the `case 1` code in a moment.)

The `mnuAnimationStart_Click()` method starts the animation process. Notice that we haven't created anything to animate the image yet and we won't—it comes as part of your application. The code verified the animation status of the bitmap before it adds the `NextFrame` event handler to the existing `ImageAnimator` object.

Remember from the Delegate example in Chapter 4 that you can continue to add new event handlers to a delegate. The delegate simply calls them each in turn. If you continue adding the same event handler to the `ImageAnimator`, the animation will continue to speed up until you can no longer see the animation—each event handler will advance the frame by one. Instead of seeing one frame per interval, you might begin seeing three or four. That's why the animated state check is so important. The `ImageAnimator` will call `NextFrame()` each time the command inside the animated GIF states it's time to display another image.

The interesting thing about the `NextFrame()` method is that the only task it performs is invalidating the display area. This action invokes the `OnPaint()` method. However, in this case, the `OnPaint()` method will use the `case 1` code. The `ImageAnimator` appears in this code as well. In this case, you're asking the `ImageAnimator` to access the next frame in the animation. When `OnPaint()` draws the image, it will actually draw the current image in the animated series, rather than the first image contained in the file as normal.

Stopping the animation is relatively easy. All you need to do is select the `case 2` image drawing routine in `OnPaint()`. The animation will stop at the current point in its execution. Theoretically, you could work with this example to slow the animation down, so you could view it one frame at a time. Figure 5.8 shows the AniDisplay application with the `Animated-Time.GIF` file loaded. You'll find `AnimatedTime.GIF` and its components in the `\Chapter 05\Animated Graphic` folder of the CD.

FIGURE 5.8:

Animated GIFs can provide extra pizzazz in a desktop application.

Application Debugging

The debugger is the most important tool in your arsenal for ensuring the code works as you intended after the application is released. The problem for some developers is that the debugger is also one of the most misunderstood parts of the IDE. The following sections provide a quick tutorial on using the debugger to your advantage while working on the examples in this book. We'll also discuss other debugging tips as the book progresses.

Using the Debugger

The most common way to use the debugger is to set a breakpoint on your code and start the debugger using the Start ➤ Debug command. Of course, you can also start the debugger and simply wait for your code to fail the first time.

Breakpoints come in two forms. The first is an unconditional breakpoint you set by clicking the left margin of the line of code. You can also right-click the line of code and choose Insert Breakpoint from the Context menu. An unconditional breakpoint always stops execution.

The second breakpoint is conditional. It relies on a specific set of circumstances to stop execution. To set a conditional breakpoint, right-click the line of code and choose New Breakpoint from the Context menu. You'll see a New Breakpoint dialog box similar to the one shown in Figure 5.9.

FIGURE 5.9:

You can set condi-
tional breakpoints
using the New Break-
point dialog box.

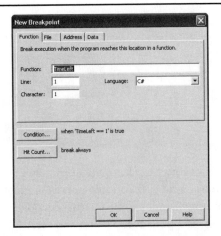

As you can see, this dialog box enables you to set a variety of conditional breakpoints, including breakpoints based on the value of a variable or even the breakpoint hit count. The hit count is the number of times the application has reached the breakpoint during normal execution. Notice the Address tab of the New Breakpoint dialog box. You can use this tab to enter the address where an application failed. The Address field will access a value in decimal or hexadecimal. Preface any hexadecimal numbers with a "0x" to ensure the debugger sees them correctly.

TIP   The Debug ➢ Start Without Debugging command enables you to run an application from the Visual Studio .NET IDE without using the debugger. This is a useful feature if you want to check for timing errors or problems that could occur when the application runs outside the debugger. Not every problem shows up when you run the application with the debugger. In fact, some resource problems only show up when you create a release version of the application. Consequently, using the Start Without Debugging command is an essential part of checking your application execution.

Once the application is running under the debugger, you have a number of choices for following the execution path. All of these actions appear on the Debug toolbar shown in Figure 5.10. These buttons (in order of appearance) are: Continue, Break All, Stop Debugging, Restart, Show Next Statement, Step Into, Step Over, and Step Out (we'll cover the other two buttons later).

FIGURE 5.10:

The Debug toolbar contains all of the buttons you'll need to perform most debugging tasks.

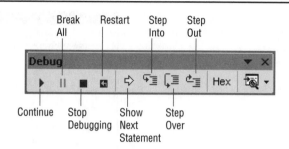

The three buttons Step Into, Step Over, and Step Out enable you to follow the execution path one step at a time. If you step into a command, you'll follow the execution path one level lower. For example, if the instruction pointer rests on a function call, you'll step into that function. Stepping over a command means that you remain at the same level. The code still executes the function call, but you only see the results of the function call, not the intermediate steps. Finally, stepping out of a function means rising one level higher. The debugger will finish executing the code at the current level and stop at the next statement of the previous (higher) level. The problem is that stepping out doesn't always work if an errant instruction at the current level prevents the code from executing.

After you've learned all you can at the current breakpoint, you can choose one of three actions. Click Continue if you want the application to execute normally until it hits the next breakpoint. Click Stop Debugging if you've finished the current debugging session. Finally, click Restart if you want to start the debugging session over again. Clicking Break All will stop application execution at the current instruction, no matter what the application might be doing at the time.

Performing Remote Debugging

Not every debugging session happens with an application loaded in the debugger or even with a local application. Sometimes you'll want to debug a running process. In some cases, this process might appear on another machine. For example, you need to perform remote debugging to check the operation of a component on a server that a local client is using. If you're using a distributed application technology such as SOAP, there's no direct connection between client and server, so you need to create a separate debugging session for the remote component.

The Debug ➤ Processes command displays the Processes dialog box shown in Figure 5.11. This dialog box enables you to perform remote debugging of an existing process such as a server-side component. All you need to do is attach to the server by supplying a Transport (Default normally works fine) and a Name value. When the debugger attaches to the server, you'll see a list of the processes on that server.

FIGURE 5.11:

Use the Processes
dialog box to attach to
a remote server in
order to debug exist-
ing processes.

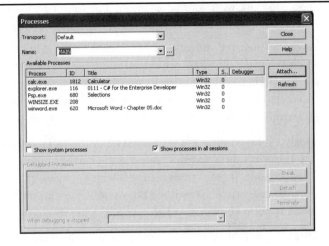

NOTE   You must be part of the Debugger Users group on the remote machine in order to use the
remote debugging features of Visual Studio .NET. In most cases, being a member of the
Administrators group doesn't automatically extend rights to the Debugger Users group.
Microsoft chose to make this security election specific in an effort to reduce the risks of
security breaches on the remote machine.

Notice that the Processes dialog box includes check boxes that show the processes in all
sessions and the system processes. Choosing the correct set of viewing options makes it easier to locate the process you want to view. When you find the process you want to view, click
Attach. You'll see an Attach to Process dialog box that contains application debug types. This
dialog box will always have the Common Language Runtime and Native options checked. If
you want to debug another application type, you'll need to check the correct option. Click
OK and you'll attach to the process.

At this point, you can click Break, in the Processes dialog box, to start the debugging session. You can use the same controls as you would with any application to start and stop application execution. In short, except for the attachment process, debugging a remote application
is much the same as debugging a local application. Of course, you can't see any visual elements of the application unless they appear through the client on the local machine. Remote
debugging is limited to work with the remote code.

Performing Standard Debugging Tasks

When you start your application, the debugger normally creates a series of seven windows
along the bottom of the display area. Each of these windows serves a different purpose in

helping you work with your application. The following list tells you about each window. We won't visit each window in detail in this chapter, but we'll discuss them as the book progresses.

Autos   Some applications can get quite complex and generate more than a few variables, which can make the windows become cluttered. The Autos window contains a list of variables associated with the current and the preceding statement. This view enables you to focus on just the current task and clears up the clutter you might otherwise have to view. The window shows the variable name, value, and type.

Locals   This window contains a list of all the variables associated with the current function. It doesn't show variables outside the current function. For example, if you have a global variable, it won't appear in this window, even if the current function performs some task with the variable. You'll see the values of any arguments used to call the function. The Locals window shows the variable name, value, and type.

Watch   You'll place variables and functions that you want to watch in this window. The easiest way to do this is to highlight the code in question and drag it to the window. The Watch window also allows you to type variables and functions by hand. You can create multiple Watch windows for a given debugging session. The Watch window shows the variable name, value, and type.

Call Stack   This window answers the question of how the application got to the current point of execution. Every time the application makes a call, the call gets added to the call stack. When the call returns, Visual Studio removes it from the call stack. In short, the Call Stack window shows you a list of pending calls, which tells you how the application accessed the current function.

Breakpoints   The Breakpoints window contains a list of breakpoints for your application. It also tells you the break conditions. You can use this window to manage breakpoints, which includes adding new breakpoints and deleting existing breakpoints. The Clear All Breakpoints button enables you to remove all of the breakpoints from your application without looking for them individually. You can also disable the breakpoints by clearing the check next to the entry. The Disable All Breakpoints button will disable all of the breakpoints in an application at once, which means the application will run as if you hadn't set any breakpoints.

Command Window   You'll use the Command Window to perform queries on your application as you debug it. For example, if you typed **? *\<Variable Name\>*** in the Command Window, Visual Studio would return the current value of the Command Window. You can also perform limited "what if" analysis by trying out various permutations of function calls within the window. The reason this option is limited is that you have to avoid certain types of calls. For example, you wouldn't want to call an event handler from within the Command Window.

Output   The Output window contains a list of the current debugger actions and any debug statements you place within the code. For example, this window tells you the names of all the DLLs loaded to service your application when it starts. The Output window also reports any return code from your application.

Generally, you'll find that the windows in this list provide everything you need in the way of information. You can learn the values of any variables in your application, interact with the application in various ways, and perform certain types of management tasks. However, there are times when you need to view an application in intense detail, and the debugger displays can help you there as well. For example, you can view the IL code for your application by selecting Disassembly from the View drop-down list box on the Debug menu (the last button in Figure 5.10). Figure 5.12 shows a typical disassembly of the Typing Buddy application we discussed earlier. The C# statements appear in bold type, while the disassembly appears in a lighter type.

FIGURE 5.12:

The Disassembly window shows you the internal workings of your application.

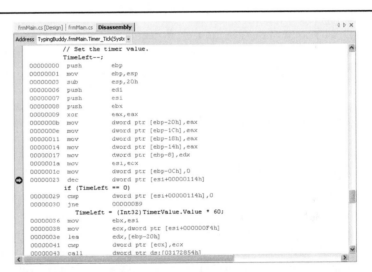

Notice the `if (TimeLeft == 0)` statement in Figure 5.12. The disassembly of this code is `cmp dword ptr [esi+00000114h],0`. It's clear that the code is performing a DWORD (double word or 16-bit) comparison of the value pointed to by the ESI register offset by 0x00000114 with 0. However, you don't believe that the code is correct. How do you validate it? The first thing you need to know is that this value supposedly points to `TimeLeft`, which has a value of 3,600 according to the Autos window. So, if `[esi+00000114h]` actually points to a value of 3,600, there's a good chance that this code is correct.

The View drop-down list box also contains a Registers entry. When you open this window, you'll see all of the registers for your machine. According to my Registers window (your window will differ), ESI contains a value of 0x00c45638. Adding 0x114 to this value means that the memory location should point to 0x00c4574c. Open the Memory 1 window using the options in the View drop-down, enter the address, and you'll see a display similar to the one in Figure 5.13. If you look at the value in the Memory window, you'll see that a hex value of 0x0e10 is equal to 3,600 decimal (remember that Intel processors use a little endian storage technique).

FIGURE 5.13:

You can even view the contents of memory within the debugger.

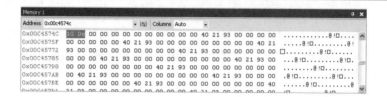

The point of this section isn't to demonstrate that you can become hopelessly mired in debugger functionality in Visual Studio .NET; it demonstrates that you can get as much detail about your application as you need. Application development boils down to knowing the details. Knowing how to use the debugger enables you to check the details, even the details of library code. In short, you might not look at the IL code for your applications every day, but it's good to know what to do if you need that level of detail somewhere along the way.

Where Do You Go From Here?

This chapter has answered the important question of what type of applications you can write using C#. The answer is that you can write all of the common Windows application types you've used in the past. If you're a Visual Basic developer, using a form to create all of your Windows applications isn't anything new, but the level of flexibility that C# provides is a welcome addition. On the other hand, Visual C++ developers will need to get past the document/view architecture of the past and realize there's only one basic Windows application project type to work with now.

The one thing this chapter presents is possibilities. You've learned that a console application commonly writes to the command prompt screen, a file, or an event log. Now is a good time to try out some alternative forms of output that you could use on remote machines. It's also good to know how to work with standard C# resources so you can create feature-rich applications with a minimum of code in a minimum of time. Spend time learning the different Windows applications types so you can create them as needed. Finally, learning to debug applications is a skill that's important for every kind of application. If you gain nothing else from this chapter, learning how to use the debugger is critical.

Chapter 6 presents you with some more opportunities to learn about the kinds of applications you can create with C#. In this chapter, you'll learn how to create both components and controls. This is an essential skills chapter because you need to know how a component works in order to create distributed applications. Controls are important because they're the building blocks of modern applications.

CHAPTER 6

Creating Controls and Components

- .NET and Components and Controls

- Creating Controls

- Creating Components

Components and controls form the building blocks of most modern applications. In an effort to reuse as much code as possible, developers create components or controls that can fulfill more than one need. For example, even though the function of each pushbutton on a form performs a different task, the underlying code required to create the pushbutton doesn't vary. Consequently, even though developers once had to code the individual pushbuttons at one time, they don't any longer because the code appears within an easy-to-use control and encapsulates the control functionality.

C# makes it easy to create both components and controls containing reusable code. It combines the low-level functionality of Visual C++ with the high-level resource management of Visual Basic. This combination of features actually works to the developer's good, because the developer still has the flexibility required to create useful components and controls but doesn't have to spend as much time coding them.

This chapter will show you how to build and use components and controls within your applications. It assumes you have at least some knowledge of component and control construction, so we won't discuss every detail. For example, you should already know the basics such as the use of properties, methods, and events.

.NET and Components and Controls

Components and controls are the basic building blocks of every application today. A developer uses these building blocks to create application elements without coding the generic elements of the component or control each time. Components offer code that defines business elements or generic functionality. Controls provide visual elements (such as pushbuttons) and nonvisual elements (such as timers) that developers use to create the user interface for an application. Both technologies appear as part of Visual Studio .NET as well as offerings from third parties.

The following sections discuss some issues regarding the use of components and controls under Visual Studio .NET in general and in C# specifically. One of the more important issues is how many compatibility problems you'll face when using your current collection of controls and components with .NET. We'll discuss the issue of working with metadata and how you read the metadata for the application.

Compatibility Issues

For many developers, .NET represents yet another way to create applications that might not provide full compatibility with existing technology. After all, .NET relies on CLR, rather than on the Win32 API. You probably have a hard drive full of components and controls that do rely on the Win32 API that you use to build applications. The existence of such a large base of unmanaged components and controls might have some developers worried. However, .NET in general works with both managed and unmanaged components and controls. The managed components and controls rely on the .NET Framework and the Common Language Runtime (CLR) to operate. Unmanaged components and controls run under the Win32 API. C# automatically handles the different environments for you in most cases.

The reason you need to think about general support is that some older components and controls might not work in the new environment. For example, many developers have reported problems using Microsoft's older database controls, such as the Microsoft ADO Data Control (MSADODC.OCX), within the Visual Studio .NET IDE, because these controls tend to produce less than acceptable results in the application. For example, the Microsoft ADO Data Control will accept your input parameters, but will refuse to access the database or act as a data source to data award controls. In fact, Microsoft doesn't supply these older controls as part of Visual Studio .NET. You need to install the components from a Visual Studio 6 installation, and then follow the instructions found in the \Extras\VB6 Controls folder of Disk 4 of the Visual Studio .NET Enterprise Architect CD set to enable them. While it might appear that the instructions would allow you to use the older controls as before, they'll fail on most systems.

Not every unmanaged component or control has problems working in the new environment. In fact, many developers have found their unmanaged controls work just as they did before. You'll find a custom pushbutton control (PButton1.OCX) in the \Chapter 06\ Unmanaged Pushbutton Control folder on the CD. Register this control by typing **RegSvr32 PButton1.OCX** at the command line and pressing Enter. To use the control, right-click the Toolbox in the Visual Studio .NET IDE and select Customize Toolbox. You'll find the PButton1.OCX entry in the Customize Toolbox dialog box, as shown in Figure 6.1. Click OK, and the control will appear in your Toolbox. You'll find a working example of how to use this control in the \Chapter 06\PButtonTest folder on the CD. The point is that although many of your old controls will work, some won't under .NET when using C#.

TIP It pays to keep your managed and unmanaged controls separated in the Toolbox. The separation makes it easier to determine when a control might not work due to compatibility problems. In addition, the separation acts as a visual cue that helps the developer keep the control types separate. You can add a new tab to the Toolbox by right-clicking the Toolbox and selecting Add Tab from the context menu. Use a distinct name for the tab, such as "Unmanaged Controls."

FIGURE 6.1:

You can find all of your
old controls on the
COM tab of the
Customize Toolbox
dialog box.

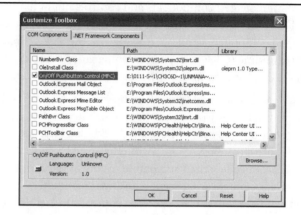

Even when a control works as anticipated, you might find some unexpected side effects from the transition from unmanaged to managed environments. Here, the example control supports an About dialog, but you can't access it from C#. This might present a problem if you place your support information in the About dialog for easy access by the developer. If you plan to use an unmanaged control in both managed and unmanaged environments, make sure the developer can access every critical feature from the control property pages.

Another oddity that you need to work with is that you won't see the unmanaged form of the control anywhere in the code. That's because C# has to build a bridge between your unmanaged control and the .NET environment. You'll likely see a reference such as this one for the control:

```
private AxPButton1Lib.AxPButton1 btnTest;
```

`AxPButton1Lib.AxPButton1` is a reference to the managed wrapper for the control. Unfortunately, your search for control information still isn't over. The code accesses the control using the `AxPButton1Lib.AxPButton1`, but if you want to view the control in Object Browser, you'll need to find the `interop.pbutton1lib` assembly, which is automatically added to your project. The use of a different nomenclature for the button will affect the method used to access elements, such as enumerations. For example, if you want to determine the current ModalResult value, you must write a comparison similar to `PButton1Lib.ModalType.mrOff`. Figure 6.2 shows an Object Browser view of the unmanaged `PButton1.OCX` control within the managed C# environment. Notice the `AboutBox()` method is still present, even if it isn't displayed as you might think.

FIGURE 6.2:

Using unmanaged
controls within the C#
environment might
mean spending time
in the Object Browser.

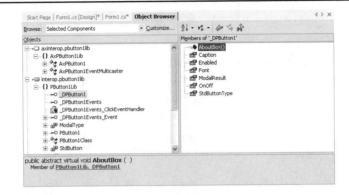

Does C# provide full compatibility with your unmanaged components and control? No, it doesn't—you'll find some situations where the Visual Studio .NET environment doesn't provide an acceptable interoperable environment. However, the vast majority of your components and controls will work with some changes in functionality due to .NET environment interoperability concerns.

Moving Unmanaged Controls to .NET

Adding an unmanaged control during design time is relatively easy—just add it to the Toolbox and use it as you would any other control. However, sometimes you need to add a control after the application is already running. The problem with unmanaged controls is that you can't access them the way you would a managed control within the .NET Framework. There's no direct access to the unmanaged environment, and coding around the various constraints is both unnecessary and problematic.

You can manually create a wrapper for your unmanaged control using several .NET utilities. The advantage of this technique is that the control ends up in the Global Assembly Cache (GAC) where it's accessible to all .NET programs. The first technique we discussed in the "Compatibility Issues" section provides a local copy of the control that only one application can use. Creating the wrapper also enables you to access the control as needed without using the Designer. The following steps show how to create the wrapper. (I'll use the PButton1.OCX file from the previous section as an example.)

1. Open the folder containing the control.

2. Type **SN -k MyKey** and press Enter. This step creates a key pair that we'll use later to create a strong name for the control. The control must have a strong name to appear in the GAC.

3. Type **AxImp PButton1.OCX /Keyfile:MyKey**. This step generates the two DLL files that the Designer created for you in the previous example. However, these files have a strong name associated with them.

4. Type **GACUtil -i AxPButton1Lib.DLL** and press Enter. This step adds the control's **AxHost** class to the GAC so you can create an instance of the control using standard C# techniques. This DLL file doesn't contain the control's definition—just the **AxHost** part of the picture (as it did for the previous example).

5. Type **GACUtil -i PButton1Lib.DLL** and press Enter. This step adds the control definition to the GAC. The control definition enables you to access control features, such as properties.

You can easily verify that the two parts of your control now appear in the GAC. Open the \WINDOWS\assembly folder on your system. You'll see a list of assemblies, such as the ones shown in Figure 6.3. Notice the highlighted entry is **AxPButton1Lib**; immediately below it is **PButton1Lib**.

FIGURE 6.3:

The \WINDOWS\ assembly folder holds all of the assemblies for the GAC.

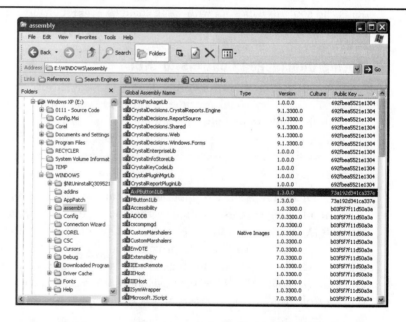

At this point, you can access the control from an application. The PButtonTest2 application in the \Chapter 06\PButtonTest2 folder on the CD contains the example for this section. Let's look at a few details of that example. The first task you'll need to perform is adding a reference for both DLLs to your application. Use the Project ➤ Add Reference command to display the Add Reference dialog box. Highlight and select the two DLLs, as shown in Figure 6.4.

FIGURE 6.4:

Be sure to add references to the two DLL files for the control.

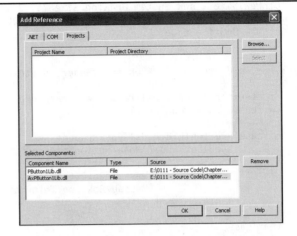

Everything's in place for creating the control dynamically. The sample application has a Test button with a Click event handler named btnTest_Click(). The dynamically created PButton1 pushbutton will also have an event handler, btnNew_Click(). Listing 6.1 shows the source code for both event handlers (the btnNew_Click() event handler is shortened for the sake of clarity).

Listing 6.1   Creating the PButton1 Control Dynamically

```
// Declare the new button.
private AxPButton1Lib.AxPButton1 btnNew;

private void btnTest_Click(object sender, System.EventArgs e)
{
    // Create a copy of the new control.
    if (btnNew == null)
        btnNew = new AxPButton1Lib.AxPButton1();
    else
    {
        MessageBox.Show("Button Already Created!",
            "Button Error",
            MessageBoxButtons.OK,
            MessageBoxIcon.Error);
        return;
    }

    // Add the control to the form.
    Controls.Add(btnNew);

    // Configure the control.
    btnNew.Name = "btnNew";
    btnNew.ClickEvent += new System.EventHandler(btnNew_Click);
```

```
        btnNew.Size = new System.Drawing.Size(75, 23);
        btnNew.Location = new System.Drawing.Point(208, 72);
        btnNew.OnOff = true;
    }

    private void btnNew_Click(object sender, System.EventArgs e)
    {
        //Determine which modal result was returned and display a message.
        switch (btnNew.ModalResult)
        {
            case PButton1Lib.ModalType.mrNone:
                MessageBox.Show("None button pressed",
                                "State of Control",
                                MessageBoxButtons.OK,
                                MessageBoxIcon.Information);
                break;
//
//Other cases
//
            case PButton1Lib.ModalType.mrOff:
                MessageBox.Show("Button is Off",
                                "State of Control",
                                MessageBoxButtons.OK,
                                MessageBoxIcon.Information);
                break;
        }
    }
```

As you can see, we create the control as we would any .NET control; the control is added to the form, and then we configure it. You might wonder why the code performs the configuration second. Many unmanaged controls react better when you configure them *after* adding the control to the form. PButton1 causes an unhandled exception if you configure the *YesNo* property before you add the control to the form.

The btnNew_Click() method simply tests the output of the button (which is set to alternate between on and off for the example). The *ModalResult* property relies on an enumeration (*ModalType*) to define the return results of a button click. The example button provides numerous modal states that enable you to use the same button for a variety of predefined tasks.

Moving Unmanaged Components to .NET

Working with unmanaged components is similar to working with unmanaged controls. However, you'll find that components come with fewer problems attached and you normally won't need to work as hard to get them to work within .NET. You can still create a local copy of the component by creating a reference to it. If you want to make the component globally available, you'll need to create a key using the SN utility as we did for the control. However, instead of using the AxImp utility to create the assembly DLL, you'll use the TlbImp command.

You'll find an example of an unmanaged component named MyAdd in the \Chapter 06\ Unmanaged Component folder of the source code on the CD. If you wanted to create a managed DLL to access this component, you'd first create a key pair using the SN utility. Next, you'd type **TlbImp MyAdd.DLL /namespace:Sample /keyfile:MyKey** at the command prompt and press Enter. This command creates a new library named MyAddLib.DLL. You can use the GACUtil utility to register the resulting DLL for public use.

Calling the DoAdd method within the MyAdd component is similar to calling any other .NET component. You need to add a reference to the project, as usual. (You can find an example in the \Chapter 06\MyAddTest folder on the CD.) Here's an example of the code you might use to call the component in this example.

```
private void btnTest_Click(object sender, System.EventArgs e)
{
    // Create the component.
    Sample.DoMathClass   DoAdd = new Sample.DoMathClass();

    // Make the call.
    txtResult.Text =
        DoAdd.DoAdd(Int16.Parse(txtValue1.Text),
                    Int16.Parse(txtValue2.Text)).ToString();
}
```

As you can see, there's no difference in the code for this example than from any other .NET component. Notice how you can avoid the use of intermediate variables by using data conversion function calls. The Int16.Parse() function converts the text values in the input text boxes to numbers. Likewise, you can use the ToString() function to convert the result into a string for the *txtResult* text box.

Working with Metadata

All .NET applications include metadata as part of the assembly. The metadata describes the assembly elements, making it easier to learn about the assembly after it's put together. One of the most common forms of metadata is the assembly information found in the Assembly-Info.CS file. Each of the [assembly:] attributes contains information about the assembly. Figure 6.5 shows an ILDASM view of the assembly information for the PButtonTest application discussed earlier.

FIGURE 6.5:

Metadata provides
descriptive informa-
tion for every assem-
bly you create.

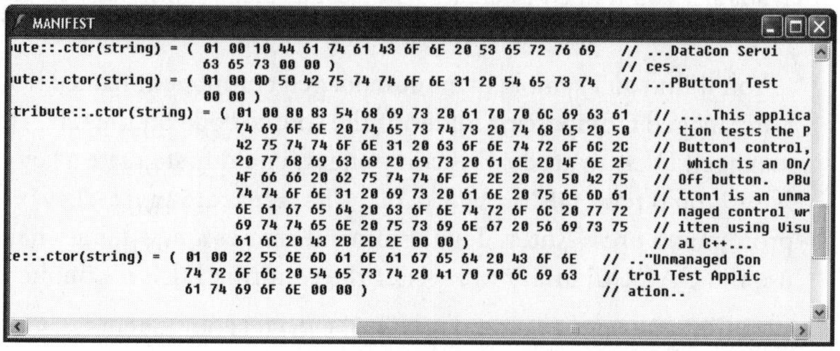

As you can see, each metadata entry consists of code and data. In this case, the data is also readable text, but there's no requirement that the entry appear in human readable form. For example, the security metadata for an assembly often appears in non-readable encrypted form for the obvious reasons.

The C# compiler automatically adds some types of metadata to your assembly. For example, it includes a list of the assemblies used to construct the current assembly. The metadata also includes information about base classes and other particulars about assembly construction.

A developer can also add metadata to the assembly. Many of the attributes you use will automatically add descriptive metadata. In addition, a developer can create custom attributes to assist in the documentation of the assembly. Custom attributes could also perform tasks such as sending application documentation to a server for storage. The idea is that metadata is another form of essential documentation.

Visual Studio .NET uses metadata to promote language interoperability and reduce application complexity. An application can use a process known as *reflect* (described in "An Overview of Reflection") to query a component about its interface requirements. Contrast this with the complex methods required by COM. In addition, you don't need a separate file to create the description, as you would with languages such as Visual C++.

One of the best ways to learn how metadata works within C# is to try the various attributes this language provides. We discussed some of these attributes as part of the "COM" section of Chapter 3. As you work with the attributes, use ILDASM to see how they affect the content of the assembly.

An Overview of Reflection

As previously mentioned, reflection provides a means for reading metadata from within your application. Obviously, this means learning everything you need to know in order to use the assembly, which means reading every form of metadata that the assembly contains. However, it's most common for developers to want to know the attributes that an assembly contains because the attributes describe assembly features. For example, you'll use an attribute to describe the interface for a component or control.

The following sections show both sides of the metadata equation. In the first section, we'll create a custom attribute that adds descriptive information to the test application. In the second section, we'll use reflection to read the content of the custom attribute entries and display them on screen. After you read through these two sections, you should have a better idea of what metadata means and why it's so useful to the .NET developer.

Creating the Custom Attribute

In Chapter 3, we discussed attributes and how you can use them within your applications to produce certain effects. .NET comes with a lot of built-in attributes that meet common needs for all developers. However, you'll find that .NET doesn't cover every base and the attributes it does supply aren't always complete. You'll also want to create some custom attributes just to ensure you can work with attributes in the way that's most convenient for you.

Interestingly enough, you use an attribute to begin creating a custom attribute. Here's an example of an attribute we'll use for the example in this section.

```
[AttributeUsage(AttributeTargets.All,
                AllowMultiple=true,
                Inherited=false)]
```

The [AttributeUsage] attribute has only one required parameter, the types that the attribute will affect. You'll find these types in the *AttributeTargets* enumeration. The optional *AllowMultiple* parameter determines if a user can have more than one attribute placed in front of a given entity. For example, you'd only want to allow one attribute that determines the configuration of a component. However, you'd want to allow multiple copies of an attribute that provides documentation for a class. The optional *Inherited* parameter determines if other attributes can inherit the features of the custom attribute. Here's a list of the types that you can support using attributes.

- Assembly
- Module
- Class
- Struct
- Enum
- Constructor
- Method
- Property

- Field
- Event
- Interface
- Parameter
- Delegate
- ReturnValue
- All

Creating a custom attribute is relatively easy once you know about the [AttributeUsage] attribute. Unlike Visual C++ .NET, you can only use classes for attributes (Visual C++ also enables you to use structs). Listing 6.2 shows the code for the custom attribute used in this section. The example will enable developers to describe entities in various ways. For example, you could use the attribute to describe additional work the assembly requires to provide a list of bugs within the entity.

Listing 6.2   Creating a Custom Attribute

```
// Attribute contains three mandatory (date, author, and purpose)
// and one optional entry (comment).
[AttributeUsage(AttributeTargets.All,
                AllowMultiple=true,
                Inherited=false)]
public class EntityDescribe : System.Attribute
{
   private String   _Date;      // The date the comment is made.
   private String   _Author;    // Comment author.
   private String   _Purpose;   // Purpose of the element.
   private String   _Comment;   // Comment about the element (optional).

   public EntityDescribe(String Date, String Author, String Purpose)
   {
      // These three values are mandatory and appear as part of
      // the constructor.
      _Date = Date;
      _Author = Author;
      _Purpose = Purpose;
   }

   // The comment field is optional,
   // so it gets treated as a property.
   public String Comment
   {
      get
      {
         return _Comment;
```

```
        }
        set
        {
            _Comment = value;
        }
    }

    // Accessors for the mandatory fields.
    public String Date
    {
        get
        {
            return _Date;
        }
    }
    public String Author
    {
        get
        {
            return _Author;
        }
    }
    public String Purpose
    {
        get
        {
            return _Purpose;
        }
    }
};
```

As you can see, the code is relatively simple. However, you need to know about a few nuances of attribute construction. Notice that only three of the properties—Date, Author, and Purpose—appear in the constructor. These three properties represent the required entries for using the attribute. The Comment property is separate and is therefore optional.

Because Comment is optional, you need to provide it with both a get and a set property, as shown in the listing. You could add anything here that you wanted, such as range checking. The main thing that the get and set routines have to provide is some means of storing the data provided by the user to the custom attribute.

The final issue is providing accessors for the three mandatory properties. The assembly will still contain the data if you don't provide an accessor, but you won't be able to read it from within your code. In short, the data will become lost within the assembly, never to see the light of day.

The custom attribute is ready to use. All we need to do is add one or more entries to another class to see it at work. The example places attributes in two places to make it easier to discuss the effect of the attribute on application metadata. However, the three most important entries appear at the class level, because we'll use reflection to read them in the next section. Here are the three entries we'll add to the class.

```
[EntityDescribe("11/27/2001",
    "John",
    "Created the new form for test application.")]
[EntityDescribe("11/28/2001",
    "Rebecca",
    "OK Button Click Event Handler",
    Comment="Needs more work")]
[EntityDescribe("11/29/2001",
    "Chester",
    "Added Attribute Test Button")]
```

As you can see, the three custom attribute entries all describe aspects of the target class, FrmAttribute. The second entry in the list also makes use of the optional Comment property. Notice that you need to provide the name of the custom property to use it by providing a <Property Name>=<Value> pair within the attribute entry. The example entry doesn't check the validity of these entries, but you'd want to add this feature to an attribute that you wanted to use for production purposes.

TIP   One of the nice features of attributes is that they always use the same presentation—no matter which development language you use. The same attribute code will work in C#, Visual C++, and even Visual Basic without modification. This makes attributes one of the only truly generic pieces of code you can use.

After you add some custom attribute entries to the application, you can compile it. Open the application using the ILDASM utility (which we've discussed in several places). Figure 6.6 shows the results of the three entries we made to the class. Notice that ILDASM doesn't make them particularly readable, but you can definitely see them in them list (starting with the highlighted entry in the figure).

FIGURE 6.6:

ILDASM displays any custom attribute additions you make to the code.

If you want to see the full effect of an attribute entry, you need to attach it to a data member, such as a pushbutton. Open the disassembly of the data member by double-clicking it in ILDASM. Figure 6.7 shows an example of the [EntityDescribe] attribute attached to the *btnOK* object. Notice that you can see all three of the default entries.

FIGURE 6.7:

Use a disassembly to see the full effect of any custom attribute you create.

It's important to realize that the compiler stores the property values as they'd appear for the constructor. In other words, the compiler doesn't change the attribute in any way. The data you add to an assembly is readable in the disassembly, even if the attribute would normally encrypt the data. This security problem means you shouldn't store company secrets in the attributes and you might want to remove attributes from applications before you send them to a customer. Figure 6.8 shows an example of the readable data for the *btnOK* object.

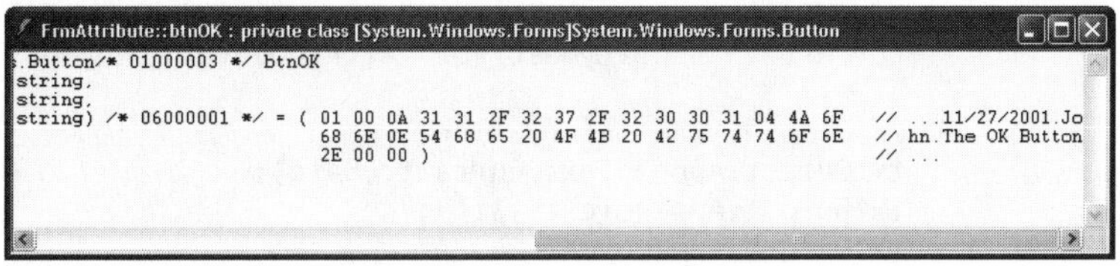

FIGURE 6.8:

Some types of metadata could represent a security risk for your application.

A source dump of your application is even more revealing. You'll find the `AssemblyDump.il` file in the \Chapter 06\Attribute\bin\Debug folder. This file contains a lot of information about the example application. While the native code executables from the Windows 32 environment weren't that much safer than the IL files used by .NET, they also didn't include as much descriptive information. It pays to create custom attributes using information that you'll only use during application construction or that you don't mind others seeing.

Accessing the Custom Attribute Using Reflection

One of the reasons to include metadata within an assembly is to document the assembly features and problems. Of course, reading these comments with ILDASM is hardly the best way to make use of the information. You could easily view the source code instead and probably save time by doing so. Reflection enables an application to read its own metadata and the metadata contained in other assemblies. This feature enables you to create utilities to read the metadata and do something with it. The nice part of this feature is that it also extends to the Microsoft assemblies, which means you can finally search them for tidbits of information.

Creating an application that relies on reflection isn't difficult, but it does look a tad strange at first. Listing 6.3 shows an example of reflection at work. In this case, clicking the Attribute button on the example application will fill the *txtOutput* text box with the content of the higher level attributes for the sample application.

Listing 6.3   Adding Reflection to an Application is Relatively Easy

```
private void btnAttribute_Click(object sender, System.EventArgs e)
{
    Object          []Attr;    // Array of attributes.
    EntityDescribe  CurrAttr;  // Current Attribute.

    // Gain access to the member information for the class.
    MemberInfo  Info = typeof(FrmAttribute);

    // Grab the custom attribute information.
    Attr = (Object[])(System.Attribute.GetCustomAttributes(Info,
                        typeof(EntityDescribe)));

    // Look at each attribute in the array.
    for (int Counter = 0; Counter < Attr.Length; Counter++)
    {
        // Obtain the current attribute.
        CurrAttr = (EntityDescribe)(Attr[Counter]);

        // Display the information.
        txtOutput.AppendText(CurrAttr.Date);
        txtOutput.AppendText("\t");
        txtOutput.AppendText(CurrAttr.Author);
```

```
        txtOutput.AppendText("\t");
        txtOutput.AppendText(CurrAttr.Purpose);
        txtOutput.AppendText("\t");
        txtOutput.AppendText(CurrAttr.Comment);
        txtOutput.AppendText("\r\n\r\n");
    }
}
```

The first task is to gain access to the member information that you want to use to search for attributes. In this case, we'll gain access to the FrmAttribute class and view the class level attributes. The *Info* variable contains this information.

The next task is to search for the attributes. You'll find a number of overrides for the Get-CustomAttributes() method. Listing 6.3 shows just one option. In this case, we'll search for all of the [EntityDescribe] attributes found in the FrmAttribute class. Notice the use of casts within the code. You need to locate the information in the order shown, or C# will display an error message during the compile cycle and not provide much in the way of a helpful answer about what's wrong with the code.

NOTE   The .NET Framework actually provides two methods for gaining access to a custom attribute's information. The first is GetCustomAttribute(), which returns a single attribute—the first one it finds. The second is GetCustomAttributes(), which returns an array of all of the attributes that fit within the search criteria.

After you gain access to the attributes, you need some way to convert them to readable or storable data. The first step in the for loop is to cast the individual attribute entry into an EntityDescribe data type. After that, you can use the data to display information on screen, send it to the printer for a report, or place it within a database for later use. In this case, we'll use the AppendText() method to place the data in the txtOutput text box. Figure 6.9 shows the output from the application.

FIGURE 6.9:

The output of the example application shows the top-level attribute entries.

Creating Controls

C# provides a number of ways to create managed controls. In fact, you'll be surprised by the variety of controls you can create using the projects supplied as part of the Visual Studio .NET IDE. The sections that follow will show you how to create some simple examples of controls using C#. You'll learn how to create additional controls as the book progresses, but these controls provide you with the basics you need to create the complex controls found later in the book.

NOTE You can't create unmanaged component and controls directly with C#. This limitation means that many of the tools you used to test your controls in the past, such as the ActiveX Control Test Container, no longer have a useful purpose. You must test the components and controls using the debugger provided by the IDE. Fortunately, you can convert the managed C# components and controls to work in the unmanaged environment. We'll discuss this technique in the "COM Component Example" section of the chapter.

Windows Control Library Overview

The Windows Control Library project enables you to create managed controls for your applications. Microsoft has made the process of creating controls much easier than the unmanaged counterpart you might have created in the past. The following sections will show that C# provides low-level support for common control needs. We'll also discuss the requirements for debugging a control. The fact that you don't have direct access to the control means you need to know how to access the control code through a client application.

User Control Example

User controls aren't controls in the same sense as controls that you might have created using Visual C++ in the past. You use them like controls, but actually they're composites of other controls. A user control represents a method of bundling some level of control functionality and then using it within a form. User controls have the same functionality as the COM controls you created in the past, but you'll notice they require a lot less work to create.

You begin developing a user control by creating a new Windows Control Library project. (The example appears in the \Chapter 06\UserControl folder on the CD.) After you name the class and files, you can begin adding controls to the Designer display. The example uses a simple pushbutton and timer. If the user doesn't click the button within the time set by the timer, the button will automatically click itself. This particular control comes in handy for slide presentations where you want to maintain a certain pace throughout the presentation. However, you can use it for other purposes.

Figure 6.10 shows the layout for the AutoButton control. Notice that the user control area is just large enough to hold the button. The reason you want to size the user control area is to prevent it from overlapping other controls when displayed in an application. In addition, the default size makes moving and placing the control cumbersome.

FIGURE 6.10:

The AutoButton control automatically clicks itself if the user doesn't click it within the specified time.

After you create the physical appearance of the control and add any non-visual controls, it's time to code it. One of the problems you'll need to consider is that none of the client control elements are accessible. For example, the AutoButton control requires some means of accessing the *Text* property on *btnAuto* or the user won't be able to change it. The same holds true for any events that you want to expose. All events require a new means of access or the user won't be able to interact with them when the control is compiled.

Of course, there are other items to consider. For example, you need to provide access to any new control functionality. User controls can provide more than just a means to bundle existing controls—you can add new functionality as well. Listing 6.4 shows the code you'll need to add to make this control functional.

Listing 6.4   **The AutoButton Automatically Clicks When Time Expires**

```
#region Exposed Properties
[Description("The text that appears on the button.")]
public String Caption
{
   get
   {
      return btnAuto.Text;
   }
   set
   {
      btnAuto.Text = value;
   }
}

[Description("The dialog result produced in a modal " +
            "by clicking the button")]
public DialogResult DialogResult
```

```csharp
{
   get
   {
      return btnAuto.DialogResult;
   }
   set
   {
      btnAuto.DialogResult = value;
   }
}

[Description("The amount of time to wait to press the button " +
            "automatically in milliseconds.")]
public int TimerValue
{
   get
   {
      return AutoTime.Interval;
   }
   set
   {
      AutoTime.Interval = value;
   }
}
#endregion

#region "Exposed Events"
[Description("Invoked when the user clicks the button.")]
public event EventHandler ButtonClick;
#endregion

#region "Exposed Methods"
[Description("Starts the button timer.")]
public void StartTimer()
{
   AutoTime.Start();
}

[Description("Stops the button timer.")]
public void StopTimer()
{
   AutoTime.Stop();
}

#endregion

private void btnAuto_Click(object sender, System.EventArgs e)
{
   // Reset the timer.
   AutoTime.Stop();
   AutoTime.Start();
```

```
    // Invoke the ButtonClick event.
    ButtonClick(this, e);
}

private void AutoTime_Tick(object sender, System.EventArgs e)
{
    // Invoke the ButtonClick event.
    ButtonClick(this, e);
}
```

The AutoButton control shows how to work with the three control elements: properties, events, and methods. Each element appears within a separate #region pair to make it easier to spot within the code. It's a good idea to use regions within your code to help hide some of the complexity when you want to work on a specific area. In addition, you can hover the mouse over a region to obtain a quick view of the code it contains without actually opening the region. Figure 6.11 shows an example of a region in use.

FIGURE 6.11:

Placing the mouse over a region shows the code it contains.

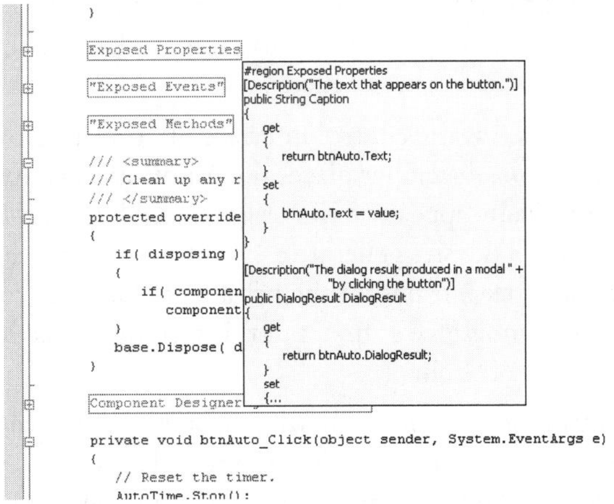

The properties include *Caption*, *DialogResult*, and *TimerValue*. Each property has an associated [Description] attribute. Not only does the [Description] attribute document the property for the control developer, it also provides the help text for the property within the Visual Studio IDE, as shown in Figure 6.12. The property code simply exchanges data between the controls used for the AutoButton control and the client.

FIGURE 6.12:

Use the [Descrip-tion] attribute to self-document proper-ties, events, and methods.

The one property needed for this example is ButtonClick(). As you can see, all you need is a public event EventHandler entry to create the event. The compiler automatically creates a class for you on the same order as it does for the delegate keyword. However, you also need code to fire the event. You'll see how this comes into play later in this section.

The two methods StartTimer() and StopTimer() enable the user to stop and start the internal timer. You have to make methods like this available. Otherwise, the AutoButton will continue to run, even when it isn't needed.

Now that we've looked at the control interface, it's time to look at the code that makes everything work. When a developer places the AutoButton control on a new project, all of the controls that originally appear on the original panel go with it. When the user clicks the AutoButton, the control doesn't generate a Click() event that the client application can trap—it generates a Click() event for the private *btnAuto* control contained on the panel. This might seem like a nuisance at first, but this technique enables you to trap the event first, and then pass it along to the client.

This use of control events is precisely what happens in the btnAuto_Click() method. The user clicks the button, your control resets its internal time, and then passes the event to the client using the ButtonClick() event. Firing the event makes it available to the client. The AutoTime_Tick() method fires the same event if time runs out before the user clicks the button.

The client works with the AutoButton much as it would any other pushbutton control. The two main requirements are setting the *TimerValue* property and ensuring the application starts the timer at some point. The code will also need to respond to the ButtonClick() event to gain any value from the AutoButton. The following code shows the code for a test application (also found in the \Chapter 06\UserControl folder on the CD).

```
private void autoButton1_ButtonClick(object sender, System.EventArgs e)
{
```

```
    // Display a message.
    MessageBox.Show("The AutoButton was clicked.",
        "Click Alert",
        MessageBoxButtons.OK,
        MessageBoxIcon.Information);
}

private void FrmMain_Load(object sender, System.EventArgs e)
{
    // Start the timer.
    autoButton1.StartTimer();
}
```

As you can see, the test application displays a message in response to a button click. The timer starts as soon as the application loads the form. If you want to test the AutoButton feature, start the application and wait 5 seconds (or set some other interval). Whenever you click the AutoButton, the timer resets and waits another 5 seconds before it clicks again.

Debugging Windows Control Library Projects

The methods you use to debug a control depend on the control element of interest. You use different techniques with each control element. A property requires different debugging procedures than a method or event. However, you can generally categorize debugging into three areas: property, method, and event.

Let's begin by looking at a method. All you need to do is place a breakpoint at the method call within the client application. Use the Step Into button to trace into the method code. It helps if you have a copy of the source code (not the entire solution) open in the IDE to make moving between method and client code easier. The debugger will try to find the source code when you step into the method code. One of the biggest problems to check with methods is to ensure the values you send to the method actually arrive in the form you anticipated.

Property checking is only a little more difficult than checking methods. Begin by setting a breakpoint within the control code at the get() or set() method. You might think that changing the property value in the IDE would give you access to the code. However, the debugger isn't active when you make such a change, so there's no process to stop. You need to create code that will exercise both get() and set() methods. Many developers find it easier to create a pushbutton for the task and add appropriate code as shown here.

```
private void btnDebug_Click(object sender, System.EventArgs e)
{
    // Set a breakpoint on the get and set methods for the Caption
    // property in the control. Trace into the property code using
    // the code shown below. A full check of a property means checking
    // both get and set code (when appropriate).
```

```
    autoButton1.Caption = "AutoButton";
    string MyCaption = autoButton1.Caption;
}
```

Tracing into the two statements (using the Step Into button) enables you to see any problems with the code you create. Obviously, you'll want to use a test application to check for bugs or remove the test code after you check a production application. Make sure you check for unexpected values to ensure range and validation code work as anticipated.

Debugging events can prove troublesome because you have no direct access to the event from the client code. When a user clicks on a pushbutton, the application environment invokes the event handler without making an intervening client code call. In short, you can't set a breakpoint within the client to see the event code.

To debug an event, you must set a breakpoint within the control code at the point where the event is fired. For example, in the AutoButton example, you set the breakpoint within the btnAuto_Click() or the AutoTime_Tick() method at the ButtonClick(this, e) call and trace the event from that point.

NOTE   You can't access the event EventHandler code directly. In most cases, you'll never need to debug this code because the compiler generates it automatically for you.

Web Control Library Overview

The Web Control Library project provides the web browser version of the control you'd create for a desktop application. In fact, you'll find that most of the Microsoft supplied desktop controls have a Web Control equivalent. The idea behind a Web Control is to bring as much of the look and feel of the desktop to the browser. In addition, Web Controls make it easier to build robust browser applications.

Controls generally help you encapsulate generic user interface functionality in a form that many applications can use, and Web Controls are no exception. The following sections show how to create a Web Control, add it as a web page, and display it in a browser. We'll also discuss some of the problems you'll encounter when debugging Web Controls. For example, there is the problem of creating a remote connection to ensure you can see how the control works in the server environment.

Simple Web Control Example

Web Controls interact with ASP .NET web pages. Creating a Web Control is different from a Windows control because the methods for rendering the control output are completely different. Consequently, little of what you know for creating a Windows control will transfer directly to the Web Control project.

TIP   Microsoft is constantly updating Visual Studio .NET components, especially those components that deal with distributed application development, because this area of development is constantly changing. As a developer, you'll want to ensure your development environment is updated before you begin a new project by visiting Microsoft's ASP .NET website at `http://www.asp.net/`. However, once you begin the project, it's usually a good idea to maintain a stable development environment by maintaining the current level of updates until project completion. Of course, you'll have to make a change if an update affects a critical development area, such as security.

This section of the chapter shows how to create a simple Web Control. In this case, you'll see how to create a switched label. In one mode it outputs Cascading Style Sheet (CSS) code that allows for absolute positioning and everything else that CSS has to offer. In the second mode, the same label will output straight HTML. A control like this is useful for a number of reasons, not the least of which is browser compatibility. A dual mode control could also help your website service the needs of those with accessibility requirements and could even enable those who don't want anything but a plain page to get their wish. The benefit to the developer is that you design the page once. A simple property change modifies the ASP.NET output, making the whole web page construction process easier.

NOTE   The ASP.NET portion of this example relies on a web server connection to open. Because Visual Studio .NET doesn't provide a means for modifying an ASP.NET Web Application project directly, you'll need to re-create the program shell and move the example code to it, or modify the project files found on the CD using a text editor. Replace all occurrences of the "`http://WinServer`" URL with the URL for your web server. The example is unlikely to open directly from the CD (unless your web server name is the same as mine).

Unlike the Windows control example earlier, you can't simply place controls on a panel to start building a Web Control. This project lacks designer support—you need to code all of the controls contained within the control. Verification of control placement and functionality occurs when you view the control on a web page. Consequently, you'll want to create the project so that you have both the control and the test web page available in the same solution. The following steps will describe how to create the dual project solution required for this example.

1. Open the New Project dialog box shown in Figure 6.13 and choose Web Control Library from the list of C# project templates. Type a name for the project—the example uses MyWebControl. Click OK to create the project.

FIGURE 6.13:

Use the New Project
dialog box to select
the Web Control
Library template.

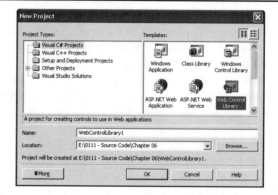

2. Select the File ➤ Add Project ➤ New Project command.

3. Select the ASP.NET Web Application template. Choose a location for this part of the project on your web server. The last part of the URL is the project name—the example uses MyWebControlTest. Click OK to create the project.

4. Change the names of any file within the project by selecting its entry in Solution Explorer and typing a new name in the File Name property. Also change the names of any class by highlighting its entry in Class View and changing the Name property. The example uses the name of SpecialHeader for the Web Control class and MainWebForm for the ASP.NET Web form.

5. Right-click MyWebControlTest and choose Set as Startup Project from the context menu. This ensures you can perform remote debugging of the project.

6. Right-click MyWebControlTest ➤ References and choose Add Reference from the context menu. You'll see the Add Reference dialog box shown in Figure 6.14.

FIGURE 6.14:

Always add a refer-
ence to the Web Con-
trol in the ASP.NET
Web Application.

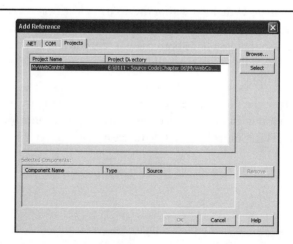

7. Select the Projects tab. Visual Studio .NET normally places the Web Control project in the list for you, but you can also use the Browse button to locate it. Highlight the Web Control project entry and click Select. Click OK. Visual Studio .NET will add the reference to the reference list for you.

Now that you have a project shell put together, it's time to add some code to MyWebControl. This example shows how to use attributes, create properties, and render the control on screen. Listing 6.5 contains the sample code. You'll find the complete source in the \Chapter 06\ MyWebControl folder on the CD; the ASP.NET Web Application source appears in the \Chapter 06\MyWebControlTest folder.

Listing 6.5   **The *SpecialHeader* Class Provides Extended Label Functionality**

```
[DefaultProperty("Text"),
   ToolboxData("<{0}:SpecialHeader " +
               "Text=\"Sample Header\" HeaderLevel=\"1\"" +
               "Centered=\"True\" AbsolutePosition=\"False\"" +
               "runat=server></{0}:SpecialHeader>")]
public class SpecialHeader : System.Web.UI.WebControls.WebControl
{
   private string _Text;          // Heading content.
   private int    _HeaderLevel;   // Heading level <H?>
   private bool   _Centered;      // Center the heading?
   private bool   _Absolute;      // Use absolute positioning?

   #region Control Properties
   [Bindable(true),
      Category("Appearance"),
      DefaultValue("Sample Header"),
      Description("String displayed by the control.")]
   public string Text
   {
      get { return _Text; }
      set { _Text = value; }
   }

   [Bindable(true),
      Category("Layout"),
      DefaultValue("1"),
      Description("Header level for the string")]
   public int HeaderLevel
   {
      get { return _HeaderLevel; }
      set
      {
         // Validate the input range, then set the property.
         if (value < 1 || value > 6)
            value = 1;
```

```csharp
        _HeaderLevel = value;
    }
}

[Bindable(true),
    Category("Layout"),
    DefaultValue("True"),
    Description("Center the string when true.")]
public bool Centered
{
    get { return _Centered; }
    set { _Centered = value; }
}

[Bindable(true),
    Category("Behavior"),
    DefaultValue("False"),
    Description("Use absolute header positioning when true.")]
public bool AbsolutePosition
{
    get { return _Absolute; }
    set { _Absolute = value; }
}
#endregion

/// <summary>
/// Render this control to the output parameter specified.
/// </summary>
/// <param name="output"> The HTML writer to write out to </param>
protected override void Render(HtmlTextWriter output)
{
    if (_Absolute)
    {
        // Create an enumerator for the WebControl.Style.
        IEnumerator keys = this.Style.Keys.GetEnumerator();

        // Provide the non-CSS output values.
        output.Write("<span id=\"" + this.ID + "\" ");
        output.Write("style=\"WIDTH: " + this.Width);

        // Move from one key value to the next until the enumeration
        // returns null.
        while (keys.MoveNext())
        {
            // Output a separator
            output.Write(";");

            // Obtain the current key value from the key enumeration.
            String key = (String)keys.Current;

            // Output the key and enumeration value to
```

```
        // the Web page.
        output.Write( key + ": " + this.Style[key]);
    }

    // Output the font configuration, if any.
    if (this.Font.Name != null)
        output.Write(";font-family: " + this.Font.Name);
    if (this.Font.Size.ToString() != null)
        output.Write(";font-size: " + this.Font.Size.ToString());
    if (this.Font.Bold)
        output.Write(";font-weight: Bold");
    if (this.Font.Italic)
        output.Write(";font-style: Italic");
    if (this.Font.Overline ||
        this.Font.Underline ||
        this.Font.Strikeout)
    {
        output.Write(";text-decoration:");
        if (this.Font.Overline)
            output.Write(" Overline");
        if (this.Font.Strikeout)
            output.Write(" Line-Through");
        if (this.Font.Underline)
            output.Write(" Underline");
    }

    // Output the text and closing tag.
    output.Write("\">" + _Text);
    output.Write("</span>\r\n");
}
else
{
    // Create the standard output, using standard HTML tags.
    if (_Centered)
        output.Write("<CENTER>");
    if (this.Font.Name != null)
        output.Write("<FONT face=\"" + this.Font.Name + "\">");
    if (this.Font.Bold)
        output.Write("<STRONG>");
    if (this.Font.Italic)
        output.Write("<EM>");
    if (this.Font.Underline)
        output.Write("<U>");
    output.Write("<H" + _HeaderLevel.ToString() + ">");
    output.Write(_Text);
    output.Write("</H" + _HeaderLevel.ToString() + ">");
    if (this.Font.Underline)
        output.Write("</U>");
    if (this.Font.Italic)
        output.Write("</EM>");
    if (this.Font.Bold)
```

```
            output.Write("</STRONG>");
        if (this.Font.Name != null)
            output.Write("</FONT>");
        if (_Centered)
            output.Write("</CENTER>");
        output.Write("\r\n");
        }
    }
}
```

The first item you should notice in Listing 6.5 is the two attributes immediately before the SpecialHeader class declaration. Both attributes affect how the Visual Studio .NET IDE interacts with the control. The [DefaultProperty] attribute tells the IDE to select the Text property as the first property when the user opens the Properties window. The [ToolBox-Data] attribute configures the HTML entry for the control. When someone creates a new control, the HTML code will include a tag, the name of the control, and some default property values.

Creating a property for a Web Control is much like creating a property for a Windows control. An internal private variable keeps track of the property value. The get() and set() methods enable the client to retrieve values. However, a Web Control requires several attributes to ensure it works properly with the website. The [Bindable] attribute ensures the client is notified every time a property change occurs. The [Category] attribute places the property in a specific category in the Properties window. The [DefaultValue] attribute ensures the property has a value, even if the client doesn't assign one. Finally, the [Description] property displays descriptive (help) text about the property in the Properties window.

Unlike most of the properties, the *HeaderLevel* property requires some custom handling. You need to ensure the input value makes sense, so this property performs some range checking in the set() method. This is a good example of how you can get around problems with invalid input. The code could also include an error message, but setting the property to a valid value is usually enough.

The Render() method is where all of the processing for this control takes place. The code begins by testing the *_Absolute* variable. If the user has set the *AbsolutePosition* property true, then the control will output CSS-compliant code. Otherwise, the control will output generic HTML code.

We'll discuss the CSS-compliant code generation first. This section of the code begins by outputting a <span> tag. This tag consumes most of the code section because it contains all of the information required to format the text of the control. The <span> tag begins with a definition of the width of the label.

One of the more interesting problems you'll face is discovering the values contained in some C# enumerations. For example, the `WebControl.Style` enumeration is one that you'll commonly use. Unfortunately, the content of this enumeration might not precisely match the input from your web page. Some items are distributed. The easiest way to discover how an enumeration is going to work is to create a quick listing of the members. For example, the code in Listing 6.5 shows how to work with the `WebControl.Style` enumeration.

Sometimes you don't need to use all of the CSS values in your control. The `while` loop code in Listing 6.5 will return the key value and associated CSS value input from the web page. The key value is case sensitive, so this technique saves time spent playing with various permutations of spelling and capitalization for the `Style[index]` value. Right-click the resulting web page and use the View Source command to display the key values. Cut and paste the keys directly into your code as needed.

The rest of the CSS portion of the code works with font attributes. In most cases, all you have to do is detect the font value, then output a keyword as needed. The `text-decoration` attribute requires special handling because it can contain any of three values (including combinations of all three values) for overline, underline, and strikethrough. The remainder of the code completes the `<span>` tag. Notice the use of a newline (\r\n pair) character in the output. If you don't include a newline character, the code is almost unreadable when you use the View ➤ Source command in Internet Explorer to view the results of your handiwork.

The HTML code portion of the `Render()` method outputs an HTML version of the CSS section. The match isn't exact because HTML offers fewer capabilities. However, the HTML version does offer some nice formatting features, and all you need to do to use it is change the value of the `AbsolutePosition` property. The same label works in both cases.

Web Controls require a few usability tweaks before they're friendly additions to your toolkit. When you add a Web Control to an ASP .NET Web Application, it relies on a tag to identify the control. The Microsoft-supplied controls use the `<asp:>` tag, but your controls will need to use something else to avoid confusion. Defining a tag for your application is easy. Just add the following code (or something similar) to the `AssemblyInfo.CS` file for your project.

```
// Special for Web Controls.
[assembly: TagPrefix("MyWebControl", "MyWebControl")]
```

The first argument for the `[TagPrefix]` attribute is the name of the namespace for your control. The entire namespace will use the same prefix. The second argument is the name of the tag. In this case, I used the same value for both namespace and tag, but this isn't a requirement.

The second addition to your control is a bitmap that will appear in the Toolbox when you add the control to the IDE. Create a new 16 × 16-pixel bitmap and give it the same name as the control class. The example uses `SpecialHeader.BMP` because that's the name of the class. Draw something interesting for the bitmap. Highlight the bitmap entry in Solution Explorer and select Embedded Resource for the *Build Action* property. This option forces the compiler to include the bitmap within the control.

Compile the control and you're ready to go. All you need to do is add the control to the toolbox. Right-click the Toolbox and choose Customize Toolbox from the context menu. You'll see the Customize Toolbox dialog box. Select the .NET Framework Components tab. Click Browse and you'll see an Open dialog box. Locate your Web Control, highlight it, then click Open. C# will add the control to the Toolbox.

Add the control to the ASPX file of your application. The first check you need to make is whether Visual Studio added the tag for your control to the top of the Web page automatically. You also need to check whether the tag value is correct. Here's what the tag entry looks like for the test application. (Note that this tag normally appears on one line.)

```
<%@ Register TagPrefix="mywebcontrol" Namespace="MyWebControl"
    Assembly="MyWebControl" %>
```

Try various control options. You'll normally see any changes you make within the Designer. However, there are some situations where the output from your website won't quite match the output in the Designer. For example, the size of the browser window will make a difference, as will the capabilities of the browser. Figure 6.15 shows some sample output from this control. The first label relies on standard HTML, while the second relies on CSS formatting.

FIGURE 6.15:

The `SpecialHeader` control works equally well in CSS or HTML mode.

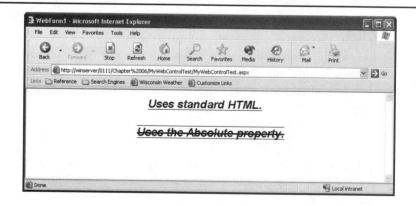

Debugging Web Control Library Projects

One of the most common problems with debugging a Web Control Library project is gaining access to the remote server. The first problem that many developers experience is not setting the startup project as we did in the previous section. The second problem is one of rights to the server. The developer must belong to the Debugger Users group or the debugger won't work properly, even if you're a member of the Administrator group (just why this happens is something that Microsoft hasn't answered). You'll also experience fewer problems if you log into the domain rather than the local machine.

TIP A Web Control renders within a browser, which means that not all browsers provide full support for them. This means you have to design the control for maximum compatibility. The runtime environment performs part of this work for you by mapping some commands and providing overrides for others, given a specific browser client. However, it pays to test your control using several browsers to ensure it will work as predicted.

Another connection problem occurs when you have the project configured for localhost debugging and you attempt to use a two-machine setup. If you can start the application using the Debug ➤ Start Without Debugging command, but not with the Debug ➤ Start command, it's likely that you have a configuration problem in the Web.CONFIG or Global.ASAX file. For example, several TCP/IP addresses in Web.CONFIG are set to 127.0.0.1, which is the localhost setting. Make sure you wait long enough for the project to start. It takes an incredibly long time for the debugger to set up all of the required connections, even with a simple project.

NOTE The Global.ASAX file is the ASP.NET replacement for the Global.ASA file used in previous versions of Visual Studio. Make sure you take this change into consideration when moving your applications from ASP to ASP.NET.

Once the program has started, you'll immediately stop at any breakpoints set within the application. In some cases, you'll need to click Refresh in the browser to force the application to reload the page before a new breakpoint will do anything. For example, you need to click Refresh every time you want to check code within the Render() method.

Creating Components

Components serve as the nonvisual building problem of application development. A component can reside on the client or the server, work in the background or the foreground, and require user input or act without it. You'll never place components in your Toolbox; you'll always refer to them and then use them within your application. In short, components are the invisible building blocks of the Visual Studio .NET environment.

The following sections discuss several component issues, and we'll create two component examples. The first example is a managed component used in a managed environment. You'll find that using components in a managed environment is extremely easy compared to experiences you might have had in the unmanaged environment. The second example will show you how to move the component from the managed environment to the unmanaged environment and use it within a native executable. As far as the native executable is concerned, it's just like using any other COM component. Of course, the ability to move between environments can't be overemphasized.

Class Library Example

The .NET Framework provides a number of text manipulation classes. However, it seems like there are always more ways to manipulate text than there are prebuilt methods to do it. The example in this section will add a few new text manipulation methods to your arsenal and show how to build a simple component as well.

You'll begin with the Class Library project. The example uses a project name of TextChange and you'll find the associated code in the \Chapter 06\TextChange folder on the CD. (The example also includes a test application as part of the project.) The project is empty when you create it, except for a bare skeleton containing a sample namespace and class name. Listing 6.6 shows the source code for this example.

Listing 6.6   **The TextChange Component Methods Modify Your Text**

```
/// <summary>
/// A class for manipulating text.
/// </summary>
public class Manipulate
{
   public Manipulate()
   {

   }

   /// <summary>
   /// A method for reversing the text.
   /// </summary>
   /// <param name="Input">Requires an input string to reverse.</param>
   /// <returns>A string containing reversed text.</returns>
   public string Reverse(string Input)
   {
      string   Temp = "";   // Temporary holding string.
      int      Counter;     // Loop control variable.
```

```
        // Create the reversed string.
        for (Counter = 1; Counter <= Input.Length; Counter++)
        {
            Temp = Temp + Input.Substring(Input.Length - Counter, 1);
        }

        // Return the string value.
        return Temp;
    }

    /// <summary>
    /// Return the last character of the string.
    /// </summary>
    /// <param name="Input">The input string.</param>
    /// <returns>The last character of the input string.</returns>
    public string GetLast(string Input)
    {
        return Input.Substring(Input.Length - 1, 1);
    }

    /// <summary>
    /// Return the last <em>n</em> characters of the string.
    /// </summary>
    /// <param name="Input">The input string.</param>
    /// <param name="NumChars">The number of return characters.</param>
    /// <returns>The last <em>n</em> characters of the string.</returns>
    public string GetLast(string Input, int NumChars)
    {
        // Validate the input.
        if (NumChars >= Input.Length)
            return Input;
        else
            return Input.Substring(Input.Length - NumChars, NumChars);
    }

    /// <summary>
    /// Return the last character of the string.
    /// </summary>
    /// <param name="Input">The input string.</param>
    /// <returns>The last character of the input string.</returns>
    /// <remarks>Used without an object.</remarks>
    public static string GetLastChar(string Input)
    {
        return Input.Substring(Input.Length - 1, 1);
    }
}
```

As you can see, the code for this component is relatively simple. However, you should notice a few features of this code. The first feature is the use of the XML-like entries at the beginning of each method. These entries are exceptionally important when working with components because they help you document the component code. When you look at the method in the Object Browser, the additional entries help identify what you need to work with the method. Figure 6.16 shows an example of how these entries look when you view them in Object Browser.

FIGURE 6.16:

Using the `<summary>` and other tags helps you document your component.

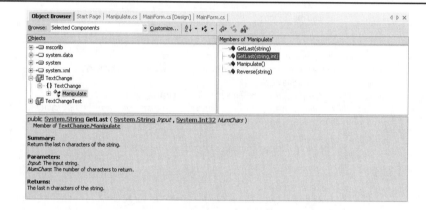

You can use common HTML formatting tags within the comments for your methods and class. The formatting won't appear in Object Browser, but it will appear in other environments. For example, you can create documentation from the source code by filling these tags out. The generated document will retain the formatting you put in place.

The second feature of note is the use of two overrides for the `GetLast()` method. It's common to provide multiple overrides when it makes sense. In this case, it's reasonable to assume the user will want both overrides. If the component user doesn't specify the number of returned characters, the first form of the method is executed and the user receives just one character in return.

The `GetLastChar()` method is also special. Notice that this method is declared as `static`. The `static` keyword enables you to use the method without creating an object (an instance of the method) first. However, you can't use static methods with object references and you can't override an existing method with a static version. The second limitation means you can't create a static version of `GetLast()`.

COM Component Example

What happens when you want to use your lovely new managed component with an older application? The component is definitely useful in the unmanaged environment, but you need to make a few minor changes first. Remember from the unmanaged component and control examples from the beginning of the chapter that you need to create a strong name to move from one environment to the other. The same holds true for unmanaged components. You'll still type `SN -k MyKey` at the command prompt to create a key pair for your component. However, unlike those previous examples, you'll compile the key directly into the component by adding it to the `AssemblyInfo.CS` file as shown here:

```
[assembly: AssemblyKeyFile("MyKey")]
```

When you recompile the component, it will have a strong name that won't affect its functionality. In fact, creating the strong name improves flexibility, because you can register the component in the GAC and make it generally available to any application that needs it. The GAC doesn't remove the need to create a reference to the component, but it enables CLR to find the component when called upon by an application. The following steps show how to make the `TextChange.DLL` accessible from an unmanaged application environment using COM.

1. Type `RegASM /tlb:TextChange.TLB TextChange.DLL` and press Enter at the command prompt. This action will register the component and create a type library that unmanaged environments can use to access the component. In some cases, you might want to run the program a second time using the **/regfile:<Filename>** switch to create a registry file for the application as well. The registry file makes it easier to move the component to other systems.

2. Type `GACUtil -i TextChange.DLL` and press Enter at the command prompt. The unmanaged application will call upon CLR to load and run the `TextChange.DLL` file. The problem is that CLR won't know where to find the component unless you make it part of the GAC.

At this point, the component is ready for use. However, you need to verify that the component is registered properly and that you can access it from an unmanaged application. The first step is easy. Open the OLE/COM Object Viewer. Open the .NET Category folder, then locate the `TextChange.Manipulate` entry. Figure 6.17 shows an example of what you'll see.

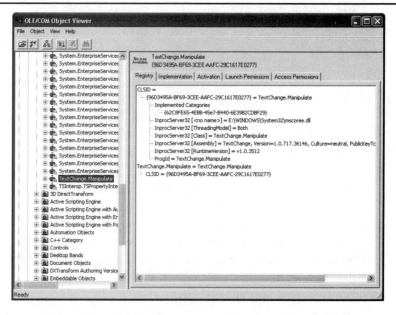

Performing the second test means creating an application in an unmanaged programming language environment such as Visual C++. You'll find a Visual C++ application that tests the component in the \Chapter 06\UnmanagedApp folder on the CD. Note that this example relies on the Dispatch ID method for instantiating the object, so it's not for the faint of heart.

Where Do You Go From Here?

This chapter has shown you how to work with managed and unmanaged controls and components in a number of ways. You've learned how to convert unmanaged components and controls for use in your managed applications and how to perform the process in reverse for your older unmanaged applications. In this chapter, you also learned about the basic component and control types. However, we'll build on that knowledge as the book progresses.

Because components and controls form the building blocks of modern applications, knowing how to create them is an essential part of your training as a developer. It's important to spend time learning to build components and controls of various types so you can learn about the intricacies of the .NET and Win32 environments. One of the ways you can learn more about both components and controls is to create a toolbox of components and controls you can use later. It's also important to begin converting your older components and controls now so you have them when you begin building larger managed applications. Likewise, you might want to develop all new components and controls using managed programming techniques, so knowing how to convert the new components and controls to work with older applications is critical.

Chapter 7 will introduce you to the concept of threads under .NET. A thread is one execution path within a process. Every process contains at least one, but perhaps more, threads of execution. We'll discuss how threads can make your applications more efficient and when too many threads can become a problem. In some cases, using fewer threads will result in better performance. You'll also learn about the thread types supported within the .NET Framework and when you should avoid using them in transitional projects.

CHAPTER 7

Working with Threads

Threads are a performance-enhancing feature of an application when they're developed correctly and used under the right circumstances. On the other hand, working with threads can become a mind-numbing exercise in application bugs, wasted developer time, and wasted resources. A thread (short for *thread of execution*) is a series of instructions executed independently of any other instructions within an application. An application always has at least one thread of execution, but may have many more.

This chapter provides you with a wealth of information about how threads work and how you can use them in your applications to make things run more efficiently. It's important to understand how threads get used in various types of projects. We'll also explore safety considerations for using threads. For example, we'll consider how critical sections ensure that two calling processes don't try to use the same portion of code at the same time. This chapter also explores the things you need to consider to ensure thread safety when working with local libraries. We'll spend time working through several example programs that demonstrate how threads work in different environments.

An Overview of Threads

Developers are constantly looking for ways to use machine resources more efficiently without spending more time developing applications. One way to do this is to write an application so that it can perform more than one task at a time. Windows provides this ability using threads. A thread is essentially a single subject of execution within an application. For example, using threads, an application could print and spell check a document in the background, while the user is typing in the foreground.

Threads don't perform any kind of magic. They won't make the user's machine any faster and the processor still won't be able to perform more than one task at a time. In other words, threads don't allow a machine to perform more than one task simultaneously unless that machine has the resources (i.e., multiple processors) to do so. However, threads can make use of resources that would otherwise go unused. A background thread can continue working while a foreground thread waits for user input. Another way to look at the issue is that the background thread frees the user interface so the user can get back to work more quickly.

NOTE You actually need to be aware of two entities when talking about threads. The term *thread* describes one set of contiguous instructions for performing a single task. A *process*, on the other hand, describes the application as a whole. Every executing application has at least one thread and one process. There's never more than one process for an application, but applications can always produce more than one thread. The distinction between processes and threads will become clear as the chapter progresses.

In some cases, an application requires threads for purposes other than efficiency. For example, a server application might need to service more than one user at a time. In this case, each thread would contain a separate user request. The threads enable the main application thread to continue accepting requests while pending requests are serviced in the background. The use of threads, in this case, ensures server availability but might not affect server performance.

Sometimes threads are simply inappropriate. For example, if an application spawns two threads, both of which require constant user interaction, the application will tend to run more slowly because the users have to divide their attention between the two threads. Likewise, adding a disk-intensive thread to an application that's already disk intensive is unlikely to increase system performance. The new thread will compete for resources with existing threads. Finally, adding threads to an overburdened server is unlikely to enhance server availability—quite the contrary—the server might cease to work at all.

Now that you have a little more information about threads, let's look at them in more detail. The following sections will help you understand how to use threads, what types of threads you can create, and how to use threads safely.

Uses for Threads

Theoretically, you can use threads in any C# application, including something as small as a component or control. Using threads in the managed environment is similar to working in the unmanaged environment in that you have the same thread types to consider and the underlying process is the same. In short, threads are a nearly universal solution to some types of problems.

Threads don't necessarily need to be large or complex either to make an application more efficient and responsive to user needs. In fact, you can use threads to perform small maintenance tasks in the background at regular intervals—something that you may not want to interrupt your main application to do. A thread can also replace timer-related tasks in some cases. In other words, threads aren't limited to performing any particular task.

TIP
One of the easiest ways to add a timed thread to your application is to use the Timer control. The Timer continues to execute in the background while your main application continues to work. Of course, this type of thread only works for tasks that execute at a regular interval, such as updating a clock or checking the status of the application environment.

However, you do need to consider some issues before you start using threads for every small task that your application may need to perform. It's important to use threads correctly in order to avoid some common problems that developers seem to face with them. The following list provides you with some guidelines on what you should think about before using threads.

Debugging   The biggest consideration from a developer perspective is that threads greatly increase the difficulty of debugging an application. A thread can actually hide bugs, or, at least, make them more difficult to find, since you'd now have to watch more than one thread of execution at a time.

Development Time   Most developers are used to thinking about application programming in a linear fashion. In other words, given a specific event, the application will perform a series of steps to handle it. Using a multiple thread approach forces the programmer to think about application processes in parallel, rather than in a linear fashion.

True Efficiency   While it's true that placing some tasks into background threads can make use of idle time in the application, there are situations when there isn't any idle time to exploit. In this situation, you'll find that the application is actually less efficient than before, because there's a certain amount of overhead and housekeeping associated with using multiple threads. In other words, only use threads in situations when you anticipate there will be some amount of idle time to exploit.

Reliability   Multiple threads of execution don't necessarily make an application failure prone, but there are more failure points to consider. Any time you add more failure points to anything, it becomes less reliable. There's a greater probability that the application will break simply because there are more things that can go wrong with it.

Unexpected Side Effects   No matter how carefully you craft a multithreaded application, there are going to be side effects that you have to deal with, especially if the threads in the application interact. Even if you make your application thread safe and use critical sections, there's a chance that two threads will try to access the same variable at the same time in an unanticipated way. Not only do these unexpected side effects increase development and debugging time, but they make it more likely that a user will come across a problem that you can't duplicate with your setup. In other words, multithreaded applications will more than likely increase application support costs.

Now that you have a good overview of the way in which you can use threads in general, let's look at some specific multithreaded usage types. The following sections will explore the four most common ways that you'll see multiple threads in use: applications, DLLs, system services, and server applications. Each of these areas represents a major application type. We'll explore some of these multithreaded usage examples later in the chapter.

Applications

We've already explored this topic to some extent. Applications can benefit from multiple threads of execution in a number of ways. In fact, some of those ways will seem quite natural from a programming perspective, because the tasks in question can be broken from the main thread of execution quite easily. The following list will give you some ideas on how you can use multiple threads with applications.

Printing   This one major task can always benefit from multiple threads in any application. Queuing a print job takes time, which means that the user is sitting at their desk, staring at the screen, doing nothing at all. In fact, some print jobs could take enough time that the user will give up trying to use the computer at all and do something else while waiting. Printing in the background in a separate thread is always an efficient way to handle this task.

As the User Types   There are many tasks that fall into the "as the user types" category, but the two most common are spelling and grammar checks. Many applications offer the ability to check the user's spelling and grammar as they type, which reduces the need to check the whole document later. Of course, there are a lot of less common tasks that fall into this category as well. For example, you could check the validity of an equation as the user types it or make sure that a database entry is correct. For that matter, you could even suggest (as some applications do) a completed entry for the user, based on past input.

Repetition   Repagination and other repetitive tasks can always occur as background threads. There isn't any need to take up the foreground task's time with things like updating the application clock. Most repetitive, continuous tasks can be relegated to background threads.

Data Saves   Most applications now include an automatic save feature simply because many users are very poor at saving data themselves. It's not hard to figure out why—the user is engrossed in completing their document and simply forget to perform the data save. An automatic data saving feature can allow the user to complete a document without worrying about power failures or other computer glitches that can cause data to disappear.

Updates   Streamlining the update process has become increasingly important, especially with more users relying on remote computing. Updates, in this case, aren't necessarily limited to data. For example, a user might check in with the company each morning for updated pricing schedules. A system administrator could use this habit to their advantage by also including a background thread that downloads any system updates the user may require. In other words, the user would receive both a data update and an application update at the same time. Of course, automatic data updates are a nice feature as well. The application could update pricing tables or other forms of application-specific information in the background at regular intervals, provided the machine has the capability of creating a remote connection to the company.

TIP You can combine multiple threads and system updates in other ways. For example, you might want to include a virus-checking thread that runs in the background and checks all of the incoming data before it actually is placed on the client machine. Another use of background threads includes running diagnostics in the background, as the user works, to ensure that their machine is fully functional. An alarm would tell the user that their machine required service and that they should save any data before it's too late. As you can see, there are a lot of ways that you can use threads to protect the user, their data, and the client machine from damage.

Calculations Math operations are notorious for consuming vast amounts of processor cycles. In some cases, you have to accept the heavy penalty of a calculation because the user requires an answer immediately. However, there are other situations when the application could complete the calculation just as easily in the background as a separate thread. In fact, many spreadsheet and graphics applications use this technique now to make foreground features more responsive to user input.

There are a few things you should consider not adding to background threads, simply because it's not feasible to do so. The one rule of thumb is that you should probably handle anything that requires direct user interaction on a constant basis as part of the main thread. On the other hand, anything the user can set once, then allow the computer to complete, is a good candidate for a separate thread. Any time you create a thread, make sure the application will realize an efficiency gain and the user an increased responsiveness. A thread that causes the entire machine to slow is somewhat counterproductive, and you should consider running the task as quickly as possible to reduce system down time.

DLLs

Dynamic link libraries (DLLs) have been around since Microsoft first introduced Windows. In fact, DLLs are actually the successors of the libraries used by DOS applications. For the most part, DLLs allow for the same uses of threads that applications do. The main difference is that you'd want to place common thread types in DLLs—threads that perform work that you may need to do in more than one application. However, developers do place some thread categories in DLLs, simply because they're major components of an application that the developer does not want to recompile every time the application is updated. Examples would include:

- Spelling and grammar checkers
- Print routines
- Non-automated data formatting

- Data processing routines

- Report builders

You could potentially add other items to the list, but this list should provide you with enough ideas to get started. The reason that these items could appear in a DLL is that the developer normally creates and debugs them separately from the main part of the application. It pays to keep these elements in a DLL to reduce debugging time for the main application and to reduce application compile time.

System Services

For the most part, users never interact with system services. System services sit in the background and perform tasks such as enabling the hardware to operate or creating network connections. Consequently, there are some specialized uses for threads within a system service. The following list will provide you with a few ideas.

Service Priority Upgrade   Some system services execute as low-priority background tasks. You normally don't want them to consume valuable processor cycles unless the machine is idle or there's some type of priority task to perform. When you use a service in the second capacity, high-priority threads come into play. Rather than change the priority of the entire service, you can simply launch a single thread to perform the high-priority task.

Discovery   Most system services are low-level applications that need to discover a great deal about the system to ensure that it's working properly. Sometimes this discovery phase can occur once during service initialization; but in other cases, it's an ongoing process. Consider the network driver that has to keep track of the current system configuration, including the status of remote resources. A good use of threads, in this case, would be to allow the service to perform multiple levels of discovery at the same time, without reducing its availability to the system as a whole.

Multiple Copies of the Same Task   Some services, such as the Indexing Service, perform a single task. However, they might need to perform this single task on multiple data streams or objects. In the case of the Indexing Service, each thread handles a separate catalog, ensuring that each catalog receives the same amount of processing power. It's important to handle some tasks like this to ensure that each data stream is handled in a timely manner.

Server Applications

Threads are generally a requirement for server applications. In fact, server applications are one place where you can use threads with impunity, if for no other reason than the need to fulfill multiple user requests simultaneously. Threads on a server are grouped into the following categories.

Availability   If several users will share the same process on a server, then you need threads to keep the user requests separated. For example, when working with an Internet Server Application Programming Interface (ISAPI) Extension, the DLL is passed a user context. The context identifies that user to the current thread of execution. Database applications represent another situation where threading is important; there's only one database management system (DBMS) process running, but multiple threads containing user requests exist.

Maintenance   Servers often run maintenance tasks on threads. For example, compacting a database will likely occur on a thread because you don't want to disturb the foreground processes. Likewise, tasks such as defragmenting the drive or checking drive status will likely occur in the background using threads monitored by a main process.

Reliability   Most companies want servers that run 24/7. This means running background tasks that check for reliability concerns before they become a problem. Diagnostic software often uses threads to meet the needs of redundant hardware. For example, fan-monitoring software could use a separate thread to monitor each fan on the system.

Security   Some applications use separate threads to monitor system security. The thread is outside the mainstream of other work occurring within the application and will react independently when a security breach occurs. Of course, each level of the system will have separate security checks. For example, the operation system uses threads to monitor the security of each application.

Performance   Interestingly enough, performance is one of the more uncommon uses of threads on a server. A server generally has few free resources that a thread can use to increase performance. In addition, the network administrator is likely to configure the system to favor background and service routine tasks anyway, making resources even less available. The one time when a thread will work for performance reasons is when the server supports a single application and the application is prone to use one resource over another. For example, a compute-intensive thread might work well on a server that supports a disk-intensive database application.

It isn't safe to assume that every application you write for a server will require threads. For example, components don't require threads, in most cases, because each user will create a new copy of the component. Only if more than one user will use the object at a time do you need to consider threads. Using COM+ is another example of when you need to look at the environment before you create a thread. In this case, the environment will manage threads for you, so long as you use single-threaded apartment (STA) components, making development easier.

Generally, it isn't safe to assume that a server can spawn endless threads and continue running. While the number of threads on the desktop is necessarily limited by the needs of the user, a server doesn't have any such limitation. Users will continue to make requests until there are no more resources. The need to monitor resources makes thread development for server applications more complicated than for the desktop. In most cases, you'll want to add monitoring software to thread-generating applications for servers to ensure that the thread will have enough resources to run without potential performance penalties.

Types of Threads

From a Windows perspective, you have threads and the processes that contain them and nothing else. In fact, the .NET Framework provides a single class that all threads use, so there's little difference between threads even from a thread-specific coding perspective. However, from an application concept perspective, there are actually two kinds of threads: worker and user interface (UI).

Worker and UI threads both perform a single sequence of execution within the application. The difference comes in the way that you implement and use these two kinds of threads. A UI thread normally interacts with the user in some way, while a worker thread executes in the background where the user might not even be aware of it. The following sections talk about these two thread types and show how they're used.

TIP   You can use the Win32 `CreateThread()` function to create a thread that doesn't rely on the .NET Framework. The advantage of doing so is that you eliminate some overhead normally encountered using the .NET Framework. In addition, this method conserves memory (unfortunately, you have to manage that memory manually). The down side, of course, is that you can't use any of the capabilities that the .NET Framework provides and you do have to consider managed-to-unmanaged boundary conversions. In most cases, you'll find that the .NET Framework `Thread` class works best for threads that perform simple repetitive tasks.

Worker Threads

Worker threads are normally used for background tasks that require no user interaction. A worker thread normally performs its work and quietly exits. If an error occurs, the worker thread must throw a `ThreadException` event. The application should include a thread exception handler to determine if the error is critical, is something the user needs to decide about, could resolve itself through a retry to the call, or is a non-critical error that the application doesn't need to worry about. Thread exception handlers are of the `ThreadException-EventHandler()` type.

Another way to end a worker thread and generate an exit code is to use the `Abort()` method of the `Thread` class. Using this function will stop thread execution and perform any required cleanup before exiting to the calling application. The `Abort()` method doesn't guarantee data integrity or that the application will remain in a stable state. Calling `Abort()` automatically generates a `ThreadAbortException`. This exception is separate from the `ThreadException`, and you need a separate handler for it.

The .NET Framework won't allow you to pass parameters to the thread method when you start it. The best way to pass data to a worker thread is through the constructor. In other words, when you create the worker thread, you also set the parameters needed to make it run. Another way to pass data to the worker thread is to use properties. This enables you to provide optional variable support without creating a lot of constructor overrides. The only other way to pass data to a worker thread is by using shared fields or variables.

If you need to pass data to a worker thread using a shared resource, be sure to protect the data using an `Interlocked` class object. The `Interlocked` class ensures that changes made by one thread complete before access by another thread is allowed. See the "Understanding Critical Sections" and "Understanding Thread Safety" discussions later in this chapter for more details.

UI Threads

As the name suggests, you normally create UI threads to provide some type of user interface functionality within application. Generally, this means creating a separate dialog box using a separate class. The UI thread can perform work once it accepts the user input, but the initial focus is on gaining any required input. In addition, a UI thread can provide user output in the form of status and completion messages. Of course, this means that UI threads are limited to applications that deal with the desktop, since there's little chance that someone would use the server console often enough to make a UI thread worthwhile.

The differentiation between a UI thread and a worker thread goes much further than the user interface element. A good example of a UI thread application is a file copy or a printing routine. The thread acquires user input, provides status messages, and then provides some type of completion message. None of these functions require support from the main thread. In short, the UI thread tends to provide self-contained support.

One of the major considerations for a UI thread is providing a user interface element that doesn't get in the way of other needs. The UI thread should only interrupt the user as necessary—when it makes sense to interrupt the user. For example, a print routine would need to interrupt the user long enough to get printer setup and document output information. Because the user expects this interaction, the UI thread isn't considered obtrusive. Likewise, most readers will want to know when the print job is done, but in this case you should provide an option to turn off the completion message because the user might sit next to the printer and know when the job is complete by simply listening to the printer.

UI threads are different enough that some languages provide a separate class to handle them. For example, Visual C++ developers have access to the CWinThread class when working with UI threads. C# and the .NET Framework provide one class, Thread, to handle all threading requirements. The lack of a separate class doesn't make C# harder to use—actually, it means you have less to remember. However, it's important to keep the philosophy behind a UI thread in mind as you develop a C# application.

Working with Threads

As previously mentioned, you'll generally use threads in specific environments for purposes suited to those environments. Threads also appear in both worker and UI varieties, with the UI variety limited to user application needs in general. (Server applications won't benefit from a UI thread, because no one is working at the server console to see the thread output.)

With these criteria in mind, the following sections present three example applications. The first uses a worker thread to create output for a desktop application. The application and thread code appear in the same file. The second application uses a UI thread, but the thread appears in a separate DLL file. Finally, the third application shows how you'd create a DLL for a server application. (Make sure you look at the example in the "Understanding Critical Sections" section later in this chapter for an example on sharing resources.)

Desktop Application Example

The worker thread is the most common type of thread you'll create for an application, because this type works in the background without user intervention. A worker thread enables you to perform work in the background while the user works in the foreground.

Creating the Thread Class

The example application consists of a worker thread that sleeps for a given number of milliseconds, then fires an event to show that it has completed its work. The use of events in this example shows just one way of interacting with threads. You can always use other techniques. The event mechanism does have the advantage of freeing the main thread and enabling the application to react to thread events as needed. Listing 7.1 shows the thread source code. (The listing only shows the thread-related code—you'll find the complete source code in the \Chapter 07\WorkerThread folder of the CD.)

Listing 7.1 **This Worker Thread Example Relies on Events for Communication**

```
public class MyThread
{
    #region Private Variable Declarations
    private int    _Interval;      // Time to wait for event.
    private bool   _CreateError;   // Create an error event?
    private string _StandardMsg;   // Standard event message.
    private string _ErrorMsg;      // Event error message.
    #endregion

    public MyThread(int Interval)
    {
        // Perform a range check and assign an appropriate value.
        if (Interval >= 100)
            _Interval = Interval;
        else
            _Interval = 1000;

        // Initialize private variables.
        _CreateError = false;
        _StandardMsg = "Hello World";
        _ErrorMsg = "An Error Occurred";
    }

    #region Public Methods
    public void DoWait()
    {
        MyEventArgs              e;   // WorkerThread Arguments.
        ThreadExceptionEventArgs fe;  // Failure Arguments.
        System.Exception         se;  // System Exception Value.

        // Wait for some interval.
        Thread.Sleep(_Interval);

        // Create and fill out the event arguments.
        e = new MyEventArgs();
        e.Message = _StandardMsg;
        e.ErrorMsg = _ErrorMsg;

        // Determine if we need to throw an error.
        if (_CreateError)
        {
            // If so, create an error.
            se = new System.Exception(_ErrorMsg);
            se.Source = this.ToString();
            fe = new ThreadExceptionEventArgs(se);
            ThreadFail(this, fe);
        }
```

```
         // Otherwise, there is no error.
      else

         // Fire the WorkerThread event.
         WorkerThread(this, e);
   }
   #endregion

   #region Public Properties
   public bool CreateError
   {
      get { return _CreateError; }
      set { _CreateError = value; }
   }

   public string StandardMsg
   {
      get { return _StandardMsg; }
      set { _StandardMsg = value; }
   }

   public string ErrorMsg
   {
      get { return _ErrorMsg; }
      set { _ErrorMsg = value; }
   }
   #endregion

   #region Public Event Declarations

   /// <summary>
   /// Standard event handler for successful completion.
   /// </summary>
   public event MyEventHandler WorkerThread;

   /// <summary>
   /// Error event handler for unsuccessful completion.
   /// </summary>
   public event ThreadExceptionEventHandler ThreadFail;
   #endregion
};
```

When you work with a thread, you need to decide which input is required and which is optional. Use the constructor to force input of mandatory inputs and properties to enable input of the optional arguments. Notice that the MyThread() constructor requires a wait interval as input. Instead of raising an error for inappropriate input, the constructor assigns a minimum value to the _Interval variable. The _CreateError, _StandardMsg, and _ErrorMsg variables receive standard values to ensure that the thread won't fail due to a lack of optional input.

The only method within the worker thread class is DoWait(). This method begins by sleeping for the number of milliseconds specified by _Interval. After the method wakes up, it checks for an error condition indicator simulated by _CreateError in this case. If the error condition is in place, the DoWait() method creates a System.Exception object that contains an error message and an error source. Complete implementations will also fill in the Target-Site and StackTrace properties for this object. The System.Exception object is turned into a ThreadExceptionEventArgs object and finally passed along to the client when DoWait() fires the first of two events, ThreadFail().

The DoWait() non-error condition is a little easier to follow. All the method does is fire the second of two events, WorkerThread(). The WorkerThread() event is actually more complex than ThreadFail() because it requires the use of a custom event message handler and delegate. You can see both event declarations near the end of Listing 7.1. Notice that Thread-Fail() relies upon the standard ThreadExceptionEventHandler, but WorkerThread() relies upon MyEventHandler. Listing 7.2 shows the specialized event delegate and event message class used for WorkerThread().

Listing 7.2   *WorkerThread()* Relies on a Specialized Delegate and Message Class

```
/// <summary>
/// The example requires a custom delegate for firing an
/// event message.
/// </summary>
public delegate void MyEventHandler(object Sender, MyEventArgs e);

/// <summary>
/// The System.EventArgs class doesn't provide the means to pass
/// data to the event handler, so we need a custom class.
/// </summary>
public class MyEventArgs : EventArgs
{
   #region Private Variable Declarations
   private string _Message;   // Message the user wants to dipslay.
   private string _ErrorMsg;  // Error message for event handler.
   #endregion

   public MyEventArgs()
   {
      _Message = "No Message Supplied";
      _ErrorMsg = "An Event Error Occurred";
   }

   #region Public Properties
   public string Message
   {
      get { return _Message; }
      set { _Message = value; }
```

```
    }

    public string ErrorMsg
    {
        get { return _ErrorMsg; }
        set { _ErrorMsg = value; }
    }
    #endregion
};
```

As you can see, MyEventHandler() is a standard delegate declaration that the compiler turns into a class for you. One of the arguments for this event handler is MyEventArgs—a special class that inherits from System.EventArgs. The only additions to this class are two properties: one for the standard message and a second for the custom error message.

Creating the Test Code

Now that you understand the thread, let's look at the code for the main form. The main form contains textboxes that enable the user to input the standard and error messages, and the interval the worker thread should wait. The Test pushbutton creates a normal thread, while the Throw Error pushbutton enables the error condition and throws an error. Listing 7.3 shows the code for this portion of the example.

| Listing 7.3 | The Pushbutton and Thread Event Handlers for the Example Application |

```
private void btnTest_Click(object sender, System.EventArgs e)
{
    // Create a new worker thread object.
    MyThread NewThread = new MyThread(Int32.Parse(txtInterval.Text));

    // Add the event handlers.
    NewThread.WorkerThread += new MyEventHandler(WorkerThreadEvent);
    NewThread.ThreadFail +=
        new ThreadExceptionEventHandler(MyThreadExceptionHandler);

    // Add the messages.
    NewThread.StandardMsg = txtStandardMsg.Text;
    NewThread.ErrorMsg = txtErrorMsg.Text;

    // Create and execute the thread.
    Thread   DoThread = new Thread(new ThreadStart(NewThread.DoWait));
    DoThread.Start();

    // Get rid of the thread.
    DoThread = null;
    NewThread = null;
}
```

```csharp
private void btnThrowError_Click(object sender, System.EventArgs e)
{
    // Create a new worker thread object.
    MyThread NewThread = new MyThread(Int32.Parse(txtInterval.Text));

    // Add the event handlers.
    NewThread.WorkerThread += new MyEventHandler(WorkerThreadEvent);
    NewThread.ThreadFail +=
        new ThreadExceptionEventHandler(MyThreadExceptionHandler);

    // Add the messages.
    NewThread.StandardMsg = txtStandardMsg.Text;
    NewThread.ErrorMsg = txtErrorMsg.Text;

    // Set the thread to throw an error.
    NewThread.CreateError = true;

    // Create and execute the thread.
    Thread   DoThread = new Thread(new ThreadStart(NewThread.DoWait));
    DoThread.Start();

    // Get rid of the thread.
    DoThread = null;
    NewThread = null;
}
#endregion

#region Thread Event Handlers
private void WorkerThreadEvent(object sender, MyEventArgs e)
{
    // Display the worker thread message.
    MessageBox.Show("This is the thread message:\r\n" + e.Message,
                    "Thread Success Message",
                    MessageBoxButtons.OK,
                    MessageBoxIcon.Information);
}

private void MyThreadExceptionHandler(object sender,
    ThreadExceptionEventArgs e)
{
    // Get user input on the error.
    DialogResult Result = new DialogResult();

    // Display the error message.
    Result = MessageBox.Show(
                    "The thread error information:\r\n\tMessage:\t" +
                    e.Exception.Message + "\r\n\tSource:\t" +
                    e.Exception.Source + "\r\n\tStack Trace:\t" +
                    e.Exception.StackTrace + "\r\n\tTarget Site:\t" +
                    e.Exception.TargetSite,
                    "Thread Error",
```

```
                        MessageBoxButtons.AbortRetryIgnore,
                        MessageBoxIcon.Error);

    // Do something based on the result.
    if (Result == DialogResult.Abort)
        Application.Exit();
    else if (Result == DialogResult.Retry)
        btnThrowError_Click(this, new System.EventArgs());
}
#endregion
```

As you can see, the btnTest_Click() and btnThrowError_Click() button event handlers follow the same process for creating the thread and starting it. Notice the use of the Int32 .Parse() method for converting text input to a number for the MyThread() constructor.

Once we have a thread object to use, it's time to configure it. You must configure the thread before you start it. As previously mentioned, the MyThread class provides two event handlers, so the next step is to assign local methods to handle both. Both button event handlers assign values to the *StandardMsg* and *ErrorMsg* properties. Only the btnThrowError_ Click() button event handler needs to set the *CreateError* property so the thread will fail.

The final three lines of code create the actual thread, start it, and assign a null value to the thread and thread object. Starting the thread isn't nearly as much work as setting it up.

Both thread event handlers display messages. The MyThreadExceptionHandler() event handler provides the most complete information based on the contents of the *Thread-ExceptionEventArgs* object. Notice the use of the *DialogResult* variable, *Result*, to handle user input. This event handler assumes that the user might want to terminate the application due to the error, but it gives the user other options as well.

Performing a Worker Thread Test

The example application helps you learn about several worker thread features. For one thing, you'd never know the worker thread even existed were it not for the event handler code. Any application can hide threads this way. The threads work in the background without notice unless an error or some other event occurs. Theoretically, the application could perform tasks on the user's behalf without the user's knowledge.

When you start the application, you'll see a dialog similar to the one shown in Figure 7.1. Try using different message and timing values. As you increase the thread sleep time, you'll see a longer interval before the event message appears. Using a long interval also enables you to start several threads at once by clicking either Test or Throw Error several times in succession. Changing the messages before each pushbutton press shows that the threads are truly independent and that no data corruption occurs due to shared data.

FIGURE 7.1:

The Worker Thread Demo enables you to test both success and error conditions.

One other test you'll want to try is viewing the application using the Spy++ utility found in the \Program Files\Microsoft Visual Studio .NET\Common7\Tools folder. You must set the Wait Time field to a high value to make this part of the test process work. I found that 12 seconds (12,000 milliseconds) works best, but your results will vary.

Start Spy++ and look for the WORKERTHREAD entry shown in Figure 7.2. The example begins by creating three threads. The first thread is the main window and it has all of the controls within it. The second and third threads are application-specific and you don't need to worry about them at this point.

FIGURE 7.2:

Use Spy++ to see the threads in your application.

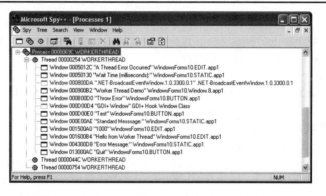

Click the Test button on the application, then quickly press F5 in Spy++ to refresh the window. You'll see another thread added to the list. This thread won't have any display elements because it's the worker thread. In fact, you'll see one new thread generated each time you click Test or Throw Error. If you create multiple threads, you'll see multiple entries added to Spy++. After the time elapses and the event message dialog box appears, press F5 in Spy++ again. This time you'll see a new thread that does include display elements—the thread for our worker thread will be gone. Close the Success or Error Message dialog boxes and the number of threads will return to the same number you started with in Figure 7.2.

Local DLL Example

This example shows how to place the threading logic for your application in a separate file—a DLL. The reason you want to know how to use this technique is that placing the thread in a DLL enables you to use it with more than one application. This principle is at the center of the common dialogs that most developers use to create applications. A single DLL can serve many generic needs, so long as you include enough configuration features to ensure complete customization, if desired.

The example in this section contains two user interface elements. The first is the main thread—a dialog-based test application. The second is the UI thread contained within a DLL. The test application will enable you to create multiple copies of the UI thread, with each UI thread providing independent operation for the user. You'll find the source code for this example in the \Chapter 07\DLLThread folder of the CD.

Configuring the Project

This example requires a little special configuration, due to the use of multiple UI elements. You'll begin creating the DLL portion of this example using the Class Library project. The example uses a project name of DLLThread. Add to this project a Windows Application with a name of DLLThreadTest.

NOTE   Make sure you set DLLThreadTest as your startup project to ensure that the example runs in debug mode. The Visual Studio .NET IDE will assume you want to use DLLThread as the startup project because it's the first project created. To set DLLThreadTest as the startup project, right-click DLLThreadTest in Solution Explorer and select Set as Startup Project from the context menu.

The Class Library project provides you with an empty shell. It doesn't even include a dialog box as part of the project. You'll need to add a dialog box by right-clicking DLLThread in Solution Explorer and choosing Add ➣ Add New Item from the context menu. Select Local Project Items\UI and you'll see a list of items similar to the one shown in Figure 7.3. You'll need to add the Windows Form option to the project. The example uses a name of Thread-Form.CS for the resulting file.

As part of the configuration process, you need to create a connection between the DLL and the test application. Right-click DLLThreadTest\References in Solution Explorer and choose Add Reference from the context menu. Select the Projects tab in the Add Reference dialog. Highlight the DLLThread project and click Select. Click OK to add the reference to the DLLThreadTest project.

FIGURE 7.3:
Visual Studio .NET
allows you to add UI
items to DLLs using
this dialog box.

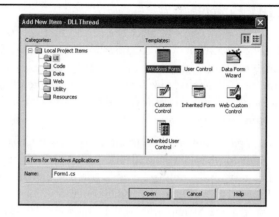

Creating the DLL

The DLL code falls into two parts. First, you need to design a dialog box. The example uses a simple dialog box with a Quit button. The Quit button closes the form when you're done viewing it. You can find the code for the form in the ThreadForm.CS file. Second, you need to create code within the DLL to manage the form. The DLLThread class code appears in Listing 7.4.

Listing 7.4   The DLLThread Class Manages Access to the ThreadForm

```
public class DLLThread
{
   // Create a dialog name variable.
   private string _ThreadDlgName;

   public DLLThread(string ThreadDlgName)
   {
      // Store a dialog name value.
      if (ThreadDlgName != null)
         _ThreadDlgName = ThreadDlgName;
      else
         _ThreadDlgName = "Sample Dialog";
   }

   public void CreateUIThread()
   {
      // Create a new form.
      ThreadForm  Dlg = new ThreadForm();

      // Name the dialog.
      Dlg.Text = _ThreadDlgName;
```

```
        // Display the form.
        Dlg.ShowDialog();
    }
}
```

As you can see, the code for the DLL is relatively simple. Notice the private variable _ThreadDlgName. In an updated version of this program in the "Understanding Critical Sections" section of this chapter, you'll see that this variable isn't thread safe. We need a critical section in order to keep this variable safe. For now, with the current program construction, this variable will work as anticipated. However, it's important to think about potential problems in your application variables before you use the code in a multithreaded scenario.

The DLL constructor assigns a value to _ThreadDlgName. The check for a null value is important because you want to be sure the dialog has a name later. Note that you'd probably initialize other dialog construction variables as part of the constructor or use properties as we did in the worker thread example.

The CreateUIThread() method creates a new instance of the ThreadForm class, which contains the Thread dialog box. Notice that this method also assigns the name of the dialog box using the _ThreadDlgName variable. It's the time delay between the constructor and this assignment that causes problems in a multithreaded scenario. CreateUIThread() finishes by calling the ShowDialog() method of the ThreadForm class. It's important to use ShowDialog() rather than Show(), so you can obtain the modal result of the dialog box if necessary.

Creating the Test Program

The test program form consists of three pushbuttons and a textbox. The Quit button allows the user to exit the application. The New Dialog button will demonstrate the DLLThread class as a single-threaded application. The New Thread button will demonstrate the DLLThread class as a multithreaded application. It's important to the understanding of threads to realize that any DLL you create for multithreaded use can also be used in a single-threaded scenario. Listing 7.5 shows the test application code.

Listing 7.5   **The Test Application Works in Both Single-threaded and Multithreaded Modes**

```
private void btnNewDialog_Click(object sender, System.EventArgs e)
{
    // Create a new thread object.
    DLLThread.DLLThread   MyThread =
        new DLLThread.DLLThread(txtDlgName.Text);

    // Display the dialog.
    MyThread.CreateUIThread();
}

private void btnNewThread_Click(object sender, System.EventArgs e)
```

```
{
    // Create a new thread object.
    DLLThread.DLLThread   MyThread =
        new DLLThread.DLLThread(txtDlgName.Text);

    // Create and start the new thread.
    Thread    DoThread =
        new Thread(new ThreadStart(MyThread.CreateUIThread));
    DoThread.Start();

    // Get rid of the variables.
    DoThread = null;
    MyThread = null;
}
```

The `btnNewDialog_Click()` method begins by creating an instance of the `DLLThread` class. Notice the inclusion of the text from the application textbox as part of the call to the constructor. The method calls `CreateUIThread()` to create a standard single-threaded application call to the DLL.

The `btnNewThread_Click()` method begins essentially the same way as `btnNewDialog_Click()`. However, in this case, the method creates a separate thread for the dialog box. Notice that there's no difference between this call and the one we used for the worker thread example earlier in the chapter. The only difference is in the implementation of the thread within the thread class.

When you run this application you'll notice that both buttons will produce a copy of the thread form when clicked the first time. However, if you try to click New Dialog a second time while the thread form is still present, the application will beep. That's because the application is waiting for the modal result from the thread form. However, you can create multiple copies of the thread form by clicking the New Thread button because each dialog resides in a separate thread. Of course, you can only continue clicking New Thread so long as you don't click New Dialog. The moment you click New Dialog, the main application thread stops and waits for the thread form to complete.

Server-Based DLL Example

Threading is used for more than a few server needs. For example, when a user accesses a website and requests service from an ISAPI Extension, the DLL must track the user identification as well as operate in a thread-safe manner. The same can be said for many server services. One or more users can send information to the service, either directly or as part of another request.

The following sections show how to create a Windows service. In this case, the service monitors user access, updates an internal variable showing the last service, and provides a command for writing the number of accesses to an event log entry. The client application generates stop, start, access, and access log requests.

Creating the Windows Service

The initial part of creating a Windows service is configuration of the Windows Service project. In fact, the wizard performs a large part of the setup for you. All you really need to worry about is the service functionality—at least if you're creating a basic service that doesn't require low-level system access such as device driver interfaces. The following steps show how to create the service. (You'll find the complete source code for this example in the \Chapter 07\ServerThread folder on the CD.)

1. Create a new Windows Service project. The example uses a name of Server Thread. You'll see an initial Designer where you can place controls for the service to use. This example won't use any special controls.

2. Select the Designer window. Note that the entries in the Properties window (shown in Figure 7.4) help you configure your service. The figure shows the settings for the example service. The main property you need to set is *ServiceName*. Notice the Add Installer link at the bottom of the Properties window—you must add an installer after completing the service configuration.

FIGURE 7.4:

The Service properties enable you to config-ure general service features.

3. Perform any required configuration of class, file, and service names. It's better to finish the service configuration before you add an installer. Otherwise, you'll need to configure both the service and the installer manually.

4. Create an installer by clicking the Add Installer link at the bottom of the Properties window shown in Figure 7.4. Notice that the wizard creates another Designer window for you. However, in this case, the Designer window contains two controls used to manage the service installation.

5. Select the serviceProcessInstaller1 control. Modify the *Password*, *Username*, and *Account* properties as needed for your service. In most cases, you'll want to leave the *Password* and *Username* properties blank, and set the *Account* property to **LocalSystem**.

6. Select the serviceInstaller1 control. Modify the *DisplayName* and *StartType* properties as needed for your service. The example uses a value of **Track Number of User Accesses** for the *DisplayName* property. Generally, you'll want to set the *StartType* to Automatic for services that will run all of the time.

At this point, you should have a generic Windows service project. If you compiled and installed the service, at this point, you could start, stop, and pause it. However, the service wouldn't do much more than waste CPU cycles, because you haven't added any commands to it. Listing 7.6 shows one of several techniques you can use to support commands in a Windows service.

Listing 7.6   **The Windows Service Performs Much of the Work**

```
protected override void OnStart(string[] args)
{
    // Set the number of accesses to 0.
    _NumberOfAccesses = 0;
}

public void DoAccess()
{
    // Increment the number of accesses.
    _NumberOfAccesses++;
}

public void GetAccess()
{
    // Write an event log entry that shows how many accesses occurred.
    this.EventLog.WriteEntry("The number of user accesses is: "
                            + _NumberOfAccesses.ToString(),
                            EventLogEntryType.Information,
                            1200,
                            99);
}

protected override void OnCustomCommand(int Command)
{
    // Execute the default command.
    if (Command < 128)
        base.OnCustomCommand(Command);

    // Increment the number of accesses.
    if (Command == 128)
        DoAccess();
```

```
    // Write an event long entry.
    if (Command == 129)
        GetAccess();
}
```

The two commands, DoAccess() and GetAccess() work with a private variable named _NumberOfAccesses. The only purpose for this variable is to record the number of times someone accesses the service since it was last started. To ensure that the variable always starts at a known value, the OnStart() method sets it to 0. The OnStart() method is one of several methods the wizard assumes you'll need to override, so it provides this method by default.

The user still can't access your service. We'll see later that accessing a service is a bit cryptic in C#, most likely because of the way Windows services work in general. You must override the OnCustomCommand() method if you expect the user to interact with the service directly. Notice that this method transfers any commands below 127 to the base class. It also supports two other commands, 128 and 129, which call the appropriate command. The service ignores any other command input number.

Compile the example and you'll end up with an EXE file. The EXE file won't run from the command prompt and you can't install it in a project. You must install the service using the InstallUtil ServerThread.EXE command. If you want to uninstall the service, simply add the -u switch to the command line. After you install the service, open the Services console found in the Administrative Tools folder of the Control Panel. Figure 7.5 shows the service installed.

FIGURE 7.5:

The InstallUtil utility will install the Windows service on any machine that will support it.

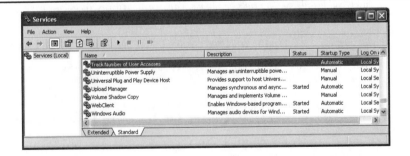

Creating the Test Application

The client application uses a standard dialog form containing buttons to exit the application, start the service, stop the service, register a service access, and display the number of service accesses since the last service start. To access the service, locate it in the Server Explorer dialog shown in Figure 7.6. Drag the service to the form in the Designer. This action will create a new *ServiceController* entry in the Designer that you can use to access the service.

FIGURE 7.6:

User the Server
Explorer to locate ser-
vices on the local or
any remote machine.

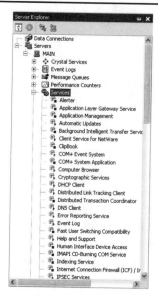

Now that you have access to the service, let's look at some code to interact with it.
Listing 7.7 shows the code you'll use to work with a *ServiceController* named *TrackAccess*.
Notice that some of the code enables and disables buttons as needed to ensure that they're
accessible only when valid. This is a big concern for the developer because attempting to
perform some actions with the service in an unknown state can have unfortunate side effects,
such as data loss. At the very least, the application will generate an exception.

Listing 7.7   The Windows Service Client Can Stop, Start, and Access Service Commands

```csharp
private void MainForm_Activated(object sender, System.EventArgs e)
{

    // Validate current service status.
    if (TrackAccess.Status == ServiceControllerStatus.Running)
    {
        btnStart.Enabled = false;
    }
    else
    {
        btnStop.Enabled = false;
        btnAccess.Enabled = false;
        btnGetAccess.Enabled = false;
    }
}

private void bntStart_Click(object sender, System.EventArgs e)
```

```
{
   // Start the service.
   TrackAccess.Start();

   // Wait for the start to complete.
   TrackAccess.WaitForStatus(ServiceControllerStatus.Running,
                             System.TimeSpan.FromMilliseconds(2000));

   // Change the button configuration to match service status.
   btnStart.Enabled = false;
   btnStop.Enabled = true;
   btnAccess.Enabled = true;
   btnGetAccess.Enabled = true;
}

private void btnStop_Click(object sender, System.EventArgs e)
{
   // Stop the service.
   if (TrackAccess.CanStop)
      TrackAccess.Stop();
   else
   {
      // We can't stop the service, so exit.
      MessageBox.Show("Service doesn't support stopping.",
                      "Service Stop Error",
                      MessageBoxButtons.OK,
                      MessageBoxIcon.Error);
      return;
   }

   // Wait for the start to complete.
   TrackAccess.WaitForStatus(ServiceControllerStatus.Stopped,
                             System.TimeSpan.FromMilliseconds(2000));

   // Change the button configuration to match service status.
   btnStart.Enabled = true;
   btnStop.Enabled = false;
   btnAccess.Enabled = false;
   btnGetAccess.Enabled = false;
}

private void btnAccess_Click(object sender, System.EventArgs e)
{
   // Access the service to increment the counter.
   TrackAccess.ExecuteCommand(128);
}

private void btnGetAccess_Click(object sender, System.EventArgs e)
{
   EventLog MyEvents;    // Event log containing service entries.
```

```
//Accesss the service to report the number of accesses.
TrackAccess.ExecuteCommand(129);

// Open the event log.
MyEvents = new EventLog("Application");

// Look at each event log entry for the correct message.
foreach (EventLogEntry ThisEvent in MyEvents.Entries)
{
    // The message will contain a category number of 99
    // and an event ID of 1200.
    if (ThisEvent.CategoryNumber == 99 &&
        ThisEvent.EventID == 1200)

        // Display the message.
        MessageBox.Show(ThisEvent.Message);
}
}
```

The application starts by validating the current service status in the MainForm_Activated() method. Any application that provides access to a service needs to make this check. Otherwise, you have no idea of what state the service is in and whether it's safe to work with it. Multiple users could attempt to access the service at the same time. If User A stops the service at the same time User B wants to access it, one or both calls could fail.

The bntStart_Click() and btnStop_Click() methods control the service status. You can always attempt to start a service, but some services won't allow you to stop them. The btnStop_Click() contains additional code that verifies that the service can stop before it attempts to stop the service. Notice that both methods contain a call to WaitForStatus(). This call ensures that the user is unable to do anything more with the application until the service reaches a stable state. The ServiceControllerStatus enumeration contains a number of standard service states. You must also use one of the members from the TimeSpan class to specify how long to wait for the service to change states. The example uses the From-Milliseconds() method, but any of the methods will work. Never use the infinite wait version of WaitForStatus() because the application could freeze. If the service hasn't changed states in the time provided, your application should display an error message and offer the user some options to overcome the problem.

The btnAccess_Click() method is the first to use the arcane command system used by Windows services. Notice that there's nothing to indicate the purpose of the command. You must simply know that executing command number 128 will update the number of accesses count in the service.

The ExecuteCommand() returns type *void*. You have no idea if the service executed the command successfully unless you look in the event log to see if there's an entry in either the

System or Application logs. The ExecuteCommand() method also provides no means for returning data from the service, so you need to provide your own method.

The btnGetAccess_Click() enables the user to learn how many times the service has been accessed since it started. As you can see from Listing 7.7, the application must go to some trouble to gain access to the required information. In this case, it uses the event log as a medium for exchange. The CategoryNumber and EventID property combination is unique and unlikely to cause problems with any other entry in the event log. (Even so, you could perform additional checks on the event entry before you process it.) Figure 7.7 shows typical event log entries from the service when accessed by the client.

FIGURE 7.7:

The client and service rely on the event log for communication.

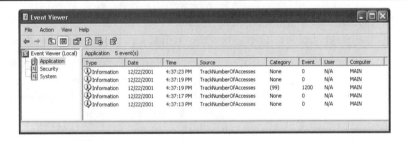

Spending time looking through the series of event log entries in both the System and Application logs will help you better understand the way services function. Notice the special event with the *Category* value of (99). Figure 7.8 shows the message associated with this entry. Notice that the service provided the number of accesses in an easy to read form.

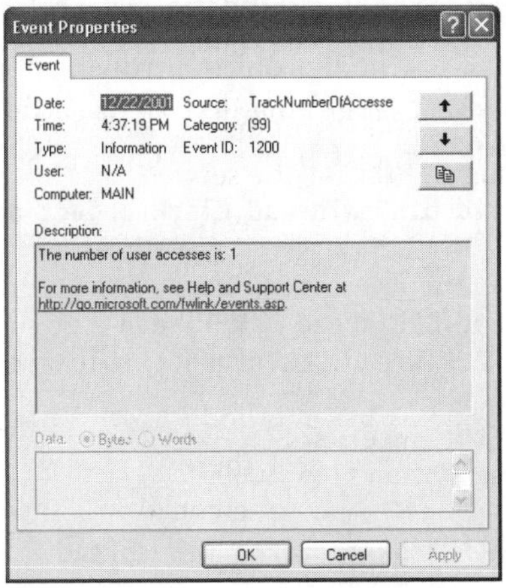

FIGURE 7.8:

Event log messages must be easy to understand because they're the sole source of service communication.

Understanding Critical Sections

A *critical section* is a piece of code or a variable that application threads can only access one thread at one time. If two applications require access to the same critical section, the first to make the request will obtain access. The second application will wait until the first application completes its task. In short, critical sections create bottlenecks in your code and can affect performance if you're not careful.

Some forms of critical section ensure that the thread completes code sequence without interruption. For example, you wouldn't want to begin a save to a database and have another thread of execution interrupt that save. The first application must complete the save before a second thread starts in order to ensure data integrity. The .NET Framework doesn't provide special calls to perform magic in this case; you must develop the thread in such a way that it saves the data safely. In short, the critical section helps ensure database integrity.

You may want to create a critical section for many different reasons; the most important of which is application data integrity. An application changes the contents of variables and the status of objects to meet the needs of a particular user. If another user suddenly decides to execute the same code, the lack of a critical section to protect the variable and object content would ruin the application for both parties.

A critical section must protect both data and code. The variables used in the thread are of equal importance to executing the code in the desired sequence. There are two methods used to create a critical section for use with threads. The first is to use the C# `lock` keyword to create a critical block. The second method is to use the `Enter()` and `Exit()` methods of the `Monitor` class. The second method is actually preferred because it provides you with greater flexibility and it isn't C#-specific because it relies on a .NET Framework class.

Let's look at a potential problem involving critical sections. Here's a modified version of the `btnNewThread_Click()` method we discussed in Listing 7.5. (You can find the source code for this example in the \Chapter 07\Critical Section folder of the CD.)

```
private void btnNewThread_Click(object sender, System.EventArgs e)
{
    // Create a new thread object.
    DLLThread.DLLThread   MyThread =
        new DLLThread.DLLThread(txtDlgName.Text);

    // Set the interval.
    MyThread.Interval = 5000;

    // Create and start the new thread.
    Thread   DoThread =
        new Thread(new ThreadStart(MyThread.CreateUIThread));
    DoThread.Start();
```

```
// Change the interval.
MyThread.Interval = 1000;

// Create and start a new thread.
Thread   DoThread2 =
    new Thread(new ThreadStart(MyThread.CreateUIThread));
DoThread2.Start();

// Get rid of the variables.
DoThread2 = null;
DoThread = null;
MyThread = null;
}
```

When you run this code, you're using the same object for two threads. There's a possibility of the two threads creating a collision if they access the same variable at the same time. Here's a slightly modified version of the CreateUIThread() from Listing 7.4. Notice that it adds a *Counter* variable that makes collisions apparent.

```
public void CreateUIThread()
{
    // Create a new form.
    ThreadForm  Dlg = new ThreadForm();

    // Wait before assigning the dialog name.
    Thread.Sleep(_Interval);

    // Name the dialog.
    Dlg.Text = _ThreadDlgName + " " + Counter.ToString();

    // Increment the counter.
    Counter++;

    // Display the form.
    Dlg.ShowDialog();
}
```

Run this application without adding a critical section and you're likely to see the results of a collision. The two Thread Form dialog boxes will have the same number appended to the dialog box names. In some cases, you'll see the anticipated result; in others, you'll see that the second thread actually has a 1 attached to its name and the first thread has a value of 2. That's because both threads access the CreateUIThread() in a haphazard manner. The fix for this problem is as follows:

```
public void CreateUIThread()
{
    // Begin the critical section.
    Monitor.Enter(this);
```

```
// Create a new form.
ThreadForm  Dlg = new ThreadForm();

// Wait before assigning the dialog name.
Thread.Sleep(_Interval);

// Name the dialog.
Dlg.Text = _ThreadDlgName + " " + Counter.ToString();

// Increment the counter.
Counter++;

// Exit the critical section.
Monitor.Exit(this);

// Display the form.
Dlg.ShowDialog();
}
```

Notice the addition of the `Monitor.Enter(this)` and `Monitor.Exit(this)` calls. These calls ensure that the first thread always finishes before the second thread gains access to the method. As a result, the first dialog always contains a 1 and the second dialog always contains a 2.

You should also note the placement of the critical section. If you place the `Monitor.Exit(this)` call after `Dlg.ShowDialog()`, the application will stop after the first dialog appears. It will wait for you to close the first dialog before it displays the second dialog. The point is that you need to place critical sections carefully or the performance hit on your system could be substantial.

Understanding Thread Safety

One of the benefits of using libraries is code reuse. Once a developer writes and tests the code, they can place it in a library and forget about it. The functionality you'll need will be available without a lot of additional work. All you need to do is access the DLL. Windows uses this technique for all of the APIs that it supports.

Unfortunately, the black box functionality of libraries can be a double-edged sword. One of the biggest problems when using libraries with threads is that the library isn't thread safe. In other words, if two threads attempt to access the same object or function at the same time, there could be a collision, resulting in a frozen application, lost data, or other unanticipated results.

Fortunately, you can protect your libraries in a number of ways. One way is to use critical sections as needed to ensure that a sequence of events takes place without interruption. A second way is to allocate variables and objects on the stack. Finally, it's extremely important to reduce the risk of collisions by not allowing more than one thread to access the same variable—use techniques that ensure that each thread will have its own set of variables to use.

Even Microsoft's libraries aren't totally thread safe. For the most part, any object provided by the .NET Framework is thread safe at the class level but not at the object level. In other words, two threads could access different objects derived from the same class but not the same object. Fortunately, Microsoft has made thread safety a major issue in the help files that accompany Visual Studio .NET. Most of the help topics will tell you if the .NET Framework object you want to use is thread safe, so you'll want to verify thread safety each time you work with a new .NET Framework namespace or class.

However, this still doesn't guarantee thread safety for your code. You need to make your code thread safe as well. We discussed some of the techniques you can use to perform this task in the "Understanding Critical Sections" section of the chapter. Even if you don't plan to use a DLL you create today in a distributed application tomorrow, adding thread safety is insurance that the application you create tomorrow will work as anticipated.

Where Do You Go From Here?

Working with multiple threads can make your workstation more efficient and your server more available. However, misuse of threading techniques can easily run counter to these goals. You need to know when threads will do the job for you and when it's better to use a single-threaded approach. This chapter has provided a good understanding of how threads work and provided a good overview of when it's best to use them. You've also seen several threading examples.

Now it's time to work with threading examples of your own design. Look for places that might cause conflicts and add a critical section to them. Try various access scenarios to ensure that your applications, components, and services are thread safe.

Chapter 8 addresses Active Directory. You'll learn how to access this vast database of user, network, and machine information. We'll also look at some techniques for expanding the Active Directory schema as needed to meet customized needs.

CHAPTER 8

Working with Active Directory

- What Is Active Directory?

- Understanding the Active Directory Service Interface (ADSI)

- Working with the ADSI API

- Working with the *System.DirectoryServices* Namespace

- Working with the Active Directory

Windows 2000 introduced a new centralized database of information called Active Directory. Essentially, Active Directory is a database manager that tracks the equipment and users on a network along with associated information such as security and policy settings. You can also expand the schema of the database to include custom information about your company and the applications that it owns. The changes made to the database on one server automatically appear on every other server on the system, making Active Directory a central storage location for all network information.

This chapter helps you understand Active Directory. We'll discuss the central database and the tools used to view and manipulate it. You'll also learn how to work with the existing database schema, as well as extend the schema for your needs. Finally, we'll discuss the features that Windows and the .NET Framework make available for working with Active Directory. The interface you use determines the level of functionality that Active Directory provides.

What Is Active Directory?

Active Directory evokes a number of impressions by developers. Some developers see Active Directory as a super-sized Registry—an accurate but limited viewpoint. Each machine still has a Registry because Active Directory is global in nature, while the Registry handles local needs. A few developers even look at Active Directory as a direct competitor to other directory services. From a management perspective, Active Directory does serve this function, but from a developer perspective, the view is different. Many developers see Active Directory as something they'd rather not use because they perceive it as overly complex. Actually, Active Directory *is* robust and large, but it's based on a relatively simple idea.

The simple way to look at Active Directory is as a massive database designed to make network management easier for everyone. However, you may not realize just how massive this database is. As you'd expect, Active Directory holds the usual network information, such as user and group security setups. In addition, Active Directory helps you manage network resources like disk drives and printers. Finally, Active Directory contains a multitude of application settings—not local applications, but those that operate at an enterprise level.

In this section of the chapter, we'll look at a few of the things that you might not expect Active Directory to do. We'll also look at a few potential pitfalls you should consider when working with any network management system like Active Directory.

NOTE   Active Directory requires a server. Windows XP isn't a server platform, it's used for the desktop alone and therefore doesn't provide Active Directory support. Because the name for Microsoft's new server product changes daily, I'll use the term Windows Server throughout the chapter to reference any Windows 2000 or newer server product.

An Overview of the Interface

Like any database application, Active Directory consists of three components: database engine, data storage, and user interface. In this section, we view the standard user interface for Active Directory; the *Microsoft Management Console (MMC)* and associated snap-ins. Microsoft put a lot of effort into creating a new management tool for Windows 2000 in the form of the MMC. Windows XP follows in this tradition, and there's no reason to expect Microsoft's latest server product to do otherwise. Consequently, any initial work with Active Directory will revolve around an MMC Console (the MMC application and one or more snap-ins). You need to use a few of the Active Directory–related consoles to work with the example in this chapter, so it's a good idea to review them now.

NOTE   MMC is a container application for specialized components. If you get the idea that MMC is some form of COM technology, you'd be right. A snap-in is really nothing more than a component that uses MMC as a container.

Figure 8.1 shows a typical Active Directory Users and Computers console. Any predefined selection of MMC snap-ins is a console. You can also create custom snap-ins (the component) and consoles for your own use—something we'll discuss in Chapter 16. As you can see from the figure, the Active Directory Users and Computers console provides access to computer and use resource information on your network. All of this information appears within Active Directory database entries on the server.

FIGURE 8.1:

Microsoft provides Active Directory–related consoles that help you modify the Active Directory database.

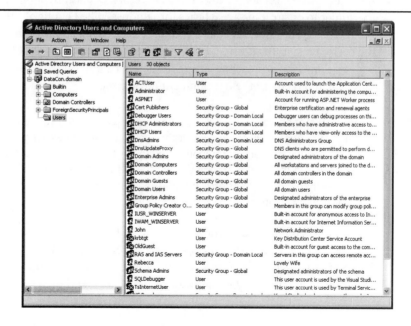

Let's spend a few minutes talking about the various components of the display shown in Figure 8.1. At the top of the tree is the Active Directory root. Below this is the single domain in this tree, DataCon.domain. If there were multiple domains, then there would be multiple entries at this level of the tree. Don't confuse the domain controller with the domain as a whole. A domain can have more than one domain controller, and these controllers would appear in the Domain Controllers folder. The Builtin folder contains all of the built-in groups for the domain. The Computers folder holds a list of all the computers that have logged into the domain. Active Directory manages these first three folders, Builtin, Computers, and Domain Controllers automatically. Normally, you won't need to add new entries, but you'll have to configure the ones that Active Directory adds for you.

The last folder, Users, is misleading because it can contain a lot more than just users. At minimum, this folder can actually contain computers, contacts, groups, printers, users, and shared folders. An administrator can create other classes of objects to add into this folder, and you can design components to work with these classes. For the most part, you'll spend the greatest amount of time in this folder, unless you create additional folders of your own. Active Directory enables you to add new entries at every level of the database including the domain level. At the domain level, you can add computers, contacts, groups, organizational units, printers, users, and shared folders. However, unless you want a messy, hard-to-follow directory, you'll usually limit the entries at the domain level to organizational units.

You may have also noticed the Saved Queries folder in Figure 8.1. This is a new feature for the .NET Server version of the Active Directory Users and Computers snap-in. You can use this folder to create and save queries for later use. The benefit of this folder to the developer is that you can test queries before you place them in an application to ensure that they return the desired result. In addition, the Query String field of the Edit Query and Add Query dialog box shows the proper formatting of the query. You can copy the contents of this field and move them directly to the development environment.

TIP   The workstation you use must have a domain connection to work with Active Directory. One of the best ways to check whether your computer has logged into the domain and exchanged the proper information is to look in the Computers folder. The client machine will appear in this folder automatically after a successful logon and the client and server have exchanged information. This information exchange is essential for many kinds of COM-related activities.

Developers often need to check the status of their development machines. For example, you may want to ensure that the operating system is up to date. A developer can use Active Directory to check on the status of any accessible machine from a remote location. Open either the Computers or Domain Controllers folder, and then double-click on a computer icon. You'll see a Properties dialog that enables you to check machine statistics, such as the fully qualified domain name of the computer and the version of the operating system installed.

There are times when you need better access to the machine than the computer Properties dialog will provide. For example, you may need to know the hardware configuration of the machine or the status of the drivers. This information is also available from Active Directory. All you need to do is right-click the computer of interest and choose Manage from the context menu; you'll see the Computer Management console for that machine. The console groups them by System Tools (hardware), Storage (the content and organization of the hard drives), and Server Applications and Services (a list of services including COM+ and MSMQ).

By this time, you should have a better idea of why Active Directory, even the interface portion, is important for you as a programmer. Given the right tools, you can manage most testing scenarios and troubleshoot most application failures without even leaving your desk. In addition, Active Directory gives you access to real-world data, something that was difficult to collect in the past. Users tend to behave differently when you watch them directly. This difference in behavior affects the results you get when running tests and ultimately results in applications with less than perfect performance characteristics. While I'm not advocating a "big brother" approach to application testing, getting real-world data is an important part of working with today's complex application programming environment.

Why Use Active Directory?

Active Directory has a lot to offer the network administrator and developer alike. One of the most important considerations is that it provides complete information security. Not only will Active Directory allow you to set the security for individual objects, but you can set security on object properties as well. This level of functionality means that you can create an extremely detailed security policy that gives users access to what they need. In addition, you can block rights at the object or the property level, which means that giving someone access to an object no longer means that they necessarily get full access. Finally, you can delegate the authority to manage security on an object or even a property level.

Policy-based administration is another feature that Active Directory provides. Policies are an implementation of role-based security. Active Directory objects always have a context that defines how a particular user is using the object and expresses the user's rights to the object. All of this information is stored in the Active Directory database, making it easy for an Administrator to create policies that dictate the rights for entire groups of users. The combination of context, role-based security, and groups means that an administrator can manage security using a few groups of users, rather than mange individual users, and still be sure that individual users are getting the access they require.

As a developer, you're already well aware of the extensibility that Active Directory provides. However, you may not know that the administrator can extend Active Directory by adding new object classes or new attributes to existing classes. For example, you may want to add the number of sick leave and vacation days an employee has to their entry in Active Directory. A component that you build could keep this value updated so that the employee and manager could track this information without relying on another resource. Instead of a simple contact list, you might create special kinds of contacts; for instance, you could keep outside consultants who are paid by the company separate from large customers that the company relies on for income.

Scalability is another feature that makes Active Directory a good choice. Active Directory enables you to include multiple domains in a single database. Each domain could contain more than one domain controller. You can organize the entire setup into a contiguous namespace that Microsoft calls a *directory tree*. If your organization is so large that a single tree would be impossible to manage, you can combine directory trees into a non-contiguous namespace called a *forest*. The ability to scale a single Active Directory database over the largest organization means that when you search for a specific domain within your application, you'll find it —as long as you have a connection and the server is online.

As previously stated, DNS and Active Directory are coupled. What this means to you as a programmer is that the domain controller and other servers could use the same name no matter how they're accessed. A user who normally accesses a server from their desktop computer within the company wouldn't need to make any adjustment when accessing that same server using an Internet connection (assuming that you've properly registered your domain name). In addition, the components you create can access the server in the same way using any connection type.

Active Directory can use two standard directory access protocols for access purposes. The most common method is the *Lightweight Directory Access Protocol (LDAP)*. You can find out more about this access method at http://www.faqs.org/rfcs/rfc2251.html. A secondary access method is *Name Service Provider Interface (NSPI)*. This is a Microsoft standard used with Microsoft Exchange version 4.0 and above. Many third-party products work with Microsoft Exchange, so from a Microsoft-specific programming perspective this second access method is just as important as LDAP. However, you'll probably use LDAP when working with multiple directory types.

The last benefit of using Active Directory is the ability to query the database using any of a number of methods. From a user perspective, you can find any object on the network using Search, My Network Places, or Active Directory Users and Computers. We'll see in the next chapter that querying the database within your application is just as easy and flexible. Finding what you need isn't a problem with Active Directory.

Active Directory Programming Pitfalls

It would be frivolous to say that Active Directory will take care of every need you've ever had or ever will have. That just isn't realistic, despite what Microsoft's marketing arm would have you believe. A network management system like Active Directory can be a hindrance in more than a few ways. The following list provides you with a few ideas.

Domain versus Workgroup   Active Directory assumes that the domain is everything and that workgroups, as such, really don't exist. Obviously, any company with more than a few employees will have workgroups, because in many situations this is the easiest way to work. Logging into the workgroup rather than the domain, though, can have unexpected results. For example, you can't set up services like MSMQ without a domain connection—at least not as an independent client.

Server Loading   Moving from Windows NT to newer Windows Server versions can create performance problems. Unfortunately, many administrators will blame the new suite of components you've developed to take advantage of Windows Server features, despite the fact that the more likely culprit is the polling and data processing that Active Directory requires. All of that information takes processing cycles and system resources to collect.

Interface Complexity   Microsoft's new MMC snap-ins may be one of the better ways to manage Active Directory, but the learning curve for this utility is astronomical and the complexity of Active Directory doesn't help. It seems as if there's a specialized snap-in for every situation. For the most part, you'll find that writing applications that take advantage of everything Active Directory has to offer greatly increases the administrative learning curve, unless you can work within the confines of the current interface.

Storage   Active Directory stores everything you can imagine and probably a few things that you don't even know exist. As a result, disk storage needs for Windows Server have greatly increased over the same setup you had for Windows NT. This means you'll have to exercise care when expanding the database schema or face the consequences of large disk usage increases.

Programmer Learning Curve   Active Directory relies on COM/COM+ components. Many developers are just learning COM and a few may be working with their first applications. The problem is that Active Directory uses some of Microsoft's most advanced technologies, making the learning curve for developers steep.

As you can see, there are many limitations when using Active Directory that you can categorize in one of two ways. Most of the limitations are due to either new resource requirements or the complexity of the Active Directory interface. It's important to keep these limitations in mind as you design projects that require Active Directory. The most important limitation now is the newness of the technology compared to other directory services on the market. For instance, Novell required several years after their initial release of NDS to make their product completely functional and make it at least moderately reliable.

Getting Support from Microsoft Newsgroups

Microsoft provides places where you can get help from peers and Microsoft support personnel. This help is free, unlike the help that you have to pay a support person to obtain, and is usually high in quality. If your ISP doesn't provide access to these newsgroups, you can access them using the news.microsoft.com news server. The Active Directory–related Microsoft newsgroups include:

- microsoft.public.active.directory.interfaces

- microsoft.public.exchange2000.active.directory.integration

- microsoft.public.platformsdk.active.directory

- microsoft.public.win2000.active_directory

Understanding the Active Directory Service Interface (ADSI)

Active Directory provides many features that make it easier to manage large networks and safeguard the information they contain. While the MMC snap-ins that Microsoft provides as part of Windows 2000 perform adequately for standard classes that come with Active Directory, customized classes may require more in the way of management capability. Consequently, it's important that Active Directory also comes with a set of services that you can access through an application program. ADSI helps you to interact with Active Directory using a single set of well-defined interfaces.

Microsoft designed ADSI to be easy and flexible to use. ADSI provides few interfaces and they're all relatively easy to understand, which means your learning curve won't be as steep as for other products currently on the market. Two completely different groups use ADSI as a means for automating directory services tasks. Network administrators fall into the first group. Because ADSI relies on COM, a network administrator could access the features that it provides with relative ease from a scripting language. Obviously, developers fall into the other group. Microsoft is hoping that developers will create Active Directory–enabled applications using the lower-level ADSI features.

Active Directory has garnered a lot of interest from non-Microsoft sources that can help you decipher what Active Directory can mean for your organization. One of the better places to look for information about the Active Directory Server Interface (ADSI) is the 15 Seconds website at: http://www.15seconds.com/focus/ADSI.htm. This site contains articles, links to other sites, a few examples, and a list of Microsoft Knowledge Base articles for ADSI-specific topics. If you want to learn about Microsoft's view of ADSI, then check out the Active Directory Services Interfaces Overview site at http://www.microsoft.com/windows2000/techinfo/howitworks/activedirectory/adsilinks.asp.

Now that I've introduced you to ADSI, let's take a more detailed look. The following sections will help you understand what ADSI can provide in the way of programming support. We'll look at the actual mechanics of using ADSI later in the chapter.

Working with a Common API

ADSI has some advantages besides working with Active Directory, if you take the Microsoft approach to performing tasks. Most organizations have more than one directory service structure in place. The three most common directory services are those used by the network, the e-mail program, and groupware. If all of the directory service products in your organization conform to either the LDAP or NSPI standards, then you can use ADSI to manage them all. Of course, ADSI won't work in some situations, because the product vendor didn't know about ADSI during development and didn't provide the required interface elements.

NOTE ADSI actually contains two levels of API support. The first level provides support for Active Directory structures that can support automation. The COM components that provide access to these structures are accessible from just about any language, as long as the language supports automation. This includes support for Java, Visual Basic, VBScript, JavaScript, and ASP. Administrators also obtain this level of support through a standard MMC snap-in. The second level of support is for structures that can't support automation. To gain access to this second level of support, you must use a programming language like Visual C++.

So, how does Microsoft hope to get these third-party directory services to work with ADSI? Most of the core logic depends on LDAP or NSPI, which are common standards for directory access. All a third-party vendor really needs to do is write an ADSI provider that allows directory services access through the components that Microsoft provides. That's why access to any directory service is theoretical at this point—Microsoft has to convince third parties to supply the required provider so you can gain access to these other directory services using one interface.

If Microsoft does successfully write ADSI providers themselves, or convince third-party vendors to perform the task, then you'll gain an important benefit. Any application designed to work with ADSI will also work with any directory service. In short, you could write a single application that would allow you to manage groupware, e-mail, and the network. What this means for developers is that you'll no longer waste time writing the same application multiple times because the directory services API for each product that your company uses is different.

Creating New Objects

Like Active Directory, you aren't limited to the objects that Microsoft provides for ADSI. You can write new objects that extend the tasks that ADSI can perform. In some respects, this means you can write your own customized programming platform. Of course, accessing the directory database won't be a problem because ADSI supports OLE-DB.

ADSI also divides the kinds of objects that you can create into two categories. Container objects can act as objects. However, in most cases, they hold other objects and help you interact with those objects in a consistent manner. Leaf objects are stand-alone components designed to perform a single task.

Working with Namespaces

Every object on a network has to have a unique identification. Depending on the directory service, this identification method might look similar to the method you use to access a file on your hard drive. However, most namespaces use the X.500 standard for naming, which consists of object type definitions, followed by the object type value. Here's an example.

```
CN=John;OU=Editorial;O=NewMagPub
```

In this example, John is the object that we want to work with. CN stands for the context name. John is located within an organizational unit known as Editorial, which is part of an organization called NewMagPub. As you can see, this method of accessing a particular object on the network is very easy to understand and use.

ADSI doesn't support every namespace, but it does support four of the most common namespaces: Active Directory services (ADs://), LDAP (LDAP://), Windows NT/2000 (WinNT://), and Novell Directory Services (NDS://). Notice that this namespace convention looks like a URL. You'll find the namespace ends up looking like an URL because of the DNS support that Active Directory provides. In fact, this is one of the reasons that Microsoft makes it so easy to find the fully qualified DNS name for the resources on your network.

Note that you can access Active Directory entries using more than one namespace. Each namespace provides certain benefits when accessing information. We'll discuss the effect of using a particular namespace later in the chapter.

Working with the ADSI API

ADSI is the API that enables you to work with Active Directory and helps you to add the new features that Active Directory provides to your applications. Like many other parts of Windows Server, ADSI relies heavily on COM components. In fact, many of your applications will require direct access to these components, despite functionality provided by the .NET Framework. We'll see one such example in the sample code for this chapter.

TIP   It's interesting to note that only Windows Server products come with Active Directory as part of the package. Microsoft does provide Active Directory support for Windows 9x, along with a setup for older versions of Windows NT. You can find links for all four levels of support at http://www.microsoft.com/NTServer/nts/downloads/other/ADSI25/. This site also includes a link for the Active Directory Services Interfaces SDK. If you want full ADSI information, check the Active Directory Service Interfaces website at http://www.microsoft.com/windows2000/techinfo/howitworks/activedirectory/adinterface.asp.

The most common ADSI API COM functionality appears in the ACTIVEDS.TLB file found in the Windows System32 folder. To add this type library to your project, right-click the References folder in Solution Explorer, and then choose Add Reference from the context menu. You'll see an Add Reference dialog box similar to the one shown in Figure 8.2. Notice that the figure shows the ACTIVEDS.TLB entry highlighted.

FIGURE 8.2:

You'll need to add COM support for Active Directory to many of your projects.

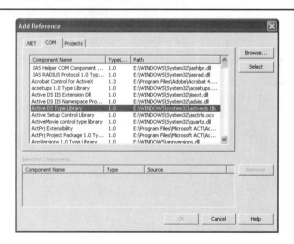

When working with COM, you need to understand the interfaces it provides. One way to see the features that the ACTIVEDS.TLB file provides is to look at them in Object Browser. However, you'll quickly notice that the list is long and there are many ADSI features that the

.NET Framework implements for you. Table 8.1 contains a list of common ADSI interfaces you might need for C# applications. You'll want to spend some additional time learning about these interfaces as you work with Active Directory using ADSI.

NOTE   Table 8.1 doesn't contain a complete list of ADSI interfaces. Some of these interfaces are in other areas of the chapter. The .NET Framework implements other interfaces, so you really don't need to worry about them when working with C#. In addition, this table doesn't include any of the NDS-specific interfaces. The table does include the more common interfaces.

TABLE 8.1: Active Directory Automation Interfaces

Interface	Description	Purpose
Core		
IADs	Defines the basic features, properties, and methods of any ADSI object.	Helps you to learn about the features common to every object such as its name, parent, class, GUID, path, and schema. Special methods enable you to work with either single-value or multiple-value properties.
IADsContainer	Enables an ADSI container to create, delete, enumerate, and manage ADSI objects.	Allows you to learn more about objects held within an ADSI container. You can count objects, create filters to exclude objects from an enumeration or count, enumerate objects, move objects to another location, or create a copy that you can modify.
IADsNamespaces	Allows you to work with namespace objects.	Contains two methods for working with namespaces. The first obtains the namespace container name, while the second modifies the namespace container name to a new value. The new namespace container name becomes the default namespace container for the user.

Continued on next page

TABLE 8.1 CONTINUED: Active Directory Automation Interfaces

Interface	Description	Purpose
Data Type		
IADsLargeInteger	Allows you to work with large (64-bit) integers.	Permits use of 64-bit integers within Active Directory. Because many compilers can't handle 64-bit integers, there are two sets of methods. The first set deals with the lower 32 bits, while the second set deals with the upper 32 bits.
Dynamic Object		
IADsComputerOperations	Manages computer operations across the network.	Contains two methods. The first helps determine the status of any computer. The second helps you shut a computer down from a remote location.
IADsFileServiceOperations	Manages file services across the network.	Enables you to work with the open and active file services sessions for the domain. The two methods include one that works with resources and another that deals with sessions.
IADsPrintJobOperations	Provides access to print jobs executing on the domain.	Obtains the status of print jobs. In addition, there are methods for pausing, reordering, and resuming print jobs.
IADsPrintQueueOperations	Provides access to print queues within the domain.	Obtains the status of the print jobs residing within the queue. There are also methods for pausing, resuming, and purging print jobs.
IADsResource	Works with open file service resources.	Permits viewing of open file service resource attributes including user, user path, resource path, and the resource lock count. A file service resource is open when the user accesses it and creates a connection to it.
IADsServiceOperations	Works with system services, active or not.	Stops, starts, pauses, or continues system services on the domain. In addition, you can determine the system service status and set the system service password.

Continued on next page

TABLE 8.1 CONTINUED: Active Directory Automation Interfaces

Interface	Description	Purpose
Dynamic Object		
IADsSession	Works with active file service sessions.	Permits viewing of user statistics for the active file service sessions. A session is active when a user creates a connection to the file system and opens one or more files. The user statistics include user name, user path, computer name, computer path, the amount of connection time for the session, and the amount of time that the connection has been idle.
Extension		
IADsExtension	Implements an application extension model.	Adds application-specific behaviors into existing ADSI objects. An application extension uses aggregation to modify the behavior of the existing object.
Persistent Object		
IADsCollection	Manages an arbitrary collection of object.	Provides methods for adding, removing, retrieving, and enumerating objects within the array. Collections are specialized arrays that can hold any type of directory services object.
IADsComputer	Allows access to any computer type.	Obtains common information about workstations, servers, or other computer types on the network.
IADsDomain	Represents a domain and helps manage accounts on the domain.	Permits account security management. You can determine password length, the age at which passwords are changed, the maximum number of bad logins allowed, lockout parameters, and other password attributes.
IADsFileService	Represents the file service and user access management.	Modifies the file service description and the number of users allowed to use the file service at the same time.

Continued on next page

TABLE 8.1 CONTINUED: Active Directory Automation Interfaces

Interface	Description	Purpose
Persistent Object		
IADsFileShare	Allows you to modify the attributes of any file share on the network.	Provides the methods to determine the user count for a file share. In addition, you can both view and set the file share description, host computer path, shared directory path, and maximum user count.
IADsLocality	Represents domain geographical location.	Views or sets the locality description, region name, postal code, or "see also" (note) information.
IADsO	Represents an Organization object within the domain.	Views or sets the organization description, locality, postal address, telephone number, fax number, and see also information.
IADsOU	Represents an Organizational Unit object within the domain.	Views or sets the organization description, locality, postal address, telephone number, fax number, see also information, and business category.
IADsPrintJob	Defines individual print jobs within the print queue.	Provides management methods for active print jobs. Methods enable you to view the host print queue location, user name, user path, time submitted, total pages, and size. In addition, you can view or set the description, priority, start time, until time, notification value, and notification path.
IADsPrintQueue	Represents a print job destination on the network.	Manages printer options. You can view or change the printer path, model, data type, print processor, description, location, start time, until time, default job priority, queue priority for processing data on the printer, banner page, print devices, and network addresses.
Property Cache		
IADsPropertyEntry	Manages attribute values as defined within the schema.	Manipulates an individual entry within a property list. The methods in this interface help you view or modify the name, data type, control code, or value of individual attribute values.

Continued on next page

TABLE 8.1 CONTINUED: Active Directory Automation Interfaces

Interface	Description	Purpose
Property Cache		
IADsPropertyList	Contains one or more property entries associated with an object attribute.	Manages the value entries associated with an object attribute. You can list the entries, obtain a total number of all entries, get or put entries, reset the values within an individual entry, or purge the entire list.
Schema		
IADsClass	Manages object descriptions within the schema.	Provides interfaces for describing Active Directory object creation including the class identifier (CLSID), object identifier (OID), mandatory and optional properties, and help file data.
IADsProperty	Manages object attributes within the schema.	Determines how Active Directory manages and creates a property. The methods in this interface include the OID, syntax object path, minimum and maximum ranges, multi-valued properties, and any additional required property qualifiers.
IADsSyntax	Manages automation data types that describe schema object property values.	Provides a single method that returns the automation value for a property. These are the virtual types like VT_BOOL (for a BOOL value) used in other parts of Visual C++ to describe the type of a variable or constant.
Utility		
IADsDeleteOps	Deletes an object from the underlying directory structure.	Contains a single method that an object can call to delete itself from the directory structure once it's no longer needed.
IADsObjectOptions	Allows you to manage provider-specific options for working with ADSI.	Contains two methods for viewing and modifying ADSI provider options. There are four standard options: server name, referrals, page size, and security mask. Individual providers may support other options.

Continued on next page

TABLE 8.1 CONTINUED: Active Directory Automation Interfaces

Interface	Description	Purpose
Utility		
IADsPathName	Parses Windows and X.500 paths within ADSI.	Enables you to work with paths provided by application programs, users, other directory services, and other objects.

Working with the *System.DirectoryServices* Namespace

The System.DirectoryServices namespace is simply a managed version of the ADSI interface we've discussed to this point. It enables you to access Active Directory using managed, rather than unmanaged, techniques in many situations. You'll run into two problems when using this namespace. First, CLR doesn't recognize some Active Directory data types, even though it seems as if it should. Second, the DirectoryServices namespace doesn't provide support for every Active Directory interface, so you'll need to resort to COM to gain access to these interfaces. We'll discuss both problems in the sample applications.

The DirectoryServices namespace includes class counterparts for the interfaces we've discussed so far (and will continue to discuss as the chapter progresses). The main focus of the classes provided in the System.DirectoryService namespace is implementation of the IADsOpenDSObject interface. Once you have an open connection to Active Directory, you can begin to manipulate the data it contains. The following list contains a description of the major classes found in the System.DirectoryService namespace.

DirectoryEntries   Provides access to the child entries for an Active Directory entry. Essential tasks include adding, removing, and finding the child entries. You'll use the DirectoryEntry class to modify the child entries.

DirectoryEntry   Provides access to a single Active Directory entry, including the root object. You can also use this class to access some of the information found in schema entries. Essential tasks include name and path modification, identification of children and parent, property modification, and obtaining the native object. When working with the native object, you must cast it to an IADs COM object. C# also has access to a Directory-Entry control that makes using this class easier. You'll learn how to use this control in the example application.

`DirectorySearcher`   Enables you to search Active Directory for specific entries. You can search for one or all matching entries, cache the entries locally, filter and sort the search results, and set the search environment. For example, you can set timeouts for both client and server. C# also provides a control version of this particular class that makes configuration easier.

`DirectoryServicesPermission`   Sets the code access permissions (security) for Active Directory. The `Assert()` method enables to you validate that the calling code can access the requested resource. You can also copy, deny, and demand permissions, as well as perform other tasks.

`DirectoryServicesPermissionAttribute`   Permits a declarative `System.DirectoryServices` permission check. You can either match a permission to a specific permission, or create a new permission.

`DirectoryServicesPermissionEntry`   Sets the smallest unit of code access security permission provided by `System.DirectoryServices`.

`DirectoryServicesPermissionEntryCollection`   Creates a strongly typed collection of `DirectoryServicesPermissionEntry` objects. You can perform all of the usual collection tasks, including counting the number of items and working with a specific item. Other methods enable you to add, remove, insert, or copy permissions.

`PropertyCollection`   Enables you to examine the properties for a single `DirectoryEntry` object. You can count the number of properties, obtain a list of property values, obtain a list of property names, or extract the value of a single property.

`PropertyValueCollection`   Enables you to examine the property values for a single `DirectoryEntry` object. You can count the number of values, set a specific property value, or set the values for the entire collection. Methods help you perform all of the usual collection tasks, including counting the number of items and working with a specific item. Other methods enable you to add, remove, insert, or copy permissions.

`ResultPropertyCollection`   Enables you to examine the properties for a `SearchResult` object. You can count the number of properties, obtain a list of property values, obtain a list of property names, or extract the value of a single property.

`ResultPropertyValueCollection`   Enables you to examine the property values for a `SearchResult` object. You can count the number of items in the collection and work with specific items. Methods enable you to perform specific tasks such as to copy the collection to an array or determine if the collection contains a specific property.

SchemaNameCollection   Contains a list of schema names that you can use with the SchemaFilter property of the DirectoryEntry object. You can count the number of items in the collection and work with specific items. Methods help you perform all of the usual collection tasks, including counting the number of items and working with a specific item. Other methods enable you to add, remove, insert, or copy permissions.

SearchResult   Contains the results of using a DirectorySearcher object to look for specific Active Directory entries. The SearchResult object contains an entire Active Directory node, beginning with the location of the first object found.

SearchResultCollection   Contains a collection of SearchResult objects. You can obtain a count of the SearchResult objects, obtain a handle to the IDirectorySearch::ExecuteSearch interface, work with a specific item, or obtain a list of properties used for the search. Methods enable you to perform specific tasks such as to copy the collection to an array or determine if the collection contains a specific SearchResult object.

SortOption   Determines how Windows XP sorts the results of a search. You can specify both the search direction and search property.

As you can see, you can perform most tasks using managed code. In the few cases where you need to perform a task using the COM interfaces, you can obtain a copy of the object using built-in method calls (see DirectoryEntry for an example). Of course, several issues remain besides ease of access. One of the most important issues is thread safety—an important consideration in a distributed application. Generally, you'll find that public static class members are thread safe while instance members aren't. This limitation means you must use class members carefully and take steps to ensure that method calls occur in a thread-safe manner.

Working with the Active Directory

Active Directory is a complex part of Windows Server. You must consider database elements, interaction with other directory services, management issues, and even a new set of programming features implemented by the COM components that make up ADSI. This section discusses the programming considerations for Active Directory.

The fact that we're managing a large distributed database changes the entire picture for the programmer. You need to consider programming requirements that other kinds of applications don't even touch. For example, how do you create a connection to an object that may reside in another city or country? Because Active Directory replicates all of the data for the entire database on each domain controller, access is faster, but replication can work against you when it comes to recording changes in the schema or object attributes.

One of the most important tools for working with Active Directory is the ADSI Viewer. This utility enables you to find data elements within the database. In addition, many developers use it to obtain the correct syntax for accessing database elements within an application.

We'll discuss three important programming considerations in this chapter. The following list tells you about each concern:

Security   Security is always a concern, especially when you're talking about the configuration data for a large organization.

Binding   Microsoft calls the process of gaining access to Active Directory objects *binding*. You're creating a connection to the object to manipulate the data that it contains.

Managing Users and Groups   One of the main tasks that you'll likely perform when working with directory objects is modifying the attributes of groups and users. Even if your application doesn't modify users or groups, you'll interact with them to determine user or group rights and potentially change those rights.

ADSI Viewer

The Active Directory Services Interface (ADSI) Viewer enables you to see the schema for Active Directory. The schema controls the structure of the database. Knowing the schema helps you to work with Active Directory, change its contents, and even add new schema elements. In order to control the kinds of data stored for the applications you create, you must know the Active Directory schema. Otherwise, you could damage the database (given sufficient rights) or, at least, prevent your application from working correctly.

When you first start ADSI Viewer, you'll see a New dialog box that allows you to choose between browsing the current objects in the database or making a specific query. You'll use the browse mode when performing research on Active Directory schema structure. The query approach provides precise information fast when you already know what you need to find.

In most cases, you'll begin your work with Active Directory by browsing through it. This means you'll select the Object Viewer at the New object dialog box. Once you do that, you'll see a New Object dialog box like the one shown in Figure 8.3. Notice that this dialog already has the LDAP path for my server entered into it. If you're using Windows 2000, you can also use a WinNT path.

The New object dialog
box enables you to
create a connection to
the server.

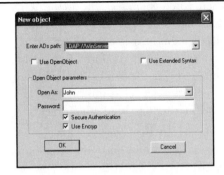

This figure shows a sample ADs Path entry. You'll need to supply Active Directory path information, which usually means typing **LDAP://** followed by the name of your server (**Win-Server** in my case). If you're using Windows 2000 to access Active Directory, you'll want to clear the Use OpenObject option when working with an LDAP path and check it when using a WinNT path.

Once you've filled in the required information in the New Object dialog box, click OK. If you've entered all of the right information and have the proper rights to access Active Directory, then you'll see a dialog box like the one shown in Figure 8.4. (Note that I've expanded the hierarchical display in this figure.)

Opening a new object
browser allows you to
see the Active Direc-
tory schema for your
server.

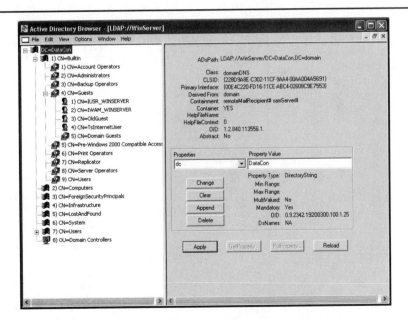

This is where you'll begin learning about Active Directory. On the left side of the display is the hierarchical database structure. Each of these elements is an Active Directory object. Clicking the plus signs next to each object will show the layers of objects beneath. Highlighting an object displays detailed information about it in the right pane. For example, in Figure 8.4 you're seeing the details about the domain object for the server. The heading for this display includes object class information, help file location, and shows whether the object is a container used to hold other objects.

Below the header are the properties for the object. You can choose one of the properties from the Properties list box and see its value in the Property Value field. Active Directory is extensible, which means that you can add new properties to an existing object, change an existing property, or delete properties that you no longer need. If you want to add a new property, all you need to do is type its name in the Properties list box and assign it a value in the Property Value field, then click Append. This doesn't make the change final; however, you still need to click Apply at the bottom of the dialog box. Deleting a property is equally easy. Just select it in the Properties list box, then click Delete. Clicking Apply will make the change final.

Leaf properties often have additional features that you can change. For example, the user object shown in Figure 8.5 helps you to change the user password and determine user group affiliation. When working with a computer object, you'll can determine the computer status and even shut it down if you'd like.

FIGURE 8.5:

Some containers and leaf objects provide special buttons that help you to perform tasks associated with that object.

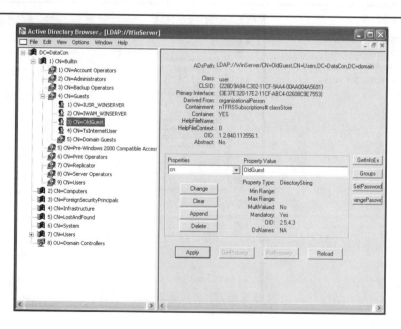

The method you use to access Active Directory affects the ADSI Viewer display. For example, Figure 8.6 shows the information for the same server using WinNT instead of LDAP for access. Notice that you garner less information in the left pane using WinNT. You'll also find that the WinNT method produces fewer property entries. The advantage of using the WinNT path is that more of the information appears in human-readable form. For example, if you want to check the date the user last logged in under LDAP, you'd better be prepared to convert a 64-bit timer tick value to the time and date. The WinNT version provides this value in human-readable form.

FIGURE 8.6:

Using the WinNT path can make some information easier to read.

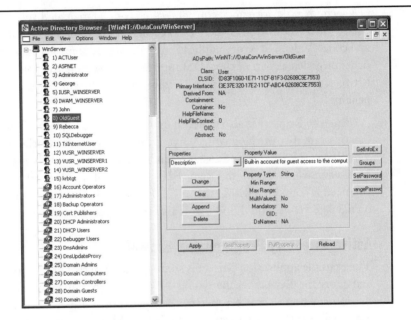

Active Directory versus the Registry

With all of the functionality that Active Directory provides, it's tempting to think that it will replace the Registry. In some respects, Active Directory does in fact replace the Registry. You should consider using it wherever an application has global importance, more than one user will require access to a single set of settings, or the information is so critical that you want to ensure that it remains safe. However, placing all your data within Active Directory also presents some problems that you need to consider.

Active Directory is a poor choice for local settings for applications that only matter to the user. For example, no one else is really concerned with a user's settings for a word processor. You gain nothing in the way of shared resource management or data security by storing these settings on the server. In fact, using Active Directory could mean a performance hit in this case because the application will need to access the server every time it needs to change a stored setting.

The performance hit for server access is relatively small for a LAN. However, you have to consider the global nature of networks today. A user on the road is going to be out of communication for some time, which means Active Directory setting changes will languish on the local machine. In short, the Registry is a better choice in many situations where the user data is non-critical.

A secondary performance consideration is one of managed versus unmanaged code and data. When you work with Active Directory, you'll often need to work with unmanaged data and code. Active Directory applications will require some access to the native COM components provided as part of the ADSI interface. Every time the application makes a transition between managed and unmanaged environments, the application suffers a performance penalty.

Using the Registry is also easier than using Active Directory. The example application will demonstrate that working with Active Directory is akin to working with a complex database. The Registry is smaller and easier to understand. It's less likely that you'll experience major bugs when working with the Registry because all of the Registry manipulation functionality you need is contained within the .NET Framework. Because C# performs extensive checks on managed code, you'll find that it also catches more potential problems with your code.

Active Directory Programming Example

The example application performs some essential Active Directory tasks. It will accept a general query for user names that you'll use to select an individual user. The application will use this information to create a specific user query, then display certain information about that user including their department and job title. Active Directory also provides a note field for each user entry that you can use to make comments. The application will enable you to view the current comment and modify it as needed.

The first task is to gain access to Active Directory generally. Listing 8.1 shows the code you'll need to create a general query. Note that this code will work with either a WinNT or an LDAP path. (It could also work with other path types, but hasn't been tested to use them.) Make sure you check the application code found in the \Chapter 08\Monitor folder on the CD.

Listing 8.1   **Accessing Active Directory**

```
private void btnQuery_Click(object sender, System.EventArgs e)
{
    // Clear the previous query (if any).
```

```
        lvUsers.Items.Clear();

        // Add the path information to the DirectoryEntry object.
        ADSIEntry.Path = txtQuery.Text;

        // The query might fail, so add some error checking.
        try
        {

            // Process each DirectoryEntry child of the root
            // DirectoryEntry object.
            foreach (DirectoryEntry Child in ADSIEntry.Children)
            {
                // Look for user objects, versus group or service objects.
                if (Child.SchemaClassName.ToUpper() == "USER")
                {
                    // Fill in the ListView object columns. Note that the
                    // username is available as part of the DirectoryEntry
                    // Name property, but that we need to obtain the
                    // Description using another technique.
                    ListViewItem lvItem  = new ListViewItem(Child.Name);
                    lvItem.SubItems.Add(
                        Child.Properties["Description"].Value.ToString());
                    lvUsers.Items.Add(lvItem);
                }
            }
        }
        catch (System.Runtime.InteropServices.COMException eQuery)
        {
            MessageBox.Show("Invalid Query\r\nMessage: " +
                            eQuery.Message +
                            "\r\nSource: " + eQuery.Source,
                            "Query Error",
                            MessageBoxButtons.OK,
                            MessageBoxIcon.Error);
        }
    }

    private void lvUsers_DoubleClick(object sender, System.EventArgs e)
    {
        // Create a new copy of the Detail Form.
        DetailForm ViewDetails  =
            new DetailForm(lvUsers.SelectedItems[0].Text,
                           lvUsers.SelectedItems[0].SubItems[1].Text,
                           txtQuery.Text);

        // Display it on screen.
        ViewDetails.ShowDialog(this);
    }
```

The application begins with the `btnQuery_Click()` method. It uses a ListView control to display the output of the query, so the first task is to clear the items in the ListView control. Notice that we specifically clear the items, not the entire control. This prevents corruption of settings such as the list headings.

You can configure all elements of the ADSIEntry (DirectoryEntry) control as part of the design process except the path. The application provides an example path in the txtQuery textbox that you'll need to change to meet your specific server configuration. You can obtain the correct path from the `ADsPath` field for the ADSI Viewer application—the application will allow you to copy the path to the clipboard using the Ctrl+C key combination. See the "ADSI Viewer" section for details.

The `ADSIEntry.Children` property is a collection of *DirectoryEntry* objects. The application won't fail with a bad path until you try to access these *DirectoryEntry* objects, which is why you want to place the portion of the code in a `try...catch` block. Notice how the code uses a property string as an index into each *DirectoryEntry* object. Even if the property is a string, you must use the `ToString()` method or the compiler will complain. This is because C# views each *DirectoryEntry* value as an object, regardless of object type.

The output of this portion of the code can vary depending on the path string you supply. Figure 8.7 shows the output for a WinNT path while Figure 8.8 shows the output for a LDAP path. Notice that the actual *DirectoryEntry* value changes to match the path type. This means you can't depend on specific *DirectoryEntry* values within your code, even if you're working with the same Active Directory entry. For example, notice how the entry for George changes from WinNT to LDAP. The WinNT entry is simple, while the LDAP entry contains the user's full name and the CN qualifier required for the path.

FIGURE 8.7:

The WinNT path tends to produce easy to read DirectoryEntry values.

FIGURE 8.8:

LDAP paths tend to
produce complex
DirectoryEntry values
that you'll need to
clean up for user
displays.

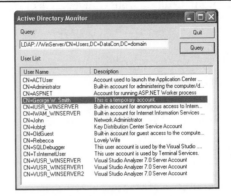

Once you have access to the user names, it's possible to gain details about a specific user. The sample application performs this task using a secondary form. When a user double-clicks on one of the names, the lvUsers_DoubleClick() method creates a new copy of the secondary form and passes it everything needed to create a detailed query. Notice that the code uses the ShowDialog() method, rather than the Show() method. This ensures that one query completes before the user creates another one.

Most of the activity for the details form occurs in the constructor. The constructor accepts the user name, description, and path as inputs so it can create a detailed query for specific user information. Listing 8.2 shows the constructor code for this part of the example.

Listing 8.2   The Details Form Displays Individual User Information

```csharp
public DetailForm(string UserName, string Description, string Path)
{
    string   UserPath;   // Path to the user object.
    bool     IsLDAP;     // LDAP provides more information.

    // Required for Windows Form Designer support
    InitializeComponent();

    // Set the username and description.
    lblUserName.Text = "User Name: " + UserName;
    lblDescription.Text = "Description: " + Description;

    // Determine the path type and create a path variable.
    if (Path.Substring(0, 4) == "LDAP")
    {
        IsLDAP = true;

        // LDAP requires some work to manipulate the path
        // string.
        int CNPosit = Path.IndexOf("CN");
```

```
        UserPath = Path.Substring(0, CNPosit) +
                   UserName + "," +
                   Path.Substring(CNPosit, Path.Length - CNPosit);
    }
    else
    {
        IsLDAP = false;

        // A WinNT path requires simple concatenation.
        UserPath = Path + "/" + UserName;
    }

    // Set the ADSIUserEntry Path and get user details.
    ADSIUserEntry.Path = UserPath;
    ADSIUserEntry.RefreshCache();

    // This information is only available using LDAP
    if (IsLDAP)
    {
        // Get the user's title.
        if (ADSIUserEntry.Properties["Title"].Value == null)
            lblTitleDept.Text = "Title (Department): No Title";
        else
            lblTitleDept.Text = "Title (Department): " +
                ADSIUserEntry.Properties["Title"].Value.ToString();

        // Get the user's department.
        if (ADSIUserEntry.Properties["Department"].Value == null)
            lblTitleDept.Text = lblTitleDept.Text + " (No Department)";
        else
            lblTitleDept.Text = lblTitleDept.Text + " (" +
                ADSIUserEntry.Properties["Department"].Value.ToString()
                + ")";
    }

    // This information is common to both WinNT and LDAP, but uses
    // slightly different names.
    if (IsLDAP)
    {
        if (ADSIUserEntry.Properties["lastLogon"].Value == null)
            lblLogOn.Text = "Last Logon: Never Logged On";
        else
        {
            LargeInteger         Ticks;      // COM Time in Ticks.
            long                 ConvTicks;  // Converted Time in Ticks.
            PropertyCollection   LogOnTime;  // Logon Property Collection.

            // Create a property collection.
            LogOnTime = ADSIUserEntry.Properties;

            // Obtain the LastLogon property value.
```

```csharp
            Ticks = (LargeInteger)LogOnTime["lastLogon"][0];

            // Convert the System.__ComObject value to a managed
            // value.
            ConvTicks = (((long)(Ticks.HighPart) << 32) +
                        (long) Ticks.LowPart);

            // Release the COM ticks value.
            Marshal.ReleaseComObject(Ticks);

            // Display the value.
            lblLogOn.Text = "Last Logon: " +
                DateTime.FromFileTime(ConvTicks).ToString();
        }
    }
    else
    {
        if (ADSIUserEntry.Properties["LastLogin"].Value == null)
            lblLogOn.Text = "Last Logon: Never Logged On";
        else
            lblLogOn.Text = "Last Logon: " +
                ADSIUserEntry.Properties["LastLogin"].Value.ToString();
    }

    // In a few cases, WinNT and LDAP use the same property names.
    if (ADSIUserEntry.Properties["HomeDirectory"].Value == null)
        lblHomeDirectory.Text = "Home Directory: None";
    else
        lblHomeDirectory.Text = "Home Directory: " +
            ADSIUserEntry.Properties["HomeDirectory"].Value.ToString();

    // Get the text for the user notes. Works only for LDAP.
    if (IsLDAP)
    {
        if (ADSIUserEntry.Properties["Info"].Value != null)
            txtNotes.Text =
                ADSIUserEntry.Properties["Info"].Value.ToString();

        // Enable the Update button.
        btnUpdate.Visible = true;
    }
    else
    {
        txtNotes.Text = "Note Feature Not Available with WinNT";
    }
}
```

The application requires two methods for creating the path to the user directory entry. The WinNT path is easy—just add the *UserName* to the existing *Path*. The LDAP path requires a little more work in that the user name must appear as the first "CN=" value in the path string. Here's an example of an LDAP formatting user directory entry path.

```
LDAP://WinServer/CN=George W. Smith,CN=Users,DC=DataCon,DC=domain
```

Notice that the server name appears first, then the user name, followed by the group, and finally the domain. You must include the full directory entry name as presented in the ADSI Viewer utility. This differs from the presentation for a WinNT path, which includes only the user's logon name.

The process for adding the path to the DirectoryEntry control, *ADSIUserEntry*, is the same as before. In this case, the control is activated using the `RefreshCache()` method. Calling `RefreshCache()` ensures that the local control contains the property values for the user in question.

LDAP does provide access to a lot more properties than WinNT. The example shows just two of the additional properties in the form of the user's title and department name. While WinNT provides access to a mere 25 properties, you'll find that LDAP provides access to 56 or more. Notice that each property access relies on checks for `null` values. Active Directory uses `null` values when a property doesn't have a value, rather than set it to a default value such as 0 or an empty string.

WinNT and LDAP do have some overlap in the property values they provide. In some cases, the properties don't have precisely the same name, so you need to extract the property value depending on the type of path used to access the directory entry. Both WinNT and LDAP provide access to the user's last logon, but WinNT uses *LastLogin*, while LDAP uses `lastLogon`.

WinNT normally provides an easy method for accessing data values that CLR can understand. In the case of the `lastLogon` property, LDAP presents some challenges. This is one case where you need to use the COM access method. Notice that the `lastLogon` property requires use of a *LargeInteger* (defined in the `ACTIVEDS.TLB` file). If you view the property value returned by the `lastLogon` property, you'll see that it's of the `System.__ComObject` type. This type always indicates that CLR couldn't understand the value returned by COM. Notice that the code converts the COM value to a managed type, then releases the COM object using `Marshal.ReleaseComObject()`. If you don't release the object, your application will have a memory leak—so memory allocation problems aren't quite solved in .NET, they just don't occur when using managed types. The final part of the conversion process is to change the number of ticks into a formatted string using the `DateTime.FromFileTime()` method.

As previously mentioned, the sample application shows how to present and edit one of the user properties. The *Info* property is only available when working with LDAP, so the code only accesses the property if you're using an LDAP path. The code also enables an Update button when using an LDAP path, so you can update the value in Active Directory. Here's the simple code for sending a change to Active Directory.

```
private void btnUpdate_Click(object sender, System.EventArgs e)
{
    // Place the new value in the correct property.
    ADSIUserEntry.Properties["info"][0] = txtNotes.Text;

    // Update the property.
    ADSIUserEntry.CommitChanges();
}
```

The application uses a double index when accessing the property to ensure that the updated text from `txtNotes` appears in the right place. All you need to do to make the change permanent is call `CommitChanges()`. Note that the change will only take place if the user has sufficient rights to make it. In most cases, COM will ignore any update errors, so you won't know the change took place unless you actually check the entry. Figure 8.9 shows the LDAP output for the sample application.

FIGURE 8.9:

The LDAP output is more complete than the WinNT output, but requires more work as well.

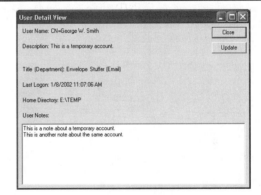

Where Do You Go From Here?

This chapter has shown you some of the intricacies of working with Active Directory in a managed C# environment. You've learned the effects of various path configurations and some of the tools you can use to research those effects. The example application also showed you how to work with values that CLR doesn't understand.

One of the best ways to learn about Active Directory is to spend time exploring it. The ADSI Viewer utility provides everything you need to perform queries and learn about the various objects. This tool also helps you modify the Active Directory schema to meet specific company needs. Because you need to rely on COM, in some cases you'll also want to view the interfaces and classes imported from the ACTIVEDS.TLB file. Finally, it's important to spend time using the online resources mentioned in the chapter.

Chapter 9 will help you understand security under Windows and the .NET Framework. Security has taken on increased importance because of the viruses and cracker break-ins that many companies experience. This chapter will show how new .NET features enable you to create a secure environment for the applications you create. Especially important is the use of role-based security to ensure that everyone gets the correct level of access to the application, but nothing more.

CHAPTER 9

Designing with Security in Mind

- Choosing a Security Strategy

- Working with Windows Security

- Working with .NET Security

At one time, PC applications resided on a local machine or a LAN, so security requirements were small or non-existent. As developers created larger applications that affected critical enterprise data, the need for security increased. Today, applications commonly service the needs of distributed environments where employees and partners log in from remote locations to manipulate critical enterprise data. The only problem is that the security provided with many applications is still at the stand-alone machine or LAN level. Adding to the problem of application security are operating system bugs, administration errors, and the forays of crackers.

> **NOTE** For the purposes of this book, the term *cracker* will always refer to an individual who's breaking into a system on an unauthorized basis. This includes any form of illegal activity on the system. On the other hand, a *hacker* will refer to someone who performs authorized (legal) low-level system activities, including testing system security. In some cases, you need to employ the services of a good hacker to test the security measures you have in place or suffer the consequences of a break-in. This book will use the term hacker to refer to someone who performs these legal forms of service.

The role for developers in managing security has changed over the years as well. A developer is now part of the security team, and management often demands that the developer provide security features as part of application design. The security emphasis, for most developers, is to prevent security breaches from occurring, provide monitoring to warn when a security breach does occur, educate in the form of warning messages and online help, and improve security through the use of new technology.

> **NOTE** Lest you think that .NET is impervious to virus attack, crackers have created a "proof of concept" virus named W32/Donut. The virus doesn't do any severe damage, but it does demonstrate .NET application vulnerability. Read more about this virus at `http://www.infoworld.com/articles/hn/xml/02/01/09/020109hndonut.xml?0110tham`.

This chapter will help you learn about new technologies, such as role-based security, that reduce the burden of creating a secure application. We'll also discuss different techniques for implementing security. For example, you'll learn when built-in security is better than using a configuration program to implement security. Finally, we'll look at some areas crackers hope you'll ignore, such as security monitoring. In some cases, you can detect usage patterns that signal security problems your application can't prevent due to holes in the operating system or other factors.

NOTE This chapter doesn't provide concrete answers that are going to work in your specific situation. A single chapter can't cover all of the technologies available today or discuss every security issue you'll ever run into. What we'll concentrate on instead is the programmer's perspective on security matters. We'll talk about the Visual Studio .NET and Windows technologies that are available to you as a programmer, but we won't get into specific solutions to a specific problem. The solution you finally decide to use will have to be based on your company's needs and the tools you have at your disposal.

Choosing a Security Strategy

Crackers depend on a certain level of disorganization within a company in order to employ their trade. That's why it's important to create a security strategy for your organization before you even begin coding the application. New programming features in Visual Studio .NET rely on your ability to define the application user. For example, you can't develop a role-based security strategy for an application until you know which roles the users could fulfill as they use the application. Some developers brainstorm roles they think an organization will need, but this leaves holes from unused roles in the application implementation and makes the application more complicated to configure.

NOTE Microsoft has produced a plethora of Windows operating system versions. For the purposes of this discussion, we'll divide those versions into two categories. I'll refer to Windows 95/98/Me as Windows 9x throughout the chapter. Likewise, I'll refer to Windows NT/ 2000/XP as Windows 2000 throughout the chapter. If I need to refer to a specific operating system version so that I can point out a new or interesting feature, I'll refer to the operating system by name. We'll discuss the reason for this operating system division in the "Working with Windows Security" section of the chapter.

The developer also needs to decide how to implement security. You can configure security at the client, the server, or both. Security can appear as an internal programmed function, something the administrator can configure using an MMC snap-in or other tool, a user-controlled application feature, or an add-on implemented as needed for distributed requirements. In many cases, an application will require several levels of security and use more than one method for implementing it. The application design should specify what type of security to implement and how to implement it. There are situations, such as data security, when the feature is an absolute and should appear as a hard-wired feature of the application. Of course, you might want to place the security feature within a DLL, so you can update it as crackers develop new ploys for gaining access to your system.

Another consideration is the type of security you want to implement. You have a choice of traditional Windows security, newer role-based security, or third-party implementations. Third-party implementations are important because Windows doesn't fill every gap in the modern application. For example, if you choose to use the SOAP or some other XML-derivative to transfer data, you'll need a third-party product to secure the information in most cases (using a secure server connection does help).

Most developers find that role-based security works best at the server. It enables the developer or network administrator to create a security policy based on the tasks the user must perform, rather than focusing on the user's job title or other personal information. Role-based security is extremely flexible because you can employ it programmatically or rely on the network administrator to configure it. A developer also has the option of enforcing a minimum security level and allowing the network administrator to enforce more stringent security measures as needed.

Standard Windows security is still the favorite on the client side, because it works with the local machine policies and security features. Windows standard security attaches an access control list (ACL) to each object. The user's security identifier (SID) acts as a key to access the object.

Working with Windows Security

This section of the chapter helps you understand standard Windows security—the type that relies on object-level access tokens. Many of the applications you create will work fine with this level of security. We'll begin with a look at the Windows Security API. Next, we'll explore a Windows security example that demonstrates Windows security features. You'll learn about Windows security programming pitfalls and how to use two security-related utilities. Finally, we'll discuss cryptography.

Understanding the Windows Security API

The Windows security API is vast and performs many functions within the operating system and the applications it supports. We're going to talk about two essential topics in this portion of the chapter.

The first section is an overview of the security API from a programmer's perspective. While the user may be faintly aware that there's a security API, they're unlikely to use it or even care that it exists. As a programmer, you need to be very aware of this part of Windows 2000 and know how to use the various API calls to make your applications secure.

Using the Biometrics API to Ease Security Concerns

One security API to consider relies on *biometrics*—the use of human body parts such as the iris and fingerprints for identification purposes. The Biometrics API (BAPI) helps programmers embed biometric technology into applications. A consortium of vendors including IBM, Compaq, IO Software, Microsoft, Sony, Toshiba, and Novell originated BAPI. Learn more about BAPI at the IO Software website (`http://www.iosoftware.com/products/licensing/bapi/`).

You can download an overview, general information, technical information, and the BAPI Software Development Kit (SDK). Lest you think that all of these APIs are vendor specific, you can also find a biometrics standards link at the Biometrics Consortium website (`http://www.biometrics.org/`). This site contains helpful information about seminars, standards progress, and public information such as periodicals. Another interesting place to look for information is the National Institute of Standards and Technology (`http://www.itl.nist.gov/div895/isis/projects/biometricsproject.html`). The main interests at this site are the publications, conferences, products, and success stories.

The second section highlights the cryptography API. This API allows you to encrypt and decrypt messages under Windows 2000. It provides the built-in cryptography support used by many applications. Of course, you can also buy third-party alternatives.

Why Worry About the Windows API?

Some developers are under the misconception that the .NET Framework is a complete solution or that it will answer every need. The problem is that the .NET Framework is new technology that extends what developers used in the past—you can't count on it to answer many of the old problems you have. In many cases, you'll find that a particular level of functionality is completely missing. The example in the section demonstrates one such instance.

However, the problem isn't limited to just missing functionality. Hidden within the .NET Framework are problems where you could assume one level of functionality when the .NET Framework provides another. Consider the `System.IO.FileStream.Lock()` method. In theory you should use this method to lock a file. In fact, it *will* lock the file if no one else is using it at the time.

Unfortunately, the `Lock()` method uses the `LockFile()` function found in `KERNEL32.DLL`, not the more functional `LockFileEx()` function. This means you don't have the option to ask `Lock()` to wait until it *can* lock the file—the method always returns immediately, even if it can't lock the file. In addition, you can't differentiate between a shared and an exclusive lock. Your only choices to get around this problem are to create a loop and continually poll the file until it locks, or use `PInvoke` to execute the `LockFileEx()` function. In short, the .NET Framework is incomplete, and you'll need to know how to work with the Windows API to overcome those limitations.

Windows Security API Overview

The Windows security API is large and cumbersome. Let's begin with the user end of the picture. It's important to understand that the user's access is limited to the combination of groups and individual rights that the administrator assigns. However, most of the configuration options available to the administrator affect Windows as a whole. If you want the administrator to set user-level access for your application, then you must provide a feature to set user access for each object or task that your application provides.

User-level access depends on a security ID (SID). When the user first logs into the system, Windows assigns an access token to the user and places the user's SID (stored on the domain controller or other security database) within it. The user object carries around both the access token and the SID for the duration of the session. An access token also contains both a DACL and an SACL. The combination of ACLs and SID within the access token is a key that allows the user access to certain system resources. Table 9.1 contains a list of the various API functions that you'll commonly use to change the user's access token. This list only provides an overview, and not a detailed description, of each API function.

NOTE   The tables in this section don't provide a complete list of all of the functions in the security API. Functions were chosen because they're unique, new, modified, or representative of a larger group of functions.

TABLE 9.1: Common User Access Token Function Overview

Function Name	Description
AdjustTokenGroups	Allows you to adjust one or more group flags that control group usage within the access token. For example, you can use this function to replace the group's owner.
AdjustTokenPrivileges	Allows you to adjust one or more privileges within the access token. This function enables or disables an existing privilege; you can't add or delete privileges from the access token.
AllocateLocallyUniqueId	Creates a new LUID. The LUID is only unique for the current computer session on a particular computer. Unlike a GUID, an LUID is temporary.
BuildExplicitAccessWithName	Creates an EXPLICIT_ACCESS data structure for the named trustee. This data structure defines the trustee's ACL information. Use this data structure with API functions like SetEntries-InAcl to define a trustee's access level to objects. The EXPLICIT_ACCESS data structure can affect either the SACL or DACL, depending on the access mode you set for it.

Continued on next page

TABLE 9.1 CONTINUED: Common User Access Token Function Overview

Function Name	Description
`BuildTrusteeWithName`	Creates a TRUSTEE data structure used to identify a specific trustee. You supply a trustee name, and Windows fills the other data structure elements with default values. You'll need to modify the data structure before using it.
`BuildTrusteeWithSid`	Creates a TRUSTEE data structure that relies on a SID, rather than a trustee name. Windows modifies the default data structure values appropriately.
`CheckTokenMembership`	Determines whether a SID appears within an access token. This can help you to determine if a user or process belongs to a particular group.
`CreateRestrictedToken`	Creates a duplicate of an existing token. The new token will have only a subset of the rights within the existing token. You can't use this function to add new rights to the resulting token.
`DuplicateToken`	Creates a copy of an existing token. Using this technique allows you to create a new token that varies from an existing token by one or two privileges.
`DuplicateTokenEx`	Creates a duplicate of a token. This function allows you to create either a primary or impersonation token. You can set access rights to the new token as part of the duplication call.
`GetAuditedPermissionsFromAcl`	Returns a list of ACL entries that result in an audit log entry for the specified trustee. This includes ACL entries that affect the trustee as well as groups to which the trustee belongs. You get a complete list of all audit-generating access events, not just those associated with the trustee. Windows returns the audited access in an ACCESS_MASK data structure.
`GetEffectiveRightsFromAcl`	Returns a list of ACL entries that list the effective rights for the specified trustee. Windows returns the effective rights in an ACCESS_MASK data structure.
`GetExplicitEntriesFromAcl`	Returns an array of EXPLICIT_ACCESS data structures that define the level of access each ACE within an ACL grants the trustee. The data structure provides information like the access mode, access rights, and inheritance setting for each ACE.
`GetTokenInformation`	Returns a data structure containing complete information about the access token. This includes the token's user, groups that appear within the token, the owner of the token, the impersonation level, and statistics associated with the token.
`GetTrusteeForm`	Returns a constant from one of the TRUSTEE_FORM enumeration values for a trustee. In most cases, the constants indicate whether the trustee is a name, a SID, or an object.
`GetTrusteeName`	Returns the name associated with a name trustee. If the TRUSTEE data structure that you provide is for a SID or an object, Windows returns a NULL value.

Continued on next page

TABLE 9.1 CONTINUED: Common User Access Token Function Overview

Function Name	Description
GetTrusteeType	Returns a constant from one of the TRUSTEE_TYPE enumeration values for a trustee. In most cases, the constants indicate whether the trustee is a user, group, domain, or an alias. There are also values to show deleted or invalid trustees.
IsTokenRestricted	Detects whether the access token contains one or more restricting SIDs.
LookupPrivilegeDisplayName	Converts a privilege name listed in WINNT.H to human-readable form. For example, SE_REMOTE_SHUTDOWN_NAME might convert to "Force shutdown from a remote system."
LookupPrivilegeName	Allows you to convert a privilege name specified by an LUID to one of the constant forms listed in WINNT.H.
LookupPrivilegeValue	Allows you to convert a privilege name as listed in WINNT.H to an LUID.
OpenProcessToken	Opens a token associated with a process (application). Like a file, you need to specify the level of access to the token. For example, the TOKEN_ALL_ACCESS constant gives you complete access to the token.
OpenThreadToken	Opens a token that's associated with a thread within an application. As with a process token, you need to request a specific level of access when making the request.
SetEntriesInAcl	Creates a new ACL by merging new access control or audit control information into an existing ACL. You can use this function to create an entirely new ACL using the ACL creation function, BuildExplicitAccessWithName.
SetThreadToken	Used mainly to implement impersonation within a thread. Use this function to give different rights to a single thread within an application. This allows the thread to perform tasks that the user may not have the rights to perform.
SetTokenInformation	Sets the information contained within an access token. Before you can set the information within the token, you have to have the required access rights. The three data structures associated with this function allow you to adjust owner, primary group, and DACL information.

Normally, you'll never work with SIDs directly, because you can address a user by their login name and make your code easier to both debug and understand. However, there are certain situations when you'll want to work with SIDs. The most important of these situations is when you're dealing with common SIDs like the one for the World, which has a SID of S-1-1-0. The SID for the World always remains the same, but the name for the World could change from country to country. Always refer to common, universal SIDs by their SID rather than their common name. With this in mind, you'll want to know about SID-related functions for times you want to work with common SIDs. Table 9.2 contains a list of SID-related functions.

TABLE 9.2: Common SID-Related Function Overview

Function Name	Description
AllocateAndInitializeSid	Creates and initializes a SID with up to eight subauthorities.
ConvertSidToStringSid	Converts a SID to a string in human-readable format. This format consists of values in the form S-R-I-SA, where S designates the string as a SID, R is the revision level, I is the identifier authority value, and SA is one or more subauthority values. Note that the dashes between SID values are always part of the SID string.
ConvertStringSidToSid	Converts a specially formatted string into a SID.
CopySid	Creates a duplicate of an existing SID.
EqualPrefixSid	Compares two SID prefixes for equality. A SID prefix is the SID value minus the last subauthority value. This test is useful for detecting two SIDs in the same domain.
EqualSid	Compares two SIDs for equality in their entirety.
FreeSid	De-allocates the memory used by a SID previously created using the AllocateAndInitializeSid function.
GetLengthSid	Returns the length of a SID in bytes.
GetSidIdentifierAuthority	Returns a pointer to a SID_IDENTIFIER_AUTHORITY data structure that contains an array of six bytes that specify the SID's top-level authority. Predefined authorities include NULL (0), local (1), world (2), creator (3), and Windows NT/Windows 2000 (5).
GetSidLengthRequired	Returns the length of a buffer required to hold a SID structure with a specified number of subauthorities.
GetSidSubAuthority	Returns the address of a specific subauthority within a SID structure. The subauthority is a relative identifier (RID).
GetSidSubAuthorityCount	Returns the address of a field used to hold the number of subauthorities within the SID. Use this address to determine the number of subauthorities within the SID.
InitializeSid	Sets the identifier authority of a SID structure to a known value using a SID_IDENTIFIER_AUTHORITY data structure. Subauthority values aren't set using this function. Use the AllocateAndInitializeSid function to initialize a SID completely.
IsValidSid	Determines the validity of a SID structure's contents. This function checks the revision number and ensures that the number of subauthorities doesn't exceed the maximum value.
LookupAccountName	Retrieves the SID (and accompanying data) for a specific account. You must supply an account and system name.
LookupAccountSid	Retrieves the name and machine associated with a given SID. It also returns the name of the SID's first domain.

Security isn't this one-sided. Once Windows determines the rights a user or other object has, it must match those rights to the access requirements of the system resource. This means working with security descriptors. A security descriptor is a lock on the object or other system resource. The key (access token) fits the lock or it doesn't. Windows only grants access when the key fits the lock. Table 9.3 is an overview of the security descriptor API functions.

TABLE 9.3: Security Descriptor Function Overview

Function Name	Description
ConvertSecurityDescriptor-ToStringSecurityDescriptor	Converts a security descriptor to string format. Flags determine the level of information returned in the string. A complete string contains the owner SID, the group SID, a DACL flag list using coded letters, a SACL flag list using coded letters, and a series of ACE entries.
ConvertStringSecurityDescriptor-ToSecurityDescriptor	Converts a specially formatted string into a security descriptor.
GetNamedSecurityInfo	Returns the security descriptor for the named object provided as input. Flags determine what kind of information to retrieve.
GetSecurityDescriptorControl	Returns the security descriptor control information and revision number for the security descriptor structure provided as input.
GetSecurityInfo	Returns the security descriptor for an object that is specified using an object handle. Windows 2000 provides flags that determine which security descriptor entries to retrieve.
SetNamedSecurityInfo	Modifies the security descriptor information for an object specified by name.
SetSecurityDescriptorControl	Modifies the control bits of a security descriptor. Functions related to this one include SetSecurityDescriptor-Dacl, which allows you to set other control bits of the security descriptor.
SetSecurityInfo	Modifies the owner, group, SACL, or DACL within the security descriptor for an object. Each information type requires a separate data structure. Flags to tell Windows 2000 which elements to change. A handle and object type descriptor identifies the object.

By now, you should have some idea of how to work within the security API Windows 2000 provides. The divisions I set up within the tables are artificial; they've been used for description purposes to make the functions easier to comprehend and use. In a real-world application, you'll combine elements of all three tables to create a complete security picture.

Cryptography API Overview

Sometimes data protection is more a matter of adding hurdles to discourage theft than preventing the theft from occurring. Encrypting data at several levels adds "doors" the cracker must pass through to get to the data. Put enough doors between your data and the cracker, and the cracker will find something easier to break. (Of course, you should always assume that anyone who has enough time and reason to break into your system will, so monitoring is extremely important.)

Microsoft's CryptoAPI provides a means of adding yet another layer of protection to your sensitive data. While a cracker could break the encryption techniques Microsoft supplies, these mechanisms do extend the time required for someone to unlock your data and read it. Using the CryptoAPI routines will help you better protect the data transferred between a client and server in any environment.

> **TIP**   You can find many of Microsoft's security solutions at `http://www.microsoft.com/technet/security/prodtech.asp`. This site includes a link for additional CryptoAPI information. You'll also find valuable operating system and other security technology links.

The CryptoAPI is a general-purpose tool that encrypts data in any environment. For example, you could build an application that stores data using the same encrypted format, whether the information is stored locally, transferred through a modem, uploaded to a website, or sent through surface mail on a disk. That's a big advantage to your company. Using encryption all the time means a cracker breaking into your system will find that the job has suddenly become harder. Yet using a common encryption technique increases user convenience because the user won't have to learn new ways to work. You can bet that a user is more likely to use encryption when it's convenient (and for the most part automatic).

Microsoft used a modular approach when designing the CryptoAPI, much as it has for other portions of Windows. You could compare the CryptoAPI to the GDI (Graphics Device Interface) API under Windows. Any vendor can add a new device driver that tells the GDI how to work with a particular display adapter. The same holds true for the CryptoAPI. It uses the idea of a Cryptographic Service Provider (CSP) that vendors can update using techniques similar to device driver replacement. Windows comes with one CSP—the one provided by Microsoft. However, if Microsoft's encryption feature set doesn't meet your needs, you could either design a new CSP yourself or buy one from a third party.

The .NET Framework provides good access to the CryptoAPI with the benefits of a managed environment. You'll learn more about this level of access in the "An Overview of the *System.Security* Namespace" section of the chapter. You can also access the CryptoAPI using the PInvoke technique we've used in several areas of the book already (see Chapters 4 and 8 for practical examples). All of the CryptoAPI functions begin with the word Crypt. For example, the `CryptAcquireContext()` function returns a handle to the default cryptographic provider, while `CryptGenKey()` creates a random key used to encrypt data.

Windows Security Example

You'll run into more than a few situations when you must gain access to one or more types of security information that the .NET Framework doesn't provide. For example, you might need to know the security information for the local user. The previous sections discussed some of this information and how you can use it to improve your applications. Unfortunately, the functions required to access those security features reside in one or more C libraries such as `ADVAPI32.LIB`. This file is only accessible from within a C application.

NOTE   The examples in this section assume a familiarity with underlying security concepts such as the use of the Security Access Control List (SACL) and Discretionary Access Control List (DACL). We'll discuss issues regarding the Access Control Entries (ACEs) and you'll learn how to manage access tokens. If you aren't familiar with these topics, make sure you read the security theory sections of the help files starting with "Windows NT Security in Theory and Practice" (`ms-help://MS.VSCC/MS.MSDNVS/dnwbgen/html/msdn_seccpp.htm`). The help file has a four-part theory section that will tell you everything you need to understand the examples.

The example application shows how to get around this access problem. You need to build a separate, managed Visual C++ DLL that handles access to the library in question, then access that DLL function from within your application. The first step is to create the required projects. Make sure you add a reference to the Visual C++ DLL in your C# project's References folder. You'll also need to add a `using` statement for the Visual C++ DLL at the beginning of your C# application. The example found in the \Chapter 09\AccessToken folder on the CD will provide you with the details of this setup.

There are a number of ways to create a connection between a C library and your C# application. In some cases, you can create a one-for-one set of function calls. For example, this works well when you want to call the console library routines because they don't exchange pointers—just data. However, the security API calls are a little more complicated, so you'll find that you need to perform a little more work to create the interface. Listing 9.1 shows the Visual C++ DLL code. Remember that this is a managed DLL, so you have access to both managed and unmanaged functionality—a real plus in this situation.

Listing 9.1   **The Visual C++ DLL Code for User Security Access**

```
// Obtain the size of the data structure for a particular
// token information class.
int GetTokenSize(TOKEN_INFORMATION_CLASS TIC,
```

```
                IntPtr *ReturnLength)
{
   HANDLE  TokenHandle = NULL; // Handle to the process token.
   DWORD   RL = 0;             // Return Length.
   HRESULT hr = 0;             // Operation Result Value.

   // Obtain a handle for the current process token.
   hr = OpenProcessToken(GetCurrentProcess(),
                         TOKEN_QUERY,
                         &TokenHandle);

   // Obtain the size of the token for the desired
   // token information class.
   hr = GetTokenInformation(TokenHandle,
                            TIC,
                            NULL,
                            0,
                            &RL);

   // Return the size of the token information.
   *ReturnLength = IntPtr((int)RL);

   // Free the token handle.
   CloseHandle(TokenHandle);

   return hr;
}

// Obtain the date for a particular token information
// class. The calling application must provide a properly
// sized buffer.
int GetTokenData(TOKEN_INFORMATION_CLASS TIC,
                 IntPtr *TokenData,
                 IntPtr TokenDataLength,
                 IntPtr *ReturnLength)
{
   HANDLE  TokenHandle = NULL;  // Handle to the process token.
   DWORD   RL = 0;              // Return Length.
   HRESULT hr = 0;              // Operation Result Value.
   VOID*   lpTokenData;         // Token Data Holder.

   // Obtain a handle for the current process token.
   hr = OpenProcessToken(GetCurrentProcess(),
                         TOKEN_QUERY,
                         &TokenHandle);

   // Allocate memory for the return data.
   lpTokenData = malloc(TokenDataLength.ToInt32());

   // Obtain the size of the token for the desired
   // token information class.
```

```
    hr = GetTokenInformation(TokenHandle,
                             TIC,
                             lpTokenData,
                             (DWORD)TokenDataLength.ToInt32(),
                             &RL);

    // Return the size of the token information.
    *ReturnLength = IntPtr((int)RL);

    // Return the token data.
    *TokenData = IntPtr(lpTokenData);

    // Free the data holder.
    //free(lpTokenData);

    // Free the token handle.
    CloseHandle(TokenHandle);

    return hr;
}

// Convert the TOKEN_USER structure to a SID string.
int ConvertTokenUserToSidString(IntPtr TokenData,
                                String **SIDString)
{
    HRESULT    hr = 0;      // Operation Result Value.
    TOKEN_USER *TU;         // Token user data structure.
    LPTSTR     SIDValue;    // The string version of the SID.
    VOID       *Temp;       // A temporary pointer.

    // Convert the IntPtr to a TOKEN_USER structure.
    Temp = TokenData.ToPointer();
    TU = (TOKEN_USER*)Temp;

    // Convert the SID to a string.
    hr = ConvertSidToStringSid(TU->User.Sid, &SIDValue);

    // Return the string value of the SID.
    *SIDString = new String(SIDValue);

    // Free the memory used by SIDValue.
    LocalFree(SIDValue);

    return hr;
}

// Convert a TOKEN_USER structure to user account information.
int ConvertTokenUserToUserData(IntPtr TokenData,
                               String **UserName,
                               String **Domain)
{
```

```
    HRESULT       hr = 0;        // Operation Result Value.
    TOKEN_USER    *TU;           // Token user data structure.
    VOID          *Temp;         // A temporary pointer.
    LPTSTR        lpUserName;    // The user name value.
    LPTSTR        lpDomain;      // The user's domain.
    SID_NAME_USE  SNU;           // Use of the SID Name.

    // Length of the data return values.
    DWORD         UserNameLength = 40;
    DWORD         DomainLength = 40;

    // Convert the IntPtr to a TOKEN_USER structure.
    Temp = TokenData.ToPointer();
    TU = (TOKEN_USER*)Temp;

    // Allocate memory for the return values.
    lpUserName = (LPTSTR)malloc(40);
    lpDomain = (LPTSTR)malloc(40);

    // Find the user account information.
    hr = LookupAccountSid(NULL,
                          TU->User.Sid,
                          lpUserName,
                          &UserNameLength,
                          lpDomain,
                          &DomainLength,
                          &SNU);

    // Return the user account information.
    *UserName = new String(lpUserName);
    *Domain = new String(lpDomain);

    // Free the local variables.
    free(lpUserName);
    free(lpDomain);

    return hr;
}
// Free unmanaged memory used by the application.
void FreePointer(IntPtr Pointer)
{
    free(Pointer.ToPointer());
}
```

One of the features of this example is that it uses as many generic function calls as possible to reduce the amount of Visual C++ code required to handle any given task. The GetToken-Size() and GetTokenData() both fall into this category. You can use them to obtain any of a number of token types. The example concentrates on the user token—the one that contains security information for the current user—but you can use these two functions to gain access to any other supported token as well.

The GetTokenSize() function begins by using the OpenProcessToken() function to retrieve the token for the current process. Every process the user opens contains a copy of the user's token. However, the system and other external processes can also open processes, so the only certain way to retrieve a copy of the user's token is to look at the current process. Notice that we've opened the token for query purposes only and that we obtain a handle to the current process by using the GetCurrentProcess() function.

Once the code obtains a token handle, it can retrieve information about the token. The purpose of the GetTokenSize() function is to tell the caller how much memory to allocate for the token information, not to actually retrieve the information. The caller must provide one of several TOKEN_INFORMATION_CLASS enumeration values as input to the GetTokenSize() function. We'll visit these values later. For now, the enumeration is used as input to the Get-TokenInformation() function, which also requires the token handle and a variable to return the length. If this were an information retrieval call, the code would also need to supply a pointer to a buffer to receive the information and the length of that buffer.

> **WARNING**   Always close all handles and free all allocated memory when working with unmanaged code. Every call you make to the Win32 API, including the security API, is a call to unmanaged code. Notice the call to CloseHandle() in the example code. This call frees the token handle before the GetTokenSize() function returns.

The GetTokenData() function works much like the GetTokenSize(). In this case, the caller must provide a pointer to a buffer used to store the data. However, you need to consider how the GetTokenInformation() function works before you proceed; the GetTokenInformation() is general purpose—it returns more than one type of data depending on the kind of token you request. As a result, it returns a VOID* that the application must typecast to another kind of information. We'll see how this works later. The point for now is that GetTokenData() must allocate the memory for the GetTokenInformation() call, and you can't free this memory within the function as you would normally (notice the commented free(lpTokenData) call within the code that shows where you'd normally free the buffer).

The data buffer returned by GetTokenInformation() contains a TOKEN_USER data structure. This data structure contains a security identifier (SID) that we'll use to obtain three pieces of information about the user. The ConvertTokenUserToSidString() function accepts the buffer as input, typecasts it to a TOKEN_USER data structure, then uses the data structure to make a ConvertSidToStringSid() call. The resulting LPTSTR, SIDValue, is used to create a String value (SIDString). Notice that the code requires a double pointer (**) to SIDString to create a reference to it. This is an idiosyncrasy of Visual C++ that you need to consider when creating wrapper functions such as this one. Also notice that the function uses LocalFree() to free the memory used by *SIDValue*. That's because the memory for *SIDValue* is actually allocated by the ConvertSidToStringSid() function. We'll see later that locally allocated memory is freed using the free() function.

The final wrapper function, ConvertTokenUserToUserData(), retrieves the user name and domain using the SID. In this case, the code relies on the LookupAccountSid() function, which requires two locally allocated buffers. Notice the use of the malloc() function with appropriate typecasting and the use of the free() function calls to free the memory later.

The example does show one instance where there's a direct correlation between a Win32 API function and the wrapper function. The FreePointer() function simply calls the free() function used earlier to free memory signified by a pointer.

The C# code required to use all of these wrapper functions is almost mundane compared to the wrapper code. The code calls the various wrappers to obtain a user token, uses it to access the user's SID, name, and domain, and then displays that information in a message box. Listing 9.2 shows the code to perform these tasks.

Listing 9.2   **Obtaining the User SID, Domain, and Name**

```
public enum TOKEN_INFORMATION_CLASS
{
    TokenUser = 1,
    TokenGroups,
    TokenPrivileges,
    TokenOwner,
    TokenPrimaryGroup,
    TokenDefaultDacl,
    TokenSource,
    TokenType,
    TokenImpersonationLevel,
    TokenStatistics,
    TokenRestrictedSids,
    TokenSessionId,
    TokenGroupsAndPrivileges,
    TokenSessionReference,
    TokenSandBoxInert
}

 private void btnTest_Click(object sender, System.EventArgs e)
{
    int             Result;
    SecurityWrapper SW = new SecurityWrapper();
    IntPtr          TokenSize = new IntPtr(0);
    IntPtr          TokenData = new IntPtr(0);
    String          SIDString = null;
    String          UserName = null;
```

```
String              Domain = null;

// Get the size of the data structure. The return value of
// this call is always 0. The call has actually failed because
// it didn't retrieve the user information token.
Result = SW.GetTokenSize((int)TOKEN_INFORMATION_CLASS.TokenUser,
                         ref TokenSize);

// Get the token data. The return value of this call should always
// be 1. The call has succeeded in returning the user token.
Result = SW.GetTokenData((int)TOKEN_INFORMATION_CLASS.TokenUser,
                         ref TokenData,
                         TokenSize,
                         ref TokenSize);

// Obtain the SID String.
Result = SW.ConvertTokenUserToSidString(TokenData, ref SIDString);

// Obtain the user account information.
Result = SW.ConvertTokenUserToUserData(TokenData,
                                       ref UserName,
                                       ref Domain);

// Free the memory used by the token data.
SW.FreePointer(TokenData);

// Display the output.
MessageBox.Show("User Name:\t" + UserName +
                "\r\nDomain:\t\t" + Domain +
                "\r\nSID:\t\t" + SIDString,
                "Local Account Information",
                MessageBoxButtons.OK,
                MessageBoxIcon.Information);
}
```

The *TOKEN_INFORMATION_CLASS* enumeration shows the types of data you can request using the GetTokenSize() and GetTokenData() methods. The example code uses *TokenUser*. However, you can also gain access to the process privileges, own, group association, statistics, and other kind of information. In short, the technique shown in this section is the tip of a much larger iceberg.

The btnTest_Click() method is straightforward. The GetTokenSize() and GetToken-Data() methods work together to obtain the *TokenData* pointer—which is a pointer to the *TOKEN_USER* data structure discussed earlier. However, as far as C# is concerned, *TokenData* is simply a pointer to some data. It could point to any of the data structures used by any of the *TOKEN_INFORMATION_CLASS* enumeration members. It's only during the call to the Convert-TokenUserToSidString() and ConvertTokenUserToUserData() functions that the code becomes specific to the TOKEN_USER data structure. Figure 9.1 shows the output of this example.

WARNING The code must free the memory the *TokenData* variable points to before it exits. Otherwise, the application will leak memory. The Visual C++ DLL contains a special function, FreePointer() for this purpose. Any DLL you create should contain a special function that accomplishes this same task.

FIGURE 9.1:

The output of the example program is simple, but demonstrates token access.

Using the Access Control Editor

The Access Control Editor is a COM control that helps you to add a standard interface to your application—allowing administrators to set application security as needed. These are the same property pages that Microsoft uses within Windows 2000 to set security. The Access Control Editor uses two sets of property pages. The user will normally see the simple property page dialog shown in Figure 9.2.

FIGURE 9.2:

The Access Control Editor is a generally accessible component.

I chose this particular example so that you'd see the dialog in action. The content of the dialog changes to meet object requirements. The Administrator will normally use the advanced property page shown in Figure 9.3.

FIGURE 9.3:

The Advanced fea-
tures of the Access
Control Editor provide
the administrator with
full access control.

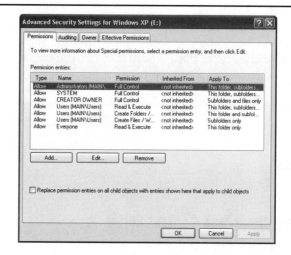

As you can see, both property pages allow the administrator to work with the security settings for an application with relative ease. Notice that the advanced dialog provides complete controls for setting every security aspect for this particular object. The Permissions tab sets the DACL, the Auditing tab the SACL, and the Owner tab the owner information. The only missing element is the group information, which isn't important at the user level in many cases.

Now that we've seen the Access Control Editor user interface, let's look at development. You create Access Control Editor property sheets using the ISecurityInformation interface. There are two main methods used to call on this interface: CreateSecurityPage() and EditSecurity(). The CreateSecurityPage() method is used to add a Security tab to an existing property sheet. You can use the PropertySheet() function or the PSM_ADDPAGE message to add the resulting property page to the existing property sheet. The EditSecurity() method displays the Security property page on a property sheet that's created specifically to display the Access Control Editor.

Some two-way communication takes place between your application and the Access Control Editor. The Access Control Editor doesn't know anything about your application when you first start it, so you have to supply this information. This means implementing several methods of the ISecurityInformation interface within your application. The following list provides a very brief description of these functions.

GetObjectInformation   Obtains the information to initialize the Access Control Editor.

GetSecurity   Obtains the object security descriptor.

SetSecurity   Returns an updated security descriptor to the object after the user completes the editing process using Access Control Editor dialog.

`GetAccessRights`   Obtains the object access rights.

`MapGeneric`   Asks the object to map the generic rights in an access mask to the standard and specific rights equivalents.

`GetInheritTypes`   Asks how child objects can inherit the ACEs owned by the requesting object.

`PropertySheetPageCallback`   Tells the object that Windows is about to create or destroy the property page.

TIP   The Access Control Editor provides you with complete control over the security environment it creates. In fact, you can set one of the flags to allow the user to only view the object security information. This means a user could look at which rights they had to an object in your application, then request help from an administrator if needed.

The `GetObjectInformation()` method implementation is important. You create an `SI_OBJECT_INFO` data structure and pass it to the Access Control Editor. The data structure includes security dialog configuration information. For example, you can choose which features the user will see. You can also disable the Advanced button, making it impossible to change auditing options or object owner. In addition, this data structure defines property page elements like the title bar contents, the name of the object, and the name of a server that the Access Control Editor uses to look up object security information.

Using the Security Configuration Editor

The Microsoft Security Configuration Editor is an administration tool that reduces both security management and analysis time. Initially you'll use this tool to configure the operating system security parameters. Once these parameters are in place, you can use the Security Configuration Editor to schedule periodic tests.

NOTE   Windows NT provides one MMC snap-in for the Security Configuration Editor called the System Configuration Manager. You can use the System Configuration Manager to work with the security database (SDB) and security configuration (INF) files you create using the Security Configuration Editor. Windows 2000 and Windows XP divide the Security Configuration Editor into two parts. The Security Configuration and Analysis MMC snap-in helps you configure the security database, while the Security Templates MMC snap-in helps you work with the security configuration files. All of these operating systems provide similar functionality. Windows 2000 and Windows XP do provide some advanced features. All screenshots in this section of the chapter depict the Windows XP setup.

The overall goal of the Security Configuration Editor is to provide a single place to manage all of the security concerns for a network. However, it doesn't actually replace all of the tools you used in the past—the Security Configuration Editor *augments* other security tools. The Security Configuration Editor also provides auditing tools that Windows has lacked in the past.

One of the unique ideas behind the Security Configuration Editor is that it's a macrobased tool. You'll create a set of instructions for the Security Configuration Editor to perform, then allow it to perform those instructions in the background. Obviously, this saves a lot of developer time since the developer doesn't have to wait for one set of instructions to complete before going to the next set. You can also group tasks, which saves input time.

At this point, you may wonder why a developer should care about this tool at all. After all, configuring network security is a network administrator's task. That idea used to be true—a network administrator was responsible for all security on the network. However, as computer networks become more complex and the technologies used with them become more flexible, part of the responsibility for network security has shifted to the developer. As a developer, you need to know how this tool works so that you can test the applications you create.

Creating a security setup begins when you choose an existing template or create a new one using the Security Templates MMC snap-in. If you want to use an existing template as a basis for creating a new one, you can right-click on the desired template and use the Save As command found on the context menu. Microsoft supplies a variety of templates designed to get your started in creating this security database, as shown in Figure 9.4.

FIGURE 9.4:

The Security Configuration Editor provides a number of standard templates for creating your security setup.

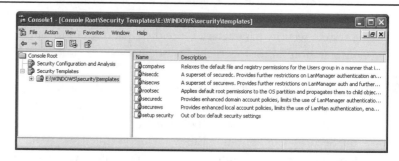

Each of the security templates is designed for a different purpose (which is indicated by its name). The one I'll use in this section is the Compatibility Workstation template (compatws), but all of the other templates work about the same as this one. All of the templates contain the same basic elements shown in Figure 9.5. The following list describes each of these elements for you.

FIGURE 9.5:

Each of the security templates contains the same security elements.

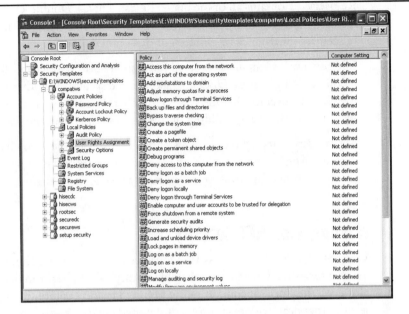

Account Policies   Defines the password, account lockout, and Kerberos policies for the machine. Password policies include items like the minimum password length and the maximum time the user can use a single password. The account lockout policy includes the number of times a user can enter the wrong password without initiating a system lockout. Kerberos policies feature elements like the maximum user ticket lifetime.

Local Policies   Defines the audit policy, user rights assignment, and security options. Audit policies determine the types of data you collect. For example, you could audit each failed user logon attempt. User rights assignments are of special interest, since this policy affects the rights you can assign to a user (the access token). The security options policy contains the elements that determine how the security system will react given a set of circumstances. For example, one policy will log a user off when their usage hours expire.

Event Log   Defines how the event log stores data and for how long. These policies also determine maximum event log size and event log viewing rights.

Restricted Groups   Defines groups that can't access the workstation or server at all or restricts the amount of access they can obtain.

System Services   Displays a list of the system services on the target machine. Double-clicking a service displays a dialog that allows you to set the policy for that service and allows you to adjust the startup mode for the service. Normally, you'll leave the icons in this policy alone. However, you can safely change any system service DLLs you create.

Registry   Contains all of the major Registry hives. Double-clicking a branch displays a dialog you use to set the security for that branch. In addition, you can choose the method of security inheritance by children of this branch.

File System   Contains protected file system entries. You can add new files to the list or modify existing entries. Double-clicking a file system entry displays a dialog you use to set the security level for that file system member. In addition, you can choose the method of security inheritance by children of this file system entity (applies only to folders).

Active Directory Objects   This entry is only available if you have Active Directory enabled (which means you must have a domain controller set up). It allows you to edit the security settings for any Active Directory objects, including users and groups.

Working with .NET Security

Visual Studio .NET can access Windows security using the techniques discussed earlier in the chapter—you'll need to use the old security calls to perform many local security tasks. However, the world of computing isn't limited to local computing anymore. You'll need security that deals with encryption, distributed environments, and web applications. It's in these areas of security where the .NET Framework excels.

The following sections provide an overview of the security provided by .NET. In many ways, you'll find that .NET makes security easier. We'll discuss the ramifications of role-based security, and you'll learn how it differs from the standard Windows security you used in the past. This section also shows an example of using .NET role-based security.

Understanding the .NET Framework Security Features

Most of the security features we'll discuss in this chapter appear in the System.Security namespace. However, it's important to realize that Microsoft attempted to order the .NET Framework for convenience. While most security features appear in the security-related namespaces, you'll find a few in odd places. For example, if you want to lock a file, you'll use the System.IO.FileStream.Lock() method. Likewise, if you want to ensure that your web page synchronizes properly, you'll want to use the System.Web.HttpApplicationState .Lock() method. There's even a System.Drawing.Design.ToolboxItem.Lock() method you can use to lock individual properties in a toolbox item. In short, if Microsoft felt that a developer would have better access to a security method within the affected object's class, the method should appear in that location.

The .NET Framework provides several levels of security. However, you can easily divide security into application and role-based security. Application security defends the code elements used to create an application. In addition, it protects the system from code elements that originate outside the system (such as code downloaded from a website) by assigning such code a lower security level. In short, the code receives a trust value based on its origin. Role-based security defines the actions a user (or other entity) is allowed to perform based on their organizational role. This differs from the older individual and group token access because a user can "change hats" (roles) based on current environmental and access conditions. Together, the two levels of security enable you to protect applications without worrying too much about low-level functionality. Of course, these features only work if you have already defined the various security elements.

NOTE   Many of the security features that the .NET Framework provides only affect managed code. If your application uses a combination of managed and unmanaged code, you'll need to implement security that works in both arenas, namely the Security API we discussed earlier.

Another way to look at .NET security is the method of code implementation. You can programmatically define a security feature using declarative or imperative syntax. Some security features require you to use a specific method, while others allow implementation using either method.

Declarative syntax relies on attributes. The attributes can appear at the assembly, class, or member levels and they can request, demand, or override the security options currently in place. Applications use requests to change their current security settings. A request can ask for more or less access to objects. Demands and overrides appear within library code. A demand protects the object from caller access, while an override changes the default security settings. Here's an example of declarative syntax in action (you can also find this example in the \Chapter 09\Declarative folder on the CD—make sure you change the file location to match your system).

```
[System.Security.Permissions.FileIOPermission(SecurityAction.Deny,
                                              All="E:\\Temp.txt")]
private void btnDeny_Click(object sender, System.EventArgs e)
{
    Stream   FS = null;  // A test file stream.

    // Try to access the file.
    try
    {
        FS = new FileStream("E:\\Temp.txt",
                            FileMode.Open,
                            FileAccess.Read);
    }
    catch(SecurityException SE)
```

```
    {
        MessageBox.Show("Access Denied\r\n" +
                        SE.Message,
                        "File IO Error",
                        MessageBoxButtons.OK,
                        MessageBoxIcon.Error);
        return;
    }

    // Display a success message.
    MessageBox.Show("File is open!",
                    "File IO Success",
                    MessageBoxButtons.OK,
                    MessageBoxIcon.Information);

    // Close the file if opened.
    FS.Close();
}
```

The btnAllow_Click() will always fail because the FileIOPermission attribute is set to deny all access to the file. The Assert() or Demand() methods would allow access to the same file (the example uses the Assert() method). As you can see, the result of this code is that the Temp.TXT file is protected, even if the user would normally have access to it.

Imperative syntax relies on security objects. An application creates a security object, then uses the object to set permissions or perform other tasks. You can use imperative syntax to perform demands and overrides, but not requests. Here's an example of imperative syntax in action (you can also find this example in the \Chapter 09\Imperative folder on the CD—make sure you change the file location to match your system).

```
private void btnDeny_Click(object sender, System.EventArgs e)
{
    FileIOPermission  FIOP;        // Permission object.
    Stream            FS = null;   // A test file stream.

    // Create the permission object.
    FIOP = new FileIOPermission(FileIOPermissionAccess.Read,
                "E:\\Temp.txt");

    // Deny access to the resource.
    FIOP.Deny();

    // Try to access the object.
    try
    {
        FS = new FileStream("E:\\Temp.txt",
                            FileMode.Open,
```

```
                    FileAccess.Read);
   }
   catch(SecurityException SE)
   {
      MessageBox.Show("Access Denied\r\n" +
                   SE.Message,
                   "File IO Error",
                   MessageBoxButtons.OK,
                   MessageBoxIcon.Error);
      return;
   }

   // Display a success message.
   MessageBox.Show("File is open!",
                   "File IO Success",
                   MessageBoxButtons.OK,
                   MessageBoxIcon.Information);

   // Close the file if opened.
   FS.Close();
}
```

The btnDeny_Click() method will always fail because the imperative security call, FIOP.Deny(), denies access to the file. Notice how the code initializes the FileIOPermission object before using it. The code requires a full path to the file in question. As with the declarative syntax, you can use the Assert() or Demand() methods to allow access to an object.

Role-Based Security Example

The idea behind role-based security isn't new. Microsoft originally introduced this idea with COM+ 1.0. However, COM+ only enabled the developer to use role-based security on the server. In addition, the use of role-based security only applied to the COM+ application, not the server in general. In short, even though role-based security is extremely helpful under COM+, it's not accessible.

The .NET Framework extends the idea of role-based security. You can use it on both the client and the server. In addition, you can use role-based security for generic needs. For example, you can use it to check a user's group membership. The group membership becomes the user's role.

Role-based security relies on two elements under the .NET Framework: the principle object and the identity object. The principle object is the security context that the application uses to run, while the identity object represents the user. The combination of these two objects represents a unique security context that identifies a specific application.

You can use the principle and identity objects for a number of purposes. In addition, the .NET Framework provides both Windows and generic versions of both the principle and the identity objects. Listing 9.3 shows one way to create a Windows principle and use it to identify the current user. (You can find this example in the \Chapter 09\Role folder on the CD.)

Listing 9.3   **The .NET Framework Enables Role-Based Security on Both Client and Server**

```
private void btnTest_Click(object sender, System.EventArgs e)
{
    WindowsPrincipal  WinPrin; // Security Principle.

    // Initialize the principle.
    WinPrin = new WindowsPrincipal(WindowsIdentity.GetCurrent());

    // Display the resulting information.
    MessageBox.Show("Name:\t\t" +
                    WinPrin.Identity.Name.ToString() +
                    "\r\nAuthentication:\t" +
                    WinPrin.Identity.AuthenticationType.ToString() +
                    "\r\nIs Authenticated:\t" +
                    WinPrin.Identity.IsAuthenticated.ToString(),
                    "Security Identity",
                    MessageBoxButtons.OK,
                    MessageBoxIcon.Information);

    // Check the user's role status.
    if (WinPrin.IsInRole(WindowsBuiltInRole.Administrator))
    {
        MessageBox.Show("The user is an administrator.",
                    "Security Role",
                    MessageBoxButtons.OK,
                    MessageBoxIcon.Information);
    }

    // Check a custom user role.
    if (WinPrin.IsInRole("Main\\Debugger Users"))
    {
        MessageBox.Show("The user is a debugger user.",
                    "Special Security Role",
                    MessageBoxButtons.OK,
                    MessageBoxIcon.Information);
    }
}
```

The example code begins by creating a *WindowsPrinciple* object. This object includes a *WindowsIdentity* object specified by the WindowsIdentity.GetCurrent() call, which is the current user. After it created the *WindowsPrinciple* object, the code displays the identification information for the user. Figure 9.6 shows an example of the output that you'll see.

Notice that Figure 9.6 shows the fully qualified user identification, which includes a user name and either the machine name or the domain name.

FIGURE 9.6:

The identification
information includes
name, domain,
authentication type,
and status.

You'll always use the IsInRole() method to verify the user's role. The two easiest methods of doing this are to use a *WindowsBuiltInRole* enumeration value or to create a role string. Notice that the string must include a fully qualified name that includes either the machine name or the domain name and the security role.

.NET Cryptography Programming Example

Cryptography, the act of making data unreadable to someone else, and then converting it back to something readable, is one of the most ancient arts in the world for keeping a secret. Of course, ancient cryptographic methods can't compete with the modern equivalent, but the idea has been the same since those early times.

One of the ways in which .NET has greatly improved the life of developers is by using cryptography to keep data safe. Unlike the CryptoAPI provided with previous versions of Windows, the .NET method is actually easy to understand and use. Listing 9.4 shows an example of the encryption portion of the process. The decryption portion is almost the same with a few minor differences. You'll find this example in the \Chapter 09\Crypto folder on the CD.

Listing 9.4   **Encrypting and Decrypting a File Requires Similar Code**

```
private void btnEncrypt_Click(object sender, System.EventArgs e)
{
    FileStream        FIn;                      // Input file.
    FileStream        FOut;                     // Output file.
    Byte[]            Data = new Byte[100];     // Temporary buffer.
    int               Counter = 0;              // Total converted.
    int               ReadByte = 0;             // Currently read counter.
    CryptoStream      CryptStream;              // Cryptographic stream.
    RijndaelManaged   RM;                       // Encryption Algorithm.
    byte[] Key = {0x01, 0x02, 0x03, 0x04,       // Encryption Key.
                  0x05, 0x06, 0x07, 0x08,
                  0x09, 0x10, 0x11, 0x12,
                  0x13, 0x14, 0x15, 0x16};
    byte[] IV = {0x01, 0x02, 0x03, 0x04,        // Initialization vector.
```

```
                    0x05, 0x06, 0x07, 0x08,
                    0x09, 0x10, 0x11, 0x12,
                    0x13, 0x14, 0x15, 0x16};

// Open the input and output files.
FIn = new FileStream(txtInput.Text,
                    FileMode.Open,
                    FileAccess.Read);
FOut = new FileStream(txtEncrypt.Text,
                    FileMode.OpenOrCreate,
                    FileAccess.Write);

// Create the cryptographic stream.
RM = new RijndaelManaged();
CryptStream = new CryptoStream(FOut,
                        RM.CreateEncryptor(Key, IV),
                        CryptoStreamMode.Write);

// Encrypt the file.
while(Counter < FIn.Length)
{
    ReadByte = FIn.Read(Data, 0, 100);
    CryptStream.Write(Data, 0, ReadByte);
    Counter = Counter + ReadByte;
}

// Close the open stream and files.
CryptStream.Close();
FIn.Close();
FOut.Close();
}
```

As you can see from the example code, the idea is to open an input and an output file. The input file contains the plain text that you want to encrypt. After you open the two files, you need to create an algorithm object to encrypt the data and a stream for handling the encryption. Notice the CreateEncryptor() method call in the CryptoStream() constructor. You would replace this with a CreateDecryptor() call in the decryption portion of the code.

After the code creates the required stream, it simply reads from the input file, encrypts the data, and sends the data to the output file. It's important to track how many bytes the input file actually contained, or you'll obtain some odd results from the encryption portion of the program. Once the output is complete, you close the stream first, and then the two files. Make sure you follow this order or you'll receive an error from the application. The output file will also lose data because the *CryptoStream* object isn't flushed until you close it.

Where Do You Go From Here?

This chapter has shown you just some of the security features provided by both the Win32 API and the .NET Framework. However, you should have enough information now to secure many, if not most, of your applications. The problem now is one of actually applying what you know to the application to make it secure, without making it slow or cumbersome.

You'll want to spend a lot more time looking at the functions provided by the Win32 API and the .NET Framework. Because of the number of flaws in Microsoft's security, you'll also want to spend time online looking for patches and updates to Microsoft's security features. These patches and updates often affect your code, so it's important to keep everything up-to-date.

The next chapter covers an important, but overlooked, area of application development—packaging. We'll discuss how to create help files, determine the type of package to use for specific scenarios, and create an application package using the tools that Microsoft provides. Visual Studio .NET actually provides a number of good packaging techniques that are easy for both you and the end user.

CHAPTER 10

Application Packaging Issues

- Building Help Files

- Working with Assemblies

- Developing a Distribution Strategy

- Creating a Distribution File

One of the most forgotten developer skills is application packaging. Many developers know how to create an application but have little or no experience in creating a package to deliver that application to the end user. The new features provided by Visual Studio .NET don't reduce the importance of this task. In fact, in the world of distributed application development, the need to create useful packaging is even greater than before.

There are a number of ways to create application packaging, including the use of third-party packaging products such as InstallShield. This chapter will help you understand the packaging features bundled with Visual Studio .NET and how to use them most effectively. We'll also discuss the content of a typical application package, including two types of help files: standard Windows and HTML-based. When you complete this chapter, you'll have a better understanding of what you need to do to package an application and what to avoid when creating the application package.

Building Help Files

Windows has gone through numerous iterations of the help file over the years. The most recent form of help file relies on HTML-based input. In fact, if you look at the MSDN help provided with Visual Studio .NET, you'll quickly discover you're using web pages to access help content. A link on an MSDN help page can lead you to either a location on Microsoft's website or your local hard drive with equal ease. The basic advantage of using HTML-based help is that it enables you to keep the information for your application updated. The basic disadvantages include the requirement for an Internet link, the need to write complex web pages, and problems with flexibility. (For instance, HTML-based help often relies on a specific version of a browser.)

Despite Microsoft's efforts, the standard Windows compiled help file (HLP) remains extremely popular and quite usable. The advantage of using this method is that the mechanisms for creating the help file are easily understood. In addition, the data is local, which means you don't need an Internet connection and the user won't have to wait long to receive critical application information. Standard Windows help files also tend to compress the help information in smaller packages than those you can create with HTML-based help. The standard Windows help file is also under full developer control—you can add new menu items to the Help program, as well as disable existing help options. The biggest disadvantage with this form of help is that you can't fix errors with ease. In addition, when it comes to large applications, HTML-based help tends to work better because it doesn't suffer the file size constraints found in standard Windows help.

TIP HTML-based help tends toward a freeform organization. Microsoft doesn't even provide a tool for creating an HTML-based help file as part of Visual Studio .NET. On the other hand, standard Windows help is quite organized, and you'll need to use the Microsoft Help Workshop to create such a file.

Both forms of help perform the same service—they teach a user how to use your application. Which type of help will work best for your organization is more a matter of style, personal taste, and individual application requirements. Some applications will never receive a help update (or might receive just one update during the course of use). Such an application won't benefit much from the flexibility of an HTML-based help file, and some users may balk at using one. On the other hand, some application help files include topical information, such as company policy, and will benefit from using an HTML-based help file. The following sections tell you how to create these two common help file types.

HTML-Based Help

HTML help is composed of web pages. However, HTML help doesn't end with a simple web page; there are other elements to consider. For example, you need to consider the organization of the help file from an access perspective. The following sections help you create a help file setup that's both efficient and practical.

NOTE The companion CD includes a complete HTML-based help file application in the \Chapter 10\HTMLHelp folder. This example shows you how to create an application that relies on HTML help, even though the application itself uses a desktop interface.

Multiple or Single-Page Files?

One of the more important considerations you'll need to make is how you want to put your help file together. When you use Windows Help, you create a single file containing many pages of information. This kind of approach won't work with HTML-based help because it doesn't use a master file approach. You have to figure out how you want to put multiple pages of information into one package, and still be assured that the package you create will contain multiple files.

Help files should rely on an outline for organizational purposes. However, outlines simply organize the information—there are multiple standards you can use to inform that organization. For example, some applications lend themselves to organization by menu option. The following list presents some common strategies for organizing your help file.

Menu Flow   The menu flow technique starts with the application menu system and works down from there. Simply list all of the menu items in hierarchical format. Once you have all the menu items listed, start listing any dialogs. List each dialog in order along with the controls that it contains. Finally, list the Main window and any components it contains.

Task   Most users I've talked to don't care about the latest feature in a program. All they know is that they have to get a particular job done in a limited amount of time. This is especially true of people who crunch numbers all day or those who perform some of the more mundane office chores in a company. They don't have time to figure out how to do something—you have to tell them. Using the task-oriented technique, you work out a list of tasks the user will perform and then explain each one in detail. It's good to start with an explanation of the task, "What will the user accomplish?" Then provide a procedure to get the job done.

Generalized Menu/Task   Some applications perform many tasks. For example, most people use a word processor for more than one task. If you wrote hard and fast rules for accomplishing tasks, in this case, you'd be doing the user and yourself a disservice. When using this organization strategy, provide a list of task explanations that demonstrates product features along with an overview of the menu system. The user gets a general feel for what the application can do without absorbing too many preconceived ideas from the developer.

Reference   Compilers and applications that provide their own macro language often include a reference-type help file. In this case, you're looking at the program not from a physical perspective but from a control perspective. It doesn't really pay to do much more than list the macro commands in alphabetical order, because there isn't any way to know how the user will use them. Describe the command, tell what each parameter will do, and then provide some kind of example of how to use the command. You can also add other information such as hints and version-specific differences.

Tutorial   Tutorials are special-purpose help files used with applications designed for novices in most cases. You'll use this type of help file to teach someone how to use your application. Most developers use this type of help file for users who haven't had much experience with the application in the past, but some developers use it for other training purposes such as "tips and techniques" aids for experienced users. In order to make this type of help file work, you must keep in mind that the user has a minimal amount of experience with the computer and operating system.

Functional Area   Some applications lend themselves to this kind of help file organization because of the way that they're used. CAD and other drawings fall into this area because you can group the tasks they perform into functional areas. For instance, a CAD program provides some commands for drawing, others that control the color palette, and still others that allow you to manipulate the drawing size and shape. Grouping like items will help users find what they need quickly. The reason is simple: When users are creating the drawing, they look for drawing commands. Later, as they embellish their work of art, they'll want to know about color- and texture-related commands.

Now that you know how to organize the data for your help file, you need to consider how to block text for placement in a file. Text blocking is important in HTML-based help, because the browser incurs download time whenever the user clicks a link or a control button. The following list describes the file layout options and considers their relative strengths and weaknesses.

Topic   Each file contains one help file topic. For example, you might have a file on data entry methods. Users who want to find information about a specific topic will get fast access since all of the information arrives in one download. Unfortunately, remote users who require information about menu-related items will end up waiting for each item to download. In addition, the information is difficult to update, since you'll need to look through several files for one menu change.

Large Menu/Dialog Control   All dialog controls or menu tree entries appear in one file. Anchors help the user move from topic to topic. Users rely on a table of contents to go directly to a topic, making it easy for first-time users to explore the application. In addition, the layout makes the help file read more like the manual it's designed to replace. The use of a table of contents makes information easy to find. The negative aspect is that the large file size will cause some users to think twice before downloading the file.

Small Menu/Dialog Control   Each menu item or dialog box control appears in a separate file. Users will benefit from the short download times, which will enable users to use help even when connected through a dial-up line. Users will find information fast since they see only one screen. Updates are faster and more reliable since the information only appears in one file. The drawback is that first-time users will find the constant download of information for each menu item or dialog control frustrating, especially when a dial-up connection is used. A table of contents won't be an automatic feature and will require separate maintenance time.

Large Task   Each file contains a complete description and procedure for performing a specific task. For example, a file might show how to create a new document. New users will find that they can learn to perform tasks more easily. You can test each task separately, reducing the possibility of mistakes. Large task files allow the writer to include specific screen shots and enhanced graphics. This is the only layout that works for tutorials. This technique is generally unacceptable for advanced users who won't want to wade through entire procedures to find one piece of information. In addition, the help files are harder to update and will require more space on the server. Remote downloads will take a long time.

Small Task   A hierarchical table of contents and a list of tasks organizes the information. Each task is broken into a series of common subtasks. A task overview page covers any special events. The table of contents makes information easy to find. The hierarchical format allows users to drill down to the information they need. Short download time encourages everyone to use help rather than call the help desk for information. Updates consist of changing the information in a single subtask folder. On the down side, there's a possibility of introducing subtle errors into the task procedures. For example, a menu entry may change in one part of the application but not in another.

Connection Type

It's interesting to note that some vendors who use HTML-based help assume that everyone has a T1 connection to the Internet. The truth is that many users rely on a dial-up connection to download their files. Help files are an essential application, unlike many sites that users surf on the Internet. This means you need to keep HTML help fast or the support desk will hear about it. The following list will help you optimize your help file for dial-up connections.

- Use graphics, sounds, and multimedia sparingly. Keep file sizes small by reducing resolution, color depth, or other features.

- Allow users to choose a text-only presentation.

- Reduce content whenever possible, but allow the user to click links that provide additional information.

- Use the right HTML file layout.

Search Capability

Searching a help file for valuable information is what most users do once they get past the novice level. They'll look for some tidbit of knowledge that they need to accomplish a task or an explanation for some control on a dialog box. You can't completely duplicate the search features of Windows Help using HTML help. However, there are ways you can mimic the search capability of Windows help. The following list provides a few ideas you can use.

- Create an index.

- Define additional links.

- Add a table of contents.

- Produce a hot topics list.

- Add a Search page that relies on the search capabilities of your server.

It's unlikely that you'll create a word-for-word index like the one provided with Windows Help. This means the user will always have some question that you didn't anticipate and the search features of your HTML-based help file won't be able to answer. It always pays to provide a comment page so users can request additional links.

Standard Windows Help

If you choose the standard Windows help file, the Microsoft Help Workshop will aid you in creating help project files and compiling them from within Windows. Standard Windows help files rely on Rich Text Format (RTF) files formatted with special footnotes. For example, the $ footnote represents a topic title, # is a topic identifier (like an anchor on a web page), K is a keyword used for searching, and @ is used for comments. Formatting includes using the outlining suggestions found in the "Multiple or Single-Page Files?" section earlier in the chapter.

We'll use the RTF files found in the \Chapter 10\Help folder on the CD in this section. Use these files as examples of the types of formatting you can use in a help file.

TIP   RTF files have a standardized format. You can find a complete breakdown of all the tags in an RTF file by looking at the Rich Text Format (RTF) Specification, version 1.6 help topic (`ms-help://MS.VSCC/MS.MSDNVS/Dnrtfspec/html/rtfspec_16.htm`). Windows Help doesn't support the full RTF specification. The Rich Text Format Subset Supported by Windows (`ms-help://MS.VSCC/MS.MSDNVS/kbwin32/Source/win16sdk/q75010.htm`) provides additional information on which RTF features you can use.

Once you create the RTF help files, the first step in creating the new help file is to create a new project. Use the File ➤ New command to display the New dialog. Select Help Project and click on OK to complete the action. The project starts out as a blank page that you fill in with the characteristics of your help file.

Adding Special Effects to a Help File

You can add many enhancements to a help file. For example, you can grab a screen shot of your application and then define hotspots on it with the Hotspot Editor utility (SHED.EXE). You can use BMP, DIB, WMF, and SHG graphics formats with the Hotspot Editor. Files containing hotspots always use the .SHG extension. (Note that you might not find SHED.EXE installed with Visual Studio .NET, but this utility always comes with the Platform SDK.)

Figure 10.1 shows a typical view of the Hotspot Editor. I've opened a screen shot of the Resource example program (from Chapter 5) that we'll use as a topic for the help file. In this case, we're looking at a picture of the main form. I'll add hotspots for each control to make it easy for the user to learn about the application. You can't use the Hotspot Editor to create a new drawing—you'll need a graphics application to do that. The purpose of using the Hotspot Editor is to add places where the user can point and expect something to happen. Every time you see the cursor change from a pointer to a pointing hand in a help file, you're seeing the effect of using the Hotspot Editor.

FIGURE 10.1:

The Hotspot Editor won't allow you to create a new drawing, but it does add hotspots to existing ones.

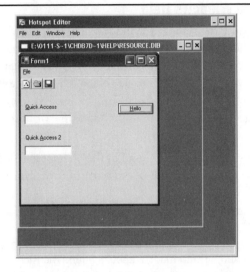

Creating a new hotspot is as easy as dragging the mouse. All you need to do is create a box, and the area within that box becomes the hotspot. Once you create a hotspot, you need to define it. Just double-click on the hotspot and you'll see the Attributes dialog shown in Figure 10.2. Notice that the Hotspot Editor automatically fills some entries in for you, but you can change them as needed.

FIGURE 10.2:

Use the Attributes dialog box to define special characteristics for a hotspot.

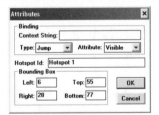

There are three mandatory entries in this dialog: Context String, Type, and Attribute. A context string acts as the second half of a hyperlink. When the user clicks on the hotspot, Windows Help will set the focus to the place in the help file that you've defined. You can choose to make the box surrounding the hotspot visible or invisible. There are three types of hotspots as described in the following list.

Jump   A jump moves the user from one area of the help file to another. Windows Help replaces the contents of the current window with the help topic pointed at by the context string. This hotspot type works well for icons that tell users about other information they can find on a given topic. You could use it to create a "See Also" icon. I also use this type of jump when creating links between a multi-page hierarchical chart. Hotspots allow the user to jump from one place to another without using the Browse buttons. I also use this jump to control pictures used to simulate the display the user will find in an application.

Pop-up   A pop-up displays the help topic associated with the hotspot in a dialog/message box window. You'll find that this kind of a jump is used most often with control descriptions or other pictorial-type hotspots. Since the user doesn't leave the picture, they can easily select other controls. I also use this hotspot in tutorial-type help files in the question-and-answer section. An Answer button displays a pop-up window containing the answer to a question, which remains visible for reference in the original window.

Macro   The macro hotspot allows you to play back a predefined macro. You'll find that macros are a powerful (and underused) feature of Windows Help. You can even use macros to call programs or reprogram the way that Windows Help works.

TIP   The Microsoft Help Compiler provides many predefined macros. For example, you can use the SetPopupColor macro to change the color of a pop-up window. Attaching macros to a button or menu will give users control over the help window and enhance their ability to use it. One way to combine a macro with a bitmap is to create a bitmap of colored squares. When a user clicks on a colored square, the color of the help windows changes.

The Attribute dialog contains a few optional entries. One is the Hotspot ID field. It tells the Hotspot Editor how to identify this particular hotspot. The other four entries define the bounding box for the hotspot. You can use these entries to fine-tune a box's position or size. However, the user won't notice if the hotspot is a pixel or two off, as long as the hotspot is available for use.

You may need to redefine a hotspot. Hotspots are easy to find if you make them visible, but most people don't. So how do you find a hidden hotspot on a complex drawing? The Edit ➤ Select command provides the answer. It displays the Select dialog.

The Select dialog lists the hotspots in the current drawing by hotspot identifier, not by context string. Selecting a particular hotspot will display its context string so that you can be sure you have the right one without going to that location on the drawing. The Select dialog also displays the jump type and attribute information.

After you define the hotspots, you may be tempted to save your graphic using the File ➤ Save command; however, you should always save it with an .SHG extension using File ➤ Save As command. The Hotspot Editor doesn't insist you do this, but if you don't, you'll find that you've overwritten your drawing with information that some drawing programs can't read. Since you can't modify your drawing within the Hotspot Editor, you're stuck with an image that you can't change.

Once you have a drawing (or other multimedia element), you can add it to your help file using Microsoft-defined commands that enable you to add graphics or other elements to your help file. The same commands provide control over the placement of these graphics, but I find the positioning mechanism is crude at best. Table 10.1 shows a complete list of the commands you'll use to add multimedia elements to your help file. Note that you can add a T (for transparent) to the three graphics commands listed in Table 10.1. Adding a T changes the background color of the image to match that of the help window.

TABLE 10.1: Multimedia Element Help Commands

Command	Description
{BMR <Filename>}	Displays a graphic on the right side of the display window. You must provide a full filename and extension. Windows Help recognizes bitmaps (BMP, DIB, and WMF files), multiple-hotspot bitmaps (SHG files), and multiple-resolution bitmaps (MRB files).
{BMC <Filename>}	Displays a graphic in the center of the display window.
{BML <Filename>}	Displays a graphic on the left side of the display window.
{MCI_LEFT [<Options>,] <Filename>}	Displays a media control interface (MCI) file on the left side of the display. There's a mistake in the Microsoft Help Workshop help file that says you can only use this option with AVI files. The current version of Windows help supports all MCI formats including WAV, MID, and AVI files. Sticking with these three formats is probably a good idea unless you know the target machine supports other formats. You can also specify one or more options with this command, including EXTERNAL, NOPLAYER, NOMENU, REPEAT, and PLAY. The EXTERNAL option keeps the file outside the help file, reducing the amount of memory the help file consumes when the user loads it. The down side of this option is that you must include the multimedia file as a separate item. Normally, Windows help displays a multimedia player when it displays the file—you can use the NOPLAYER option to prevent this. This option comes in handy if you want to automatically play or repeat a multimedia file. The NOMENU option displays a play bar without the menu button, effectively keeping the display elements of the play bar but removing the user's ability to control playback. The REPEAT option tells Windows Help to play the file again when it finishes playing the first time. The PLAY option automatically plays the file.
{MCI_RIGHT [<Options>,] <Filename>}	Displays an MCI file on the right side of the display.

Defining a Project's Options

By the time you begin a help project, you should have all of the data files created and the graphics files edited using the Hotspot Editor. You'll start a project by defining some of the project options. For example, you should give your help file a name and add copyright information. I always use "Contents" as my main topic, so adding that entry at the beginning is a good idea as well. Click Options and you'll see the Options dialog shown in Figure 10.3.

FIGURE 10.3:

The Options dialog enables you to define the help file project options.

The General tab contains the default topic for the help file. This is an essential entry because the help file might not work properly otherwise. You can also give the help file a title, add copyright and trademark information, and determine what level of output you want to receive from the compiler. In most cases, you'll want to check both Notes and Progress to ensure that you receive complete information about the help file compilation process.

The Compression tab contains options for compressing the content of the help file into a manageable size. In most cases, you'll want to set the compression level to None as you build the help file for testing. Leaving compression off reduces compile time. Once you're satisfied with your help file, you'll want to set compression on. Using the Maximum option ensures that the help file is as small as possible. However, you might want to choose one of the lesser compression options to ensure good help file performance.

The Sorting tab of the Options dialog contains several options that determine how to sort entries. The Non-spacing marks option allows you to ignore non-spacing characters. For example, the circumflex (^) that appears in ê would affect the sort order if you didn't select this option. Another option tells the help compiler to ignore any symbols in the help file when sorting. This is handy if you want to create a non-specialized index for a data entry program or other general application. On the other hand, it would actually get in the way when creating an index for a reference help file. Many C functions begin with an underscore.

Ignoring those underscores would make the function difficult to find. Finally, you can choose something other than commas and colons to separate index entries. The only time you'd need this feature is if you wanted to create a help file based on the output of another application that doesn't support the standard separators.

The Files tab of the Options dialog, shown in Figure 10.4, determines which files you use for a given task. You can change the name of the help file by changing the contents of the Help File field. The help compiler uses the name of the project file as a basis for naming the help file. The Log File field contains the name of a log file. This option isn't required with the help compiler since it also displays errors on screen.

FIGURE 10.4:

Use the Files tab to list the files used in your project.

One of the most important fields on the Files tab is the Rich Text Format (RTF) Files list box. You'll find a list of the files for the current help project here. Clicking the Change button next to the field displays the Topic Files dialog. This is where you add and remove topic files from the list in the FILES section of the project file. The two check boxes at the bottom of this dialog control how the help compiler reacts to your RTF files. The first option tells the help compiler to automatically implement any changes you make to the RTF files during the next compile. If you leave this box unchecked, the help compiler will ignore any changes. The second option is important if you use a double-byte character set (DBCS) within your help file. This option changes the way the help compiler works with your file and allows it to preserve the special characters.

Windows Help offers full text search (FTS)—a database created when you select the Find page of the Help Topics dialog. FTS allows you to search an entire help file word-by-word. The FTS tab of the Options dialog contains an option to generate this file at the time you compile the help file. Since Windows automatically generates the GID file, most developers leave this option blank. The GID file that the help compiler creates takes up a lot of room on the distribution disks and increases compile time considerably.

You'll want to spend some time learning to use the Macros tab. It helps you to define keyword macros to use on a file-wide basis. These macros also appear on the Index page of the Help Topics dialog when the user searches for a particular topic.

Clicking Add displays a Keyword Macros dialog containing three fields. The first field contains the name of the macro. The second field contains the macro itself. The third field contains a string that tells Help Workshop how to display the macro on the Index page. Use this entry when you have more than one help file and want to display a particular keyword file-wide. For example, I often place the glossary and list of acronyms in a separate file and then use the JI macro to create a file-wide jump to them. The keyword macro is the method I use to do this. The user never even realizes that he or she has loaded another file—it's that transparent.

The Build Tags tab of the Options dialog helps you use build (*) tags found within the RTF files. The main idea is to provide Help Workshop with a list of build tags that you want to include in a help file. Even if an RTF file contains other topics, it won't include them in the help file if you don't include the build tag. If you leave this page blank, Help Workshop assumes you want to include all RTF file topics as part of the final help file.

The Fonts tab of the Options dialog customizes the fonts used for the help file. The Character Set field selects a character set for your help file; the default is ANSI. You can also choose from language types such as Arabic. The Font in WinHelp Dialog Boxes field defines a default font type. Click Change and you'll see a Font dialog containing three fields. The first defines the font name, the second the font point size. The third field defines the character set. The list box below the Font in WinHelp Dialog Boxes field changes the general fonts used within the Windows help file—substituting one font for another. The Add button displays an Add/Edit Font Mapping dialog that contains two groups of three fields. The three fields are the same as the ones used in the Font dialog. The settings on this tab won't work if your word processor overrides the settings—something that generally happens if you use a product like Word for Windows.

Defining Windows

Defining options is only the first phase of creating a project file—you need to define some windows to display your data. The example uses one window called Main. Ancillary windows may include a Glossary window to display terms. To create a window, click Windows in the Main window to display the Window Properties dialog shown in Figure 10.5.

FIGURE 10.5:

The Window Proper-
ties dialog enables
you to define new win-
dows for your project.

FIGURE 10.5:

The Window Proper-
ties dialog enables
you to define new win-
dows for your project.

The General window is where you'll start. Click Add and you'll see an Add a New Window dialog with two fields. One field contains the name of the window; the other field contains the window type. Help Workshop creates three window types: procedural, reference, and error message. There's little difference between the procedural and reference windows. Both auto-size and contain the three system buttons. The big difference between the two is their placement on screen. The error message window differs from the other two in that it doesn't include the three system buttons. It looks somewhat like a dialog.

The Title Bar Text field on the General tab determines what Windows Help places on the title bar. This entry doesn't affect the appearance of the topic title area of the Help window. The Comment field places a comment next to the entry in the project file. There are also three attribute check boxes. Help Workshop may disable one or more of these checkboxes, depending on the situation. For example, you can't make the main help window auto-sizing. If you make an ancillary window auto-sizing, you can't maximize it when it opens. Most procedural windows default to staying on top.

You'll usually want to spend some time working with the Position tab of the Window Properties dialog. There are four fields on the Position tab: Left, Top, Width, and Height. These control the size and position of your window. I normally position my first help window in the upper-left corner and use a size of either 640 X 480 or 800 X 600, depending on the capabilities of the target machine for my application. This may seem a bit small, but the user can always resize the window as needed. Trying to find a help window on an older display when the programmer positions it near one of the edges is frustrating, to say the least. I really like the Adjust for User's Screen Resolution option on this page, because it prevents the help window from becoming totally hidden when the user has a low-resolution display.

There's one special feature on the Position tab that you may not notice at first. Look at the Auto-Sizer button. Clicking on this button displays an example window. If you change the window's position, the Left and Top field values also change. Resizing the window changes the value of the Width and Height fields. This graphic method of changing window size reduces the number of times you have to recompile the help file to take care of aesthetic needs.

There are situations where you may not want to add all of the default buttons normally provided by Windows Help to your help file. For example, the Browser buttons aren't important if you don't define a browse (+ footnote) in one of your RTF files. The Buttons tab shown in Figure 10.6 permits you to define the buttons used with your help window. Note that Microsoft Help Workshop automatically disables and enables options as needed for specific window types.

The Color tab contains two fields: Nonscrolling Area Color and Topic Area Color. Each has a Change button. Click Change to display a color palette. Selecting a different color from the palette changes the appearance of the help window.

The Macros tab displays the macros defined for your help file. The Main window always uses the macros in the CONFIG section of the project file. The macros you see in this section are self-executing—that's why Help Workshop adds the macros in the CONFIG section to the Main window. Adding a new macro to the Main window always adds it to the CONFIG section of the help project file. Adding macros to other windows changes the way those windows appear in comparison to the Main window. For example, if you add a browse to one of the ancillary windows, you might need to add macros to handle new conditions. Each ancillary window has a special CONFIG-<window name> section in the help project.

Mapping Help Topics

If you don't map the topic identifiers in your help file to a help context number, you can't attach context-sensitive help to the controls in your application. You'll see how this works in the section that follows on adding context-sensitive help to your application.

Adding a map is easy. Click Map to display the Map dialog. This is where you define the relationship between a topic identifier and a context number. The topic identifier is set equal to a help context number. It's followed by a comment that describes the entry.

There are many ways to keep the context numbers straight. I usually start at 1 and count up until I reach the last topic identifier for small help files. Large help files require something a bit more complex, or you'll find yourself reusing numbers. Use a three- or four-digit number in this case. The first two numbers are the position of the control or menu item described by the help context within the application. For example, the File menu is normally 01 and the Edit menu is 02. A description of the File ≻ New command would receive a help context number of 0101, since the New option is usually the first entry on the File menu. I assign a value of 0001 to the first non-application topic. (For example, the glossary would fall into this category.) The first two numbers for a control on the form of an application would be one greater than the last menu item. I use the tab order for the last two numbers since it's unlikely that a label or other non-active component would ever appear in the help file.

Add a new map entry by clicking Add. You'll see the Add Map Entry dialog. This dialog contains three fields: topic identifier, mapped numeric value (help context number), and a comment. Fill out the three fields and click OK to add a new map to the project.

You'll want to include an HM file with your help file to reduce the amount of work you do and to provide a quick and easy method for checking your work. Nothing is more frustrating than to release a help file that you thought was complete at the time of testing but turns out to be missing one or more crucial entries after you release it. Click Include to include a file. You'll see an Include File dialog. This dialog provides a Browse button so you can search for your include file on the hard drive. The Browse button opens a standard Open dialog, just like the ones you've used with other applications.

Compiling Your Help File

Once you get a help project file put together, it's time to try to compile it. Click Save and Compile at the bottom of the Main window. The Help Workshop window will minimize while it compiles the help file. This allows you to work on something else (compiling a large help file can take a long time). Once the compilation is complete, you'll see a window similar to the one shown in Figure 10.7.

Figure 10.7 shows what happens when your help file compiles correctly. You'll see which files Microsoft Help Workshop processed, some statistics about the help file, the effects of compression, and the compile time. You'll also see notes if the help compiler found errors in the help files or associated project. (For example, you might see an error message for missing file maps or missing jumps.)

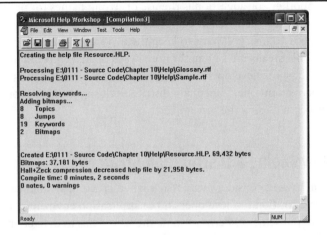

FIGURE 10.7:

This compilation screen shows the current status of the help file and any error messages.

Working with Assemblies

The .NET way of development applications presents several new challenges when you want to distribute your application. For one thing, as we discussed previously, .NET avoids DLL hell by tying the application you create to a specific version of the .NET Framework. The same policy holds true for any public assemblies (those registered in the GAC) that you create for distribution with the application. The only problem is that the user might not have a copy of your version of the .NET Framework and public assemblies installed on their drive. We'll see in the "Creating a Distribution File" section that this change in development strategy means that your distribution disks will consume more space. The application package must include the common as well as the unique files in order to run.

Private assemblies require special handling as well. The installation program must install any private assemblies in the same directory as the application. Unlike previous development products, .NET looks for assemblies in specific locations. If it doesn't find the assembly, it won't load it and the application will fail. This means you can't place a private assembly in a central location and allow more than one application to use it. Each application must have its own copy of the private assembly.

Installation programs commonly use compressed files to save space on the distribution media. Windows must decompress any assemblies that appear in compressed form (such as a CAB file) into a temporary directory. The next step is to move the assembly to its final location. In the case of a public assembly, this means using a utility such as GACUtil to register the assembly in the GAC.

Another consideration is the use of strong names for public assemblies. (We discussed this issue in several places in Chapter 6.) Creating a strong name means signing it with a private key. Of course, you want to keep the private key in a safe place to ensure that no one else uses it. This means the key might not always be in a convenient location for development. As a result, some developers will delay signing their assemblies—using a temporary key in place of a permanent one. When you distribute the application, you must ensure that all assemblies are signed using the private key.

Developing a Distribution Strategy

You have to consider many issues when creating an application package. The most important consideration for developers is the application environment. An in-house developer won't have the same concerns as someone who plans to deliver an application for use by someone else. For one thing, the in-house developer probably won't have much time to get an installation program together—time becomes a factor in most in-house situations.

This section looks at the three most common types of installation environments: corporate, shareware, and shrink-wrap. You'll likely fall into one of the three categories, but you may want to look at the other categories since they contain a lot of helpful tips and hints.

Corporate

Corporate programmers have the least to do to beautify their packaging and the most to do to customize it. Let's face it, the corporate programmer doesn't have to impress anyone with fancy graphics or impressive sound effects. A user-friendly and functional interface is enough.

The corporate programmer is often engaged in creating a custom application. It's common for custom applications, especially database applications, to require specialized files. You'll likely need custom settings as well. Creating a custom installation program that works on all the workstations in a corporate environment with little help from the programmer is quite an undertaking. Plan to spend a lot of time hand-tuning the installation program you create.

Media is another category where most corporate installation programs differ from the other two categories. Unless the company you're working for is living in the dark ages, you'll probably use a LAN for distribution purposes. Use this feature to your benefit to create the application package; select the most efficient storage method possible—a large LAN-based file.

Once you've packaged your application on the LAN, add an instruction to the main logon batch file for your server to install the program. The next time the user logs on, your logon batch file will check for the installed application. If it doesn't find the application, the batch file will call the installation program that you've placed on the LAN.

TIP   The corporate setting is one place where using Universal Naming Convention (UNC) paths in place of standard drive identifiers comes in handy. Using a UNC path for the source directory ensures that everyone can access the required source files for your application without too much effort.

The following list has some other packaging issue suggestions to consider. Just select those that fit your programming style and organizational needs.

Absolute Preferences   A shareware or shrink-wrap application author can't assume anything about the application environment. You don't have that problem. All you need to worry about is the differences between the machines on your network. If you set all the machines up the same way, you can assume a default destination. Using UNC paths means you can assume an absolute source since the server path name won't change. You can assume a certain amount about the workstation if your network is small and all the machines have similar capabilities. In sum, this means that you don't have to present the user with as many installation choices and you can substantially reduce the complexity of the installation program.

No Configuration Choices Needed   Just about every shrink-wrap program offers you a choice between three installation configurations: Custom, Typical, and Compact. The Custom choice allows you to choose specific program elements; the Typical configuration is designed for desktop users; the Compact configuration is intended for people who own laptops. In most cases, you can limit your configuration options to two choices: Laptop (Compact) and Desktop (Typical). In fact, you may want to use those terms to keep user confusion to a minimum.

Shareware

Shareware programmers probably have the most challenging job when it comes to packaging their application. One of the main problems is installation size. Unlike the developer who has a high-speed network connection to use or who can distribute an application on CD, the shareware developer usually has to make do with a low-speed modem connection to a BBS, online service, or the Internet. It's hard to convince someone to download a huge file.

NOTE   The file sizes in this section are guidelines only. The disk space or time that a potential user will invest in your product depends on many factors including perceived value and the current level of product exposure. For example, my favorite shareware graphics package takes up a whopping 7MB of hard disk space and is well over 1MB in size when compressed. I still download it because this program is well worth the investment.

Okay, so you're a little limited on space. How do you get around this problem? The key is in how you market your product. Most of the successful shareware products use the same graphics and sounds repeatedly. Instead of using one graphic for the installation program and a totally different graphic for the application itself, the shareware programmer is content to use the same graphic for both the installation program and the application. Using subtle programming techniques could allow you to use the application's icon in several places.

Can a shareware developer create installation programs without graphics or sound? Not likely. If you want someone to pay for the application you've created, you'll need to add a little polish. No one will pay for a drab application, even if it provides good functionality. Obviously, trying to weigh the amount of pizzazz a feature provides against the space it takes up is difficult.

Another problem that a shareware developer runs into is resources. Many shareware developers start out as one-person shops. The developer takes on consulting jobs and other ventures. Time isn't on your side, and it's unlikely you'll have an artist or sound person at your disposal to create the multimedia presentations provided by companies who create shrink-wrap applications. Most people are satisfied if they see a shareware product that's well designed, space-conscious (consumes 10MB or less of hard disk space), and provides at least a modicum of polish.

We haven't yet discussed the biggest problem for shareware developers—compatibility. The installation program is the first place you'll have to deal with compatibility problems such as the level of installation support provided by various versions of Windows. For example, newer versions of Windows include support for MSI (Microsoft Installation) files and vendor information, while older versions of Windows still require the use of InstallShield in many situations. Differences in machine configurations come in place, with some installation programs performing a compatibility check before they do anything else. Corporate developers can get by with a minimum of machine checks and configuration options. Shrink-wrap developers come next—they can print a set of requirements on the box to ensure that no one will use their application without sufficient hardware. The shareware developer has no such guarantees. A user of your program could have just about any kind of machine ever made—including an old 8088 PC.

What does this lack of control mean? First, you'll have to build extra detection routines in your installation program to ensure that the client meets minimum hardware requirements. Users will rarely read the README file you provide (the one stating the minimum requirements for using the application) and are unlikely to pay attention to them if they do. When the installation fails, users are going to blame you, not their lack of attention. Therefore, you have to build in some type of hardware detection. You'll also need to include application configuration flexibility. For example, you may decide to let the user configure the application for text mode only and forgo those fancy graphics or sounds on an older-technology machine.

The shareware developer does have a few tricks for making the installation program easier to use. While the following list isn't inclusive of everything you could try, it does provide some ideas on what might work. You'll need to try a variety of packaging techniques with your application before you come up with something that works all the time.

Granular Packaging   One way to get around hard disk-space and download-time problems is to package the application in several pieces. For example, you could place the main program in one package, the graphics in another, and the sounds in a third package. The users can choose what level of support they're willing to pay for in download time and hard disk space. This concept doesn't come without a price, though. You have to write your application to work without graphics and sounds—or whatever elements you decide to place in a separate package. Your installation program has to provide similar flexibility. It has to know what do to if a user decides to download one packaging element but not another.

Amplified Help   We discussed the idea of creating separate packages for help files earlier in this chapter. One of the ways you can do this is to make a main and an amplifying help file. The main help file would contain explanations for basic commands, while the amplifying help file could contain user tutorials, macro language descriptions, and detailed command descriptions. Again, the user could decide what level of help to pay for in the form of download time and disk space.

Shrink-Wrap

This section concentrates on what you can learn from shrink-wrap vendors. One of the factors that set a shrink-wrap product apart from shareware is the size of the company producing the application. Larger software companies usually concentrate on one or more products and they have a large professional group of people to help put the packaging together. However, the average programmer can learn a few things by looking at these shrink-wrap packages.

I've taken notes whenever I installed a shrink-wrap or shareware product over the last few years. Recently, I decided to look over those notes. The results were surprising. For example, the previous section mentions using the installation program as a means to sell your product if you're a shareware vendor, since you have a captive audience and fewer sales resources at your disposal. It may surprise you to find that shrink-wrap software commonly uses the installation program for this purpose, but in a different way than a shareware vendor would use it. The user has already purchased the product they're installing, but how about add-on products? Shrink-wrap vendors commonly use the installation program to sell add-on products that relate to the application the user is installing.

In many cases, large companies will supply demonstration versions of other products on the same CD as the product the user is currently installing. The installation program will often ask if the user would like to install these demonstration programs. This technique enables the vendor to use CD space more efficiently and advertise other products. The end user gains by having a better understanding of the vendor's product line.

Shrink-wrap software commonly tells the user what's new about the program during the installation process. They figured out long ago that most users don't read the README file, and the installation program is usually the last part of the product to get finished. The shrink-wrap vendor has a captive audience, so it uses the installation program to give users an overview of what they would learn if they'd actually read the README file.

Vendors pack shrink-wrap installation programs with lots of multimedia presentation materials. Even if you don't have the resources to duplicate the presentation provided by a shrink-wrap vendor, you can make notes to determine what works and what doesn't. Providing a smaller version of the same type of presentation in your installation program is one way to make it look more polished. Creating a nice-looking installation program won't make your application work better, but it will affect the user's perception of your application, which is a very important part of getting the user up and running with a minimum of support.

There are some negative lessons you can learn from shrink-wrap vendors as well. For example, you can make your installation program too complex to test thoroughly. I recently tried installing one product and found that the help screens for the program were for the previous version. The vendor had forgotten to update the screens as needed for the new version of its product. The result? Since the product didn't come with any printed documentation, I didn't have a clue as to whether I should install certain product features. If the vendor had tested the program fully, I would have had the information needed to make an informed feature installation decision.

Creating a Distribution File

Visual Studio .NET includes several projects for distributing your application. The easiest project is the Setup Wizard. This project leads you through the process of creating a simple distribution package that will work for most simple applications and a few of the complex application types. The following steps show how to use the Setup Wizard.

1. Start the Setup Wizard by selecting the Setup Wizard project in the Setup and Deployment Projects dialog box shown in Figure 10.8. Type a name for the project, then click OK. Note that the example uses a name of ResourceSetup1 and you'll find this project in the \Chapter 10\ResourceSetup1 folder on the CD. You'll see the Setup Wizard (Step 1 of 4) dialog box.

FIGURE 10.8:

FIGURE 10.8:

Visual Studio .NET provides several methods for creating an application package.

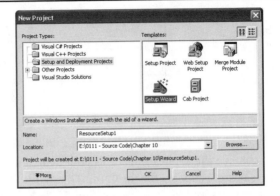

2. Click Next. The Setup Wizard will ask you to select a project type. The first set of radio buttons enables you to choose between a Windows (desktop) and a Web installation. Select between these two options if you want to create an installation file for a complete application. The second set of radio buttons lets you select between a MSI (Microsoft Installer) or a CAB file. The CAB file tends to be smaller, but doesn't offer the features and flexibility of an MSI file. Select between these two options to create an installation file for an application component, such as optional application features or common files used in more than one application. The example uses the Windows option.

> **TIP** If you decide to use MSI file distribution for most of your projects, you'll want to install the Windows Installer SDK (`http://msdn.microsoft.com/downloads/sample.asp?url= msdn-files/027/001/530/msdncompositedoc.xml`). The SDK includes several tools not found in Visual Studio .NET, including the ORCA tool used to modify the MSI database. In addition, the SDK contains a wealth of documentation about MSI files and presents a few concepts not found in the Visual Studio .NET documentation.

3. Select a project option, and then click Next. The Setup Wizard will ask which files you want to include in your project. You must select all of the files used for the application. This includes all private assemblies but no public assemblies. The example uses the `Resource.EXE` file from Chapter 5 and the `Resource.HLP` file we created earlier in that chapter.

4. Select the files required for the project by clicking Add. Use the Remove button to remove any unneeded files. Click Next. The Setup Wizard will display a summary of your project. Make sure the summary includes all of the project files you'll need.

5. Click Finish. You'll see a File System window similar to the one shown in Figure 10.9. Notice that the Setup Wizard automatically creates three folders for application files. You can create other folders, rearrange the files, and otherwise set up the application as needed.

FIGURE 10.9:

Even a simple installation program requires that you check the location of each installed file.

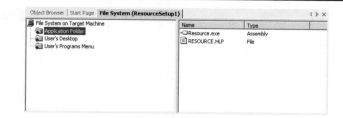

6. Arrange the files as required, and then compile the application.

If you compile the application at this point, you'll notice an error message stating that the package is missing support for the DOTNETFX.EXE file. This file contains the .NET Framework version required for your application. If you're designing a package for corporate use and know that everyone already has the .NET Framework installed, you can safely ignore this message. A shareware distributor will probably want to make the .NET Framework a separate download and definitely include it as a separate install. The elimination of the .NET Framework reduces the size of the installation package considerably. (In fact, a shareware developer will likely want to provide the MSI file alone and tell the user how to install by right-clicking the file.) Of course, a shrink-wrap developer will want to include the .NET Framework as part of the distribution disk and as part of the standard application installation.

You can compare a package that includes the .NET Framework to one that doesn't by looking at the \Chapter 10\ResourceSetup2 folder on the CD. This project does include support for the .NET Framework. Adding this support is easy; just right-click dotnetfxredist_x86_enu.msm entry under the Detected Dependencies folder in Solution Explorer and clear the Exclude entry on the context menu. As an alternative, you can also create a custom merge module containing only the .NET Framework elements your application needs. Exercise care if you use this option, because assemblies are often interdependent.

Where Do You Go From Here?

This chapter has taught you about help files, packaging strategies, and the packaging methods provided by Visual Studio .NET. The art of packaging an application is one that many developers never learn. However, as you can see from this chapter, creating a good application package is important to ultimate user acceptance of your application.

Unfortunately, the art of creating an application package is highly subjective. A technique that works well for one application might not work particularly well for another. As a result, you need to perform actual user testing with the entire application package, including the help file. This is one task you'll need to perform with each application you develop. It's also one of the areas where you'll constantly learn as you develop new applications.

Chapter 11 moves from working with individual applications and components to the larger world of the database. The database application is the most common application created by developers today, and there is no sign that another application type will take its place in the future. Databases come in all shapes and sizes; they store data in many ways and in many formats.

PART III

Database Application Development with C#

CHAPTER 11

Using Databases

- ODBC, ODBC.NET, OLE-DB, ADO, and ADO.NET Essentials

- An Overview of the System.Data Assembly

- Writing an ODBC.NET Application

- Troubleshooting Techniques for LAN-Based Applications

- Performance Tips for LAN-Based Applications

- Writing an OLE-DB Application

- Working with Crystal Reports

Database applications represent the single largest application category that developers create today. In fact, database management has been a major category of application development almost from the time that the computer first appeared on the scene. Companies have huge quantities of data to manage, and computers provide the best way to perform that task efficiently.

Because databases represent such an important area of application development, they've also undergone the most significant amount of change. Every day someone comes out with a new database technology that promises better data protection, faster data transfer, and more efficient storage. Microsoft is no exception to the rule, which is why we'll look at so many database technologies in this chapter.

Of course, simply managing the data isn't enough. There are many people who will never use your database application, yet the impact of your application on their daily work is profound. Most of these people will judge the quality of your application by the reports that it outputs to the printer. This chapter will also discuss the issue of reports by showing how to work with Crystal Reports.

ODBC, ODBC.NET, OLE-DB, ADO, and ADO.NET Essentials

Microsoft has produced so many database technologies over the years that many of them have faded into obscurity—used by a few hardy souls who have to maintain existing applications. For example, those of you who rely on Data Access Objects (DAO) technology will need to move to something new if you want to work with .NET.

NOTE   You can find additional details about this problem in the Microsoft Knowledge Base topic, "INFO: Microsoft .NET Framework Does Not Support Data Access Object (Q311058)." This article is found at `http://support.microsoft.com/default.aspx?scid=kb;en-us;` `Q311058`.

However, there are five existing technologies that you should know about. Why so many? Each of these technologies has a different purpose in life and each has different strengths. Some developers will attempt to use a single technology for all of their needs, and they might even succeed; but generally, you should use the technology best suited to meet the needs of a particular application. This section of the chapter will explore each technology and help you understand the situations where a particular technology works best.

The sections that follow do concentrate on Open Database Connectivity (ODBC), ODBC.NET, and Object Linking and Embedding–Database (OLE-DB). ActiveX Data Objects (ADO) and ADO.NET are such important technologies that we'll explore them in much greater detail in Chapters 12 and 13. However, because the technologies are interrelated, you'll find out a little bit of information about all of them here.

We'll also explore some of the tasks you'll need to perform in order to use these technologies in an application. For example, if you want to use ODBC or ODBC.NET, you'll need to create a data source. The sections that follow not only show you how to create a data source, but they also show how to log ODBC transactions as well. In short, this is the section that will prepare you for the examples that follow.

When Should You Use ODBC, ODBC.NET, OLE-DB, ADO, or ADO.NET?

It's never easy to figure out which database connection technology to use, especially when the usage environment changes constantly. You may need a common utility to handle more than one database type; part of your data may appear on a local hard drive, part on a network, and still other parts on a mainframe. There's also the question of database management system (DBMS) support for the access technology you want to use. Not all DBMS vendors have providers that work with newer technologies such as ADO.

Even the products that a client normally installs on their machine may make the choice more difficult. For example, the level of ODBC support you can expect might rely on which version of Microsoft Office is installed, since this product does provide ODBC support. You'll also find that ADO classes offer more objects and methods than ODBC classes do. ADO may offer some features you absolutely have to have in your program—for example, you'll find that both OLE-DB and ADO support the currency data type, which has no counterpart in ODBC—but you'll pay a penalty in speed to get them.

There are a few general rules of thumb you can use for making the choice between OLE-DB and ODBC. Since ADO is actually a wrapper for OLE-DB, these same rules apply to it. You'll find the .NET choices make good sense as extensions to existing technology. The following list provides some guidelines you can use to help make the decision between the various database technologies.

Non-OLE Environment   If you're trying to access a database that already supports ODBC and that database is on a server that doesn't support OLE, then ODBC is your best choice.

Non-SQL Environment   Microsoft designed ODBC to excel at working with SQL. However, many vendors provide ODBC drivers now, making ODBC the best compatibility choice. If your vendor does supply an OLE-DB provider, OLE-DB might be the better choice, especially for new coding projects.

OLE Environment   The choice between OLE-DB and ODBC may be a toss-up when looking at a server that supports OLE. Normally, it's a good idea to use ODBC if you have an ODBC driver available; otherwise, OLE-DB may be your only choice.

Interoperability Required   If you need interoperable database components, OLE-DB is your only choice. OLE-DB provides a broad range of low-level methods that enable a developer to create robust applications that don't rely on DSNs and do offer maximum flexibility.

Distributed Application Environment   If you need to service users on the road, you have two good choices. Use ADO.NET if you're working with new code and want to gain the maximum benefit from new .NET Framework features. On the other hand, use ODBC.NET if you need to update older code or require maximum compatibility with existing databases.

Extended Application Environment   Many companies today find themselves with a fully developed database application that works fine on a LAN, but fails when working with partners over an Internet connection. Because the Internet has become such a big part of business-to-business communication, you need to use matching technologies to extend the existing application. For example, you'd use ODBC.NET with an application that already uses ODBC.

Disconnected Application or Real-Time Connection   All of the .NET database technologies focus on the distributed environment, disconnected application scenario. The reason for this orientation is that older Microsoft technologies already provide for the scenario where you want to maintain the database connection. You must choose between technology types based on the kind of connection your application requires. For example, use ADO if you need to maintain the connection in the background, but use ADO.NET if the disconnected application scenario is more important.

Other issues tend to compound the problem, or, at least, complicate the rules that you use to differentiate the two technologies. For example, ADO and ODBC have many of the same features in common. One of these is that Visual C++ allows you to access either technology directly. (The access you gain from C# depends on the technology you choose to use, the provider vendor, and the type of access you require—some types of access will require you create a wrapper in Visual C++, then use the resulting DLL in C#.) This means you'll always have full access to every feature that both ADO and ODBC can provide.

Some of these technological similarities actually help you move your application from ODBC to ADO, or vice versa, if you make a wrong decision. Both technologies rely on database objects to manage the underlying DBMS, while recordset objects contain the results of queries made against the DBMS. In addition, both ODBC and ADO use database and recordset objects with similar members. Even though you'll need to make some changes to class and member names, you'll find that the code for ODBC and ADO programming is remarkably similar.

There's one place where you absolutely can't use ADO. If you need 16-bit data access, ADO is out. You'll have to use ODBC whether you want to or not. However, very few people are even working with 16-bit databases anymore. Most of your new projects will use 32-bit interfaces, which means you'll have a choice. Since old projects already have a data access method embedded in the code, you really won't need to make a decision there either.

One area where ODBC falls short is that you can't follow transactions as precisely as you can with ADO. When using ADO, you get workspace-level support for transactions. ODBC only offers transaction support at the database level, which means that you could be tracking transactions from several different workspaces at once. (This lack of functionality makes debugging very difficult, and it could cause other kinds of problems as well.)

The biggest rule of thumb to remember is that you need to study your options and not assume anything about a database technology. When it comes to database technology, .NET isn't an all-inclusive option. If you relied on ADO in the past, you'll very likely rely on ADO now. Only if you want to create a distributed application will you need to move to ADO.NET. Microsoft oriented ADO.NET toward the Internet and made the disconnected application a focal point.

An Overview of ODBC.NET

ODBC has been one of the mainstays of database connectivity for Microsoft developers for a long time. When Visual Studio .NET appeared on the scene without a hint of ODBC connectivity, developers were understandably concerned (irate is more like it). After a lot of consideration, Microsoft determined that ODBC connectivity might be a good idea after all and began development of ODBC.NET. Unfortunately, ODBC.NET appeared on the scene well after the rest of Visual Studio .NET and won't ship with the product—you'll need to download it as a separate product and install it on your system separately.

At the time of this writing, ODBC.NET is still in beta. Some of the issues I raise in this chapter might not exist when you use the release version of ODBC.NET. However, the ODBC.NET beta has been around long enough that it's feature-complete and you should be able to use the code in the chapter without making any tweaks.

NOTE   You won't see ODBC.NET in the Visual Studio .NET package because ODBC.NET got a late start. It appeared in released form a few months after the release of Visual Studio .NET. Download the current released version at `http://msdn.microsoft.com/downloads/sample.asp?url=/MSDN-FILES/027/001/668/msdncompositedoc.xml` or `http://www.microsoft.com/data/`. You can also learn about the latest ODBC.NET developments on the `microsoft.public.dotnet.framework.odbcnet` newsgroup. Make certain that you read the online documentation for any late breaking news before you download and install the product. Otherwise, you might find that the current product implementation breaks some part of your development environment.

After you install the ODBC.NET provider, you'll find a new namespace on your system: `System.Data.Odbc`. The new namespace uses the same four objects as ADO.NET, so you have access to a `Connection`, `Command`, `DataReader`, and `DataAdapter` object. Working with the namespace is similar to working with the two ADO.NET namespaces. However, you have the same options that you would with any ODBC implementation. For example, you can use Data Source Names (DSNs) to create a connection to a data source.

Windows supports three basic types of DSNs: User, System, and File. The User and System DSNs are essentially the same. However, the User DSN affects only the current user, while the System DSN affects everyone who logs onto the current machine. The File DSN is a text representation of a DSN. You can open a File DSN in a program like Notepad and see how it's put together. The following sections provide an overview of ODBC.NET, show you how to create the three DSN types, and discuss logging the ODBC activities on your system.

Now that you have some idea of what ODBC.NET can do for you, let's look at it in detail. You'll find out how ODBC.NET compares to standard ODBC, how to install ODBC.NET on your system, how to create DSNs, and how to log ODBC transactions.

ODBC versus ODBC.NET

The biggest plus of using ODBC.NET is that you gain all of the benefits of a managed environment. You won't have to worry about memory management. In addition, ODBC.NET appears as part of the .NET Framework after you install it. You'll use the `System.Data.Odbc` namespace. ODBC.NET relies on the same techniques that you use with ADO.NET and OLE-DB to create code. Of course, the connection technology still relies on the Data Source Names (DSNs) that you've used in the past.

ODBC.NET doesn't add any new features to the world of ODBC. In fact, you'll find ODBC.NET imposes some new and not so exciting limitations because of the managed environment. For example, you'll have limited access to ODBC providers, (which begs the question of why Microsoft changed this functionality). One of the big reasons to use ODBC in the past was that it's compatible with so many vendor products. (Even though Microsoft's website states that ODBC.NET will work with all compliant ODBC drivers, they also state that the product had only been tested with Microsoft specific offerings. Initial testing shows that many third party drivers do experience problems such as reduced functionality with ODBC.NET.) ODBC.NET is only compatible with these providers:

- Microsoft SQL ODBC Driver

- Microsoft ODBC Driver for Oracle

- Microsoft Jet ODBC Driver

NOTE   The problem of provider support is universal in the .NET Framework. OLE-DB .NET (and by extension, ADO.NET) also suffers loss of functionality due to a lack of provider support. You can find out more about this problem in the Microsoft Knowledge Base article entitled, "INFO: OLE DB .NET Managed Provider Does Not Support Some OLE DB Providers in Visual C# .NET (Q312794)" found at `http://support.microsoft.com/default.aspx?scid=kb;en-us;Q312794`.

In many cases, the providers supplied with ODBC.NET are less capable than their unmanaged counterparts. While testing the ODBC.NET version that was available at the time of writing, I found that many functions that would normally provide me with some content from the database would return the infamous `E_NOTIMP` (error, not implemented) or `E_NOTIMPLEMENTED` errors. Theoretically, Microsoft will fix these and many errors during a future ODBC.NET release.

ODBC.NET provides access to four data access components that reflect its managed orientation. These are the same four objects that you use with other .NET database technologies:

Connection   Creates a connection between the application and the data source. You must establish a connection before doing anything else.

Command   Executes some action on the data source. You'll use this object after you create a connection to obtain data access. Commands also enable you to perform actions, such as adding new records and performing database maintenance.

DataReader   Obtains a read-only, forward-only stream of data from the database. This is the object to use for disconnected application scenarios. You also use the DataReader when you want to display data without editing it.

DataAdapter   Obtains a read/write data stream from the database. The application can perform updates and add new records using this object. However, a DataAdapter requires a live connection to the database.

The ODBC.NET help file appears in the \Program Files\Microsoft.NET\Odbc.NET directory of your hard drive. Right now, you can't access it from the Start menu unless you add the link manually. The help file contains a good overview of ODBC.NET, but you'll want to augment this information with some Microsoft Knowledge Base articles. Here's the list of articles that I found most helpful:

- "HOW TO: Use the ODBC.NET Managed Provider in Visual C# .NET and Connection Strings" (`http://support.microsoft.com/default.aspx?scid=kb;EN-US;q310988`).

- "HOW TO: Execute SQL Parameterized Stored Procedures Using the ODBC.NET Provider and C# .NET" (`http://support.microsoft.com/default.aspx?scid=kb;EN-US;q310130`).

- "PRB: Error Unhandled Exception of Type 'System.NotSupportedException' Occurred in System.Data.dll" (`http://support.microsoft.com/default.aspx?scid=kb;en-us;Q310374`).

Installation Requirements for ODBC.NET

You must install a compatible version of Visual Studio .NET before you install ODBC.NET. The ODBC.NET installation program relies on the existence of the .NET Framework, and you'll want the installation program to install any special features in the Visual Studio .NET IDE. ODBC.NET will also require Microsoft Data Access Components (MDAC) version 2.7 or above. Microsoft provides the MDAC support as part of the Visual Studio .NET installation, so you won't need to perform a separate update of this product as indicated on the ODBC.NET download page.

One of the problems you could run into when working with ODBC.NET is that the installation program fails to update the providers correctly. The ODBC.NET installation program not only installs new providers, it updates the Microsoft ODBC Administrator to use the new providers as well. It's important to verify the presence of the new providers by opening the Microsoft ODBC Administrator and viewing the version numbers on the Drivers tab (Figure 11.1). Here's an example of a Microsoft ODBC Administrator display with updated providers.

FIGURE 11.1:

Make sure you have
the correct ODBC dri-
vers installed before
you begin a project.

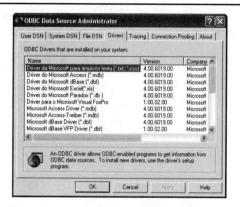

Working with User and System DSNs

Designing a database is the first step of any database application. You need to know how you plan to store and access data for your application. After you have a database designed, you need to create an ODBC DSN for it. That's what we'll look at in this section. The following procedure shows one technique for getting a data source configured.

WARNING　You'll normally need to create an entry on the User DSN tab for single user databases and on the System DSN tab for machine databases. Under no circumstances create entries that use the same name on both the User DSN and System DSN tabs. In that situation, what will normally happen is that you'll attempt to access the database remotely and get really strange and inconsistent error messages from your server. In fact, the ODBC applet is one of the first places you should look if you get strange error messages during remote database access.

1. Double-click the 32-bit ODBC applet in the Control Panel. (Some versions of Windows use a simple ODBC applet if there are no 16-bit drivers installed on the current system. Windows 2000 and Windows XP place the Data Sources (ODBC) applet in the Administrative Tools folder.) You'll see the ODBC Data Source Administrator dialog.

2. Click the Add button. You'll see a Create New Data Source dialog like the one shown in Figure 11.2.

TIP　You can ensure that you're using the most current ODBC drivers available by checking the Drivers and About tabs of the ODBC Data Source Administrator dialog. These tabs contain the version numbers of the various ODBC DLLs, the name of the vendor who created them, and the name of the file as it appears in the SYSTEM folder. In most cases, you'll be able to use the version number as a method for verifying that your ODBC driver is up-to-date.

The Create New Data
Source dialog box con-
tains a list of all
providers installed on
your machine.

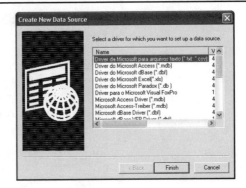

3. Choose one of the data sources. For this exercise, I chose an Access data source.

4. Click Finish and you'll see a configuration dialog similar to the ODBC Microsoft Access
   Setup dialog shown in Figure 11.3. Note that the dialog will contain unique information
   for each database provider because each DBMS requires different configuration information.

ODBC configuration
information varies by
vendor, but every ven-
dor will need some
common information.

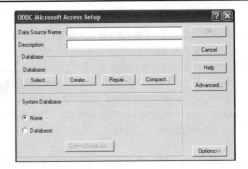

NOTE Steps 5 through 11 only work with the Microsoft Access provider. If you select a data
source different from the one I've chosen in this example, the steps required to configure
it will differ from the ones shown here—each ODBC driver requires a different type of configuration. However, some types of information are always the same. For example, you
must always provide the name of the database and a description of the DSN.

5. Type a data source name in the Data Source Name field. Make sure you choose something descriptive but not overly long. The example uses "Address Database" because the
   DSN will eventually create a link to a simple Address database.

6. Type a description in the Description field. You'll want to make this entry a bit longer than the previous one since it describes the purpose of your database. On the other hand, you don't want to write a novel the size of *War and Peace*. The example uses the following description: "This database contains a contact management list."

7. Click Select. You'll see a Select Database dialog where you can choose an existing database. The example uses the MyData.MDB database found in the \Chapter 11\DSN folder on the CD. The ODBC driver will automatically choose the correct file extension for you.

TIP You don't have to design your database before you create a DSN for it. Notice that the Access ODBC driver also includes a button to create a new database. Most, but not all, ODBC drivers provide this feature. Clicking this button will start the database manager application and help you to design the database. It's interesting to note that the Access ODBC driver also provides options to compress or repair the database from this dialog.

8. Choose a system database option. In most cases, you'll choose None unless you specifically created a system database for your application.

9. Click the Advanced button and you'll see a Set Advanced Options dialog, like the one shown in Figure 11.4. You won't need to modify many of the entries. However, it usually pays to add the Guest user name to the Login Name field and the Guest password to the Password field. This enables a guest to access your database without really knowing anything about the access at all—not even the name the guest used to log in.

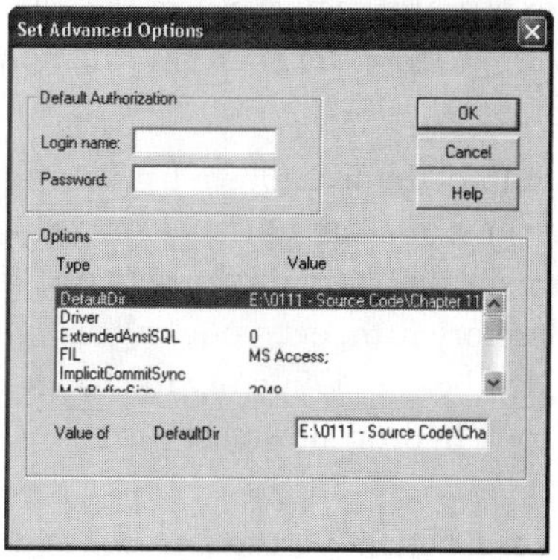

FIGURE 11.4:

The Set Advanced Options dialog box includes features such as the login name and password.

TIP You may want to look through the list of advanced options provided by your ODBC driver for potential areas of optimization. For example, the Access ODBC driver allows you to change the number of threads that the DBMS uses. The default setting of 3 usually provides good performance, but you may find that more threads in a complex application will make foreground tasks run faster. However, using too many threads does have the overall effect of slowing your application down, since Windows uses some processor cycles to manage the thread overhead.

10. Click OK once you've set any advanced options that you need.

11. Click OK again to close the ODBC Microsoft Access Setup dialog. You should see your new entry added to the ODBC Data Source Administrator dialog. If you need to change the settings for the database later, simply highlight it and click on Configure. Getting rid of the database is equally easy. Just highlight the DSN and click on Remove.

Working with File DSNs

You may have noticed a problem with the example in the previous section. It works fine if you want to configure every machine on your network individually, which probably isn't your idea of a good time. There's another way to store the information needed to create a data source: the File DSN. That's what we'll look at in this section. The following procedure will give you a general idea of how to set up a File DSN.

1. Double-click the 32-bit ODBC applet in the Control Panel. You'll see the ODBC Data Source Administrator dialog. Select the File DSN tab. The first thing you'll need to do is choose a place to store the DSN information. The example uses the \Chapter 11\DSN folder on the CD.

2. Click on the Look In drop-down list box. You'll see a list of directories and drives for the current machine. You can use any storage location for the DSN. I normally choose the database storage directory on the network. If you choose a UNC (universal naming convention) directory path, everyone will access the DSN file using the same path. Note that you'll need to click Set Directory to change the default directory to the one you select using the Look In drop-down list.

TIP The Up One Level button (next to the Look In drop-down list) works just the way it does in Explorer. You can use this button to go up one directory at a time. Eventually, you'll end up at My Computer and see a listing of all the drives on your machine.

3. Click Add. You'll see a Create New Data Source dialog.

4. Choose one of the ODBC drivers in the list, and then click Next. For this example, I again chose Access. You'll see the next page of the Create New Data Source dialog. This is where you'll choose a name and storage location for your data source. Click Browse and you'll see a File Open–type dialog box where you can choose a storage location. Type a filename, and the ODBC wizard will automatically add DSN as the extension. I chose SAMPLE.DSN as the name for the DSN file in this example.

5. Click Next and you'll see a summary dialog like the one shown here. It tells you the parameters for the DSN you're going to create.

6. Click Finish. At this point, you'll see a modified version of the ODBC Microsoft Access Setup dialog. You won't be able to add information in the Data Source Name or Description fields like we did in the previous section. However, everything else will work the same way as before.

7. Make sure you enter the name of a database by clicking the Select button and then choosing the database you want to use. (You can also click Create if you want to create a new database.)

8. Click OK when you complete the configuration process. You'll see a new DSN file entry in the ODBC Data Source Administrator dialog.

Unlike the previous DSN that we created, this one actually creates a file that you can view and edit with a text editor. Figure 11.5 shows what the example file looks like. Notice that it follows a standard INI file format. You can see the [ODBC] heading at the top. All of the settings I chose follow. This file will allow application code to choose a data source from C#, yet it's very easy to transfer from machine to machine. The installation code could even change the locations as required during the installation process—this is a real plus when you don't know what kind of setup the user will have.

FIGURE 11.5:

The SAMPLE.DSN file contains all of the settings required to use my database from within C#.

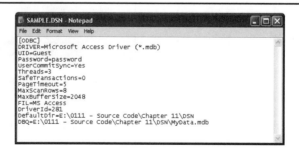

WARNING   There's a bug in the ODBC Administrator. Whenever you create a file DSN, it automatically sets the username value (*UID*) to Admin and the password to blank. If you want to change this value, you must open the file and change it manually. Set the *UID* to any name you wish and add a *Password* entry. Figure 11.5 shows the correct entries for a Guest login. Notice that the password appears in plain text and that anyone could open this file, which is one reason to use it for Guest logins only. This bug has appeared in several versions of Windows, including both Windows 2000 and Windows XP.

Logging ODBC Transactions

It's always nice to have a log of whatever you're doing when it comes time to debug an application. The ODBC Data Source Administrator dialog offers this capability as well as the configuration options we visited earlier. You can choose to track the various transactions you make to a database through ODBC. Of course, these logs can get rather large, so you won't want to use them all the time. Most developers use the logs only during development time, then turn them off for a production application (unless the user sees a bug that you want to track).

To start logging transactions, open the ODBC Data Source Administrator dialog by double-clicking the 32-bit ODBC applet in the Control Panel. Choose the Tracing tab. You'll see a dialog like the one shown Figure 11.6.

FIGURE 11.6:

The Tracing tab contains options for logging each ODBC action on a particular DSN.

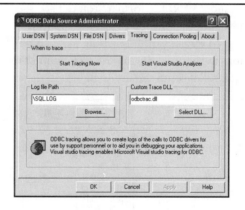

The trace won't start automatically. You'll need to click Start Tracing Now. The push button caption will change to Stop Tracing Now as soon as tracing starts. Click on the button again to turn tracing off.

NOTE   You might see variations in the content of the Tracing tab based on the version of Windows that you use and the Visual Studio features you install. The version shown is for Windows XP with Visual Studio Analyzer installed. In some cases, you'll see three radio buttons that determine when you'll trace the ODBC calls. The default setting is Don't Trace. You'd select All the Time if you were going to work on debugging a single application. The One-Time Only traces the ODBC calls during the next connection—tracing gets turned off as soon as the connection is broken. This is a good selection to choose when a user calls in with a specific problem. You can monitor the connection during one session and then use that information to help you create a plan for getting rid of the bug.

The only other setting that you'll need to worry about is the Log File Path. ODBC normally places the transaction information in the SQL.LOG file in your root directory. However, you may want to place the logging information on a network drive or use a location hidden from the user. The default location normally works fine during the debugging process.

NOTE   Unless you want to create your own logging DLL, don't change the setting in the Custom Trace DLL field. The DLL listed here, ODBCTRAC.DLL, is responsible for maintaining the transaction log.

An Overview of OLE-DB and ADO

One of the more confusing things about working with ADO is understanding that it's not the lowest rung on the ladder. OLE-DB is the basis for anything you do with ADO; it provides the basis for communication with the database. ADO is simply a nice wrapper around the services that OLE-DB provides. In fact, you can even bypass ADO and go right to OLE-DB if you want to. However, using ADO will help you to develop applications much faster. The following sections will help you understand both OLE-DB and ADO.

Understanding OLE-DB

So, what is OLE-DB? As the name implies, it uses OLE (or more specifically, the component object model—COM) to provide a set of interfaces for data access. Just like any other COM object, you can query, create, and destroy an OLE-DB object. The source of an OLE-DB object is a provider. The .NET Framework includes only a few of OLE-DB providers found in the unmanaged version of the product. More will likely arrive as vendors upgrade their database products. The nice thing about OLE-DB is that the same provider works with any Visual Studio product: Visual C++, Visual Basic, and C#.

OLE-DB also relies on events, just as any COM object would. These events tell you when an update of a table is required to show new entries made by other users or when the table you've requested is ready for viewing. You'll also see events used to signal various database errors and other activities that require polling right now.

Microsoft defines four major categories of OLE-DB user. It's important to understand how you fit into the grand scheme of things. The following list breaks the various groups down and describes how they contribute toward the use of OLE-DB as a whole.

Data Provider   A developer who creates an OLE-DB provider using the OLE-DB SDK (Software Development Kit). The provider user interfaces to interact with the database and events to signal special occurrences.

Data Consumer   An application, system driver, or user that requires access to the information contained in a database.

Data Service Provider   A developer who creates stand-alone utilities (services) that enhance the user's or administrator's ability to use or manage the contents of a database. For example, a developer could create a query engine that allows the user to make natural language requests for information in the database. A service works with the OLE-DB provider and becomes an integral part of it.

Business Component Developer   A developer who creates application modules or components that reduce the amount of coding used to create a database application. A component could be something as generic as a grid control that allows you to display a subset of the records in the database at a glance or something specific to the type of database being accessed.

Microsoft designed OLE-DB as an upgrade to ODBC. The fact is that many people still use ODBC because they perceive it as easier to use than OLE-DB or ADO. Note that this view is so pervasive that Microsoft finally created ODBC.NET for those developers who refuse to make the change. In addition, more database vendors provide ODBC access (although this is changing now). So, how does OLE-DB differ from ODBC? Table 11.1 shows the major differences between the two products. We'll discuss how these differences affect your usage decisions later in this chapter.

TABLE 11.1: OLE-DB to ODBC Technology Comparison

Element	OLE-DB	ODBC	Comments
Access type	Component	Direct	OLE-DB provides interfaces that interact with the data. User access to the data is through components designed to interact with OLE-DB.

Continued on next page

TABLE 11.1 CONTINUED: OLE-DB to ODBC Technology Comparison

Element	OLE-DB	ODBC	Comments
Data access specialization	Any tabular data	SQL	Microsoft designed ODBC to use SQL as the basis for data transactions. In some cases, that means the programmer has to make concessions to force the data to fit into the SQL standard.
Driver access method	Component	Native	As mentioned earlier, all access to an OLE-DB provider is through COM interfaces using components of various types. ODBC normally requires direct programming of some type and relies heavily on the level of SQL compatibility enforced by the database vendor.
Programming model	COM	C/C++	OLE-DB relies on COM to provide the programmer with access to the provider. This means that OLE-DB is language independent, while ODBC is language specific.
Technology standard	COM	SQL	OLE-DB adheres to Microsoft's COM standard, which means that it's much more vendor- and platform-specific than the SQL technology standard used by ODBC.

Don't get the idea that OLE-DB and ODBC are two completely separate technologies meant to replace each other. Microsoft provides an ODBC OLE-DB provider that enables you to access all of the functionality that ODBC provides through OLE-DB or ADO. In other words, the two technologies complement each other and don't act as complete replacements for each other. (Unfortunately, this cross compatibility doesn't translate well to the .NET Framework where OLE-DB and ODBC are separate entities.)

Can you replace ODBC with ADO or OLE-DB? Yes, but you won't get the very best performance from your applications if you do. The whole idea of OLE-DB is to broaden the range of database types that you can access with your C# applications. Obviously, if you do need to access both ODBC and tabular data with a single application, OLE-DB provides one of the better solutions for doing so.

Understanding ADO

Now that you have a little better handle on OLE-DB, where does ADO fit in? As previously mentioned, ADO provides an easy method for accessing the functionality of an OLE-DB provider. In other words, ADO helps you to create applications quickly and enables C# to take care of some of the details that you'd normally have to consider when using OLE-DB directly. ADO is a wrapper for OLE-DB and reduces the number of steps required to perform common tasks.

ADO represents a new way to provide database access through the combination of data-bound ActiveX controls and five specialty classes. You can divide the classes into two functional areas: data provider and dataset.

The data provider contains classes that provide connection, command, data reader, and data adapter support. The connection provides the conduit for database communications. The command enables the client to request information from the database server. It also enables the client to perform updates and other tasks. The data reader is a one-way, read-only, disconnected method of viewing data. The data adapter provides the real-time connection support normally associated with live data connections.

The dataset is the representation of information within the database. It contains two collections: `DataTableCollection` and `DataRelationCollection`. The `DataTableCollection` contains the columns and rows of the table, along with any constraints imposed on that information. The `DataRelationCollection` contains the relational information used to create the dataset.

ADO provides several advantages over previous database access methods. The following list will describe them for you.

Independently Created Objects   You no longer have to thread your way through a hierarchy of objects. This feature permits you to create only the objects you need, reducing memory requirements and enhancing application speed.

Batch Updating   Instead of sending one change to the server, you can collect them in local memory and send all of them to the server at once. Using this feature improves application performance (because the data provider can perform the update in the background) and reduces network load.

Stored Procedures   These procedures reside on the server as part of the database manager. You'll use them to perform specific tasks on the dataset. ADO uses stored procedures with in/out parameters and a return value.

Multiple Cursor Types   Essentially, cursors point to the data you're currently working with. You can use both client-side and server-side cursors.

Returned Row Limits   You only get the amount of data you actually need to meet a user request.

Multiple Recordset Objects   Helps you to work with multiple recordsets returned by stored procedures or batch processing.

Free-Threaded Objects   This feature enhances web server performance.

There are two databinding models used for ActiveX controls. The first, simple databinding provides the means for an ActiveX control like a text box to display a single field of a single record. The second, complex databinding enables an ActiveX control like a grid to display multiple fields and records at the same time. Complex databinding also requires the ActiveX control to manage which records and fields the control will display. C# comes with several ActiveX controls that support ADO, including the following:

- DataGrid
- DataCombo
- DataList
- Hierarchical Flex Grid
- Date and Time Picker

Like OLE-DB, Microsoft based ADO on COM. ADO provides a dual interface: a program ID of ADODB for local operations and a program ID of ADOR for remote operations. The ADO library itself is free-threaded, even though the registry shows it as using the apartment-threaded model. The thread safety of ADO depends on the OLE-DB provider that you use. In other words, if you're using Microsoft's ODBC OLE-DB provider, you won't have any problems. If you're using a third-party OLE-DB provider, you'll want to check the vendor documentation before assuming that ADO is thread safe (a requirement for using ADO over an Internet or intranet connection).

You'll use seven different objects to work with ADO. Table 11.2 lists these objects and describes how you'll use them. Most of these object types are replicated in the other technologies that Microsoft has introduced, although the level of ADO object functionality is much greater than that offered by previous technologies.

TABLE 11.2: ADO Object Overview

Object	Description
Command	A command object performs a task using a connection or recordset object. Even though you can execute commands as part of the connection or recordset objects, the command object is much more flexible and allows you to define output parameters.
Connection	Defines the connection with the OLE-DB provider. You can use this object to perform tasks like beginning, committing, and rolling back transactions. There are also methods for opening or closing the connection and for executing commands.
Error	ADO creates an error object as part of the connection object. It provides additional information about errors raised by the OLE-DB provider. A single error object can contain information about more than one error. Each object is associated with a specific event, like committing a transaction.

Continued on next page

TABLE 11.2 CONTINUED: ADO Object Overview

Object	Description
Field	A field object contains a single column of data contained in a recordset object. In other words, a field could be looked at as a single column in a table and contain one type of data for all of the records associated with a recordset.
Parameter	Defines a single parameter for a command object. A parameter modifies the result of a stored procedure or query. Parameter objects can provide input, output, or both.
Property	Some OLE-DB providers will need to extend the standard ADO object. Property objects represent one way to perform this task. A property object contains attribute, name, type, and value information.
Recordset	Contains the result of a query and a cursor for choosing individual elements within the returned table. C# gives you the option of creating both a connection and a recordset using a single recordset object or using an existing connection object to support multiple recordset objects.

Writing an OLE-DB Application

The OLE-DB example will rely on a contact database that contains name and address information for the customers in a company. You'll find the database in the \Chapter 11\DSN folder as MyData.MDB. The example code appears in the \Chapter 11\OLEDB folder on the CD. The following sections show you how to create and code an application that provides both grid and detail views.

> **NOTE**   The examples in this chapter rely on a Microsoft Access database for input. I chose this product because many people ask for Access-specific examples on the various Visual Studio newsgroups and because I've received e-mails asking for this type of example. The examples in Chapters 12 and 13 will rely on SQL Server 2000. The combination of the two database sources should provide you with a better view of how well .NET works for a variety of database application needs. Please feel free to contact me at JMueller@mwt.net with comments.

Creating the Grid View

This example requires more setup than examples in previous chapters. You have to create a connection to the database, provide commands for manipulating the database, use a data adapter to create a place to store the data, and finally, generate a dataset to store the results of the data query. As you'll learn, the Server Explorer in the Visual Studio IDE helps make application creation faster and easier. The following steps show how to use Server Explorer to set up your application.

1. Open the Server Explorer toolbar shown in Figure 11.7 by clicking on the top (rather than the bottom) of the toolbar area on the left side of the Visual Studio IDE. As you can see, this display provides immediate access to local machine resources and data connections. You can also create connections to remote machines.

FIGURE 11.7:

The Server Explorer enables you to create new connections or use existing resources.

2. Right-click Data Connections and choose Add Connection from the context menu. You'll see the Data Link Properties dialog box shown in Figure 11.8. Note that you might have to manually select the Provider tab. Selecting the right provider is an essential part of the application configuration process.

FIGURE 11.8:

Visual Studio .NET includes the list of providers shown in this figure.

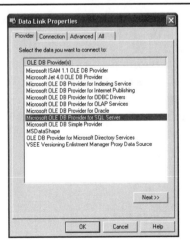

3. Select the Microsoft Jet 4.0 OLE-DB Provider option, and then click Next. You'll see a Connection tab that includes the name of the database and logon credentials.

4. Select the database you want to use (the example uses the `MyData.MDB` file), and then click Test Connection. It's essential to perform the connection test to ensure errors you see in the application aren't due to a lack of access. You should see a Test Connection Succeeded message. If not, try to create the connection again.

NOTE   The Advanced tab contains options that may increase your chances of accessing a database, especially a remote resource. This tab contains options for selecting an impersonation level, protection level, connection timeout, and type of access. The connection timeout value is especially important for Internet resources, because the default timeout assumes a LAN connection. Likewise, the wizard assumes you want to create a Share Deny None connection when you really need a Share Exclusive connection for the application.

5. Click OK to create the connection. The Visual Studio IDE may pause for a few seconds, at this point, to establish the connection. When the IDE establishes the connection, you'll see a new connection in the Server Explorer. An Access database typically provides tables, views, and stored procedures, but you might see other entries within the connection.

6. Locate the Address table in the Tables folder. Drag the Address table to the form. Visual Studio will automatically generate a connection and data adapter for you. Make absolutely certain the data adapter contains entries for the *DeleteCommand*, *InsertCommand*, *SelectCommand*, and *UpdateCommand* properties or the example won't work properly. You'll want to rename the connection and data adapter—the example uses `AddressConnection` and `AddressDA`.

7. Right-click `AddressDA` and choose Generate Dataset from the context menu. You'll see a Generate Dataset dialog box.

8. Type **AddressDataset** in the New field, then click OK. Visual Studio .NET will automatically generate the dataset for you.

The example application uses a menu driven system and includes a toolbar for quick access to commands. It relies on a `DataGrid` control to display the data. One of the `DataGrid` configuration tasks is to ensure the *DataSource* property points to `foDataSet1` and the *DataMember* property points to the `FoodOrders` query. Check the project on the CD for the remaining configuration items.

TIP The toolbar uses standard icons for the Print and Print Preview menu options (among others). You can find a list of standard icons in the \Program Files\Microsoft Visual Studio .NET\Common7\Graphics\bitmaps\OffCtlBr\Small\Color folder of your Visual Studio installation. Add these icons to an `ImageList` control, which you can then access within the `ToolBar` control as a source of images. The example also uses arrows from the \Program Files\Microsoft Visual Studio .NET\Common7\Graphics\icons\arrows folder and modified versions of the arrows found in the \Chapter 11\Graphics folder for record movement icons.

You'll want to pay special attention to the *DataGrid* configuration because some elements aren't obvious. Look at the *TableStyles* property and you'll notice that it's a collection not a single value. Click the ellipses button next to the property and you'll see a DataGridTableStyle Collection Editor dialog, similar to the one shown in Figure 11.9. Notice that this dialog already has an entry in it. You need one entry for each table or query that you want to add to the data grid.

FIGURE 11.9:

The DataGridTable-Style Collection Editor enables you to configure a table for display.

TIP Any modifications you make to the DataGridTableStyle Collection Editor or DataGrid-ColumnStyle Collection Editor dialog box entries will appear in bold type. The use of bold text makes it easy to find any changes you've made.

As you can see, the properties in this dialog box help you set table attributes, such as the default column width and the cell selection color. To make these settings work, you must set the *MappingName* property to the table or query that you want to configure for display. You also need to configure the *GridColumnStyles* property, which is another collection. Click the ellipses button and you'll see a DataGridColumnStyle Collection Editor dialog box, like the one shown in Figure 11.10. This figure also shows the columns required for the example application.

Configuring the table also implies that you'll configure the associated columns.

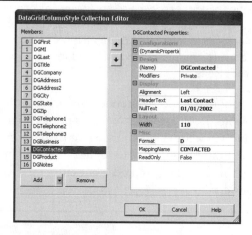

Figure 11.10 shows a typical *DataGridColumnStyle* object entry. You must provide a *MappingName* property value. In this case, the *MappingName* refers to a single column within the table or query. Generally, you'll find that you need to provide values for the *HeaderText*, *NullText*, and *Width* properties. The *Format* property is a special entry that you'll want to use for special value types such as dates and currency. Because the *DataGridColumnStyle* object entry in Figure 11.10 is for a date value, the *Format* property contains an uppercase **D** for a long date format. You'd use a lowercase **d** for a short date format. The .NET Framework provides a wealth of format string values that you can learn about in the Formatting Types (ms-help://MS.VSCC/MS.MSDNVS/cpguide/html/cpconformattingtypes.htm) help topic.

Coding the Grid View

Coding database applications can become quite complex depending on the number of tables and application features you want to provide. However, there are certain coding tasks that every Grid view application will have. The first requirement is some means of filling the grid with data. You'll find the following line of code in the GridView class constructor.

```
AddressDA.Fill(addressDataset1);
```

This line of code tells the data adapter to fill the data set with data. The connection to the data grid is automatic because of the *DataSource* and *DataMember* property entries. The various *MappingName* entries ensure the data appears in the correct order and in the correct format.

While the connection between the dataset and the data grid is automatic, the connection between the dataset and the data adapter isn't. Changing a value in the data grid doesn't guarantee that it will appear in the database as well. In fact, there are a number of conditions that will prevent the data from ever appearing in the database. For example, you can configure the dataset as read-only, which would prevent changes at a basic level. However, for any change to take place, you must detect the change using the CurrentCellChanged() event and then update the data adapter with the new data. Listing 11.1 shows the code you'll need to perform data grid updates.

Listing 11.1   Updating the Data Adapter

```
private void AddrDataGrid_CurrentCellChanged(object sender,
                                            System.EventArgs e)
{
    DialogResult DR;  // Used to store the result of a dialog.

    try
    {
        // Update the record to reflect user changes.
        AddressDA.Update(addressDataset1);
    }
    catch (DBConcurrencyException DBCE)
    {
        // If an error occurs, see if the user wants
        // to exit the application.
        DR = MessageBox.Show("Concurrency Error\r\n" +
                            DBCE.Message + "\r\n" +
                            DBCE.Source + "\r\n" +
                            DBCE.Row + "\r\n" +
                            "Exit Application?",
                            "Database Update Error",
                            MessageBoxButtons.YesNo,
                            MessageBoxIcon.Error);

        if (DR == DialogResult.Yes)
            // Exit the application.
            Close();
        else
        {
            // Otherwise, reject the user changes.
            addressDataset1.RejectChanges();
            addressDataset1.Clear();
            AddressDA.Fill(addressDataset1);
        }
    }
    catch (OleDbException ODBE)
    {
        // If an error occurs, see if the user wants
```

```
                 // to exit the application.
                 DR = MessageBox.Show("OLE-DB Error\r\n" +
                                   ODBE.Message + "\r\n" +
                                   ODBE.Source + "\r\n" +
                                   "Exit Application?",
                                   "Database Update Error",
                                   MessageBoxButtons.YesNo,
                                   MessageBoxIcon.Error);

              if (DR == DialogResult.Yes)
                 // Exit the application.
                 Close();
              else
              {
                 // Otherwise, reject the user changes.
                 addressDataset1.RejectChanges();
                 addressDataset1.Clear();
                 AddressDA.Fill(addressDataset1);
              }
         }
     }
```

The actual update process is easy. All you need to do is call the Update() method of the AddressDA data adapter and supply the data set, *addressDataset1*, as input. However, this can be an error-prone process. The two common exceptions are DBConcurrencyException and OleDbException. You handle both exceptions in the same way. The application displays an error message that tells the user what went wrong and offers a choice of exiting the application or attempting to recover from the error. The update is lost, in either case, and you shouldn't attempt to retry the update.

The three-step recovery process works in most cases. First, you reject the current changes in the dataset using the RejectChanges() method to ensure they don't remain in memory and threaten the stability of your application again. Second, you clear the dataset to return it to its original state using the Clear() method. At this point, the dataset is clear and ready for data. It's empty, so you must provide new data to display or the application will generate an index range exception. The third step is to use the Fill() method of the data adapter to replace the missing data. At this point, the application is stable again and should continue processing data as before.

You might wonder how this simple piece of code could possibly perform every type of update the data adapter is capable of performing. Remember that the data adapter includes the *DeleteCommand*, *InsertCommand*, *SelectCommand*, and *UpdateCommand* properties. These properties contain the commands that actually perform the work. When the code calls the Update() method, the data adapter calls upon the correct command to process the data updates.

Moving from record-to-record is another Grid view concern. The example application supports the four common record movement commands to move to the first, previous, next, and last records. However, it supports these commands from both the Record menu and the toolbar, so creating a common set of methods makes sense. The Record menu and toolbar event handlers simply call the correct common method for the desired record movement. Listing 11.2 shows the record movement command code.

Listing 11.2   Record Movement Commands

```csharp
private void DoFirst()
{
   // Move to the first record.
   AddrDataGrid.CurrentRowIndex = 0;
   AddrDataGrid.Select();
}

private void DoNext()
{
   // Move to the next record.
   if (AddrDataGrid.CurrentRowIndex !=
      addressDataset1.Tables[0].Rows.Count - 1)
   {
      AddrDataGrid.CurrentRowIndex++;
      AddrDataGrid.Select();
   }
   else
      // Display an error message.
      MessageBox.Show("Already at last record!",
                  "Data Grid Pointer",
                  MessageBoxButtons.OK,
                  MessageBoxIcon.Exclamation);
}

private void DoPrevious()
{
   // Validate pointer location.
   if (AddrDataGrid.CurrentRowIndex != 0)
      // Move to the previous record.
      AddrDataGrid.CurrentRowIndex--;
   else
      // Display an error message.
      MessageBox.Show("Already at first record!",
                  "Data Grid Pointer",
                  MessageBoxButtons.OK,
                  MessageBoxIcon.Exclamation);
   AddrDataGrid.Select();
}

private void DoLast()
```

```
    {
        // Move to the last record.
        AddrDataGrid.CurrentRowIndex =
            addressDataset1.Tables[0].Rows.Count - 1;
        AddrDataGrid.Select();
    }
```

DoFirst() is the easiest of the record movement commands. Simply set the *Current-RowIndex* property to 0, then use the Select() method to change the row pointer. The DoNext() and DoPrevious() method both validate the current row index using the *Current-RowIndex* property. If the row index isn't at the end of the dataset for DoNext() or beginning of the dataset for DoPrevious(), the code increments or decrements the *CurrentRowIndex* property as appropriate and uses Select() to make the change permanent. Otherwise, a message box appears to tell the user that they're at the beginning or end of the dataset. The DoLast() and DoNext() methods both require some means to find the end of the dataset. Theoretically the data grid should have an end of dataset event, but it doesn't, so the code uses addressDataset1.Tables[0].Rows.Count - 1 as the means for determining the last row.

At this point, we have a data Grid view that can position the record pointer. It can also delete, add, and modify records. Modern database applications have a lot of gizmos we haven't covered here, such as search and replace, spelling and grammar checkers, and a variety of other useful utilities. However, the example does provide everything you'd need from a basic application. Figure 11.11 shows the resulting application.

FIGURE 11.11:

An example of a basic Grid view application.

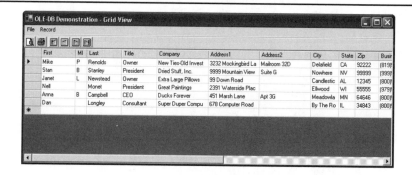

Printing in Grid View

The database application shown in Figure 11.11 is still incomplete. While this application will provide essential data management functionality, it doesn't provide any type of printed output. This section looks at a custom print job. The "Working with Crystal Reports" section of this chapter tells you about an easier, but less custom, method of creating printed output.

Most applications provide three essential pieces of print functionality: printer setup, print preview, and print output. Listing 11.3 shows the implementation of these three key pieces of functionality for the example application.

Listing 11:3   Print, Print Preview, and Printer Setup Functionality

```
// Print object
PrintDialog        PrnDialog;
PrinterSettings    PrnSettings;

private void mnuFilePageSetup_Click(object sender, System.EventArgs e)
{
   // Use the current printer settings (default if not set).
   PrnDialog.PrinterSettings = PrnSettings;

   // Show the printer setup dialog.
   PrnDialog.ShowDialog();
}

void DoPrintPreview()
{
   // Create a printer document and a dialog to display it.
   PrintDocument       PD = new PrintDocument();
   PrintPreviewDialog   ShowPreview = new PrintPreviewDialog();

   // Add an event handler for document printing details.
   PD.PrintPage += new PrintPageEventHandler(PD_PrintPage);

   // Assign the printer document to the dialog and then display it.
   ShowPreview.Document = PD;
   ShowPreview.ShowDialog();
}

void DoPrint()
{
   PrintDialog    Dlg = new PrintDialog();    // Print Dialog
   PrintDocument  PD = new PrintDocument();    // Document Rendering

   // Add an event handler for document printing details.
   PD.PrintPage += new PrintPageEventHandler(PD_PrintPage);

   // Set up the Print Dialog.
   Dlg.PrinterSettings = PrnSettings;

   // Obtain the print parameters.
   if (Dlg.ShowDialog() == DialogResult.OK)
   {
      // Set up the document for printing.
      PD.PrinterSettings = Dlg.PrinterSettings;
```

```
        // Print the document.
        PD.Print();
    }
    else
    {
        // Exit if the user selects Cancel.
        return;
    }
}

void PD_PrintPage(Object sender, PrintPageEventArgs ev)
{
    Font      docFont;       // Document Font
    Font      headFont;      // Heading Font
    Font      columnFont;    // Column Font
    float     yPos = 20;     // Position of text on page.
    int       Counter;       // Loop counter.
    DataTable Current;       // Data table array.

    // Create the font.
    docFont = new Font("Arial", 11);
    headFont = new Font("Arial", 24);
    columnFont = new Font("Arial", 12, FontStyle.Bold);

    // Print the heading.
    ev.Graphics.DrawString("KATZ! Corporation Contact List",
                           headFont,
                           Brushes.Black,
                           20,
                           yPos);
    yPos = yPos + headFont.GetHeight() + 20;

    // Print the column headings.
    ev.Graphics.DrawString("Name",
                           columnFont,
                           Brushes.Black,
                           20,
                           yPos);
//
// See the source code CD for additional headings.
//
    ev.Graphics.DrawString("Home Phone",
                           columnFont,
                           Brushes.Black,
                           695,
                           yPos);
    yPos = yPos + columnFont.GetHeight() + 15;

    // Continue printing as long as there is space on the page and
    // we don't run out of things to write.
    Current = addressDataset1.Tables[0];
```

```
    for (Counter = 0; Counter < Current.Rows.Count; Counter++)
    {
        // Print the line of text.
        ev.Graphics.DrawString(AddrDataGrid[Counter, 0].ToString()
                               + " " +
                               AddrDataGrid[Counter, 1].ToString()
                               + " " +
                               AddrDataGrid[Counter, 2].ToString(),
                               docFont,
                               Brushes.Black,
                               20,
                               yPos);
        ev.Graphics.DrawString(AddrDataGrid[Counter, 3].ToString(),
                               docFont,
                               Brushes.Black,
                               175,
                               yPos);
//
// See the source code CD for additional code.
//
        ev.Graphics.DrawString(AddrDataGrid[Counter, 12].ToString(),
                               docFont,
                               Brushes.Black,
                               695,
                               yPos);

        // Determine the next print position.
        yPos = yPos + docFont.GetHeight() + 10;
    }

    // Tell the application there are no more pages to print.
    ev.HasMorePages = false;
}
```

PrnDialog and *PrnSettings* are two objects that many of the methods in this section share. *PrnSettings* contains the settings for the currently selected printer. If you want to use a different printer, then you need to regenerate the printer settings. As shown in the mnu-FilePageSetup_Click() method, the *PrnSettings* object appears as input to the *PrnDialog*. The property settings within *PrnSettings* control the options that *PrnDialog* will present to the user. As Figure 11.12 shows, the default settings are minimal, but usable.

FIGURE 11.12:

The Print dialog contains a minimal set of options unless you change the printer setting object options.

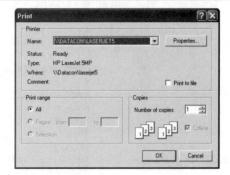

Because the Print Preview and Print options appear on the File menu as well as the toolbar, the example uses a common set of methods to implement both. The `DoPrintPreview()` method begins by creating a new print document, *PD*, and a print preview dialog, *ShowPreview*. *PD* has an event named `PrintPage()` that your code must handle or the application won't output any data. Both the print preview and the print methods can use the same event handler. In fact, you'll definitely want to use the same event handler for both to ensure that what the user sees on screen is what they'll see in the printed output. Once the event handler is in place, the code assigns *PD* to *ShowPreview*, then uses the `ShowDialog()` method to display the printed output.

It's important to remember that the print process relies on the printer settings stored in *PrnSettings*. If the user hasn't selected printer options, then the print routine will fail, no matter what else you want to do. The `DoPrint()` method performs essentially the same tasks as `DoPrintPreview()`. The big difference is that it must also ensure that *PrnSettings* contains valid information.

The `PD_PrintPage()` event handler performs the grunt work of outputting data to the printer. The print routine always handles one page at a time. Printing means drawing the image on a virtual screen, and then sending that screen to the output device. The .NET Framework makes printing somewhat easier than it was under the Win32 API by providing some items for you, such as the device context used for drawing. The `PrintPageEventArgs` object, *ev*, contains a *Graphics* object that you use for drawing purposes. The example uses the `DrawString()` method to output text to the display using one of three font objects. Notice that you must track the position of the drawing cursor on the virtual screen at all times to ensure the data remains within the page borders. Figure 11.13 shows the output from the drawing routine.

FIGURE 11.13:

The print event handler draws the text and other visual elements on screen.

The final piece of code in the `PD_PrintPage()` method looks simple enough, but it's an essential part of the print routine. You must set the *ev.HasMorePages* property to `false` if the print routine is done printing, or the application will continue to call the print routine forever. This property ensures that the application continues to call the print routine until it runs out of pages to print, so you need to set it to `true` or `false` as needed.

Creating the Detail View

The Grid view is great for looking at a group of records at one time, but it also hides information for individual records. There are too many entries to see each record in its entirety all at once, so the application also requires a Detail view. The Detail view will show one record at a time, but it will show all of the data in that record.

Creating the Detail view means adding another Windows Form to the project using the Add ➤ Add New Item command in Solution Explorer. The example uses textbox controls for all data fields, except for the *Business* field, which requires a checkbox. The *Notes* field contains multiple lines of text. You'll need to set the *Multiline* property of the `txtNotes` object to true, and then resize the textbox to fill the lower part of the display area.

The example application could have used a menu system and toolbar similar to the Grid view, but it uses buttons in this case. You need to supply a button to close the Detail view and at least four buttons for controlling the record pointer. Figure 11.14 shows the final output of the Detail view. Notice the use of the toolbar buttons as part of the record buttons—this addition helps the user see the relationship between the buttons on this page and the buttons on the toolbar.

FIGURE 11.14:

The Detail view enables you to see an entire record at one time.

Coding the Detail View

The Detail view doesn't require quite as much code as the Grid view for display purposes because the Detail view is actually easier to develop and much of the data manipulation work is already complete. However, we do need a way to open the Detail view. Most users will expect to double-click on the row selector to open a Detail view, so we'll handle it with the AddrDataGrid_DoubleClick() method. When a user double-clicks a row, the code will need to create an instance of the DetailView class then use the ShowDialog() method of that class to display the Detail view. (We'll see in the "Synchronizing the Grid View and Detail View" section that you need to perform some additional work before the Detail view is ready to display.)

The constructor of the DetailView class will create the components as usual. It then needs to fill those components with data from the GridView class using some type of data exchange. Unfortunately, the data grid on the Grid view is inaccessible, even if you make it public. This means you have to find some one other means of exchanging data with the Detail view. The first technique is to send the information to the Detail View constructor. This approach only works if you want to create a Detail view that handles a single record at a time with no record movement. A second method is to provide some form of intermediate variable, which is the technique we'll use with the example.

Synchronizing the Grid View and Detail View

Data synchronization is an essential consideration when you have two views of the same data to work with. You'll need to perform several tasks to ensure the data in the first view remains in synchronization with data in the second view. Generally, you won't require more than two views because most users relate well to a Grid and Detail view combination; but there are times when you might require three or even four views, making the synchronization task even harder.

The first task is to get the data into the Detail view from the Grid view. In some cases, maintaining two connections to the database might work, but normally its better to rely on the Grid view as a source of data to conserve resources, improve performance, and maintain reliability. Listing 11.4 shows the GridView class code for filling static variables with data. These variables must be static or you won't be able to access them from the DetailView class.

Listing 11.4   **Creating Static Variables to Hold Grid Data**

```
private void ExchangeFill()
{
    // Fill the static variables with data.
    ExchFirst = AddrDataGrid[AddrDataGrid.CurrentCell.RowNumber,
        0].ToString();
//
// See the source code CD for additional code.
//
    ExchNotes = AddrDataGrid[AddrDataGrid.CurrentCell.RowNumber,
        16].ToString();
}
```

As you can see, the code relies on the Item enumerator of the AddrDataGrid control to access each cell in the current row. The Item enumerator takes the form AddrDataGrid[row, column] in this example. The code obtains the current row using the *AddrDataGrid.Current-Cell.RowNumber* property. The code selects each column in the row in turn to obtain the current cell value for the column and places it in the static string.

It might be tempting to access the static variables directly from the DetailView class. However, in this case, you'll want to use an accessor method to aid in smooth application performance, debugging, and data integrity. The DetailView class contains the ExchangeData() method shown in Listing 11.5.

Listing 11.5   **The DetailView Class Provides a Central Data Exchange Method**

```
private void ExchangeData()
{
    string   IsBusiness; // Business if true.
```

```
   // Obtain all of the data fields.
   txtFirst.Text = GridView.GetData("First");
//
// See the source code CD for additional code.
//
   txtTelephone3.Text = GridView.GetData("Telephone3");
   IsBusiness = GridView.GetData("Business");
   if (IsBusiness == "True")
   {
      cbBusiness.Checked = true;
   }
   DateTime TempDate = DateTime.Parse(GridView.GetData("Contacted"));
   txtContacted.Text = TempDate.ToLongDateString();
   txtProduct.Text = GridView.GetData("Product");
   txtNotes.Text = GridView.GetData("Notes");
}
```

Notice that the ExchangeData() method calls upon the static GetData() method in the GridView class to obtain each static string. You could accomplish this task in a number of ways, but the example uses an access string to make the GetData() method a single solution for all fields in the database. Notice the special handling required for both the *cbBusiness* and the *txtContacted* fields. The *cbBusiness* field requires a bool value, while the *txtContacted* field requires special formatting to obtain a usable display. The GetData() method is a simple case statement as shown in Listing 11.6.

Listing 11.6   **The GetData() Method Acts as an Accessor**

```
public static string GetData(string FieldName)
{
   // Determine which field the calling program wants, then
   // return the appropriate static value.
   switch (FieldName)
   {
      case "First":
         return ExchFirst;
//
// See the source code CD for additional code.
//
      case "Notes":
         return ExchNotes;
   }

   // If the FieldName didn't match any of the entries,
   // return a default value.
   return "Value Not Found";
}
```

You should notice something peculiar about this switch statement. In previous chapters, I always included a break or a goto after each case statement. In this case, if you add the break or goto after each case statement, the compiler will complain about inaccessible code; the return statement takes the place of the break or goto. The GetData() method also includes a default return value in case the developer provides an inaccurate input value.

At this point, the Detail view will display data when you first create it, but there's no functionality for updating the data as the user moves from one record to the next. The record update task is actually a two-part process. First, the GridView class must move the record pointer and update the static variables. Second, the DetailView class must recognize that the change has occurred and update the data displayed on the form. Listing 11.7 shows the Grid-View class portion of the code.

Listing 11.7   The GridView Class Updates Local Variables During a Record Change

```
public delegate void DataChangeDelegate();
public static event DataChangeDelegate DataChanged;

private void GoFirst(object sender, System.EventArgs e)
{
   // Move to the next record.
   DoFirst();

   // Fill the AddrDataGrid variables.
   ExchangeFill();

   // Fire the DataChanged event.
   DataChanged();
}
private void GoPrevious(object sender, System.EventArgs e)
{
   // Move to the next record.
   DoPrevious();

   // Fill the AddrDataGrid variables.
   ExchangeFill();

   // Fire the DataChanged event.
   DataChanged();
}
private void GoNext(object sender, System.EventArgs e)
{
   // Move to the next record.
   DoNext();

   // Fill the AddrDataGrid variables.
   ExchangeFill();
```

```
    // Fire the DataChanged event.
    DataChanged();
}
private void GoLast(object sender, System.EventArgs e)
{
    // Move to the next record.
    DoLast();

    // Fill the AddrDataGrid variables.
    ExchangeFill();

    // Fire the DataChanged event.
    DataChanged();
}
```

The code begins by creating the DataChangeDelegate delegate and the DataChanged event. Notice that both DataChangeDelegate and DataChanged are public so the DetailView class can access them. In addition, the DataChanged event is static, making it accessible directly from the GridView class.

Notice that each event handler performs three steps. First, it moves the record pointer. Second, it fills the static variables with data. Third, it fires the DataChanged event so the DetailView class knows that a data update occurred. This code brings up the question of which event it handles. You can make the events of the pushbuttons on the DetailView form public by changing their *Modifiers* property to Public. The AddrDataGrid_DoubleClick() method creates the connection to the DetailView class using the following code:

```
// Create event handlers for the record movement keys.
DetailDlg.btnFirst.Click += new EventHandler(GoFirst);
DetailDlg.btnPrevious.Click += new EventHandler(GoPrevious);
DetailDlg.btnNext.Click += new EventHandler(GoNext);
DetailDlg.btnLast.Click += new EventHandler(GoLast);
```

Whenever the user clicks a record movement button in the DetailView (*DetailDlg*), it actually passes control to the appropriate event in the GridView code, shown in Listing 11.7. The DataChanged() event fires and passes control to the ExchangeData() method in the DetailView class, which then updates the detail form.

There's one more synchronization item to consider. What happens if the user types a new value into the detail form? If that change doesn't appear in the Grid view, then the change is lost. By now, you should know that the first step in resolving this issue is to change the *Modifiers* property of all the data entry fields to Public. Once the fields are public, you can access their TextChanged event as shown here:

```
// Create event handlers for the data change events.
DetailDlg.txtFirst.TextChanged +=
    new EventHandler(FirstChanged);
```

```
//
// See the source code CD for additional code.
//
DetailDlg.txtNotes.TextChanged +=
   new EventHandler(NotesChanged);
```

You'll add this code to the AddrDataGrid_DoubleClick() method so that the text change events occur as soon as the *DetailDlg* form appears on screen. Note that the TextChanged event distinguishes between changes the user makes and those made by application code. In other words, you won't need any special code to detect updates made by the ExchangeData() method.

This brings us to the final piece of synchronization code for this example. The changes in the Detail view must appear within the Grid view. We've already created connections to the event handlers in the GridView class for the Detail view. Here's an example of the most common method for handling the changes.

```
private void FirstChanged(object sender, System.EventArgs e)
{
   AddrDataGrid[AddrDataGrid.CurrentCell.RowNumber, 0] =
      DetailDlg.txtFirst.Text;
}
```

As you can see, this technique works fine as long as you're working with text. It even works well with bool and int values. However, it won't work with date values. To transfer a date, you must validate the date value first as shown here:

```
private void ContactedChanged(object sender, System.EventArgs e)
{
   // The user might not enter a valid date, so we need to
   // verify the date.
   DateTime TempDate;
   try
   {
      // Create a temporary date holder.
      TempDate = DateTime.Parse(DetailDlg.txtContacted.Text);
   }
   catch
   {
      // If the date is invalid, return without making a change.
      return;
   }

   // Otherwise, make the appropriate change.
   AddrDataGrid[AddrDataGrid.CurrentCell.RowNumber, 14] = TempDate;
}
```

As you can see, if the Detail view sends an invalid date, the event handler will return rather than report an error. Notice the data conversion that occurs every time the Detail view sends a value. This conversion is important because the event handler receives a text value, when it really needs a date value. When the user does provide a valid date, the event handler stores the converted value in the data grid.

Writing an ODBC.NET Application

The actual mechanics of the ODBC.NET application are the same as the OLE-DB application we just discussed. For example, you'll experience the same synchronization issues between the Grid view and the Detail view. However, the ODBC.NET namespace doesn't provide the same level of automation as the OLE-DB namespace, so you'll need to perform additional configuration.

NOTE   This section of the chapter discusses the additional configuration required for an ODBC.NET application. We won't discuss elements that are the same as the OLE-DB equivalent application. You'll find the full source code for this example in the \Chapter 11\ODBCNET folder on the CD.

Let's begin with the objects that you'll use. Like the previous example, you'll need a connection, data adapter, and data set. However, you'll use the ODBC versions of these objects, which means adding them to the toolbox. In addition, you'll need to configure all of these objects by hand. The data adapter requires four commands: delete, insert, select, and update. You'll need to configure all four commands by hand using the `OdbcCommand` object. The example uses the objects shown in Figure 11.15.

FIGURE 11.15:

An ODBC.NET application relies heavily on manually configured components.

AddressConnect is the first object you need to configure. All you need to change, in this case, is the `ConnectionString` property. Type **DSN=Address Database** in the field, and you'll have everything needed to create the connection.

Create the four commands next. The easiest command to configure is `SelectData`. Select AddressConnect in the `Connection` property. Type **Select * From Address** in the *Command-Text* property. This is a SQL statement that selects all of the data from the Address table in the database pointed to by AddressConnect. If you want to order the data in a certain way, you'd need to add the Order By clause and add the name of one or more fields that you want to use for sorting.

The InsertData command object is the next most difficult command to configure. In this case, we don't know what data the user will want to insert into the table in advance, so we need to create some parameters that the application will use to pass the data to the database. You create parameters as a collection and they must appear in the order in which you plan to use them. The order is an absolute. You can't do anything later to change the order in the command, so the parameters must appear in the correct order. Figure 11.16 shows the parameters used for this example—there's one parameter for each field in the table.

FIGURE 11.16:

Make certain that you place the parameters for your command in the proper order.

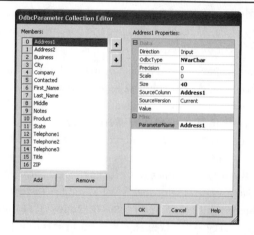

NOTE   Make certain you select the proper connection in the *Connection* property for all four commands. Otherwise, the command will fail.

You'll need to know a few bits of information to make some of the entries work properly. ODBC.NET doesn't support a bool type, so you'll use the bit type for Boolean values instead. Memo fields use the standard character field type. However, you won't provide a Size property value. You must supply a SourceColumn property value for any value that you want to pass from the data grid. The Value property is always blank, unless you want to provide a calculated value as input.

The *CommandText* property value is a little longer this time. Type **INSERT INTO Address(Address1, Address2, Business, City, Company, Contacted, First_Name, Last_Name, Middle, Notes, Product, State, Telephone1, Telephone2, Telephone3, Title, ZIP) VALUES (?, ?, ?, ?, ?, ?, ?, ?, ?, ?, ?, ?, ?, ?, ?, ?, ?)** to provide the complete command. This command tells the database to insert a new record with the following fields and the associated field values. The field names must follow the same order as the parameter list shown in Figure 11.16.

The `DeleteData` command is similar to the `InsertData` command in that you need to use input parameters. However, the properties are different this time. In most cases, you only need to provide the list of fields that make up the primary key, since the primary key is supposed to point to a unique value in the table. Some developers provide a full list of fields in order to ensure only one record is deleted. The example uses the first method, it relies on the unique value of the primary key to ensure that only one entry in the database is deleted. This means creating three parameter entries for the *Last_Name*, *First_Name*, and *Company* fields. Because you have fewer properties to consider, the *CommandText* property value is much shorter this time: **DELETE FROM Address WHERE (Last_Name = ?) AND (First_Name = ?) AND (Company = ?)**. Make sure you use the parenthesis as noted to ensure the database interprets the `delete` command correctly.

The `UpdateData` command is unique in that it requires multiple versions of the same parameter. You need to know both the current and the original value of some fields in order to update the database correctly. If you don't identify the record correct, the database will attempt to change the value of every record to match the user's input, resulting in errors. Like the `DeleteData` command, you can generally identify a unique record for the `UpdateData` command using the primary key fields. You'll need to change the *SourceVersion* property for the original values to `Original`. Make sure you identify the original values by using a unique *ParameterName* property value such as **Original_Last_Name**. The *CommandText* property value for this command is **UPDATE Address SET Address1 = ?, Address2 = ?, Business = ?, City = ?, Company = ?, Contacted = ?, First_Name = ?, Last_Name = ?, Middle = ?, Notes = ?, Product = ?, State = ?, Telephone1 = ?, Telephone2 = ?, Telephone3 = ?, Title = ?, ZIP = ? WHERE (Last_Name = ?) AND (First_Name = ?) AND (Company = ?)**.

We now have everything needed to create a data adapter. The `AddressDA` data adapter doesn't require much in the way of configuration. All you need to do is add the four commands to the *DeleteCommand*, *InsertCommand*, *SelectCommand*, and *UpdateCommand* properties.

If you were wondering about automated dataset generation, it won't happen when using ODBC.NET. As with everything else, you need to manually configure a dataset for this application. Configuration isn't difficult. All you need to do is specify a name for the *DataSetName* property and create a *Tables* property collection. The example uses a *DataSetName* value of **AddressDataSet**.

Setting up the Tables property does require a bit more work. The following steps lead you through the process of setting up a table.

1. Click the ellipses next to this property and you'll see a Tables Collection Editor.

2. Click Add. You'll see a new table added to the list. Type **ADDRESS** in the *TableName* property and **Address** in the *(Name)* property. This creates a table similar to the one used for the OLE-DB example. Now we have to define columns for the table.

3. Click the ellipses in the *Columns* property. You'll see a Columns Collection Editor dialog. Figure 11.17 shows the list of columns for this example and provides an example of how you need to fill out each column property. The six essential properties include *Caption*, *ColumnName*, *DataType*, *DefaultValue*, *MaxLength*, and *(Name)*. You must also set the *AllowDBNull* property for every primary key or essential column to *False*. Otherwise, the user can enter a *null* value and cause an error.

FIGURE 11.17:

Define columns for each column in the table or query used for the dataset.

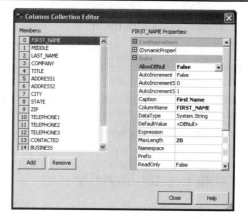

4. Click Close to close the Columns Collection Editor dialog. We can now define a primary key for the table. Defining a primary key helps display the data properly and can reduce the number of errors the user will experience by giving the ODBC provider cues about the database setup.

5. Click the *PrimaryKey* property drop-down list box. You'll see a list of columns defined for the table as shown in Figure 11.18. Click next to the gray square for each column you want to add to the primary key. The IDE will number each entry in order. The first key value is considered first when ordering the data.

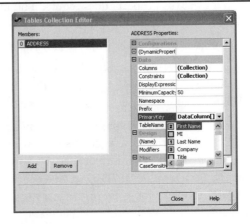

The *PrimaryKey* property enables you to define the primary key for your table or query.

6. Click Close to close the Tables Collection Editor dialog. The connection, data adapter, and dataset are now configured for use.

As previously mentioned, the ODBC version of the address database application works very much like the OLE-DB version. There's only one small quirk that you need to consider. Because of the way we created the dataset, you need to change the Fill() and Update() methods as shown here to work with the table we've just set up in the dataset.

```
AddressDA.Fill(AddressData, "Address");
AddressDA.Update(AddressData, "Address");
```

Working with Crystal Reports

Previously, we looked at how you could create a simple report using drawing commands. Obviously, even a simple report isn't for the faint of heart, and the complex reports that management often requires may prove nigh on to impossible to create within a reasonable timeframe. Unfortunately, the reports your application outputs will form the basis of management's opinion of your application in many cases. That's why a product like Crystal Reports is so important. It enables you to create complex reports in a modicum of time in many cases. The tradeoff is application overhead, resource usage, and size. That's why there's also still a place for custom print routines.

> The example in this section uses the OLE-DB example we created earlier as a starting point. You'll find the updated code in the \Chapter 11\CrystalReports folder on the CD.

Using Crystal Reports is relatively easy. Begin by right-clicking the Project entry in Solution Explorer and selecting the Add ➤ Add New Item command to display the Add New dialog box. Select the Crystal Report icon, type a name for the report (the example uses

MyReport) and click Open. (If this is your first time using Crystal Reports, the product will ask you to perform a registration—you can choose to perform the registration or not at this point.) If you use the Report Expert, the Crystal Report Gallery shown in Figure 11.19 enables you to select from several project types (the recommended choice for most reports). You can also choose to create a blank project or start a new report based on an existing report.

FIGURE 11.19:

The Crystal Report Gallery is the starting point for report projects.

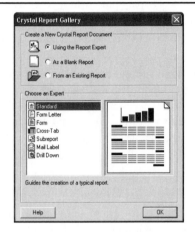

The example application will create a Standard Report using the Report Expert. (You'll also find a Mail Label report included on the companion CD.) The following steps tell how to use the Report Expert to create a Standard Report.

1. Select the Report Expert and Standard Report options in the Crystal Report Gallery, and then click OK. You'll see the Standard Report Expert shown in Figure 11.20. Note that the figure shows the dialog with the data source configured.

FIGURE 11.20:

The first task is to choose a source of data for your report.

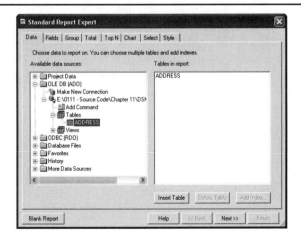

2. Create a new database connection using the Make New Connection option in the OLE-DB folder if necessary. Otherwise, you'll see the needed connection as shown in Figure 11.20. Select the ADDRESS table entry and click Insert Table. The new table entry will appear in the Tables in Report pane.

3. Click Next. The Report Expert will ask which table fields you want to appear in the report. You can choose one or all of the fields. The fields will appear in the order shown in the Fields to Display pane when you create the report, so use the up and down arrows to position the fields as needed. The example uses all of the fields in the database except Company, which we'll use as a means for grouping information in the report.

TIP The Column Heading field on the Fields tab helps you to customize headings for each data item in the report. You can also add calculated data by clicking Formula.

4. Select the fields you want to use and ensure they appear in the order that you want them to appear in the report. The example report includes the user name first, title, address, telephone, and miscellaneous information in order. Click Next. The Report Expert will ask if you want to group report information.

5. Select one or more fields for grouping purposes. The example uses the Company field for grouping. At this point, there are a number of optional report entries you can make. The example doesn't include numeric information, so we don't need totals or graphs in the report. However, these features are available if you need them.

6. Click the Style tab. This tab contains a list of report styles. It also enables you to type a title for the report. Type **Contact List Grouped by Company** in the Title field. Select the **Executive, Trailing Break** style.

7. Click Finish. The Report Expert will create the report for you.

8. Rearrange the report elements as needed so each report element has enough space to print.

Of course, a report doesn't do much if you can't view it in some way. We'll add a new Windows form to the project. This form will contain a single component, the Crystal Report Viewer. You don't need to configure anything for the report, except to set the *Dock* property to Fill. The constructor for the form accepts a single input string that the code assigns to the Crystal Report Viewer like this:

```
ReportView.ReportSource = ReportName;
```

All you need to do now is create an instance of the dialog and pass it the name of the report you want to print as part of the constructor. The report must appear in the same directory as the application, or you'll need to provide a full path to the report. Figure 11.21 shows a typical Crystal Report.

FIGURE 11.21:

Crystal Reports are easy and fast to create and the results speak for themselves.

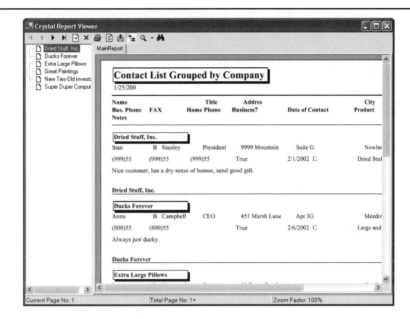

Where Do You Go From Here?

This chapter has started you on your way to a better understanding of the database capabilities provided by C# and the .NET Framework. We've discussed both OLE-DB and ODBC applications for the Microsoft Access database. You've also learned about the power of both custom and Crystal Reports output.

Obviously, we haven't covered every aspect of database programming. More than a few authors have tried to discuss the topic in an entire book and failed. However, you do know enough to start creating database projects of your own. Try tables with other data formats and create applications that rely on more than one table. Using Access keeps everything local and helps you get around some of the problems that larger DBMSs can cause.

Chapter 12 will continue the database discussion using ADO. We'll begin using SQL Server 2000 for the examples in this chapter and you'll see examples of more complex database design.

ADO Application Development

- Using Server Explorer

- An Overview of the ADO Classes

- Writing an ADO Application

- Troubleshooting Techniques for ADO Applications

In Chapter 11, we looked at both OLE-DB and ODBC .NET application development for Microsoft Access databases. However, many developers don't use Access for their development projects and want something higher-level than OLE-DB, so they don't have to perform most of the work. ADO is one answer to this question. It enables you to perform data access tasks at a higher level. This chapter also uses SQL Server 2000 as the DBMS. SQL Server enables a developer to create enterprise-level database applications that will scale as needed.

This chapter shows you how to use more of the automation provided by Server Explorer to create applications quickly. The emphasis in this chapter is on development speed, reliability, and flexibility, rather than on supporting older applications, application size, or application speed, as was the focus in Chapter 11. Because processing cycles are so cheap today and developer time is so precious, many developers are looking for ways to improve productivity despite the loss of a little speed and increase in application size. This chapter has the answers you're seeking.

Using Server Explorer

Server Explorer replaces a lot of tools that you used to get as extras on the Visual Studio disk. It also creates new tools for exploring your network in ways that you might not have thought possible in the past. In fact, the name Server Explorer is a bit of a misnomer, because Server Explorer provides access to any resource on any machine to which you have access. This feature alone makes using the Visual Studio .NET IDE more useful than any previous IDE you might have used. The ability to explore and use resources without leaving the IDE makes application development a lot easier. We've already seen one way to use Server Explorer in the OLE-DB example in Chapter 10. This section provides an in-depth view of this essential tool.

Server Explorer shares the same area of your IDE as the Toolbox. Click on the upper icon and you'll see Server Explorer; click on the lower icon and the Toolbox appears. Figure 12.1 shows a typical example of the Server Explorer with connections to two machines. Because I have administrator privileges on both machines, all of the resources of both machines are at my disposal.

Notice that I opened the SQL Server connection to the server, WinServer. If you get the idea that you won't need to use the server-side tools much anymore, you'd be correct. You can perform most (but not all) tasks right from Server Explorer. If you need to make a new database, reconfigure a table, or create a query, Server Explorer does it all. In fact, we'll take a quick look at these features when creating the example in the "Creating a SQL Server Database" section of the chapter.

FIGURE 12.1:

Server Explorer not
only gives you the
grand view of your net-
work to start but
allows you to drill
down as needed.

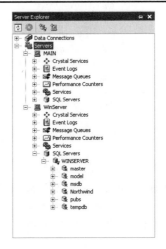

Working with the Event Log

One of the features that developers come to appreciate about Server Explorer is that it helps
you categorize information. You can drill down to the information you need but ignore
everything else. For example, when you open the Application Event Log, you need to connect to the remote server, locate the log, and then search through the list of messages for the
particular message you need. Server Explorer categorizes event messages by type, so all you
see is the message you want.

If you want to build a quick application to monitor just certain types of messages, all you
need to do is drag the requisite folder to a form and add some quick code to monitor it.
(You'll find examples of Server Explorer usage in the \Chapter 12\ServerExplorer folder on
the CD.) Here's a short example of how you could use this feature in an application.

```
private void btnCreateEvent_Click(object sender, System.EventArgs e)
{
   // Create an event entry.
   ApplicationEvents.WriteEntry("This is a test message",
                                EventLogEntryType.Information,
                                1001,
                                1);
}

private void ApplicationEvents_EntryWritten(object sender,
   System.Diagnostics.EntryWrittenEventArgs e)
{
   // Respond to the entry written event.
   MessageBox.Show("The Application Generated an Event!" +
```

```
                            "\r\nType:\t\t" + e.Entry.EntryType.ToString() +
                            "\r\nCategory:\t" + e.Entry.Category.ToString() +
                            "\r\nEvent ID:\t\t" + e.Entry.EventID.ToString() +
                            "\r\nSource:\t\t" + e.Entry.Source.ToString() +
                            "\r\nMessage:\t\t" + e.Entry.Message.ToString() +
                            "\r\nTime Created:\t" +
                            e.Entry.TimeGenerated.ToString(),
                            "Application Event",
                            MessageBoxButtons.OK,
                            MessageBoxIcon.Information);
    }
```

You could place such code in a Taskbar Tray (Notification Area) application, such as the Typing Buddy example in Chapter 5. The application will continuously monitor the event log in the background and let you know if something happens. This particular feature is even good for debugging, because many server-side controls only log errors in the event logs.

NOTE   The Event Log entry created by dragging the event log from the Server Explorer will have a default configuration. The *EnableRaisingEvents* property will enable your application to detect changes to the log and notify you. However, this feature only works on the local machine. If you want to monitor events on a remote machine, your application will have to perform some form of polling or use a remote component that connects to your local application.

Working with Performance Counters

While event logs are an essential part of the Windows experience, monitoring them isn't so difficult that you'd want to spend a lot of time doing it. However, one type of monitoring that's a little more difficult involves the performance counters. Working with performance counters has been notoriously difficult in the past. Server Explorer makes it almost too simple to monitor all of the performance counters on your machine. Again, all you need to do is drag the counter of interest from Server Explorer to the application form. This example uses a *DataSet* to store the intermediate values and a *DataGrid* to show the values. A *Timer* provides the means for obtaining constant data updates. Listing 12.1 shows the code you'll need for this example (note that it doesn't include the report setup, which you can view in the source code on the CD).

Listing 12.1   **Server Explorer Makes It Easy to Use Performance Counters**

```
private void DataTimer_Elapsed(object sender, System.Timers.ElapsedEventArgs e)
{
    DataTable    CounterTable;
    DataRow      NewRow;
```

```
        // Create the data table object.
        CounterTable = CounterData.Tables["UserProcessorTime"];

        // Create a new row for the data table.
        NewRow = CounterTable.NewRow();

        // Obtain the current performance counter value.
        NewRow["Total Percent User Time"] =
            UserProcessorTime.NextValue();

        // Store the value in the data table.
        CounterTable.Rows.Add(NewRow);

        // Verify the size of the data table and remove
        // a record if necessary.
        if (CounterTable.Rows.Count >= CounterDataView.VisibleRowCount)
            CounterTable.Rows.RemoveAt(0);
}

private void btnStopCounter_Click(object sender, System.EventArgs e)
{
    // Start and stop the timer as needed.  Change the
    // caption to show the current timer state.
    if (btnStopCounter.Text == "Stop Counter")
    {
        DataTimer.Stop();
        btnStopCounter.Text = "Start Counter";
    }
    else
    {
        DataTimer.Start();
        btnStopCounter.Text = "Stop Counter";
    }
}

private void txtTimerInterval_TextChanged(object sender, System.EventArgs e)
{
    try
    {
        // Verify the timer change value has a number in it.
        if (Int64.Parse(txtTimerInterval.Text) == 0)
            // If not, reset the value.
            txtTimerInterval.Text = DataTimer.Interval.ToString();
        else
            // If so, use the new value.
            DataTimer.Interval = Int64.Parse(txtTimerInterval.Text);
    }
    catch
    {
        // Catch invalid values.
```

```
        MessageBox.Show("Type Only Numeric Values!",
            "Input Error",
            MessageBoxButtons.OK,
            MessageBoxIcon.Error);
        txtTimerInterval.Text = DataTimer.Interval.ToString();
    }
}
```

Notice that most of the code in this part of the example relates to the presentation of data. For example, the txtTimerInterval_TextChanged() method modifies the display speed of the application, while the btnStopCounter_Click() method enables and disables the timer. Disabling the *DataTimer* has the effect of stopping the display so you can see the current data value, along with the value history.

The DataTimer_Elapsed() method contains the code that updates the display at the interval specified by *DataTimer.Interval. CounterTable* contains the entire data table used for the example. The NewRow() method of this object creates a new row represented by *NewRow*. The *Item* property, *Total Percent User Time* is a particular column within the table, and we'll fill it with the current processed value for the *UserProcessorTime* performance counter using the NextValue() method. The final step is to add the new row to the data table using the Add() method. Figure 12.2 shows an example of the output from this application.

FIGURE 12.2:

The Server Explorer example shows how easy it is to use performance counters in C#.

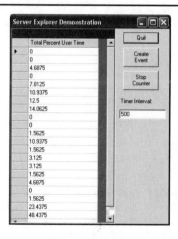

One of the interesting things about this example is that this view isn't available using the System Monitor component of the Performance console. The Report View of the utility shows the current counter value, but doesn't provide any history. The Graph View and Histogram View might prove less than accurate for developer needs. So this report view with history fulfills a developer need. It enables you to capture precise counter values over a period of time in a way that helps you look for data patterns. The fact that the table automatically sizes itself ensures that you won't end up with too much data in the table. Of course, you can always change the method used to delete excess records to meet specific needs.

> **TIP** It's interesting to note that Visual Studio installs a number of .NET CLR–specific performance counters for you. For example, you have access to memory, network, and data-related counters to adjust the performance of your application. A special *Interop* object contains counters that measure the impact of external calls on application performance. Not only do these counters help you work on performance issues, but you can also use them to locate bugs or enable an application to tune itself. For example, you could monitor memory usage and get rid of non-essential features when application memory is low. In addition, a special *Exceptions* object contains counters that help you monitor application exceptions, including those that your application handles without any other visible signs.

Creating a SQL Server Database

The ADO programming example in this chapter will require use of a SQL Server 2000 database. Normally, you'd use the tools provided with SQL Server to create and manage your database. In some situations, you'll still need those tools, because they provide essential functions that the Visual Studio .NET IDE can't provide. However, in many cases, you can at least begin the design process and perform some testing without ever leaving the IDE. The following steps show how to create the database used for this example and for databases in general. (You'll find a script for creating this database in the \Chapter 12\Data folder on the CD. This folder also contains some exported data used for the example.)

1. Open Server Explorer, locate the server with SQL Server installed on it, open the SQL Servers folder, and open the SQL Server instance of interest. In most cases, you'll only see one. My server is named WinServer—your server will probably have a different name.

2. Right-click the SQL Server instance and choose New Database from the context menu. You'll see a Create Database dialog box.

3. Type a name in the New Database Name field. The example uses **MovieGuide** as the database name.

4. Choose between Windows NT integrated security and SQL Server authentication. The example uses SQL Server authentication with the **sa** username and appropriate password. (See the "Database Security in Focus" sidebar for some thoughts on which type of security to use.)

5. Click OK, and SQL Server will create a new database for you (which will appear in the Visual Studio .NET IDE). Now it's time to create a table for the database.

TIP   If you click on the new MovieGuide entry, you'll notice that one of the properties in the Properties window is *ConnectString*. You can normally use this value as a starting point when configuring the ADO connection. Simply double-click the property and press Ctrl+C to copy it to the clipboard, then paste as needed in your application code.

6. Right-click Tables and choose New Table from the context menu. You'll see a blank table form similar to the one shown in Figure 12.3. (Note that this table is already filled out and ready for use.)

FIGURE 12.3:

This form shows the table structure for the database in the ADO example.

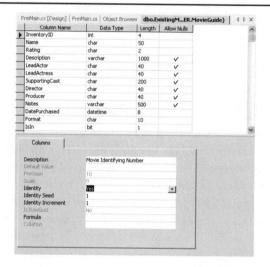

7. Fill in the required table entries.

8. Save the table and close it. The example uses a table name of ExistingMovies. You're ready to create the ADO application.

This is obviously the short tour of working with Server Explorer to create a database. You'll also need to add indexes, primary keys, queries, and other entries to make a complete database. In fact, the example application does use the *InventoryID* column as the primary key and has indexes for the Name, LeadActor, LeadActress, Director, Producer, and DatePurchased columns. Of course, the database will require some data as well.

> **TIP**　To add a primary key to the table, Ctrl-click the columns you want to use for the primary key, right-click the table, and choose Set Primary key from the context menu. To add new indexes to the table, right-click the table and choose Indexes/Keys from the context menu. Use the Property Pages dialog to add new indexes to the table. Note that you'll have the same index creation tools as in SQL Server, but some of the dialog boxes may look slightly different.

The example does show what you can do without leaving the IDE. The most important consideration is that using Server Explorer saves time and effort by making the database creation and usage process easier.

Database Security in Focus

Database applications represent the most critical applications for most organizations. The data stored in the database is often worth more than anything the company might possess, including all of the computer equipment used to store that data. Needless to say, pressure to maintain the security of company data is high for the database developer, making the choice of security policies difficult at best. A developer must satisfy the security requirements of today, as well as anticipate the needs of tomorrow.

The decision of which type of security to use begins early in the SQL Server design process and is often difficult (or impossible) to change later. The innocuous question of whether to use Windows NT–integrated security or SQL Server authentication means more than many developers think, because this choice could mean the difference between a secure computing environment and one that crackers overcome quickly.

In general, you'll find that the Windows NT–integrated security option is better for distributed applications, because it offers single sign-on security and you have more options for implementing the security. However, the SQL Server authentication can actually work better for local applications where you want to provide a single sign-on for classes of users that differs from their standard logon. The use of groups in SQL Server transcends those groups that the user might ordinarily participate in.

The importance of flexible security implementation is becoming greater as more companies use alternatives to the standard username and password. For example, St. Vincent Hospital and Health Services in Indianapolis has begun a pilot program that depends on biometric authentication for enterprise users. Imagine you're a doctor making your rounds. Logging in at every terminal to learn patient statistics would become a painful experience, an ordeal that the use of biometric authentication overcomes (not to mention making the authentication process more secure). The hospital's authentication system relies on Saflink (http://www.saflink.com/), a product that can tie-in with Windows security but not directly to SQL Server authentication (at least not without a lot of work).

Continued on next page

Microsoft is also making an effort to create better connectivity between third-party security products and the operating system. For example, Windows XP includes functionality that makes biometric security integration easier. DigitalPersona's (http://www.digitalpersona.com/) U.Are.U personal fingerprint system directly integrates with Windows XP security to create a seamless solution. Several organizations such as California Commerce Bank and Coca-Cola are already using this technology in their database development projects. Unfortunately, this is another solution where Windows-integrated security reigns supreme over SQL Server authentication.

Lest you think that you'll need to continue working in the dark on database security issues, the National Information Assurance Partnership (NIAP) (http://niap.nist.gov/) and many IT vendors are currently working on a set of common criteria for testing and evaluating security products—especially those used for databases. Members of the National Institute of Standards and Technology (NIST) and the National Security Agency (NSA) are taking the lead in NIAP. The current security standards include the Trusted Computer System Evaluation Criteria (TCSEC) introduced as the "Orange Book" in 1985, the Information Technology Security Evaluation Criteria (ITSEC) introduced in 1991, and the Canadian Trusted Computer Product Evaluation Criteria (CTCPEC) introduced in 1993. One of the major recent security events was the signing of an agreement between the US, Canada, France, Germany, and the United Kingdom that details a need for common security criteria. Hopefully, the wheels of government will begin turning swiftly enough that you as a developer will have some guidelines to use in the near future when developing applications.

An Overview of the ADO Classes

We've partially discussed the ADO classes as part of the discussion in Chapter 11. For example, in the "Understanding ADO" section, you learned about the basic object types used by ADO. In addition, that section provided you with some basic information on how ADO makes data access easier. However, you also need to know about the mechanics of ADO access. For one thing, ADO is a COM technology, not a .NET Framework technology. Like OLE-DB, Microsoft provides wrappers for the various ADO classes. Unlike OLE-DB, you can't access ADO objects from the Toolbox; they're part of an import library.

You'll find ADODB.DLL in the \Program Files\Microsoft.NET\Primary Interop Assemblies folder. You'll need to add a reference to this DLL in your application by right-clicking the References folder in Solution Explorer and choosing Add Reference from the context menu. The ADODB.DLL reference appears on the .NET tab of the Add Reference dialog box, as shown in Figure 12.4.

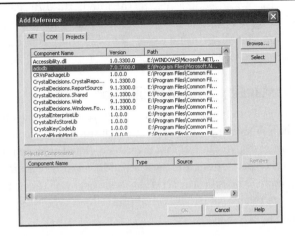

FIGURE 12.4:

The .NET Framework provides an interoperability DLL you can use for ADO.

It's important to note that this isn't your only way to access ADO and that you might have to use another technique in the future. You can also use the Browse button on the COM tab to locate the type library (TLB) files found in the \Program Files\Common Files\System\ ado folder. These TLB files contain everything you'll need to use ADO in an application. At some point, the TLB files found on your drive might provide better input than the .NET Framework files, so it's best to know how to use both access techniques.

Writing an ADO Application

This section of the chapter shows how to create a basic ADO application that relies on a detail form for display purposes. We'll create the connection and recordset by hand, and you'll see how using ADO differs from using other database technologies. The application includes the capability to add and delete records, as well as a print routine. By the time you complete the example, you'll have a good idea of why Microsoft sees ADO as a better technology for many database applications. You'll also understand why ADO isn't the best answer when you need complete control over the data management environment.

NOTE   You'll find an OLE-DB test application for the MovieGuide table in the \Extras\DataFill folder on the CD. This application is an extra example that you can use for comparison purposes. It shows how to access a SQL Server database using OLE-DB, rather than the ADO methods used in this chapter. Make sure you view the README file in the folder for additional details.

The following sections discuss the important differences between ADO and OLE-DB application development. This includes manipulating the data, moving between records, and some (but not all) printing issues. The full source code appears in the \Chapter 12\ADO folder on the CD.

Understanding Data Manipulation

Before you can manipulate application data, you need a recordset and a connection to the database. Developers use different techniques for gaining access to the data they require; but, in most cases, you'll find that creating a global connection and recordset is the easiest method of performing this task. In addition, this technique generally produces the most efficient code. The following code shows what you'll need to add to the MainForm() constructor to create the global database and print objects required for the example.

```
public MainForm()
{
    // Required for Windows Form Designer support
    InitializeComponent();

    // Initialize the database components.
    // Open the database connection.
    DBConnect = new Connection();
    DBConnect.Open("Provider=SQLOLEDB;" +
                   "Data Source=WINSERVER;" +
                   "Initial Catalog=MovieGuide",
                   "sa",
                   "",
                   0);

    // Create and open the recordset.
    DBRecordset = new Recordset();
    DBRecordset.Open("Select * From ExistingMovies " +
                     "Order By InventoryID",
                     DBConnect,
                     CursorTypeEnum.adOpenDynamic,
                     LockTypeEnum.adLockOptimistic,
                     (int)ExecuteOptionEnum.adOptionUnspecified);

    // Fill the dialog with data.
    DoFill();

    // Initialize the print elements.
    PrnDialog = new PrintDialog();
    PrnSettings = new PrinterSettings();
}
```

As you can see, the process of creating and using both *DBConnect* and *DBRecordset* is about the same. First, you instantiate the object, and then you use the Open() method to activate it.

Notice the three items supplied as the first argument to the DBConnect.Open() method. You must always supply a data provider, the data source (even for a local data source), and the catalog or database that you'll use. Some DBMS might require more information, but you'll never provide less than that. Notice that the example supplies a username and a blank password. In this case, we don't require any of the optional parameters for the DBConnect.Open() method, so the final argument is a 0 (not a null as you might expect).

The DBRecordset.Open() method requires a query string of some type as the first entry. The example uses a SQL query, but you can also choose to use a table name or a stored procedure name for most DBMS. Notice that you must provide *DBConnect* or another connection as the second argument. One of the reasons to use ADO instead of ADO.NET is that you have full control over the type of cursor used to manage the record pointer. ADO.NET won't allow you to use server-side cursors, so you'll have to use ADO in this case. (See the "Comparing ADO to ADO.NET" section of Chapter 13 for more details about differences between ADO and ADO.NET.)

> **NOTE**   The execution option, the last argument in the DBRecordset.Open() method call, requires a typecast as shown here: (int)ExecuteOptionEnum.adOptionUnspecified. This is due to an error in the COM implementation of the ADO object. You're going to find that some methods won't compile unless you perform the typecast. The enumeration still works, but the method expects an integer value, rather than the enumeration as input.

Now that we have a connection and a recordset to use, there are four tasks that we need to perform: update, delete, add, and fill. Interestingly, this comes very close the same four functions provided by a data adapter (update, delete, insert, and select). In fact, you could substitute those terms if desired. Listing 12.2 shows the data manipulation source code for this example.

Listing 12.2   The Data Manipulation Methods for the ADO Example

```
private void DoFill()
{
   // Create a list of fields to retrieve.
   Object   []FieldArray =
      new Object[] {0, 1, 2, 3, 4, 5, 6, 7, 8, 9, 10, 11, 12};

   // Locate the current record.
   Object   Retrieved = DBRecordset.GetRows(1, 0, FieldArray);

   // Getting the record moves the record pointer, so we need
```

```csharp
    // to move it back.
    DBRecordset.MovePrevious();

    // Convert the object into an array.
    Object   [,]Data = new Object[13, 1];
    Array.Copy((Array)Retrieved, Data, 13);

    // Fill the text fields with data.
    txtInventoryID.Text = Data[0, 0].ToString();
    txtName.Text = Data[1, 0].ToString();
    txtRating.Text = Data[2, 0].ToString();
    txtDescription.Text = Data[3, 0].ToString();
    txtLeadActor.Text = Data[4, 0].ToString();
    txtLeadActress.Text = Data[5, 0].ToString();
    txtSupportingCast.Text = Data[6, 0].ToString();
    txtDirector.Text = Data[7, 0].ToString();
    txtProducer.Text = Data[8, 0].ToString();
    txtNotes.Text = Data[9, 0].ToString();
    txtDatePurchased.Text = Data[10, 0].ToString();
    txtFormat.Text = Data[11, 0].ToString();

    if ((bool)Data[12, 0])
        cbIsIn.Checked = true;
    else
        cbIsIn.Checked = false;
}

private void DoDataUpdate()
{
    // Change the field values using the easy, set_Collect()
    // method. You must provide a valid name and update value.
    DBRecordset.set_Collect("Name",
                            txtName.Text);
    DBRecordset.set_Collect("Rating",
                            txtRating.Text);
    DBRecordset.set_Collect("Description",
                            txtDescription.Text);
    DBRecordset.set_Collect("LeadActor",
                            txtLeadActor.Text);
    DBRecordset.set_Collect("LeadActress",
                            txtLeadActress.Text);
    DBRecordset.set_Collect("SupportingCast",
                            txtSupportingCast.Text);
    DBRecordset.set_Collect("Director",
                            txtDirector.Text);
    DBRecordset.set_Collect("Producer",
                            txtProducer.Text);
    DBRecordset.set_Collect("Notes",
                            txtNotes.Text);
    DBRecordset.set_Collect("DatePurchased",
                            DateTime.Parse(txtDatePurchased.Text));
```

```
        DBRecordset.set_Collect("Format",
                                txtFormat.Text);
        DBRecordset.set_Collect("IsIn",
                                cbIsIn.Checked);

}

private void DoAdd()
{
    // Create a list of fields to retrieve.
    Object   []FieldArray =
        new Object[] {1, 2, 3, 4, 5, 6, 7, 8, 9, 10, 11, 12};

    Object   []DataArray =
        new Object[] {"No Name Assigned",
                      "NR",
                      "No Description Supplied",
                      "No Lead Actor",
                      "No Lead Actress",
                      "No Supporting Cast",
                      "No Director",
                      "No Producer",
                      "No Special Notes for this Film",
                      DateTime.Today,
                      "VHS",
                      true};
    // Add a new record to the table.
    DBRecordset.AddNew(FieldArray, DataArray);

    // Update the recordset to reflect the new record.
    DBRecordset.Requery(0);
    DBRecordset.MoveLast();

    // Display the record on screen for editing.
    DoFill();
}

private void DoDelete()
{
    // Delete the current record.
    DBRecordset.Delete(AffectEnum.adAffectCurrent);

    // Update the recordset to reflect the deleted record.
    DBRecordset.Requery(0);

    // Display the next record on screen.
    DoFill();
}
```

You'll find that ADO provides more than one way to perform every task. The example uses the hard way for the DoFill() method, simply as a counterpoint to the easy method shown for the DoDataUpdate() method. Either method of working with the recordset is viable and completely correct, but the first method we'll discuss is more time consuming to implement—something you should consider if you don't require the additional flexibility that it provides. In short, always look for the easy ADO method for accomplishing any given task.

The DoFill() method begins by retrieving the data using the GetRows() method. We only need to retrieve one record at a time, but the GetRows() method enables you to retrieve any number of records. The advantage of using this technique is that you could build in-memory databases of static data using arrays. Notice that you must reposition the record pointer after using GetRows() because this call always positions the record pointer at the next record.

We also need to perform an odd data transition when using the GetRows() method because it will only return an *Object*, not an *Object Array*. You can view the returned data in the *Retrieved* object using the debugger, but you can't access the individual array elements until you convert the *Object* to an *Object Array*. Of course, you can't perform this transition directly, so you need to use the Array.Copy() method to accomplish the task. Once the code performs the conversion, placing the resulting data in the form fields is easy.

As previously mentioned, the DoDataUpdate() method shows the easy way of working with *DBRecordset*. Here's the problem with the second method—it isn't documented. You can look in the help file (or even the MSDN subscription for that matter) and you'll never find the set_Collect() method. Unless you spend time working with the ADODB namespace in Object Explorer, you'll never find gems like this undocumented method and you'll face endless hours of misery developing an application the hard way. The set_Collect() method sets the data, while the get_Collect() method gets the data for any accessible field in the current record. Notice that the DoDataUpdate() method lacks a call to the DBRecordset.Update() method. You'll find that you don't need to make the call to update the database and that it won't work, in most cases, if you do.

The DoAdd() method relies on two arrays to add a record to *DBRecordset*. The first array contains a list of field numbers (don't try to use field strings—they won't work in some cases), while the second array contains default values for those fields. You must assign a value to every field in the new record except for automatically numbered fields (such as *InventoryID* in the example).

After you add the new record, you must use Requery() to fill *DBRecordset* with the actual new record from the database. If you don't query the database, *DBRecordset* will only contain the default values provided as part of the AddNew() call and the DoFill() method will fail with a *null* value error. Unfortunately, using the Requery() method positions the record pointer to the first record in *DBRecordset*, so we need to reposition the record pointer to the new record (the last record in every case for the example). The last step of adding the new record is to display it on screen. Notice that the DoAdd() method lacks any code for updating the new record with user input from the form—the application takes care of this automatically as part of the update process.

It's interesting to note that ADO makes it easier to delete an existing record than to add a new one. The DoDelete() method uses the DBRecordset.Delete() method to delete the current record, and then it simply displays the first record of the database on screen after a Requery() call. You can delete something other than the current record, so it's important to add a value from the *AffectEnum* enumeration.

Moving Between Records

One of the best features of using ADO is that it makes moving between records simple. All you need to do is use one of a number of Move() methods to change the record pointer position. From this perspective alone, using ADO is a lot easier than using OLE-DB. Listing 12.3 shows the code you'll need to move from record-to-record in this example.

Listing 12.3   **ADO Makes Moving Between Records Easy**

```
private void DoFirst()
{
    // Update the data.
    DoDataUpdate();

    // Move to the first record.
    DBRecordset.MoveFirst();

    // Update the screen.
    DoFill();
}

private void DoNext()
{
    // Update the data.
    DoDataUpdate();

    // Move to the next record.
    DBRecordset.MoveNext();

    // If we are at the end of the database,
    // move back one and display a message.
    if (DBRecordset.EOF)
    {
        DBRecordset.MovePrevious();
        MessageBox.Show("Already at last record!",
                        "Dataset Pointer",
```

```
                        MessageBoxButtons.OK,
                        MessageBoxIcon.Exclamation);
    }

    // Update the screen.
    DoFill();
}

private void DoPrevious()
{
    // Update the data.
    DoDataUpdate();

    // Move to the previous record.
    DBRecordset.MovePrevious();

    // If we are at the beginning of the database,
    // move forward one and display a message.
    if (DBRecordset.BOF)
    {
        DBRecordset.MoveFirst();
        MessageBox.Show("Already at first record!",
                        "Dataset Pointer",
                        MessageBoxButtons.OK,
                        MessageBoxIcon.Exclamation);
    }

        // Update the screen.
        DoFill();
}

private void DoLast()
{
    // Update the data.
    DoDataUpdate();

    // Move to the last record.
    DBRecordset.MoveLast();

    // Update the screen.
    DoFill();
}
```

As you can see, all four of the record movement methods share three elements in common. First, they update the data so that any changes the user makes will appear in the current record before the code changes to the next record. Second, the code uses one of four record movement commands: MoveFirst(), MoveNext(), MovePrevious(), or MoveLast() to change the record pointer. Third, the code calls DoFill() to show the changed record pointer position on screen.

The `DoNext()` and `DoPrevious()` methods require additional code to ensure the user doesn't attempt to move past the end or the beginning of the recordset. Two special properties, *EOF* (end of file) and *BOF* (beginning of file) tell the application when the record pointer is pointing to a special phantom record that marks the beginning and end of the recordset. All DBMS have a BOF and EOF concept, but ADO makes it easy to determine when this event occurs. It's educational to compare the implementation of an ADO record movement method to the OLE-DB equivalent because OLE-DB lacks any means of checking for either EOF or BOF.

Now that we've discussed the important differences in the user interface and recordset manipulation code for ADO, it's time to see what the application looks like in operation. Figure 12.5 shows the output of this application. After looking at the amount of data displayed for each record, it's easy to understand why this example relies on a Detail view, rather than a Grid view. The Grid view would hide important details that the user would need to know in order to make any decisions about the movie. Of course, a Grid view add-on would make it easier to perform movie searches based on specific criteria.

FIGURE 12.5:

The ADO Demonstration application uses an efficient Detail view for data access.

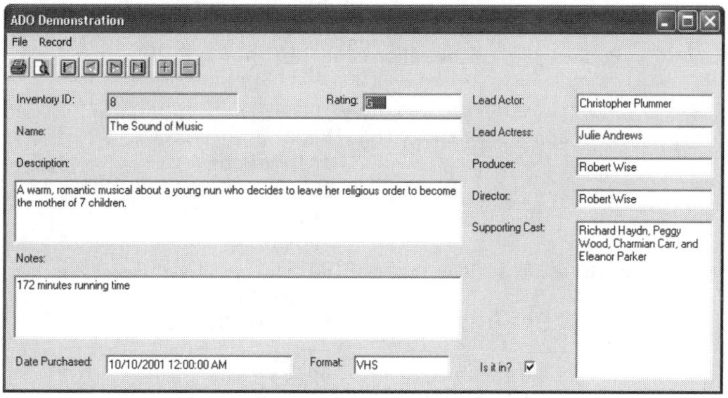

Printing the Data

Most of the print routines for any given application are the same no matter what type of database access technology you use, so we won't look at everything required for printing in this chapter because we've already visited the topic in detail in Chapter 11. (In fact, I cut and paste the routines from Chapter 11 into the example for this chapter in order to demonstrate there are few differences you need to consider.) However, the one item that will always change is the `PrintPageEventHandler()`. The data access technology you choose for your application will have a very big impact on the method assigned to handle print page events. Listing 12.4 shows the event handler for this example.

```csharp
void PD_PrintPage(Object sender, PrintPageEventArgs ev)
{
    Font        docFont;            // Document Font
    Font        headFont;           // Heading Font
    Font        columnFont;         // Column Font
    float       yPos = 20;          // Position of text on page.
    DateTime    PurchaseDate;       // Purchase date of the film.
    string      IsItIn;             // Is the movie in stock?

    // Create the font.
    docFont = new Font("Arial", 11);
    headFont = new Font("Arial", 24);
    columnFont = new Font("Arial", 12, FontStyle.Bold);

    // Print the heading.
    ev.Graphics.DrawString("Movies 'R Us Movie Listing",
                            headFont,
                            Brushes.Black,
                            20,
                            yPos);
    yPos = yPos + headFont.GetHeight() + 20;

    // Print the column headings.
    ev.Graphics.DrawString("Name",
                            columnFont,
                            Brushes.Black,
                            20,
                            yPos);
    ev.Graphics.DrawString("Rating",
                            columnFont,
                            Brushes.Black,
                            240,
                            yPos);
    ev.Graphics.DrawString("Format",
                            columnFont,
                            Brushes.Black,
                            320,
                            yPos);
    ev.Graphics.DrawString("Purchase Date",
                            columnFont,
                            Brushes.Black,
                            420,
                            yPos);
    ev.Graphics.DrawString("Is It In?",
                            columnFont,
                            Brushes.Black,
```

```
                              580,
                              yPos);

    yPos = yPos + columnFont.GetHeight() + 15;

    // Go to the first record in the recordset.
    DBRecordset.MoveFirst();

    // Continue printing as long as there is space on the page and
    // we don't run out of things to write.
    while (!DBRecordset.EOF)
    {
        // Print the line of text.
        ev.Graphics.DrawString(DBRecordset.get_Collect("Name").ToString(),
                              docFont,
                              Brushes.Black,
                              20,
                              yPos);
        ev.Graphics.DrawString(DBRecordset.get_Collect("Rating").ToString(),
                              docFont,
                              Brushes.Black,
                              240,
                              yPos);
        ev.Graphics.DrawString(DBRecordset.get_Collect("Format").ToString(),
                              docFont,
                              Brushes.Black,
                              320,
                              yPos);
        PurchaseDate =
            DateTime.Parse(DBRecordset.get_Collect("DatePurchased").ToString());
        ev.Graphics.DrawString(PurchaseDate.ToShortDateString(),
                              docFont,
                              Brushes.Black,
                              420,
                              yPos);
        if ((bool)DBRecordset.get_Collect("IsIn"))
            IsItIn = "Yes";
        else
            IsItIn = "No";
        ev.Graphics.DrawString(IsItIn,
                              docFont,
                              Brushes.Black,
                              580,
                              yPos);


        // Determine the next print position.
        yPos = yPos + docFont.GetHeight() + 10;

        // Move to the next record.
        DBRecordset.MoveNext();
```

```
    }

    // Tell the application there are no more pages to print.
    ev.HasMorePages = false;

    // Make sure we're at a valid record.
    DBRecordset.MoveFirst();
    DoFill();
}
```

There are similarities between the code in this chapter and the code in Chapter 11. For example, you still need to print headers for the report and provide other static functionality that doesn't change much in concept from application to application. Once you get past these obvious similarities, however, everything changes.

The code begins by moving to the first record position in *DBRecordset* using the Move-First() method. Unlike the data grid used in Chapter 11, *DBRecordset* only points to one record at a time, so we need to ensure the record pointer is in the right position.

Unlike the print routine in Chapter 11, you don't need to know how many records *DBRecordset* contains before you begin printing detail rows. *DBRecordset* includes the *EOF* property you can use to validate the end of the recordset. The detail row routine will continue printing pages until it runs out of records. Of course, the example shows a simple implementation that you can expand to meet specific needs.

Notice that the print routine uses the same DrawString() method found in Chapter 11 for displaying detail rows. However, the method for accessing the data differs. In this case, the code uses the simple method of accessing the individual field values for the current record— the get_Collect() method. As you can see, all you need to provide is the name of the field of interest.

The single record orientation of ADO comes into play again near the end of the routine. First, you need to use the MoveNext() method to ensure the recordset always points to the next record. Second, once the print routine completes, the code uses MoveFirst() method to position the record pointer to a valid record. Remember that the print routine continues until the *EOF* condition is true. This means *DBRecordset* would point to an invalid record unless you move the recordset at the end of the routine.

In all other ways, this example works the same as the example in Chapter 11. When you run the Print Preview code, you'll see a movie listing similar to the one shown in Figure 12.6.

FIGURE 12.6:
The Print Preview view of the data contains a listing of the facts most users will need to locate a specific title.

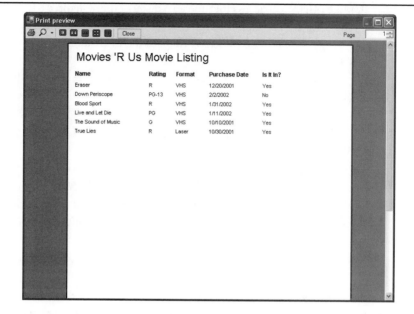

Troubleshooting Techniques for ADO Applications

Most developers find that ADO is easier to use than OLE-DB, even though it does hide some of the database transaction details (or perhaps *because* it hides the details). Of course, the ease of using ADO doesn't means you'll have an error-free environment in which to work. While errors are less common when using ADO because the underlying components take care of most of the work for you, finding an error can be more difficult because you can't see what's going on in many cases. The following sections discuss common problems you'll encounter as you create ADO applications using C#.

General

One of the most general rules to remember about ADO is that Microsoft provides multiple ways of performing any given task. However, as we saw in the "Understanding Data Manipulation" section of the chapter, one method is normally easier to use than any of the other available methods. Consequently, if you want to reduce development time, it pays to look for the easy way to accomplish a task. While the *Recordset* object doesn't provide enumeration, it usually provides some means of gaining access to individual data values, such as the get_Collect() method used for printing in this example.

Unlike other data access methods we discussed in Chapter 11, ADO does provide a means for detecting the EOF and BOF conditions. In some respects, this makes the job of writing code much easier. You don't have to use the weird end-of-data methods we used in Chapter 11 to move to the last record in the dataset. On other hand, ADO is also susceptible to EOF and BOF error conditions. Code can't manipulate the phantom records at the beginning or end of the database. Therefore, if you're having an odd, poorly defined error crop up during a data manipulation, check for the EOF or BOF condition as part of your troubleshooting.

Method Calls

One of the oddities of working with ADO is that it uses COM objects and the .NET Framework doesn't always provide the best translation of COM object methods. You'll notice that all of the method calls in this chapter include entries for every possible argument, even though many arguments are optional. The reason for including all arguments is that the application won't compile without them.

Of course, the requirement to provide an entry for every argument means you can't assume any default values when making a method call. One way around this problem is to provide *null* values for optional arguments. This technique works in many cases, but not in others. If you find that your code is failing for some "unknown" reason, it's probable that you've used a *null* value where an actual argument is required.

Another problem with method call arguments is that you'll often need to provide a value of type Variant. Unfortunately, this type isn't available in .NET, so you need to substitute the Object type. Always assume that you must provide an Object, not a string or some other value type, when working with any argument that includes an optional Variant argument. For example, the *Recordset* object GetRows() method can accept either a string or a Variant in the second argument. The only type that will work under .NET is the Variant (Object) type. Likewise, when the documentation states that you can provide a string, numeric value, or an array of either a string or a numeric value for the third argument for the GetRows() method call, what you really need to do is provide an Object. Nothing else will work, in this case, and the error message you receive from ADO is confusing at best.

ADO and the Garbage Collector

It's important to remember that ADO is a COM technology. This fact means that CLR can't release resources used by ADO automatically—you need to remember to release them. In addition, you'll need to use some bizarre techniques at times to ensure the accessibility of application data to ADO. This means pinning values when you run into problems with ADO access to the memory (the Garbage Collector releases the resource before ADO can use it).

Let's discuss one of the most important tasks you can perform when it comes to ADO and that Garbage Collector. You'll need to close the handles to the ADO objects and then set the objects to a `null` reference before the application closes. Otherwise, the application will leak memory and other resources—the Garbage Collector is unable to help with this particular chore. Here's an example of the code you'll use.

```
private void MainForm_Closing(object sender,
                              System.ComponentModel.CancelEventArgs e)
{
    // Close the recordset and the connection.
    DBRecordset.Close();
    DBConnect.Close();

    // Set the objects up for deletion.
    DBRecordset = null;
    DBConnect = null;
}
```

As you can see, there's nothing mysterious about this code, but you need to include it with your application. Notice that the code appears as a form `Closing()` event handler. You can theoretically place this code in other areas, but releasing global variables in the `MainForm_Closing()` method seems to work best.

You might be tempted to close and release the various ADO objects after each use, but this would incur a huge performance penalty in your application. The forte of ADO is the live database connection. In addition, you'd have to reposition the record pointer every time the user decided to perform any task. Tracking the current record will prove troublesome to say the least. However, it's a good idea to release local resources as soon as you finish using them. For example, an intermediate data result is a good candidate for immediate release.

Where Do You Go From Here?

This chapter has shown you how to work with Server Explorer, one of the more important developer productivity aids in the Visual Studio .NET IDE. You've learned how to use Server Explorer to gain access to a variety of data types and how to use it to build your own databases. We've also discussed ADO, an important database technology in that it enables you to create quick connections to databases with less work than using OLE-DB. Of course, ADO doesn't provide the level of automation that OLE-DB does in C#.

The Server Explorer is complex enough that you won't learn about everything it can provide in one or two sessions. Yet, this tool is an essential productivity aid, so learning everything it can do is important. One of the ways to develop a better appreciation of the Server

Explorer is to spend time developing small projects with it. Of course, you'll want to create projects that could yield usable code for larger applications later.

Combining Server Explorer with database technologies such as ADO makes a simple tool more powerful. We used this approach in the performance counter example in the chapter, but it's useful in many other projects. Spend the time required to learn how to manage the data exposed by Server Explorer with datasets and how to store the resulting data in databases for future use.

Chapter 13 will show you how to use the latest Microsoft database technology, ADO.NET. This new technology combines ease-of-use, fast development time, and a high-level view of the data management process in a managed application package. As you'll learn, ADO.NET does have limitations that you'll need to consider when designing your next database application, but the technology does represent a giant leap forward for the developer.

CHAPTER 13

ADO.NET Application Development

- Comparing ADO to ADO.NET

- Using OleDbDataAdapter for Data Transfer to ADO.NET

- Writing a DataReader Application

- Writing a Dataset Application

- Importing and Exporting XML Example

- Using StringBuilder to Improve Performance

The previous two chapters have taken you through Object Linking and Embedding-Database (OLE-DB), Open Database Connectivity (ODBC), and ActiveX Data Objects (ADO). Now it's time to look at the final piece of the database puzzle for .NET—ADO.NET. This is Microsoft's latest and greatest database access offering. However, unlike previous Microsoft database technologies, ADO.NET isn't designed to provide an all-inclusive solution to every database need; ADO.NET is designed with distributed application requirements exclusively in mind.

This chapter tells you about ADO.NET and shows you several ways to use this new technology. Of course, the big news for ADO.NET is the disconnected application scenario, where a user on the road downloads the data they need for a particular purpose, and then disconnects from the company Internet connection while continuing to work. However, ADO.NET makes just about every type of distributed application programming easier, because it supports the latest connection technologies. We'll also look at what passes for a live connection in ADO.NET. (Of course, you won't see any server-side cursor support with this technology.)

As part of the distributed and disconnected application scenarios, we'll also begin to look at technologies that might make your online communication events easier. Most notably, this chapter will look at techniques for working with XML data. XML is the current solution for distributed application program connectivity because it enables an application to communicate with a web server through a firewall. Future chapters will take remote connectivity further and show you how to use some of the latest communication technologies including the Simple Object Access Protocol (SOAP).

TIP   Microsoft is making a concerted effort to XML-enable all of their products, which includes the XML support found in SQL Server 2000. A large part of this effort is directed toward making it easier to create web services using Microsoft products. In fact, Microsoft recently released a Web Services Toolkit (`http://msdn.microsoft.com/downloads/sample.asp?url=/MSDN-FILES/027/001/872/msdncompositedoc.xml`) for SQL Server 2000 that makes it easier to create web service applications. The Web Services Toolkit site includes a link for the toolkit, white papers, webcasts, demonstrations, and the SQL Server–related newsgroups. Coupled with the SQL Server offering is an offering for BizTalk Server that links it with .NET. The Microsoft BizTalk Server 2002 Toolkit for Microsoft .NET includes a wealth of examples in addition to the required assemblies. You can find this toolkit at `http://msdn.microsoft.com/downloads/default.asp?url=/downloads/sample.asp?url=%20/msdn-files/027/001/870/msdncompositedoc.xml`.

Comparing ADO to ADO.NET

ADO.NET has had a rough childhood in some respects. It began as ADO+; the new and improved form of ADO, but Microsoft quickly changed the name when it became obvious that ADO.NET was going to become something different. In fact, ADO and ADO.NET are very different technologies, despite the similarities in names. Of course, this begs the question of why Microsoft used the term at all if the technologies are so different. The answer lies in the few similarities between the two technologies and not in their differences.

NOTE   This section of the chapter assumes you've read Chapter 12 and worked through the example application. You should also have a good understanding of how ADO works. For example, you need to understand terms like *recordset* to understand the material in this section.

Both ADO and ADO.NET are high-level database access technologies. This means you do less work to accomplish any given task than you would with a low-level technology such as OLE-DB, but you also lose some flexibility and control. In addition, both of these technologies rely on OLE-DB as the low-level technology that performs most of the behind-the-scenes work. (We discussed OLE-DB in Chapter 11.) The final point of similarity between these two technologies is that they both rely on similar access techniques, such as the use of cursors and an in-memory data representation. This feature is hardly surprising considering both technologies come from the same company.

You learned in Chapter 12 that the basic in-memory representation for ADO is the *Recordset* object. This object contains a single table that can come from a query, individual table, stored procedure, or any other source of a single table of information. In some respects, this representation is limited, because you can only work with one set of information per *Recordset* object. However, nothing prevents you from creating more than one *Recordset* object, so in reality, the limit is more of perception than anything else. In fact, some developers state that using recordsets makes their code more readable than the ADO.NET alternative.

The ADO.NET alternative is to use a *Dataset* object. This is the same object that OLE-DB uses under .NET. A *Dataset* can contain multiple tables, which means you don't need exotic queries to gain access to precisely the information you need. The *DataTable* objects within the *Dataset* can have relations, just as they would within the database. The result is that you can create complex database setups within your application. Of course, this assumes you have so much data that you require such a complex setup for a single application. Some companies do have that much data, which is why this approach is so valuable. We'll see how to use the multiple table and relations feature of the *DataSet* object later in the chapter.

The simple, single-table *Recordset* object used by ADO means that it can also use simple commands to move between records. We saw in Chapter 12 that the Move(), MoveFirst(), MovePrevious(), MoveNext(), and MoveLast() functions do all the work required to move from one record to another. In addition, you can easily determine the EOF and BOF conditions using the associated *Recordset* property values. This means that moving to the beginning or end of a table is easy and you can always determine your current position within the table. The record pointer associated with all of this movement is called a *cursor*. ADO supports cursors that reside on both the server and the client, which means that an application can track the current record position wherever it makes sense within a LAN application environment.

ADO.NET makes use of collections within the dataset. Actually, there are groups of collections, and collections-within-collections. The advantage of this technique is that you can examine records using a foreach statement—the same technique you'd use to enumerate any other collection. Using collections also makes it easier to transfer data to display elements such as the *DataGrid* object. (Although, the *Recordset* object is actually easier to use with detail forms.) The use of collections means that it's easier to read a *Dataset* object from end-to-end than it is to address an individual record or to move backward within the collection. For example, let's say you want to address a single record field within the dataset; you'd probably require code similar to the code shown here:

```
MyString = MyData.Tables[0].Rows[0].ItemArray.GetValue(1).ToString();
```

The equivalent code for ADO is simpler and easier to understand. Here's an example:

```
MyString = DBRecordset.get_Collect("Name").ToString()
```

As you can see, a Recordset object does have an advantage in requiring less code to access an individual value because it isn't buried in multiple layers. In addition, notice that you can access the field by name when using a Recordset object—the Dataset object offers you an integer value that you must derive from the field's position within the data result. Still, there are significant advantages to using ADO.NET, as we'll see in the sections that follow.

This brings us to the *DataReader* object, which uses a read-only, forward-only cursor. The main purpose of the *DataReader* object is to enable disconnected mode operation for applications. A user can download data from the company database while connecting using an Internet (or other) connection. The data is then available for viewing offline (but not for modification because the connection to the database is lost).

While both ADO and ADO.NET rely on OLE-DB as their connectivity technology, they each use different techniques to accomplish their goal. Both database technologies do rely on a connection. However, ADO provides little flexibility in the way data updates occur once the connection is established. As we saw in the ODBC.NET example in Chapter 11, you can create the individual update elements of the *DataAdapter* object or rely on automation, as we did for the OLE-DB example. The point is that ADO.NET also relies on a *DataAdapter*, which means it also provides you with this flexibility in performing updates.

The final point for consideration, now, is the issue of connectivity. ADO does provide remote connectivity features, but like all other COM-based technologies, it uses DCOM as the basis for data exchange across a remote network. This means the connection port number changes often and the data itself is in binary form. The benefit of this approach is that few crackers have the knowledge required to peer at your data. The disadvantage is firewall support—most firewalls are designed to keep ports closed and to restrict binary data.

ADO.NET gets around the firewall problems by using XML to transfer the data using HTTP or some other appropriate data transfer technology. The point is that the data is in pure ASCII and relies on a single port for data transfers. Unfortunately, many people criticize XML as a security risk and vendors have done little to make it more secure. Any attempt to encrypt the data would open the Pandora's box of binary data transfer again, making the use of XML questionable. In short, XML is a good, but not perfect, solution to the problem of remote connectivity.

Using OleDbDataAdapter for Data Transfer to ADO.NET

As previously mentioned, ADO.NET relies on OLE-DB to perform low-level database connectivity chores. You're already familiar with the two objects that ADO.NET uses for this task, the *OleDbConnection* and the *OleDbDataAdapter*. The *OleDbConnection* object creates the actual connection between the application and the database management system (DBMS). The *OleDbDataAdapter* performs tasks like inserting new records, updating existing records, and deleting old records. We created a set of these commands for the ODBC.NET example in Chapter 11.

NOTE   The *OleDbDataAdapter* comes in more than one flavor. Visual Studio .NET comes with a form of this object that's optimized for SQL Server—the *SqlDataAdapter*. The difference between the two objects is that the SQL Server version is optimized for use with SQL Server, which means your application gains a performance benefit. Microsoft anticipates that other vendors will eventually create specialized connection and data-adapter objects for .NET. In fact, the first add-on for this technology is the ODBC.NET technology we discussed in Chapter 11.The performance you receive from a custom object will normally be better than the performance you obtain from the standard objects. However, the only thing you gain, in some cases, is some additional flexibility in accessing the data.

Once the data appears within the data adapter, you can access it in a number of ways. For example, it's possible to fill a *Dataset* object with information from the data adapter using the

Fill() or the FillSchema() command. A *Dataset* object can contain more than one table, so it's possible to create relations and perform other tasks normally performed by a DBMS.

The *Dataset* object contains the whole table found in the data adapter in a raw form that you can manipulate as needed. Sometimes you don't need the raw data; you need something that's sorted, filtered, or otherwise manipulated in some way. That's where the *DataView* object comes into play. The *DataView* object can present a particular view of the information found in the data adapter. For example, you can choose to ignore specific fields or rows with certain attributes (such as deleted rows). Two *DataViews* that use the same data adapter can contain vastly different information, which makes the *DataView* somewhat limiting but also adds a level of automation to the database application.

Writing a DataReader Application

Previous examples in the book have discussed the use of the *Dataset* object because it provides the type of connectivity that most developers are used to using in an application. You'll also find a new *DataReader* object with Visual Studio .NET that enables you to create a read-only, forward-only stream of data from a database. The main benefit of using a *DataReader* object is that the application saves memory (only a single record resides in memory) and the technique can help enhance application performance.

The *DataReader* object is useful for a number of purposes. For example, you can use it to create fast print routines and display lists. A *DataReader* also enables you to download data to a laptop or PDA for later use. Because the *DataReader* doesn't need a connection to the database once you complete the download, you can use it to create disconnected applications.

The following sections describe one use for the *DataReader*. We'll build a list view and a print routine based on the *DataReader* for the MovieGuide database discussed in Chapter 12. You'll also find a new type of construct in this section, the *StringBuilder* object. The "Using StringBuilder to Improve Performance" section describes when and where you'll use this object.

Creating the Application Shell

The application we'll create in this section uses a standard dialog box. You'll need to add a *SqlConnection* named MovieConnect and a *SqlCommand* named GetMovie. The easiest way to create the *SqlConnection* is to drag the ExistingMovies database from Server Explorer to the form.

To configure *GetMovie*, you'll need to select MovieConnect in the *Connection* property. Click the ellipses in the *CommandText* property for the *GetMovie* command and you'll see a

Query Builder dialog box. Figure 13.1 shows how to format the query for this example. The graphical display at the top of the dialog box enables you to create relations and choose fields. The next section contains options for sort order and criteria. You'll see the current query listed in the third section. The fourth section of the dialog box contains parameters for the command. You should end up with a *CommandText* property value of SELECT Name, Rating, Description, LeadActor, LeadActress FROM ExistingMovies ORDER BY Name.

FIGURE 13.1:

Use the Query Builder to create text for the GetMovie command.

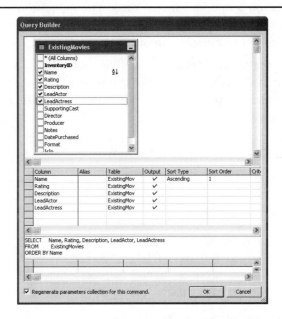

The application also includes three buttons: Quit, List Data, and Print Data. A textbox (*txtOutput*) will hold the data that the application produces when the user clicks List Data. Figure 13.2 shows typical application output.

FIGURE 13.2:

The application will list or print data using a DataReader instead of a Dataset.

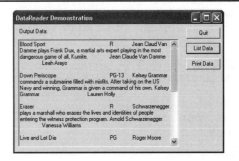

Adding Some Code

The *DataReader* application differs from other database applications covered in this book, because it concentrates on output rather than full database functionality. The use of a *SqlCommand* object enables the developer to add flexibility in the form of query support— changing the query will always create a different output. Consequently, you could easily use a configuration dialog to provide query input. For instance, one of the uses for this type of application is an informational kiosk. The application is actually safer than most, because it's impossible for the user to send new data or modify existing data—the *DataReader* limits interaction to requests for information only.

The first task is to create a list of the data in the database. Listing 13.1 shows the code for the btnListData control. Notice the use of a **StringBuilder** (*MovieList*) to improve performance and the special control requirements for this example, such as opening and closing the connection.

Listing 13.1   **Use a DataReader When Application Security is Paramount**

```
private void btnListData_Click(object sender, System.EventArgs e)
{
   // Open the connection.
   MovieConnect.Open();

   // Create and initialize the DataReader.
   SqlDataReader  MovieGuide = GetMovie.ExecuteReader();

   // Create and initialize the StringBuilder.
   StringBuilder  MovieList = new StringBuilder();

   // Build the display string.
   while (MovieGuide.Read())
   {
      MovieList.Append(MovieGuide.GetString(0));
      MovieList.AppendFormat("\t{0}", MovieGuide.GetString(1));
      MovieList.AppendFormat("\t{0}", MovieGuide.GetString(2));
      MovieList.AppendFormat("\t{0}", MovieGuide.GetString(3));
      MovieList.AppendFormat("\t{0}\r\n\r\n", MovieGuide.GetString(4));
   }

   // Display the data in the textbox.
   txtOutput.Text = MovieList.ToString();

   // Close the data objects.
   MovieGuide.Close();
   MovieConnect.Close();
}
```

The first task the code performs is creating the *DataReader*. The easiest and most flexible way to do this is to call upon the ExecuteReader() method of the command we created earlier.

As you can see, you use a *DataReader* in a loop. Each call to Read() brings in another row of data. Remember that MovieGuide will contain only one row of data at a time and that you can't go back to a previous record. Therefore, you must perform any data processing on the current row while the row is in MovieGuide or store the information for future use. The *DataReader* object uses a 0-based index for storing the data fields in the order they appear in the query string for the *SqlCommand*. After you process all of the rows of data the query can provide, Read() will return false, which ends the processing loop and displays the data on screen.

If you'll remember from previous chapters, print routines follow a specific pattern .NET. What you really need is a *PrintPageEventHandler*. The other basics of printing remain the same in all but a few instances. Consequently, Listing 13.2 shows the *PrintPageEvent-Handler* for the example. Notice that PD_PrintPage() follows a pattern very different from previous chapters.

Listing 13.2   **The PrintPageEventHandler PD_PrintPage() Uses a StringBuilder for Output**

```
void PD_PrintPage(Object sender, PrintPageEventArgs ev)
{
    Font            docFont;     // Document Font
    Font            headFont;    // Heading Font
    float           yPos = 20;   // Position of text on page.
    StringFormat    Format;      // Drawing format for details.
    Rectangle       PrintArea;   // Printing area.

    // Create the font.
    docFont = new Font("Courier New", 10, FontStyle.Bold);
    headFont = new Font("Arial", 15);

    // Create the StringFormat.
    Format = new StringFormat();
    Format.FormatFlags = StringFormatFlags.NoClip;
    Format.Trimming = StringTrimming.None;

    // Determine a print area.
    PrintArea = new Rectangle(0,
        (Int32)yPos,
        (Int32)ev.Graphics.VisibleClipBounds.Width,
        (Int32)docFont.GetHeight() * 4);

    // Print the heading.
    ev.Graphics.DrawString("Movie Guide Output",
                    headFont,
                    Brushes.Black,
```

```
                          0,
                          yPos);
yPos = yPos + headFont.GetHeight() + 20;

// Open the connection.
MovieConnect.Open();

// Create and initialize the DataReader.
SqlDataReader  MovieGuide = GetMovie.ExecuteReader();

// Create and initialize the StringBuilder.
StringBuilder  MovieList = new StringBuilder();

// Continue printing as long as there is space on the page and
// we don't run out of things to write.
while (MovieGuide.Read())
{
    // Build the display string.
    MovieList.AppendFormat("{0, -51}", MovieGuide.GetString(0));
    MovieList.AppendFormat("{0, -6}", MovieGuide.GetString(1));
    MovieList.AppendFormat("{0, -1001}", MovieGuide.GetString(2));
    MovieList.AppendFormat("{0, -41}", MovieGuide.GetString(3));
    MovieList.AppendFormat("{0, -41}", MovieGuide.GetString(4));

    // Set the Y position.
    PrintArea.Y = (Int32)yPos;

    // Output the data.
    ev.Graphics.DrawString(MovieList.ToString(),
                          docFont,
                          Brushes.Black,
                          PrintArea,
                          Format);

    // Determine the next print position.
    yPos = yPos + (docFont.GetHeight() * 4) + 10;

    // Clear the StringBuilder object.
    MovieList =  new StringBuilder();
}

// Close the data objects.
MovieGuide.Close();
MovieConnect.Close();

// Tell the application there are no more pages to print.
ev.HasMorePages = false;
}
```

The process of creating various fonts and using `DrawString()` to create a header is the same as before. However, this is where the similarity to other print output routines we've studied ends. The first thing you should notice is that the detail lines rely on a rectangle, not a single point, as a means for determining the output range. The upper left corner is determined by the preferred x and y values (0 and $yPos$ for the example). We have no way to determine the width of the page because each printer is different. Fortunately, you can retrieve this value at runtime using the `ev.Graphics.VisibleClipBounds.Width` property. It's also necessary to determine a print height based on the font used by the print routine. The example allocates 4 lines of text for each database entry, so the rectangle height is `docFont.GetHeight() * 4`.

Because each entry in the report can contain multiple lines of data, it's also important to create a `StringFormat` object. This object determines the formatting characteristics of the output. The example tells the CLR not to clip the output text and not to use any string trimming. These two entries are essential or the CLR will attempt to clean up your output in some cases—an undesirable trait if you want to preserve the formatting of your text.

The detail portion of the output routine looks very similar to the routine we used for the textbox on screen. However, notice the complete lack of formatting (escape) characters in the text. The example also uses the second parameter of the formatting string to force each string to occupy one more character than its maximum length, which ensures the printed entries will line up. The use of a `StringBuilder` object isn't only a performance enhancement, in this case; it's a necessary part of the print routine and we'd need a lot more code to duplicate what this object does automatically.

There are some additional pieces of code you need to consider. `StringBuilder` objects have no `Clear()` method, so you need to create a new object after each line of printed text. The `StringBuilder` object is still more efficient than using a string alternative, but not quite as efficient as the textbox portion of the example.

Note, also, that you need to change the `Y` property of `PrintArea` after each row of text, or the data won't print in the right area. The need to keep track of two row variables is a nuisance and could lead to errors in a complex print routines, but it's a necessity in this situation. In short, you must update both $yPos$ and `PrintArea` to position the text on the printer.

Testing Using NUnit

As you create more application code and the code becomes more complex, it becomes important to have a good testing tool. Microsoft does provide some rudimentary testing tools with Visual Studio .NET, but most of these tools appear with the Enterprise Architect Edition and don't provide much in the way of automation. Consequently, third-party developers have filled in the gaps by creating automated tools for the developer. NUnit represents one of the tools that fill this gap. You'll find this product in the \NUnit folder of the CD.

NUnit provides two forms of testing application. The GUI version is accessible from the NUnit folder of the Start menu. The GUI version enables you to run the application test immediately after adding new code and provides a neater presentation of the logged errors. You'll also find a command-line version of the program called NUnitConsole in the \Program Files\NUnit\ folder of your hard drive. The console version lets you place several testing scenarios in a single batch file and perform automated testing on more than one application at a time. You can also schedule testing using the Task Scheduler.

The product works by examining test cases that you create for your application. A test case is essentially a script that compares the result from your code to an anticipated result (what you expected the code to do). The test case can also check the truth-value of a return value. The software author, Philip Craig, recommends creating a section of code, and then creating a test case for that code. For example, you'll want to create a minimum of one test case for each method within a class. In this way, you build layers of code and tests that help locate problems quickly and tell you when a piece of code that previously worked is broken by a new addition to the application.

NUnit provides the means to perform individual tests based on a single test case or to create a test suite based on multiple test cases. The use of a special function, `Assert()` or `AssertEquals()` enables NUnit to test for the required condition. When NUnit sees a failure condition, it logs the event so you can see it at the end of the test. The point is that you don't have to create test conditions yourself—each test is performed automatically. Of course, the test cases still need to address every failure condition to provide complete application testing.

Let's look at a simple example. (You'll find the source code for this example in the \Chapter 13\NUnitDemo folder of the CD.) The example code performs simple math operations, but the code could perform any task. The `DoAdd()` and `DoMultiply()` methods both work as written. However, there's an error in the `DoSubtract()` method as shown below.

```
public static string DoSubtract(string Input1, string Input2)
{
    int    Value1;
    int    Value2;
    int    Result;

    // Convert the strings.
    Value1 = Int32.Parse(Input1);
    Value2 = Int32.Parse(Input2);

    // Perform the addition.
    Result = Value2 - Value1;
```

```
    // Output the result.
    return Result.ToString();
}
```

Obviously, most developers would catch this error just by looking at the code, but it isn't always easy to find this type of error in complex code. That's why it's important to write a test routine as part of your application (or in a separate DLL). Creating the test routine consists of five steps:

1. Include the NUnitCore.DLL (located in the \Program Files\NUnit\bin folder) as a reference to your application.

2. Create a class that relies on the NUnit.Framework.TestCase class as a base class.

3. Add a constructor that includes a string input and passes the string to the base class such as: public MathCheckTest(String name) : base(name).

4. Add a test suite property to your code formatted as: public static ITest Suite.

5. Create one or more public test scenarios.

There are a number of ways to create the test suite for your application. The two main methods are dynamic and static, with the dynamic method presenting the fewest problems for the developer. Here's an example of the dynamic test suite declaration:

```
// You must define a suite of tests to perform.
public static ITest Suite
{
    get
    {
        return new TestSuite(typeof (MathCheckTest));
    }
}
```

As you can see, it's a simple read-only property. The property returns the type of the test. In this case, it's the MathCheckTest class. The example actually includes two classes, so you can see how the classes appear in the test engine. If you don't include this property, the test engine will claim that there aren't any tests—even if you've defined everything else correctly.

The test can be as complex or simple as you need in order to verify the functionality of the application. The simpler you can make the test, the better. You don't want errors in the test suite to hide errors in your code (or worse yet, tell you there are errors when its obvious the code is working as anticipated). Here's an example of a simple test method.

```
// Test the add function using a simple example.
public void TestAdd()
{
    string   Expected = "5";
    string   Result = MathCheck.DoAdd("2", "3");
```

```
    Assert(Expected.Equals(Result));
}
```

Sometimes you need two or more test methods to fully examine a method. For example, the DoDivide() method requires two tests as a minimum. First, you must examine the code for proper operation. Second, you must verify that the code can handle divide-by-zero scenarios. It's never a good idea to include both tests in one test method—use a single method for each test as shown in the example code.

Now that you know what the code looks like, let's see the code in action. When you first start the NUnitGUI application, you'll see a dialog containing fields for the Assembly File and the Test Fixture. Select an assembly file using the Browse button and you'll see the test suites the assembly contains in the Test Fixture field. Each test suite is a separate class and the name of the class appears in the field, as shown in Figure 13.3.

FIGURE 13.3:

An application can contain more than one test suite, but each suite must appear in a separate class.

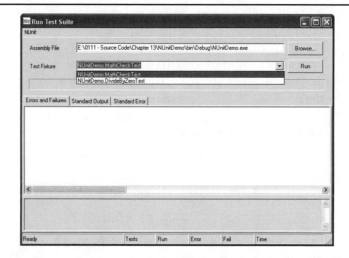

If you select a test suite and click Run, NUnitGUI will run all of the tests in that suite. However, you might only want to run one test in the suite. In this case, use the NUnit ≻ Show Test Browser command to display the Show Tests dialog box shown in Figure 13.4. Highlight the individual test you want to run and click Run. The results of the individual test will appear in the main window as usual.

FIGURE 13.4:

Use the Show Tests dialog box to select individual tests from a suite.

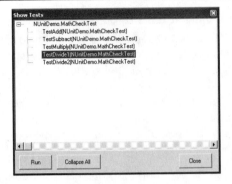

So, what happens when you run the tests? As the tests run, a bar will move across the window to show the test progress. If the tests run without error, you'll see a green bar on the main window; a red bar appears when the application has errors. Figure 13.5 shows a typical example of an application with errors.

FIGURE 13.5:

This application contains two errors that the test suite found with ease using simple tests.

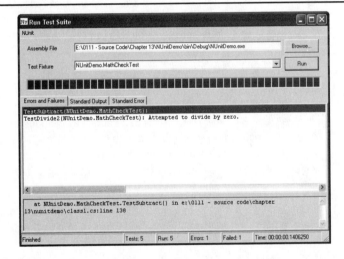

As you can see, the test found two errors. The first is the subtraction error that I mentioned earlier in the section. Notice that the lower pane of the main window provides you with enough information to locate the error in the source code. The second error is one of omission. The DoDivide() method lacks any means for detecting a divide-by-zero error. This second error points out that NUnit can help you find errors of commission, as well as errors of omission, given a good test suite.

Other Development Tools to Consider

Visual Studio .NET, like versions of Visual Studio before it, will rely heavily on third-party tools to enable the developer to perform certain tasks. For example, some developers find the profiling support in Visual Studio .NET lacking. Fortunately, DevPartner Profiler from Compuware Corporation enables you to perform a line-by-line analysis of your code. The best news is that this product is fully integrated with the Visual Studio .NET IDE, and you can download it free. You'll find DevPartner Profiler at the Compuware website (http://www.compuware.com/products/numega/dps/profiler/).

Another developer of performance testing tools is Mercury Interactive. LoadRunner (http://www-svca.mercuryinteractive.com/products/loadrunner/) enables the developer to place various types of loads on a system. For example, you could simulate 1,000 network users and 200 Internet users to create a mixed execution environment. You receive feedback about the effects of the load on the system as a whole through performance monitors. Astra LoadTest (http://astratryandbuy.mercuryinteractive.com/cgi-bin/portal/trynbuy/index.jsp) is one of a suite of tools you can use to perform website testing. Other tools in the suite include Astra QuickTest (automated web testing), Astra FastTrack (defect management), and Astra SiteManager (an application management tool). You can download demonstration versions of all four of these tools.

If the four database technologies we've studied so far have left you with more questions than answers, you might consider looking at Dataphor from Alphora (http://www.alphora.com/tiern.asp?ID=DATAPHOR). Dataphor is a data access alternative to the solutions that come with .NET. You'd use this technology in place of a technology such as OLE-DB or ADO.NET. The website currently includes a series of white papers explaining the product and a sign-up for the beta (the product will likely be released by the time you read this). Dataphor solves problems we've discussed in the various chapters including: non-updateable queries, lack of navigational access, join information loss, static data types, schema duplication, and three-valued logic.

Finding information in a large application can be difficult, to say the least. For example, you might remember that you defined a variable, but finding the definition can prove challenging. FMS provides a series of .NET–related tools, such as Total .NET XRef (http://www.fmsinc.com/dotnet/default.asp) that make it easier to manage your applications. The Total .NET series includes XRef (cross-reference variables and objects in your code), SourceBook (an extensive collection of source code examples), Analyzer (automated error and performance problem detection), and Renamer (a smart alternative to find and replace). Only the XRef product was available for preview at the time of writing.

Writing a Dataset Application

The *Dataset* object enables you to store data from a variety of sources, including *DataAdapters* and *DataTables*. The point is that it doesn't really care where the data comes from, as long as it can store the data in a *DataTable*. Every *Dataset* contains zero or more *DataTables*. We've discussed how you can create relations between the various tables in previous chapters. However, one of the points of the example in this chapter is that the source of the data is unimportant.

TIP   Many developers want to incorporate controls other than the standard string or check box into their *DataGrid*. The only problem is that Microsoft doesn't provide any additional controls as part of Visual Studio .NET. If you want to create other input forms, such as a drop-down list box, then you need to create a custom class that implements the Data-GridColumnStyle. Fortunately, some third-party developers are already working on this problem. For example, Axxias.ColumnStyles (http://www.columnstyles.com/) provides several types of controls you can incorporate into your *DataGrid* without a lot of additional programming.

This example relies on a database similar in design to the one found in Chapter 11 for the OLE-DB example. In fact, I simply exported the Access database in Chapter 11 to a SQL Server database on my Windows 2000 server and then made a few small changes to accommodate the additional functionality that SQL Server 2000 provides. One of the big differences between the two examples is that this example relies on SQL Server. You'll find the scripts for creating the database and adding data to it in the \Chapter 13\Data folder on the CD.

When you run the example, you'll find that it bears a striking similarity to the example in Chapter 11 (except for changes made to accommodate the new data source). While the Grid view code required some changes to make it run under the *SqlConnection* and *SqlDataAdapter*, I was able to move the Detail view code from the OLE-DB example directly to this example without a single change. Even though the source of the data changed drastically, the code required to access the data remained essentially the same—a real difference from coding in the past. (We'll discuss the Grid view code changes in the "Coding the Grid View" section.)

This example will also add new capabilities to the example found in Chapter 11. For example, you'll be able to add records to the Address table from the Detail view and also print from the Detail view. This chapter won't discuss some setup elements that are the same whether you use an Access database or a SQL Server database. For example, you still need to create the connection and data adapter objects (see the "Creating the Grid View" and "Creating the Detail View" sections of Chapter 11 for details). The following sections help you focus in on some new database application functionality, especially new functionality provided by the SQL Server 2000 provider.

Coding the Grid View

Because all of the data for this example goes through the Grid view, you'll need to make some minor changes to the code from Chapter 11. The first change is adding the proper using statements to the beginning of the FrmGridView.CS file. The example draws from the SQL Server provider, so we need to use namespaces for that provider. Unlike OLE-DB, you actually need two namespaces to gain full functionality to SQL Server 2000 features:

```
using System.Data.SqlClient;
using System.Data.SqlTypes;
```

The SqlClient namespace takes the place of the System.Data.OleDb namespace used for the previous example. You'll find all of the same functionality that the OLE-DB provider included, plus some additional functionality unique for SQL Server (not to mention the enhanced performance you'll receive). The SqlTypes namespace contains special data types you can use when working with SQL Server 2000 (previous versions of the product might not support all of the types shown in the namespace).

You'll also need to change some of the object names. For example, instead of an OleDbException, you'll need to check for a SqlException. The actual functioning of the exception object is the same—it still produces the same error and for the same reason. You'll still receive the same information and you'll use it in the same way. The only thing that's changed is the exception object name.

At this point, you should have a duplicate of the example in Chapter 11. The only difference is that you're using SQL Server instead of Access as the database. Of course, this is an important change because many database applications start out small and eventually outgrow their original DBMS. It's important to know how to transition from one DBMS to another.

Now that we have the preliminaries completed, let's look at some ways to augment the Grid view in the following sections.

TIP   It's interesting to note that you can't always create project names and namespaces that are conflict-free on the first try. For example, as an experiment for the example in this chapter, I tried naming the project "DataSet." The name should have worked given Microsoft's documentation, but it caused all kinds of odd conflicts, including a disappearing *DataSet* object problem. However, renaming the project files and changing the namespace entry to namespace MyDataSet didn't fix the problem. It seems the automatic code generation features of the Visual Studio IDE will continue to use the old namespace value until you change two values in the project Property Pages dialog. To view these properties, right-click the project name in Solution Explorer and choose Properties from the context menu. Open the \Common Properties\General folder and you'll see two properties: *Assembly Name* and *Default Namespace.* You must change both of these property values to the new namespace name in order to ensure that the automatic code generation features of the IDE work as intended.

Moving the Cursor on Screen

One of the first changes you'll see for the Grid view portion of this example is a new method for selecting rows. Some developers want something easier to see than the row pointer used for the first example. The most common way to make the row selection more visible is to highlight the entire row as shown here:

```
private void DoNext()
{
    // Move to the next record.
    if (AddrDataGrid.CurrentRowIndex !=
        addressDataset1.Tables[0].Rows.Count - 1)
    {
        AddrDataGrid.UnSelect(AddrDataGrid.CurrentRowIndex);
        AddrDataGrid.CurrentRowIndex++;
        AddrDataGrid.Select(AddrDataGrid.CurrentRowIndex);
    }
    else
        // Display an error message.
        MessageBox.Show("Already at last record!",
                        "Data Grid Pointer",
                        MessageBoxButtons.OK,
                        MessageBoxIcon.Exclamation);
}
```

Notice that this version of DoNext() relies heavily on the *CurrentRowIndex* property to ensure proper row selection. The UnSelect() method removes the highlight from the current row, the *CurrentRowIndex* value is incremented, and then the Select() method is called with the new *CurrentRowIndex*. (For comparison, see the DoNext() method in Chapter 11.)

It's possible to expand this process to enable the user to select more than one row—simply leave the UnSelect() method call out and the *DataGrid* will continue highlighting rows as needed.

Of course, you might not want to select an entire row. Perhaps you just want to select the current cell. You can perform this task in a number of ways, but this code will provide you with some general ideas:

```
private void DoLast()
{
    DataGridColumnStyle  DGCS; // The column we want to view.

    // Move to the last record.
    AddrDataGrid.UnSelect(AddrDataGrid.CurrentRowIndex);
    AddrDataGrid.CurrentRowIndex =
        addressDataset1.Tables[0].Rows.Count - 1;

    // Select the cell we want to highlight.
    AddrDataGrid.CurrentCell =
        new DataGridCell(AddrDataGrid.CurrentRowIndex, 0);
    DGCS = AddrDataGrid.TableStyles[0].GridColumnStyles[0];

    // Begin an edit to highlight the cell.
    AddrDataGrid.BeginEdit(DGCS, AddrDataGrid.CurrentRowIndex);
}
```

The first thing you should notice is that the code uses UnSelect() to remove the highlight from the current row, but doesn't rely on Select() to add a highlight to the next row. The code initially selects a new cell by creating a new value for the *CurrentCell* property using a *DataGridCell* object. The example assumes the user will want to select the first column in the *DataGrid*, but you can use the code to select any column, including the current column.

Simply selecting the cell won't highlight it. You could press Tab, at this point, and see the next cell highlighted, but it won't highlight the current cell, which is what we want the code to do. When the user clicks Tab, the *DataGrid* goes into edit mode, so that's what the example code will need to do as well. This means creating a *DataGridColumnStyle* object and then using it as input to the BeginEdit() method. Notice that the code doesn't call EndEdit() because the user hasn't made any changes to the data yet—the edit has only begun. At this point, you have two more ways to move the cursor around on the *DataGrid*.

Adding and Removing Records

The Grid view comes with the capability to add and remove records due to the connectivity between the *DataGrid* and the *DataAdapter*. However, the functionality is difficult to access outside of the *DataGrid* and assumes the user actually understands the results of pressing the control keys. For example, pressing Del will remove a record without one note of caution from the *DataGrid*, which opens the database to accidental data loss.

The example includes both menu entries and toolbar buttons for adding and removing records. One special note for the Record ➢ Delete menu entry is that you also need to add the Del key as a shortcut to ensure the user can't delete a record without using the proper routine. As with many other parts of this example, the menu and toolbar event handlers merely reroute the call to a centralized routine we can use for multiple purposes (not the least of which is adding the same support to the Detail view). Listing 13.3 shows the code you'll need to add for adding and removing records.

Listing 13.3   Adding and Removing Records from the Grid View

```
private void mnuRecordAdd_Click(object sender, System.EventArgs e)
{
   // Add a record.
   DoAddRecord();
}

private void mnuRecordDelete_Click(object sender, System.EventArgs e)
{
   // Delete a record.
   DoDeleteRecord();
}

private void DoAddRecord()
{
   // The column we want to view.
   DataGridColumnStyle  DGCS;

   // Create a new data row.
   DataRow  NewRow = addressDataset1.Tables[0].NewRow();

   // Fill required fields with default information.
   NewRow["LAST_NAME"] = "";
   NewRow["FIRST_NAME"] = "";
   NewRow["COMPANY"] = "";
   NewRow["BUSINESS"] = true;
   NewRow["CONTACTED"] = DateTime.Today.ToString();

   // Begin the editing process.
   NewRow.BeginEdit();

   // Place the cursor in the data add row.
   addressDataset1.Tables[0].Rows.Add(NewRow);

   // Select the new row and prepare to edit it.
   DoLast();
}
```

```
private void DoDeleteRecord()
{
   DialogResult    Result = DialogResult.No;
   DataRow         RemoveRow;

   // Display a message asking the user if they really want to
   // delete the record.
   Result =
      MessageBox.Show("Are you sure you want to remove the record?",
                      "Permanent Record Deletion Warning",
                      MessageBoxButtons.YesNo,
                      MessageBoxIcon.Warning);

   // If the user is sure about the record deletion, remove it.
   if (Result == DialogResult.Yes)
   {
      // Get the current data row.
      RemoveRow =
         addressDataset1.Tables[0].Rows[AddrDataGrid.CurrentRowIndex];

      // Mark the row as deleted.
      RemoveRow.Delete();

      // Update the data adapter.
      AddressDA.Update(addressDataset1);
   }
}
```

Adding a row to the database isn't a one step process—you need to modify the dataset first. To add a row to the dataset, you need to create a new *DataRow* object (*NewRow* in this case) based on the current table schema using the addressDataset1.Tables[0].NewRow() method. Note that you must select the proper table to ensure the schema of the new row is correct.

NewRow is blank when you create it, which means that even the primary key fields are empty. If you insert the new row into the dataset immediately, the application will raise an error. Consequently, the code assigns values to the new *DataRow*. In this case, it also assigns a value to the *BUSINESS* field because the database won't allow null values and the *CONTACTED* field for the convenience of the user. The Add() method completes the process of adding a new record to the dataset. The code calls DoLast() to position the cursor and open the first field of the *DataGrid* for editing.

Notice the call to BeginEdit(). The record addition will still work even without this call. However, the user won't see the familiar blinking cursor on the first entry in the new record if you don't provide this call. The call to DoLast() won't accomplish the same purpose in this case.

The code doesn't call `AddressDA.Update()` when adding a record. The act of creating the record automatically calls `AddrDataGrid_CurrentCellChanged()`. This method contains the required `AddressDA.Update()` call.

Deleting a record is a three-step process. The code still uses the dataset to perform the task. As with the record addition, the code creates a *DataRow* object that holds the record to delete. It marks the record for deletion using the `Delete()` method. The call to `AddressDA.Update()` completes the process. The code must call the `AddressDA.Update()` method, in this case, because the user isn't editing the record.

Notice that the `DoDeleteRecord()` method includes a `MessageBox.Show()` call that gives the user a chance to change their mind about deleting the record. This is an important addition, because it helps keeps the database intact by reducing the chance of an accidental deletion.

There's a potential problem with all of the modifications the code performs—it's possible that a change could occur and not get recorded. Even though this event is unlikely, it's important to consider it anyway. The following event handler reduces the likelihood that a database-damaging event will occur when the application closes.

```
private void GridView_Closing(object sender,
System.ComponentModel.CancelEventArgs e)
{
    // Create a series of data check objects.
    DataSet DeletedData =
        addressDataset1.GetChanges(DataRowState.Deleted);
    DataSet AddedData =
        addressDataset1.GetChanges(DataRowState.Added);
    DataSet ModifiedData =
        addressDataset1.GetChanges(DataRowState.Modified);

    // Check for pending updates and update the database as required.
    if (DeletedData != null ||
        AddedData != null ||
        ModifiedData != null)
        AddressDA.Update(addressDataset1);
}
```

The `GridView_Closing()` event occurs before the main application form closes and any of the data sources close. The code checks for *DataSet* conditions that could cause data loss, including the existence of modified, added, or deleted records. If the *DataSet* contains any records of this type, the code calls `AddressDA.Update()` to ensure the change is recorded.

Adding Copy, Cut, and Paste

The Copy, Cut, and Paste commands are somewhat tricky to add to a database application. The default setup for the *DataGrid* object enables you to cut, copy, or paste single cells. However, a row can only be copied. The reason you can't cut a row is that would delete the row and the *DataGrid* already provides a method for accomplishing that task. Likewise, pasting a row is akin to adding a new row to the database, which is handled by another method. Unfortunately, the only way to use Copy, Cut, and Paste in a *DataGrid* is to rely on the control key combinations of Ctrl+C, Ctrl+X, and Ctrl+V. If you want the convenience of using menus or toolbars, then you need to add the commands separately. Listing 13.4 adds this functionality to both the menus and toolbar.

Listing 13.4	Adding Copy, Cut, and Paste to the Example Program

```
private void mnuEditCut_Click(object sender, System.EventArgs e)
{
    // Perform the cut function.
    DoCut();
}

private void mnuEditCopy_Click(object sender, System.EventArgs e)
{
    // Perform the copy function.
    DoCopy();
}

private void mnuEditPaste_Click(object sender, System.EventArgs e)
{
    // Perform the paste function.
    DoPaste();
}

private void DoCut()
{
    DataGridColumnStyle  DGCS;        // The column we want to view.
    int                  Column;      // Data grid column.

    // Place the current data on the clipboard.
    Clipboard.SetDataObject(AddrDataGrid[AddrDataGrid.CurrentCell]);

    // Place a blank value in the data grid.
    AddrDataGrid[AddrDataGrid.CurrentCell] = "";

    // Begin the editing process.
    Column = AddrDataGrid.CurrentCell.ColumnNumber;
    DGCS = AddrDataGrid.TableStyles[0].GridColumnStyles[Column];
    AddrDataGrid.BeginEdit(DGCS, AddrDataGrid.CurrentRowIndex);
}
```

```csharp
private void DoCopy()
{
   StringBuilder   SelectedText = new StringBuilder();
   int             Row;
   int             Column;

   // Get the current row.
   Row = AddrDataGrid.CurrentCell.RowNumber;

   // If true, copy the entire row.
   if (AddrDataGrid.IsSelected(Row))
   {
      // Set the column value to 0.
      Column = 0;

      // Copy every entry in the row to the SelectedText
      // string.
      for(Column = 0;
         Column < AddrDataGrid.TableStyles[0].GridColumnStyles.Count;
         Column++)
      {
         SelectedText.Append(AddrDataGrid[Row, Column].ToString());

         // If this isn't the last entry, then add a tab.
         if (Column <
            AddrDataGrid.TableStyles[0].GridColumnStyles.Count - 1)
            SelectedText.Append("\t");
      }

      // Copy the composite string to the clipboard.
      Clipboard.SetDataObject(SelectedText.ToString());
   }

      // If only a single cell is selected, copy just
      // that cell.
   else
   {
      // Set the column value to the current cell.
      Column = AddrDataGrid.CurrentCell.ColumnNumber;

      // Place the data on the clipboard.
      Clipboard.SetDataObject(AddrDataGrid[Row, Column]);
   }
}

private void DoPaste()
{
   IDataObject          ClipboardData;  // Contents of the clipboard.
   string               PasteData;      // Data to paste.
   DataGridColumnStyle  DGCS;           // The column we want to view.
   int                  Column;         // Data grid column.
```

```
    // Verify the data is text.
    ClipboardData = Clipboard.GetDataObject();
    if (ClipboardData.GetDataPresent(DataFormats.Text))
    {
        // Get the data and place it in a string.
        PasteData = ClipboardData.GetData(DataFormats.Text).ToString();

        // Paste it in the current data grid cell.
        AddrDataGrid[AddrDataGrid.CurrentCell] = PasteData;

        // Begin the editing process.
        Column = AddrDataGrid.CurrentCell.ColumnNumber;
        DGCS = AddrDataGrid.TableStyles[0].GridColumnStyles[Column];
        AddrDataGrid.BeginEdit(DGCS, AddrDataGrid.CurrentRowIndex);
    }
}

private void AddrDataGrid_CursorChanged(object sender,
                                        System.EventArgs e)
{
    int         Row;             // Current data grid row
    IDataObject ClipboardData;   // Contents of the clipboard.

    // Get the current row.
    Row = AddrDataGrid.CurrentCell.RowNumber;

    // Ensure everything is enabled to start.
    mnuEditCut.Enabled = true;
    mnuEditCopy.Enabled = true;
    mnuEditPaste.Enabled = true;
    GridViewToolbar.Buttons[11].Enabled = true;
    GridViewToolbar.Buttons[12].Enabled = true;
    GridViewToolbar.Buttons[13].Enabled = true;

    // Determine if the row is selected. If so, then turn off the cut
    // and paste buttons since we can't perform either task on a row.
    if (AddrDataGrid.IsSelected(Row))
    {
        mnuEditPaste.Enabled = false;
        mnuEditCut.Enabled = false;
        GridViewToolbar.Buttons[11].Enabled = false;
        GridViewToolbar.Buttons[13].Enabled = false;
    }

    // We also need to check for an empty clipboard. An empty clipboard
    // means we can't paste anything. It's also possible the clipboard
    // contains an incompatible data type, so we need to check that as
    // well.
    ClipboardData = Clipboard.GetDataObject();
    if (ClipboardData == null ||
```

```
        !ClipboardData.GetDataPresent(DataFormats.Text))
    {
        mnuEditPaste.Enabled = false;
        GridViewToolbar.Buttons[13].Enabled = false;
    }
}
```

The DoCut() method only works with a single cell. It uses the Clipboard.SetDataObject() method call to place the current text on the clipboard. Notice how this example uses a cell, rather than individual row and column references for the *AddrDataGrid* indexer. After it saves the contents of the cell to the clipboard, DoCut() places a null string in the current cell. However, placing the value in the cell doesn't make it permanent—an update must occur before that happens. The final three lines of code place the current cell in the editing mode. These steps ensure the user notices a change in the appearance of *AddrDataGrid*. At this point, if the user presses Escape, the change on *AddrDataGrid* is reversed. However, the clipboard will still retain the new string value.

Because the DoCopy() method has to work for both single cells and entire rows, the code is actually a little more complex than DoCut(). The code initially determines if the user has selected an entire row or a single cell. The selection of a single cell means the DoCopy() method can simply place the value of the current cell on the clipboard without further processing. However, when working with a row of data, you must create a string containing all of the column values first. The default copy function places a tab between each field entry, but you can alter this technique to suit any requirements your application might have.

This is another situation where you can improve the performance of your application using a *StringBuilder* object in place of a standard string. The code appends each column value to *SelectedText*. If the code detects that this isn't the last column, it also adds a tab to *Selected-Text*. The processing continues until all of the columns have been processed and DoCopy() places the value in *SelectedText* on the clipboard.

Creating the DoPaste() method is the most difficult part of the coding process. Placing data on the clipboard isn't hard because you don't have to worry about problems such as data type—the clipboard takes care of the issue for you. However, when you're pasting data from the clipboard, you need to know that the data is the correct type. The first task the DoPaste() method performs is checking the data type of the clipboard data. If the data type isn't text, then the method exits without doing anything else.

NOTE   Notice that *ClipboardData* is of the IDataObject type. Most developers who have worked with COM know that this is a common COM interface. However, the IDataObject in the .NET Framework isn't a substitute for the COM interface. It does work in this situation, but probably won't work if you're creating a DLL to interact with COM in some way.

The DoPaste() method obtains the current clipboard contents using the GetData() method. Notice that you must specify a data format using the DataFormats enumeration. DoPaste() follows a process similar to DoCut() at this point. It makes the current cell value equal to the *PasteData* value obtained from the clipboard, and then places the cell in edit mode. If the user presses Escape, AddrDataGrid will reverse the change.

There's one last problem to consider for this scenario. The user depends on visual cues from the menu and toolbar to determine when it's possible to cut, copy, or paste data. This user assumption means you need some way to enable and disable both the toolbar buttons and the menu commands. You could select a number of ways to detect changes in the settings, but I chose to attach the code to the AddrDataGrid CursorChanged() event.

The code begins by enabling all of the affected buttons and menu entries. This step ensures the menu command and toolbar buttons are accessible. The code then checks for a selected row. If the user has selected a row, the code disables the cut and paste options because they only work with a single cell. Finally, the code checks the data type of the clipboard data. If the clipboard is empty or it contains data of the wrong type, then the code disables the paste function. The application can only accept text as input.

Coding the Detail View

The Detail view found in Chapter 11 is functional, but barely. You can move between records and edit existing records. Any change in the Detail view is also synchronized with the Grid view. However, if you want to add or remove records, you need to do it in the Grid view. Printer support is likewise limited.

This section of the chapter discusses a few enhancements you can add to the Detail view to make it more functional. We'll discuss what you need to do in order to add and remove records. You'll also learn about a single-record print routine that's based on data in the Detail view, instead of the data found in the Grid view. These customizations move the Detail view from barely functional to quite practical.

Adding and Removing Records in Detail View

As with other database operations for the Detail view, the Grid view already has the required code. What you really need is a means of accessing that code through the Detail view controls. Of course, the first task is to add the required controls to the form so that the user can click them as needed. Make sure you change the *Modifiers* property to Public so the button's Click() event is accessible from the Grid view.

All of the code for *btnAdd* and *btnDelete* appear in FrmGridView.cs file, not the FrmDetail-View.cs file as you might expect. The first task is to create a connection to the Detail view buttons by adding event handlers. The following code appears in the `AddrDataGrid_Double-Click()` method to ensure the event handlers aren't created unless actually needed.

```
// Create event handlers for adding and removing records.
DetailDlg.btnAdd.Click += new EventHandler(DoDetailAdd);
DetailDlg.btnDelete.Click += new EventHandler(DoDetailDelete);
```

The event handlers have to do more than their Grid view counterparts. We discussed the synchronization issues in the "Synchronizing the Grid View and Detail View" section of Chapter 11. In addition to synchronization issues, you also need to consider data update issues. The event handler must ensure that the data that the Detail view sees is the same as the data in the Grid view. Here's the code for the two event handlers.

```
private void DoDetailAdd(object sender, System.EventArgs e)
{
    // Add a new record.
    DoAddRecord();

    // Ensure the record is recorded.
    AddressDA.Update(addressDataset1);

    // Fill the AddrDataGrid variables.
    ExchangeFill();

    // Fire the DataChanged event.
    DataChanged();
}

private void DoDetailDelete(object sender, System.EventArgs e)
{
    // Remove the current record.
    DoDeleteRecord();

    // Ensure the record is recorded.
    AddressDA.Update(addressDataset1);

    // Fill the AddrDataGrid variables.
    ExchangeFill();

    // Fire the DataChanged event.
    DataChanged();
}
```

As you can see, the code calls upon the same `DoAddRecord()` or `DoDeleteRecord()` methods used by the Grid view to add or remove a record. The code then calls `AddressDA.Update()` to ensure the dataset contains the correct information. This might seem like overkill, but the need is real. The last two steps place data in a location where the Detail view can see it and then fires an event that will force the Detail view to perform an update.

Printing in Detail View

We've already looked at quite a few printing techniques in the book. However, it's important to realize that users will anticipate certain types of print jobs when looking at specific views of their data. For example, when looking at the Detail view, users are likely to want an individual record printout, rather than a list of contacts in the database. The example code contains such a report. We'll discuss some of the highlights of that report in this section.

Individual report records are somewhat easier to print than multiple record reports because you don't need to consider any complex looping structures. All you need is the data for a single record. Of course, the user is likely to want complete information for that single record, so you'll need to address the full range of data input. The formatting is going to be different as well. Using a structure similar to the Detail view for this example works well in most cases.

One of the first changes that you'll notice in this version of the print routine is that the heading is smaller and relies on both bold and italic font attributes. It's easy to combine font attributes by or-ing them together. Here's an example of multiple attribute use:

```
headFont = new Font("Arial", 14, FontStyle.Bold | FontStyle.Italic);
```

Another problem with individual record reports is that you need to print items on single lines. This change from the tabular view used in the Grid view portion of the application means you'll calculate the *yPos* value more often. Rather than incur the cost of constant recalculation of the incremental difference between lines, you should calculate it once as shown here:

```
// Determine the yIncrement value.
yIncrement = columnFont.GetHeight() + 10;
```

Users will also expect friendly text in the report. For example, you wouldn't want to place a check box on the printed report for the BUSINESS field. Likewise, a value of true or false is unattractive. You can solve the problem by using a simple comparison and printing out the desired text as shown here:

```
ev.Graphics.DrawString("Business Contact?",
                       columnFont,
                       Brushes.Black,
                       20,
                       yPos);
if (cbBusiness.Checked)
    ev.Graphics.DrawString("Yes",
                       docFont,
```

```
                              Brushes.Black,
                              180,
                              yPos);
else
    ev.Graphics.DrawString("No",
                           docFont,
                           Brushes.Black,
                           180,
                           yPos);
yPos = yPos + yIncrement;
```

Finally, you'll need some large text areas to contain notes and other memo fields in your database. The way to perform this task is to specify a rectangular area as part of the Draw-String() call as shown here:

```
ev.Graphics.DrawString("Notes:",
                       columnFont,
                       Brushes.Black,
                       20,
                       yPos);
ev.Graphics.DrawString(txtNotes.Text,
                       docFont,
                       Brushes.Black,
                       new Rectangle(
                           180,
                           (Int32)yPos,
                           (Int32)ev.Graphics.VisibleClipBounds.Width -
                               180,
                           (Int32)ev.Graphics.VisibleClipBounds.Height -
                               (Int32)yPos));
yPos = yPos + yIncrement;
```

Because the print routine only needs the rectangle one time, the code declares the rectangle directly, rather than as a separate object. This technique tends to reduce resource usage and the time before the CLR frees the rectangle. Notice how the various rectangle boundaries are calculated. Make sure you take any offsets into consideration when designing your print routine.

Importing and Exporting XML Example

As applications develop into distributed systems, the need for some method of data exchange becomes more important. Microsoft has become convinced that various forms of XML are the answer, so they're making every effort to make their applications and application development platforms XML-enabled. This XML development extends Visual Studio .NET and the .NET Framework. You'll find a gold mine of XML development capabilities that you can easily access using C#.

This section provides a quick overview of one XML capability—the ability to import and export data in XML format using a dataset. We'll study XML in more detail in Chapter 16. However, this section is important now because it creates the first link between the world of distributed applications and the world of the desktop. This section provides you with a glimpse of the possibilities for applications that you wouldn't normally associate with the Internet. You'll find this example in the \Chapter 13\XMLInOut folder on the CD.

Writing the Code

The example performs two tasks. First, it enables the user to export the data found in the Movie database used earlier in the chapter to an XML file. Second, it enables the user to import data from a second XML file named SampleData.XML. The input and output files will appear in the \Chapter 13\XMLInOut\bin\Debug folder on the CD. Listing 13.5 shows the code we'll use in this case.

Listing 13.5   **Importing and Exporting XML is Easy in .NET**

```
private void btnImport_Click(object sender, System.EventArgs e)
{
   // Create a data stream.
   StreamReader  SR = new StreamReader("SampleData.xml");

   // Create a dataset and associated table.
   DataTable   DT = new DataTable("NewDataElement");
   DataSet     DS = new DataSet("NewData");

   // Configure the table.
   DT.Columns.Add(new DataColumn("Data1", typeof(string)));
   DT.Columns.Add(new DataColumn("Data2", typeof(string)));
   DT.Columns.Add(new DataColumn("Data3", typeof(string)));

   // Configure the dataset.
   DS.Tables.Add(DT);

   // Import the data.
   DS.ReadXml(SR);

   // Display the new data.
   dataGrid1.DataSource = DS;
   dataGrid1.DataMember = "NewDataElement";
   dataGrid1.Update();

   // Close the stream.
   SR.Close();
```

```
    }

    private void btnExport_Click(object sender, System.EventArgs e)
    {
        // Create a data stream.
        StreamWriter    SW = new StreamWriter("MovieExport.xml");

        // Output the data.
        movieDS1.WriteXml(SW);

        // Close the stream.
        SW.Close();

        // Create a second data stream.
        SW = new StreamWriter("MovieExportSchema.xml");

        // Output the schema.
        movieDS1.WriteXmlSchema(SW);

        // Close the second stream.
        SW.Close();
    }
```

The btnImport_Click() method begins by creating a *StreamReader* object (*SR*). *SR* will open the XML file for reading. The code then creates the *DataTable* (*DT*) and the *DataSet* (*DS*) objects used to cache the data locally. Configuring the table consists of adding three columns, one of each of the columns in the sample XML file. Once *DT* is configured, the code adds it to *DS*. Reading the data is as easy as calling the ReadXml() method.

As we'll see later, the name of the *DataTable* must match the name of the XML elements within the sample file. Likewise, the column names must match the names of the XML child elements used to store the data. Otherwise, you'll find that the reading process works as anticipated, but you won't see any data on screen.

The final part of the process is to modify the *DataSource* and *DataMember* properties of *dataGrid1*. The call to Update() ensures the new data appears on screen, as shown in Figure 13.6.

FIGURE 13.6:

Modifying the Data-Source and DataMem-ber properties enables dataGrid1 to display the imported data.

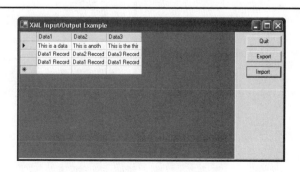

The btnExport_Click() method begins by creating a *StreamWriter* object (*SW*). The WriteXml() method of *movieDS1* outputs the data in XML format to the file opened by *SW*. Note that all you need to change to output the dataset schema instead of the data is call WriteXmlSchema().

Using the Microsoft XML Notepad

XML is almost, but not quite, readable by the average human. Reading simple files is almost trivial, but once the data gets nested a few layers deep, reading it can become tiresome. That's why you should have a tool for reading XML in your developer toolkit. The only problem is that some of these tools cost quite a bit for the occasional user. Microsoft has remedied this problem a little with the introduction of XML Notepad (http://msdn.microsoft .com/library/default.asp?url=/library/en-us/dnxml/html/xmlpaddownload.asp). This utility is free for the price of a download and does a reasonable job of reading most XML files. (Microsoft hasn't bothered to update the date for this site, but be assured that XML Notepad runs fine under both Windows 2000 and Windows XP.)

When you start XML Notepad, you'll see a blank project. Use the File ≻ Open command to display an Open dialog that allows you to open XML files from a local drive or from a website. All you need is a filename (and path) or a URL to get started.

Figure 13.7 shows the output of the sample XML application. Notice that the name of the elements matches the name of the table for the movie database. Likewise, each of the child elements matches the name of one of the fields within the table. The right pane shows the data contained within each one of the child elements.

FIGURE 13.7:

The names of the elements are important when working with exported data in XML format.

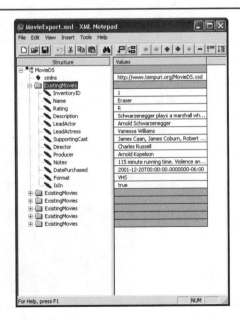

Creating new data for testing purposes is relatively painless once you see the exported data from an existing database. Create a blank project using the File ➤ New command. Type the name of the dataset in the Root object. Rename the first element to reflect the new table. Add a new child element using the options on the Insert menu. You'll notice that the first element changes into a folder. Type the name of the first data column in this element. Add additional columns as needed until you complete one record's worth of entries. Finally, type values for each of the child elements.

Now that you have one complete record, you can use the Duplicate command to create copies of it. Each copy will become one record within the XML database. Figure 13.8 shows the structure and contents of the SampleData.XML file.

FIGURE 13.8:

Creating an XML database using XML Notepad is relatively easy as long as you follow a few rules.

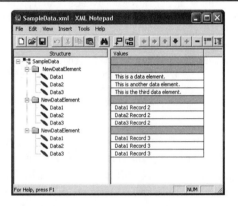

As you can see, XML Notepad doesn't have some of the bells and whistles of high-end products such as XML Spy (http://www.xmlspy.com/), but it's a good alternative if you only use an XML editor occasionally and don't want to spend a lot of money. The important consideration is that you have an XML editor that you can use to view the output from your applications.

Using StringBuilder to Improve Performance

Strings are unusual objects in C# in that they're immutable—you can't change them. Whenever you assign a new value to a string, C# deletes the old string and creates a new one. This includes any additions to the string. For example, the following event handler actually contains eight unique copies of *MyString*, even though all of the strings have the same name and you can't access them individually. (You'll find the test application shown in this section in the \Chapter 13\StringBuilder folder on the CD.)

```
private void btnTest1_Click(object sender, System.EventArgs e)
{
```

```
// Create some objects and values.
string   MyString = "Hello";
string   NewString = " World";
int      NewInt = 3;
float    NewFloat = 4.5F;
bool     NewBool = true;

// Append values to the StringBuilder.
MyString = MyString + NewString;
MyString = MyString + "\r\nInteger Value: ";
MyString = MyString + NewInt.ToString();
MyString = MyString + "\r\nFloat Value: ";
MyString = MyString + NewFloat.ToString();
MyString = MyString + "\r\nBoolean Value: ";
MyString = MyString + NewBool.ToString();

// Display the result.
MessageBox.Show(MyString.ToString(),
                "Standard String Output",
                MessageBoxButtons.OK,
                MessageBoxIcon.Information);
}
```

C# will destroy the copy of *MyString* on the right side of the equation before it creates the new copy of *MyString* on the left side in each case. Your code only sees one *MyString*, but eight copies actually exist at different times, which makes this form of the code relatively resource intensive. In short, making string assignments could become costly if you perform this task more than a few times in your code. While the Garbage Collector will automatically recover the memory used by the old versions of a string, creating, deleting, and managing the strings does incur a performance penalty.

It's unlikely that you'll ever see the performance penalty of using strings in a desktop application (unless you literally handle hundreds of strings in the application), but the performance cost is real enough that you can notice the penalty in a server application. A StringBuilder object helps you get around this performance problem by enabling your application to use a single object to handle string manipulations. For example, the following code uses one copy of *MyString* in place of the eight that we used earlier.

```
private void btnTest2_Click(object sender, System.EventArgs e)
{
    // Create some objects and values.
    StringBuilder   MyString = new StringBuilder("Hello");
    string          NewString = " World";
    int             NewInt = 3;
    float           NewFloat = 4.5F;
    bool            NewBool = true;
```

```
        // Append values to the StringBuilder.
        MyString.Append(NewString);
        MyString.Append("\r\nInteger Value: ");
        MyString.Append(NewInt);
        MyString.Append("\r\nFloat Value: ");
        MyString.Append(NewFloat);
        MyString.Append("\r\nBoolean Value: ");
        MyString.Append(NewBool);

        // Display the result.
        MessageBox.Show(MyString.ToString(),
                        "StringBuilder Output",
                        MessageBoxButtons.OK,
                        MessageBoxIcon.Information);
    }
```

It's interesting to note that a StringBuilder object also has greater flexibility than a standard string. You must convert all other objects to a string before you can add them to a standard string. Notice that the StringBuilder example has no such requirement, you can Append() any of data types that StringBuilder supports directly (which includes most value types). StringBuilder supports the AppendFormat() method that enables you to add other object types to the string without prior conversion. For example, the following code adds a number in several formats to a StringBuilder object.

```
    private void btnTest3_Click(object sender, System.EventArgs e)
    {
        // Create a StringBuilder object and a value.
        StringBuilder  MyString = new StringBuilder("Number Formats:\r\n");
        float          NewFloat = 1004.5F;
        int            NewInt = 1005;

        // Append float values to the StringBuilder.
        MyString.Append("\r\nFrom Float:\r\n");
        MyString.AppendFormat("Custom Format: {0:#,###.0000}\r\n",
                        NewFloat);
        MyString.AppendFormat("Currency Format: {0:C}\r\n", NewFloat);
        MyString.AppendFormat("Exponential Format 1: {0:E}<End>\r\n",
                        NewFloat);
        MyString.AppendFormat("Exponential Format 2: {0, 20:E}<End>\r\n",
                        NewFloat);
        MyString.AppendFormat("Exponential Format 3: {0, -20:E}<End>\r\n",
                        NewFloat);
        MyString.AppendFormat("Fixed Point Format: {0:F}\r\n", NewFloat);
        MyString.AppendFormat("General Format: {0:G}\r\n", NewFloat);
        MyString.AppendFormat("Numeric Format: {0:N}\r\n", NewFloat);
        MyString.AppendFormat("Percentage Format: {0:P}\r\n", NewFloat);
```

```
        // Append int values to the StringBuilder.
        MyString.Append("\r\nFrom Int:\r\n");
        MyString.AppendFormat("Custom Format: {0:#,###.0000}\r\n", NewInt);
        MyString.AppendFormat("Decimal Format: {0:D}\r\n", NewInt);
        MyString.AppendFormat("Hexadecimal Format: {0:X}\r\n", NewInt);

        // Display the result.
        MessageBox.Show(MyString.ToString(),
                        "AppendFormat() Output",
                        MessageBoxButtons.OK,
                        MessageBoxIcon.Information);
    }
```

This is just a small sampling of the formatting methods you can use with `StringBuilder`. The custom format is especially useful and you can perform some tricks with the standard formatting methods. Figure 13.9 shows the output from this example. Notice how the various output values look.

FIGURE 13.9:

The `StringBuilder` object provides more than a few methods for formatting data output.

One of the more important techniques you can learn is defining the number of digits an entry will consume. Look at the three Exponential Format entries in Figure 13.9. The first entry shows what happens if you use the E format by itself. The second entry shows the effects of right justification—the entry will consume 20 digits worth of space, but the padding appears on the left side. Likewise, the third entry shows the effects of left justification. In this case, the padding appears on the right side of the number.

Where Do You Go From Here?

Database technology is an essential part of every business today. In fact, database technology is an essential part of many home installations too. Over the last three chapters, we've looked at the four essential database technologies that you'll use with .NET. More database technologies will likely appear on the horizon as technology changes, but for now, you've seen what Microsoft has to offer.

This chapter has helped tie up some loose ends with Visual Studio .NET database support. You've learned the difference between a *Dataset* and a *DataReader* and how each object can help you create applications. You've also learned about the *DataView* object and how it can make the job of displaying data easier. Obviously, we've only scratched the surface of this topic. You'll definitely want to visit the websites listed in various places in the chapter, as well as try some of the performance techniques in your own code. Make sure you spend plenty of time experimenting with the new database features that the .NET Framework has to offer before you begin your first project.

Chapter 14 begins a series of chapters that discuss remote communications, distributed application programming scenarios, and some of the difficult requirements for working with partners over an Internet connection. In this chapter, we'll discuss programming strategies for Internet Information Server (IIS). The chapter will show you how to create web applications (those that serve data to end users directly) and web services (mini-applications that provide services to other applications on the Internet). Both technologies are exciting because they expand on what you as a developer can do when writing applications for use by those in your company, clients, and partners.

PART IV

Distributed Application Development with C#

CHAPTER 14

Working with Internet Information Server

- Working with Web Applications

- Working with Web Services

- Using the Antechinus C# Editor

Internet Information Server (IIS) represents part of the Web portion of Microsoft's development strategy. Over the years, developers have used a myriad of technologies to work with Microsoft's web server. For example, Microsoft originally introduced the Internet Server Application Programming Interface (ISAPI) as a means for creating robust web applications. The only problem with these early attempts is that they required a knowledgeable developer. In addition, the complex technology was difficult to modify and debug, resulting in a high level of frustration for developers.

Microsoft finally hit on a popular idea when it introduced Active Server Pages (ASP), which is a technology that relies on scripting instead of native code. The use of interpreted text files does impose a performance penalty, but most developers find the ease of modification and troubleshooting well worth the price. This chapter will examine the role of various Microsoft technologies in making IIS a useful development platform. Of course, this is just the first look at web technology—we'll discuss both ASP and ASP.NET in greater detail in Chapter 15, and you'll learn about other web technologies in Chapter 16.

NOTE   Due to differences in machine and web server configuration, some or all of the examples in this chapter may require configuration adjustments to run on your system. In some cases, you'll want to follow the instructions for creating the example and simply copy the source code from the existing projects on the CD. Each dual machine project will include folders for both the server side and the local code, in order to make it easier to determine where each type of code should appear on your system.

Working with Web Applications

Web applications are a first step in distributed application development for many programmers. A web application enables the developer to begin working in the distributed environment without creating a lot of code. In addition, web applications provide almost instant feedback, which helps a developer locate and fix errors quickly during the learning process. Finally, many companies seek to support users on the road during their initial foray into distributed application development, so web applications form the basis of these initial efforts.

Whatever your reason for working with web applications, Visual Studio .NET provides a wealth of resources for creating them. The first ASP.NET example for the book actually appears in the "Active Server Pages" section of Chapter 2. This simple example showed some basics of web page creation. Of course, it's an extremely basic example, so this section builds on what we've discussed in the past.

NOTE The term *web application* is going to be new for many developers and somewhat confusing, as well, because many other web terms are so ill-defined. Consequently, it's important to differentiate between a web application and a web service. For the purposes of this book, a *web application* always provides a complete solution to a computing problem and includes some type of user interface. In short, a web application is simply an application that executes across the Internet. On the other hand, a *web service* is a component of a larger application. The component might be part of a service offered to another company, or it might fulfill some internal needs for your company. The bottom line is that a web service is only part of a computing solution. Obviously, my definition won't always match that of other developers or the media, so you need to consider what someone means when they use the terms web application or web service.

The following sections explore several types of web applications—applications that will do more than just say "Hello World" when you try them out. You'll learn about some of the capabilities that web applications have and how you can use them to support both in-house users and users on the road. Most importantly, you'll learn about the features that Visual Studio .NET provides for web application development.

Simple Empty Web Application Example

One of the first web projects that developers will try after the requisite "Hello World" example is the Empty Web Project, because it provides a blank canvas a developer can use to experiment. Yes, you have to add all of the files manually, but using this project also frees you from any preconceptions fostered by other project types. You can add and remove items as desired, just to see what effect they have on the project and final application. In addition, this project begins teaching you about dependencies between applications elements. (You'll find the source for this example in the \Chapter 14\EmptyWeb folder on the CD.)

NOTE Some of the projects in this chapter aren't available to users of the Standard Edition of Visual Studio .NET. This version doesn't include support for either the Empty Web Project or the Web Control Library. In short, you can use the Standard Edition to create standard ASP.NET projects, but you can't extend it in other ways.

As developers become more advanced, they also turn to this project because it enables them to configure the project in any way needed in order to meet specific application objectives. This is the use of the Empty Web Project that Microsoft concentrates on for the most part. The Empty Web Project does help an advanced developer create complex projects, but don't limit yourself to this particular view of the project.

Like most of the web projects you'll create, the Empty Web Project resides on a web server. When you select the Empty Web Project entry in the New Project dialog box, the IDE will ask you to provide a URL for the new project, as shown in Figure 14.1. Enter a location and click OK to create the project. What you'll see is literally an empty project—one without any extras.

FIGURE 14.1:

Most web projects begin by asking for a project location on the web server.

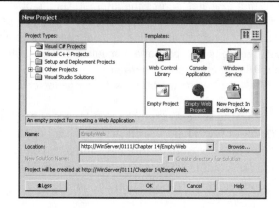

The first order of business is to add something to the project. To perform this task, right-click the project name (EmptyWeb) in Solution Explorer and choose Add ➤ Add New Item from the context menu. You'll see an Add New Item dialog box similar to the one shown in Figure 14.2. This dialog contains a list of the major components of any web application—including those that don't rely on ASP.NET. For example, you can use this project to build a simple web page using the HTML Page item or add frame support using the Frameset item. The point is that you can build whatever you'd like using the Empty Web Project.

FIGURE 14.2:

The Add New Item dialog box will contain a list of web items that Visual Studio .NET supports.

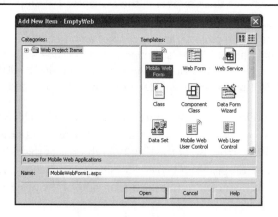

Because this is a simple project, the example includes an HTML Page item (if for no other reason than to show that Visual Studio .NET can support the mundane as easily as it can support the esoteric projects that Microsoft's marketing department keeps pushing). This is the only time you'll see old technology in the chapter. However, it's important to realize that old technology is still viable and quite useful for static information. Once you add the HTML page, you'll see a Designer display similar to the one you'd see for any web form. Of course, the controls you'll see in the Toolbox are limited to those that a simple HTML page will support.

> **TIP** You might wonder why we're wasting time with such a simple project. A project such as this one serves more than one purpose. You can use it to learn what Visual Studio provides in the way of application support. This is also a good project to test the server connection, because there's little that can go wrong. Adding an error to the code enables you to check the remote debugging connection with the server (a requirement for complex projects). Make sure you check the various IDE features as you debug the error using the remote connection. Try the Command Window and other application features. Make sure the application environment automatically detects the open Visual Studio .NET session and offers to use it for debugging purposes. Simple projects offer an opportunity to test development options, the development environment, and your system setup.

Now that we have a sample HTML page to use, it's time to do something with it. Figure 14.3 shows the simple layout for this example. Notice that it's just a simple calculator, but we'll need to add some script to make it functional.

FIGURE 14.3:

You can even create simple web pages with Visual Studio .NET.

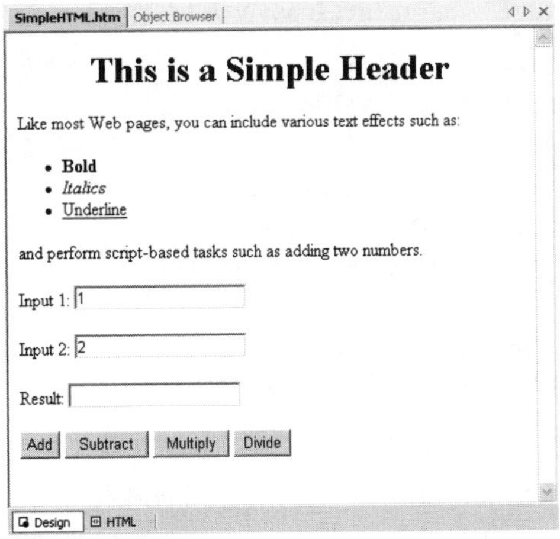

There are a number of ways to interact with the IDE, but you'll find that double-clicking a button creates an OnClick() event handler for it. Interestingly enough, the IDE does provide a list of events that the various objects will support, so you'll need to determine the level of support from the JScript reference contained in the help files. Listing 14.1 shows the simple source code for this example.

Listing 14.1   The Code for the Four-Function Calculator Web Page

```jscript
function btnAdd_onclick() {
   // Convert the inputs to numbers.
   Value1 = parseInt(Input1.value);
   Value2 = parseInt(Input2.value);

   // Return a result.
   Result.value = Value1 + Value2;
}

function btnSubtract_onclick() {
   // Convert the inputs to numbers.
   Value1 = parseInt(Input1.value);
   Value2 = parseInt(Input2.value);

   // Return a result.
   Result.value = Value1 - Value2;
}

function btnMultiply_onclick() {
   // Convert the inputs to numbers.
   Value1 = parseInt(Input1.value);
   Value2 = parseInt(Input2.value);

   // Return a result.
   Result.value = Value1 * Value2;
}

function btnDivide_onclick() {
   // Convert the inputs to numbers.
   Value1 = parseInt(Input1.value);
   Value2 = parseInt(Input2.value);

   // Return a result.
   Result.value = Value1 / Value2;
}
```

As you can see, this is simple JScript code that performs the requested math function and returns it to the web page. The point is that you can create code easily using this technique. The IDE provides everything required to work on old projects as well as new.

Remote Access Database Example

Web applications don't commonly consist solely of a little text and a few controls that exercise simple JScript code. (Although, I do use such a website for converting between metric and English values—check the Unit Conversion Calculators site at http://www.granite-rock.com/calculators/calcconv.htm for details.) This section looks at an application that most developers will work with, the database application. You'll find the source code for this example in the \Chapter 14\RemoteDB folder of the CD.

Configuring the Grid View

A great-looking database web project begins with the project configuration. The following steps show you how to configure a project based on the movie database we've used in previous chapters. You'll find the scripts and data required to create the database in the \Chapter 12\Data folder on the CD.

1. Create an ASP.NET Web Application project. The example uses a name of RemoteDB, but you can use any name you'd like.

2. Use Sever Explorer to locate the ExistingMovies table of the MovieGuide database on your database server. Right-drag the ExistingMovies table to the web form in order to generate a connection and data adapter. Name the two objects `MovieConnect` and `MovieDA`.

3. Generate a dataset for the database. Use MovieDS as the dataset name. You'll see the `movieDS1` dataset object appear in the Web Form view. At this point, you have everything needed to create a connection to the database. We'll create a Grid view of the application to begin.

4. Add a Label and a DataGrid to the form. Rename the DataGrid as `MovieDG`. These two controls are all you'll need to display the data for now.

5. Type `Welcome to the Movie Guide` in the Text property of Label1. Type `Arial, X-Large` in the Font property for Label 1 (or make the appropriate selections in the property listing).

6. Set the `AllowSorting` property of MovieDG to `True`. Select `movieDS1` in the DataSource property, `ExistingMovies` in the DataMember property, and `Name` in the DataKeyField property.

The view is essentially set up and ready for viewing. Remember from previous database examples, though, that you need to add some code to fill the dataset with information. Web applications also require that you bind MovieDG to the data it will display. Modify the Page_Load() method as shown below to activate the view.

```
private void Page_Load(object sender, System.EventArgs e)
{
   // Fill the dataset.
   MovieDA.Fill(movieDS1);

   // Update the data grid.
   MovieDG.DataBind();
}
```

What you'll see, at this point, is something that most website developers would want to avoid. For one thing, there's too much data to display in the typical browser window. In addition, the field names are directly copied from the database table and not particularly user friendly. Finally, the IsIn field uses True and False to display the availability of movies—hardly useful for anyone looking for information. Fortunately, the vast majority of the required changes don't require any coding—you can configure them using dialog box entries.

The Columns property of MovieDG is a collection that you access by clicking the ellipsis button. You'll see a MovieDG Properties dialog box similar to the one shown in Figure 14.4. (The figure shows the properties dialog in a configured state.)

FIGURE 14.4:

The MovieDG Properties dialog helps you configure the columns for the Grid view display.

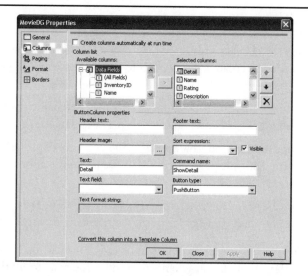

You'll want to clear the Create Columns Automatically at Runtime option. Otherwise, the IDE assumes you want to use the columns as they appear in the database. Next, select each of the fields in turn and click the right arrow to move them into the Selected Columns list. Of course, you don't need to make all of the fields visible, so it's important to remove check boxes from fields that we'll use for the Detail view but won't need for the Grid view display. The example makes the Name, Rating, LeadActor, LeadActress, SupportingCast, Format, and IsIn data fields visible.

It's important to include a method for selecting a row. When a user selects a row, we want to create a Detail view so they can see all of the information for that row. Scroll down the list of Available Columns and you'll see a Button Column option. Select the Select suboption, then click the right arrow. You'll see the button added to the Select Columns list. Move the Select button to the top of the list using the up arrow.

The IsIn column presents special problems because it doesn't lend itself to friendly text output—at least not without extensive coding. However, if you click Convert this Column into a Template Column, you'll find that you can change the presentation into a perfectly acceptable check box. Make sure you select **IsIn** in the Sort Expression field or the user won't be able to sort by this column. At this point, the data grid is configured and you can click OK.

At this point, you're going to have to perform some coding to make the IsIn column work correctly. Click HTML so you can view the code for the form. Notice the two entries within the `<asp:TemplateColumn>` tag. You'll need to modify the `<ItemTemplate>` tag to use a check box. Since this example won't include editing capability, you can remove the `<EditTemplate>` tag. The new entry should look like this:

```
<asp:TemplateColumn SortExpression="IsIn" HeaderText="Is It In?">
   <ItemTemplate>
      <asp:CheckBox id=CheckBox1 runat="server"
         Checked='<%# DataBinder.Eval(Container, "DataItem.IsIn") %>'>
      </asp:CheckBox>
   </ItemTemplate>
</asp:TemplateColumn>
```

Notice that the `Checked` value isn't equal to True or False—it's equal to the output of the `DataBinder.Eval()` method, which returns True or False based on the content of the `DataItem.IsIn` field. This is the common method for creating a connection between a Template Column and the underlying database. Figure 14.5 shows the completed Grid view presentation. Of course, we still need to make the Detail buttons functional.

The completed Grid view presents an overview of the movie that will display well in most browsers.

Coding the Detail Button

The Detail button requires the application to transfer control from one web page to another. Unlike a form in a desktop application, transferring between pages on a website isn't always easy and there's always the matter of data to consider. However, ASP.NET does reduce the programming you'll need to do by performing some tasks in the background.

You'll need to add an event handler for the `ItemCommand()` event for `MovieDG`. This event fires whenever the user clicks a control on the grid. Because there's only one control to consider (the Detail link), coding is relatively easy. Listing 14.2 shows the code you'll need to transfer control to the detail view.

Listing 14.2   Grid View Detail Button Source Code

```
private void MovieDG_ItemCommand(object source,
    System.Web.UI.WebControls.DataGridCommandEventArgs e)
{
    // Create cookies for each of the values stored in the DataGrid,
    // even those values not currently displayed on screen.
    Response.SetCookie(
        new HttpCookie("Name", e.Item.Cells[1].Text));
    Response.SetCookie(
        new HttpCookie("Rating", e.Item.Cells[2].Text));
    Response.SetCookie(
```

```
            new HttpCookie("Description", e.Item.Cells[3].Text));
    Response.SetCookie(
            new HttpCookie("LeadActor", e.Item.Cells[4].Text));
    Response.SetCookie(
            new HttpCookie("LeadActress", e.Item.Cells[5].Text));
    Response.SetCookie(
            new HttpCookie("SupportingCast", e.Item.Cells[6].Text));
    Response.SetCookie(
            new HttpCookie("Director", e.Item.Cells[7].Text));
    Response.SetCookie(
            new HttpCookie("Producer", e.Item.Cells[8].Text));
    Response.SetCookie(
            new HttpCookie("Notes", e.Item.Cells[9].Text));
    Response.SetCookie(
            new HttpCookie("PurchaseDate", e.Item.Cells[10].Text));
    Response.SetCookie(
            new HttpCookie("VideoFormat", e.Item.Cells[11].Text));
    if (((CheckBox)e.Item.Cells[12].Controls[1]).Checked)
            Response.SetCookie(new HttpCookie("IsItIn", "Yes"));
    else
            Response.SetCookie(new HttpCookie("IsItIn", "No"));

    // Display the values using the detail view.
    Response.Redirect("DetailView.ASPX");
}
```

As you can see, the code is relatively straightforward. The code uses the `Response.Set-Cookie()` method to build a cookie collection that the Detail view will receive. Once the cookies are stored, the Detail view has everything it needs to display data on screen. The final step in transferring control is to use the `Response.Redirect()` method to call on the `DetailView.ASPX` file.

Obtaining data from most of the `MovieDG` cells is easy—all you need to do is pass the content of that `e.Item.Cells` property to the cookie. However, remember that the `IsIn` field is a `bool` value and that we needed to convert it to a `<asp:TemplateColumn>`. This presents problems when transferring the data to the Detail view.

The code actually accesses the `CheckBox` control within the cell in order to determine its state. Determining the control status is exacerbated by the presence of three controls within the `<asp:TemplateColumn>`. (You might find more in situations where the control provides both viewing and editing capabilities.) Notice that you must perform an odd-looking cast in order to access the `Checked` property. Now that you know whether the control is checked, it's possible to create a text value for the Detail view.

The Detail view performs two tasks. First, it populates the form controls with the data passed in the cookies. Second, it provides a means for "closing" the form and transferring control back to the Grid view. The second task is interesting because the code isn't actually closing the form—it's reloading the Grid view. Listing 14.3 shows the code for the Detail view.

Listing 14.3   The Detail View Performs Two Tasks

```
private void Page_Load(object sender, System.EventArgs e)
{
    // Load all of the data previously stored in cookies.
    txtName.Text = Request.Cookies["Name"].Value;
    txtRating.Text = Request.Cookies["Rating"].Value;
    txtDescription.Text = Request.Cookies["Description"].Value;
    txtLeadActor.Text = Request.Cookies["LeadActor"].Value;
    txtLeadActress.Text = Request.Cookies["LeadActress"].Value;
    txtSupportingCast.Text = Request.Cookies["SupportingCast"].Value;
    txtDirector.Text = Request.Cookies["Director"].Value;
    txtProducer.Text = Request.Cookies["Producer"].Value;
    txtNotes.Text = Request.Cookies["Notes"].Value;
    txtPurchaseDate.Text = Request.Cookies["PurchaseDate"].Value;
    txtFormat.Text = Request.Cookies["VideoFormat"].Value;
    txtIsItIn.Text = Request.Cookies["IsItIn"].Value.ToString();
}

private void btnClose_Click(object sender, System.EventArgs e)
{
    // Go back to the Grid View form.
    Response.Redirect("GridView.ASPX");
}
```

The Page_Load() method is where the code populates the on-screen controls with data from the Grid view. Because all of the data is in string format, all the code needs to do is access the cookie of interest using the Request.Cookies collection. Note that you can use a string, as shown in Listing 14.3, or a number. In this case, it's easier to access the value using a string because you can't be sure about the order of the cookies in the collection.

The Detail view relies on the Response.Redirect() method to close the form. As previously noted, the code actually opens a copy of the GridView.ASPX file. Notice that the code doesn't pass any data back to the Grid view. If this application allowed data editing, you'd need to pass cookies both ways. Figure 14.6 shows the output from the Detail view. As you can see, the data from a single record fits nicely within an average browser window. Note the inclusion of scrollbars for properties such as Supporting Cast. You can obtain this effect by changing the TextMode property to MultiLine.

FIGURE 14.6:

The Detail view shows
a complete record in a
typical browser
window.

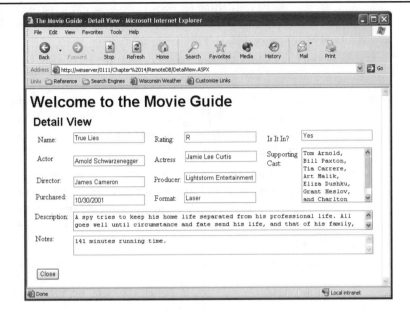

Adding Sort Support

When you create a `DataGrid` for a Windows Form, the ability to sort the columns is included by default. Unfortunately, sorting isn't part of the `DataGrid` for Web Forms—you must include it as a separate feature. However, you also need to remember that sorting takes place as a post back operation, which means that the web page instantly forgets anything it knew in the past. After a lot of trial and error, it appears that using cookies is the best way to get the sort information from the current iteration of the Grid view to the next iteration.

There are three steps required to add sorting to the current example. First, you must create a `SortCommand()` event handler. Second, you'll need to add some filtering to the `MovieDG_ItemCommand()` method. Otherwise, the method will continue to generate cookies every time a user clicks a button on `MovieDG`, even for changes in sort order. Third, you need to modify the `Page_Load()` method to accommodate the new sort functionality. Here's the code you'll need for the `SortCommand()` event handler.

```
private void MovieDG_SortCommand(object source,
    System.Web.UI.WebControls.DataGridSortCommandEventArgs e)
{
    // Save the sort order in a cookie.
    Response.SetCookie(new HttpCookie("SortOrder", e.SortExpression));
}
```

As you can see, the only thing we need to do is save the user-selected sort order in a cookie. The application passes the string value that corresponds to the Sort Expression field in the MovieDG Properties dialog. This string tells which database field to use for sorting—theoretically you could allow the user to select multiple sort fields, but this would become cumbersome to code.

Filtering the `MovieDG_ItemCommand()` method is as easy as adding an `if` statement to surround the existing code. The filter criteria is `e.CommandName.ToString() == "Select"`, where *Select* is the name of the command that we want to process. The method will now ignore the *Sort* command orders.

The final modification would be a little difficult to understand at first if you tried to follow the Microsoft documentation. It turns out that the example won't sort properly no matter how often you create a separate view and modify the *Sort* property. However, the following code works well and you'll find it quite effective for almost any type of database that relies on a data adapter.

```
private void Page_Load(object sender, System.EventArgs e)
{
    string SortOrder = "";  // Holds the sorting information.

    // Determine if there is a request for sorting the data.
    try
    {
        SortOrder = Request.Cookies["SortOrder"].Value;
    }
    catch
    {
    }

    // Change the sort order if necessary.
    if (SortOrder != "")
    {
        MovieDA.SelectCommand.CommandText =
            MovieDA.SelectCommand.CommandText +
            " ORDER BY " +
            SortOrder;
    }

    // Fill the dataset.
    MovieDA.Fill(movieDS1);

    // Update the data grid.
    MovieDG.DataBind();
}
```

There are two main areas of interest in this code. First, the code uses a `try` block to obtain a sort order from the cookie that we saved previously. The only problem with this technique is that the cookie doesn't exist until the user selects a sort order. That's why you have to encase the code in a `try` block. Second, notice how the code modifies the `CommandText` property of the `MovieDA.SelectCommand`. This is the easiest way to change the sort order. However, you must ensure the `ComandText` property doesn't have an `ORDER BY` clause if you want to use this technique. The method ends as usual by filling the dataset with information and binding it to the data grid.

Web Control Example

A web control is the Internet equivalent of a Windows control. You use a web control in the same way that you would a Windows control. Web controls include the same categories of controls that Windows controls include, such as buttons, text boxes, and labels. In short, a web control is similar enough in concept to a Windows control that many developers don't consciously think about the differences.

TIP   You'll find a wealth of web service–oriented sites on the Internet. One of the more interesting sites for developers enables anyone with Internet Explorer 6 to create ASP.NET web pages visually, using online development techniques. FormBuilder.NET (http://www .xmlforasp.net/content.aspx?content=formBuilder.NET) accepts a number of forms of input, including SQL Server databases, and outputs code in either Visual Basic .NET or C#. The best part of FormBuild.NET is that it's free (at least for now). The same site offers links for books and a variety of training options.

This example will show you a simple way to create a button that alternates between states such as On and Off. You begin this example by creating a Web Control Library project. The example uses a name of MyControls, but any name will work. This is a local project, which means that you can access it from your hard drive, even if you're using a two-machine setup. The control will appear as part of a static application in most cases, and not reside on the server as a web service. (You'll find the source code for this example in the \Chapter 14\MyControls folder on the CD.)

The IDE will suggest that you subclass your control from `System.Web.UI.WebControls` `.WebControl`, which is a good choice if you plan on creating a generic control. However, you can gain quite a bit by using a different base class. For example, the example application uses `System.Web.UI.WebControls.Button` as its base class.

Starting with a pre-built class has other advantages. For example, the default project assumes that you'll need to render (draw) the control on screen. If you comment out the

Render() method code, you'll find that the compiled button draws itself on screen without any problem.

The example does use properties that we must set as part of creating the control within the web page. The only way to perform this task is to change the [ToolboxData] attribute that normally resides with the [Default] attribute immediately before the class declaration. Here's the modified version we use for this example. Notice that the arguments don't include any double quotes—the IDE automatically adds them for you.

```
[DefaultProperty("Text"),
    ToolboxData("<{0}:MyButton Text=On FirstText=On " +
                "SecondText=Off runat=server></{0}:MyButton>")]
```

The example includes three properties not found in a normal button: FirstText, Second-Text, and IsSecond. The FirstText and SecondText properties track the two values the button will display. The button will always begin with the FirstText property value and use the SecondText property value as the alternate. The IsSecond property tracks which of the two values currently appears on screen, and the client can use this value to perform one of two tasks, depending on the current setting.

The piece of code that performs all of the work for this control is the OnClick() override. The OnClick() method fires the Click() event. The default button merely fires the event without doing much else. The modified form for this example alternates the text and then fires the Click() event. Here's the code you'll need to perform a task of this nature.

```
protected override void OnClick(EventArgs e)
{
    // Obtain the current view state.
    try
    {
        _IsSecond = (bool)ViewState["IsSecondValue"];
    }
    catch
    {
    }

    // Determine which caption to use. Alternate
    // between the two text values.
    if (_IsSecond)
    {
        _IsSecond = false;
        Text = _FirstText;
    }
    else
    {
        _IsSecond = true;
```

```
        Text = _SecondText;
    }

    // Save the current state.
    ViewState["IsSecondValue"] = _IsSecond;

    // Perform the standard action.
    base.OnClick(e);
}
```

You might wonder what the call to the ViewState property accomplishes. This property is a collection of values that must remain intact between calls to a particular control. It's akin to the property bag used by COM controls. Because web pages have no state information, we must save the value of the IsSecond property between component calls. Otherwise, the control will always stay in one state. Of course, the first time the user clicks the button, there's no ViewState["IsSecondValue"] property value to retrieve, which is why the code appears within a try block.

The actual mechanism for switching between captions is relatively simple. The value changes based on the current value of _IsSecond. Note that the last step is to call base.OnClick(). If you don't call the base.OnClick() method, the Click() event won't occur because we haven't added code for it.

The text application appears within the same project as the control. Figure 14.7 shows the layout for the test application. As you can see, it's browser-based and includes a textbox for displaying the current button state.

FIGURE 14.7:

The test application shows the current button state.

The client also requires some simple code to handle the Click() event. Here's the code you'll need to use.

```
private void MyButton1_Click(object sender, System.EventArgs e)
{
    // Set the button state indicator.
    if (MyButton1.IsSecond)
        txtState.Text = "The Button is Off";
    else
        txtState.Text = "The Button is On";
}
```

As you can see, the code relies on the value of the IsSecond property to determine which message to display. Of course, the code could easily perform other tasks, such as turning a printer or other device on or off based on the button state.

Understanding the Advantages of Data Caching in Web Applications

One of the most popular techniques for improving the performance of ASP applications is data caching. For example, if the contents of a database are fairly static, an application can improve its performance by caching the data locally, rather than incurring the cost of requesting a fresh copy of the database for each user request. In addition to saving the time required to make the call to the database, using data caching techniques can save resources on the back-end server. You can find out more about the basic process at http://www.aspfaqs .com/aspfaqs/ShowFAQ.asp?FAQID=142. In addition, you might want to review the features for third-party products such as XCache (http://www.xcache.com/home/) that make the process of storing data locally even easier.

TIP   One of the major problems that developers cite when working with IIS is security. Over the past few years, IIS has received constant cracker attention, which means it's constantly failed to work as bugs and viruses conspire to take web servers offline. Microsoft has become a little more serious about security recently and even started to consider following the advice of third parties regarding IIS configuration. One major about-face is the automatic configuration of IIS features. This latest version of IIS begins with all of its features locked down and isn't even installed by default—you must install it manually. Of course, now an equally boisterous group of detractors claim that IIS isn't user friendly. You can read more about these new security features as part of an article entitled, "Trustworthy IIS" on the WebTrends site (http://www.iisadministrator.com/Articles/ Index.cfm?ArticleID=23838).

Of course, one of the problems with data caching is that the information can change between the time the data is cached and the time the user requests it. Consequently, most caching techniques also include some type of time-out mechanism that invalidates the stored information after a specific interval. For example, an application developer could assume that a database query is valid for one day, which means the DBMS receives a request just once a day, rather than one for each user request.

While caching data locally was a chore in ASP, Microsoft has provided several cache-related classes for ASP.NET that make things relatively easy for the developer. In fact, ASP.NET supports three levels of data caching, so you can choose the type of caching that works best in a particular situation, as described in the following list.

Page Level (Output)   This level of caching stores the dynamic output of an HTML page. In short, the page is only generated once for each caching interval and future requests rely on the stored HTML page. You should use this type of caching for static content where the information is unlikely to change quickly and there's little or no customization to consider. Implementing this form is caching is easy—simply add the `<%@OutputCache Duration="60"%>` to your ASP.NET page. The `Duration` argument tells how long to store the page in the cache in seconds. You can also add other attributes such as `VaryByParam` that vary the output from the cached page using the `GET` query string or `POST` parameters. The server will cache multiple versions of each page type requested. Other attributes include `VaryByHeader` (caches versions of the page based on header content), `VaryByControl` (caches versions of the page based on a particular control's settings), and `VaryByCustom` (caches versions of the page based on custom settings, such as browser type). An optional `Location` attribute determines where the ASP.NET page is cached: anywhere, client, downstream, or server. You can see a live demonstration of this form of caching at `http://aspnet.4guysfromrolla.com/demos/OutputCaching.aspx`.

Page Fragment (Partial-Page Output)   In most cases, you can't cache an entire page because it contains some amount of customization that's unique for each viewer. You can still cache partial pages—the static content of a page that's the same for every viewer. ASP.NET uses control-based caching to implement the page-fragment technique. One of the easiest ways to tell ASP.NET that you want to cache a particular control is to add the `<%@OutputCache>` directive to the top of the control. You can also use the `[Partial-Caching]` attribute found in the `System.Web.UI` namespace. The advantage of using the attribute is that you can use reflection to read the attribute settings and using the attribute appears to give you better control over the caching mechanism. The `<%@OutputCache>` directive is easier to use and read for many developers.

Programmatic or Data Fragment   In rare instances, you can't define a specific control to cache, but you can define the data you need to cache. In this case, you can use programmatic or data-level caching. The biggest problem with data caching is that the cache continues to exist for the life of the application. This limitation means you must actually stop and then restart the application to clear the cache—a problem for modern websites. In addition, you must limit the data cache to items that definitely won't change or use up resources on other servers. For example, you wouldn't want to cache a database connection because caching the database connection would needlessly tie up resources on another machine and not garner much in the way of performance benefit. You add an item to the cache using the Cache[*Variable Name*] call. The Cache class, found in the System .Web.Caching.Cache namespace, includes methods for getting, adding, inserting, and removing cache members. Code accesses the various members using the variable name as a string, since the cache stores items in an array.

As you can see, ASP.NET provides a number of ways to improve application performance using caching. The method you choose depends on the level of caching your application can support, with the page fragment technique being the most common and the page level technique being the easiest to implement. No matter which level of caching you use, it's important to balance the caching requirements of your application with the resources it needs to perform useful work. If your application is resource-starved because the cache consumes too many memory or processor resources, the performance gain you'll see is going to be small or even non-existent. In short, caching isn't actually a cure for anything—it's simply a tool that can provide a performance gain when used properly.

Working with Web Services

A web service is an application fragment—part of an application that some other application will use to create a complete solution. For some people, web service is just another name for component, but it's really not the same thing. Web services are more functional than components, in most cases, and use a different form of communication than components do. One of the best ways to look at a web service is as a super-charged component designed for distributed application use; it enables you to garner the benefits of code written by someone else.

The sample application in this section is going to rely on the four-function calculator we've used in the past. The web service will provide the math functions while a browser-based application creates a connection and uses the functions to perform calculations. The following sections create the web service and then test it using the browser-based application. You'll find the source code for this example in the \Chapter 14\WebServe folder of the CD.

Creating the Web Service

You'll begin the web service by creating an ASP.NET Web Service project. The example uses a project name of WebServe and a class name of MathStuff. Remember that there's no user interface in this example; although, Visual Studio certainly provides the functionality required to add user interface elements to your web service. (The inclusion of user interface elements is one of the reasons that a web service doesn't really fall into the component category.)

The code for this example begins with an attribute you should include as part of the class declaration for every web service. The [WebService] attribute defines the namespace and provides a description of your web service. Here's the code used for the example.

```
[WebService(Namespace="http://winserver",
            Description="This is a simple Web Service that performs " +
                        "four math functions.")]
```

Notice the *Namespace* argument is a URL. ASP.NET provides a default URL if you don't supply one. The default URL works fine for local applications, but will very likely cause problems in a distributed application, especially one that you share with corporate partners or with the public. The *Description* argument isn't required, but it does help identify the purpose of the web service to others who might not be familiar with it. You can make the description as long or short as you like.

The four methods for this example are relatively straightforward. However, they do point out a few items that you need to consider. Here's one of the four functions (they're all pretty much the same—see the source code on the CD for differences).

```
[WebMethod (Description = "This is a simple method for " +
                          "adding two numbers")]
public string DoAdd(string Input1, string Input2)
{
   // Convert the two input values.
   int   Value1 = Int32.Parse(Input1);
   int   Value2 = Int32.Parse(Input2);

   // Calculate the sum.
   int   Result = Value1 + Value2;

   // Return the result.
   return Result.ToString();
}
```

Any web service method you create must begin with a [WebMethod] attribute. In most cases, you can use this attribute by itself, but it's best if you add the *Description* argument as shown. The point of the *Description* argument is to make the method relatively self-documenting. The [WebMethod] attribute also accepts other optional arguments, such as BufferResponse, that affect the performance or functionality of the method. Generally, you'll only add these other arguments in special circumstances. For example, you might want to track session information, so you'd need to provide the EnableSession argument. At this point, you can compile the web service.

TIP   Even though you can transfer most value types from point-to-point using technologies such as SOAP, you'll find that using strings is advantageous because it's least likely to cause data-translation problems. An integer on one platform isn't necessarily an integer on another platform, but a string is always a string (at least, in the pure ASCII format used by SOAP). String values are also easier to debug. Consequently, the conversion cost from a numeric (or other) data format is small compared to the gains you'll receive from using string data.

Taking a Test Drive with a Browser

Now that you have a web service, it's time to see how it works. The files that your web service project creates don't just sit in the dark and wait until someone stumbles upon them. You can access the web service directly with a browser. In fact, that's the method you should use for an initial web service test, because it's the most direct and the most likely to work.

The WebServe application created two "discovery" files on the web server. The first has a DISCO file extension and is used by applications for automated discovery. We won't use that file in this example. The second file is MathStuff.ASMX, and we can access it directly using a browser. When you access this file through a web connection through a web server, you'll see a display similar to the one shown in Figure 14.8.

FIGURE 14.8:

Accessing the ASMX file is the first step in testing your web service.

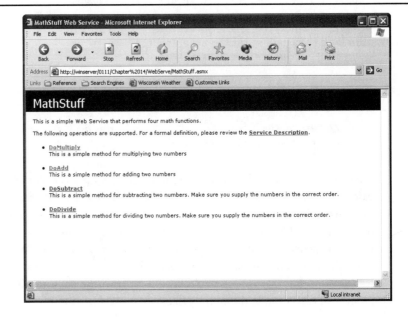

Notice that the web service includes a description, as do each of the methods. You can use the Service Description link to view the XML used to describe the service to ensure it's correct. Generally, you'll find that the automated Web Services Description Language (WSDL) code provided by the IDE works fine. We'll discuss the inner workings of WSDL and SOAP in more detail throughout Chapter 16.

The point of interest now is the four method links. Each of these links will help you test and use the associated web service method. Click on the DoAdd link and you'll see a dialog similar to the one shown in Figure 14.9.

FIGURE 14.9:

Each web service provides a testing area on the website.

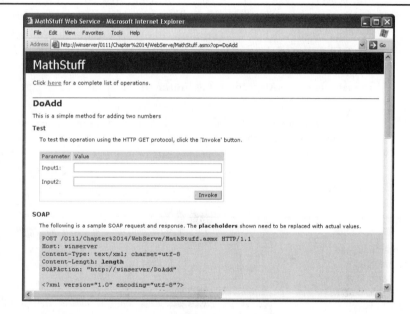

Notice that there are actually two sections to this dialog. First is the testing section. You can enter two values into the fields provided, then click Invoke to see the result. Second is an advice section for accessing the web service from an application using SOAP, HTTP GET, or HTTP POST access techniques. The information shows how to format your message, and you can use this information for troubleshooting the messages as they pass from machine-to-machine.

Using the Antechinus C# Editor

Many developers have expressed dissatisfaction with the editor provided with Visual Studio .NET for C# development, which isn't a surprise for anyone who's developed applications for long. The editor, along with other tools such as third-party libraries, represents the developer's custom tool for creating code. Since each one of us is different, it's not surprising that a one-size-fits-all approach to the editor doesn't work.

More than a few developers are also looking for alternatives to the rather steep purchase price of Visual Studio .NET. Not every developer is convinced that .NET programming is in their future and the Visual Studio .NET package could represent an expensive experiment. Because the .NET Framework and the .NET Framework SDK are free for the price of a download, all that a developer really needs is a good editor to get started coding C#.

Of course, using a general editor deprives the developer of the features that a C#-specific editor can provide, such as context-sensitive help and keyword highlighting, so any alternative a developer chooses must provide some basic level of functionality. The Antechinus C# Editor (http://www.c-point.com/download2.htm) from CPoint Pty Ltd does provide all of the required functionality for a C# editor, yet has a different interface from the one provided by Visual Studio .NET. This section will briefly explore the Antechinus C# Editor. You'll also find a copy of this product in the \Antechinus folder of the CD. The example code used in this section appears in the \Chapter 14\Antechinus folder of the CD. Figure 14.10 shows an example of the Antechinus C# Editor with a project file loaded.

> **NOTE** The Antechinus C# Editor relies on the .NET Framework, so you'll need to install the released version of the .NET Framework to use it. The installation program provided on the CD won't install the .NET Framework for you. However, if you install Visual Studio .NET or the .NET Framework SDK before you install the Antechinus C# Editor, you'll have the required support.

FIGURE 14.10:

The Antechinus C# Editor provides a simpler interface than the one provided by Visual Studio .NET.

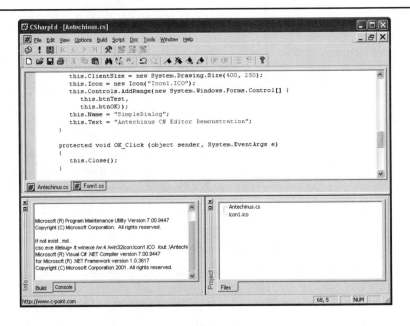

The first difference you'll notice when using the Antechinus C# Editor is that it deals with source code files and doesn't rely on a solution file as the center of the application universe. This is actually a big plus, because many of the examples you'll see online lack any kind of solution file, so the Visual Studio .NET IDE has to build one as part of "importing" the application. You do have complete control over the project settings using the Project Options dialog box shown in Figure 14.11. Many developers find this method of setting project options easier than the relatively complex set of dialogs and folders provided with Visual Studio .NET.

FIGURE 14.11:

The Project Options dialog box gives you complete control over the project options.

Some of the options demonstrated in this section are only available to registered users. For example, the trial version lacks support for using projects. However, even with the trial version you can create individual files and compile them into an executable. (You can't create multiple file examples without project support.) The trial version will also show features such as key word highlighting. In short, the editor itself is fully functional, but you'll find some of the functionality required to create complete applications is missing.

The Antechinus C# Editor is missing what some developers would consider an exceptionally important feature—there's no designer support. This means you have to code the forms by hand. Some developers actually find this easier, but you'll need to consider this omission from a productivity standpoint. Moving objects around in a graphical environment is easier than moving them around by modifying coordinates in source code. Still, not every project involves a visual interface. You can create a multitude of components and controls without worrying too much about graphics. Listing 14.4 shows an example of the code required to create a simple dialog box application. I followed some of the techniques employed by the Visual Studio .NET IDE, but also made the application cleaner whenever possible.

Listing 14.4   **The Antechinus Can Work on Any Application Type**

```
namespace Sample
{
    using System;
    using System.Drawing;
    using System.Collections;
    using System.ComponentModel;
    using System.Windows.Forms;
    using System.Data;

    public class SimpleDialog : System.Windows.Forms.Form
    {
        // Declare the components for the dialog box.
        private System.Windows.Forms.Button btnTest;
        private System.Windows.Forms.Button btnOK;

        public SimpleDialog()
        {
            // Required for Windows Form Designer support
            InitializeComponent();

        }

        private void InitializeComponent()
        {
            // Initialize the components. Start with btnTest.
            this.btnTest = new System.Windows.Forms.Button();
            this.btnTest.Location = new System.Drawing.Point(325, 35);
            this.btnTest.Name = "btnTest";
            this.btnTest.Size = new System.Drawing.Size(70, 20);
            this.btnTest.TabIndex = 1;
            this.btnTest.Text = "Test";
            this.btnTest.Click +=
                new System.EventHandler(this.Test_Click);

            // Initialize btnOK.
            this.btnOK = new System.Windows.Forms.Button();
            this.btnOK.Location = new System.Drawing.Point(325, 10);
            this.btnOK.Name = "btnOK";
            this.btnOK.Size = new System.Drawing.Size(70, 20);
            this.btnOK.TabIndex = 0;
            this.btnOK.Text = "OK";
            this.btnOK.Click += new System.EventHandler(this.OK_Click);

            // Create the dialog box.
            this.ClientSize = new System.Drawing.Size(400, 250);
            this.Icon = new Icon("Icon1.ICO");
            this.Controls.AddRange(new System.Windows.Forms.Control[] {
                this.btnTest,
```

```
            this.btnOK});
        this.Name = "SimpleDialog";
        this.Text = "Antechinus C# Editor Demonstration";
    }

    protected void OK_Click (object sender, System.EventArgs e)
    {
        this.Close();
    }

    protected void Test_Click(object sender, System.EventArgs e)
    {
        MessageBox.Show("This is a test message.",
                        "Test Message",
                        MessageBoxButtons.OK,
                        MessageBoxIcon.Information);
    }
}

class DialogExample
{
    static void Main() // Entry point
    {
            Application.Run(new SimpleDialog());
    }
}
}
```

The code begins by creating the two controls you'll see on the dialog box. The constructor calls InitializeComponent(), which initializes the two components and adds them to the form. Notice that the code doesn't contain any of the extras you'll find in a similar Visual Studio .NET application (see the Simple2 application example in Chapter 1 for comparison).

There are a few extras in this listing. For example, the code loads an icon from disk to display on the form. Normally, Visual Studio .NET would place the icon in a resource and load it from there. If you want the icon to also appear within Windows Explorer, you'll need to add it to project options using the /win32icon:Icon1.ICO switch.

In sum, the Antechinus C# Editor is a good alternative to the Visual Studio .NET IDE—*if* you don't plan to work on large applications that require a lot of graphics. This is the perfect editor for someone who writes a lot of component and control code or works on website code. It's also a good way to get to know C# without a lot of extra widgets to get in the way. Using this editor forces you to learn about the code that the Visual Studio .NET editor creates (and sometimes botches) in the background.

Where Do You Go From Here?

This chapter has concentrated on web applications and web services that run under IIS. By now you realize that most developers will need to learn both types of programming projects to work in the distributed application environment of today. Of course, the type of project you concentrate on will depend on the company you work for. Many companies are more interested in supporting users on the road right now, which makes the web application more appealing. However, once users gain the support they need, you can bet that companies will begin developing web services to leverage the resources they have available to offer to other companies. This is especially true of companies that are already service-oriented.

We did look at more than just programming principles in this chapter. While your first task is to learn how to create the two types of distributed applications, you'll also need to learn how to optimize the applications. For example, it's important to experiment with various types of page caching. Using a cache can significantly improve the performance of your application. You'll also want to try the Antechinus C# Editor to see if it helps you become more productive—a developer's personal tools can make the difference between high productivity and frustration.

Chapter 15 will move away from the general web development discussed in this chapter and onto the benefits of using specific technologies—ASP.NET in this case. In fact, you'll find the next three chapters all help you develop strategies for using specific technologies. We'll look at XML and SOAP in Chapter 16. Chapter 17 will tell you how to work with mobile devices. In short, once you finish this series of chapters, you'll have a better idea of how to use specific Microsoft technologies to accomplish the goals your company has for distributed application development.

CHAPTER 15

ASP and ASP.NET Application Development

- An Overview of the Controls and Components

- Working with the *DataGrid*

- Understanding Code Behind

- *DataGrid* Editing Example

There was a time that Microsoft introduced a technology called the Internet Server Application Programming Interface (ISAPI) and deemed it the next big programming platform. ISAPI still exists, but has never seen the light of day for many developers because it proved difficult to use and manage. Active Server Pages (ASP), while less robust and efficient, is extremely popular because it's both easy to develop and to manage. In sum, many developers use ASP today because it's the path of least resistance—a development methodology that's easy to understand.

Unfortunately, ASP is far from a perfect technology. Performance is a major concern, as is flexibility. ASP.NET is designed to make life better by adding functionality that you won't find in ASP. This chapter helps you understand the differences between ASP and ASP.NET. You'll learn how these new features will help you create better applications in less time.

We'll also look at several programming examples in this chapter. It's interesting to note that some developers see ASP.NET as a browser-only technology. However, the lines between browser and desktop applications have continued to blur as Internet content continues to find its way into desktop applications. For example, many desktop applications now rely on help data stored on a website, rather than on the local hard drive, to ensure the information the user gets is current.

TIP	Visual Studio .NET doesn't always place your Web Solution files in an easy-to-find location. You can change this location by opening the Options dialog using the Tools ➤ Options command. Open the \Environment\Projects and Solutions folder within the Options dialog, and you'll see a Visual Studio Project Location field. Type the location for your project in this field or use the Browse button to locate the correct location using an Explorer-like interface. Note that other settings in this dialog include use of the Task List and Output windows, as well as the method used to save changes to your source files prior to building the application. Make sure you set the Visual Studio Project Location field value before you begin a project, so the solution file ends up in the right location.

An Overview of the Controls and Components

Working with ASP.NET requires an understanding of the controls and components that Microsoft provides. This difference isn't always clear because controls for the desktop environment often have the same names as controls for ASP.NET. The functionality of the two controls might be similar, but the behavior of the two controls is likely to be different. In addition to control, programming, and environmental differences, you'll also run into some new controls—some of which are indispensable in the distributed application environment.

The following sections provide you with an overview of ASP.NET controls and components from the desktop developer perspective. In short, given that you know about the controls used on the desktop, this section tells you what you need to know in order to use the controls in the web environment. Of course, the big issue is learning how ASP.NET differs from both the desktop environment and the ASP programming environment that preceded it.

Understanding the Environmental Differences

Controls and components under ASP.NET differ from those used in desktop applications, but they also have many similarities. As you saw in the simple control example in the "Web Control Example" section of Chapter 14, controls used for ASP.NET development share many similarities with their desktop counterparts. Both control types include features such as properties, methods, and events. You also have to render the control to see it on screen in both environments.

Likewise, the "Creating the Web Service" section of Chapter 14 provided a basic understanding of how components work under ASP.NET. Components seldom present a user interface of any type—it doesn't matter if the component resides on the desktop or as part of a web application. Components generally perform grunt work in an application, such as accessing databases or performing intricate calculations. In addition, both web and desktop components can reside on the client or the server—it all depends on where you install the component for a desktop application or where you cache it in a web application.

However, to say that the controls and components you use with ASP.NET are precisely the same as their desktop counterparts is absurd. The most obvious difference is utility—a web application has different developmental and environmental requirements than a desktop application. For one thing, there's no state storage in a web application. You have to pass a property bag, which is just a glorified cookie, to ensure your web application retains some sense of state from call to call.

The limitations of the browser display also have an important role to play in the functionality of controls. Unlike desktop screens, which normally provide a 1024×768 display area as a minimum, developers for browser displays might have to contend with something as small as 640×480 in the desktop. With more users requesting data from Personal Digital Assistants (PDAs) and cellular telephones, the display area is becoming miniscule indeed.

One of the best ways to see the differences between desktop and web controls is to compare the two versions of the `DataGrid` control (discussed in the "Working with the DataGrid" section of the chapter). You'll immediately notice some significant differences in the two control implementations, even though both controls purportedly perform the same task and were created by the same vendor. For example, the web version of the `DataGrid` provides public properties for controlling the use of paging—something that the desktop version doesn't even support. Unfortunately, this means you can't just move a copy of your code from one environment to the other and expect it to work—moving from the desktop to the Web means changing your code, even if the control does have the same name.

Understanding Coding Differences

Let's look at some specific implementation differences for web components and controls. (You'll find the source code for this section of the chapter in the \Chapter 15\CompControl folder on the CD.) The first problem is to record control and component property values in a persistable manner. ASP.NET accomplishes this task using entries within the ASPX page (rather than as part of the Code Behind, explained in the "Understanding Code Behind" section of the chapter). Here's an example of a label, pushbutton, and textbox using default settings.

```
<asp:TextBox id="TextBox1" style="Z-INDEX: 101; LEFT: 31px;POSITION:
    absolute; TOP: 51px" runat="server"></asp:TextBox>
<asp:Button id="Button1" style="Z-INDEX: 103; LEFT: 31px;POSITION:
    absolute; TOP: 95px" runat="server" Text="Button"></asp:Button>
<asp:Label id="Label1" style="Z-INDEX: 102; LEFT: 31px; POSITION:
    absolute; TOP: 17px" runat="server">Label</asp:Label>
```

NOTE   The code for each control in an ASPX file normally appears on a single line. The source code lines in the book are split to make them easier to read. Consequently, instead of seeing six lines in the source code file as you do in the book, you'd see three. Because the IDE automatically reformats the code in the ASPX file, there wasn't any way to format both the book and the source file so they'd appear the same.

As you format these controls, the text in the ASPX file changes to reflect the new control settings. This is the technique that ASP.NET uses to persist the control properties for each call to the application. Here's the code for the same three controls. The only difference is that I've formatted them for use in the sample application.

```
<asp:textbox id="txtInput" style="Z-INDEX: 101; LEFT: 31px; POSITION:
    absolute; TOP: 51px" runat="server" ToolTip="Type a larger or
    smaller number to create an error.">0</asp:textbox>
<asp:button id="btnTest" style="Z-INDEX: 103; LEFT: 31px; POSITION:
    absolute; TOP: 95px" runat="server" Text="Test" ToolTip="See if
    there are any errors."></asp:button>
<asp:label id="Label1" style="Z-INDEX: 102; LEFT: 31px; POSITION:
    absolute; TOP: 17px" runat="server">Enter a number between 0 and
    9:</asp:label></form>
```

The settings now reflect some changes in configuration from the base control setup. All of the basic settings are still in place, but the ASPX page now contains new settings to ensure the page displays as intended. Something you should note is that the <asp:button> tag lacks any entry for the event handler for the button, even though the page had an event handler at the time. Only property values appear in the ASPX file—ASP.NET looks into the Code Behind page to find non-property entries, such as event handlers and methods. You'll find the event handler entry in the `InitializeComponent()` method, as shown here. (Contrast this code with the `InitializeComponent()` code for a desktop application, and you'll notice that the desktop application uses this method to handle all component initialization needs.)

```
private void InitializeComponent()
{
    this.btnTest.Click += new System.EventHandler(this.btnTest_Click);
    this.Load += new System.EventHandler(this.Page_Load);

}
```

An Overview of Validators

The Windows Forms control list also differs from the Web Forms control list. For example, you'll find a list of basic dialog box types in the Windows Forms control list that doesn't make sense for inclusion in the Web Forms list. However, some control entries aren't quite as clear cut. For example, Microsoft includes a series of validator controls in the Web Forms list that could possibly see use in a Windows Forms project.

A validator ensures the user enters the right type of data and in the proper range. All validators require an error message found in the *Text* property that the user will see and use to correct the error on the web page. In addition, all validators provide a *ControlToValidate* property that you use to associate the control with the validator. Visual Studio .NET supports several validator types, but here are the four types you'll commonly use for applications.

CompareValidator The `CompareValidator` accepts two controls as input and then compares the value of each control. If the two controls don't match the condition you specify, the `CompareValidator` displays an error message. The name of the second control appears in the *ControlToCompare* property. The *Operator* property defines the comparison between the two controls. For example, if you choose the *GreaterThan* option, the value of the control listed in the *ControlToValidate* property must be greater than the value of the control listed in the *ControlToCompare* property. A *Type* property ensures the second control contains data of the correct type, but this is almost superfluous because the two controls won't compare if their types don't match.

RangeValidator The `RangeValidator` ensures that the input in a control falls within a range of values. The *MinimumValue* and *MaximumValue* properties contain the limit of values the user can input. You'll use the *Type* property to determine what type of data the control will accept. The `RangeValidator` accepts common types including string, integer, double, date, and currency. If the input doesn't fall within the selected range of values or is of the wrong type, the control will display an error message.

RegularExpressionValidator   The `RegularExpressionValidator` uses an expression to validate the content or format of the input. You'll find that the Microsoft help topics at `ms-help://MS.VSCC/MS.MSDNVS/script56/html/jsgrpRegExpSyntax.htm` tend to focus on the format of the expression, as do the built-in expressions. However, the example in this section will show you how to build an expression that defines the content of the expression. The expression used for comparison with the input of the target control appears in the *ValidationExpression* property. Click the ellipses in this property to display the Regular Expression Editor dialog box shown in Figure 15.1.

FIGURE 15.1:

The Regular Expression Editor helps you choose a predefined expression or create one of your own.

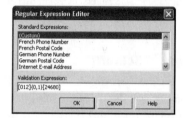

RequiredFieldValidator   This is the easiest of validators to understand. If the target control is blank, the validator displays an error message. Some developers will use an asterisk in place of the error message and simply display one error message for all required fields. However, the use of a custom error message for each control means that you can provide example input for each data entry control.

Notice that I haven't mentioned any need for application code. All four validators perform their job without any coding on your part. The only work you need to perform is configuring the validator as described in the list. The validator performs the rest of the work for you at that point.

All of the validators provide client-side support. This feature will force the client to fix any errors in the form before the browser will send it to the server. Using a validator means that your server will have to react to fewer poorly formatted messages and that the server will work more efficiently. Of course, validators can only check for problems that they're designed to detect.

You can use multiple validators on one field to ensure the application detects as many problems as possible. In addition, the `CustomValidator` enables you to create special validators that can react to some unique conditions. Unfortunately, the `CustomValidator` requires you create code to make it functional, which makes a `CustomValidator` the custom programming solution for special situations only.

A Validator Example

Now it's time to apply what you've learned so far. This example concentrates on using validators under various conditions. In fact, we'll use all four of the common validators described in the previous section. Figure 15.2 shows the layout for a web page.

FIGURE 15.2:

Using validators means setting aside space for text that might never appear on screen.

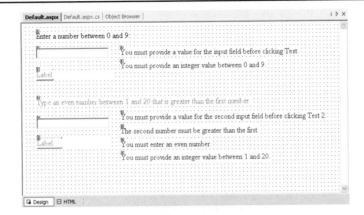

Notice the form contains two textboxes. You can't see it very well in the figure, but there are two pushbuttons that appear beneath two labels immediately below the two textboxes. Overlapping controls enables you to display more information on screen if the information has a short life span. The first textbox has a `RequiredFieldValidator` and a `RangeValidator` associated with it.

The second textbox uses all four validators to ensure the input is correct. The `Required-FieldValidator` ensures the user enters some data. The `RangeValidator` ensures the data is within the specified range limit. The `CompareValidator` ensures that the second textbox contains a value greater than the first textbox. Finally, the `RegularExpressionValidator` ensures that the input value is even. We'll use the following regular expression to perform this task.

```
[012]{0,1}[24680]
```

The first set of numbers in square brackets indicates that the user can enter a 0, 1, or 2 as the first input value. The `{0,1}` part of the expression indicates that this first number can appear 0 or 1 times. The second set of square brackets indicates that the second input value must be even. Note that this second input value must appear once, and only once, in the textbox.

The code for this example is relatively simple. The buttons control the appearance of secondary data on screen. Listing 15.1 shows the code for the two test pushbuttons.

Listing 15.1   **This Code Demonstrates the Use of Data Hiding**

```
private void btnTest_Click(object sender, System.EventArgs e)
{
    //Enable the output, display a value, and disable the Test button.
    lblOutput1.Text = "You Typed: " + txtInput.Text;
    lblOutput1.Enabled = true;
    lblOutput1.Visible = true;
    btnTest.Enabled = false;
    btnTest.Visible = false;
    txtInput.ReadOnly = true;

    // Enable the second group of controls.
    Label2.Visible = true;
    Label2.Enabled = true;
    btnTest2.Enabled = true;
    btnTest2.Visible = true;
    txtInput2.Enabled = true;
    txtInput2.Visible = true;

    // Enable the validators for the second group of controls.
    RequiredFieldValidator2.Enabled = true;
    RequiredFieldValidator2.Visible = true;
    CompareValidator1.Enabled = true;
    CompareValidator1.Visible = true;
    RegularExpressionValidator1.Enabled = true;
    RegularExpressionValidator1.Visible = true;
    RangeValidator2.Enabled = true;
    RangeValidator2.Visible = true;
}

private void btnTest2_Click(object sender, System.EventArgs e)
{
    //Enable the output, display a value, and disable the Test button.
    lblOutput2.Text = "You Typed: " + txtInput2.Text;
    lblOutput2.Enabled = true;
    lblOutput2.Visible = true;
    btnTest2.Enabled = false;
    btnTest2.Visible = false;
    txtInput2.ReadOnly = true;
}
```

You should notice a few features about this code. First, it sets both the *Enabled* and the *Visible* properties for the affected controls. If you don't set both properties, the form can fail in unanticipated ways. In addition, you want to ensure that the validators don't begin checking for valid input before the control is active.

Second, the code sets the input values to *ReadOnly* after the user inputs and accepts the value. This step ensures that the user won't change the value of previous inputs and therefore change the validation conditions of the form. This is an important consideration when you use data-hiding, as we do in this example, because one change in a previous step can cascade into errors in the current step—errors you can't easily fix or repeat.

Finally, notice that the overlapped controls are displayed one at a time. When the user clicks the first Test button, it disappears and a label appears in its place. This step ensures the user can't go back to a previous step with any ease or click the Test button more than once (causing potential cascade errors). The use of data-hiding is also key in making maximum use of screen real estate. This is an important consideration when using validators, because the validator will use screen real estate even if the user never needs the error message it provides. Figure 15.3 shows initial output of this example with an error message in view.

FIGURE 15.3:

The initial screen hides much of the data this application will present from view.

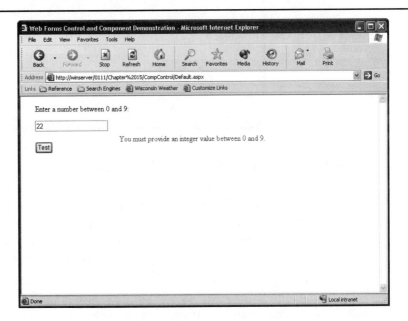

You can test the application out with various input values to see the error messages it will present. One thing you should notice is that only one of the error messages will appear in most cases—an important feature if you want to avoid confusing the user. One exception to the rule is if the user types something absurd in the second input value. For example, try typing 99 in the second input, and you'll see two error messages; the first says that the input value must be even, while the second says it must be in the correct range. Figure 15.4 shows the final output of the application. Notice how the data-hiding clears the pushbuttons from view and presents only the output values.

FIGURE 15.4:

The final output hides both pushbuttons and shows only the answers.

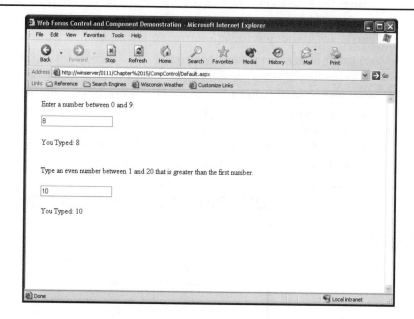

Some Other Interesting ASP.NET Controls

ASP.NET provides access to a number of other interesting controls. For example, you'll find the SpecialHeader control indispensable when you want to create a web page with impact. The AdRotator control from ASP is still available (and enhanced) in ASP.NET. You'll also find the Literal control, which displays text like a Label, but doesn't allow text formatting. The main purpose for this control is to reduce the memory footprint of static text display.

You'll also find some new versions of existing controls. For example, the CheckBox and RadioButton controls are augmented by the CheckBoxList and RadioButtonList controls. Instead of creating control group members individually, the CheckBoxList and RadioButtonList controls enable you to create list members within one control.

Chatty versus Chunky Design

Developers realize that there's normally more than one way to design a component. However, one design normally performs better than another in a given situation. One of the

Continued on next page

biggest performance indicators for applications that run on the Internet is the number of trips required to complete a task. A chatty design requires more trips with small data payloads, while a chunky design requires fewer trips with a larger data payload. For example, consider the following two class designs:

```
public class Chatty
{
    string _Name;
    string _Password;
    public string Name
    {
        get {return _Name;}
        set {_Name = value;}
    }
    public string Password
    {
        get {return _Password;}
        set {_Password = value;}
    }
    public void LogOn()
    {
    }
}
public class Chunky
{
    string _Name;
    string _Password;
    public void LogOn(string Name, string Password)
    {
    }
}
```

Both of these designs accomplish the same task—log a user into the system. However, the Chatty class requires three trips to the server in place of the single trip used by the Chunky class. If you view this situation from a pure performance perspective, the Chunky class is the correct method to use when creating a class. On the other hand, you might require the additional flexibility provided by the Chatty class in some situations. Notice that Chatty enables you to retrieve user name and password information—something that Chunky doesn't provide. This is a simplification of an important design principle, but one you need to consider. Perhaps your solution doesn't rest in using either Chatty or Chunky, but something in between that uses elements of both.

Working with the *DataGrid*

The most common use of the DataGrid is as a means for displaying information from a database on screen. In some cases, you'll also need to provide a means for editing the data and storing it within the database. We'll explore this use of the DataGrid in the "DataGrid Editing Example" section of the chapter. However, using the DataGrid exclusively for database applications misses the point of the DataGrid—you can use it for all types of data display.

> **TIP**
>
> You can use the PlaceHolder control to reserve space on a web page for controls that you intend to create programmatically. The PlaceHolder control acts as a container for the controls you want to display.

This section of the chapter looks at another way to use the DataGrid. We'll create an application that uses the DataGrid as a replacement for the common HTML table. This smart table replacement will display text and graphic links, allow the user to sort the information as needed, and even offer a level of data-hiding. We'll use an Access database for this example (located in the \Chapter 15\Data folder on the CD). Of course, the end result of this example is that you'll learn some new techniques for using the DataGrid in your web applications.

Creating a *DataGrid* with Hyperlinks

We'll begin with a standard web application that includes a DataGrid and a bit of text. Figure 15.5 shows the output of this example.

FIGURE 15.5:

The DataGrid Demonstration creates a static table of information based on database content.

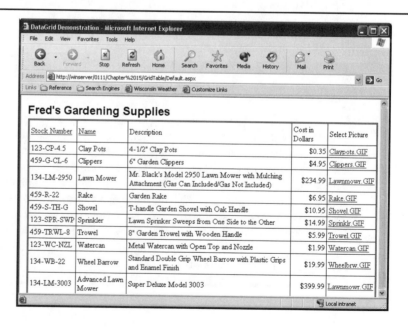

As you can see, the example contains links for changing the sort order by the Name or the Stock Number fields. It isn't always necessary to allow sorting by all fields in the DataGrid, even though the code for doing so isn't that difficult to create. The last column of the table provides links to pictures of the product. These links appear as text within the database. You could also store the actual pictures in the database, but this proves problematic in some cases. The DataGrid doesn't provide any easy method for displaying graphics directly, which is why the link option is often your best choice.

Now that we've gotten some of the basics out of the way, let's look at the application code. Listing 15.2 shows the code you'll need to make this web page functional. Notice that this example emphasizes the use of Code Behind, rather than ASXP code, to create the web page. The results are essentially the same, but Code Behind offers more flexibility in some areas (and less in others). For example, try creating a TemplateColumn using Code Behind, and you'll find that it isn't nearly as easy as using ASPX. In short, each technique has advantages and you need to select the method that best meets your application needs.

Listing 15.2   **An Example of a *DataGrid* that Relies on Code Behind**

```
// Create some database connectivity objects.
protected    OleDbConnection    FGSConnect;
protected System.Web.UI.WebControls.DataGrid DataDisplay;
protected    OleDbDataAdapter    FGSAdapter;

private void Page_Load(object sender, System.EventArgs e)
{
    BoundColumn        NewColumn;        // Data column in table.
    HyperLinkColumn    PictureColumn;    // Link to picture of product.
    string             SortOrder = "";   // Holds sorting information.

    // Determine if there is a request for sorting the data.
    try
    {
        SortOrder = Request.Cookies["SortOrder"].Value;
    }
    catch
    {
    }

    try
    {
        // Create a connection to the database.
        FGSConnect = new OleDbConnection(
            "Provider=Microsoft.Jet.OLEDB.4.0;" +
            "Password='';" +
            "User ID='Admin';" +
            "Data Source=D:\\Data\\Garden.mdb;" +
            "Mode=Share Deny None");
```

```
        FGSAdapter = new OleDbDataAdapter("Select * From Implement",
                                          FGSConnect);

     // Change the sort order if necessary.
     if (SortOrder != "")
     {
        FGSAdapter.SelectCommand.CommandText =
           FGSAdapter.SelectCommand.CommandText +
           " ORDER BY " +
           SortOrder;
     }

     // Fill the dataset with data.
     FGSAdapter.Fill(GardenDS);
  }
  catch (System.Exception error)
  {
     // Clear the buffer.
     Response.ClearContent();

     // Send a response.
     Response.Write("<HTML>\r\n<HEAD>\r\n");
     Response.Write("<TITLE>Database Error Message</TITLE>\r\n");
     Response.Write("</HEAD>\r\n<BODY>\r\n");
     Response.Write("<H1><CENTER>Database Error</CENTER></H1>\r\n");
     Response.Write("Couldn't Create the Database Connection!\r\n");
     Response.Write("<P><B>Details</B>");
     Response.Write("<P>Message: " + error.Message);
     Response.Write("\r\n<BR>Source: " + error.Source);
     Response.Write("\r\n<BR>Stack Trace: " + error.StackTrace);
     Response.Write("</BODY>\r\n</HTML>");

     // End the message.
     Response.End();
  }

  // Name the table to make it easy to access.
  GardenDS.Tables[0].TableName = "Implement";
  DataDisplay.DataMember = "Implement";

  // Enable sorting.
  DataDisplay.AllowSorting = true;

  // Change the display characteristics.
  DataDisplay.BorderStyle = BorderStyle.Double;
  DataDisplay.BorderWidth = 3;
  DataDisplay.BorderColor = Color.Black;
  DataDisplay.CellPadding = 3;

  // Create Data Grid Columns-map a database field to
  // each of the standard columns.
```

```
    NewColumn = new BoundColumn();
    NewColumn.DataField = "StockNumber";
    NewColumn.HeaderText = "Stock Number";
    NewColumn.SortExpression = "StockNumber";
    NewColumn.ItemStyle.Wrap = false;
    DataDisplay.Columns.Add(NewColumn);

    NewColumn = new BoundColumn();
    NewColumn.DataField = "Name";
    NewColumn.HeaderText = "Name";
    NewColumn.SortExpression = "Name";
    DataDisplay.Columns.Add(NewColumn);

    NewColumn = new BoundColumn();
    NewColumn.DataField = "Description";
    NewColumn.HeaderText = "Description";
    DataDisplay.Columns.Add(NewColumn);

    NewColumn = new BoundColumn();
    NewColumn.DataField = "Cost";
    NewColumn.DataFormatString = "{0:C}";
    NewColumn.HeaderText = "Cost in Dollars";
    NewColumn.ItemStyle.HorizontalAlign = HorizontalAlign.Right;
    DataDisplay.Columns.Add(NewColumn);

    PictureColumn = new HyperLinkColumn();
    PictureColumn.DataTextField = "Picture";
    PictureColumn.DataNavigateUrlField = "Picture";
    PictureColumn.HeaderText = "Select Picture";
    DataDisplay.Columns.Add(PictureColumn);

    // Fill the grid view with data.
    DataDisplay.DataBind();

    // Close the connection.
    FGSConnect.Close();
}

private void DataDisplay_SortCommand(object source,
    System.Web.UI.WebControls.DataGridSortCommandEventArgs e)
{
    // Save the sort order in a cookie.
    Response.SetCookie(new HttpCookie("SortOrder", e.SortExpression));
}
```

Most of the action in this example takes place in the Page_Load() method because we need to set the DataGrid functionality before the application displays it on screen. The code begins with a check for a SortOrder cookie because it uses the same sorting technique as the example in Chapter 14. However, in this case, we have to build the database connection before the SortOrder cookie becomes useful, so you won't find the ordering code immediately.

The next step is to create a database connection. However, this is an error-prone process that you'll want to place within a try...catch structure. Notice that the catch portion isn't empty in this case. It contains a generic error message and then uses the *error* object to further define the problem. We'll discuss a more generic version of this message-sending technique in the "Understanding Code Behind" section of the chapter. What you need to consider for now is that this is the standard MessageBox replacement for a web application.

Opening the data connection is much like the desktop equivalent. The code creates a connection containing all of the connection information including the actual source of data on the server's hard drive. The DataAdapter selects data from the database using the selection string. Notice that the code doesn't include any update, delete, or insert logic because we're simply displaying data. If you want to create an interactive web page, you'll need to include these three commands and any associated parameters. We discussed these issues as part of the ODBC.NET example in Chapter 11.

Once you have a DataAdapter, you can modify the selection command to reflect any sort order information passed by a previous iteration of the web page through a cookie. The final step is to fill GardenDS (the DataSet) with data. At this point, we could close the connection and free the DataAdapter, because GardenDS contains everything it needs for the data presentation on screen. The remaining code focuses on the task of presenting the information on screen. This type of data access is great for static information. If you set the web page up for caching, it might be days before the application actually accesses the database again.

The code begins the data presentation process by giving the GardenDS DataTable a name. It uses this name to assign the DataTable to the DataDisplay.DataMember property. At this point, DataDisplay could present information in the DataGrid, except the example has set the AutoGenerateColumns property to false. It's important to set this property to false if you want to create a custom information display as we will in this example.

DataDisplay also needs to have the AllowSorting property set to true so that any columns with SortExpression property values will appear on screen with a link and the DataGrid will activate the SortCommand() event. The example also sets various DataDisplay border style properties, which includes the CellPadding property. Setting CellPadding is important if you plan to highlight the DataGrid lines or if you have data that aligns to both the left and right side of the cells.

When working with a BoundColumn, you must create a new copy of the object, provide a DataField property value, and add the column to the DataGrid. It's also a good idea to use the HeaderText property to give the BoundColumn a name. If you want the user to be able to sort on the BoundColumn, it's also essential to provide a SortExpression value.

Providing the bare minimum for a BoundColumn isn't always optimal. For example, consider the Stock Number column. Generally, you won't want this column to wrap unless the stock number is exceptionally long. Setting the `ItemStyle.Wrap` property `false` ensures the column won't wrap (the property is `true` by default). There are a number of other `ItemStyle` property settings such as the `HorizontalAlign` property used for the Cost in Dollars column. Note that, in some cases, you'll need to use the enumerated value associated with a property, as in the case of `HorizontalAlign`.

The final `BoundColumn` consideration for this example is the `DataFormatString`. You'll normally need to set this property value when working with currency, time, or date values. It also comes in handy for numeric types where you want to control the output. For example, you might want to use scientific notation or limit the number of decimal point values.

This example makes use of a `HyperLinkColumn` to create a link between the picture placeholder and the actual picture. It would be nice to display the pictures directly within the table, but you'd need to perform some custom coding to do it. In most cases, displaying a link to a large view of the item is preferable to shrinking the picture down to fit within the confines of a table anyway.

A `HyperLinkColumn` always requires a new copy of the object, a text version of the link, and the URL that the link points to. As with the `BoundColumn`, you'll want to include a `HeaderText` value so the user knows what the column represents. Once you create the `HyperLinkColumn`, you add it to the `DataGrid` as you would a `BoundColumn`.

Notice how the example uses the same database field for both the `DataTextField` and the `DataNavigateUrlField` property values. If you use this technique, you'll need to restrict the entry to a simple filename in most cases. The `DataGrid` assumes that you want to use the application directory as a base URL and that the filename points to an object within the application directory. If you want to see any other behavior, you'll need a minimum of two database fields to hold the data value and the associated URL for the resource.

Adding Graphics to a *DataGrid*

Let's get back to the Select Picture column again. Remember that I mentioned there's a way to code the example so it will display pictures. Our example is relatively simple, so the coding isn't difficult. However, it can become quite a task when working with complex databases. The following code (commented out in the source code found in the \Chapter 15\GridTable folder on the CD) will enable the application to display pictures on screen.

```
// Create column and row objects for the dataset. Add a calculated
// column to the dataset.
DataColumn  DC = GardenDS.Tables[0].Columns.Add("Picture2");
DataRow     DR;

// Parse each row in the dataset. Create a calculated column
// entry that contains an <img> tag.
```

```
for (int Counter = 0;
     Counter < GardenDS.Tables[0].Rows.Count;
     Counter ++)
{
   DR = GardenDS.Tables[0].Rows[Counter];
   DR["Picture2"] = "<img src=" + DR["Picture"] + ">";
}

// Display the column using the calculated column in place
// of the standard text column.
PictureColumn = new HyperLinkColumn();
PictureColumn.DataTextField = "Picture2";
PictureColumn.DataNavigateUrlField = "Picture";
PictureColumn.HeaderText = "Select Picture";
DataDisplay.Columns.Add(PictureColumn);
```

As you can see, the code begins by creating a calculated column in the dataset. The calculated column will contain an <img> tag that directs the DataGrid to display an image instead of text. The application must create a calculated entry for every row in the dataset, so large datasets could impose a huge performance penalty. Notice that the DataTextField property relies on the calculated field value in place of the standard database entry. Figure 15.6 shows the new output from the application.

FIGURE 15.6:

Using graphics in a DataGrid is possible, but can prove a performance burden.

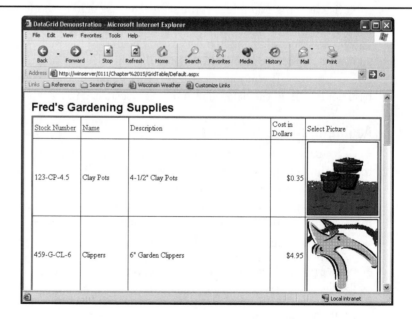

There are many things that can go wrong with this or any other approach to the problem of displaying the graphics. The method shown in this section is the least error-prone because the <img> tag value is calculated immediately before the image is displayed. However, this method also presents the greatest performance penalty. You can get around the problem by creating the <img> tag in a separate database field during data entry. Unfortunately, while this technique does improve application performance, it also requires that the application track two versions of the same data. In addition to errors that the dual entry tracking could produce, using the dual entry method also increases the size of the database.

Understanding Code Behind

Code Behind is one of the most requested features for ASP.NET. It enables the developer to separate the user interface of a web application from the underlying code. The end result is that applications are easier to understand and maintain. In addition, using Code Behind helps an organization use developer resources more efficiently. Developers who know how to create web interfaces can work on the HTML code independently of those who create the low-level code. One group can consider the needs of the interface, while a second group makes the interface usable and functional. You've already learned a little about Code Behind in the "Understanding Coding Differences" section of the chapter. This section discusses the topic in greater detail.

In many respects, Code Behind works the same as the applications you create for the desktop. The Code Behind portion of a web application relies on namespaces, uses the .NET Framework, works within classes, and even uses the same coding constructs. As a result, you'll find a lot of familiar elements in a web application that relies on Code Behind. Of course, one of the big differences is that Code Behind is merely the back end of the HTML front end. Consequently, there's little display code within a Code Behind module—the display code appears within the ASPX file.

A Code Behind file always has the same name as the ASPX file with a suitable extension added for the programming language. When using C#, you'll find that the Code Behind file has a CS extension. An ASPX file named Default would have a Code Behind file with a name of Default.ASPX.CS. Notice the use of dot syntax in the filename. The same naming convention holds true for other support files in the application. For example, the resource file would have a name of Default.ASPX.RESX.

TIP   When working with remote projects, you'll want to enable the remote error-messaging capability of the application. The Web.CONFIG file contains a <customErrors mode= "RemoteOnly" /> entry. You need to change this entry to read <customErrors mode="Off" /> in order to see the error messages from your remote desktop.

There are some limitations to the techniques you can use with Code Behind. For example, the ubiquitous message box is unavailable. If you want to send a special message to the user, then you need to create the message as a new web page or part of the existing web page. We've seen how to redirect a user to another web page in Chapter 14. However, you have other means at your disposal. For example, the following method will create a custom response (you can find the source code in the \Chapter 15\SendMessage folder on the CD).

```csharp
private void btnPressMe_Click(object sender, System.EventArgs e)
{
    // Clear the buffer.
    this.Response.ClearContent();

    // Send a response.
    this.Response.Write("<HTML>\r\n<HEAD>\r\n");
    this.Response.Write("<TITLE>Simulated Message</TITLE>\r\n");
    this.Response.Write("</HEAD>\r\n<BODY>\r\n");
    this.Response.Write("<H1><CENTER>A Message Box</CENTER></H1>\r\n");
    this.Response.Write("This is a message.\r\n");
    this.Response.Write("</BODY>\r\n</HTML>");

    // End the message.
    this.Response.End();
}
```

This isn't necessarily the best way to create a message substitute, but it does work. You'll find that the page switches to the sample message without a sign of the previous form. Of course, anything you want to display, including the requisite tags, must appear as part of a this.Response.Write() call. Unfortunately, if you simply write the information to screen, all of the information from the previous message will also appear. The magic is in the call to this.Response.End(), which ensures that none of the previous content appears on screen.

This technique points to the flexibility that ASP.NET provides. You have more than one solution to any given problem when using Code Behind—some solutions are simply better than others are in a given situation. This solution works best when you need to display a simple custom message that won't appear in other applications or requires some added level of flexibility that standard techniques can't provide.

Unlike a standard application, you won't find a Main() method in a web application. In addition, web application elements won't call the constructor for the web page class, nor can you use multiple constructors to handle command-line input because there's no command-line input to handle. The substitute for this entire group of entities is the Page_Load() method. You can use the Page_Load() method to initialize variables and perform other setup tasks before the application outputs the initial web page. However, the Page_Load() method still doesn't provide quite the flexibility of the constructor, because you can't create alternative versions of it.

DataGrid **Editing Example**

The application we created in Chapter 14 was a good start—it showed you how to create a basic DataGrid application that also includes a Detail view. However, it's far from complete. The most notable exclusion is the ability the edit the data. The example in this section will show you how to add editing capability to the web application we created in Chapter 14.

> **TIP** If you copy an existing application from one directory to another, make sure you set the application up as an application in Internet Information Server (IIS). Copied applications appear as standard folders in the Internet Information Services MMC snap-in. Application folders use a special icon that differentiates their use from a standard folder. To set a copied application as an application folder, open the folder Properties dialog. Click Create on the Directory tab of the dialog. The Properties dialog will now have an Application Name entry that matches the name of the application folder.

The first task is to enhance the capability of the template used to display the Is It In? column information. To begin the process, right-click anywhere on the DataGrid, then choose Edit Template ➤ Columns[12] - Is It In? from the context menu. You'll see a template-editing window similar to the one shown in Figure 15.7. Notice that the figure shows a new template added to the Edit Item Template portion of the window. The template includes helpful text that only appears when the application is in edit mode.

FIGURE 15.7:

The template-editing window enables you to add new template functionality by dragging and dropping controls.

After you create the visual portion of the template, you'll still need to associate it with the database. You can make this change by clicking the HTML tab and modifying the `<Edit-ItemTemplate> <asp:CheckBox>` tag. This tag requires the same `Checked='<%# DataBinder .Eval(Container, "DataItem.IsIn") %>'` entry used by the `<asp: CheckBox>` tag in the `<ItemTemplate>`.

The example also needs a new Edit, Update, Cancel button that you can add using the MovieDG Properties dialog box shown in Figure 15.8. Notice the example uses the *Link-Button* option. As with the Select button, you can use the standard *PushButton* option. However, the *PushButton* option often proves troublesome and doesn't work as anticipated. The *LinkButton* option appears to work more consistently and is the option that you should use unless graphic appearance is a requirement for the application.

FIGURE 15.8:

Add an Edit, Update, Cancel button to the application to enable the user to change the record content.

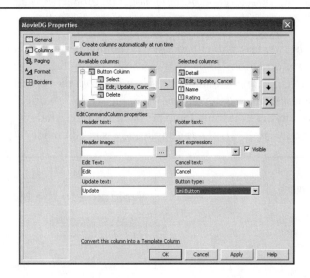

To make the three links functional, you'll need to add three event handlers to the code. The Edit, Update, and Cancel commands have separate event handlers, as shown in Listing 15.3. Notice that the Edit and Cancel commands are relatively simple compared to the Update command.

Listing 15.3   **Adding the Edit, Update, and Cancel Commands to the Example Application**

```
private void MovieDG_EditCommand(object source,
    System.Web.UI.WebControls.DataGridCommandEventArgs e)
{
    // Select the record for editing.
    MovieDG.EditItemIndex = e.Item.ItemIndex;
```

```
      // Rebind the data grid.
      MovieDG.DataBind();
}

private void MovieDG_CancelCommand(object source,
   System.Web.UI.WebControls.DataGridCommandEventArgs e)
{
      // Deselect the record for editing.
      MovieDG.EditItemIndex = -1;

      // Rebind the data grid.
      MovieDG.DataBind();
}

private void MovieDG_UpdateCommand(object source,
   System.Web.UI.WebControls.DataGridCommandEventArgs e)
{
      // Obtain the current data row.
      DataRow DR = movieDS1.Tables[0].Rows[MovieDG.EditItemIndex];

      // Remove the row from the dataset.
      movieDS1.Tables[0].Rows.Remove(DR);

      // Create a row with updated values.
      TextBox Temp = (TextBox)e.Item.Cells[2].Controls[0];
      DR[1] = Temp.Text;
      Temp = (TextBox)e.Item.Cells[3].Controls[0];
      DR[2] = Temp.Text;
      Temp = (TextBox)e.Item.Cells[4].Controls[0];
      DR[3] = Temp.Text;
      Temp = (TextBox)e.Item.Cells[5].Controls[0];
      DR[4] = Temp.Text;
      Temp = (TextBox)e.Item.Cells[6].Controls[0];
      DR[5] = Temp.Text;
      Temp = (TextBox)e.Item.Cells[7].Controls[0];
      DR[6] = Temp.Text;
      Temp = (TextBox)e.Item.Cells[8].Controls[0];
      DR[7] = Temp.Text;
      Temp = (TextBox)e.Item.Cells[9].Controls[0];
      DR[8] = Temp.Text;
      Temp = (TextBox)e.Item.Cells[10].Controls[0];
      DR[9] = Temp.Text;
      Temp = (TextBox)e.Item.Cells[11].Controls[0];
      DR[10] = Temp.Text;
      Temp = (TextBox)e.Item.Cells[12].Controls[0];
      DR[11] = Temp.Text;
      CheckBox LTemp = (CheckBox)e.Item.Cells[13].Controls[1];
      DR[12] = LTemp.Checked;

      // Add the row to the dataset.
      movieDS1.Tables[0].Rows.Add(DR);
```

```
    // Update the database.
    MovieDA.Update(movieDS1);

    // Deselect the record for editing.
    MovieDG.EditItemIndex = -1;

    // Rebind the data grid.
    MovieDG.DataBind();
}
```

The code uses a simple concept to place the web page in editing mode. If the `MovieDG`.`EditItemIndex` property has a value of –1, then the web page remains in normal mode. However, if the property has a positive value, then the web page appears in edit mode. Figure 15.9 shows a typical example of edit mode in action. Notice that the various database fields have been replaced with `TextBox` controls that enable the `DataGrid` to detect when the user makes a change. The links for the selected row also change from Edit to Update and Cancel.

FIGURE 15.9:

A typical example of a web page in edit mode.

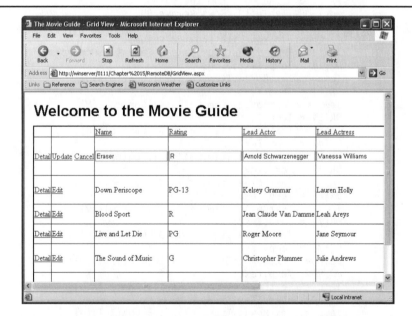

Updating a record is a process of removing the old record and inserting a new record. You'll want to perform both of these actions on the dataset, and then submit the dataset using the `Update()` method of the `DataAdapter`. Remember to use the `DataBind()` method to rebind the `DataGrid` to the dataset when you complete the update or the `DataGrid` won't reflect the changes.

The code relies on the data passed to the event handler in the System.Web.UI.Web-Controls.DataGridCommandEventArgs object (e). You need to drill down to the individual controls within the cells of the DataGrid to obtain the current value of each field. Notice that text fields use the first control in the set passed for that cell. A CheckBox always resides in the second control, however, because the first control contains the label of the CheckBox. As you can see from the code, all of the columns for the dataset are present in the DataGrid, even though the user sees only a subset of the columns. You need to include all of the columns in the update, because the act of removing the row from the dataset also removes all of the previous data from the DataRow object.

Where Do You Go From Here?

This chapter has helped you understand the benefits of using ASP.NET for application development. Hopefully, you agree that features such as Code Behind turn what was good in ASP to great in ASP.NET. The key reason to use ASP.NET for development is flexibility—it helps you create better applications because you have access to more operating system features. Of course, the new IDE features that Visual Studio .NET provides are a big help too.

We've only begun looking at the types of things you can do with ASP.NET. You'll definitely want to explore some of the websites provided in this chapter for additional information about this exciting technology. Creating a few new applications will help, as will moving some current applications from ASP to ASP.NET. You'll find that the task can be difficult due to the problems of separating code and presentation, but well worth the effort because of the additional features you gain. Finally, make sure you look at productivity issues such as chunky versus chatty design. Applications can always use better performance and access to more resources.

Chapter 16 focuses on SOAP and XML development. While ASP.NET provides the means to create a user interface, SOAP and XML can help you move data from point to point on a network. Consider this chapter the second half of the discussion we've started here. After all, an application is both presentation and data management. While ASP.NET provides a great presentation, you still need to find a way to move the data to another location once the user is finished working with it.

CHAPTER 16

XML and SOAP Application Development

- An Overview of the System.Xml Namespace

- Creating a Simple Monitor Example

- Creating Distributed Applications Using SOAP

Getting data from one point of a network to another is hard; performing the same task on the Internet is nearly impossible, especially if you have to worry about working with other companies. Data movement problems include data schemas, the use of binary versus text formats, firewalls, incompatible operating systems, and applications that simply won't recognize each other. Before you can consider an application ready for distributed use, you need to consider a wealth of problems, some of which might not be known at design or development time.

This chapter isn't going to solve all of your distributed data transfer problems; no one book can provide such an in-depth solution. Some problems, such as which data schema to use, are more a matter of negotiation between companies than problems with absolute solutions. However, this chapter will help you solve at least a few of the data transfer problems. The eXtensible Markup Language (XML) and Simple Object Access Protocol (SOAP) are two solutions to the data transfer problem that really work and can already be found in a few commercial applications.

Both XML and SOAP exist outside of Microsoft—they're supported by a variety of standards groups and third parties. From a technology perspective, Visual Studio .NET isn't doing anything new or different. However, what you'll find in this chapter is that the .NET Framework can make working with XML and SOAP easier. We've already had a glimpse at what the .NET Framework can do with XML in the "Importing and Exporting XML Example" section of Chapter 13—this chapter builds on that example and shows you a lot more.

An Overview of the *System.Xml* Namespace

Microsoft groups the System.Xml namespace with other data-oriented namespaces such as System.OleDb. Essentially, the System.Xml namespace provides classes oriented toward the management and control of data. You've already seen some of the System.Xml classes at work as part of the example in Chapter 13. In that example, the application imported and exported XML data. However, the System.Xml assembly has a lot more to offer than simple data import and export functionality.

XML has a basic structure that lends itself to distributed application development, because every computer out there can interpret text. XML relies on a formal use of tags to delineate data elements and format them in a way that two machines can understand. Formatting requires the use of attributes that define the type, scope, and use of the data in question. An XML file usually contains a header that shows the version of XML in use. In some cases, XML also requires special constructs such as the CDATA section to ensure the recipient interprets the XML-formatted code directly. It's also possible to add comments to an XML file to help document the content (although the use of comments is relatively uncommon, except as a means of identifying the data source.) Finally, you need some way to read and write XML to a data stream (be it a file or an Internet connection).

Now that you have some idea of what an XML namespace would have to include, let's look at some class specifics. The following list doesn't tell you about every class within System.Xml, but it does tell you about the classes you'll use most often. We've used some of these classes in Chapter 13 and will use many more of them throughout this chapter.

XmlAttribute and XmlAttributeCollection   Defines one or more data features such as type. Attributes normally appear as part of a database schema or within a Document Type Definition (DTD). Applications need attribute data to convert the text representation of information such as numbers to their locally supported type.

XmlCDataSection   Prevents the XmlReader from interpreting the associated text as tag input. An application could use a CDATA section for a number of purposes, including the transfer of HTML or other tag-based code. CDATA sections are also used with escaped or binary data.

XmlComment   Represents a comment within the XML document. Generally, vendors use comments to include data source information or standards-adherence guidelines. However, comments can also document XML data or serve any other human-readable text need the developer might have.

XmlDataDocument, XmlDocument, and XmlDocumentFragment   Contains all or part of an XML document. The XmlDataDocument class enables the developer to work with data found in a dataset. Data stored using an XmlDataDocument can be retrieved, stored, and manipulated using the same features provided by a dataset. Use the XmlDocument to represent the Worldwide Web Consortium (W3C) Document Object Model (DOM) that relies on the typical tree representation of hierarchical data. An XmlDocumentFragment represents just a part of an XML document. Developers normally use an object of this class for data insertions into an existing tree structure.

XmlDeclaration   Contains the XML declaration node. The declaration node includes information such as the XML version, encoding level, read-only status, and namespace. An XML document usually contains a single declaration node, but it's possible to use multiple declaration nodes to provide multiple layers of data support.

XmlNode   Represents a single leaf of the XML data hierarchy. A XmlNode usually consists of a single tag pair with associated data (contained within a XmlText object). The XmlNode is the root object for many other classes in the System.Xml namespace. For example, the Xml-Document and XmlDocumentFragment container classes are derived from XmlNode. At the lower end of the scale, XmlAttribute and XmlEntity are both leaf nodes based on XmlNode. In some cases, developers will use XmlNode directly to parse an XML document.

XmlNodeReader, XmlReader, XmlTextReader, and XmlValidatingReader   Performs a read of XML data from a document, stream, or other source. The XmlReader is the base class for all other readers. This reader provides fast, forward-only access to XML data of any type. The XmlNodeReader reads XML data from XmlNodes only—it doesn't work with schema or DTD data. The XmlTextReader doesn't perform as quickly as other readers, but it does work with DTD and schema data. This reader checks the document and nodes for well-formed XML, but doesn't perform any validation in the interest of speed. Use the XmlValidatingReader when the validity of the data is more important than application speed. This reader does perform DTD, XML-Data Reduced (XDR) schema, and XML Schema definition language (XSD) schema validation. If either the XmlTextReader or XmlValidatingReader detects an error in the XML, both classes will raise a XmlException.

TIP   Using the correct reader is the most important way to improve application reliability and performance. Using the slow XmlValidatingReader on simple node data ensures your application will perform poorly (much to the consternation of the user). On the other hand, using the XmlNodeReader on mission-critical data could result in data loss and unreliable application operation. In fact, due to the need to resend missing or incorrectly resolved data, application performance could suffer as well.

XmlResolver and XmlUrlResolver   Resolves external XML resources pointed to by a Uniform Resource Identifier (URI). For example, many common data types appear as definitions in external, standards-maintained resources. In addition, external resources on your company's website, such as a DTD or schema, will also appear in this list. Most developers will use the default resolution capabilities provided by XmlUrlResolver. However, you can also create your own resolver using the XmlResolver class as a basis.

XmlTextWriter and XmlWriter   Performs a write of XML data to a data stream, file, or other output. The XmlWriter provides a means of manually controlling the output stream—a requirement in some cases. For example, the XmlWriter provides control over the start and stop of each data element and enables you to declare namespaces manually. However, the XmlTextWriter greatly simplifies the task of outputting data by performing some tasks automatically and making assumptions based on the current application environment.

Creating a Simple Monitor Example

Now that you have a better idea of how the System.Xml namespace works, it's time to look at a practical example. This section of the chapter provides you with a better understanding of where XML fits in today's distributed application environment through coding examples. We'll look at a typical DOM example.

XML and Security

XML is an important part of the security efforts for distributed applications. The need for security is greater in distributed applications than in desktop or LAN applications, yet security efforts have lagged in this distributed application arena. Many companies cite the lack of good security as one of the main reasons their distributed application plans are on hold, so, obviously, the computer industry has to do something to address the problem.

The Worldwide Web Consortium (W3C) and Internet Engineering Task Form (IETF) released the XML Signature specification as an industry standard shortly after the release of Visual Studio .NET. This means you won't find this important security feature as part of Visual Studio .NET until Microsoft adds it as a service pack or part of a subsequent release.

XML security is an important issue because the standard XML transmission relies on pure text, which means data is open to the casual observer. Using an XML Signature means that the recipient can validate the sender of XML data and verify that the data is unmodified. Look for third-party vendors to offer products that add XML Signature support to Visual Studio .NET. You can read about this standard at http://www.w3.org/TR/2002/REC-xmld-sig-core-20020212/. The W3C and IETF are still working on two other XML security standards: XML Encryption and XML Key Management.

The use of biometrics is also becoming an important part of local application security. Biometrics make it difficult for a third party to steal passwords because the password is based on a body feature such as a fingerprint, facial component, voiceprint, or the construction of the iris. Previous biometric encoding techniques relied on binary technology, which doesn't work well with XML—a text-based technology designed to overcome the limits of binary data transfer. The XML Common Biometric Format (XCBF) is a new standard designed to make biometrics accessible to XML communication. You can see an overview of this technology at http://www.eweek.com/article/0,3658,s=1884&a=23693,00.asp, http://www .infoworld.com/articles/hn/xml/02/03/07/020307hnoasis.xml?0308fram, and http://www.internetnews.com/dev-news/article/0,,10_987001,00.html. You can find a more comprehensive discussion of this topic at http://www.oasis-open.org/committees/xcbf/.

XML represents a new way to store data. Sure, the method is verbose, but it's also nearly platform-independent. A developer can place information on a website that an administrator in another location can use to monitor the local machines. Imagine for a moment that the Typing Buddy example in Chapter 5 is designed to monitor local machine performance instead of someone's typing time. Storing the information in a local database might make sense if everyone who manages the system were in the same building. However, with larger companies, this is seldom the case and you need to consider other means of connecting the administrator to the information.

The Typing Buddy application idea will still work locally, but the information needs to appear on the company's website in a secure area and in a format that a remote administrator can use. That's the example we'll explore in this section of the chapter. It doesn't matter what you want to monitor; the principle is the same. The goal is to store the data in such a manner that anyone who needs it can retrieve it—XML is a perfect match.

The example will require two output files. The first is the XML file created by the example application. This file contains the data that the % User Time Performance Counter generates. The second is a style sheet (XSL) file used to format the data so the average human can read it. Even though XML is in text format, it's hardly readable by the average human without a lot of effort. Style sheets enable a developer to format the data in a pleasing form. The following sections show how to create both the example application and the associated style sheet.

NOTE   Database Management Systems (DBMSs) that work with XML have become quite common. You can currently find solutions from Microsoft, Oracle, and IBM that provide the means to import and export data in XML format. However, some companies are working on ways to store XML natively, so an application won't take a performance hit every time it needs to translate data to or from XML format. Unfortunately, vendors are already seeking proprietary answers to customer's XML woes. When you look for a database capable of working with XML data, look at the feature set the vendor is offering. For example, the DBMS should offer both schema and data XML support. The DBMS should also support the Worldwide Web Consortium (W3C) XML Data Schema (`http://www.w3.org/TR/1998/NOTE-XML-data-0105/`) if maximum compatibility is a requirement. (For an overview of tools that support the XML Data Schema, check `http://www.xml.com/pub/a/2000/12/13/schematools.html`.) It's also important to ensure the product will support full SQL queries and not just a subset of the SQL language. In fact, you might want to look for W3C XML Query (`http://www.w3.org/XML/Query`) standard support to ensure future applications can access your DBMS.

Designing the Application

The test application has the simple interface shown in Figure 16.1. All you need to do to generate data is click Start. The counter shows how many entries will appear in the XML data file. Once you have enough entries, click Stop, then Quit. The application will automatically store the XML data in the location you specify.

FIGURE 16.1:

The sample application will generate performance data information and store it in XML format.

This dialog-based application doesn't actually minimize to the Taskbar tray as the Typing Buddy does, but you could easily add this feature. It does output an XML message that you can view in a browser using the style sheet we'll create later. The message contains two parts: a header and a body. The message header contains the elements required to identify the file as XML-formatted data. It includes an XML declaration, style sheet processing instructions, and the root node of the XML message, as shown in Listing 16.1.

Listing 16.1   Building the XML Header

```
public frmMain()
{
    XmlDeclaration XD;   // The XML declaration.
    XmlElement     Root; // The root note of the XML document.
    XmlNode        Node; // A node in the XML document.

    // Required for Windows Form Designer support
    InitializeComponent();

    // Open the XML document for use. The program will
    // create a new copy of the file every time you start it.
    XMLDoc = new XmlDocument();

    // Load some XML
    XMLDoc.LoadXml("<Performance></Performance>");

    // Create the document declaration.
    XD = XMLDoc.CreateXmlDeclaration("1.0", "utf-8", null);
    Root = XMLDoc.DocumentElement;
    XMLDoc.InsertBefore(XD, Root);

    // Create the stylesheet declaration.
    Node = XMLDoc.CreateNode(XmlNodeType.ProcessingInstruction,
                             "xml-stylesheet",
                             "");
    Node.Value = "type=\u0022text/xsl\u0022 href=\u0022PFormat.XSL\u0022";
    XMLDoc.InsertAfter(Node, XD);
}
```

The basis of an XML message is the XmlDocument object. The code creates a root node for the document using the LoadXml() method. Actually, this method will accept as much XML as you want to provide, so it's possible to use this as your only document creation step. The point is that you need to load some amount of XML into the document before you perform any other steps in creating the XML document. Note that the application will ensure the code is well formed as it adds data to the XML document, so it's normally a good idea to place the code within a try...catch block (omitted here for clarity).

After the code creates the initial document and root node, it adds to other important pieces of XML information. The first is the XML declaration created using the CreateXmlDeclaration() method. The three inputs to this method are the XML version number, encoding method, and whether this is a stand-alone document. The declaration must appear as the first header item in the XML document, so the code uses the InsertBefore() method to place the declaration before the root node. Here's what the XML declaration looks like. Notice that since the stand-alone element is null in the CreateXmlDeclaration() call, it doesn't appear in the declaration.

```
<?xml version="1.0" encoding="utf-8"?>
```

The second important piece of XML information is a processing instruction. A processing instruction can perform any number of tasks. However, it's never considered part of the data of the XML message—a processing instruction always tells the interpreter how to react to the document. In this case, the processing instruction contains the xml-stylesheet declaration, which tells the interpreter which XML Stylesheet Language (XSL) file to use to interpret the content of the XML message. Notice the use of the \u Unicode escape sequences to create double quotes within the declaration. The xml-stylesheet declaration must appear after the XML declaration, but before the root node in the message. Here's how the xml-stylesheet declaration appears within the XML message.

```
<?xml-stylesheet type="text/xsl" href="PFormat.XSL"?>
```

As you can see, the style sheet uses a combination of text and XSL script to format the document. The name of the style sheet document is PFormat.XSL and the interpreter will look for it in the same folder as the XML message document. The href attribute can include path information so that the style sheet can appear anywhere on the web server.

Now that we have an XML document and associated header information, it's time to create some content for the document. The example uses a performance counter dragged and dropped from Server Explorer. It also relies on a timer to check the counter content at regular intervals. The data entries consist of the time that the counter was checked and the percentage of user CPU time at that moment. Listing 16.2 shows how these various elements work together to create the XML document data.

Listing 16.2   **Creating Data and Saving the Document**

```
private void btnToggle_Click(object sender, System.EventArgs e)
{
   // Set the timer on or off.
   if (btnToggle.Text == "Start")
   {
      btnToggle.Text = "Stop";
      CounterTimer.Start();
   }
   else
   {
      btnToggle.Text = "Start";
      CounterTimer.Stop();
   }
}

private void frmMain_Closing(object sender,
                            System.ComponentModel.CancelEventArgs e)
{
   // Close the XML Document before the application exits.
   XMLDoc.Save(txtXMLFileLoc.Text);
}

private void CounterTimer_Tick(object sender, System.EventArgs e)
{
   XmlNode  Item;       // The current XML item.
   XmlNode  Time;       // The Time element within the item.
   XmlNode  Data;       // The Data element within the item.
   XmlNode  PerfNode;   // The container for all item nodes.
   int      EntryCount; // The number of item entries in the file.

   // Get the Performance node.
   PerfNode = XMLDoc.DocumentElement;

   // Create the Item element.
   Item = XMLDoc.CreateNode(XmlNodeType.Element, "Item", "");

   // Create the time and data entries.
   Time = XMLDoc.CreateNode(XmlNodeType.Element, "Time", "");
   Time.InnerText = DateTime.Now.ToLongTimeString();
   Item.AppendChild(Time);
   Data = XMLDoc.CreateNode(XmlNodeType.Element, "Data", "");
   Data.InnerText = UserTimeCounter.NextValue().ToString();
   Item.AppendChild(Data);

   // Add the Item element to the document.
   PerfNode.AppendChild(Item);

   // Update the counter.
```

```
        EntryCount = Int32.Parse(txtFileEntries.Text);
        EntryCount++;
        txtFileEntries.Text = EntryCount.ToString();
    }
```

The btnToggle_Click() handles the Stop/Start button click event. This event handler performs two tasks. First, it changes the button caption to reflect the current status of the timer. If the timer is stopped, then the button caption changes to Start so that the user can start the timer again. Second, the code stops or starts the timer. Starting the timer generates Tick() events that record performance data.

The frmMain_Closing() ensures the application saves the XML message to disk. The Save() method creates the XML message at whatever disk location appears in the txtXML-FileLoc textbox. Note that the Save() method is a requirement because the XML document exists only in memory until you save it to disk. This means that if the application exits suddenly, the XML document is lost. Considering the non-critical nature of the data the application produces, this is an acceptable risk.

The CounterTimer_Tick() is the most complex part of the application. The code begins by gaining access to the root node using the DocumentElement property of the XML document. The code then creates the three nodes that make up a single data entry: Item, Time, and Data.

The Item node is a wrapper for the two actual data entries. XML relies on a hierarchical structure, so using a container node is important. Otherwise, you'll have a hard time parsing the data later. The CreateNode() method creates a new node entry of a specific type. The code selects the proper type using the XmlNodeType enumeration. The second required entry is the node name. The code could also specify a namespace, but this entry is optional.

Both of the data nodes (Time and Data) rely on the InnerText property to hold their respective values. Because we're monitoring the time in seconds, it's important to use the DateTime.Now.ToLongTimeString() method to convert the current time to a string—the short format only includes the minutes. The UserTimeCounter.NextValue().ToString() method converts the current performance counter value to a string. Note that you want to use the calculated, not the raw data value, to create XML message entries.

All three of the nodes rely on the AppendChild() method to add their entries to the message. Note the order in which the AppendChild() calls appear in the code. You must complete the Item node before adding it to the root node, which means adding the Data and Time elements to it first.

The final step is to update the item counter. Because we add a new <Item> tag for every timer tick, all the code needs to do is increment the txtFileEntries textbox. The code could have used a number of methods to perform this task, but converting the text value to an integer using the `Int32.Parse()` method seemed like the fastest way. Of course, the code also needs to convert the integer back to a string before updating the `txtFileEntries` textbox.

The actual XML data isn't very complex—at least not when compared with some XML data you'll find online. Figure 16.2 shows an example of the data created by the test application. Notice it follows the format anticipated by the code we discussed in this section. Of course, the data will be a lot easier to read once we have a style sheet in place to read it using a browser.

FIGURE 16.2:

The XML output is somewhat readable, but most administrators will want something better.

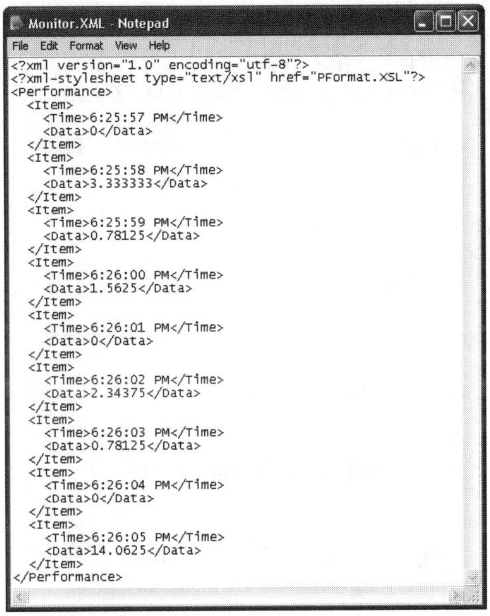

```
<?xml version="1.0" encoding="utf-8"?>
<?xml-stylesheet type="text/xsl" href="PFormat.XSL"?>
<Performance>
  <Item>
    <Time>6:25:57 PM</Time>
    <Data>0</Data>
  </Item>
  <Item>
    <Time>6:25:58 PM</Time>
    <Data>3.333333</Data>
  </Item>
  <Item>
    <Time>6:25:59 PM</Time>
    <Data>0.78125</Data>
  </Item>
  <Item>
    <Time>6:26:00 PM</Time>
    <Data>1.5625</Data>
  </Item>
  <Item>
    <Time>6:26:01 PM</Time>
    <Data>0</Data>
  </Item>
  <Item>
    <Time>6:26:02 PM</Time>
    <Data>2.34375</Data>
  </Item>
  <Item>
    <Time>6:26:03 PM</Time>
    <Data>0.78125</Data>
  </Item>
  <Item>
    <Time>6:26:04 PM</Time>
    <Data>0</Data>
  </Item>
  <Item>
    <Time>6:26:05 PM</Time>
    <Data>14.0625</Data>
  </Item>
</Performance>
```

Defining a Style Sheet

There are a number of ways to read XML data once you create it, but one of the most common scenarios today is creating the data with some type of desktop application and then reading it with a browser. The previous section showed how to create the data using a monitoring application. This section shows how to create the `PFormat.XSL` style sheet used to read the data. The style sheet code appears in Listing 16.3.

Listing 16.3 Formatting the XML Data Using a Style Sheet

```
<?xml version='1.0'?>
<xsl:stylesheet version='1.0'
xmlns:xsl='http://www.w3.org/1999/XSL/Transform'>
<xsl:output method="xml" indent="yes" />
```

```
<xsl:template match="/">

<!-- Create the HTML Code for this stylesheet. -->
<HTML>
<HEAD>
    <TITLE>Remote Performance Monitor</TITLE>
</HEAD>

<BODY>
<CENTER><H3>Performance Monitor Results</H3></CENTER>

<TABLE BORDER="2">
    <TR>
        <TH>Time</TH>
        <TH>Percent User Time Value</TH>
    </TR>
        <xsl:apply-templates select="//Item"/>
</TABLE>

</BODY>
</HTML>
</xsl:template>

<!-- XSL template section that describes table content. -->

<xsl:template match="Item">
    <TR>
        <TD>
            <xsl:value-of select="Time"/>
        </TD>
        <TD>
            <xsl:value-of select="Data"/>
        </TD>
    </TR>
</xsl:template>

</xsl:stylesheet>
```

As you can see, the style sheet contains three main sections: header, HTML code, and XSL template. Not every XSL file contains these three sections—in fact, it's quite safe to assume otherwise, given the freeform nature of XML. However, it's safe to say that most browser style sheets will contain these three sections.

The XSL header begins with the XML declaration—a requirement for all XML-based documents. It also includes an XSL declaration that includes a namespace for the XSL-specific declarations. Again, this is a requirement for all XSL documents. The `<xsl:output>` tag determines the type of output the style sheet will create as well as output attributes, such as the use of indentation to make the resulting code easier to read. The `<xsl:template>`

defines the beginning of the template used to interpret the input file, as well as the attributes the interpreter will use. In this case, we're telling the template to match everything in the source file, but this isn't a requirement.

The HTML code includes the usual sections. However, notice the special `<xsl:apply-templates>` tag. This tag creates a connection between the HTML code and the XSL template that follows. It tells the interpreter where to place the template output within the HTML data stream. The `select` attribute determines which of the templates the interpreter places in the HTML output stream.

The final section is the XSL template, which begins with the `<xsl:template>` tag. Notice that this tag contains a match attribute, which selects the data container nodes within the XML message document. The template will parse each `<Item>` tag within the XML message document until it runs out of tags to parse. The code that follows includes a combination of HTML tags and `<xsl:value-of>` tags. As you can see, each of the `<xsl:value-of>` tags selects one of the data items in the XML message and places it within the HTML table. Figure 16.3 shows the output from the XSL template.

FIGURE 16.3:

The XSL output is easy to read using any browser that includes XSL support.

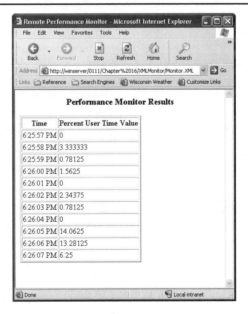

Creating Distributed Applications Using SOAP

SOAP represents one of the best technologies for moving data on the Internet because it defines a protocol for organizing the information and responding to it. In addition, SOAP defines a method for passing error information back to the message sender, so the sender knows if the data arrived safely.

However, like XML, the composition of the data payload will vary. This means that you still need to establish a schema with the recipient in order to exchange information. The organization of your data payload must match the organization the remote machine is expecting.

Another problem with SOAP is that it doesn't provide any security. The various SOAP supporters and standards organizations are currently working on a solution for this problem. In the meantime, you should plan on establishing a Virtual Private Network (VPN) with the remote location when using SOAP. Using data encryption doesn't hurt either, but it does detract from one of the benefits of using SOAP—the lack of binary data in the data stream.

The following sections will tell you more about SOAP, discuss the SOAP support you'll find in the .NET Framework, and provide a SOAP application demonstration. As you read these sections, remember that SOAP is a protocol—essentially a set of rules—for organized data transfer across any type of network. The organization is in the data transfer technique employed by SOAP, as demonstrated by the example application.

NOTE   SOAP is still a young technology, even by computer standards. The form of SOAP used by Visual Studio .NET relies on the Remote Procedure Call (RPC) model that other Microsoft technologies such as the Distributed Component Object Model (DCOM) use. RPC makes it appear that the source of a resource is the local client, rather than force the client to see remote resources as something on another computer. A few vendors such as IBM see RPC as outmoded and incapable of supporting distributed application in the future. Consequently, they've created new models such as Resource Description Framework (RDF) to handle the needs of distributed resource sharing. You can read about RDF at http://www-106.ibm.com/developerworks/library/ws-soaprdf/?n-ws-372. We won't discuss alternatives such as RDF in the book because you can't easily use them within Visual Studio .NET.

Dissecting the SOAP Message

You can divide SOAP messages into two basic categories: requests and responses. The client sends a request to the server. If the server can fulfill the request, then it sends a data message back to the client. Otherwise, the server sends an error message indicating why it couldn't send a response back to the client. In most cases, the problem is one of security, access, equipment failure, or an inability to find the requested object or data.

SOAP messages don't exist within a vacuum. If you send just a SOAP message, it will never reach its destination. SOAP is a wire protocol—it relies on another protocol such as HTTP or SMTP for transport. This is the same technique used by other wire protocols, so there's nothing strange about SOAP when it comes to data transfer needs. The most common transport protocol in use today is HTTP, so that's what we'll look at in this section. Keep in mind, however, that SOAP can theoretically use any of a number of transport protocols and probably will do so in the future.

SOAP messages look and act like XML messages. Therefore, in addition to the HTTP wrapper, a SOAP message requires an XML wrapper. All that the XML wrapper does, in this case, is tell the data receiver that this is an XML-formatted message. The SOAP part of the message contains all of the data; however, SOAP uses XML-like tags to format the data.

Figure 16.4 shows a common SOAP message configuration. Notice the SOAP message formatting. This isn't the only way to wrap a SOAP message in other protocols, but it's the most common method in use today.

FIGURE 16.4:

An illustration of how a SOAP message is commonly encased within other protocols.

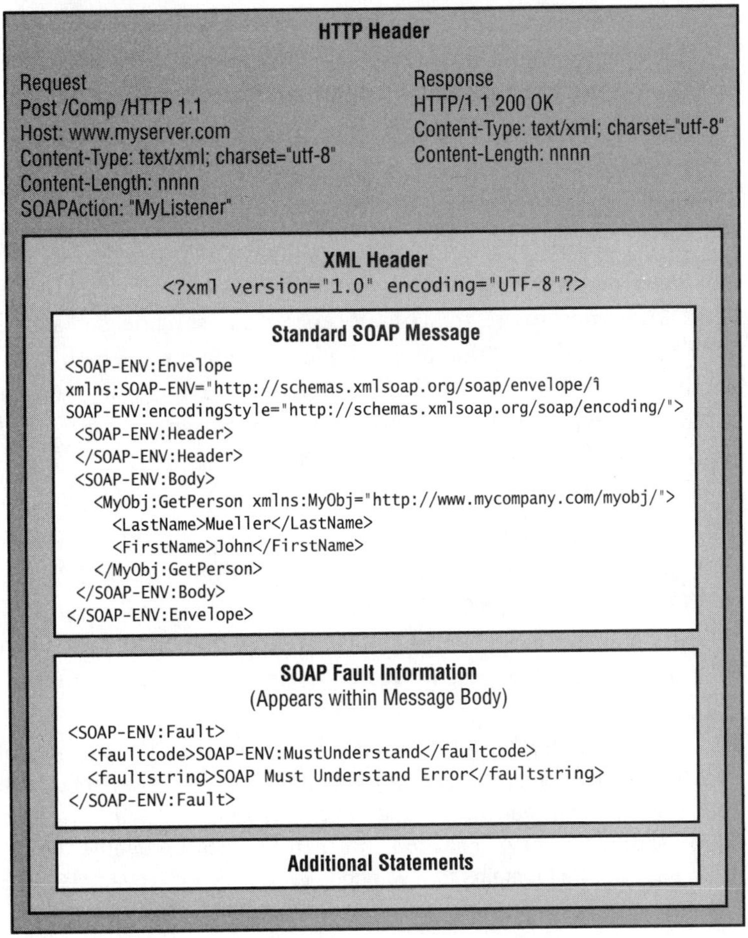

HTTP Header

Request
Post /Comp /HTTP 1.1
Host: www.myserver.com
Content-Type: text/xml; charset="utf-8"
Content-Length: nnnn
SOAPAction: "MyListener"

Response
HTTP/1.1 200 OK
Content-Type: text/xml; charset="utf-8"
Content-Length: nnnn

XML Header

```
<?xml version="1.0" encoding="UTF-8"?>
```

Standard SOAP Message

```
<SOAP-ENV:Envelope
xmlns:SOAP-ENV="http://schemas.xmlsoap.org/soap/envelope/î
SOAP-ENV:encodingStyle="http://schemas.xmlsoap.org/soap/encoding/">
 <SOAP-ENV:Header>
 </SOAP-ENV:Header>
 <SOAP-ENV:Body>
   <MyObj:GetPerson xmlns:MyObj="http://www.mycompany.com/myobj/">
     <LastName>Mueller</LastName>
     <FirstName>John</FirstName>
   </MyObj:GetPerson>
 </SOAP-ENV:Body>
</SOAP-ENV:Envelope>
```

SOAP Fault Information
(Appears within Message Body)

```
<SOAP-ENV:Fault>
 <faultcode>SOAP-ENV:MustUnderstand</faultcode>
 <faultstring>SOAP Must Understand Error</faultstring>
</SOAP-ENV:Fault>
```

Additional Statements

The next three sections tell you how a SOAP message appears during transmission. We'll use Figure 16.4 as an aid for discussion. It's the only time we'll explore a complete request or response in the book, since in most other cases you'll only need to worry about the SOAP message itself.

TIP Working with the new capabilities provided by technologies like XML and SOAP means dealing with dynamically created web pages. While it's nice that we can modify the content of a web page as needed for an individual user, it can also be a problem if you need to troubleshoot the web page. That's where a handy little script comes into play. Type `javascript:'<xmp>'+document.all(0).outerHTML+'</xmp>'` in the Address field of Internet Explorer for any dynamically created web page, and you'll see the actual HTML for that page. This includes the results of using scripts and other page construction techniques.

Viewing the HTTP Portion of SOAP

The HTTP portion of a SOAP message looks much the same as any other HTTP header you may have seen in the past. In fact, if you don't look carefully, you might pass it by without paying any attention. As with any HTTP transmission, there are two types of headers—one for requests and another for responses. Figure 16.4 shows examples of both types.

As with any request header, the HTTP portion of a SOAP message will contain an action (POST, in most cases), the HTTP version, a host name, and some content length information. The POST action portion of the header will contain the path for the SOAP listener, which is either an ASP script or an ISAPI component. Also located within a request header is a Content-Type entry of *text/xml* and a charset entry of *utf-8*. The utf-8 entry is important right now because many SOAP toolkits don't support utf-16 and many other character sets. The SOAP specification also uses utf-8 for all of its examples.

You'll also find the unique SOAPAction entry in the HTTP request header. It contains the Uniform Resource Identifier (URI) of the ASP script or ISAPI component used to parse the SOAP request. If the SOAPAction entry is " ", then the server will use the HTTP Request-URI entry to locate a listener instead. This is the only SOAP-specific entry in the HTTP header—everything else we've discussed could appear in any HTTP formatted message.

TIP UTF stands for Unicode Transformation Format. UTF represents one standard method for encoding characters. One of the better places to learn about UTF-8 is `http://www.utf8.org/`. You can find a good discussion of various encoding techniques at `http://www.czyborra.com/utf/`. This website presents the information in tutorial format. The fact remains that you need to use the utf-8 character set when working with SOAP.

The response header portion of the HTTP wrapper for a SOAP message contains all of the essentials as well. You'll find the HTTP version, status, and content length as usual. Like the request header, the response header has a Content-Type entry of *text/xml* and a charset entry of *utf-8*.

There are two common status indicators for a response header: 200 OK or 500 Internal Server Error. While the SOAP specification allows leeway in the positive response status number (any value in the 200 series), a server must return a status value of 500 for SOAP errors to indicate a server error.

Whenever a SOAP response header contains an error status, the SOAP message must include a SOAP fault section. We'll talk about SOAP faults later in this chapter. All you need to know now is that the HTTP header provides the first indication of a SOAP fault that will require additional processing.

A message can contain other applicable status errors codes in the response header. For example, if the client sends a standard HTTP header and the server wants to use the HTTP Extension Framework, it can respond with a status error value of 510 Not Extended. The 510 error isn't necessarily fatal; a client can make the request again using the mandatory HTTP Extension Framework declaration. In this case, an error message serves to alert the client to a special server requirement.

Viewing the XML Portion of SOAP

All SOAP messages are encoded using XML. SOAP follows the XML specification and can be considered a true superset of XML. In other words, it adds to the functionality already in place within XML. Anyone familiar with XML will feel comfortable with SOAP at the outset—all you really need to know is the SOAP nuances.

Although the examples in the SOAP specification don't show an XML connection (other than the formatting of the SOAP message), most real-world examples will contain at least one line of XML-specific information. Here's an example of an XML entry:

```
<?xml version="1.0" encoding="UTF-8" standalone="no"?>
```

As you can see, the tag is quite simple. The only bits of information that it includes are the XML version number, the character set (encoding), and whether the message is stand-alone. As with the HTTP header, the XML portion relies on the utf-8 character set for now. The version number will change as new versions of XML appear on the scene. The standalone attribute determines if external markup declarations could affect the manner in which this XML document is processed. A value of no means external documents could affect the processing of this document.

We won't discuss all of the XML tag attributes (declarations) in this chapter. You can find a complete listing of these attributes at `http://www.w3.org/TR/REC-xml`. For those of you who don't read specifications very well (or prefer not to), look at Tim Bray's annotated XML specification website at `http://www.xml.com/axml/testaxml.htm`. Another good place to look is the XML.com website at `http://www.xml.com/`. Finally, if you want to see the tools and other resources available for XML, look at `http://www.projectcool.com/developer/xmlz/xmlref/examples.html`.

Some developers don't include all of the XML tag attributes in their SOAP messages. So far, I haven't seen any problems with leaving the encoding and `standalone` attributes out of the picture. You should, however, always include the XML version number—if for no other reason than the need to document your code and ensure there are no compatibility problems with future SOAP implementations.

Working with the SOAP Message

A simple SOAP message consists of an envelope that contains both a header and a body. The header can contain information that isn't associated with the data itself. For example, the header commonly contains a transaction ID when the application needs one to identify a particular SOAP message. The body contains the data in XML format. If an error occurs, the body will contain fault information, rather than data.

Now that you have a summary of the SOAP message content, let's look at some particulars you'll need when working with SOAP. The following sections will fill you in on some technical details needed to understand the SOAP message fully.

HTTP and the SOAP Transfer

SOAP is essentially a one-way data transfer protocol. While SOAP messages often follow a request/response pattern, the messages themselves are individual entities. They aren't linked in any way. This means that a SOAP message is stand-alone—it doesn't rely on the immediate presence of a server, nor is a response expected when a request message contains all of the required information. For example, some types of data entry may not require a response since the user is inputting information and may not care about a response.

The envelope in which a SOAP message travels, however, may provide more than just a one-way transfer path. For example, when a developer encases a SOAP message within an HTTP envelope, the request and response both use the same connection. The connection is created and maintained by HTTP, not by SOAP. Consequently, the connection follows the HTTP way of performing data transfer—using the same techniques as a browser uses to request web pages for display.

Testing Your SOAP Knowledge

Microsoft maintains two websites to check your SOAP messages. The first accepts SOAP messages, parses them, and provides a check of their validity. You'll find it at `http://www` `.soaptoolkit.com/soapvalidator/`. Figure 16.5 shows what this website looks like. (You'll find this message as the `Test.XML` file in the \Chapter 16 folder on the CD.)

FIGURE 16.5:

The SOAP Message Validation site tests your SOAP knowledge.

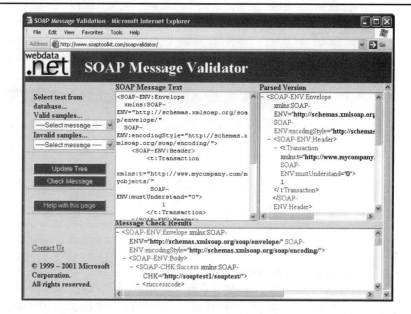

As you can see, there are three panes in this display. The SOAP Message Text window contains the message you want to verify. You can also choose one of the valid or invalid samples from the drop-down boxes. These samples can teach you quite a bit about SOAP by showing what you can and can't do within a message and the results that you'll get when performing certain actions. You don't need to include the HTTP or XML headers in the SOAP Message Text window, just the SOAP message.

The Parsed Version window shows what the message looks like after the SOAP listener parses it. This window doesn't tell you about the validity of the message, but it does help you understand the XML formatting better. You can use this window to determine if the message is well formed. The use of text coloring also helps you to distinguish between specific text elements.

The Message Check Results window will show the results of diagnostics the site performs on your SOAP message. You'll see error messages in places where the SOAP message doesn't contain required entries or the entry format is incorrect. When all of the error messages are gone, the SOAP message is ready for use. Of course, the website doesn't check the validity of the data within the SOAP message. You can create a perfect SOAP message that still doesn't work because the server-side component is expecting the data in a different format or it even requires other arguments.

The second website is a generic SOAP listener. You can send a SOAP message to it using an application. The site will test the message much like the Message Check Results window of the SOAP Message Validation site. You'll find this website at `http://www.soaptoolkit` `.com/soapvalidator/listener.asp`. Figure 16.6 shows an error output from this site. This is also an example of the SOAP fault message that we'll discuss in the next section of the chapter.

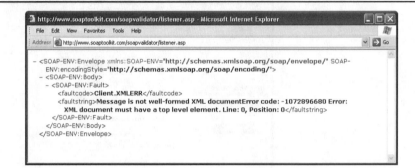

FIGURE 16.6:

The SOAP Message Listener site will validate requests from your applications.

SOAP Fault Messages

Sometimes a SOAP request will generate a fault message instead of the anticipated reply. The server may not have the means to answer your request, the request you generated may be incomplete, or bad communication may prevent your message from arriving in the same state in which you sent it. There are many reasons that you may receive a SOAP fault message. However, you can generally categorize them into four general areas, as described in the following list.

Client   The client generated a request that the server couldn't process for some reason. The most common problem is that the XML format of the SOAP message is incorrect (malformed). Another common problem is the server can't find the requested component or the client doesn't provide all of the information the server needs to process the message. If the client receives an error message of this type, it must recreate the message and fix the problems of the original. The server usually provides amplifying information if it can determine how the request is malformed or otherwise in error.

mustUnderstand   This error only occurs when you set the SOAP message `mustUnderstand` attribute to 1. The error occurs when the client sends a request that the server can't understand or obey for some reason. The server may not understand a request when the client relies on capabilities of a version of SOAP that the server's listener doesn't provide. A server may not obey a client request due to security or other concerns.

Server   The server couldn't process the message even though the request is valid. A server error can occur for a number of reasons. For example, the server could run out of resources for initializing the requested component. In a complex application environment, the server may rely on the processing of another server that's offline or otherwise inaccessible. The server usually provides amplifying information if it can determine the precise server-side error that occurred.

VersionMismatch   SOAP doesn't have a versioning system. It does rely on the name-spaces that you define to perform useful work. This error message occurs when the SOAP envelope namespace is either incorrect or missing.

When a server returns a fault message, it doesn't return any data. Look at Figure 16.6 and you'll see a typical client fault message. Notice the message contains only fault information. With this in mind, the client-side components you create must be prepared to parse SOAP fault messages and return the information to the calling application in such a way that the user will understand the meaning of the fault.

Figure 16.6 shows the standard presentation of a SOAP fault message. Notice that the fault envelope resides within the body of the SOAP message. A fault envelope will generally contain a `faultcode` and `faultstring` element that tells you which error occurred. All of the other SOAP fault message elements are optional. The following list tells you how they're used.

`faultcode`   The `faultcode` contains the name of the error that occurred. It can use a dot syntax to define a more precise error code. The `faultcode` will always begin with a classification. For example, the `faultcode` in Figure 16.6 consists of a client error code followed by an XMLERR subcode. This error tells you that the request message is malformed because the XML formatting is incorrect. Since it's possible to create a list of standard SOAP `faultcode`s, you can use them directly for processing purposes.

`faultstring`   This is a human-readable form of the error specified by the `faultcode` entry. This string should follow the same format as HTTP error strings. You can learn more about HTTP error strings by reading the HTTP specification at `http://www.normos.org/ietf/rfc/rfc2616.txt`. A good general rule to follow is to make the `faultstring` entry short and easy to understand.

`faultactor`   This element points to the source of a fault in a SOAP transaction. It contains a Uniform Resource Identifier (URI) similar to the one used for determining the destination of the header entry. According to the specification, you must include this element if the application that generates the fault message isn't the ultimate destination for the SOAP message.

detail   You'll use this element to hold detailed information about a fault when available. For example, this is the element that you'd use to hold server-side component return values. This element is SOAP message body–specific, which means you can't use it to detail errors that occur in other areas like the SOAP message header. A detail entry acts as an envelope for storing detail sub-elements. Each sub-element includes a tag containing namespace information and a string containing error message information.

Desktop Application Example

If you worked with the Microsoft SOAP Toolkit under Visual Studio 6.0 and found yourself disappointed from an ease-of-use perspective, Visual Studio .NET makes life a lot easier. Creating a SOAP application no longer requires you to create a myriad of objects that are unlikely to work the first time. In addition, creating a connection to the server is so easy that you'll wonder if there's some hidden problem waiting to jump out from the dark recesses of the SOAP support mechanism.

We won't discuss the component end of this example, except to say that it's a simple component that adds two numbers together. You'll find the component in the \Chapter 16\AddIt folder on the CD. This same component works fine on the local machine, or you could access it using DCOM. In short, it's a typical component representative of hundreds of components already on the market.

The example also relies on a Web Services Description Language (WSDL) and associated Web Services Meta Language (WSML) files. You can generate the files in a number of ways. For example, you can use the WSDL Generator utility that comes with the Microsoft SOAP Toolkit (`http://msdn.microsoft.com/downloads/default.asp?URL=/code/sample.asp?url=/msdn-files/027/001/580/msdncompositedoc.xml`). Third-party vendors such as PhalanxSys, the makers of psSOAP (`http://www.phalanxsys.com/soap/wsdlwiz.htm`) have created WSDL generator utilities. Finally, you can create the two required files as part of your project. The \Chapter 16\AddIt folder on the CD also contains the WSDL and WSML files for this example. You'll need to edit the WSDL URLs to match your web server setup as needed.

After you complete the component requirements, you can begin creating the desktop application to access the web service provided by the component. Previous versions of Visual Studio made this task relatively difficult. When working with Visual Studio .NET, the task is easy because you create a special type of web reference to the web service. The web reference forces the IDE to generate some additional local code automatically, making the task of accessing the service automatic. The following steps tell how to create the web reference.

(You'll find the source code for this example in the \Chapter 16\SOAPAdder folder on the CD.)

1. Right-click References in Solution Explorer and choose Add Web Reference from the context menu. You'll see an Add Web Reference dialog box. This is actually a special type of browser you'll use to locate the WSDL file on the web server (local or remote—it doesn't matter).

2. Type the URL for the web service in the Address field of the Add Web Reference dialog box.

3. Locate the WSDL file. The Add Web Reference dialog box will display the content of the WSDL file in the left pane and the reference information in the right pane, as shown in Figure 16.7.

FIGURE 16.7:

The Add Reference dialog box contains information about the WSDL file associated with a component.

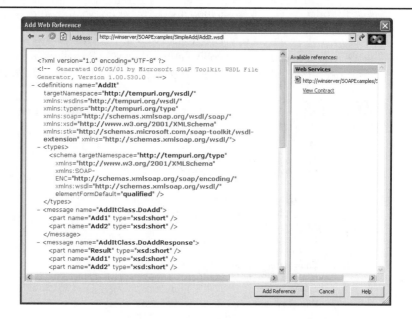

NOTE Notice that the WSDL file is just another form of XML file. It includes an XML declaration at the beginning. Each of the `<types>` tags contains a description of any custom data types used by the component. The `<message>` tags each contain one path that a message can take between client and server. Consequently, if a method provides a return value, it will produce two `<message>` tags within the WSDL file—one to transmit the data and another to transmit the result. The two messages are transparent to the client and server. As far as the client and server are concerned, the message traffic occurs as normal. The WSDL file also contains port, binding, and service information that the Visual Studio .NET IDE will use to create a connection.

4. Click Add Reference. You'll see a new Web Reference added to Solution Explorer. The Web Reference folder will include a reference to the web server and the WSDL file on the server. Double-click the WSDL entry, and you'll see a copy of the WSDL information for the service. You'll also see a Reference Map entry that describes the contract between the client and the server.

5. Add a using statement to the source code that describes the new Web Reference. The example program uses SOAPAdder.winserver;, which is a combination of the application name and the web server name. The reference isn't optional in this case—the application will likely fail to work without it because of the additional files the IDE generates for you.

Now that we have a reference to the web service, it's time to write some code to use it. Forget everything you know if you've used other SOAP toolkits in the past; Visual Studio .NET uses an entirely different technique to access the web service. Listing 16.4 shows you how.

Listing 16.4   **Using SOAP in Visual Studio .NET Is Extremely Easy**

```
private void btnTest_Click(object sender, System.EventArgs e)
{
    // Create a reference to the object.
    AddIt AddObj = new AddIt();

    // Create some intermediate variables.
    short Input1 = Int16.Parse(txtValue1.Text);
    short Input2 = Int16.Parse(txtValue2.Text);
    short Results = 0;

    // Call the Web service using SOAP.
    Results = AddObj.DoAdd(ref Input1, ref Input2);

    // Display the results on screen.
    txtResults.Text = Results.ToString();
}
```

If you're thinking this is a mistake, it's really this easy to use a web service. All you need to do is create a reference to the web service, define any intermediate variables, and then call the method you want to use within the associated component. Figure 16.8 shows the output from this example.

FIGURE 16.8:

The SOAP example
adds two numbers
together using a web
service.

Where Do You Go From Here?

This chapter has taught you about new data movement methods offered by Visual Studio .NET. While you don't have a complete solution to every problem that the distributed environment will present (such as the infamous data schema problem) you do have enough information to begin experimenting with distributed application development. We've looked at the two technologies most likely to make your next project doable: XML and SOAP.

In Chapter 13, we looked at a method for importing and exporting data from a desktop application using XML. Actually, this is a good place to start working with this new technology. SQL Server 2000 includes features that enable you to work with XML data. All you need to do is set the connection up slightly differently and you're ready to go.

After you get a desktop application working, try using XML with a web application. Combine XML and SOAP functionality to transfer data to a browser or a browser-like desktop application. If you have a Pocket PC available, try one of the third-party SOAP solutions, such as PocketSOAP (http://www.pocketsoap.com/) to move your application from the desktop to a portable device.

Speaking of portable devices, Chapter 17 is your introduction to coding on a Pocket PC and other portable devices. We'll discuss various methods you can use to create applications for your mobile devices. Unfortunately, the mobile form of the .NET Framework wasn't released at the time of this writing, so we won't discuss that option, but you'll find many other useful programming techniques in the chapter.

CHAPTER 17

PDA Application Development

- Special Needs for PDAs

- Addressing PDA Display Issues

- Writing a Microsoft Mobile Internet Toolkit (MMIT) PDA Application

- Writing a SOAP PDA Application

- Beyond PDAs to Telephones

- Understanding PDA Security Issues

- Troubleshooting PDA Application Problems

The Personal Digital Assistant (PDA) started out as a handheld contact manager and appointment scheduler. It included a black and white display and very little in the way of application functionality. Memory, processing speed, and data entry options were all so limited that few people were excited about the device for use as anything but a toy.

Today the PDA is the number one tool for many users on the road. It's lighter and easier to carry than a laptop. The handwriting interface enables a user to input data without the clack of keys during a meeting. (You use a PDA as you'd use pen and paper—the only difference is a digital result.) The Pocket PC even makes it possible to use miniature versions of Word, Excel, Access, and Internet Explorer. More than a few developers have used these capabilities to implement full-blown distributed applications that rely on technologies such as Simple Object Access Protocol (SOAP). (Admittedly, most of these applications are still in the experimental stage—I know of only one fully functional production system that relies on both the power of the Pocket PC and SOAP.)

Working with PDAs in the past meant working with arcane toolkits or jumping through hoops to accomplish even basic tasks. The .NET Framework has taken some of the sting out of working with PDAs by hiding some implementation details from the developer and providing web-based tools for automation. This chapter discusses several alternatives for PDA development. It's important to note that some solutions will work better than others for a given task, so you need to know more than one way to accomplish your desired task.

TIP   Just in case you feel that the new web technologies such as SOAP are a dead end, consider that Google recently opened its search engine to the public using a SOAP interface. That's right, you can now add Internet search engine capability to your PDA (or desktop) application using SOAP. You'll find a general article about this topic at `http://www` `.infoworld.com/articles/hn/xml/02/04/11/020411hngoogleapi.xml?0412fram`. The technical article at `http://www.ruby-talk.org/cgi-bin/scat.rb/ruby/ruby-talk/` `37623` provides development details you'll need to create your first PDA application with built-in search engine.

Special Needs for PDAs

There's no free lunch—I often wish I had been the first one to say that because it's so true. Companies that want to gain the advantages of using PDAs also have to decide how to handle the special needs of these devices. A PDA isn't a single-purpose device like a radio, but it isn't a full-fledged computer either; it's somewhere in between. A PDA has more to offer than the cell phones that some developers will eventually target as data sources. However, a PDA can't process data as quickly as your desktop or laptop machine, it has severe memory constraints, and it has only a small space for semi-permanent storage—which means you have to scale your applications down to fit within the hardware confines of the PDA.

> **TIP** The easiest way to create a single application that will run on both laptops and PDAs is to use a browser front end and a component or ASP.NET back end. Using SOAP combined with components offers greater flexibility and better performance. Using ASP.NET enables you to perform changes on-the-fly and develop the application faster.

When I first began looking at PDA development, a developer had a limited number of not-so-pleasant choices. Microsoft provided a Windows CE development kit, but not much for remote application development. It wasn't long before someone had developed a toolkit or two for creating distributed applications on a PDA using SOAP as a conduit for exchanging information. None of these choices were from Microsoft. You can see my favorite choice in the "Getting SOAP for Your PDA" sidebar.

Even now, your choices for development of PDA software are somewhat limited. You can still use Microsoft Embedded Visual Tools 3.0 (see the "Obtaining the Required Tools" section for details). There are also third-party tools for adding SOAP capability to your PDA. (Microsoft doesn't currently provide a SOAP toolkit for the Pocket PC or any of the other PDA offerings on the market.) Finally, the .NET Framework can enable you to create applications for your PDA, but you'll need to download the Microsoft Mobile Internet Toolkit (MMIT), which is also discussed in the "Obtaining the Required Tools" section.

It might seem like I'm hitting SOAP very hard, and that's because it provides one of the truly transparent development alternatives for PDA development. However, don't get the idea that SOAP is a perfect solution—it still has plenty of warts, partly because the SOAP specification is still in a state of flux. The issues regarding PDA application development using SOAP also make sense, because software of this sort normally appears on the desktop first. However, it also means that you need to consider your PDA development plans carefully, because there are many pitfalls. In all cases, you'll want to build a desktop version of your application before you attempt to create one for your favorite PDA.

> **TIP** It's impossible to know, at this point, just how many SOAP-related specifications will eventually appear on the horizon. One of the best places to learn about new specifications is the XML Web Service Specifications page at GotDotNet (`http://www.gotdotnet .com/team/xml_wsspecs/default.aspx`). Vendors are now trying to make all of these variations on a theme fit within a framework (`http://www.w3.org/2001/03/WSWS-popa/ paper51`). The idea of a framework is to show how the pieces fit together into a cohesive whole. You can monitor progress on the framework as well as other XML projects at `http://www.w3.org/2001/04/wsws-proceedings/ibm-ms-framework/`.

You can create a SOAP application for your favorite PDA; it just takes a little more planning. However, it's also important to note that the Microsoft Mobile Internet Toolkit (MMIT) provides an easy-to-use framework for creating mobile applications using the standard features of .NET. The following sections examine the special needs of PDAs. It's important to note that most of these special considerations are in addition to what you need to consider for a desktop application.

Getting SOAP for Your PDA

If you're the lucky owner of a Pocket PC, getting a SOAP toolkit is relatively painless. Unfortunately, none of the other PDA choices on the market has a SOAP toolkit available as of this writing. (There are rumors of a SOAP toolkit for the Palm, but none of the potential toolkits have appeared on the market yet.) However, given the newness of this technology, you can expect other vendors to provide SOAP toolkit offerings for other platforms eventually. The SOAP::Lite site (`http://www.soaplite.com/`) contains a section of SOAP toolkit links you can check periodically for new additions. This list tells which toolkits will work with PDAs.

Despite the long list of SOAP toolkits you find on the SOAP::Lite site, most aren't ready for prime time. The vast majority are in beta or not in any released state at all. The choices of usable toolkits for SOAP are extremely limited now, but you should see more choices as SOAP becomes entrenched within the corporate environment. The bottom line is that you not only need to find a SOAP toolkit for your PDA, but you need to find one that's fully functional.

Three new specifications recently appeared on the standards groups agenda including Web Services Routing Protocol (WS-Routing), Direct Internet Message Encapsulation (DIME), and XLANG. Each of these three specifications is so new that there's little in print about them yet. Here's the short overview of the three new specifications.

- XLANG (`http://www.gotdotnet.com/team/xml_wsspecs/xlang-c/default.htm`) will allow developers to model business processes using a standardized syntax. Microsoft uses XLANG with their BizTalk Server product. You'll find the XLANG discussion group at `http://discuss.develop.com/xlang.html`.

- WS-Routing (`http://msdn.microsoft.com/ws/2001/10/Routing/`) makes it easier to move data using SOAP over transports such as TCP, UDP, and HTTP in one-way, request/response, and peer-to-peer scenarios. You'll also want to check the discussion group for WS-Routing (formerly known as SOAP-RP) at `http://discuss.develop.com/soap-rp.html`.

- DIME (`http://gotdotnet.com/team/xml_wsspecs/dime/default.aspx`) is used to package data using a binary format in a form called payloads. You'll find the DIME discussion group at `http://discuss.develop.com/dime.html`.

Continued on next page

Of course, you'll still need a toolkit for developing a SOAP application for your PDA if you decide to use something more generic than .NET. One called pocketSOAP is the best choice if you own a Pocket PC. The same developer, Simon Fell, produces Simon's Soap Server Services for COM (4S4C) and pocketSOAP (`http://www.pocketsoap.com/`). You'll find desktop and PDA versions of pocketSOAP, making it easy to develop applications on your desktop machine and move them to your PDA later. This is especially true if you use scripts within a web page, as we will for one of the examples in this chapter. The Pocket PC version is easy to install and works just as well within the confines of the Pocket PC's feature set.

Although this product is still in beta, you'll find that most applications work with few problems. The only major problem that I experienced during testing was an occasional HTTP time-out error. The developer has promised to keep working on the kinks, so you'll likely find this product an optimum choice for PDA development.

The only caveat when using pocketSOAP is that you need to create the message by hand. It doesn't support a high-level API like the Microsoft SOAP Toolkit or the tools provided with the Visual Studio .NET IDE. However, this actually turned out to be beneficial when working with more than one platform (as we'll see in the examples). The bottom line is that you need to be prepared to spend a little more time coding when working with pocketSOAP, but the outcome is well worth the effort.

The Case for PDAs

Developing applications for PDAs will require considerable work. SOAP applications provide the greatest flexibility, native embedded applications provide the best performance and smallest resource usage, and MMIT uses developer time most productively. None of the current solutions are perfect, but some work better than others do in a given situation. Many developers are unused to working with devices that have small screens; the memory limitations are problematic at best, and there's a limit to the number of available development tools. However, the need for PDA development is strong.

Consider the case of Sears. They recently purchased 15,000 PDAs for their business. The deal is worth between $20 million and $25 million. That's a lot of PDA power for their staff. Each PDA is equipped with a built-in bar-code scanner and a wireless modem. The company plans to use these new devices for inventory management, price changes, and merchandise pickups. Some developer has a large programming task in the works as I write this. You can bet that such a serious investment comes with an equally serious need to affect the bottom line. In short, PDAs are becoming mainline systems for many different tasks.

Companies often cite two main reasons for switching to PDAs after using other devices. The first reason is that PDAs cost less to buy, operate, and maintain than many other devices.

A PDA equipped with the right add-on devices can perform a myriad of tasks in an intelligent manner.

The second main reason is ease of use. PDAs have a limited number of buttons on them and the functions of each button are easy to understand. The user writes on the screen the same as they would using pen and paper—the PDA uses handwriting recognition to convert the handwritten information into text.

Sears may be looking toward the future as well. A customer could come into the store with their PDA, beam the information to a sale clerk's PDA, and get their merchandise faster than ever before. Of course, this scenario is in the future; most shoppers today don't place their orders via PDA. The point is that Sears and other companies like K-Mart are already planning for this eventuality.

Unlike older, single-function devices, PDAs are completely programmable. This means an investment in hardware today won't become an albatross tomorrow. Companies can extend the life of an investment by using the same PDA in more than one way. As the PDAs age, they'll handle applications with lower programming requirements.

Special Add-ons

Most vendors design PDAs as electronic versions of the calendar, address book, and personal note taker. Early versions of these products didn't include the mini-word processors and spreadsheets you'll find in modern versions. In fact, with special add-ons, you can now extend many PDAs to double as cameras, scanners, and other devices.

The PDA isn't exactly a standard device to begin with. There are many hardware implementations, more than a few operating systems, and even different capabilities to consider. When users start adding features to their PDA, you may find that it's nearly impossible to determine what features you can rely on finding. In short, standardization within the company is essential, even if there's chaos outside.

These special add-ons can also work to your advantage. Imagine creating an application to work with one of the camera attachments for a PDA. Each picture is automatically transferred to a remote-processing center as the photographer takes pictures. SOAP could make this task relatively easy and automatic. The pictures would be ready for viewing by the time the photographer reaches the home office.

In sum, special PDA add-ons present problems because they create a non-standard programming environment. On the other hand, these add-ons can create new productivity situations where a developer can provide functionality that no one has ever seen before. The optimum setup is to standardize features required to make SOAP work, such as the type of network interface card (NIC). On the other hand, it's important to consider specialization.

Adding a camera to a PDA turns it into a direct image transfer device. PDAs provide the means to extend what computers can do, as long as you configure them with application connectivity in mind.

Networking

Distributed application development relies on a connection between the client and the server. Because PDAs have limited processing capability, distributed applications are especially important in this situation. It's easy to create a connection when you're working with a desktop machine. If you can't create a direct connection using a LAN, there are always alternatives, such as using dial-up support. However, networking with a PDA can prove problematic.

A PDA may not offer much in the way of a network connection. In many cases, they'll offer a method to synchronize the PDA with the desktop. The synchronization process works with static data and won't provide you with a live connection to the network. It helps to have a wireless network setup when working with a PDA since many vendors design PDAs to use this connection type. I was able to find a third-party product for connecting a Pocket PC directly to the network using a special NIC.

Every PDA that I looked at does provide some type of modem support, but the modem is usually an add-on and doesn't come with the device. Again, you'll need to standardize on the kind of modem support you need for your application. You'll also want to be sure that you can create the desired connection and view material using a browser. if you decide to go that route.

The bottom line is that the original purpose of a PDA conflicts with the ways that some people use them today. Vendors design the PDA to provide electronic versions of calendars and address books. Yes, you can run distributed applications on a PDA, but only if you have the required live network connection. Obtaining that connection can prove difficult, to say the least.

Operating System

You probably know about the major PDA operating systems on the market today. PDA vendors supply their own operating system. Windows CE is a favorite because it looks and acts much like Windows for the desktop. What you should realize is that the operating system the PDA package says it uses isn't the operating system you'll get. Small variations between machines make the difference between a distributed application (or application support such as a SOAP toolkit) that works and one that won't even install.

Windows CE allows for multiple levels of development. The operating system provides a subset of the features found in the Windows API. This means that you can use the programming techniques you learned in the past, if you're already a Windows developer. There's even a special toolkit for working with Windows CE devices (see the "Obtaining the Required Tools" section for details).

Because Windows CE also contains Internet Explorer, you can interact with it using a browser application. In fact, this is the method that I recommend, because it opens a number of time-saving possibilities; not the least is developing the application on your desktop system before you move it to the PDA. Be warned, though, that the version of Internet Explorer that ships with Windows CE doesn't include full scripting support. You can use JScript (Microsoft's form of JavaScript), but not VBScript (see Internet Programming with Windows CE at http://www.microsoft.com/mind/0599/webce/webce.htm for details).

Windows CE will simply ignore any script commands that it doesn't understand in the HTML file. In addition to JScript, you also have access to some Internet Explorer functions such as Alert() and you can use standard HTML tags. The Windows CE version of Internet Explorer will also work with Java applets. This means that you can create complex browser applications that don't rely on VBScript.

NOTE   You might wonder where the C# connection is for a PDA if the client can't run much more than JScript. Microsoft is currently working on a version of the .NET Framework for the Pocket PC, so you'll eventually be able to move .NET applications to your PDA. Of course, they'll likely have the same limitations as current embedded applications have. In addition to developing applications that run only on the client, you can run the required mobile code on the server and use it to create content acceptable to the PDA. That's the purpose of MMIT discussed in this chapter.

Addressing PDA Display Issues

Most developers realize that working with a PDA is going to be a challenge before they begin their first project. The problem is that the challenge usually turns out even larger than expected. Small displays with limited color capability are something that most developers consigned to the past. The old techniques that developers used to conserve screen space on desktop computers are suddenly appearing again in the form of PDAs.

The following sections discuss several important display issues you'll confront when working with a PDA. This section won't provide an in-depth treatise on the subject, but you'll walk away with some fresh ideas for your next PDA application.

Screen Size

Many users have 17″ or 19″ monitors capable of a minimum of 1280 × 1024 resolution today. Developers have taken advantage of the screen real estate to create better applications that display more data at one time. Even Microsoft uses higher resolutions as a baseline for applications—many of their application screens won't fit on an 800×600 display anymore.

Everything you want to do with your PDA has to fit within a small screen space (320×200 pixels if you're using a Pocket PC model like the Casio Cassiopeia). That's a lot smaller than the typical computer screen. In addition, some PDAs use black and white displays in place of color, so you can't even use some of the modern tricks to make the display look nicer. In short, PDA screens tend to look a bit plain and developers normally find themselves feverishly cutting their application screens down to size.

No matter what you do, it's impossible to fit 1280×1024 worth of application screen in a 320×200 space in many cases. When this happens you'll find that you need to make some compromises in the display. For example, I created a SOAP application to test the capabilities of a third-party toolkit on my PDA. The example retrieves computer name information from the server. Unfortunately, while the information fits fine on my desktop monitor, it doesn't fit on a PDA screen, so I had to get creative in cutting and pasting the data to fit the PDA screen. Figure 17.1 shows the results of screen configuration I performed in order to make the application data fit and still look reasonably nice.

FIGURE 17.1:

You'll need to size the data to fit within the PDA screen real estate limits.

In this case, I indented the second line of each data entry to allow enough space for long entries. Notice that the data is still readable, and the user won't have to guess about the formatting. Of course, this is still a less-than-perfect solution since the data does appear on two lines.

It's important to keep every application element on a single screen if possible. The example application does this by sacrificing application data display space. The user can scroll through the data in the Result values field without moving other screen elements around. The stylus provided with a PDA doesn't lend itself to mouse-like movement.

Make sure you consider XHTML for complex applications with many elements. It helps you to display your application in segments with relative ease. Other options include using the Handheld Device Markup Language (HDML) (http://www.w3.org/TR/NOTE-Submission-HDML-spec.html) or Wireless Markup Language (WML) (http://www.oasis-open.org/cover/wap-wml.html). Both of these technologies use the concept of cards and decks to break information up into easily managed pieces. Of course, the PDA you use has to provide support for these standards before you can use the tags within a document. As with XHTML, using either HDML or WML will prevent your page from appearing properly on a desktop machine.

Using Color

Developers have gotten used to seeing colors on their applications. Color dresses up a drab display and makes the application more fun to use. In addition, using color presents cues to the user about the information provided. For example, many users associate green with a good condition and red with something bad. Color can also make it easier to pick out specific application elements. In short, most applications rely heavily on color today and with good reason.

Depending on the PDA you use, you may not have any color at all. For example, many Palm models present the world in shades of gray. Even if a PDA does provide color support akin to the Pocket PC, the developer still has to use color carefully.

The problem for PDA users is that the screen is already small. If they get into an area with bright sunlight, seeing the screen might become impossible, especially if it's filled with colors that don't work well in such an environment. Notice that the PDA screenshots in this chapter are mainly black and white. The actual screens contain some color for the icons, but that's about it. Since these applications don't need color to present the information they can provide, it's possible to rely on a black and white image.

Using color to display icons or to convey a message is still a good idea, even in the world of the PDA. For example, a red icon could signal danger or tell the user to wait without using up screen real estate for words. Of course, you need to explain the meaning of the color changes within a manual or help file (preferably both).

Pointer Pointers

Most PDA users rely on a pointer to do all of their work. Sure, a few PDAs do offer a keyboard and mouse as separate items, but most of these offerings are bulky and difficult to use. Pointer use is one of the reasons that you want to keep your application on one screen, or use multiple screens when necessary. Scrolling on a PDA screen is less than intuitive and requires some level of skill to master.

The applications that you move from the desktop to the PDA will require some modification for screen size in many cases. While you're working on the screen, it might be a good time to add some pointer-friendly features as well. For example, try to make as many tasks into single-pointer options as possible. The user should be able to point to what they want and allow the PDA to complete it for them.

You can also build intelligence into the application. A distributed application normally has a direct connection to the server. You can use some of the server's processing power to make things easier on the user. Most PDAs already include predictive logic as part of their setup. For example, as you write something, the PDA tries to guess the entire word. When it guesses the correct word, you can click on it and save some writing time. The same principle works for other activities as well. For example, a distributed application could automatically display a data screen that the user needs most often, rather than force the user to dig through several screens to find it. Pointer-friendly programs also make tasks yes or no propositions. Again, this allows the user to accomplish the task with a single click, rather than have to write something down. The point is to make the PDA as efficient as possible so the user doesn't get frustrated trying to do something that should be easy.

Writing a Microsoft Mobile Internet Toolkit (MMIT) PDA Application

The MMIT is a new addition to the list of tools you can use to create an application for a PDA. MMIT has the advantage of relying on the .NET Framework, which means you can use C# to write the code. However, you still need to rely on skills that you developed for other platforms. The fact that you're using new technology doesn't change the need for emulators and local programming elements, such as controls and components. The following sections provide an overview of the PDA development process when using MMIT. We'll take some quick departures into other areas as needed, simply to show the tools you'll need to use for development purposes.

Obtaining the Required Tools

The example application in this section relies on C# and the MMIT. The MMIT enables you to create ASP.NET applications for a wide range of mobile devices including cellular telephones, HTML pagers, and PDAs using several standardized access methods. Download this toolkit from Microsoft's website at `http://msdn.microsoft.com/downloads/default .asp?url=/downloads/sample.asp?url=/msdn-files/027/001/817/msdncompositedoc.xml` and install it prior to creating the example. Note that MMIT is very dependent on the version of the .NET Framework you've installed. At the time of this writing, the two versions of MMIT supported either the release candidate (RC1) or the released version of the .NET Framework.

You may also want to download the Microsoft Embedded Visual Tools from `http://www.microsoft.com/mobile/downloads/emvt30.asp`. (Note that the download size for this toolkit is 304MB, which means you'll have a bit of a wait when using a dial-up connection.) This toolkit provides an array of development tools including a special IDE for Visual Basic and Visual C++ developers. The tool of greatest interest for C# developers is the Pocket PC emulator. You can place this utility on your development machine and use it to emulate the handheld device. The result is time saved in transferring a test application from your desktop machine to the handheld device. Of course, you still need to perform final testing on the Pocket PC or handheld of your choice.

The Microsoft Embedded Visual Tools also comes with both a Visual Basic and a Visual C++ compiler for embedded applications. The IDEs for these two products look similar to the IDEs found in Visual Studio 6. The Visual Basic compiler seems oriented toward proto-typing applications for a particular platform quickly, while the Visual C++ compiler provides a wealth of non-platform specific projects oriented toward low-level needs such as compo-nents. Even if you decide to use MMIT or SOAP for your application, you might find the need to write local desktop applications or support components using this compiler. Here's a simple example of a Visual Basic application for the Pocket PC (found in the \Chapter 17\ PocketPC folder on the CD).

```
Private Sub cmdClickMe_Click()
    'Determine the button type.
    If cmdClickMe.Caption = "Click Me" Then

        'Display some text.
        txtTest.Text = "This is some text."

        'Change the button caption.
        cmdClickMe.Caption = "Display Message"

    Else
        'Display a message box.
        MsgBox txtTest.Text

        'Change the button caption.
        cmdClickMe.Caption = "Click Me"

    End If

End Sub

Private Sub Form_OKClick()
    App.End
End Sub
```

As you can see, the example isn't anything spectacular, but it does get the point across. Writing an application for the Pocket PC (or any other platform supported by the Microsoft Embedded Visual Tools) need not be difficult. Notice the Form_OKClick() method. This is one example of a special addition for the Pocket PC. The form has a *ShowOK* property that controls the display of the OK circle button on the title bar. When the user clicks this button, the application ends. Figure 17.2 shows the output of this application.

FIGURE 17.2:

This simple application shows that embedded programming can be as easy as the desktop version.

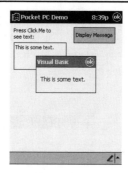

NOTE   You'll also find versions of the text application for the Palm-size and Handheld PC Pro emulators in the \Chapter 17\PalmSize and \Chapter 17\HPCPro folders on the CD. We'll view these versions in the "Using Emulators" section of the chapter.

Using the Emulators

The Microsoft Embedded Visual Tools actually comes with three emulators: Pocket PC, Handheld PC Pro, and Palm-size. Each of these emulators has a different target platform and different size screen. None of the emulators match an actual PDA implementation precisely, because each vendor adds a few features to their handheld and you also need access to PDA controls that don't appear on your desktop machine. The emulators do serve an important function in that they help you debug your application so you don't waste a lot of time working with the real device. Normally, an application that runs on the emulator also runs on the device.

You can run the emulators individually, or as part of the embedded IDE. Starting Debug also starts a copy of the appropriate emulator for your application. The emulators present the application in about the same amount of screen space that the actual device will provide. Consequently, the Handheld PC Pro has the most amount of screen real estate, as shown in Figure 17.3, while the Palm-size has the smallest amount of screen space to offer as shown in Figure 17.4.

FIGURE 17.3:

The Handheld PC Pro provides the greatest amount of screen space.

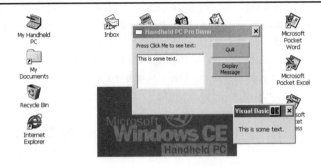

FIGURE 17.4:

Likewise, the Palm-size screen is the smallest that you'll use when developing applications.

Notice that Figures 17.3 and 17.4 have different sizes than the screen from the Pocket PC shown in Figure 17.2. In addition, you'll find that the Pocket PC is the only device that supports the *ShowOK* property, so the examples for the other two devices contain Quit buttons. It's little differences like these that will drive a developer crazy, but these are also the differences you need to observe when working on PDA applications.

Creating the Project

Creating a Mobile Web Application is akin to creating an ASP.NET project in that you create it directly on the test server and not on the local machine. We discussed ASP.NET development in Chapter 15, so I won't reiterate the need to use a two-machine setup, if at all possible, to realistically model an actual web application setup. This section of the chapter will discuss the nuances of creating a Mobile Web Application project. (The project also appears in the \Chapter 17\MobileWebApp folder on the CD—you'll need to change the web server information to match your server setup.)

To create the Mobile Web Application project, select the project in the Visual C# Projects folder on the New Project dialog box. Instead of a project name and directory, you'll need to supply a Location field value for a location on your local server. The sample application uses `http://WinServer/0111/Chapter 17/MobileWebApp` for the Location. You'll need to change this value to match your server setup. Click OK. You'll see a Create New Web dialog box while the IDE creates the project on the web server for you. The Create New Web dialog box will go away, but the wizard will continue working for a while—be patient and you'll eventually see a MobileWebForm designer appear on screen.

NOTE   There are some situations when the IDE mysteriously displays a message that it can't find one or more of the `Mobile` namespaces. Make sure you install the MMIT on both machines. If you still receive the message, make sure that the `System.Web.Mobile.DLL` appears in the `\Microsoft.NET\Framework\`*Version* folder (where *Version* is the version number of the .NET Framework). If you have multiple versions of the .NET Framework installed, try manually selecting the `System.Web.Mobile.DLL` by right-clicking References in System Explorer and choosing the Add Reference option from the context menu. You might also need to use the Browse button on the .NET tab to select the DLL manually. If all else fails, reinstall the MITT before you proceed with the example.

An MMIT project doesn't look at all like an ASP .NET project. The Designer is set up to allow multiple forms on the same page. This enables you to break up content that might not fit on a single mobile device screen into multiple screens without having to work with multiple pages. Figure 17.5 shows an example of this process at work with the example for this chapter. Notice that the figure shows some database objects already in place—we'll use the SQL Server 2000 MovieGuide database from Chapter 12 for this example.

The user will see these forms one at a time, but you'll work with them as if they appeared on a single page. This technique provides definite advantages to the developer who needs to transfer existing ASP.NET projects to MMIT, because you can move the code for your application without rewriting it in many cases. The biggest part of the effort involves redrawing the content so it fits within the confines of the mobile device display area.

FIGURE 17.5:

The design environment for MMIT enables you to have multiple forms on a single page.

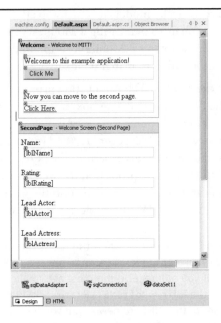

TIP Microsoft installs the MMIT with default settings that might not match your web server. As a result, the example application will fail to run. Make sure you check the event log for clues about errors in your MMIT setup. For example, if you see a mysterious error about the *username* and *password* being wrong in the processModel section of the config file, the error is probably in the Machine.CONFIG file located in the \WINNT\Microsoft.NET\ Framework\v1.0.3705\CONFIG folder on your server. The Machine.CONFIG file also contains settings that determine how long cookies last and other session timeout values (a constant source of problems during IIS tuning). Microsoft has provided copious notes within this file that explain the various configuration options.

Coding Techniques

Except for screen real estate, the coding techniques you use for MMIT are the same as the ones you'd use for an ASP.NET application. The problem is getting the information that normally appears on a full browser to appear on the screen of a PDA (or even worse, a wireless telephone). One of the techniques you can use to get around this problem is data hiding—the data is fully formed and ready to display, the user just doesn't see it until necessary. For example, the linking information on the first form of the example remains hidden until the application displays it using the following code.

```
private void cmdContinue_Click(object sender, System.EventArgs e)
{
```

```
    // Create some output for the application based on the button click.
    lbl2ndPageMsg.Visible = true;
    lnkSecondPage.Visible = true;
}
```

Using local scripting would enable the client to display the information as needed locally. The only problem with this approach is that it assumes the client has enough processing power to perform this task. Depending on the target client, you might need to use the post back method illustrated in this example to ensure the client actually sees the data once the user decides to display it.

TIP   It usually pays to create a prototype of your product using standard ASP.NET programming techniques so you can judge how well a particular scenario will work. You'll find the prototype for the application in this section in the \Chapter 17\WebApp folder on the CD.

The database development portion of the applications follows very closely with the process for ADO.NET found in Chapter 13. Because this application displays a single record at a time, you won't need the fancy DataGrid object manipulation code, nor will you need to synchronize the Detail and Grid views. Consequently, the code is much simpler and executes more quickly (a good feature, since MMIT applications seem to run relatively slow). Listing 17.1 shows the code you'll need to add to the second form.

Listing 17.1   **The Data Viewing Code for This Example**

```
// Keep track of the current record.
int    CurrRec;

private void SecondPage_Load(object sender, System.EventArgs e)
{
    // Get the current record counter pointer.
    CurrRec = Int32.Parse(lblCurrentRecord.Text);

    // Fill the dataset with data.
    sqlDataAdapter1.Fill(dataSet11);

    // Display the initial record.
    DoFill();
}

private void DoFill()
{
    // Fill the labels with data.
    lblName.Text =
    dataSet11.Tables[0].Rows[CurrRec].ItemArray.GetValue(1).ToString();
```

```csharp
    lblRating.Text =
    dataSet11.Tables[0].Rows[CurrRec].ItemArray.GetValue(2).ToString();

    lblDescription.Text =
    dataSet11.Tables[0].Rows[CurrRec].ItemArray.GetValue(3).ToString();

    lblActor.Text =
    dataSet11.Tables[0].Rows[CurrRec].ItemArray.GetValue(4).ToString();

    lblActress.Text =
    dataSet11.Tables[0].Rows[CurrRec].ItemArray.GetValue(5).ToString();
}

private void btnFirst_Click(object sender, System.EventArgs e)
{
    // Go to the first record.
    CurrRec = 0;

    // Set the current record label.
    lblCurrentRecord.Text = CurrRec.ToString();

    // Fill the display with data.
    DoFill();
}

private void btnPrevious_Click(object sender, System.EventArgs e)
{
    // Validate the current record pointer and change if necessary.
    if (CurrRec > 0)
        CurrRec--;

    // Set the current record label.
    lblCurrentRecord.Text = CurrRec.ToString();

    // Fill the display with data.
    DoFill();
}

private void btnNext_Click(object sender, System.EventArgs e)
{
    // Validate the current record pointer and change if necessary.
    if (CurrRec < dataSet11.Tables[0].Rows.Count - 1)
        CurrRec++;

    // Set the current record label.
    lblCurrentRecord.Text = CurrRec.ToString();

    // Fill the display with data.
    DoFill();
}
```

```
private void btnLast_Click(object sender, System.EventArgs e)
{
   // Go to the last record.
   CurrRec = dataSet11.Tables[0].Rows.Count - 1;

   // Set the current record label.
   lblCurrentRecord.Text = CurrRec.ToString();

   // Fill the display with data.
   DoFill();
}
```

The code begins in the usual manner by filling a dataset, *dataSet11*, with information from the data adapter, *sqlDataAdapter1*. In this respect, it doesn't matter what type of ADO.NET application you want to create, you still need to create the necessary links. Given the way that MMIT applications run, however, you'll want to ensure the application makes maximum use of data pooling by setting it up correctly in IIS.

As you can see from Listing 17.1, data movement is approximately the same as in any database application. A current record variable, *CurrRec*, tracks the current record position. Of course, there's one major difference: MMIT applications, like ASP.NET applications, lack any type of state storage information. Therefore, the application relies on a hidden label to store the current record position so that clicking Next actually displays the next record.

Testing

Unlike an ASP.NET application, you won't see multiple pages when working with an MMIT application, so getting the forms in the right order is essential. Testing means checking the form order as well as the application execution. The first form you should see when you begin this application is the one that asks the user to click the button. Figure 17.6 shows the output of this form.

FIGURE 17.6:

The first form is the one that asks for user input, so that's the first form you should see.

You might wonder how IIS keeps track of the various mobile sessions. Unlike ASP.NET, MMIT uses a special cookie embedded directly into the URL for the website after the first use of the URL. For example, here's the URL that resulted on my first visit to the example website from using the Cassiopeia: `http://winserver/0111/Chapter%2017/Mobile-WebApp/(1tsrsbnjrsOfct45ckOjxm55)/Default.aspx`. As you can see, everything is the same as on the first visit, except for the addition of a cookie (in parentheses).

Clicking the link displays the second page shown in Figure 17.7. Notice that the page includes a link for getting back to the first page. Because mobile users will look at a multitude of screens, you should always provide some means of getting back to the base page for a series of screens. Note that the four record positioning buttons are fully functional, so you can move from record to record using a PDA or other mobile device.

FIGURE 17.7:

The database screen provides a summary of the movies found in the MovieGuide database.

Writing a SOAP PDA Application

The SOAP PDA example relies on the same CompName component we used in Chapter 16. The big difference is in the client for this example. Microsoft doesn't provide a client yet for the PDA, so we need to rely on the third-party client found in the "Getting SOAP for Your PDA" sidebar.

The client code for this section is somewhat complex compared to other SOAP examples in the book, because we have to use a third-party toolkit. For one thing, we need to service two buttons instead of one. However, the Microsoft SOAP Toolkit also requires slightly different input than pocketSOAP, so there are differences in the message formatting code as well. Listing 17.2 shows the client source code for this example.

Listing 17.2   pocketSOAP Helps You Create PDA SOAP Applications

```
<HTML>
<HEAD>
<TITLE>CompName JScript Example</TITLE>
```

```jscript
<SCRIPT LANGUAGE="JScript">
function cmdGetSingleName_Click()
{
    var SOAPEnv;     // SOAP envelope
    var Transport;   // SOAP transport
    var Param;       // Parameter list
    var SOAPParam;   // SOAP method call parameters.
    var RecData;     // Received data holder

    // Create the envelope.
    SOAPEnv = new ActiveXObject("pocketSOAP.Envelope");
    SOAPEnv.MethodName = "GetCompName";
    SOAPEnv.URI = "http://tempuri.org/message/";

    // Create a parameter to place within the envelope.
    Param = SOAPEnv.CreateParameter("NameType",
        window.document.SampleForm1.comboName.value, "");

    // Send the request and receive the data.
    Transport = new ActiveXObject("pocketSOAP.HTTPTransport");
    Transport.SOAPAction =
        "http://tempuri.org/action/NameValuesProc.GetCompName"
    Transport.Send(
        "http://WinServer/soapexamples/ComputerName/CompNameProc.WSDL",
        SOAPEnv.Serialize());
    RecData = Transport.Receive();
    SOAPEnv.Parse(RecData);

    // Display the result.
    RecData = SOAPEnv.Parameters.Item(0);
    window.document.SampleForm1.Results.value = RecData.Value;
}

function cmdGetAllNames_Click()
{
    var SOAPEnv;     // SOAP envelope
    var Transport;   // SOAP transport
    var Param;       // Parameter list
    var SOAPParam;   // SOAP method call parameters.
    var RecData;     // Received data holder

    // Create the envelope.
    SOAPEnv = new ActiveXObject("pocketSOAP.Envelope");
    SOAPEnv.MethodName = "GetAllNames";
    SOAPEnv.URI = "http://tempuri.org/message/";

    // Create a parameter to place within the envelope.
    Param = SOAPEnv.CreateParameter("NameType",
        window.document.SampleForm1.comboName.value, "");

    // Send the request and receive the data.
    Transport = new ActiveXObject("pocketSOAP.HTTPTransport");
```

```
        Transport.SOAPAction =
            "http://tempuri.org/action/NameValuesProc.GetAllNames"
        Transport.Send(
            "http://WinServer/soapexamples/ComputerName/CompNameProc.WSDL",
            SOAPEnv.Serialize());
        RecData = Transport.Receive();
        SOAPEnv.Parse(RecData);

        // Display the result.
        RecData = SOAPEnv.Parameters.Item(0);
        window.document.SampleForm1.Results.value = RecData.Value;
    }
</SCRIPT>

</HEAD>

<BODY>
<!Add a heading->
<CENTER><H1>Computer Name Component Test</H1></CENTER>

<!Use a form to test out the VBScript.->
<FORM NAME="SampleForm1">

<!Create a text entry control.->
Select a single computer name if needed:<BR>

<select name=comboName>
<option value=0>ComputerNameNetBIOS
<option value=1>ComputerNameDnsHostname
<option value=2>ComputerNameDnsDomain
<option value=3>ComputerNameDnsFullyQualified
<option value=4>ComputerNamePhysicalNetBIOS
<option value=5>ComputerNamePhysicalDnsHostname
<option value=6>ComputerNamePhysicalDnsDomain
<option value=7>ComputerNamePhysicalDnsFullyQualified
<option value=8>ComputerNameMax
</select><P><P>

<!Define a place to put the results.->
Result values: <BR>
<TEXTAREA ROWS=11 COLS=60 NAME="Results">
</TEXTAREA><P><P>

<!-Create the two required buttons.->
<INPUT TYPE=button
        NAME=cmdGetSingleName
        VALUE="Get Single Name"
        ONCLICK=cmdGetSingleName_Click()>
<INPUT TYPE=button
        NAME=cmdGetAllNames
        VALUE="Get All Names"
        ONCLICK=cmdGetAllNames_Click()>
```

```
</FORM>
</BODY>
</HTML>
```

This example uses a five-step process for each function. First, you create an envelope. Second, you place data within the envelope. Third, you need to initialize the data. Fourth, you send and receive the data. Finally, you display the data on screen. The HTML code is difficult to optimize for a small screen, in this case, because of the amount of data we need to display. We'll see later how you can overcome these problems without modifying the server-side component.

The Computer Name example doesn't work quite the same on a PDA as it does on the desktop. The reason is simple—a PDA lacks the screen real estate to display this application fully. Part of the testing process is to ensure the screen remains close to the original (to keep training costs down) while ensuring readability. Figure 17.1 shows the output from this example if you click Get All Names.

The application does work the same as a desktop application would from a functionality perspective. You still use a drop-down list box to select a computer name type. The buttons still produce the same results as before. Maintaining this level of compatibility between a desktop and PDA application is essential to the success of the application. Any application that requires the user to relearn a business process is doomed to failure, no matter how nice the display looks.

Fortunately, this example is reasonably small. Your testing process must include resource usage and other factors that affect PDA application performance. Complex database applications won't run very well on a PDA because they require too many resources. Of course, you can always get around the problem by using more server-side processing and presenting the PDA with semi-finished, rather than raw results.

Beyond PDAs to Telephones

You won't find any telephones that run distributed applications today, but many developers are experimenting with telephones because they represent a potential not found with other devices. In fact, I was surprised to find that some vendors are already creating distributed applications for embedded devices. Embedded applications reside within toasters, your car, and even your television set. As distributed applications move from the desktop to the PDA, it's only logical that they'll move to the telephone as well.

The interesting thing about telephones is that we already use them for so many business and personal purposes. For example, it's possible to check your bank statement or send correspondence to your credit card company using the telephone. All you need to know how to do, in most cases, is push buttons. In addition, many companies now offer e-mail access and limited website access using a telephone; although the uses for such applications are understandably limited.

Of course, speaking into the telephone or entering some numbers for an account is hardly the same thing as using an application on a desktop computer. Eventually, technologies such as SOAP will enable two-way communications in a way that users haven't seen before. For example, an employee could enter order information using a telephone (assuming the orders are small and relatively simple).

Will telephone distributed applications appear overnight? Probably not. Will we use the telephone to accomplish the same things we do on the PC? Again, probably not. However, the telephone does present some interesting opportunities for application developers in the future.

Understanding PDA Security Issues

Many network administrators view the PDA with more than a little suspicion and for good reason. The media has painted the PDA as a device that it so open that anyone can access it at any time. Smart users keep all of their sensitive data on the company computer and just place lists of tasks on their PDA. Of course, such a view defeats the purpose of having a PDA in the first place. A PDA should be an extension of your workplace, not a hindrance to avoid.

Many of the security issues surrounding PDAs today come from a perception that they're all wireless devices. Many PDAs use network or modem connections, not wireless connections. The PDAs that do provide wireless access tend to err on the side of safety whenever possible. Vendors realize that wireless access is both a blessing and curse for many companies. However, the wireless issue probably isn't much of an issue for the SOAP developer. Count on many of your users to rely on modem or direct network interface card (NIC) connections. For example, the Pocket PC provides a slot that will accommodate an Ethernet card that provides a direct network connection.

One of the biggest security issues for all PDA users is data storage. There are actually two threats to consider. The first is that someone could access sensitive data if they stole your PDA (or, at least, borrowed it for a while). Wireless or not, the person who has the PDA also has access to the data it contains. The second threat is data loss. Many PDAs lose all of their information once the main battery is exhausted. (Some PDAs provide a backup battery that retains the contents of memory until the user replaces or recharges the main battery.) Unless the user backs up on a regular basis while on the road, the data is lost.

A distributed application can come to the rescue, in this case, by allowing the user to store all data on a central server in a secure location. The application remains on the client machine, but the data remains secure at the main office. Of course, there has to be some level of flexibility built into the security plan, so that users can operate their PDA in a disconnected mode. PDA vendors will likely add some form of biometric protection to their PDAs in the future. For example, the user might have to press their thumb in a certain area in the back when starting the PDA so the PDA can check their identity.

Some security issues involve limitations in the PDA itself. For example, when working with a desktop application, you can ask the user to enter their name and password. The application asks the server for verification before it requests any data access. The pointer a PDA user must use to enter data hampers the security effort. It's possible that they'll end up entering the password more than the three times that good applications normally allow. The next thing you'll hear is a frustrated user on the telephone asking why they can't get into their application. Security is required, but any attempt to implement security that causes user frustration is almost certain to fail.

Another PDA-specific security issue to consider is one of resources. Heavy security consumes many resources. A desktop user notices some slowing of their computer when they're working with a secure application. The slowing is due to the work of the security protocol in the background. With the limited resources of a PDA, you probably can't implement any level of heavy security because the application would run too slowly. The PDA already runs distributed applications slower because it uses a browser-based application over a relatively slow connection. Adding to this problem is one way to lose user confidence in your application.

PDAs do suffer from every other security problem that distributed applications that rely on any form of XML (such as SOAP) normally experience. A lack of built-in security will allow prying eyes to see the data that the user transfers to the home office (at least if someone is actually looking). Unfortunately, the list of available security add-ons for PDAs is extremely limited. Theoretically, you can use technologies such as Secure Sockets Layer (SSL) with a PDA. We've already discussed the limitations of some of these technologies in previous chapters, so I won't go into them again here. Needless to say, using a PDA involves some security risk that you'll need to overcome.

Troubleshooting PDA Application Problems

PDAs present some interesting challenges no matter which programming language you use to develop a client and no matter how you transfer data. Fortunately, most distributed application environments allow you to preserve the server side of your development investment. If you use a PDA such as the Pocket PC, you can also reuse some of your client code. In short, distributed application development solves significant PDA development problems. The following sections will examine some of the problems developers have when creating browser-based distributed applications for the PDA and hopefully provide the answers you need to add distributed application development to your PDA application toolkit. (Always feel free to contact me at `JMueller@mwt.net` if you have additional questions.)

Missing Screen Data or No Display at All

The number one problem for PDAs running applications from a web server is security. The PDA will often run into an access problem and simply ignore it. You won't see any kind of an error message in many cases. All that will happen is that the PDA will perform whatever local tasks it can perform and then stop when the error happens.

You'll also see this problem if you use a scripting language the PDA doesn't understand. Again, the PDA will try to accomplish all that it can locally, and then it'll simply stop. Remember that Windows CE doesn't provide VBScript support, but it does provide JScript support. Other PDA setups have similar limitations, and you need to check for them during the project definition stage.

Some developers ignore the small screen that a PDA provides; you may not see a result because it appears off screen. Moving the scroll bar up and down may show an answer that you couldn't see before. Unfortunately, users will normally complain about the lack of data long before they move the display. In short, make sure that your application fills a single screen at a time so the user doesn't have to look for the information.

In a very few cases, you'll find that all of the client files need to appear on the PDA instead of the web server. For example, downloading a web page so that the PDA can access the scripts may not work. Test all of the machines your application targets to ensure you won't run into a problem of this type.

Lack of Support for More Than One PDA

During the development process for the examples in this chapter and a few personal projects, I found that even though a PDA runs the same operating system as another PDA, there are differences for which you need to account. For example, PDAs use different processors, so you can't assume anything about low-level code. Consequently, it's important to use high-level languages if you plan to work with the code on more than one type of machine.

You'll also find that PDAs require driver and other software updates, just as desktop machines do from time to time. Make sure you download and install all patches for your PDA before you begin development.

Some toolkit implementations (especially those for SOAP) require support files. Make sure you install all of the required support before you attempt to run an application on the PDA. For example, a Windows CE machine will likely require a copy of pocketSOAP (or other SOAP toolkit) before they can run a SOAP application. The Palm systems required both the SOAP toolkit and the XML parser. Palm systems require two separate installations, so leaving one part of the support mechanism out of the picture is relatively easy.

Client Messaging Problems

Most messaging problems appear when you use more than one toolkit to accomplish a task. The server may expect something other than the normal client output. However, you can normally modify the data stream enough to accommodate the requirements of client or server. The various tracing tools allow you to compare message formats and change the standard code as needed to create a message the server will understand. Likewise, you can normally modify the server output to accommodate client needs.

Another problem is live connection confusion. A PDA requires a live connection with the server, not a synchronized connection. A live connection allows data exchange between client and server, while a synchronized connection allows the host workstation to update the PDA's files. In some cases, a synchronized connection may look live, but it isn't. PDAs always require some type of direct network connection to provide data connectivity, plus a driver that allows network configuration. In short, don't assume all wireless connections are live simply because they tap into the network—many simply provide a better way to perform synchronization.

Always double-check a failed PDA connection using a desktop client that you know works. PDA connections can fail in numerous ways that a desktop connection won't. In at least a few cases, you'll find that the server has stopped responding and the desktop application will provide an error message to this effect. PDAs often suppress error messages, making debugging especially difficult.

Where Do You Go From Here?

By now, you have a better idea of how PDA development will shape the world of distributed applications. While PDA applications currently perform mundane tasks such as reading e-mail, they'll eventually provide the basis for distributed applications. For example, a salesperson might use a PDA to enter client contact information that appears instantly on the company database and helps the company deliver products faster. In some cases, PDAs could represent the new laptop device—a laptop that fits in your pocket.

We've looked at a simple PDA example in this chapter. However, this example forms the basis of most of the code that you'll eventually write for distributed PDA applications. While many PDA applications today are of the utility type used to enhance PDA functionality, you'll eventually want to write applications that exchange data with a remote server. Enhancing the application in this chapter is one way to gain additional insights into PDA development.

Now that you have a better idea of what PDA development is like, you might want additional information about what .NET can do for you. *.NET Wireless Programming* by Mark Ridgeway (Sybex, 2002, see `http://www.sybex.com/sybexbooks.nsf/` `2604971535a28b098825693d0053081b/bafc7295f4222914882569fa003710fb!OpenDocument` for more information) provides additional insights into this new type of application development. This book includes five case studies that show various types of applications you can create using the .NET Framework.

This is the last chapter of the book. However, the content isn't over yet. You'll find several appendices after this chapter that help you learn more about how C# compares to the rest of the world. You'll also find an interesting example of how to build an MMC snap-in using a combination of C# and Visual C++. Finally, make sure you check the Glossary when you have questions about terms and acronyms in the book.

PART V

Appendices

APPENDIX A

C# for Visual C++ Developers

- An Overview of the Differences

- Language Gotchas for Visual C++ Developers

- Converting Your Existing Code to .NET

C# promises much for Visual C++ developers who need the low-level support that Visual C++ provides, but also need to become more productive. Some people have said that C# is Microsoft's answer to Java. In some respects, it probably is. Other people have pointed to C# as the mid-point between Visual Basic and Visual C++. This view is also partially true. However, C# is also a new language that has a lot to offer in its own right, so those of you converting from Visual C++ to C# should look at C# as a new language, not as the next step for Visual C++ developers.

This appendix presents information about how you can make your C# experience better if you already know how to use Visual C++. There are some obvious similarities between the two languages that make C# easier for the Visual C++ developer to learn. However, these similarities can become a trap for the unwary developer who assumes that everything will work as it did in the past. C# is a distinct language and you need to consider it as such. While you can't port all of your Visual C++ code to C# (especially considering your Visual C++ code is written for an unmanaged environment) you will be able to port some of it. We'll discuss the issues in porting code in this appendix as well.

An Overview of the Differences

If you take a cursory look at C#, it bears many similarities to Visual C++. In fact, it might be easy to confuse the two in some circumstances, because you use curly braces and other features that people associate with C in general and Visual C++ in specific. The fact is that the cursory glance doesn't tell the whole story. You'll find that while C# and Visual C++ do have some features in common, you'll also see many differences.

Differences on the Surface

The first difference is that Visual C++ programmers are used to working in an unmanaged environment, while C# always relies on a managed environment. The differences between a managed and unmanaged environment are many. Using the managed environment implies working with the .NET framework, which means the compiler doesn't create native EXE files. Any application you develop with C# will have to run on a machine that has the .NET framework installed, because C# compiles to intermediate language (IL) code. This won't be much of a problem as more machines have the .NET framework installed, but it could be a problem today; many older machines won't have the required level of support installed.

NOTE   Visual C++ .NET offers a managed environment as an option. However, many developers will likely continue using the unmanaged environment or a mixed environment for projects because of the large base of code available for Visual C++. In addition, using the unmanaged environment does provide certain benefits for the developer. For example, the developer, not the runtime environment, determines memory management policies.

Working with managed code also makes a difference to the developer. It enables you to concentrate on creating code, rather than managing memory. As mentioned in Chapter 1, one of the biggest problems that Visual C++ developers have is with memory management. Applications with memory leaks are problematic. C# answers this problem by managing the memory for you. That's what it means to provide a managed environment. Of course, developers will still require time to adjust to the new way of working with Windows.

The use of global variables is also a problem for many Visual C++ developers because global variables are at the heart of many Visual C++ projects. C# doesn't support global variables for good reason—the use of global variables leads to poor programming habits. In addition, consider that everything in C# is somehow related to an object. This means that everything must appear within a class—including variables. In short, C# enforces good programming habits and provides better object support than Visual C++ ever will.

One of the benefits of using C# is that it has no order of dependence. You don't have to make forward declarations of methods within the classes. In addition, the methods can appear in any order, and you can call them in any order. The lack of order dependence means that you can organize the code in the way that best suits your needs and personal tastes. If you want to place the code in alphabetical order, C# doesn't care and you won't suffer any kind of penalty for doing so.

A final surface difference is the fact that C# is a higher level language than Visual C++. It might look like Visual C++, but you don't have direct access to the hardware or the operating system. (While you can gain access to both hardware and operating system using PInvoke or Visual C++ wrapper code, the fact remains that you must do something special to gain this access.) Some Visual C++ developers find the loss of control over their environment difficult until they have worked with C# for a while. In some respects, this is the same transition that developers made when they moved from writing code in assembler to working with C.

Conceptual Differences

One of the major differences between C# and Visual C++ is conceptual. When you work with C#, everything is an object. Everything you use in C# ultimately derives from a base class named objects. This includes items that have some other basis in Visual C++, such as variables. In C#, you can box an integer and treat it as an object. You can manipulate it without calling on library routines. If you want to convert an integer into a string, you don't need to create a second variable and call upon itoa() to do it. The conversion process occurs with the integer and the methods associated with it.

Unlike Visual C++, C# has no need for a runtime library. Many developers are used to working with a combination of the runtime library and one of several APIs, such as the Win32 API. C# relies exclusively on the functionality provided by the .NET Framework.

This lack of libraries means that you no longer need to worry about include files and that C# only needs to reference the centralized functionality of the .NET Framework.

The loss of libraries also means the loss of arcane return codes. When a C# application experiences an error, CLR raises and exception. The use of a `try...catch` statement ensures the C# application can handle the exception and possibly recover from it. The point is that errors always use the same reporting mechanism and you never have to worry about where to find error information. This feature makes the whole issue of error handling easier.

The whole idea of versioning is also new. Because CLR handles member layout based on the versioning information contained within the assembly, C# developers won't run into as many compatibility issues. If CLR can't find the correct version of a .NET Framework or other support assembly, it will provide an error message stating the problem and the application will fail to run. This solution might not provide the perfect world that developers hope for, but it's better than allowing a user to start an application that acts strangely because it lacks support from the correct DLLs (also known as DLL hell).

Properties are first-class citizens of C#. In Visual C++ a developer creates a property, but makes it private. A user accesses the property through accessor methods that change the value of the property. C# changes this by making the accessor methods a part of the property declaration. Every property can have a `get` and/or a `set` method. If you use `get` alone, the property is read-only. Using `set` alone means that the property is write-only.

An array in Visual C++ is a pointer to a sequence of data elements. In C# an array is an object. This difference between array implementations means that arrays can provide more functionality in C#. For example, you can't write past the end of an array in C# because CLR will raise a bound error. Arrays also come in single dimensional, multi-dimensional, and ragged (or jagged) varieties.

In general, you'll find that C# supports both synchronous and asynchronous operations on most objects that handle data. The use of object methods determines whether the action is synchronous or asynchronous. For example, if you want to perform a synchronous write to a file, you would use the `Write()` method. On the other hand, if you want to perform an asynchronous write, you would begin the action with `BeginWrite()` and end it with `EndWrite()`.

New Statements

The statements that will cause developers the most trouble are those that have equivalents in Visual C++. For example, many developers rely on fall-through behavior for the `switch` statement. A `switch` statement in C# has no fall-through behavior. Every case must end with either a break or a `goto`. Of course, the `goto` statement has had a less than stellar history, so some developers will approach it caution. However, if you want to implement a fall-through behavior, you must do it explicitly using a `goto`.

Some statement differences will come as a relief to Visual C++ developers who've spent many hours scratching their heads over a problem. For example, the foreach statement is simple in concept, yet Visual C++ never had it (and doesn't have it in the latest release). The foreach statement reduces coding requirements by helping the developer work with enumerated data. For example, you could use the foreach statement to parse the contents of the drives on a network without writing complex code to do it.

Visual C++ developers share some new features with C# developers. For example, attributes are a new feature that both categories of developer can enjoy. However, even in this arena you can see differences between the world of Visual C++ and C#. Visual C++ developers will use attributes as a matter of convenience. After all, for a Visual C++ developer, attributes simple replace code that the developer would have written anyway. A C# developer needs attributes to work effectively with the .NET platform. Not only do attributes provide a means for writing boilerplate code quickly, but they also provide a means for performing tasks such as documenting code behavior. You also use attributes to perform tasks such as including declarative security within your application.

NOTE   Attributes are an extremely useful feature in C#. We discussed how to create your own custom attributes in Chapter 6. See the Attribute example in that chapter for details. In some cases, you must use attributes to accomplish specific security goals. We discussed the use of declarative security in Chapter 9. Make sure you look at the declarative programming example in that chapter, because it shows the mandatory use of attributes for security purposes.

The checked and unchecked keywords provide for additional math function validation not found in Visual C++. When a math operation is checked, CLR verifies that the operating doesn't result in an overflow. If an overflow does occur, the application will generate an exception that the code must handle. Using unchecked means that CLR won't check for overflows, but that the results of math operations are also less certain that that you might experience unpredictable results.

C# provides the concept of an indexer, which is essentially a specialized form of an array. The indexer is a means of addressing a particular element of a collection—an array of objects. You'll use this particular feature regularly with the foreach statement. For example, if you wanted to poll the device drivers supported by the system, you'd first gain access to a system object and then use an indexer to list each device object individually. Note that an object must support the IEnumerable interface before the foreach statement will work with it. The concept of an enumerator is also new to C#.

Working with Objects

It's important to note that C# has a distinct method for working with objects. Of course, you need to differentiate first between an object and a value. Objects always rely on references to memory allocated from the heap, while values always appear directly on the stack. C# makes it easy to turn any value into an object using the concept of boxing, but you can only unbox objects as specific value types.

You'll also find that C# supports only single inheritance, while Visual C++ supports multiple inheritance. All objects ultimately derive from a base class named `object` and can only inherit from a single base class derived from `object`. However, C# classes can implement multiple interfaces. (See the "Creating Interfaces" section of Chapter 3 for details on creating and working with interfaces.) Whenever an object uses an interface it must implement the methods within the interface, but it also derives the benefit of the structure the interface provides. Needless to say, C# doesn't provide support for templates, making some of the benefits (and the problems) of templates a thing of the past.

NOTE   There were rumors that Microsoft would add template support to C# sometime in the future. Unfortunately, Microsoft isn't saying much about template support at the time of this writing, so it's hard to tell if this feature will ever appear in C#. Even if Microsoft (or ECMA) adds template support, the support is unlikely to match the type of template support provided in Visual C++. In addition, the use of templates would require the addition of generics to the .NET Framework, a problematic addition at best, and an impossible one at worst.

C# had a distinct meaning for the new keyword. When you use new, you're requesting a new copy of an object. The compiler creates the object and calls its constructor with any arguments you provide. In short, the object is ready to use after you create it. In addition, the object has a definite value before you use it for the first time. Of course, you might need to provide additional information before the object will actually do something useful.

For Those Who Work with Both Languages

Even after you consider all of these differences, some people might be tempted to say that Visual C++ and C# share more than they differ. The fact is that you can't use Visual C++ one day and immediately begin using C# the next. Developers will need time to overcome old habits. For example, one of the nicer features that I'm getting used to is not worrying about header files all the time. You can write C# applications using a single file if desired.

TIP The differences between C# and other languages has become a major topic of discussion for many people. The existence of a new language intrigues many people enough that they'll spend hours in detailed comparisons. You can benefit from their researches. One of the better-detailed comparisons of C# with other languages is at `http://genamics .com/developer/csharp_comparative.htm`. The author provides detailed comparisons of C# with other languages at 26 different levels, including date types, versioning, and interoperability. Another good place to look for comparisons is `http://www.softsteel .co.uk/tutorials/cSharp/lesson2.html`. This site takes a tutorial approach and discusses the differences one language at a time.

If you're like me and work with a variety of coding projects, you'll likely find that you need to keep both your Visual C++ and your C# skills current. Sometimes that means working on a project like the security example in Chapter 9 where you use both languages in the same project. Moving back and forth between languages in that project really kept me on my toes and helped reinforce the differences between the two languages. In many cases, this technique is the one that will help you learn C# in the fastest way possible—constant exposure to the differences between the two languages tends to reinforce the advantages and disadvantages of each language in your mind.

Language Gotchas for Visual C++ Developers

Working with any new language requires a lot of flexibility. Developers, like anyone else, get into a rut—they learn to do things a certain way, so anything new proves difficult. Of course, becoming proficient at coding means learning the techniques well enough that you can write code in your sleep. In short, the developmental rut is a requirement for efficient programming. However, a developmental rut is also the best way to run afoul of new programming language features. With this in mind, the following list tells you about programming features that developers seem to use improperly most often when moving from Visual C++ to C#.

NOTE I'd like to make an effort to keep this list current. If you have a particular problem with the move from Visual C++ to C# and would like to share it, please feel free to write me at `JMueller@mwt.net`. Significant problems experienced by more than one reader could also appear in my Pinnacle newsletter, .NET Tips, Trends & Technology eNewsletter (`http://www.pinnaclepublishing.com`). I plan to provide an update to this list on my website at `http://www.mwt.net/~jmueller/`. Check my website for further details.

Using `Struct`   A difference that will almost certainly trap some Visual C++ developers making the move to C# is the `struct`. In Visual C++, a `struct` is functionally the same as a class. In fact, C++ uses `structs` as lightweight classes. In C#, a `struct` is a means for passing data from one place to another and nothing more. Yes, a `struct` can still contain code in C#, but the whole concept of the struct is different from Visual C++. If you want to create code, then you need to create a class. The best way to look at a struct in C# is as a complex value allocated on the stack—classes are references allocated on the heap. Struct also has limitations not found with classes. For example, you can't derive from a struct and a struct can't use any base class except those found in System.ValueType.

Using Bool   Sometimes, the little things count the most. Consider the Boolean value. In Visual C++, you can use an integer as a replacement for a bool. In C#, however, you must use a bool at all times. This means that if you use an int, it must end as a bool. For example, you'd need to write for (!MyInt) as for (MyInt != 0). Many Visual C++ developers will have to break habits they learned while working with Visual C++ before they can effectively work with C#, and it will be due to these small differences.

Understanding Non-deterministic Finite Automation (NFA)   The managed environment provided by C# caused one problem that most Visual C++ developers notice right away. Most C# classes don't have destructors. It's not that a developer can't add a destructor to a class; it's that the developer never knows when the Garbage Collector will call the destructor. This lack of control over the calling of the destructor is called Non-deterministic Finite Automation (NFA). This relatively complex term describes an equally problematic situation for the developer. It means that the developer must now find a way to ensure the class will work as intended without relying on the destructor to perform any required cleanup. Given the way C# and CLR works, the problem is actually less than you might think—consider that there's no need to release memory because the Garbage Collector takes care of the problem for you.

Overcoming the Lack of macro support   Many Visual C++ developers live on macros when coding their applications. While C# does support a preprocessor for conditional code, you won't find any support for macros. This means the developer must rethink some ways of writing code and that some operations might not be possible (at least not possible in the same way they were in Visual C++). The lack of macros tends to make code easier to understand, but also means that some of the shortcuts that Visual C++ developers used in the past are gone.

Overcoming the lack of Typedef support   A Typedef in Visual C++ gives an existing type a new name that better describes the function of the type within the code. The Typedef doesn't actually create a new type, it simply renames the existing type. When used properly, a Typedef can make code more readable. Unfortunately, the use of Typedef more often confuses anyone attempting to read the code. C# doesn't support Typedef, which means any inadvertent renaming of variable types the developer performs will cause errors during compilation. While the compiler does catch this particular error, it's still inconvenient and many developers will do it almost as a reflex action.

Understanding language oddities There are many changes that fall into the nuisance category. While the compiler will catch any error you make in this area, the source of the problem isn't always clear. For example, you must capitalize the Main() method for your application (unlike Visual C++, which uses lowercase). You also won't require a semicolon after a class declaration. If you add one, the C# compiler will identify an error, but not necessarily the correct error, which means checking the code line-by-line until you locate the errant semicolon.

Understanding the definite assignment requirement Normally, when you create an object in C#, you'll use new to create a new copy of the object. However, C# doesn't require that you create a new object—you can also assign an existing object to a new object. C# does require that you make some type of assignment to every object before you use it, so you must either use the new keyword to create a new copy of an object or assign an existing object. Any other action will result in errors.

It's important to realize this list contains the most common gotchas for developers moving from Visual C++ to C#. However, it doesn't include your personal list of learning curve problems. There are many ways to overcome these problems. A personal favorite is creating a checklist of problem areas, then checking those areas after each coding session. Eventually, I find that I don't make that mistake anymore and can take it off the list. As my coding proficiency increases, other problems appear and I add them to the list. Eventually, the list is empty—the learning process is complete and gotchas are a thing of the past.

Converting Your Existing Code to .NET

Most Visual C++ developers have hundreds of thousands, perhaps millions, of lines of code that they have polished to perfection over the years. Giving up such a vast amount of code to move to another language is going to be hard. In fact, in some cases I recommend you don't even consider the move. There are many ways around the whole issue of moving your code from one language to another. In fact, I'm a strong advocate of using multiple languages within a single application. Every language has something special to offer—combining languages often enables you to create code that runs faster, with fewer bugs, in less time. Consequently, the first option you need to consider is not converting the code at all.

There are situations when a customer will request a specific language for an application for the sake of future maintainability. In addition, C# is one of the few languages that will eventually execute untouched on more than one platform—or, at least, we hope it will. You might have to move your existing code to .NET in order to enjoy all of the benefits that C# can provide. However, the very concept of moving code so it can execute on another platform means you'll need to leave some code, such as Win32 API calls, behind so that your code executes entirely within the bounds of the .NET Framework.

The following sections will help you understand the options for moving your code from Visual C++ to .NET. Some of these options will enable you to continue using the features that you need in the Win32 API. Other options will help you start fresh so that you use the .NET Framework to the exclusion of everything else. The options you choose depend on the goal for moving the code. If the goal is simply to bring all of your applications under one roof, then you'll be able to use more of the options. However, be careful of anything that accesses non–.NET Framework features if interoperability is your final destination.

Using Existing Code

Use wrappers and other techniques to make your existing code palatable for the .NET environment. This book contains several examples on how to do this—from the PInvoke demo in Chapter 4, to the unmanaged component example in Chapter 6, to the library example in Chapter 9. All of these examples point out that it's possible for C# and Visual C++ to coexist in peace.

The biggest impediment to moving code from Visual C++ to C# isn't the language differences. The biggest impediment is the fact that most of your Visual C++ code is written for an unmanaged environment and C# works in a managed environment. However, it's important to remember that Visual C++ allows you to mix managed and unmanaged code in the same package. Therefore, converting your code for use with C# could be as easy as slightly reconfiguring a Visual C++ DLL and recompiling it. The new DLL functions would reside within a namespace and class as methods. The whole transition could be as easy as cutting and pasting the requisite code.

Working with the *Unsafe* Keyword

The unsafe keyword represents one of the best ways to promote interoperability between your C# code and your Visual C++ code. While using an IntPtr object enables you to work with pointers, in most cases, there are situations when you need to manipulate the pointer in ways that defies using an IntPtr. That's where using pointers comes into play. In fact, there are three well-defined situations where you'll use pointers in your C# code.

- Accessing data structures you can't replicate using managed code.

- Low-level COM or PInvoke scenarios, especially if you work with device drivers or directly with the display.

- Situations where you need the ultimate in performance and using a large number of *IntPtr* objects will slow the code significantly.

You'll want to keep `unsafe` code sections extremely small because CLR can't verify the code as safe. This has some odd ramifications in the execution of your code. For one thing, it means that the compiler won't catch as many programming errors, so you'll spend more time debugging the code. However, `unsafe` code also has ramifications for security (the code will often fail to execute in remote applications). In addition, you'll find that you need to watch memory allocation carefully. Using `unsafe` code means that you can create and delete pointers that reference memory that CLR might not deallocate automatically.

Moving Your Business Logic

At the lowest rung of the conversion ladder is your business logic. Often a routine that performs calculations, exercises rules, or performs other business logic tasks contains few, if any, calls to the Windows API. Theoretically, you can cut this code out of your Visual C++ application and paste it into a C# application. The only caveat is that you need to watch for type differences in variables. If you used good programming techniques, it should be relatively easy to locate the variable declarations and redefine them in terms that C# can understand.

The bottom line is that your Visual C++ code investment isn't lost when you move to C#. You should be able to move at least some of it directly to the new environment and access most of it using standard techniques such as component import or PInvoke. Using wrapper code as appropriate will help you access the remaining code that C# can't access directly because it appears in a library (LIB) file or some other format that C# can't understand.

Where Do You Go From Here?

One of the premises for .NET is to make life easier for the developer. In large part .NET does succeed in this goal. You'll find that you can create code faster and with fewer errors. While initial .NET projects can prove difficult, eventually you'll find that you work faster and that the learning curve for new areas is relatively small. With this in mind, your first stop after reading this book is putting some of your new-found knowledge to use in creating new C# applications.

After you have some basic knowledge of how C# works, try porting some of your existing code. Make sure you keep the problems that cause most Visual C++ developers in mind as you port the code. In addition, try using some of the tricks in the "Converting Your Existing Code to .NET" section to make the conversion process easier.

You have seen several examples of where .NET isn't quite as a complete solution as Microsoft would have you believe. For example, we had to rely entirely on a Visual C++ LIB to work with some security features in Chapter 9. In many cases, you'll find that you need both your Visual C++ and your C# skills to remain competitive today. Eventually, Microsoft will port the rest of the code you need to .NET (or find alternative solutions). However, today's development needs will still require you to work with both Visual C++ and C# at times to accomplish specific goals.

APPENDIX B

C# for Visual Basic Developers

- An Overview of the Differences

- Language Gotchas for Visual Basic Developers

- Converting Your Existing Code to .NET

V isual Basic is one of the most popular programming languages in the Windows community today. It enables developers to write applications quickly and to use prototyping to design an application interface long before the developer commits to coding. In fact, Visual Basic is so popular that its rise to fame surprised even Microsoft. In short, Visual Basic is the success that every language development company would like to see in a language.

Of course, this begs the question of why someone who develops applications with Visual Basic would even consider using C# for application development. In most respects, if you know the .NET Framework (a requirement for using Visual Basic .NET), then you also know a great deal about C#. Visual Basic .NET is a new language in many ways—a new language with extended capabilities and functionality.

However, C# brings a lot of more to the application development environment than a simple means of accessing the .NET Framework. Special keywords, such as `unsafe`, make C# a little lower level language than Visual Basic, but not quite as low-level as Visual C++. This intermediate orientation makes C# more accessible to Visual Basic developers who need to write some low-level code. C# also offers a terseness not found in Visual Basic. Put simply, C# is another tool for your toolbox that meets specific needs.

This appendix isn't designed to convince anyone of the need to use one language or another for development purposes. What you will learn is how C# differs from Visual Basic, which may provide reasons for adding C# to your language toolkit. The sections that follow will also enable you to learn how to work with C# faster. You'll also learn how to perform tasks such as moving your existing Visual Basic code to C# when the situation warrants. Of course, the reasons and goals for working with C# when your main language is Visual Basic is entirely a personal choice.

An Overview of the Differences

One of the best ways to understand when to use C# for development over Visual Basic is to understand how the two languages differ. Knowing that Visual Basic and C# have many similarities (despite the curly braces found in C#), makes it easier to transition between the two languages as needed. However, it's the differences between the two languages that make one language more appropriate than the other is for some types of development. The ability to use pointers in C# makes a big difference when you need to access Windows API functions (something that happens more often than you might expect). On the other hand, Visual Basic is still faster to use in some cases, because it hides some of the details from the developer.

NOTE   Visual Basic readers might want to look at the "An Overview of the Differences" section in Appendix A as well. This section discusses some common differences between C# and other languages. For example, both Visual Basic and Visual C++ users will gain from the inclusion of the `unsafe` keyword in C#. This particular feature is discussed in Appendix A.

Differences in Syntax

At least a few of the oddities that Visual Basic programmers will experience when using C# deal with the language constructs. For example, when you want to check if an object is empty in Visual Basic, you compare it to the keyword Nothing. On the other hand, C# uses the NULL keyword, which is the same as Visual C++. Some Visual Basic programmer somewhere will probably spend hours trying to determine the error in their code due to small language differences such as this one. The small differences cause more problems than the large ones at times.

One area where Visual Basic and C# developers have a high level of agreement is in data types and variables. It's true that C# developers don't use the Dim statement to create variables, but in many other ways, assignment and usage are the same. The big difference between Visual Basic and C# in this area, is that C# enforces data types. Type conversions follow strict rules in C#, when such conversions are possible. C# also follows strict rules for variable usage. A developer must declare a variable and assign it a value before using it. You could consider C# the strict cousin of Visual Basic.

Just how strict C# becomes about some types of type conversion depends on the use of the checked versus unchecked state of computations and data conversions. You can perform certain types of conversions using C# where the data is truncated if you maintain an unchecked environment. The moment that you begin using a checked environment, C# considers any form of truncation or other unsafe data conversion to be an error. In some cases, it won't even compile the application. Here is a simple example of the differences between checked and unchecked code.

```
public static int Main(string[] args)
{
    // Create an integer.
    int   MyInt = 355;
    byte  MyByte1 = 0;
    byte  MyByte2 = 0;

    // Try to create a byte form with checked on.
    try
    {
        // The conversion will fail.
        MyByte1 = checked((byte) MyInt);
    }
    catch
    {
        // Display an error message if the
        // conversion fails.
        Console.WriteLine("Can't convert int to byte.");
    }
```

```
try
{
   MyByte2 = unchecked((byte)MyInt);
}
catch
{
   // Display an error message if the
   // conversion fails.
   Console.WriteLine("Can't convert int to byte.");
}

// Display the results.
Console.WriteLine("MyInt Equals: {0}", MyInt);
Console.WriteLine("MyByte1 Equals: {0}", MyByte1);
Console.WriteLine("MyByte2 Equals: {0}", MyByte2);
Console.ReadLine();
return 0;
}
```

When you run this code, you'll see output similar to the text shown in Figure B.1. Notice that only the checked code registers an error. The unchecked code assumes that the conversion from int to byte is fine, even though it does result in truncation as indicated by the differences in value.

FIGURE B.1:

Use checked code to ensure that a data translation is safe and won't result in truncation.

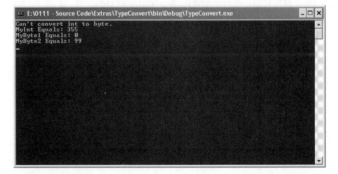

Some data types serve the same purpose between Visual Basic and C#, but the two languages use different names. For example, Visual Basic uses Integer and Long for 16-bit and 32-bit integer values, while C# uses short and int for the value data types. A point of confusion for the Visual Basic user is the fact that the long in C# is actually a 64-bit value.

Visual Basic provides developers with many string-handling features. In fact, I often consider this one of the better reasons to use Visual Basic for some tasks. C# provides more string handling features than Visual C++, but far fewer than Visual Studio. It appears that

Microsoft is still trying to find the right mix of features for the language. Hopefully, they'll err on the side of providing too much, rather than too little. C# does provide some nice string conversion features. For example, you can use the ToString() method with most data types and convert them to a string. C# handles concatenation using the + (plus sign) rather than the & (ampersand). Actually, this should cause fewer problems with people adding ampersands into a string by mistake.

Differences in Appearance

The general appearance of the code is going to be a big difference to Visual Basic developers. A Visual C++ developer sees something familiar in C#, but to Visual Basic developers both languages look like something completely different. (Admittedly, C# borrows some from Visual Basic and developers will begin to see these similarities as they begin working with the language—this discussion concentrates on the first impression and early developer use.) C# does use some friendly constructions, such as attributes, that will decrease the learning time for a Visual Basic developer, but the coding techniques are still significantly different.

Early in the Visual Studio .NET beta, Microsoft decided that everyone should use 0-based arrays. This caused no end of confusion for some Visual Basic users. Essentially, the arrays for .NET are still 0-based, even for Visual Basic users, but the IDE handles Visual Basic arrays as 1-based arrays. Needless to say, C# uses a 0-based array in the same way that Visual C++ does. Because arrays are such a handy construct, Visual Basic developers are likely to experience problems with them when they make the move to C#.

The obstacle that I think most Visual Basic developers will have a difficult time overcoming is organization. A C# program uses a completely object-oriented approach to application development. In this case, the Visual Basic and Visual C++ developer will have an equally hard time because neither language enforces the structural constraints found in a C# application. For one thing, you can't use a global variable in C# and there isn't any such thing as global code. Every line of code you write nestles safely in the confines of a class.

As previously mentioned, C# does tend to look more like Visual C++ than it does Visual Basic. Nowhere is this more apparent than in the construction of conditional statements. For example, an If statement doesn't require Then in C#. You'll use curly braces for If statements that require it. In short, Visual Basic developers will need to learn a new way of working with statements if they make the move to C#.

Missing Functionality

As previously mentioned, Visual Basic hides some implementation details from the developer. Detail hiding enables a Visual Basic developer to create code more quickly and with fewer errors. C# is the middle ground between Visual Basic and Visual C++, so it doesn't have all of the amenities that Visual Basic provides. In some cases, this means the loss of some key words. For example, the Beep function is missing from C#. The fact that developers use Beep fairly often is apparent when you visit the Microsoft newsgroups and find more than a few messages asking how to produce a beep in C#. Actually, it's possible to do so, but the method is not obvious. Here are four ways to generate a beep in C#:

```csharp
// Import the Windows Beep() API function.
[DllImport("kernel32.dll")]
private static extern bool Beep(int freq, int dur);

// Define some constants for using the PlaySound() function.
public const int SND_FILENAME = 0x00020000;
public const int SND_ASYNC = 0x0001;

// Import the Windows PlaySound() function.
[DllImport("winmm.dll")]
public static extern bool PlaySound(string pszSound,
                                    int hmod,
                                    int fdwSound);

[STAThread]
static void Main(string[] args)
{
   // Create a sound using an escape character.
   Console.Write("\a");
   Console.WriteLine("Press Any Key When Ready...");
   Console.ReadLine();

   // Create a sound using a Windows API call.
   Beep(800, 200);
   Console.WriteLine("Press Any Key When Ready...");
   Console.ReadLine();

   // Create a sound using a Visual Basic call.
   Microsoft.VisualBasic.Interaction.Beep();
   Console.WriteLine("Press Any Key When Ready...");
   Console.ReadLine();

   // Create a sound using a WAV file.
   PlaySound("BELLS.WAV",
             0,
             SND_FILENAME | SND_ASYNC);
   Console.WriteLine("Press Any Key When Ready...");
   Console.ReadLine();
}
```

You must add a reference to the Microsoft Visual Basic .NET Runtime to your application to make the Visual Basic `Beep` call work. In fact, this method represents one way to make Visual Basic and C# work together as needed, whenever needed.

As you can see, C# enables you to use the `"\a"` escape character or call on the `Beep()` function found in the Windows API (but only after you import the required function from `Kernel32.DLL`). The Windows API `Beep()` function is flexible in that it allows you to determine both the frequency and duration of the beep. Notice that you can use the Visual Basic `Beep()` function if you want to use it. Of course, you can always go for the ultimate `beep`, a call to the Windows API `PlaySound()` function (which requires an import and two constants). The point is that you'll find some Visual Basic features missing in C#.

In many cases, the best way around the problem of missing features is to determine if the Visual Basic feature is actually a wrapper around a common Windows API function. To do this, you'll need to look at the Platform SDK documentation provided with Visual Studio. Microsoft generally uses a Visual Basic function name that closely matches the Platform SDK equivalent.

Of course, there's one missing feature that you can't replace. Visual Basic includes a *Variant* data type. The *Variant* data type can hold any data value. You use it when you don't know what type a function will pass at the time you write the code. A *Variant* doesn't care about what type of data it holds, so some developers use it to coerce data from one type to another.

C# provides the *Object* data type. Like the Visual Basic equivalent, an *Object* can hold any data type. However, unlike a *Variant*, an *Object* always knows the type of data it contains, which means you can't use it to perform some coding tricks. In short, C# is still the strict brother of Visual Basic, and even the *Object* data type doesn't change anything.

Operators and Expressions

Many people view the use of operators and expressions in C# as a major obstacle for Visual Basic developers. Actually, this is unlikely to cause problems because the operators work the same in every language. The order of precedence is even the same in most cases. Of all the elements that you need to consider in between one language and another, you can usually count on there being the same set of operators.

Visual Basic developers will need to learn to use new symbols for the same operators they use today. For example, the `And` operator in Visual Basic is the `&&` operator in C#, while the Visual Basic `Mod` operator equates to the C# `%` operator. In this respect, C# follows the terse pattern of Visual C++. Visual Basic developers will also see five missing operators in C#: `^` (caret), `Like`, `Is`, `Eqv`, and `Imp`.

You can get around some of the missing Visual Basic operators when using C#. It's possible to replace the ^ operator with the Math.Pow() function. In some situations, you can replace the Like operator with the *System.Text.RegularExpressions.Regex* the object. It's possible to simulate the Is operator using the Equals() method, but the results aren't the same (for reasons we'll discuss later in this section). Here's an example of the replacement operators.

```
static void Main(string[] args)
{
   double   A, B, Result = 0;

   // Simulate the use of the ^ operator.
   A = 3;
   B = 4;
   Result = Math.Pow(A, B);
   Console.WriteLine("The result of 3^4 is: {0}", Result);

   // Simulate the Like operator.
   Regex MyRegEx = new Regex("A*");
   if (MyRegEx.IsMatch("ABC"))
      Console.WriteLine("The second string matches the pattern.");

   // Simulate the Is operator.
   Object   AType1 = A;
   Object   AType2 = A;
   Object   AType3 = (double)3;
   A  = 10;
   if (AType1.Equals(AType2))
      Console.WriteLine("The first two objects are equivalent.");
   if (AType1.Equals(AType3))
      Console.WriteLine("The third object also equals the first.");
   Console.WriteLine("AType1 = {0}, AType2 = {1}, and AType3 = {2}",
                     AType1.ToString(),
                     AType2.ToString(),
                     AType3.ToString());

   // Simulate the Imp operator.
   bool  Log1 = true;
   bool  Log2 = false;
   bool  Log3 = true;
   bool  LogResult;

   // Would evaluate to false using Imp.
   LogResult = (!Log1) || Log2;
   Console.WriteLine("The output of the Imp comparison is: {0}",
                     LogResult);
```

```
        // Would evaluate to true using Imp.
        LogResult = (!Log1) || Log3;
        Console.WriteLine("The output of the Imp comparison is: {0}",
                          LogResult);

        Console.ReadLine();
    }
```

As you can see in Figure B.2, each of the operators has an equivalent in C#, except for the Eqv operator.

Now that you've seen the code, let's discuss some of the implications of operator substitution. The Is operator implies that two new objects point to the same object—change the original object, and the derived objects change as well. However, when you use the Equals() method, you know that the type and value are the same, but that's it. The reason is simple: C# objects don't point to each other. Change the value of A after you assign it to AType1 and AType2 and the values don't change—they're new objects.

There's no reason to replace the Eqv and the Imp operators because even Visual Basic .NET doesn't include them. The Eqv operator is easily replaced with the = or the == operators. Likewise, it's easy to replace the Imp operator using a combination of the ! (not) and the || (or) operators. The example code shows how you can simulate the Imp operator.

Visual Basic .NET does include two new operators that you won't find in C# and you won't be able to implement in C#. The AndAlso and OrElse operators provide the means to short circuit Boolean expressions. If the first expression in an AndAlso statement is false, then CLR won't bother to evaluate the second expression. Likewise, if the first expression in an OrElse statement is true, then CLR won't bother to evaluate the second expression. Theoretically, these two operators give Visual Basic developers more control over the execution of their code—hopefully, the optimizations performed by the C# compiler also provide this type of functionality, even if it isn't under the control of the developer.

Error Handling

One of the areas in which C# greatly improves on Visual Basic is error handling. No longer do you have to worry about the OnError statement. C# uses a try...catch structure that enables you to catch only the errors that you want to catch as part of error handling. Even so, some developers will find the change in error handling from Visual Basic to C# a little difficult to understand. This topic is important enough that it received extensive coverage in the "Error Handling" section of Chapter 4. Make sure you read this chapter for more details on how C# handles errors and how you can use error handling in your applications. (There are numerous other examples of error handling throughout the book.)

Understanding the Cost of CLR

In the minds of many developers, C# is the only new language in .NET—or is it? Early in the Visual Studio .NET beta, the differences between Visual Basic and Visual Basic .NET were so vast that any attempt to use existing Visual Basic code in Visual Basic .NET met with failure. In many cases, the changes to Visual Basic .NET enabled it to run within the confines of CLR. The cost of developing a common runtime for all languages is apparently high.

Visual Basic developers were naturally upset to learn that moving applications to Visual Basic .NET would mean a complete rewrite, so Microsoft condescended to rewrite parts of the beta to make application transition easier. The process is still far from seamless. In fact, this is one time when Visual Basic developers are at a distinct disadvantage because Visual Studio .NET still supports a native form of Visual C++ and many Visual C++ applications will run as a result.

The reality of CLR is that it makes language interoperation much easier and removes many of the barriers developers had to overcome in the past. However, the cost of CLR is massive changes to existing languages, a new set of restrictions, and the removal some of the flexibility developers experienced in the past. In short, Visual Studio .NET includes three new languages, not just one.

Does this mean that your move to .NET is going to be fraught with agonizing hours of rewriting code to meet some new Microsoft marketing goal? No, the move isn't as hard as it might seem at first, but don't fool yourself into thinking that you won't have to work very hard to make the move either. Microsoft has made an effort to reduce the culture shock of .NET whenever possible, but there are still many hurdles to overcome.

With this revelation in mind, learning to use C# might not be as hard as you think. Once you know the .NET Framework, almost all of the .NET languages become more accessible. The problem of using CLR is that it forces all languages to observe new restrictions; the benefit of using CLR is that all languages now have a common basis. The developer still benefits in the long run, but the price is having to learn something new in the interim.

Language Gotchas for Visual Basic Developers

Working with any new language requires a lot of flexibility. Developers, like anyone else, can get into ruts—they learn to do things a certain way, so anything new proves difficult. Of course, becoming proficient at coding means learning the techniques well enough that you can write code in your sleep. In a sense, the developmental rut is a requirement for efficient programming. However, a developmental rut is also the best way to run afoul of new programming language features. With this in mind, the following list tells you about programming features that developers seem to use improperly most often when moving from Visual C++ to C#.

NOTE   I'd like to make an effort to keep this list current. If you have a particular problem with the move from Visual Basic to C# and would like to share it, please feel free to write me at JMueller@mwt.net. Significant problems experienced by more than one reader could also appear in my Pinnacle newsletter, .NET Tips, Trends & Technology eNewsletter (http://www.pinnaclepublishing.com). I plan to provide an update to this list on my website at http://www.mwt.net/~jmueller/. Check my website for further details.

Data Conversions   In the past, developers had little choice but to remember how various languages treated numeric types. The confusion caused by simple types such as int was immense, and many applications ran into difficulty because developers didn't use the proper type for the situation. .NET developers don't need to worry about type conversions between languages if they use the types found in the .NET Framework System namespace. For example, a System.Int32 type is the same in Visual C++, Visual Basic, or C#; it doesn't matter which language you use.

Similar Keywords, Different Meanings   There's at least one case where both Visual Basic and C# support the same keyword, Is, but the meaning is different in each of the two languages. When you use Is in Visual Basic, it determines if two objects point to the same object. If both objects are essentially the same, then the return value is true. The C# is keyword returns true if the expression isn't *null* and the object can be cast to a type in the form (type)(expression) without throwing an exception.

Assuming Anything Works the Same as Visual Basic 6   Visual Basic was the most changed language in Visual Studio. The modifications were so severe that developers forced Microsoft to make changes, but you'll still need to rewrite significant portions of your code. For example, the ParamArray statement in Visual Basic (which isn't supported directly in C#) has changed from a ByRef argument to a ByVal argument. In addition, the entries to the array must be of the same type in Visual Basic .NET. The C# params keyword provides similar functionality to the Visual Basic .NET version of the ParamArray. This book isn't the proper place to look at Visual Basic changes, but it's something you'll need to look at before you begin writing code in C#, with the understanding that anything you wrote in Visual Basic 6 still works that way in Visual Basic .NET.

Visual Basic Is Inaccessible   Visual Basic is far from inaccessible. If you need some Visual Basic functionality, you can (within limits) still use the functionality within C#. Look at the example in the "Missing Functionality" section for some ideas on how you can add Visual Basic functionality to your C# application. A worst-case scenario for the Visual Basic developer who needs to use C# is having to create a DLL with the required functionality in one language and using it within the second language.

Array Differences   When you create an array in C#, the size of the array is set in stone. You can't change the upper or lower bounds. There's no support for the redim statement to resize the array. Whenever you make a change to an array, C# deletes the old array reference and creates an entirely new array. However, the .NET Framework provides the ArrayList class that contains much of the functionality provided by Visual Basic arrays. If you want to work with extensible arrays, then create an *ArrayList* object.

Flow Control Differences   C# and Visual Basic have similar flow control structures, but the two languages often use different names for the same structure. For example, I mentioned earlier that you don't need to include Then with an If statement. The For statement is the same in both C# and Visual Basic, but the C# form looks more like Visual C++. C# actually has two forms for the Do loop. The first form is the While loop, which only executes if a condition is true. The second form is the Do While loop, which executes at least once, even if the condition is false. C# uses the switch statement in place of the Visual Basic Select Case. You'll also find that C# lacks any form of the With, Choose, or Switch statements. However, you can call the some of these statements directly, as with the Switch statement example in the \Appendix B\DoSwitch folder on the CD.

Converting Your Existing Code to .NET

Most of your existing Visual Basic applications will require some level of rewrite in order to work in .NET. The problem for the Visual Basic developer isn't one of deciding whether to upgrade or not, but one of which language to use when rewriting a specific application. Some of the complex Windows API access code of the past won't work in Visual Basic .NET due to a lack of pointer support. In other cases, C# makes more sense than using Visual Basic, because you can perform the same task using a lot less code.

The following sections don't necessarily provide exact rules for converting your existing application to .NET. However, these sections do provide some ideas you can use to make the transition easier. The bottom line for the developer is to make the transition to .NET with the least amount of effort possible, which means changing your language in some cases.

Changing Difficult API Calls

Visual Basic developers have always faced immense hurdles when making calls in the Windows API. Using the .NET Framework does alleviate this problem somewhat. In some cases, however, the developer still needs to call a Windows API function because the .NET Framework doesn't provide the required functionality. Unfortunately, Visual Basic .NET makes the job harder than it was in the past, because you now have a managed environment that doesn't support pointers to work with.

C# isn't the cure for every Windows API access problems. There are still a number of important functions stored in C libraries that you can only access using Visual C++. However, in those cases where you can make the Windows API call directly using a standard Windows DLL, C# does make a good choice because it does support pointer and translating the necessary structures is easier when working C# than when you work with Visual Basic .NET.

Generally, a Windows API call like `Beep()` that takes few, if any, arguments is still a good bet for Visual Basic. It's those calls that require a handle or other pointer type as input that begin to cause problems for the Visual Basic developer. When you get to calls that require complex structures, you can safely bet that C# is the best choice for the job.

Moving Your Business Logic

Normally, you won't need to move your business logic from Visual Basic to C# because Visual Basic already provides a good model for making business decisions. For example, you won't need to move a routine that performs calculations, exercises rules, or performs other business logic tasks, if the routine contains few (or any) calls to the Windows API.

In a few cases, however, moving your business logic makes sense. A Visual Basic routine that relies on functionality that the .NET Framework doesn't support directly is a good candidate for C#. For example, we looked at some missing security functionality in Chapter 9. If your routine relies on access tokens or other direct user security information, it might be better to move it from Visual Basic to C#. Unfortunately, you can't cut this code out of your Visual Basic application and paste it into a C# application, so you need to consider the cost of the move in developer time.

Where Do You Go From Here?

The premise of this appendix is that few Visual Basic developers will completely give up on their favorite language to move to C#. Visual Basic has a lot to offer the developer—too much to make the move feasible for most developers. However, C# does offer a great deal to the Visual Basic developer in the form of low-level access. This low-level access comes in a package that's incredibly easy to use. In short, C# and Visual Basic are natural partners for the developer who doesn't have the time or the need to learn Visual C++.

One of the exercises you might try is converting some difficult Visual Basic code to C# to see if you can simplify the code and make it less error prone. Any code that accesses the Windows API directly is a good candidate for the move because Visual Basic .NET offers fewer capabilities than Visual Basic 6 for managing this type of code. You might also try mixing Visual Basic as C# code as shown in the "Missing Functionality" section example.

Some developers claim that Microsoft has made all languages pretty much the same under .NET. The one thing you should have learned from this appendix is that while changes were made (some drastic), each language still has a specific place in the developer's toolbox. For Visual Basic developers, adding C# to their toolbox might mean easier access to some of the functionality that Visual Basic developers have always had a hard time obtaining in the past.

APPENDIX C

Accessing C Library Routines

It would be nice to think that everything you'll ever need to develop an application appears in the .NET Framework. Unfortunately, we've seen several cases in the book where the .NET Framework falls short. A short example of this problem appears in the MakeSound example in the \Appendix B\MakeSound folder on the CD, which shows how to get around the problem of not having a `Beep()` method in C# by using the Windows API.

Theoretically, everything you'll need to create a Windows application appears somewhere in the Windows API; but theory isn't fact. If you want to create certain classes of application, you need the services of a C library. We saw one such example in the form of the Access-Token example in Chapter 9. However, that example required that we create a complete set of methods in Visual C++ and then access them from C#.

There's a middle ground in external access. Sometimes, all you really need to do is access the C library, because C# can do everything else that you need to do. In that case, creating a wrapper code (a means of access using Visual C++) and placing it in a managed DLL would be sufficient—you don't need to use Visual C++ for anything else.

In these cases, you can create a Visual C++ wrapper DLL once, and then use it for every project where it's needed afterward. That's the purpose of this appendix—to show you how to access C library routines with the fewest problems and gain the greatest level of access. In this case, we'll examine what you need to do to create a Microsoft Management Console (MMC) snap-in, since there's little support for this management tool in Visual Studio .NET.

NOTE   The example in this appendix is an extremely simple MMC snap-in based on an unmanaged MMC snap-in written in Visual C++ used for comparison purposes. You'll find the unmanaged version MMC snap-in code in the \Appendix C\ComputerName folder on the CD. This version is provided for comparison purposes when examining the example, so you can see how unmanaged Visual C++ code translates into managed C# code. An advanced form of this MMC snap-in will appear in my upcoming book, *In Search of the Lost Win32 API: .NET Framework Solutions* (coming late 2002 from Sybex, ISBN: 0-7821-4134-X). The advanced version will include support for MMC snap-in elements like context menus and property pages.

The Case for an MMC Snap-In

We'll work on a MMC snap-in example in this appendix, because I consider it the most common example of a specialty application that requires use of C library calls. A lot of developers have asked how to create an MMC snap-in on Microsoft's various newsgroups, and I'm sure that many more are wondering how to perform this task. The lack of any MMC projects in Visual Studio .NET and the changes to the MMC snap-in in Windows XP have led some developers to believe the MMC snap-in is going to become history very soon. That may be; but for today, the MMC snap-in still represents the best way to write a configuration utility.

MMC is the application used by Windows 2000 and Windows XP to manage operating system functionality. You'll find it in the \System32 folder as MMC.EXE. MMC is a container application that hosts snap-ins—the container doesn't do much more than provide a place for the snap-in to perform its work. Of course, the container does lend a consistency to the user interface and ensures that each snap-in behaves in a certain way. Each configuration of snap-ins is called a *console*, and you'll find a list of these consoles in the Administrative Tools folder of the Control Panel. Figure C.1 shows a typical example of a console—the Performance console.

FIGURE C.1:

MMC consoles pair one or more MMC snap-ins with the MMC container application.

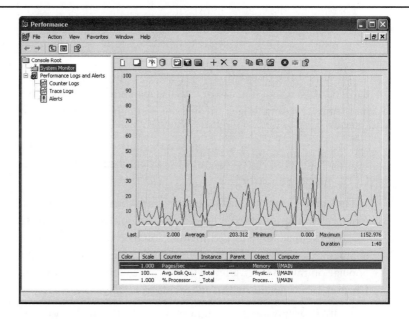

In this case, the System Monitor and the Performance Logs and Alerts are actually two separate MMC snap-ins that appear together in this console. You can use the File ➢ Add/Remove Snap-in command to display the Add/Remove Snap-in dialog box, which contains a list of snap-ins used to create a particular console, as shown in Figure C.2. Note that the folders beneath the Performance Logs and Alerts entry are actually part of a single MMC snap-in.

FIGURE C.2:

Many consoles appear
to contain just one
control, but are actu-
ally made of several
controls.

You should also notice that the System Monitor is an ActiveX Control snap-in, not a standard MMC snap-in. You can always use standard ActiveX controls as MMC snap-ins, but
most ActiveX controls lack the interfaces required to interact with the MMC container
application. For example, I created a special type of pushbutton and inserted in MMC (just to
see what it would do); yes, I could see the button and it reacted when I clicked it, but that's it.
However, my pushbutton example does demonstrate that MMC is just another way to use
COM, nothing more or less.

The "magic" for the MMC application is the MSC file. This file contains the information
required to create a console. In fact, if you look in the \System32 folder, you'll find the Perf-
Mon.MSC file that contains the information to create the Performance console. Interestingly
enough, this file uses XML to store information and has used it long before XML was very
popular on the Internet. Figure C.3 shows a view of the MSC file using XML Notepad (see
Chapter 13 for details on this useful utility).

Figure C.3 shows an important bit of information about the MMC application. The first
and third MMC snap-in Globally Unique Identifier (GUID) entries correspond to the
MMC snap-ins for the console. (You can validate this information by looking the GUIDs up
in the registry using RegEdit.) The third entry actually points to the control responsible for
handling ActiveX controls. If you look up the GUID for the second GUID entry, you'll
notice that it's for a folder snap-in, the Console Root folder in Figure C.1.

FIGURE C.3:

MMC relies on MSC files that contain information in XML format to store configuration information.

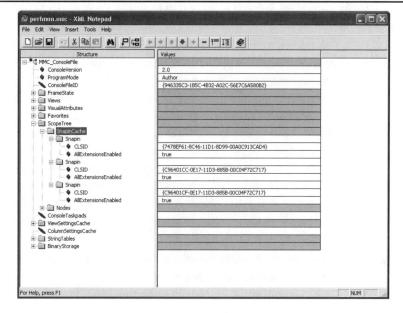

MMC does have quite a bit to offer in the way of control organization and presentation. While this appendix won't explore every MMC feature, you'll learn about quite a few of them. We'll explore the MMC application in more detail later as part of the example. For now, you have enough information to understand some MMC basics and why I chose this particular example for the appendix.

Why Library Code?

Visual Studio .NET and the .NET Framework were originally supposed to alleviate many of the problems that developers had with Windows code. No longer would you need to manage memory, and the fear of DLL hell would be a thing of the past. Microsoft has achieved that goal to a large extent. I have written more than a few applications that never call on anything but the functionality provided by the .NET Framework. In fact, it's the specialty applications that require the use of Windows API or C library calls—they are the exception to the rule.

There probably isn't a succinct answer to the question of why Microsoft chose to incorporate some functionality within easily accessible DLLs in the Windows API and hide other functionality within C library files. Because Microsoft uses C/C++ to write Windows, the use of C library files for some types of functionality doesn't present a problem. Consequently, the developers at Microsoft probably used whatever form of storage looked most convenient at the time. For the C# developer, a function that appears in a C library file always requires an external wrapper DLL for access.

The use of two methods of storing functions for the Windows API begs the question of whether there's an easy way to determine which access method to use. The answer to the question comes from the Platform SDK documentation in at least some cases. Near the bottom of the page documenting a function, you'll find that the listed functionality appears within a certain library and you need to use a specific C header (H) file to access it. The implicit addition of a library file often signals the need to use an external DLL to access the required functionality. However, the documentation fails to include the requisite LIB file entry for the MMC, so you either need to know that there's no DLL with which to perform the task or search fruitlessly for hours to locate the information. In some cases, a quick check of the `\Program Files\Microsoft Visual Studio .NET\Vc7\PlatformSDK\lib` folder will provide clues about the form of access you'll need to use for a given function.

In the end, you'll find that the combination of DLLs and C library files provides you with complete access to all of the functionality that Windows has to offer. You need to use both in order to gain complete access, but you'll normally find that you use the .NET Framework first, DLLs second, and C library files as a third (and occasional) option.

A Short View of Data

Working with C library files means converting data from the managed environment into a form that the library functions will understand. Of course, C# doesn't provide support for an *HRESULT* or a *LPTSTR*, which are the standard fare of C library routines. This means that you need to know the underlying data type for the C library types that you'll encounter. For example, you'll find that an *HRESULT* converts quite easily to a *System.Int32* value.

The following sections will provide you with some guidelines for working with various C library data types. You'll find additional examples and help in the example program for this appendix.

Working with Variables and Pointers

The difference between reference and value types becomes critical when working with C libraries. You can pass most value types such as `int` directly to a C library routine without any problem. In fact, the example will pass several value types to the C library. Enumeration also falls into the value category. Unless an enumeration contains both positive and negative values, use the `uint` type to represent it in your code.

Once you get past basic value types, it's time to convert the C library data type into something C# can understand (and vice versa). Generally, you'll find that pointers convert well to the IntPtr type. For example, you can convert a HANDLE to an IntPtr in most cases. Pointers to numeric values such as the LPARAM also convert to the IntPtr with relative ease. Sometimes odd-looking types like MMC_COOKIE are actually long pointers in disguise, so you can use IntPtr to represent them.

TIP Hover the mouse over a value in the header file to discover how Visual C++ defines it. In most cases, you'll see a typedef in the balloon that makes the base type of the value clear. For example, the balloon for MMC_COOKIE contains typedef LONG_PTR MMC_COOKIE, which makes it clear that you can use an IntPtr to represent the MMC_COOKIE.

There are some situations where there's less of a need to use an IntPtr; if a function only requires an integer value as input, you don't need to use an IntPtr. The int will transfer the cookie value to the C library just as easily as the IntPtr will. For example, if you want to destroy a snap-in component, you need to provide a cookie (MMC_COOKIE type) as either an int or an IntPtr. Using an int reduces the overhead of your code but may leave other developers scratching their heads, since the use of an int is inconsistent with the use of an IntPtr in other cases. If in doubt, always use an IntPtr, but be aware that there are some situations where an int will work just as well.

TIP The typedefs used within C headers help make the code easier to read by documenting the data type. Needless to say, when you convert a variety of pointers to the IntPtr type, some of that documentation is lost. Generally, this means you'll have to provide additional comments in the code. Because you're replicating a documented interface, function, or enumeration, you'll want to avoid changing the variable names. The help file provided with Visual Studio can still help the user, if you maintain the same basic function name and argument names as part of your code.

Objects can prove troublesome to convert because of the way that the C language handles classes and structures. Remember that classes and structures are somewhat interchangeable under C and that C views both of them as reference types. C# views classes as reference type and structures as value types. Consequently, conversion can prove difficult.

As a general rule of thumb, if the C library call defines the argument as an interface or other pure reference type, you can use the Object data type in your code. On the other hand, if the C library defines the object as a structure, you'll need to replicate the structure in your code and then pass the structure to the calling routine. In some cases, you'll need to marshal the object to ensure that the C library views it correctly. For example, if the object is an interface, then you'll need to add the following attribute to your object definition:

```
[MarshalAs(UnmanagedType.Interface)]
```

As part of the data conversion process, you need to consider the direction of data travel between your application and the C library. The C header files commonly mark arguments as [IN], [OUT], or [OUT][IN]. When working with values marked as [OUT] you need to add the out (for uninitialized values) or the ref (for initialized values) keyword to ensure your application sees the return value. Any argument marked as [OUT][IN] must use the ref keyword. In addition, you must initialize the argument before you pass it to the C library.

It's important to differentiate between ref and out values. Remember that the application must provide an initialized argument for ref values, but can include an uninitialized argument for out values. While C# makes the distinction clear through the use of native keywords, you'll find that other languages such as Visual C++ aren't quite as adept. For example, when working with Visual C++, you'll find that a double pointer will create a ref value, while the [Out] attribute is used to create an out value, as shown here. Notice that out values begin as ref values because they also require a double pointer. Also notice that the [Out] attribute is captialized—using the lowercase [out] attribute will result in errors.

```
// Create a ref value.
MMCHelper::IDataObject **ppDataObject

// Create an out value.
[Out]MMCHelper::IDataObject **ppDataObject
```

One final concern about Windows library calls is that they often use keywords for arguments. For example, the Notify() method shown here normally uses *event* as one of the argument names.

```
virtual /* [helpstring] */ HRESULT Notify(
        /* [in] */ MMCHelper::IDataObject *lpDataObject,
        /* [in] */ MMCHelper::MMC_NOTIFY_TYPE *aevent,
        /* [in] */ IntPtr arg,
        /* [in] */ IntPtr param) = 0;
```

Notice that the source code changes the name to *aevent*. If you don't make this change, the argument name will appear in a decorated form within the managed environment. For example, C# decorates the event as *@event*, making the argument difficult to read.

Working with Data Structures

Sometimes you can't easily convert a C library input into a type that C# will understand. This is especially true when working with structure. Windows relies on structures to pass large amounts of data between an application and the operating system as part of a system call. Consequently, any wrapper you create will also need to work with the plethora of data structures that Windows uses. Ultimately, the content of the structure must break down into types that C# will understand, as shown in the following code.

```
[StructLayout(LayoutKind::Sequential)]
public __gc struct DVTARGETDEVICE
```

```
{
public:
   UInt32   tdSize;
   short    tdDriverNameOffset;
   short    tdDeviceNameOffset;
   short    tdPortNameOffset;
   short    tdExtDevmodeOffset;
   char     tdData;
};
```

Notice that the structure relies on native Visual C++ types in many cases, because these types translate well into standard .NET Framework types. However, there are some situations where a native Visual C++ type could cause problems, as in the case of an unsigned integer (UINT). In this case, make sure you use the .NET Framework equivalent type directly (UInt32).

There are other problems to consider when working with structures. For example, a structure must include the [StructLayout] attribute so CLR knows how to work with the data it contains. Generally, you'll use the *LayoutKind::Sequential* argument for Windows function calls. This value ensures that CLR doesn't rearrange or optimize the structure in any way. Note that Visual C++ requires the use of the __gc keyword for managed structures and that you must make all of the data elements public so they appear within C#.

Structures become problematic in some situations. For example, you'll find that some structures contain other structures. The level of nesting can become absurd in some situations. In these situations, you need to determine if the level of nesting is warranted. If not, you can usually provide a substitute value. For example, if the code you create will never pass the structure to Windows (in other words, the structure is always passed as a NULL value), you can normally use an int as a substitute for the structure. Make sure you document any deviations within the DLL source code and as part of the DLL documentation.

Working with Enumerations

Windows relies extensively on enumerated data types. These data types normally begin with the enum keyword. Unfortunately, duplicating enumerated types with the .NET Framework proves difficult for a number of reasons. The most important reason is that the enum will never appear in the Object Browser and the DLL user won't be able to access it. Consequently, you need an alternative for creating enumerated types. In most cases, using a class is the best answer because you have good control over how the class will appear to the end user. Here's an example of the class version of the enumerated data type.

```
public __gc class DATA_OBJECT_TYPES
{
public:
```

```
    static const CCT_SCOPE        = 0x8000;
    static const CCT_RESULT       = 0x8001;
    static const CCT_SNAPIN_MANAGER = 0x8002;
    static const CCT_UNINITIALIZED = 0xffff;
};
```

Notice that you still declare the enumerated type as before using hexadecimal notation, but the enum is gone and there are some new keywords involved in the declaration. As with all managed elements of a DLL, you must declare the class as a public __gc. The entries appear as static const values.

When you use this new enumeration within interfaces or structures, you'll need to access it as a class. This means adding a pointer for Visual C++ DLLs. Generally, you'll find that C# will view the enumeration as a class with constant values, similar to enumeration values within the .NET Framework.

Creating the Visual C++ Wrapper DLL

You could create the wrapper DLL for this example using any of a number of languages, including C#. However, using other languages would prove difficult, in this case, because there are so many items you have to access from within Windows itself. Even though a C# DLL would work, using Visual C++ to write the DLL is more efficient in this case, because you'll experience fewer interface issues. The following sections provide an overview of the Visual C++ DLL used for this example. You'll find the complete source code in the \Appendix C\ MMCHelper folder on the CD.

NOTE   This discussion assumes the reader is familiar with Visual C++. If you only want to know the C# portion of the example, you can safely skip this section. The DLL on the CD is complete enough to create simple MMC snap-ins with any .NET language. However, it isn't a full implementation of the MMC snap-in DLLs that come with Windows, so you'll find that some advanced functionality is missing. The MMCHelper.DLL is the only extra DLL required for the MMC snap-in example under Windows 2000/XP.

Special Considerations for *#include* Directives

When you write an unmanaged application in Visual C++, you normally place all of the #include directive statements in the file where they're used. In many cases, such as the example in Chapter 9, this also works for a managed DLL. However, in some cases, you'll receive an ambiguous reference error when you try to compile a header in a managed DLL. This is true with the MMC.H header used in this example. To see what this error looks like, create a Managed C++ Class Library project and add this simple statement to the top of the project CPP file:

```
#include <MMC.H>
```

Compile the DLL project and you'll receive a list of errors similar to the ones shown in Figure C.4. Looking at this list of errors doesn't tell you anything about the actual problem. In fact, the error message would lead you to believe that the header file is incompatible with the managed DLL project.

FIGURE C.4:

The placement of header files in your managed DLL makes a difference in the error messages you receive.

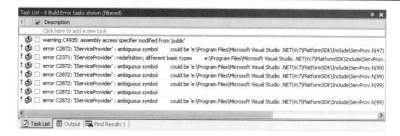

Now, move the `#include <MMC.H>` statement from the top of the CPP file to the top of the `STDAFX.H` file (before the `#using <mscorlib.dll>` statement). Compile the code again. The build should succeed without error. The only difference is the placement of the header file within the code.

This little trick works, in many cases, when you can't compile the managed DLL any other way. Unfortunately, it doesn't work in every case. There are some situations where you'll need to build an unmanaged DLL to create a wrapper for C library code. Even if you have to go the unmanaged route, the wrapper will work fine. The only difference is that you might need to work a little harder to create the interface with C#, and you'll have to remember to compensate for the lack of automatic variable handling within the unmanaged DLL.

Adding the Library Reference

Generally, you'll find that you need to add a library reference to your project if you're working with a specialty library such as `MMC.LIB`. Visual C++ includes some libraries by default when the project inherits from the project defaults (the standard configuration). However, `MMC.LIB` isn't in the list, so you need to add it by right-clicking MMCHelper in Solution Explorer and then selecting Properties from the context menu. Locate the \Linker\Input folder shown in Figure C.5 and type **MMC.LIB** in the Additional Dependencies field. The IDE will now link the `MMC.LIB` file with the rest of the DLL.

FIGURE C.5:

Make sure you add
any special libraries to
your project before
you compile it.

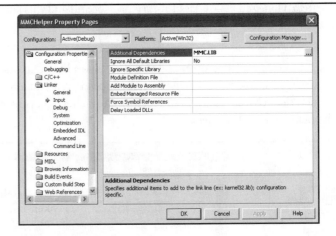

NOTE   If you don't know which libraries Visual C++ supports by default, click the ellipsis button
next to the Additional Dependencies field. You'll see an Additional Dependencies dialog
box. The Inherited Values field of this dialog box contains the default list of libraries that
Visual C++ links into the DLL.

Creating an Interface

There are a few problems you need to address when creating wrapper interfaces using Visual
C++. We've already addressed the problems of values, structures, and enumerated types in
previous sections. It's important to reiterate, however, that you must construct .NET Framework equivalents of all the data types used for the Windows calls, which might mean deriving
a creative alternative in some cases.

One of the first problems that you'll need to consider is how to create a managed version
of a COM interface. The best way to do this is to add three attributes to the interface
description. The following list tells you about each of the attributes.

[ComImport]   This attribute tells the compiler that the interface is based on a COM interface with the same name.

[InterfaceType]   This attribute describes the type of exposure to provide for the interface when it's exposed to COM. The acceptable values include *dual*, *IUnknown*, and
IDispatch.

[Guid]   This attribute assigns a globally unique identifier (GUID) to the interface. This
must be the same GUID used by the COM unmanaged counterpart.

Now that you know how to identify a COM interface substitute, let's look at a typical interface example. Here's the ISnapinHelp2 interface used to add help support to an MMC snap-in. The ISnapinHelp2 interface was introduced for MMC 1.1 and includes a second method for adding web-based help to your snap-in.

```
[ComImport,
    InterfaceType(ComInterfaceType::InterfaceIsIUnknown),
    Guid("4861A010-20F9-11d2-A510-00C04FB6DD2C")]
public __gc __interface ISnapinHelp2
{
public:
    virtual /* [helpstring] */ HRESULT GetHelpTopic(
        /* [out] */ [Out]IntPtr *lpCompiledHelpFile) = 0;

    virtual /* [helpstring] */ HRESULT GetLinkedTopics(
        /* [out] */ [Out]IntPtr *lpCompiledHelpFiles) = 0;
};
```

The first thing you need to notice about the interface is the __interface keyword. Visual C++ will compile an interface that uses the interface keyword without a single word of complaint, until you attempt to use attributes with it. Because you won't always need to use attributes with interfaces, it's possible to create an interface that relies on the interface keyword instead of the __interface keyword. The interface version will never work properly in a managed environment.

If you're familiar with the ISnapinHelp2 declaration in MMC.H, you'll know that it derives from ISnapinHelp and lacks the GetHelpTopic() method declaration shown in the example code. It's impossible to derive a managed interface from an unmanaged interface. Consequently, it's often easier to create a combined managed interface as shown in the example. (That is, unless, you expect someone to use the older interface for some reason; in which case, you should implement both.)

Because an MMC snap-in is normally an unmanaged COM object, your managed MMC snap-in will have to mimic its behavior. This means implementing at least the minimal subset of interfaces to create an operational MMC snap-in. The following list shows which interfaces the example will use.

- IDataObject
- IComponent
- IComponentData
- ISnapinAbout

NOTE The smallest possible MMC snap-in implementation must contain four interfaces: `IDataObject`, `IComponent`, `IComponentData`, and `IClassFactory`. You don't need to implement `IClassFactory`, but the other three interfaces must appear within your code.

A fully functional MMC snap-in will include several other interfaces. These interfaces aren't required to make the MMC snap-in work—you implement them to ensure the user can access features such as help and context menus. In other words, these are helpful user interface features. Generally, you'll want to implement the following list of interfaces to ensure the MMC snap-in will meet all users needs.

- `ISnapinHelp2`
- `IDisplayHelp`
- `IExtendContextMenu`
- `IExtendControlbar`
- `IExtendPropertySheet`

There are a number of other interfaces you can implement as part of an MMC snap-in; all of which appear in the MMC.H file. MMC also implements a number of interfaces for you. While you can override these interfaces to provide special behavior, you don't need to create them for a simple MMC snap-in. These MMC provided interfaces include:

- `IPropertySheetProvider`
- `IPropertySheetCallback`
- `IConsoleNamespace2`
- `IHeaderCtrl`
- `IResultData`
- `IImageList`
- `IConsole2`
- `IContextMenuCallback`
- `IControlbar`
- `IToolbar`
- `IConsoleVerb`

As you can see, creating a wrapper DLL for COM is often a matter of knowing which interfaces to implement. Ultimately, the interfaces you implement affect the functionality of the resulting component and determine the utility of the component you create. For example, you don't have to implement the ISnapinAbout interface to create a functional MMC snap-in, but this interface is required if you want to provide at least some information to the user about the purpose of the MMC snap-in.

Even the optional interfaces will have a place in the wrapper DLL. For example, the IConsole2 interface provides the means to access the MMC environment. Therefore, even though you don't have to implement the IConsole2 interface, you'll need to include it in the DLL so that you can gain access to required MMC functionality. Another example is the IControlbar interface. This interface is used by the IExtendControlbar interface to add and remove toolbars and other controls to the MMC environment. Even though you don't need to implement the IControlbar interface, the IExtendControlbar interface requires access to it. These reference interfaces are clearly identified in the source code so you can see how they interact with the snap-in as a whole.

One of the best ways that I've found to learn about COM interfaces is to view implementations of similar controls using the OLE/COM Object Viewer utility. This utility shows which interfaces are implemented by an existing control and therefore provides valuable clues for implementing similar controls when working with .NET. You'll also find clues in the various C/C++ header files, because they normally define the interfaces for a particular type of control or component. The Microsoft documentation and online sources often point to the interface requirements for certain types of components as well. All it takes is a little detective work to learn which interfaces you must implement to create a basic component and which interfaces to add in order to gain some level of component functionality.

TIP   Even though you don't have to create multiple files when working with Visual Studio .NET, it's often helpful to do so when working with moderate- to large-sized wrapper DLLs, such as the one used in this example. Dividing code by type makes it easier to locate a specific piece of code. The example uses separate files for function implementations, structures, enumerations, and interfaces.

Adding the MMC Functions

One of the reasons for using a wrapper DLL is to access the Windows functions used to perform a specific task. There are a number of MMC-related functions, but all we need for this example is a way to determine when the user has changed object settings and a method for freeing notification handles. Listing C.1 shows both MMC function implementations.

Listing C.1   **MMC Example Functions**

```
public __gc class MMCFunctions
{
```

```
public:

    // Allows the property sheet to notify the MMC snap-in component
    // that the user has made a change to the object settings.
    HRESULT DoMMCPropertyChangeNotify(long INotifyHandle,  LPARAM param)
    {
        return MMCPropertyChangeNotify(INotifyHandle, param);
    }

    // Frees the handle to an MMCN_PROPERTY_CHANGE message. The system
    // sends this message as the result of a MMCPropertyChangeNotify()
    // call by the property sheet.
    HRESULT DoMMCFreeNotifyHandle(long lNotifyHandle)
    {
        return MMCFreeNotifyHandle(lNotifyHandle);
    }
};
```

As you can see, the functions provide a direct pass through to Windows. You could implement these functions from within C#, but it's better to place them within the DLL used to wrap the interfaces, structures, enumerations, and other MMC specific code.

Developing the MMC Snap-In

Now that we have a wrapper DLL that contains all of the resources required to build an MMC snap-in, it's time to create the snap-in itself. As previously mentioned, an MMC snap-in must implement certain COM interfaces in order to interact with the MMC container application and the user. You can also divide the MMC snap-in into several functional areas, such as the About dialog, help system, component, property pages, and document data. The following sections describe several of these functional areas. You can find the complete application source code in the \Appendix C\MMCSample folder on the CD.

WARNING   During the development of this example, I noted that the example often failed to compile properly within the IDE. The code would compile, but the snap-in would fail to initialize within the MMC. The command-line version of C#, CSC.EXE, provides a simpler interface without all of the usual command-line switches that the IDE includes by default. The example code on the CD includes the MAKEFILE text file that contains instructions for the NMAKE utility. You can use the make file by opening a command prompt in the example directory on your hard drive and typing **NMAKE**. The make file will automatically generate the DLL, register it, add it to the global assembly cache (GAC), and register it as an MMC snap-in. You normally need to perform these three steps by hand when using the IDE, so using NMAKE is actually easier than using the IDE in this case.

Obtaining a GUID

As with all COM objects, MMC snap-ins rely on Registry entries to provide information about component configuration. The use of Registry entries means that you need some way to uniquely identify your component, which means using a globally unique identifier (GUID). Because Visual Studio .NET doesn't provide this information automatically as the older, native code versions of the product did, you need to obtain the GUID manually. Fortunately, you can use a utility named GUIDGen to create the required GUIDs. You can access this utility using the Tools ➤ Create GUID command from within the Visual Studio .NET IDE or from within the \Program Files\Microsoft Visual Studio .NET\Common7\Tools folder. Figure C.6 shows how this tool looks.

FIGURE C.6:

The GUIDGen utility enables you to create GUIDs for your components.

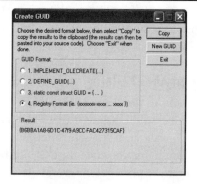

Notice that the figure shows Option 4, Registry Format, selected. Make sure you always use this format for components created in C#. Click Copy to place the GUID on the clipboard. You can then place it within the application using the following code:

```
[Guid("B6BBA1A8-6D1C-47f9-A9CC-FAC427315CAF")]
public class MySnapInData : IComponentData, IExtendPropertySheet
{
};
```

Of course, the class will contain other information. The important piece here is the placement of the [Guid] attribute. You need to provide GUIDs for both the component and the About dialog. The GUIDs also appear in the Registry entry and serve to identify the snap-in to MMC. Here are the Registry entries for the example MMC snap-in. (Note that the entry wraps in some cases and that the actual entry would appear on a single line, as shown in the source code.)

```
REGEDIT4

[HKEY_LOCAL_MACHINE\Software\Microsoft\MMC\Snapins\{B6BBA1A8-6D1C-47f9-A9CC-
FAC427315CAF}]
```

```
"About" = "{BACD4F1D-8338-41ee-9D55-DDECE3D8BBCE}"
"NameString" = "An Example of an MMC Snap-In"
"Provider" = "DataCon Services"
"Version" = "1.0"

[HKEY_LOCAL_MACHINE\Software\Microsoft\MMC\Snapins\{B6BBA1A8-6D1C-47f9-A9CC-
FAC427315CAF}\StandAlone]
```

There are a few notes about this part of the example. I began by adding a new Text File to the project and simply renamed it with a REG extension. The file must begin with REGEDIT4 as shown, and you need to add the main GUID key. Notice the use of curly brackets around the GUID entry (they don't appear in the [Guid] attribute entry). Only provide the About value if your snap-in has an About dialog. The NameString, Provider, and Version values are also optional. You must provide the StandAlone key (as shown) if you're following this example—snap-in extensions require different programming techniques from the ones shown for this example.

Developing an About Dialog

Of all the elements of the example snap-in, create the About dialog was the easiest from a coding perspective, so I'll discuss it first. The purpose of the ISnapinAbout interface is to create the data for an About dialog—the methods within the interface don't actually create the About dialog. You'll find the code for this interface in the MySnapInAbout class. MMC uses the data this interface provides in several places, not the least of which is the Add Standalone Snap-in dialog box.

In addition to text, the MySnapInAbout class provides four icons to MMC for use with the snap-in entry—don't confuse these icons with the ones you'll use for the nodes later on. The four icons include: a main icon used for elements such as the About dialog box, a large 32 × 32 icon used for display in the Results pane when the user selects the root node, a small 16 × 16 icon that shows the snap-in in its closed state, and a small 16 × 16 icon that shows the snap-in in its open state. In many cases, you can use the same icon for both open and closed states. Most snap-ins create the required icons in the constructor and destroy them in the destructor.

The About dialog is one of the few places where you actually need a destructor, because we're using Windows resources. MMC doesn't understand managed resources, so you need to convert the embedded bitmap into an icon handle that MMC will understand. Because the resources aren't managed by the Garbage Collector, you need to destroy them manually. Listing C.2 shows the code used to create and destroy the image resources required for this example.

Listing C.2   Working with MMC Means Creating and Deleting Unmanaged Resources

```
public MySnapInAbout()
{
    // Retrieve an embedded bitmap from the current assembly.
    Assembly Asm = Assembly.GetExecutingAssembly();
    Stream   Strm = Asm.GetManifestResourceStream("MMCSample.Main.bmp");
    Bitmap   Temp = new Bitmap(Strm);

    // Place a handle for an icon based on the bitmap in MainIcon.
    MainIcon = Temp.GetHicon();

    // Create compatible bitmaps for the two bitmap images.
    BMap16 = new Bitmap(Temp, 16, 16).GetHbitmap();
    BMap32 = new Bitmap(Temp, 32, 32).GetHbitmap();
}

~MySnapInAbout()
{
    // Deallocate the memory used by the three images.
    if (MainIcon != IntPtr.Zero)
        WindowsFunctions.DestroyIcon(MainIcon);
    if (BMap16 != IntPtr.Zero)
        WindowsFunctions.DeleteObject(BMap16);
    if (BMap32 != IntPtr.Zero)
        WindowsFunctions.DeleteObject(BMap32);
}
```

Notice that the example obtains the required bitmap from an embedded resource using reflection. The code creates a main icon handle using the GetHicon() method and two bitmap handles using the GetHbitmap() method. Each image resource type appears in a different place within MMC. Because the image types are different from each other, you also need to use the correct Windows API calls to destroy them. Icons require use of the DestroyIcon() function, while bitmaps rely on the DeleteObject() function.

Creating the Component

This example shows you how to create a simple single node MMC snap-in that displays Get-ComputerNameEx() outputs. As a result, we won't be doing anything with the MMC Scope Pane.

There are two main sections of code for the component portion of this example. The first processes event MMC requests. The second displays the requested data. In most circumstances, you could combine these two tasks into one method call. However, MMC uses a callback mechanism to display items within the Result View Pane. Each item is processed on a column by column basis. The callback function will need to detect the current column and provide only the string required for that column, rather than fill in all of the columns at one time. Listing C.3 shows how to create the MMCN_SHOW event handler in the MySnapInData.Notify() method.

Listing C.3   Handling MMCN_SHOW Events in an MMC Snap-In

```
public int Notify(IDataObject lpDataObject,
                  uint aevent,
                  IntPtr arg,
                  IntPtr param)
{
   MySnapInDO   TestDataObject;   // The test data object.
   IntPtr       BMap16;           // Handle for the 16 X 16 bitmap.
   IntPtr       BMap32;           // Handle for the 32 X 32 bitmap.

   // Create the TestDataObject.
   TestDataObject = (MySnapInDO)lpDataObject;

   switch(aevent)
   {

      case MMC_NOTIFY_TYPE.MMCN_SHOW:
         RESULTDATAITEM Item; // Result data variable.

         // Create two headers.
         MMCHeader.InsertColumn(0, "Name Type", 0, 250);
         MMCHeader.InsertColumn(1, "Name Value", 0, 150);

         // Initialize the result data variable.
         Item = new RESULTDATAITEM();

         // Create entries required for first item.  Include
         // constants for relevant items in mask.  Make sure
         // you use a callback for strings.  Set the image to
         // the 16 X 16 pixel image.
         Item.mask = RDI.STR | RDI.IMAGE | RDI.PARAM;
         Item.str = new IntPtr(-1); // MMC_CALLBACK
         Item.nImage = 0;
         Item.lParam = 0;
         Item.nCol = 0;

         // Display the first item.
         MMCResultData.InsertItem(ref Item);

         // Modify lParam member for second query.
         Item.lParam = 1;
```

```
        // Display the second item.
        MMCResultData.InsertItem(ref Item);

        // Perform the same two steps for subsequent items.
        Item.lParam = 2;
        MMCResultData.InsertItem(ref Item);
        Item.lParam = 3;
        MMCResultData.InsertItem(ref Item);
        Item.lParam = 4;
        MMCResultData.InsertItem(ref Item);
        Item.lParam = 5;
        MMCResultData.InsertItem(ref Item);
        Item.lParam = 6;
        MMCResultData.InsertItem(ref Item);
        Item.lParam = 7;
        MMCResultData.InsertItem(ref Item);

        break;

    case MMC_NOTIFY_TYPE.MMCN_EXPAND:
        // Normally you'd place some code here for the
        // scope pane, but we're not doing anything special
        // with the scope pane for this example.
        break;

    case MMC_NOTIFY_TYPE.MMCN_ADD_IMAGES:

        // Add Images
        Object    TempObj = arg;
        IImageList  ImageList = (IImageList)TempObj;

        // Load bitmaps associated with the scope pane
        // and add them to the image list

        // Retrieve an embedded bitmap from the current assembly.
        Assembly Asm = Assembly.GetExecutingAssembly();
        Stream    Strm =
                Asm.GetManifestResourceStream("MMCSample.Main.bmp");
        Bitmap    Temp = new Bitmap(Strm);

        // Create compatible bitmaps for the two bitmap images.
        IntPtr Translate = new Bitmap(Temp, 16, 16).GetHbitmap();
        BMap16 = MMCFunctions.TranslateBitmap(Translate);
        WindowsFunctions.DeleteObject(Translate);

        if (BMap16 != IntPtr.Zero)
        {
            // If the 16 X 16 bitmap worked, load a 32 X 32 bitmap as
            // well.
            Translate = new Bitmap(Temp, 32, 32).GetHbitmap();
            BMap32 = MMCFunctions.TranslateBitmap(Translate);
            WindowsFunctions.DeleteObject(Translate);
```

```
                // Only if both bitmaps load successfully do we want to
                // create the image list.
                if (BMap32 != IntPtr.Zero)
                {
                    int Result = ImageList.ImageListSetStrip(ref BMap16,
                                                             ref BMap32,
                                                             0,
                                                             0x00FFFFFF);

                    if (Result != RESULT_VAL.HR_OK)
                        return Result;
                }
            }
            break;

        default:
            // The snap-in doesn't support any other messages.
            return RESULT_VAL.HR_FALSE;
    }

    return RESULT_VAL.HR_OK;
}
```

Responding to the MMC's request to show the component's data is straightforward. The code begins by adding two headers to the MMC display. It doesn't matter which view MMC is currently using; you'll definitely want the headers to be available if the user decides to use the Detail view rather than one of the other views like Large Icon. In fact, the Detail view is the only useful view for this component, since the other views hide the data and we haven't implemented a dialog that could be used to display the data instead.

Once the two column headings are displayed, the next step is to initialize the RESULT-DATAITEM data structure variable, *Item*. Notice that this is accomplished in two steps. First, the code creates the object using a standard constructor. Then, the code fills in the data structure elements. A special data structure element named mask contains constants that indicate which of the other data structure elements contain information. In this case, we'll use the *str*, *nImage*, and *lParam* data members to hold information. You'll also initialize *nCol* to 0 to ensure the component starts displaying information at the right column.

Notice the *str* input value is MMC_CALLBACK (although we don't use the actual C++ constant in this case). The Microsoft documentation seems to say you could place a string in this data member if the output consists of a single column of data, rather than rely on a callback function. However, it's safer and more flexible to rely on a callback function. You must use a callback function when displaying more than one column of data.

Adding the data to the MMC display comes next. You'll use the InsertItem() method to add new data items to the display. This method requires a single argument as input, a pointer to the item that you want to add, which must be a RESULTDATAITEM data structure. There are also methods for removing and modifying existing items should you wish to do so.

The rest of the code performs two tasks. First, it places a new value in *lParam* to indicate which kind of data to display. Second, it uses `InsertItem()` to add the item to the display.

The ATL COM AppWizard doesn't automatically provide a callback function to use for displaying the items on screen, so you'll need to add it. However, you must add the callback function, `GetDisplayInfo()`, to the class that implements the `IComponent` interface. Normally, this function appears in your main component class. However, this interface could appear anywhere (as witnessed by the Microsoft examples provided with products like MSDN). Since there isn't any consistent place for this interface to appear, you'll need to check your source code before adding the `GetDisplayInfo()` function.

Once you do find the class that implements the `IComponent`, you'll need to add the `GetDisplayInfo()` function to it. Listing C.4 shows the code you'll need to implement the new member function. Note that the listing only shows the code required for one result type— the application actually supports eight different types. However, the other cases work much the same as the first case shown.

Listing C.4   **The *GetDisplayInfo ()* Method Provides Data Output for the MMC Snap-In**

```
public unsafe int GetDisplayInfo(ref RESULTDATAITEM ResultDataItem)
{
    String    ComputerName;        // Buffer to hold computer name data.
    int       BufferSize = 15 + 1; // Buffer size, plus a null.
    String    Temp;                // A temporary conversion buffer.

    // If the caller sent some information.
    if (ResultDataItem != null)

        // If that information contains a string.
        if ((ResultDataItem.mask & RDI.STR) == RDI.STR)
        {

            // Check which string the caller is requesting.
            switch (ResultDataItem.lParam)
            {
                case 0:

                    // Display the NetBIOS name item.
                    if (ResultDataItem.nCol == 0)
                    {
                        // Create the temporary data value, convert it
                        // to a pointer, and then pass it to MMC.
                        Temp = "NetBIOS Name";
                        fixed (char* ResultData = Temp)
                        {
                            ResultDataItem.str = new IntPtr(ResultData);
                        }
                    }
```

```
                            // The requester is asking for the second column.
                            else
                            {
                                // See if there is a NetBIOS name for this item.
                                if (WindowsFunctions.GetComputerNameEx(
                                    COMPUTER_NAME_FORMAT.ComputerNameNetBIOS,
                                    out ComputerName,
                                    ref BufferSize))

                                    // Output the contents of the string buffer.
                                    fixed (char* ResultData = ComputerName)
                                    {
                                        ResultDataItem.str = new IntPtr(ResultData);
                                    }

                                    // If not, display a failure string.
                                else
                                {
                                    Temp = "Value Not Available";
                                    fixed (char* ResultData = Temp)
                                    {
                                        ResultDataItem.str = new IntPtr(ResultData);
                                    }
                                }
                            }
                            break;
                    }
                }

                // Return a success value.
                return RESULT_VAL.HR_OK;
            }
```

While this code may appear long in the source file, it actually contains a few processing steps that get repeated over and over using different values, depending on the item that the caller wants to display. This example requires two variables, one of which is initialized to MAX_COMPUTERNAME_LENGTH + 1 (15 + 1 for a PC or 31 + 1 for a Macintosh). You need to initialize the buffer length to the maximum computer name string size and then add 1 for a null termination in order to ensure you can display the entire computer name. In addition, the Microsoft documentation warns that using a shorter string can have unexpected results under Windows 95.

The next task is to check whether the caller has provided a filled (or at least initialized) RESULTDATAITEM data structure. The code also verifies that the data structure contains an initialized *str* data element. The reason is simple: This component provides text output, so the *str* data element is absolutely essential. Figuring out what to display comes next; as previously stated, there are eight different computer name values that you can obtain using the `GetComputerNameEx()` function.

The processing sequence for all eight outputs is the same, so I'll only describe one of them. There are two columns for data output. The first column contains a string that shows what type of computer name data we're displaying. Since this value is constant, we can simply place it into the *str* data element for immediate display. Notice the use of pointers (unsafe code) and `fixed` blocks in this example. Make sure you perform any required data conversions before you place a value in the data structure, or you'll get memory read errors when using MMC.

The second column contains the actual value for the computer name type that we want to display. This means using the `GetComputerNameEx()` function, which requires three inputs: a constant containing the type of name we want to retrieve, a pointer to a buffer that can accept the name, and size of the buffer provided. The code converts the string variable contents to a pointer for output.

Not every attempt to get a computer name is going to be successful. In most cases, there isn't a name to get. With this in mind, you'll need to provide an alternative string for the user. In this case, the component displays a simple, "Value Not Available" string.

Working with IDataObject

Every MMC snap-in must implement the `IDataObject` interface. However, you'll find the vast majority of the methods for `IDataObject` return a "not implemented" value (`RESULT_VAL.HR_NOTIMPL` in the example). You must tell MMC that these methods aren't implemented, so it knows that the snap-in answered the call and simply doesn't provide the required functionality.

In most cases, you'll need to implement the class constructor in order to initialize data values. The data values will generally include the clipboard formats the class will handle and a private variable to hold the snap-in node. The snap-in node is especially important because it provides a context for all other activities performed in the class.

You'll also need to implement the `GetDataHere()` method to perform data conversions within the snap-in. This method contains a wealth of unsafe code—code that requires use of pointers and use of system memory that the Garbage Collector can't move. Consequently, you need to mark this method as unsafe and compile the snap-in using the `/Unsafe` command-line switch like this:

```
public unsafe int GetDataHere(ref FORMATETC pFormatEtc,
                              ref STGMEDIUM pMedium)
```

The GetDataHere() method uses some of the same techniques as other parts of the example. For example, we need to create a data buffer using the Windows CreateStreamOnHGlobal() API call. If this call fails, you'll need to throw an exception indicating the failure and exit the snap-in.

The main purpose of the method is to provide certain types of output data, including the node's display name and the GUID for both the snap-in and node. Typically, performing this task requires that the method place some data into the data buffer, create a data stream, and write the data out to the requestor. Here's an example of this activity.

```
// Determine if we need to output a name string for this node. The
// example doesn't support the zero deliminated node type, so send
// nothing in that case.
if (ClipFormat == CBDisplayName || ClipFormat == CBSZNodeType)
{
    // Assign a value to the data buffer.
    if (ClipFormat == CBDisplayName)
        DataBuffer = TheNodeData.DisplayName;
    else
        DataBuffer = Nothing;

    // Determine the data buffer length.
    DataLength = DataBuffer.Length;

    // Write the data to the data stream. Notice that you need to
    // create a fixed block in order to perform the write. This
    // ensures the snap-in writes the data without interference from
    // the garbage collector.
    fixed(byte* pData = DataBuffer)
    {
        DataStream.Write((IntPtr)pData, (uint)DataLength, out DataSent);
    }

}
```

As you can see, the code detects the requested clipboard format. If the format is the correct type, it assigns a value to *DataBuffer*. Once the data is in place, we also need to obtain the length of the data and place it in *DataLength*. The final step is to write the data using the DataStream.Write() method. This part of the task occurs within a fixed block to ensure the Garbage Collector doesn't attempt to collect the *DataBuffer* or move the memory in some way.

Testing the Snap-In within MMC

At this point, you're ready to compile the MMC snap-in and place it on the target server. The following procedure will help you test the MMCSample component.

NOTE   You must register both the `MMCSample.DLL` and the `MMCHelper.DLL` using the RegAsm and GACUtil utilities. Otherwise, CLR won't find everything it needs to display the MMC snap-in. The error you receive when this happens is that MMC couldn't instantiate the object. Rather than spend hours checking your code or the Registry entries by hand, simply ensure that you have registered both DLLs.

1. Start MMC using the Start ➤ Run command. Type **MMC** in the Open field and click OK. You'll see a blank MMC window.

2. Use the Console ➤ Add/Remove Snap-In command to display the Add/Remove Snap-In dialog.

3. Click Add. You'll see an Add Standalone Snap-In dialog. Look for the proper name, icon, provider information, and version when you view the component. All of these items are provided by the `ISnapinAbout` interface.

4. Click Add, then Close. You'll see the new snap-in added to the Add/Remove Snap-in dialog. Highlight the snap-in and you'll see text added to the Description field.

5. Click OK. You'll see the CompName component added to the Component Services display. Figure C.7 shows an example of this component in action.

FIGURE C.7:

The Component Services display is one good place to see your MMC snap-in in action.

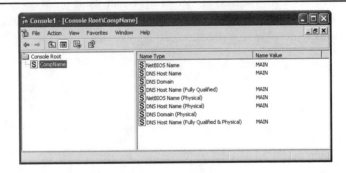

6. Select Console ➤ Exit to exit MMC. MMC asks if you want to save the current settings.

7. Click No. The Component Services dialog will close.

Where Do You Go From Here?

It's hard to believe that you still need to perform some tasks using C library files, but the example in this appendix clearly demonstrates that fact. The Windows API itself is huge and Microsoft used C to write the Windows code for many years, so the C library code is huge as well. All you need to do is spend some time in the Platform SDK documentation to realize just how many Windows features still rely on library files. It will require years of effort to move all of the functionality found in these old Windows files to the .NET Framework, which means you'll need the techniques found in this chapter for quite some time to come. Of course, you'll want to verify the functionality is actually missing in the .NET Framework before writing wrapper code.

Of course, the question now is how you deal with the problem of missing functionality. Some developers will start examining the .NET Framework documentation in detail and comparing it to the functionality offered by the Platform SDK. This is a waste of time since there are features of the Windows API and the C libraries included with Windows that you might never use.

However, it does pay to be thorough when you do find some missing functionality. Instead of merely placing a few calls into a DLL that will lack features later on, convert all of the calls that you'll need for a particular task—such as the MMC calls found in this appendix—into a comprehensive DLL. This method will enable you to use the same DLL for all projects that require the missing functionality.

You'll also find that it pays to provide input to Microsoft about the missing functionality. To some extent, Microsoft relies on input from product users to determine which features are critical for the next update of a product. Your input on missing functionality will help shape future versions of the .NET Framework. Make sure your voice is heard when it comes time to develop new product features.

Glossary

This book includes a glossary so that you can find terms and acronyms easily. It has several important features of which you need to be aware. First, every acronym in the entire book is listed here—even if there's a better than even chance you already know what the acronym means. This way, there isn't any doubt that you'll always find everything you need to use the book properly.

Second, these definitions are specific to the book. In other words, when you look through this glossary, you're seeing the words defined in the context in which the book uses them. This might or might not always coincide with current industry usage, since the computer industry changes the meaning of words so often.

Finally, the definitions here use a conversational tone in most cases. This means they might sacrifice a bit of puritanical accuracy for the sake of better understanding. The purpose of this glossary is to define the terms in such a way that there's less room for misunderstanding the intent of the book as a whole.

What to Do if You Don't Find it Here

While this Glossary is a complete view of the words and acronyms in the book, you'll run into situations when you need to know more. No matter how closely I consider the terms throughout the book, there's always a chance I'll miss the one acronym or term that you really need to know. Additionally, I've directed your attention to numerous online sources of supplemental information throughout the book, and a few those website owners may use terms that will not appear here unless I also chose to use them in the book. Fortunately, many sites on the Internet provide partial or complete glossaries to fill in the gaps:

Acronym Finder   `http://www.acronymfinder.com/`

Microsoft Encarta   `http://encarta.msn.com/`

University of Texas Acronyms and Abbreviations   `http://www-hep`
`.uta.edu/~variable/e_comm/pages/r_dic-en.htm`

Webopedia   `http://webopedia.internet.com/`

yourDictionary.com (formerly A Web of Online Dictionaries)   `http://www.yourdictionary.com/`

Let's talk about these websites a little more. Websites normally provide acronyms or glossary entries—not both. An acronym site only tells you what the letters in the acronym stand for, it doesn't provide definitions to explain what the acronym means in the context everyday computer use. The two extremes in this list are Acronym Finder (acronyms only) and Webopedia (full-fledged glossary entries).

The owner of Acronym Finder doesn't update the site as often as the University of Texas site does, but Acronym Finder does have the advantage of providing an extremely large list of acronyms from which to choose. At the time of this writing, the Acronym Finder sported 164,000 acronyms. The University of Texas site receives updates often and provides only acronyms (another page at the same site includes a glossary).

Most of the websites that you'll find for computer terms are free. In some cases, such as Microsoft's Encarta, you have to pay for the support provided. However, these locations are still worth the effort because they ensure you understand the terms used in the jargon-filled world of computing.

Webopedia has become one of my favorite places to visit, because it provides encyclopedic coverage of many computer terms and includes links to other websites. I like the fact that if I don't find a word I need, I can submit it to the Webopedia staff for addition to their dictionary, making Webopedia a community-supported dictionary of the highest quality.

One of the interesting features of the yourDictionary.com website is that it provides access to more than one dictionary and in more than one language. If English isn't your native tongue, then this is the website of choice.

A

abstract class   A limited form of nonfunctional class. Abstract classes are very close to interfaces. A developer can't instantiate an abstract class and the class doesn't need to provide implementations for any of the methods it contains. However, unlike an interface, an abstract class has the option of providing some implementation details. In addition, while a class can inherit from multiple interfaces, it can inherit from only one class. This means that an abstract class provides the perfect means to create a base class—one that a developer would never actually use directly, but one that the developer could use to create other classes.

accelerator   A shortcut key combination. An accelerator enables a user to access a menu or other command using a key combination, rather than the menu hierarchy. Like menu setups, most applications use specific accelerators for the same task. For example, you can usually access the Print feature of an application by pressing Ctrl+P.

access token   A definition of the rights that a service or resource requestor has to the operating system. This is the data structure that tells the security system what rights a user has to access a particular object. The object's access requirements are contained in a security descriptor. In short, the security descriptor is the lock and the access token is the key.

Active Directory (AD) A method of storing machine, server, and user configuration within Windows 2000 that supports full data replication so that every domain controller has a copy of the data. This is essentially a special-purpose database that contains information formatted according to a specific schema. Active Directory is designed to make Windows 2000 more reliable and secure, while reducing the work required by both the developer and network administrator for application support and distribution. The user benefits, as well, since Active Directory fully supports roving users and maintains a full record of user information, which reduces the effects of local workstation down time.

Active Directory Services Interface (ADSI) A set of APIs used to access Active Directory, the central repository of information in Windows 2000. Active Directory is a hierarchical database used to store many types of information in a somewhat freeform format. ADSI allows access to both Active Directory data and the schema, which means you can use it to create new database elements, as well as remove elements that are no longer in use.

Active Server Pages (ASP) A special type of scripting language environment used by Windows servers equipped with Internet Information Server (IIS). This specialized scripting language environment allows the programmer to create flexible web pages that include server scripts written in a number of languages, such as VBScript, JScript, and PerlScript. The use of variables and other features, such as access to server variables, allows a programmer to create scripts that can compensate for user and environmental needs, as well as security concerns. ASP uses HTML to display content to the user.

ActiveX Data Object (ADO) A local and remote database access technology that relies on *OLE-DB* to create the connection. ADO is a set of "wrapper" functions that make using OLE-DB and the underlying OLE-DB provider easier. ADO is designed as a replacement for DAO and as an adjunct to *ODBC*.

AD See *Active Directory*.

ADO See *ActiveX Data Object*.

ADO.NET A managed form of the *ActiveX Data Object (ADO)* database technology. The main difference between ADO and ADO.NET is that ADO.NET provides better support for distributed applications through disconnected datasets. See *ADO* for more details on this topic.

ADSI See *Active Directory Services Interface*.

aggregate 1). The combination of two or more components into a single entity. The components must provide aggregation support to enable use as a single component; 2). The application code or attribute used to create an aggregatable component; 3). A collection of facts or figures used to create a graph. Some presentation graphic programs use these numbers to create a graph showing both the component parts and their sum. For example, the individual wedges in a pie chart represent the components; the entire pie represents their sum.

American Standard Code for Information Interchange See *ASCII*.

API See *Application Programming Interface*.

Application Programming Interface (API) A method of defining a standard set of function calls and other interface elements. It usually defines the interface between a high-level language and the lower level elements used by a device driver or operating system. The ultimate goal is to provide some type of service to an application that requires access to the operating system or device feature set.

argument   A value passed to a procedure or function. The procedure or function recognizes the value by using the `Parameters` command to retrieve it.

array   A freeform structure that acts much like a database with a single field. An array lets you randomly or sequentially access each element by number.

ASCII (American Standard Code for Information Interchange)   A standard method of equating the numeric representations available in a computer to human-readable form. For example, the number 32 represents a space. There are 128 characters (7 bits) in the standard ASCII code. The extended ASCII code uses 8 bits for 256 characters. Display adapters from the same machine type normally use the same upper 128 characters. Printers, however, might reserve these upper 128 characters for nonstandard characters. For example, many Epson printers use them for the italic representations of the lower 128 characters.

ASP   See *Active Server Pages*.

attribute   An attribute expresses some feature peculiar to an object. When referring to a database, each field has an attribute that expresses what type of information it contains, the length of the field, the field name, and the number of decimals. When referring to a display, the attribute expresses pixel color, intensity, and position.

attributed programming   The use of special syntax within application code to modify the result of a statement, document the code, or add functionality. An attribute normally appears immediately before the statement it modifies within square brackets. The attribute could also rely on one or more required or optional arguments to augment its functionality.

B

BAPI   See *Biometrics Application Programming Interface*.

base class   A class that defines the attributes for one or more child (derived) classes. The concept of the base class is universal to all languages with object-oriented design capabilities. In many ways, this is the most generic class-creation feature. When the developer creates a new class, the new class can inherit the capabilities of a base class. Depending on the construction of the base class, the developer can customize class behavior by overriding base class methods.

Basic Input/Output System (BIOS)   A set of low-level computer interface functions stored in a chip on a computer's motherboard. The BIOS performs basic tasks like booting the computer during startup and performing the power-on startup tests (POST). DOS relied heavily on the BIOS to perform all types of low-level device interface tasks. Newer versions of Windows rely on the BIOS less or not at all.

BBS   See *Bulletin Board System*.

binding   The process of creating a connection between a data user and a data provider. For example, when working with a database, the control on a form would bind with a specific field within the dataset or recordset produced as a result of a query on the database. This process could also refer to other database-like objects, such as the objects within Active Directory.

Biometrics Application Programming Interface (BAPI)
A special set of programming constructs that help developers embed biometric technology into applications. A consortium of vendors including IBM, Compaq, IO Software, Microsoft, Sony, Toshiba, and Novell originated BAPI.

BIOS See *Basic Input/Output System*.

Boolean A method of determining whether a statement is true or false using rules of logic. Boolean values are often used to help a computer determine whether it needs to take a certain course of action based on current system or application conditions.

BOF Beginning of File.

browse A special application interface element designed to show the user an overview of a database or other storage media (for example, the thumbnail sketches presented by some graphics applications). Think of the browse as the table of contents for the rest of the storage area. A browse normally contains partial views of several data storage elements (records or picture thumbnails, in most cases) that a user can then zoom to see in their entirety. A browse form normally contains scroll bars or other high-speed interface elements to make it easier for the user to move from one section of the overall storage media to the next.

browser A special application normally used to display data downloaded from the Internet. The most common form of Internet data is the *HTML (HyperText Markup Language)* page. However, modern browsers can also display various types of graphics and even standard desktop application files, such as Word for Windows documents, directly. The actual capabilities provided by a browser vary widely depending on the software vendor and platform.

buffer The area in memory where program variable or other data is stored. For example, applications will normally read more than one page at a time from a word-processed document to improve performance. The application stores pages in addition to the one currently viewed by the user in the buffer until needed.

Bulletin Board System (BBS) A form of electronic message center that relies on a dial-up connection. BBSs normally provide services for special interest groups, software, or hardware vendors. The BBS server allows reading and upload of messages, as well as download of software and text. The Internet has largely supplanted the need for the BBS, but some vendors and private concerns still maintain them.

C

CAD See *Computer-Aided Drafting*.

Cascading Style Sheets (CSS) A method for defining a standard web page template. This may include headings, standard icons, backgrounds, and other features that would tend to give each page at a particular website the same appearance. The reason for using CSS includes speed of creating a website (it takes less time if you don't have to create an overall design for each page) and consistency. Changing the overall appearance of a website also becomes as easy as changing the style sheet instead of each page individually.

CCW See *COM Callable Wrapper*.

CGI See *Common Gateway Interface*.

client The recipient of data, services, or resources from a file or other server. This term can refer to a workstation or an application. The server can be another PC or an application.

CLR   See *Common Language Runtime*.

CLS   See *Common Language Specification*.

Code Behind   A web page coding technique in which the display (user interface) code resides in a file that is separate from the file that contains the code required to make the Web page functional. Code Behind helps promote code reuse by keeping code and user interface separate. The use of a separate code file also means that the same code file could serve multiple web pages through the use of generic routines.

COM   See *Component Object Model*.

COM Callable Wrapper (CCW)   A proxy for managed applications that enables managed code to call functions found in unmanaged code. The CCW makes unmanaged code appear to be managed code to the calling application.

command   1). An application name and associated arguments typed at the DOS or command prompt. Pressing enter executes the command; 2). An instruction the user chooses from the application menu; 3). A keyword entered within application code and executed programmatically during runtime.

Common Gateway Interface (CGI)   One of the more common methods of transferring data from a client machine to a web server on the Internet. CGI is a specification that defines how a web server can launch EXEs and communicate with them. A GCI application is normally written with a low-level language like C and is designed to receive input through the standard input device and output data through the standard output device. There are two basic data transfer types. The user can send new information

to the server or can query data already existing on the server. A data entry form asking for the user's name and address is an example of the first type of transaction. A search engine page on the Internet (a page that helps the user find information on other sites) is an example of the second type of transaction. The web server normally provides some type of feedback for the user by transmitting a new page of information once the CGI application is complete. This could be as simple as an acknowledgment for data entry or a list of Internet sites for a data query.

Common Language Runtime (CLR)   The engine used to interpret managed applications within the .NET Framework. All Visual Studio .NET languages that produce managed applications can use the same runtime engine. The major advantages of this approach include extensibility (you can add other languages) and reduced code size (you don't need a separate runtime for each language).

Common Language Specification (CLS)   A set of rules governing the underlying functionality of tools or components. Every CLS-compliant tool or component is guaranteed to interoperate with every other CLS-compliant tool or component.

Common Object Request Broker Architecture (CORBA)   A protocol that is used to describe data and application code in a way that a variety of computer types can use. It will eventually allow you to go to a web page and download a mini-application (applet) as part of that page. This is the Object Management Group's (OMG) alternative to Microsoft's ActiveX. CORBA was originally designed by IBM for inclusion with OS/2, but other companies such as Sun Microsystems now support this standard as well.

Component Object Model (COM) A Microsoft specification for an object-oriented code and data encapsulation method and transference technique. It's the basis for technologies such as *OLE* (*Object Linking And Embedding*) and ActiveX (the replacement name for OCXs—an object-oriented code library technology). COM is limited to local connections. DCOM (Distributed Component Object Model) is the technology used to allow data transfers and the use of OCXs within the Internet environment.

Computer-Aided Drafting (CAD) A special type of graphics program used for creating, printing, storing and editing architectural, electrical, mechanical or other forms of engineering drawings. CAD programs normally provide precise measuring capabilities and libraries of predefined objects, such as sinks, desks, resistors, and gears.

constructor The special method that the operating environment calls during object instantiation to ensure the object is functional. Developers often use the constructor to initialize global variables, set operating environment conditions, and perform other object creation tasks.

cookie One or more special files used by an Internet browser to store site-specific settings or other information specific to web pages. The purpose of this file is to store the value of one or more variables so that the web page can restore the information the next time the user visits a site. A webmaster always saves and restores the cookie as part of some web page programming task using a programming language such as JavaScript, Java, VBScript or CGI. In most cases, this is the only file that a webmaster can access on the client site's hard drive. The cookie could appear in one or more files anywhere on

the hard drive, depending on the browser currently in use. Microsoft Internet Explorer uses one file for each site storing a cookie and places them in the Cookies folder that normally appears under the main Windows directory. Netscape Navigator uses a single file named COOKIE.TXT to store all of the cookies from all sites. This file normally appears in the main Navigator folder.

CORBA See *Common Object Request Broker Architecture.*

cracker A hacker (computer expert) who uses their skills for misdeeds on computer systems where they have little or no authorized access. A cracker normally possesses specialty software that allows easier access to the target network. In most cases, crackers require extensive amounts of time to break the security for a system before they can enter it.

cryptography The process of changing text or other data into an unreadable form (cipher text) to protect the information during a transfer or other transition, and then changing the unreadable form back into the original format. The first part of the process is known as data encryption, while the second part of the process is called decryption. A recipient can only decrypt the data with a secret key or by using code-breaking techniques (cryptanalysis) to retrieve the data without the key.

CSS See *Cascading Style Sheets.*

D

DACL See *Discretionary Access Control List.*

DAO See *Data Access Objects.*

Data Access Objects (DAO)   An older data access technology introduced by Microsoft that relies on the Microsoft Access JET engine for local data access. DAO doesn't provide remote access features, although some programmers have been able to establish unreliable connections with it. *ADO* and *OLE-DB* have largely replaced this technology.

Data Source Name (DSN)   A name assigned to an *Open Database Connectivity (ODBC)* connection. Applications use the DSN to make the connection to the database and gain access to specific database resources like tables. The DSN always contains the name of the database server, the database, and (optionally) a resource like a query or table. *OLE-DB* connections may also use a DSN.

data stream   One of several methods used to access information in either local or remote storage. A data stream consists of a series of bits taken from any location within a data storage unit (such as a file). The information can flow continuously (as in an Internet transfer for music) or in blocks (as occurs when reading data from a file on the local hard drive). The reading and writing sequence need not use blocks of any given size and the transfer often works with individual bits rather than characters or words.

data type   The nature of the information contained in a variable or database field. Some systems recognize five major data types. The date type contains a number representing a date. The character type contains ASCII characters that some systems interpret literally. The numeric type contains numbers. The logic type is a single bit representing true or false (some systems use more than one bit, but the duality of the Boolean value remains the same). The memo type is a special instance of the character type.

Some systems limit the length of variables and database fields using the character type. Some systems don't limit the length of database fields using the memo type. Some systems support other types, such as currency, which are based on the major types.

dataset   The result of a query on one or more tables of a database. A dataset can contain a single set of records or the content of several tables (also known as data tables). In addition, a dataset is normally used to store data in a disconnected cache that doesn't rely on a connection to the DBMS. Datasets can accept input from a number of sources including data adapters, recordsets, and XML files.

DBCS   See *Double-Byte Character Set.*

DCOM   See *Distributed Component Object Model.*

Delegate   A method of handling function pointers. However, the term delegate isn't simply a replacement for function pointer. Delegates can make class creation simultaneously easier and more difficult. The delegate object encapsulates a reference to a method within a class. Consequently, the developer must consider additional levels of redirection during application development, but also isn't bothered with as many details because the environment handles many of the details automatically.

DIME   See *Direct Internet Message Encapsulation.*

Direct Internet Message Encapsulation (DIME)   An Internet media of the dime/application type. It encapsulates multiple application-defined entities, also known as payloads, into a single package. Each package can be of arbitrary size and type. The payload description includes data type, length, and an optional payload identifier.

Discretionary Access Control List (DACL)   A Windows security component. The DACL controls access to an object. You can assign both groups and individual users to a specific object.

Disk Operating System (DOS)   The underlying software used by many PCs to provide basic system services and allow the user to run application software. The operating system performs many low-level tasks through the basic input/output system (BIOS). The revision number determines the specifics of the services that DOS offers; check your user manual for details.

distributed application   An application that resides on more than one machine—normally a client and server, but not necessarily limited to this configuration. The application is composed of multiple interchangeable elements. For example, a server component could service more than one application type. The application elements are loosely coupled, and the developer can replace each element with updates as needed, as long as the new element provides the same interface to the client.

Distributed Component Object Model (DCOM)   The advanced form of the *Component Object Model (COM)* used for distributed application development. This protocol enables data transfers across the Internet or other non-local sources, but is usually limited to a local area network (LAN) or wide area network (WAN) environment. DCOM adds the capability to perform asynchronous, as well as synchronous, data transfers—which prevents the client application from becoming blocked as it waits for the server to respond. See *COM* for more details.

DLL   See *Dynamic Link Library*.

DNS   See *Domain Name System*.

domain   An area of control in a network. Members of a domain can share resources controlled by one or more member servers. One or two servers normally control the security of the network; these servers are normally called domain controllers.

Domain Name System (DNS)   An Internet technology that allows a user to refer to a host computer by name rather than using its unique IP address.

DOS   See *Disk Operating System*.

Double-Byte Character Set (DBCS)   A non-ASCII method of formatting characters that requires two bytes for each character instead of one. The DBCS allows an application to display words using character sets from non-English-speaking countries.

DS   Directory Service.

DSN   See *Data Source Name*.

Dynamic Link Library (DLL)   A specific form of application code loaded into memory by request. It's not executable by itself. A DLL does contain one or more discrete routines that an application may use to provide specific features. For example, a DLL could provide a common set of file dialogs used to access information on the hard drive. More than one application can use the functions provided by a DLL, reducing overall memory requirements when more than one application is running.

E

EOF   End of File.

event handler   A special method or function that reacts to specific system or user events, such as clicking a button on a form or the loss of focus for a textbox.

extensibility   A measure of the flexibility of a data or programming element. It reflects the ability of the data or programming element to respond to situations outside the parameters of its original design.

eXtensible Markup Language (XML)   A standardized web page design language used to incorporate data structuring within standard HTML documents. For example, you could use XML to display database information using something other than forms or tables. It's actually a lightweight version of the *Standardized Generalized Markup Language (SGML)* and is supported by the SGML community. XML will also support tag extensions that will allow various parts of a web-based application to exchange information. For example, once a user makes a choice within a catalog, that information could be added to an order entry form with a minimum of effort on the part of the developer. Since XML is easy to extend, some developers look at it as more of a base specification for other languages, rather than a complete language unto itself.

F

flow control   The use of programming constructs, statements, or other methods to modify the transfer and manipulation of data, or to change the path of execution, within an application.

FTS   See *Full Text Search*.

Full Text Search (FTS)   The capability of a help or other documentation system to provide word-by-word search capabilities without repeating the entire document within the index. FTS enables a user to find information quickly, yet without loss of search functionality.

G

GAC   See *Global Assembly Cache*.

Garbage Collector (GC)   A special component of the *Common Language Runtime (CLR)* used to free resources after an application no longer requires them. The GC runs automatically when certain conditions exist, such as low memory. An application can also initiate a garbage collection sequence, at the loss of some immediate performance.

GC   See *Garbage Collector*.

GDI   See *Graphics Device Interface*.

Global Assembly Cache (GAC)   A central repository for storing public managed components. The GAC contains only components with strong names, ensuring the integrity of the cache.

Globally Unique Identifier (GUID)   A 128-bit number used to identify a *Component Object Model (COM)* object within the Windows Registry. The GUID is used to find the object definition and allow applications to create instances of that object. GUIDs can include any kind of object, even non-visual elements. In addition, some types of complex objects are actually aggregates of simple objects. For example, an object that implements a property page will normally have a minimum of two GUIDs: one for the property page and another for the object itself.

Graphical User Interface (GUI) 1). A method of displaying information that depends on both hardware capabilities and software instructions. A GUI uses the graphics capability of a display adapter to improve communication between the computer and its user. Using a GUI involves a large investment in both programming and hardware resources; 2). A system of icons and graphic images that replace the character mode menu system used by many machines. The GUI can ride on top of another operating system (like DOS and Unix) or reside as part of the operating system itself (like OS/2 and Windows). Advantages of a GUI are ease-of-use and high-resolution graphics. Disadvantages consist of higher workstation hardware requirements and lower performance over a similar system that uses a character mode interface.

Graphics Device Interface (GDI) One of several components in the Windows operating system. The GDI controls the way that artistic graphic elements are presented on-screen. Every application must use the API provided by this component to draw or perform other graphics-related tasks.

GUI See *Graphical User Interface*.

GUID See *Globally Unique Identifier*.

H

hacker An individual who works with computers at a low level (hardware or software), especially in the area of security. A hacker normally possesses specialty software or other tools that allow easier access to the target hardware device, software application, or network. The media defines two types of hackers: those who break into systems for ethical purposes and those who do it to damage the system in some way. The proper term for the second group is crackers (see *cracker* for details). Some people have started to call the first group "ethical hackers" to prevent confusion. Ethical hackers normally work for security firms that specialize in finding holes in a company's security. However, hackers work in a wide range of computer arenas. For example, a person who writes low-level code (like that found in a device driver) after reverse engineering an existing driver is technically a hacker. The main goal of a hacker is to work for the benefit of others in the computer industry.

hierarchical 1). Referring to a method of arranging data within a database that relies on a node structure, rather than a relational structure; 2). Referring to a method of displaying information on-screen that relies on an indeterminate number of nodes connected to a root node.

hotspot An area within a graphic or other visual element that a user can click and obtain a response. For example, many Internet graphics contain one or more hotspots that link the current page with other pages on the website. Windows help files and other forms of local documentation also rely on hotspots to create linkage with additional information.

HTML See *HyperText Markup Language*.

HTTP See *HyperText Transfer Protocol*.

HyperText Markup Language (HTML) 1). A scripting language for the Internet that depends on the use of tags (keywords within angle brackets < >) to display formatted information onscreen in a non-platform-specific manner. The non-platform-specific nature of this scripting language makes it difficult to perform some basic tasks, such as placement of a screen element at a specific location. However, the language does provide for the use of fonts, color, and various other enhancements on-screen. There are also tags for displaying graphic images. Scripting tags for using more complex scripting languages such as VBScript and JavaScript were recently added, although not all browsers support this addition. The latest tag addition allows the use of ActiveX controls; 2). One method of displaying text, graphics, and sound on the Internet. HTML provides an ASCII-formatted page of information read by a special application called a *browser*. Depending on the browser's capabilities, some key words are translated into graphics elements, sounds, or text with special characteristics, such as color, font, or other attributes. Most browsers discard any keywords they don't understand, allowing browsers of various capabilities to explore the same page without problem. Obviously, there's a loss of capability if a browser doesn't support a specific keyword.

HyperText Transfer Protocol (HTTP)   One of several common data transfer protocols for the Internet. This particular protocol specializes in the display of on-screen information such as data entry forms or information displays. HTTP relies on HTML as a scripting language for describing special screen display elements, although you can also use HTTP to display non-formatted text.

I

IDE   See *Integrated Development Environment.*

IL   See *Intermediate Language.*

ILASM   See *Intermediate Language Assembler.*

ILDASM   See *Intermediate Language Disassembler.*

Integrated Development Environment (IDE)   A programming language front end that provides all the tools you need to write an application through a single editor. (Older DOS programming language products provided several utilities—one for each of the main programming tasks.) Most (if not all) Windows programming languages provide some kind of IDE support.

interface   The physical connection between two programs, a person and a machine, or any other two entities.

Intermediate Language (IL)   The common language that all .NET compilers output. The *Common Language Runtime (CLR)* interprets the IL. The use of a tokenized output ensures that all languages can share the functionality provided by the .NET Framework.

Intermediate Language Assembler (ILASM)   A utility that accepts an *Intermediate Language (IL)* text file as input and outputs a compiled assembly. A developer can use the ILDASM utility to create the IL text file.

Intermediate Language Disassembler (ILDASM)   A utility that enables a developer to examine code within a .NET assembly. The disassembler shows the *Intermediate Language (IL)* code created by a compiler and interpreted by the *Common Language Runtime (CLR)*. A developer can also use this utility to create a text file containing the IL code within the assembly.

Internet Server Application Programming Interface (ISAPI)   A set of function calls and interface elements designed to make using Microsoft's Internet Information Server (IIS) and associated products, such as Peer Web Server, easier. Essentially, this set of API calls provides the programmer with access to the server itself. Such access makes it easier to provide full server access to the Internet server through a series of ActiveX controls, without the use of a scripting language. There are two forms of ISAPI: filters and extensions. An extension replaces current script-based technologies like CGI. Its main purpose is to provide dynamic content to the user. A filter can extend the server itself by monitoring various events like user requests for access in the background. You can use a filter to create various types of new services like extended logging or specialized security schemes.

interoperability A measure of an application's ability to run in more than one environment, compatible or not. This term often refers to the ability of an application to run on more than one operating system or hardware platform. In some cases, this term refers to middleware's ability to overcome interoperability problems between platforms.

ISAPI See *Internet Server Application Programming Interface*.

L

LAN See *Local Area Network*.

LDAP See *Lightweight Directory Access Protocol*.

Lightweight Directory Access Protocol (LDAP) A set of protocols used to access directories that's based on a simplified version of the X.500 standard. Unlike X.500, LDAP provides support for TCP/IP, a requirement for Internet communication. LDAP makes it possible for a client to request directory information like e-mail addresses and public keys from any server. In addition, since LDAP is an open protocol, applications need not worry about the type of server used to host the directory.

Local Area Network (LAN) Two or more devices connected together using a combination of hardware and software. The devices, normally computers and peripheral equipment such as printers, are called nodes. An NIC (network interface card) provides the hardware communication between nodes through an appropriate medium (cable or microwave transmission.) There are two common types of LANs (also called networks). Peer-to-peer networks allow each node to connect to any other node on the network with shareable resources. This is a distributed method of files and peripheral devices. A client-server network uses one or more servers to share resources. This is a centralized method of sharing files and peripheral devices. A server provides resources to clients (usually workstations). The most common server is the file server, which provides file-sharing resources. Other server types include print servers and communication servers.

M

managed code A .NET programming term that infers the code runs under the Common Language Runtime (CLR) and relies on an *Intermediate Language (IL)* rather than native code. A managed application requires less programming effort on the part of the developer and reduces the amount of resource management the application must perform because the CLR performs, the required managed automatically. Many applications do run slower in a managed environment than they would in an unmanaged environment.

MDI See *Multiple Document Interface*.

metadata   Literally data about data, metadata is information that's known about an object or assembly. Metadata often describes how the information was collected and by whom. The metadata could also include formatting information. All .NET applications include metadata as part of the assembly. The metadata describes the assembly elements, making it easier learn about the assembly after it's put together.

Microsoft Management Console (MMC)   A special application that acts as an object container for Windows management objects like Component Services and Computer Management. The management objects are actually special components that provide interfaces that allow the user to access them within MMC in order to maintain and control the operation of Windows. A developer can create special versions of these objects for application management or other tasks. Using a single application like MMC helps maintain the same user interface across all management applications.

Microsoft Mobile Internet Toolkit (MMIT)   An add-on toolkit for the .NET development environment that enables a programmer to create applications for alternative computing devices, such as cellular telephones and personal digital assistants (PDAs).

MMC See *Microsoft Management Console*.

MMIT See *Microsoft Mobile Internet Toolkit*.

monolithic application   An application type in which all of the component parts appear on a single machine or within a single machine environment. A monolithic application forms a single, self-contained, entity that often employs customized code. In general, most users associate monolithic applications with mainframe or older desktop computer development.

Multiple Document Interface (MDI)   A method for displaying more than one document at a time within a parent window. The Program Manager interface is an example of MDI. You see multiple groups within the Program Manager window.

N

Name Service Provider Interface (NSPI)   A Microsoft standard used with Microsoft Exchange version 4.0 and above. This protocol is also one of two ways to access *Active Directory*; although, the *Lightweight Directory Access Protocol (LDAP)* represents the more common technique. However, many third-party products work with Microsoft Exchange; so from a Microsoft-specific programming perspective, this NSPI is just as important as LDAP.

National Information Assurance Partnership (NIAP)   A government organization that helps discover and fix security issues in both business and government. It provides testing, evaluation, and needs-assessment for both public and private industry. NIAP is a collaboration between the *National Institute of Standards and Technology (NIST)* and the *National Security Agency (NSA)*.

National Institute of Standards and Technology (NIST)   A government agency that helps business develop and apply technology, measurements, and standards.

National Security Agency (NSA)   A government agency that specializes in cryptography, but also works in other areas of security.

NDS See *Novell Directory Services*.

Network Interface Card (NIC)   The device responsible for allowing a workstation to communicate with the file server and other workstations. It provides the physical means for creating the connection. The card plugs into an expansion slot in the computer. A cable that attaches to the back of the card completes the communication path. Some newer NICs also use a USB, FireWire, or other interface.

NIAP   See *National Information Assurance Partnership*.

NIC   See *Network Interface Card*.

NIST   See *National Institute of Standards and Technology*.

Novell Directory Services (NDS)   An object-oriented approach to managing network resources. (Novell originally called this technology NetWare Directory Services, but subsequently renamed it.) It includes a set of graphical utilities that allows the network administrator to view the entire network at once, even if it includes more than one server or more than one location. There are a variety of object types including servers, printers, users, and files. NDS not only allows the administrator to manage the resource, but it provides security as well. As with any object-oriented management approach, NDS gives each object a unique set of properties that the administrator can change as needed.

NSA   See *National Security Agency*.

NSPI   See *Name Service Provider Interface*.

O

object   When used in the *OLE* sense of the word, a representation of all or part of a graphic, text, sound, or other data file within a compound document. An object retains its original format and properties. The client application must call on the server application to change or manipulate the object. When used in the *Component Object Model (COM)* sense of the word, object refers to the encapsulation of data and code into one file. COM objects don't allow direct manipulation of the data they contain. Data is manipulated through the use of methods that the object contains. In most cases, data manipulation is limited to a list of properties exposed by the object that define the object's operation and other characteristics. Some objects generate events in response to certain types of stimuli by either the system or user. Objects can also receive event notifications through the use of sinks. See the entry for *COM* for additional details.

Object Linking and Embedding-Database (OLE-DB)
A low-level database access technology that relies on *COM* and a vendor supplied OLE-DB provider rather than the SQL used by *ODBC*. OLE-DB is designed to work with both remote and local databases. In addition, it can access database managers that don't rely on SQL, like those found on mainframe computers. OLE-DB and ODBC are cooperative, rather than competing, data access technologies. OLE-DB, when coupled with *ADO*, is designed to replace older database technologies like RDO and DAO.

Object Linking and Embedding (OLE)   The process of packaging a file name, application name, and any required parameters into an object, then pasting this object into the file created by another application. For example, you could place a graphic object within a word processing document or spreadsheet. When you look at the object, it appears as if you simply pasted the data from the originating application into the current application (similar to DDE). The data provided by the object automatically changes as you change the data in the original object. Often you can start the originating application and automatically load the required data by double-clicking on the object.

OCX   See *OLE Custom eXtension*.

ODBC   See *Open Database Connectivity*.

ODBC.NET   A managed form of the *Open Database Connectivity (ODBC)* database technology. This technology is supported by a special addition to the .NET Framework. The main difference between ODBC and ODBC .NET is that ODBC .NET provides better support for distributed applications through disconnected datasets. See *ODBC* for more details on this topic.

OLE   See *Object Linking and Embedding*.

OLE Custom eXtension (OCX)   A component or control designed to make adding OLE capabilities to an application easier for the programmer. Essentially, an OCX is a DLL with an added programmer and OLE interface. Component technology has evolved to include a wide variety of uses including both client-side and server-side application elements. A component differs from a control in that a component is usually used for a processing task and lacks a user interface. Controls include application elements such as pushbuttons and textboxes.

OLE-DB   See *Object Linking and Embedding-Database*.

Open Database Connectivity (ODBC)   One of several methods for exchanging data between

DBMSs. In most cases, this involves three steps: installing an appropriate driver, adding a source to the ODBC applet in the Control Panel, and using SQL statements to access the database. See also *ODBC.NET*.

P

parameter   A value received by a function or procedure from another function or procedure, the DOS command line, or some other source.

parse   The act of reducing a string or other data structure to its constituent parts. For example, spreadsheets normally break words and numbers apart using the spaces between them as the break point. Developers use a multitude of application programming techniques to perform data element parsing and some object technology even includes a `Parse()` method.

PDA   See *Personal Digital Assistant*.

Personal Digital Assistant (PDA)   A very small PC normally used for personal tasks, such as taking notes and maintaining an itinerary during business trips. PDAs normally rely on special operating systems and lack any standard application support.

Q

queue   Commonly, a programming construct used to hold data while it awaits processing. A queue uses a FIFO (first in/first out) storage technique. The first data element in is also the first data element that gets processed. Think of a queue as a line at the bank or grocery store and you'll have the right idea. There are also hardware queues, which emulate the processing capability of their software counterparts.

R

RCW See *Runtime Callable Wrapper*.

RDO See *Remote Data Objects*.

recordset The result of a query on one or more tables of a database. A recordset contains a single result set consisting of a single table. The recordset relies on a connection with the DBMS in order to perform data exchange and update.

reflection The technique used to read metadata within a .NET application. In general, reflection is used to read application attribute values. It's most common for developers to want to know the attributes that an assembly contains because the attributes describe assembly features. For example, a developer could use an attribute to describe the interface for a component or control.

Registry A freeform database used to hold settings, configuration, and other information for Windows. The Registry is a hierarchy or tree consisting of keys and associated values. The operating system searches the Registry tree for keys that it requires, then requests values for those keys in order to perform tasks like configuring an application. The Registry is organized into hives. Each hive contains settings for a particular operating system element, such as user information and hardware configuration. Users share common hives such as those used for hardware, but have they separate hives for their information as long as Windows is configured to provide separate desktops for each user.

Remote Data Objects (RDO) An older Microsoft database technology that provides access to remote data using a set of objects similar to those found in technologies such as DAO and *ODBC*.

Rich Text Format (RTF) A file format originally introduced by Microsoft that allows an application to store formatting information in plain *ASCII* text. All commands begin with a backslash. For example, the \cf command tells an RTF-capable editor which color from the color table to use when displaying a particular section of text.

role-based security A method for controlling access to an object based on the requestor's job function within an organization. In other words, if the requestor has a specific job function (or role), then they're allowed to access the object. This method of maintaining security is an extension of groups. However, unlike groups, a requestor must perform a specific job function before access is granted. This security methodology is normally used with COM+ applications.

RTF See *Rich Text Format*.

Runtime Callable Wrapper (RCW) A proxy for unmanaged applications that enables the unmanaged code to call managed code functions. The RCW makes it appear to the calling application that the managed code is unmanaged code.

S

SACL See *Security Access Control List*.

scalability A definition of an object's ability to sustain increases in load. For example, companies often rate networking systems by their ability to scale from one to many users. Software scalability determines the ability of the software to run on more than one machine when needed, without making it appear that more than one machine is in use.

schema   A formal method for describing the structure of a database, storage technology, or data transfer technique such as XML. The schema defines the requirements for constructing the object in question. For example, a schema for a relational database would include information on the structure of tables, fields, and relations within the database.

SDI   See *Single Document Interface.*

SDK   See *Software Development Kit.*

sealed class   A special form of class implementation with inheritance restrictions. Sealed classes always provide a full implementation of all the methods they contain. A developer can instantiate a sealed class and use the resulting object in the same way as any other object. However, other classes can't inherit from a sealed class. In addition, all methods within a sealed class are static, which means that they can't be changed or overridden in any way. Sealed classes are useful because they enable a developer to create a specific class implementation without concern that someone else will misuse the class in some unforeseen way.

Secure Socket Layer (SSL)   A digital signature technology used for exchanging information between a client and a server. Essentially an SSL-compliant server will request a digital certificate from the client machine. The client can likewise request a digital certificate from the server. Companies or individuals obtain these digital certificates from a third-party vendor like VeriSign, who can vouch for the identity of both parties.

Security Access Control List (SACL)   One of several specialized access control lists (ACL) used to maintain object integrity. This list controls Windows' auditing feature. Every time a user or group accesses an object and the auditing feature for that object is turned on, Windows makes an entry in the audit log.

Security Identifier (SID)   The part of a user's access token that identifies the user throughout the network—like an account number. The user token that the SID identifies tells which groups the user belongs to and what privileges the user has. Each group also has a SID, so users' SIDs contain references to the various group SIDs that they belong to, not a complete set of group access rights. You'd normally use the User Manager utility under Windows NT to change the contents of this access token. You'll use the Active Directory Users and Computers console when working with Windows 2000.

SGML   See *Standard Generalized Markup Language.*

SID   See *Security Identifier.*

Simple Object Access Protocol (SOAP)   A Microsoft-sponsored protocol that provides the means for exchanging data between COM and foreign component technologies like *Common Object Request Broker Architecture (CORBA)* using *XML* as an intermediary.

Single Document Interface (SDI)   A method of displaying information where each window is independent of the other—there's no main window.

Single Threaded Apartment (STA)   A method of defining how object methods get executed. STAs include three restrictions not found in multi-threaded apartments (MTAs). The first is that an STA contains one, and only one, object. This ensures that once a component is instantiated, the resulting object doesn't share memory space with any other object, which could result in corruption. The second restriction is that one, and only one, thread can enter the apartment to interact with the object inside. The reason for this restriction is obvious. A single-threaded object can only handle the requests of one thread at a time, which means that COM must protect the object from access by more than one thread. Ensuring that only one thread can enter the apartment at a time is the easiest way to accomplish this task. Finally, a thread can execute only one object method at a time. This restriction ensures that there won't be any data corruption due to shared variables within the object. As a result of these restrictions, a single process could contain multiple STAs; one for each STA object that the application instantiated.

snap-in Refers to a component that's designed to reside within another application. Component technologies allow one application to serve as a container for multiple sub-applications. The snap-in performs one specific task out of all of the tasks that the application as a whole can perform. The *Microsoft Management Console (MMC)* is an example of a host application. Network administrators perform all Windows 2000/XP management tasks using snap-ins designed to work with the MMC.

SOAP See *Simple Object Access Protocol*.

Software Development Kit (SDK) A special add-on to an operating system or an application that describes how to access its internal features. For example, an SDK for Windows would show how to create a File Open dialog box. Programmers use an SDK to learn how to access special Windows components, such as OLE.

SSL See *Secure Socket Layer*.

STA See *Single Threaded Apartment*.

Standard Generalized Markup Language (SGML) A specification for defining document format originally created for the publishing industry.

Most developers consider SGML too complex for standard display purposes. However, both *XML* and *HTML* are based on SGML.

string Two or more characters connected to form a word or other character-based information.

T

TCO See *Total Cost of Ownership*.

TCP/IP See *Transmission Control Protocol/Internet Protocol*.

thread One executable unit within an application. Running an application creates a main thread. One of the things the main thread does is display a window with a menu. The main thread can also create other threads. Background printing may appear as a thread, for example. Only 32-bit applications support threads.

token The representation of data, an object, database element, programming syntax, or other information using a code word, phrase, number, or object. For example, in programming, a token could represent a statement, punctuation mark, argument, or other syntactical element. Users often receive tokens describing their rights as part of the security features of an operating system. Networks also use tokens to control data flow and perform other tasks.

Total Cost of Ownership (TCO) A measure of the investment required to keep a device or group of devices operational. TCO normally measures the cost of an individual workstation on a network, but companies can use the information for other purposes.

Transmission Control Protocol/Internet Protocol (TCP/IP)   A standard communication-line protocol developed by the United States Department of Defense. The protocol defines how two devices talk to each other. Think of the protocol as a type of language used by the two devices.

U

UDP   See *User Datagram Protocol*.

UI   See *User Interface*.

UNC   See *Universal Naming Convention*.

Uniform Resource Locator (URL)   A text representation of a specific location on the Internet. URLs normally include the protocol (`http://`, for example), the target location (world wide web or `www`), the domain or server name (`mycompany`), and a domain type (`.com` for commercial). It can also include a hierarchical location within that website. The URL usually specifies a particular file on the web server, although there are some situations when a web server will use a default filename. For example, asking the browser to find `http://www.mycompany.com`, would probably display the `DEFAULT.HTM` file at that location.

Universal Naming Convention (UNC)   A method for identifying network resources without using specific locations. In most cases, a user will employ this convention with drives and printers, but the user can also apply it to other types of resources. A UNC normally uses a device name in place of an identifier. For example, a user might refer to a disk drive on a remote machine as "`\\AUX\DRIVE-C.`" The advantage of using UNC is that the resource name won't change, even if the user's drive mappings do.

Universally Unique Identifier (UUID)   Another name for a *Globally Unique Identifier (GUID)*. The two terms are interchangeable.

unmanaged code   A .NET programming term for natively compiled code that runs directly under DOS or Windows. Native code executes without the benefit of the *Common Language Runtime (CLR)*.

URL   See *Uniform Resource Locator*.

User Datagram Protocol (UDP)   Allows applications to exchange individual packets of information over a TCP/IP network. UDP uses a combination of protocol ports and IP addresses to get a message from one point of the network to another. More than one client can use the same protocol port as long as all clients using the port have a unique IP address. There are two types of protocol port: well-known and dynamically bound. The well-known port assignments use the ports numbered between 1 and 255. When using dynamically bound port assignments, the requesting applications queries the service first to see which port it can use.

user interface (UI)   The portion of an application that contains user accessible controls and data manipulation elements. The user interface for a Windows application is commonly composed of buttons, text boxes, static text, graphics, and other design elements.

UUID   See *Universally Unique Identifier*.

V

variable   An identifier used to point to an area of memory containing a value.

variant   A special data type that can hold any of a number of other data types. The variant data type is typically used when the type of an argument or return value isn't known at design time.

Virtual Object System   An object execution technique originally found in COM+ applications in which each object executes within a specific context. The use of a context enables the server to differentiate between objects in large distributed applications. A context also allows the developer to use advanced programming techniques, such as role-based security.

W

Web Services Routing Protocol (WS-Routing)
Helps applications move data using SOAP over transports such as TCP, UDP, and HTTP in one-way, request/response, and peer-to-peer scenarios.

Windows Management Instrumentation (WMI)   A special set of Windows features that reduce total cost of ownership (TCO) by allowing the network administrator to remotely monitor, control, and configure workstations. This particular technology falls into the agent category and is very common on many network operating systems. An agent (special files executing on the client machine) allows the server to gain access to client machine resources and configuration information. Obviously, only machines that have the agent installed will be accessible to the network administrator.

WMI   See *Windows Management Instrumentation*.

WS-Routing   See *Web Services Routing Protocol*.

X

XML   See *eXtensible Markup Language*.

Index

Note to the Reader: Throughout this index **boldfaced** page numbers indicate primary discussions of a topic. *Italicized* page numbers indicate illustrations.

N

X

Y

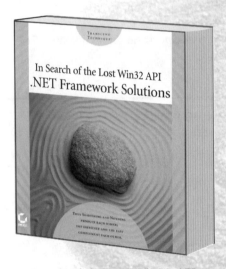

The quotation on the bottom of the front cover is taken from the fifteenth chapter of Lao Tzu's Tao Te Ching, *the classic work of Taoist philosophy. This particular verse is from the translation by D. C. Lau (copyright 1963) and begins an exploration of the qualities of the sage, who is "too profound to be known." For Lao Tzu, humility is the greatest virtue; the true leader does not call attention to himself.*

It is traditionally held that Lao Tzu lived in the fifth century B.C. in China, during the Chou dynasty, but it is unclear whether he was actually a historical figure. It is said that he was a teacher of Confucius. The concepts embodied in the Tao Te Ching *influenced religious thinking in the Far East, including Zen Buddhism in Japan. Many in the West, however, have wrongly understood the* Tao Te Ching *to be primarily a mystical work; in fact, much of the advice in the book is grounded in a practical moral philosophy governing personal conduct.*